Complete Theatre

Oscar Mandel

Complete Theatre
Oscar Mandel

© Insert Press, 2024
ISBN: 978-1-947322-10-3
Library of Congress Control Number: 2023947673

This book is also available as an ebook ISBN: 978-1-947322-11-0

All performance rights, including professional, amateur, motion pictures, animated cartoons, recitations, lecturing, public reading, radio broadcasting, television, and electronic dissemination, are strictly reserved by the Publisher.

Contact Insert Press for Actor's Editions of individual plays from this volume and with any requests for performance rights.

Cover and interior page design by HR Hegnauer.

Complete Theatre
Oscar Mandel

twenty plays, forty-three fables

LOS ANGELES

NON-DRAMATIC WORKS BY THE AUTHOR

The Book of Elaborations [essays]: New Directions
Fundamentals of the Art of Poetry: Continuum
A Definition of Tragedy: New York University Press
Philoctetes and the Fall of Troy: University of Nebraska Press
Ariadne: University of Florida Press
The Theatre of Don Juan: University of Nebraska Press
Otherwise Fables: Chi Po and the Sorcerer, Gobble-Up Stories,
   Sigimund Prince of Poland: Turner Publishing
Otherwise Poems: Turner Publishing
Last Pages [novellas, essays, poems]: Turner Publishing
The Art of Alessandro Magnasco: Leo S. Olschki
The Cheerfulness of Dutch Art: Davaco Publishers

"Hold it! said Goethe, don't talk to me about the Public, I don't care to hear anything about it. The chief point is that the piece is written; let the world handle it and make use of it as best as it is competent to do."

—*Conversations with Eckermann,* 20 December 1829

TABLE OF CONTENTS

I Modern

- 3   Living-Room With 6 Oppressions
- 23   Honest Urubamba
- 57   Water From an Italian Pump
- 83   How Alootook Came to Dance a Gavotte
- 131   A Splitting Headache
- 159   The Fatal French Dentist: a heart-rending tragedy
- 177   Professor Snaffle's Polypon: an extravanza
- 221   A Beautiful Investment: a script for stage and screen
- 243   The One Who Didn't Die

II Historical

- 259   The Rebels of Nantucket: a romantic comedy of the American Revolution
- 345   Sigismund, Prince of Poland
- 395   General Audax: a Play in Seven Scenes Concerning the Roman Invasions of Spain

III Classical

- 437   Amphitryon (after Molière)
- 469   The Summoning of Philoctetes
- 497   Agamemnon Triumphant

IV Biblical

- 527   And the Lord God Planted a Garden
- 561   An Unpleasantness in Jerusalem

V Imaginary

- 579   Prince Poupon Needs a Wife (after Marivaux)
- 623   The Virgin and the Unicorn
- 661   The Friar, the Peddler and the Witch

VI Fables

- 687   The Kukkurrik Fables: 43 mini-plays

- 753   Appendix: Table of plays translated by the author

ABOUT THIS BOOK

The present volume brings together all the plays I have published either in literary journals or under book covers since 1961, the year *The Massachusetts Review* printed *Island*, now called *The Summoning of Philoctetes*. The rounding up of these many plays, so late in life, is of course an act dictated by plain vanity, but it is also motivated by a normal paternal wish to invite all my offsprings under one roof, and also, let me confess, by a conviction that my plays, or, at worst, most of my plays, are of lasting interest.

To present these works in chronological order either of conception or of publication seemed to me to make little sense, because I have revised them — improved them, I am bold enough to claim—for the present edition, some of them a little here and there but most of them amply. This recent playwriting activity has made them all to some extent works of 2020-2021. I have therefore arranged my plays in clusters. The first of these consists of plays modern or near modern in their settings. The settings of the second are quasi- or pseudo-historical. The third cluster houses subjects from Ancient Greek lore. The fourth, biblical matter. In the fifth I placed tales with fanciful settings. My *Kukkurrik Fables* are housed in the sixth cluster.

I have omitted from this volume all references to the productions a number of these plays have enjoyed over the years. Productions come and go, texts remain. I give them here as *literature*, dramas to be read as one reads novels. Yet at the same time they stand firm as immediately producible scripts. Not that I ever dreamed that the vaster of these plays—plays crowded with actors and actresses and demanding machinery or multiple sets—would attract the funds needed to get them staged. But even these lie on the page as if some eccentric producer, tired of musical comedies, were about to finance my monsters. In the meantime, these monsters, along with the plays of modest dimensions, are here to be read as good yarns (for no "experiments" will ever replace a good yarn) *and* as playscripts addressed to the imagination, which is often, after all, a finer director than the living one.

Although *Island* is the first of my plays to have appeared in print, *The Monk Who Wouldn't*, published a year later (it is now rebaptized *The Friar, the Peddler and the Witch*) had been written several years earlier, in 1954 or 1955, along with several other plays which have gone mercifully lost. So this is the true first-born of the comedies and tragedies printed here, as its young lyricism would anyway suggest. The most recent is *Agamemnon Triumphant*, here slightly revised from its original appearance in my *Reinventions* of 2002.

One more remark. It is not my business to analyze my own work, yet I should warn the reader that not a single one of my plays—except just possibly *The One Who Didn't Die*—can be called "realistic". My plays are, in the largest sense of that word, "poetic"—poetic-funny or poetic-tragic. They are products of what I have called elsewhere the high imagination. This is nothing more than a statement of fact; it does not inhibit another fact, namely that poetic plays can be as bad as realistic ones. Good and bad are, of course, for readers and spectators to judge.

I

I

LIVING ROOM
WITH 6 OPPRESSIONS

CHARACTERS

Matthew Available, in his thirties
Nanny, in her sixties
Smiggins
The Capitalist
José Garcia
Dr. Lubumbo
Slotnik
The Innocent Bystander

(The action takes place in Matthew Available's comfortable living room. One of its doors leads directly to the street, another one leads to the kitchen. Matthew wears a lounging robe)

MATTHEW. Sunday afternoon. Fair weather, my pulse regular, all my rhythms in order, my mind alert, informed and compassionate. *(He sits down with a ledger and rings a little bell)* Nanny!
(Nanny appears)
NANNY. You rang, Mr. Matthew?
MATTHEW. Yes I did. Bring my coffee, will you? And a muffin with cinnamon.
NANNY. It's all ready in the kitchen; I'll just heat the muffin a bit.
MATTHEW. Fine. Be sure not to burn it. *(Exit Nanny. Matthew turns to his ledger)* Let's see. A hundred dollars for the Cancer Society. Fifty for the Orphanage. Fifty for the blind. Poor people. I'd rather be deaf, dumb, anything. Another twenty for Aid to the War Refugees. A hundred, fifty and fifty, twenty—that adds up to two hundred twenty for this week. I should be able to do better. I'm a bachelor, damn it, and Nanny doesn't cost much. I'll cut down on luxuries like restaurants and concerts. Just last week there was an earthquake, an invasion, an epidemic, a religious massacre, and here I am with my steady pulse and my slippers. Come to think of it, I've got my shoes on. On a Sunday afternoon! Nanny! *(Impatient)* Nanny!!
NANNY *(from the kitchen)*. What now?
MATTHEW. Why haven't I got my slippers on?
NANNY. The muffin will burn if I go for your slippers now!
MATTHEW. All right all right. *(To himself)* Always ready with an excuse.
(Enter Nanny with a tray)
NANNY. I'll get your slippers in a minute, but I've got to look—
MATTHEW. Damn damn damn. I've told you a million times—damn! Look at that lump of sugar.
NANNY. Well? I'm looking.
MATTHEW. It's wet!
NANNY. A bit of coffee spilled into the saucer.
MATTHEW. I *know* a bit of coffee spilled into the saucer! And yet I've told you a million times to bring me the sugar in a bowl. Do you know what I mean? A bowl, a crystal bowl, the way it's done in every bloody civilized household on earth.
NANNY. But why? Always the same story! Why all the fuss? You've been taking two lumps in your coffee for the last twenty years, Mr. Matthew, and you were taking two lumps in your hot milk when you were four years old,

so what's the use my carting in a bowl full of useless lumps of sugar?
MATTHEW. The use is that the sugar won't get soggy. I hope it's not too much to expect—two dry lumps of sugar picked up with a pair of sugar tongs. Now what? What's this? What's going on?
(The entrance door is flung open, and Smigginss rushes in, more on all fours than on his two feet. He is bloody, abject, emaciated and exhausted)
SMIGGINS. Help me, hide me, he's going to kill me!
MATTHEW. Who? What? Who are you?
NANNY. Get out of here, this is Mr. Available's private house!
SMIGGINS. I'll explain later! Mr. Available, I'm beggin' you—save me—have a heart—I'm an honest working man and the owner is after me, I smashed his machine.
NANNY. Well! I advise you—
MATTHEW. Shut up, Nanny! Here, give me your hand, here's a closet—
SMIGGINS. Too late! Oh Jesus!
(The Capitalist rushes in)
CAPITALIST. Where's the swine?
SMIGGINS. Protect me!
MATTHEW. Now wait a minute!
NANNY. This is private property!
CAPITALIST. *I* am private property. Don't hide behind chairs, you slum-bum, I'll rip you to pieces, striker, machine-breaker, drunkard, collective bargainer—
MATTHEW. Now wait a minute! This man is under my protection.
CAPITALIST. Who are *you?*
MATTHEW. What do you mean? This is *my* house. Kindly take your capitalist hide out of here, skinflint, blood-sucker, gouger, golfplayer.
SMIGGINS. That's tellin' him.
CAPITALIST. Hold it, feller.
MATTHEW. Nanny, show the gentleman the door,
NANNY. I keep telling you to lock that door of ours, Mr. Matthew.
MATTHEW. Never. Let nobody say that he found Matthew Available's door locked in his face. Good day, sir.
CAPITALIST. Good day my pink toe. I'll have that bolshevik gangster in manacles before I leave the house. Out of my way!
MATTHEW. What did he do to you?
CAPITALIST. He smashed my machine.
SMIGGINS *(at the same time)*. I smashed his machine.
NANNY. Why, look at him. He's so weak he couldn't smash an egg-shell.
SMIGGINS. I smashed it all the same, and I'll keep smashing it till I get a

living wage.

CAPITALIST. Scum! Ten years in the clink is what you'll get! Come out of there! *(To Matthew)* Let me go, or I'll slug you too!

MATTHEW. Stop bawling. You bloated oppressor, how much longer are you going to live off the work of the poor?

CAPITALIST. As long as I can, you bet your life. I've smashed six unions in my time. And I'm not bloated, I'm well fed.

NANNY. Oh the wicked man.

SMIGGINS. It's off of us the likes of him feed their faces. Me and my starvin' wife and my three sick kids, and a paycheck that ain't enough to feed the flies in our stinking two rooms. I wish I'd have smashed *him* instead of his machine.

CAPITALIST. Open threats!

MATTHEW. I'll say. And I'm the man to execute them. *(He takes a poker from the fireplace)* See this? Solid brass. Nanny, give me a hand.

(Nanny picks up the abstract sculpture)

SMIGGINS. Hit him!

CAPITALIST. Oh yeah? I'm not leaving without this anarchist in custody.

MATTHEW. Yes you are.

CAPITALIST. No I ain't.

NANNY. Yes you are.

CAPITALIST. Out of my way, granny, I'll have you both up for rioting.

MATTHEW. Get out!

CAPITALIST. Get out yourself!

MATTHEW *(To Nanny)*. Hold him!

CAPITALIST. I'll knock your teeth into your windpipe.

SMIGGINS. Hit him! Hit him!

(Matthew hits the Capitalist)

CAPITALIST. Ouch!

NANNY. Parasite! *(She picks up the abstract sculpture, hits him with it and lays him out flat)*

SMIGGINS. That's the ticket! *(He comes out from behind a chair and kicks the Capitalist)* I wish I was stronger.

MATTHEW. Sit down, my poor man. Nanny will give you something to eat. And I'll drag this carcass out.

CAPITALIST *(opens an eye)*. What hit me?

NANNY *(shows him the sculpture)*. Justice Unbound.

CAPITALIST. Damn. *(He faints away)*

MATTHEW. Give me a hand, Nanny. All that blubber. *(They drag the Capitalist outdoors)* So much for that. The world can stand a little improvement. How

are you feeling, Mr.—?
SMIGGINS. Smiggins. Josh Smiggins. And real grateful to the both of yous.
NANNY. I'll fix you something to eat, Mr. Smiggins. You look like you're about to become extinct.
SMIGGINS. Gee, I'd appreciate a little somethin'. Just anything will do, ma'am; I ain't used to much.
NANNY. Leave it to me. *(She goes to the kitchen)*
MATTHEW. It's about time somebody stood up to these robbers.
SMIGGINS. Without you I'd a been in jail by now, Mr. Available.
MATTHEW. Well, I did my best. I may be an intellectual, but you don't find *me* playing a harp in an ivory tower.
SMIGGINS. Doin' what?
MATTHEW. I mean, refusing to fight.
SMIGGINS. Refusin' to fight? You? Don't you believe it. That poker o' yours coulda laid out five of him. Boy, if I wasn't a wreck—
MATTHEW. Nanny! Hurry up!
NANNY *(within)*. Coming, coming!
SMIGGINS. I don't want to be no trouble to you.
MATTHEW. Trouble? I ought to apologize to you for living in ease and comfort while you and your wife and those poor children—God, it makes me choke.
SMIGGINS. Me too. This sure is nice lodgins you got here. A reglar nest, bless you all.
(Enter Nanny with a tray full of bread, butter, cold cuts and cheeses)
SMIGGINS. Oh gee, thanks, thanks a million. I'm so hungry, I can't hardly keep my head up.
MATTHEW. Heartbreaking. Here, eat, make yourself at home.
SMIGGINS. Mmmm. Good.
MATTHEW. More butter, Mr. Smiggins?
SMIGGINS. Good idea. What do you know! I'm feeling stronger already.
MATTHEW *(to Nanny)*. It's a pleasure to watch him.
NANNY. Why don't I put something in a paper bag for your children, Mr. Smiggins?
SMIGGINS. Gee, would you? They'll be real happy, the poor kids.
MATTHEW. Let's hope that your children will see a brighter future. No exploitation, a decent wage, a good education.
SMIGGINS *(his mouth full)*. You said it. Boy oh boy, do I feel better! Lemme wash this down with a cup of coffee, do you mind? Smells great. "Good to the last drop." Yes, sir, I'm gonna put the kids through college, right along with the board of directors, the jet set an' all.

MATTHEW. Let them read Sophocles, study the sciences, hear chamber music.

SMIGGINS. You bet. I'll see them at the top o' the heap if I ever get half a break at my lousy job. Gee, this here ham is the best I ever ett. Thanks for the bag, granny.

(While eating, Smiggins has become remarkably stronger, larger, ruddier)

MATTHEW. This meal has really propped you up, Mr. Smiggins. I hope today will mark a new beginning, and you know you can always count on me. Well now, listen to this!

(Music is heard)

SMIGGINS. What's that?

MATTHEW. I don't know. Nanny, why don't you take a peek outside.

NANNY. I will. *(She goes out)*

SMIGGINS. Sure sounds foreign to me.

MATTHEW. I think it's Latino.

SMIGGINS. Oh yeah? Them foreigners upset my appetite.

MATTHEW. I don't see why. *(Nanny reappears)* Well Nanny?

NANNY. It's the Virgin of Guadalupe's birthday, and they're all coming this way, bless 'em, dancing and banging on things.

SMIGGINS *(roars)*. I don't like foreigners!

MATTHEW. Mr. Smiggins! We're all Americans here. Remember the melting pot.

SMIGGINS *(roars)*. I don't like foreigners!

NANNY *(aside to Matthew)*. We gave him too much to eat.

MATTHEW. Mr. Smiggins, all kinds of people went to the building of this nation—the English, the Poles, the Swedes, the Chinese, the—

SMIGGINS *(roars)*. They grab our jobs for half pay and what do they do? They take a plane back home first chance they get, and jabbering away jabber jabber in their lingo that ain't even white. *(At the door)* Cut out that noise! Jesus, lemme take a crack at them!

MATTHEW. Wait, hold it, hold it!

SMIGGINS. Out o' my way! This place is for hundred percent Americans! I ain't gonna stand for no heathen celebrations!

MATTHEW. Nanny, help me!

SMIGGINS. I'll moider em!

NANNY. Watch the gueridon!

MATTHEW. Mr. Smiggins!

(Smiggins has thrown Matthew off and flings himself into the street. Suddenly the music stops. Sounds of a fight, curses, trumpets blaring off-key. Then a man rushes into the house, more on all fours than on his two feet. He is mauled, enfeebled, astonished and

LIVING-ROOM WITH 6 OPPRESSIONS

terrified)

GARCIA. Help me, hide me, Jesus Maria, he's going to kill me, the Yankee has gone loco!

MATTHEW. Close the door, Nanny, quick!

NANNY. Can I lock it, Mr. Matthew?

MATTHEW. Never! Here, sir, here, sit down, you're safe, believe me, we'll protect you. Here's a handkerchief.

GARCIA. Thank you, señor, muchas gracias. Oh I can't breathe, I'm dying.

MATTHEW *(to Nanny)*. Get him a glass of wine, hurry, and food. *(Exit Nanny)* Gently, my friend, you're not dying, you're only scared. My name is Matthew Available. You're safe under my roof, and I am going to give you all the help I can.

GARCIA. Mucho gusto. My name is José Garcia. I don't even know what happened. It's the feast of the Virgen de Guadalupe today. *(He crosses himself)* She is our holy guardian. We were singing and dancing. I was one of the men chosen to carry her on my shoulders.

(Enter Nanny with a tray full of bread, butter, cold cuts and cheeses)

GARCIA. Thank you, señora, kind lady. *(He eats and drinks)*

NANNY. I don't see how you could carry a statue, Mr. Garcia, you're so thin and weak I could break you in two by throwing a glance at you.

MATTHEW. Nanny!

GARCIA. There were six of us carrying her, señora, before that wild bull fell on us. Who was he, anyway? Why did he start knocking peaceful people down?

MATTHEW. Prejudice, prejudice; every people thinks itself better than other people, alas.

GARCIA. I thought I saw him coming out of here.

MATTHEW and NANNY. Did you?

GARCIA. We weren't doing anything wrong.

MATTHEW. I should say not. It's marvelous to see so many of you keeping faith with your traditions and beliefs. It's beautiful. Look at Mexican history—Aztecs, Olmecs, Toltecs—Mayan civilization—Orozco.... Mr. Garcia, I'm proud to have you as a guest in my house. I own several books on Mexican murals you might be interested in looking at.

GARCIA. Wonderful. Mexican what?

NANNY. Have another sandwich.

GARCIA. Delicious. My compliments, señora. I'm already feeling much better.

NANNY. Don't eat too fast.

MATTHEW. Café con leche?

LIVING-ROOM WITH 6 OPPRESSIONS

GARCIA *(laughing)*. Por favor, amigo. Muchas gracias.

MATTHEW. We'll put you on your feet again. If only people could understand the idea of brotherhood, regardless of race, religion, nationality, and what not. I try my best as an individual, señor Garcia. I contribute, I sympathize, I join, I fight—literally fight, you know—look at this bruise.

GARCIA. Caramba!

MATTHEW. Fighting a brutal capitalist, defending a poor workingman.

GARCIA. You mean the one who almost killed me?

MATTHEW. Maybe he was the one. I couldn't stop him, Mr. Garcia.

GARCIA. You did your best, amigo.

(While eating, GARCIA has become remarkably stronger and larger)

NANNY. You're looking ever so much fitter, Mr. Garcia.

GARCIA. Thanks to you both. The Virgen will bless you. Oh look! Your door!

(In fact, the door has been pushed open. On the floor we see the head of a black man, followed by its body. He is dusty, shriveled, sweating and enfeebled, but impeccably dressed, and speaks with the best Oxford accent)

LUBUMBO. Help, good people....

(Matthew rushes toward the door)

MATTHEW. Come in, in God's name, come in, my brother!

NANNY. Another lunch coming up. Thank God it's Sunday only once a week.

GARCIA *(glumly, to Nanny)*. This is his brother? This?

NANNY. Oh no, Mr. Garcia, only a visitor.

GARCIA *(indignant)*. A visitor!

MATTHEW *(bending over Lubumbo)*. What's the matter, sir? Are you injured? Don't worry, you're safe in this house. Nanny, give me a hand, damn it!

NANNY. Sure, sure.

LUBUMBO. I can't speak.... Whoever you are, if there's any pity left....

MATTHEW. Come on, let me help you get on your feet. *(To Nanny)* Take the other arm. One, two, three! Here we are! To the leather chair. There now. Easy, easy. My God, he's bleeding in the neck.

GARCIA *(aside)*. Trouble-makers. Monkeys.

MATTHEW. Feeling better?

LUBUMBO. A bit better. Whoever you are, thank you, thank you. But you must hide me; there's a lynching mob on my trail!

GARCIA *(aside)*. Muy bien.

MATTHEW. I thought as much. But no lynching mob is going to cross my threshold.

GARCIA *(muttering)*. Musta raped a white virgin.

MATTHEW. Did you say something, Mr. Garcia?
GARCIA. Nothing, amigo, I was belching.
MATTHEW. Nanny, don't forget our guest while I attend to Mr.—
LUBUMBO. Nguyo Lubumbo. member of the Senate of Mubanga.
MATTHEW. The Senate of Mubanga! I don't know what to say. I'm honored! How did you—how did this—?
NANNY. Here's a cup of coffee, Mr. Lubumbo.
LUBUMBO. *Doctor* Lubumbo.
GARCIA *(between his teeth)*. Zulu.
LUBUMBO. Please conceal me somewhere, I implore you. I'm too weak to fight back. If they find me I'm done for.
MATTHEW *(to Nanny)*. Take a quick look outside.
NANNY *(looking out)*. Nothing yet. A bit of dust in the distance, that's all.
LUBUMBO. It must be the mob! Oh my God, if only I had strength enough to blow this whistle. *(He has a whistle around his neck)* Nobody is going to help me.
MATTHEW. Of course we're going to help you. You're in the house of Matthew Available—
LUBUMBO *(weakly)*. Delighted.
MATTHEW. —who will fight for the downtrodden till the last flake of his body turns to dust. But tell me, Mr. Lubumbo, why this vicious mob is hunting you.
LUBUMBO. *Doctor* Lubumbo. I hardly know.
GARCIA *(under his breath)*. I bet.
LUBUMBO. I was standing on a street-corner with the Cultural Attaché of the Cameroon, reminiscing about our days at Balliol, when a pretty girl walked by in front of us.
GARCIA *(setting his lunch tray down and standing up)*. White?
LUBUMBO. Yes. I laughed and said, "What a pretty girl." A policeman happened to overhear me. He yelled Rape! and suddenly it seemed as if the entire population was down on us, howling, shaking sticks, spitting, throwing stones.
NANNY. How did you get away?
LUBUMBO. Tom Boyo, my Cameroonian friend, had his open sports coupe parked at the curb. He jumped in and drove off. This diverted the mob long enough for me to run the other way. I ran, I ran, I ran, and now I'm almost dead, I can't even blow this whistle.
MATTHEW. Why the whistle?
LUBUMBO. To rally my people.
GARCIA *(aside to Matthew)*. Are you gonna stand for this?

MATTHEW. No, Mr. Garcia. We'll all defend him against that mob.
GARCIA *(roaring)*. That ain't what I meant!
MATTHEW. What's the matter, Mr. Garcia? You look mighty upset.
GARCIA. Sangre de Dios! He don't even knock to come in, he's steaming hot after assaulting a white virgin, he talks about whistling for his Africans—
MATTHEW. Gently, amigo, we're all equal, black, white, and, if I may say so, brown, like you.
GARCIA. Brown? Brown? Who's brown? I'm pure Spanish, I'm white, pure white, you're slandering me.
MATTHEW. All right, Mr. Garcia, you're any color you choose. Nanny, go to the kitchen. I want you to fix a good solid lunch for Mr. Lubumbo. Dr. Lubumbo.
NANNY. I hate to tell you, Mr. Matthew.
MATTHEW. To tell me what?
NANNY. All I've got left is a few steaks in the freezer, and it'll take two hours to thaw them out.
LUBUMBO. My dear, dear lady, I assure you I don't need a thing. Just hide me, or let me die in peace.
MATTHEW. No sir; there's going to be a fight, and we must give you strength for it. There's enough left on Mr. Garcia's tray for two lunches.
GARCIA. That's *my* tray!
MATTHEW and NANNY. Mr. Garcia!
GARCIA. *My* tray!
MATTHEW *(trying to seize the tray)*. If you don't mind—
GARCIA *(roaring)*. No black man is gonna eat offa my tray!
MATTHEW. May I point out—
GARCIA. Who they think they are? Go back to Africa! This country is for white men!
MATTHEW. And here I thought that you Latin Americans were free of these prejudices.
GARCIA. Sure, prejudices is for Yankees. We're not good enough to have 'em.
MATTHEW. You're becoming offensive, Mr. Garcia, now that I've fed you. Give me that tray.
GARCIA. Over my dead body. Wait! I'll call that mob myself! And let the blacks stay where they belong. Under *us*. D'you hear? Down on their knees, up in the trees, back to the plantations!
MATTHEW. Give me that tray and shut up.
GARCIA. Back to slavery!
LUBUMBO *(feebly)*. We'll kill you all.
GARCIA *(flinging himself on Lubumbo)*. Like hell you will! Hijo de puta!

LUBUMBO. Help! He's killing me!
MATTHEW. Nanny, help!
NANNY. Mr. Garcia, you're a Christian!
GARCIA. Damn right I'm a goddam Christian! That's why I'll murder the voodoo heathen!
LUBUMBO. Arghhh !
MATTHEW *(fighting Garcia)*. Take your hands off my guest! *(They exchange blows)* Nanny, he's bloodied my eye!
NANNY. Watch the gueridon!
GARCIA. Ouch! White Hottentot!
MATTHEW. Nanny, hit him with the Justice Unbound!
NANNY. I will. *(She does so and lays the Garcia out flat)*
MATTHEW *(staggering to a chair)*. Fighting for the oppressed is no holiday.
LUBUMBO *(feebly)*. Jolly good work, Mr. Available. If only I could have helped.
MATTHEW. Don't mention it, Dr. Lubumbo. Nanny, give me that glass of water.
NANNY. I'm bleeding too.
MATTHEW *(bathing his eye)*. My robe is torn.
LUBUMBO. I can only apologize for the untimely intrusion.
MATTHEW. Oh no, I assure you, I'm honored to have you in my house, Senator.
LUBUMBO. You are an honor to your country, to your race, and to mankind.
NANNY. What'll we do with Mr. Garcia?
MATTHEW. The ruffian. Let's drag him out. Is he still breathing?
NANNY. I'm afraid so.
MATTHEW. Come on, Nanny, do your bit for a change, will you?
NANNY. Sorry, Mr. Matthew, my arm hurts.
(They drag him out the door)
NANNY. May I lock the door now?
MATTHEW. Never. Go on, feed our guest.
NANNY. I don't know that we should, Mr. Matthew.
MATTHEW. Why not?
NANNY. Do I have to remind you what happened when you fed the others?
MATTHEW. Isn't that just like you? I don't know why I'm even answering you. Now, Dr. Lubumbo, can we induce you to take a little refreshment?
LUBUMBO. The mob, Mr. Available, the mob. Won't you try to hide me in a cellar or an attic?
MATTHEW. The mob has no earthly reason to stop at this particular house. But if they do, I'll beat them back, don't worry. Come now, take some food.

LIVING-ROOM WITH 6 OPPRESSIONS

You said yourself you needed strength to blow your whistle.
LUBUMBO. True.
MATTHEW. Of course, I'd gladly blow it for you.
LUBUMBO. Oh no! That's for me to do. I *will* have a bite after all. Very good of you.
(He begins to eat)
MATTHEW. Nanny, stop fiddling with your wound and prepare some fresh coffee.
LUBUMBO. Oh, splendid.
(Exit Nanny)
MATTHEW. I recommend this brie.
LUBUMBO. Excellent. I feel the vital spirits starting to course again in my veins.
MATTHEW. You are here on a mission, Dr. Lubumbo?
LUBUMBO. Yes, I am. My country is seeking military aid—the usual hardware, I'm afraid—aircraft—tanks.... One day, you know, we shall have to fight for access to the diamonds. Oh my, I'm still very weak. Quite dizzy and all that.
MATTHEW. Nanny, hurry the coffee!
NANNY *(from the kitchen)*. Coming up!
MATTHEW. Another slice of ham will help, Dr. Lubumbo. You know, it's simply thrilling to think of all these proud new independent nations. Only a few years ago, you were smarting under the boot of us white colonials, and now here you are, Malawi, Cameroon, the Congo, Gabon, Zambia, Botswana, and so on. I love to roll the exotic names off my tongue.
LUBUMBO. You are a well-informed man, Mr. Available. *(Nanny has come in with the coffee)* Thank you so much, my good woman. Two lumps, that's it. Smashing lunch. What was I saying? Oh yes, that you are a well-informed man.
MATTHEW. I try to be.
LUBUMBO. And well disposed toward us.
MATTHEW. Indeed I am.
LUBUMBO. Ours is a hard struggle.
MATTHEW. But a splendid one too. Already, I believe, free Mubanga has prospered as it never did under *us*.
LUBUMBO. Appreciably. And today, when a Mubangan starves, at least he starves at the hands of another Mubangan.
MATTHEW. Nice.
NANNY. I don't call that much of an improvement.
MATTHEW. Don't meddle in what's beyond you, Nanny. I think it's

encouraging.
LUBUMBO. Most encouraging.
NANNY. What about that posse that's out looking for you, Mr. Dr. Lubumbo? Ain't you afraid of it anymore?
LUBUMBO *(fingering his whistle)*. No, I'm no longer afraid.
(He has grown noticeably larger and stronger)
MATTHEW. You do look remarkably improved, I'm happy to say.
LUBUMBO. Perhaps I'd better go. You've been most helpful, and I shan't forget it.
MATTHEW. Please don't mention it. Nanny, take a look outside again to make sure those maniacs have scattered.
NANNY. Sure. *(She looks outside)* I guess you'd better hide Mr. Lubumbo in the basement. There's a mob closing in on us. They're banging on doors and raising the devil.
MATTHEW *(grabbing the poker)*. Here's the door to the basement, Dr. Lubumbo.
LUBUMBO. That won't be necessary anymore. I believe I can manage now.
(Shouts outside)
A VOICE. If he's anywhere in town, that's where he's got to be, fellers. Do-Gooder House.
VOICES. Let's go in and get him out. Lynch the guy! Bash in the door!
LUBUMBO. Steady on, Mr. Available. Courage, madam. I shall manage.
NANNY. There's a sturdy oak tree in front of the house, Dr. Lubumbo; that's what scares me.
LUBUMBO. I'm glad you mentioned it, my good woman; I intend to make use of it.
VOICE. Easy there, don't jostle, one guy is all we need. Go on in, Slotnik.
(Violent entrance of a burly SLOTNIK)
SLOTNIK. Where's that—? *(He sees Lubumbo and shouts to the people outside)* Don't nobody need to foller me. I got him. I got him good. *(Uproar outside. Slotnik whips out a couple of pistols)* Okay, mister, come out quiet, no use puttin up a fight. You got a date with a noose.
MATTHEW *(standing in front of Lubumbo)*. Over my dead body.
SLOTNIK. I'll sure be glad to oblige.
NANNY *(screams)*. No!
LUBUMBO *(moving Matthew aside)*. Let me handle this. Here I am, mister. Remember I enjoy diplomatic immunity, but I'm ready to follow you.
VOICE. What's going on in there, Slotnik?
VOICE. Need any help?
SLOTNIK. Relax, boys, lemme handle this my own way. *(To Lubumbo)* All right, black boy, get your black ass out through that door, and we'll converse

about your diplomatic unity from the end of a rope.

MATTHEW. Stop, for God's sake! This gentleman is a Mubangan senator! He is here on an official mission!

SLOTNIK. If he needs help with his mission, let him call his pals out.

LUBUMBO. That is precisely my plan. *(He blows his whistle)*

SLOTNIK. Whadda ya think you're doin? Calling a fucking taxicab? Take hold of him, fellers! Here he is!

(He shoves Lubumbo out, leaves after him, slams the door. Uproar outside, shots)

VOICE. Don't shoot the guy before we've strung him up!

VOICE. Smith, hold the rope!

VOICE. Yippee!

VOICE. No more white girls for the black bastard!

(Other shouts ad libitum)

MATTHEW. I'm sick. What can we do? Where are the police? Nanny, look out the window, I can't, tell me what's going on.

NANNY. Oh Jesus Christ, oh Jesus Christ, save him, they've bound his wrists, they've torn off his necktie. Now what? Merciful God! What's this? What's this? Mr. Matthew, oh oh oh oh, come here, quick—

MATTHEW: I can't....

NANNY. Come here I tell you! Dozens of Blacks running to the rescue! Hundreds! Thousands! Millions!

(Matthew rushes to the window)

MATTHEW. Ha! The whistle! Nanny, the whistle did it! Hurrah!

NANNY. Don't go out, Mr. Matthew, please!

(A new kind of uproar outside)

VOICE. They're comin' down from every side!

VOICE. Run for your lives!

VOICES. Shoot! Shoot! Don't wait!

VOICE. Hold it!

VOICE. Africans! Forward! Lynch 'em! Don't let the white bastards escape! Shoot into the groins! Shoot into the eyes!

(Shots)

VOICES. Help, help! Stop!

NANNY. They're stringing up Slotnik!

SLOTNIK *(outside)*. Men, they're lynchin' me. Call out the National Guard! Tell mother I love her.... Aaargh....

(Shouts of triumph. More shots. Matthew's windows are shattered)

VOICE. Destroy the white man!

NANNY. Behind the sofa, Mr. Matthew! Oh Jesus Christ, the world's coming to an end!

LIVING-ROOM WITH 6 OPPRESSIONS

(Enter Lubumbo. He smashes all the furniture)
LUBUMBO. Nothing personal you understand. This is purely symbolic.
NANNY. The gueridon!
LUBUMBO. Personally, I'm most grateful to you both. *(He knocks down a last vase and leaves)*
VOICE. How many are swinging, men?
VOICE. Fifteen!
VOICE. Down with white imperialism!
VOICE. Fifteen in a row. Ain't they handsome!
VOICE. Here's another one!
VOICE. Don't let him get away! Fire!
NANNY. Don't move, Mr. Matthew!
VOICE OF INNOCENT BYSTANDER. Not me!
(A shot, and then a white man's body is tossed into Matthew's house)
NANNY. Oh Jesus Christ!
MATTHEW. I think they're finished, Nanny.
(The roars have diminished. Presently all is silent. Matthew and Nanny come out of hiding and examine the body)
MATTHEW. Is he dead?
NANNY. Must be.
MATTHEW. Let's lay him on the rug. Maybe we can still help. Oh God, what a Sunday afternoon!
NANNY. Oh, Mr. Matthew, there's a card in his coat pocket.
MATTHEW. Let me see it. "Innocent Bystander." What do you make of that?
NANNY. I think it's odd.
MATTHEW. I don't know. I'm beginning to feel, I don't know, as if I needed to do more thinking.
(The Innocent Bystander sits up)
INNOCENT BYSTANDER. I'm glad to hear you say that, Mr. Available. *(He gets up and shakes hands with Matthew and Nanny)* Glad to meet you both. I hope I haven't been too much bother.
MATTHEW *(dazed)*. No, not at all. Lunch?
INNOCENT BYSTANDER. Most certainly not. I only dropped in, so to speak. But now I'd better be on my way. No need to see me out, thank you. Oh yes. After I'm gone, I suggest— *(he makes a gesture)*
NANNY. Lock the door?
INNOCENT BYSTANDER. Uhuh.
MATTHEW. My door?
INNOCENT BYSTANDER. Your door.

MATTHEW. And then? What then?
INNOCENT BYSTANDER. Tat tat tat. Somebody knocks. Who's there? You take a look through the peephole. Another look. And then another look. And then maybe you open sometimes a little.
MATTHEW. And the lunches?
INNOCENT BYSTANDER. Small lunches. So long, good people. *(The handle comes off the door; he tosses it away)* Quite a junkheap you've got here. Lots of repairs.
(He leaves. There is a long pause. Matthew hesitates. He looks at Nanny, who is beginning to take in the shambles, then he goes to the door and locks it)
MATTHEW. We'll replace the doorknob and fix the windows. *(Nanny picks up the gueridon and begins to cry)* It's a junk heap all right.
NANNY. Your mother and me bought it together.
MATTHEW. There, there now.
NANNY *(sobbing)*. And look at the cupboard, Mr. Matthew, your grandad's it was, lousy Victorian he always called it, every leg broken. Look at our clock. Look at the table. Look at these chairs. Look, look, look. I can't believe it. All your things, Mr. Matthew, every day for thirty-five years I dusted everything.
(Matthew is staring at Nanny)
MATTHEW *(in a small voice)*. You're bleeding.
NANNY *(still crying)*. I don't care. They even ripped the carpet.
MATTHEW. Sure you care, with all that dust and dirt.
NANNY. I've got a clean handkerchief.
MATTHEW. Give it to me. *(He bandages her)* But you've got to stop crying.
NANNY. I'll try.
MATTHEW. We have to pick up the pieces, you and me.
NANNY. Thirty-five years of work wasted.
MATTHEW. You promised to stop crying, though.
NANNY. I'll stop, Mr. Matthew.
MATTHEW. How's this for a bandage?
NANNY. Fine.
MATTHEW. We should have used an antiseptic.
NANNY. I don't care.
MATTHEW. Sit down a bit. Here's an undemolished chair. You've had a rough day. Sit down.
NANNY. Me?
(He stares at her)
NANNY. Anything the matter with you, Mr. Matthew?
MATTHEW. Why?

NANNY. You're staring at me funny.
MATTHEW. Nanny....
NANNY. Yes, Mr. Matthew?
MATTHEW (in a very small voice). What's your name?
NANNY (dumbfounded, remembers). Bertha. Bertha Robbins.

The End

Notes

Living Room With 6 Oppressions appeared in *Drama & Theatre*, volume 8, Spring 1970, and shortly thereafter in Volume 1 of my *Collected Plays* (1971-1972). It was reprinted in *The Scene 2 (Plays from Off-Off Broadway)* in 1974, an anthology edited by Stanley Nelson.

The opening soliloquy of Matthew Available is to be treated as flexible with regard both to the names of the charities and the amounts he provides. His gifts should be felt as reasonably generous. Also flexible: the items of Matthew's furniture, except the gueridon.

HONEST URUBAMBA

CHARACTERS

A crowd of men, women and children
A Newshawk (Blodgett)
Another Newshawk (Pimpkin)
A Fat Man
A Small Man
The Virgins of La Paz
A Boy in a vision
Soldiers
A General
Major Cucuchabaz
Two Farmer Lads
A Foreigner
Fortunato Concepcion Urubamba
The Wounded Soldier
Several Delegates to the United Nations
The President of the Assembly
Onesto Morales
A Reporter
Daniel Salamanca, *President of Bolivia*
San Martín, *Minister of the Exterior*
Prado, *Minister of the Interior*
Ayala, *Minister of Transportation*
Carrion, *Minister of Defense*
Ortiz, *Minister of Commerce*
Gomez, *Minister of Information*
Aides
A Nurse
The Messenger
A Cherub
The CIA agent
Mrs. Urubamba
Pepe, *her little son*
Aunt Urubamba
General Cochón
A Beggar, *formerly* Chocolate Man
The Crippled Veteran

SCENE ONE

(The stage is bare except for a few platforms, a Bolivian flag, and a conspicuous loudspeaker. Another loudspeaker is located in the theatre itself. The curtain rises on a cacophony of rumba music and military marches. Jolly atmosphere of frenzy throughout this scene. A siren ululates above and under the music as a joyous colorful crowd dances and waggles across the stage. Bells peal. Soldiers march in and out. Automobile horns give the V toot. The music is on or off in this scene as convenient. Additional dialogue can be improvised)

A LITTLE BOY. Bolivian flags! Ten cents each, worth at least twenty-five! Bolivian flags! Made in Bolivia! Bolivian cotton!
CROWD. Here! Give me one! I'll take two! Etc.
BOY. One at a time! Wait for your change! No personal checks! Five pesos each! List price is fifteen pesos! Here you are, here you are....
MAN. On a day like this, young man, a flag is worth fifty pesos! *(He brandishes a coin)* Fifty loyal native pesos!
(Hurrahs from the crowd)
BOY. Thank you, sir. *(He has sold out his flags)* Long live Bolivia! Down with Paraguay!
(Crowd cheers)
BOY. More flags coming soon! *(He leaves)*
RADIO. Citizens of Bolivia!
CROWD. The radio! Quiet! Shhhh.
RADIO. Here is the voice of our Minister of Defense, Dr. Constantino Carrion.
VOICE OF CARRION. Citizens! Descendants of Simón Bolivar! These are historic hours! Hours that challenge the greatness of a nation! The government of Paraguay threatens to unleash its brutal hordes against our sacred territory, our national inheritance, our Chaco! Bolivia longs for peace, but when Bolivian land is invaded, Bolivia stands up and fights!
CROWD. Bolivia fights!
VOICE OF CARRION. While this administration will take every honorable measure in its constant striving for peace, you, the people of Bolivia, have the solemn pledge of your freely elected government that we shall not rest until the last Paraguayan hireling is driven out of the Chaco, the land of

our inheritance. Bolivians! This is a time for heroic sacrifice and patriotic rededication. Our dead shall not be dying in vain!
(Wild cheers)
RADIO. You have heard the voice of the Minister of Defense, Dr. Constantino Carrion, in an informative broadcast on the true facts of the border crisis.
(Music resumes. Two newshawks appear on either side of the stage. Both sport mustaches)
NEWSHAWK 1. War imminent! Read it in the *Observer*!
NEWSHAWK 2. Showdown at the United Nations tomorrow! Read it in the *Sun of the Andes*!
NEWSHAWK 1. Bolivian delegate to the United Nations, Dr. Fortunato Concepcion Urubamba, flies to New York this evening, carrying emergency instructions from President Salamanca!
NEWSHAWK 2. Second Division called to arms! Paraguay refuses to evacuate Fort Vanguardia!
NEWSHAWK 1. President Salamanca discloses Argentine oil interests are urging Paraguay behind the scenes to provoke an armed conflict!
NEWSHAWK 2. Paraguayan atrocities! Read the second installment of "I was defiled in Paraguay," told by a Bolivian maiden! More sensational disclosures! Breath-taking dirty photographs in full color!
(Crowd buys papers. Roar of planes)
CROWD. The air force! Bomb the navels off their bellies! Good boys! Over the Chaco and away!
WOMAN. Lookeee—the pilot is waving!
MAN. Off he goes! Bomb the pants off of them!
MAN. Bolivian bombs are sacred bombs!
(Cheers. A large fat man dashes across the stage, pursued by a small man swinging an axe)
SMALL MAN. Filthy Paraguayan! *(Uproar)* No—leave him to me!
(Both off)
RADIO. The entire world has witnessed this example of Paraguayan cowardice. *(More music)*
NEWSHAWK 1. The federation of Bolivian Miners affirms its solidarity!
(Cheers)
NEWSHAWK 2. The Football League of Bolivia rallies to the fair cause!
(Cheers)
NEWSHAWK 1. The Women's Volunteer Organization reveals it has stocked 10,000 bandages for our brave soldiers at the front!
(Cheers)
(The fat man, pursued by the small man, rushes across the stage in the other direction)
FAT MAN *(bawling)*. My grandmother was born in Nicaragua!
SMALL MAN. Foreigner!

(Both off)
CHOCOLATE MAN. Chocolates! Bolivian chocolates! Instant energy for the coming struggle!
(Churchbells on the right)
WOMAN. The bells of the Holy Virgin.
WOMAN. They're celebrating a solemn mass for peace.
(Bells on the left)
MAN. Bravo! The bells of the Sacred Blood!
MAN. They're celebrating a solemn mass for victory.
(Martial music)
CROWD. The army!
(Four ragged soldiers, led by a brilliant general, march in and about)
MAN. Look at him: the hero of Huachacalla with his dreaded Bullies of the Pampas!
MURMURS. The hero of Huachacalla....
GIRLS. And our soldiers, our sons, our lovers, our brothers, our husbands, our fathers.
(They throw flowers on the soldiers and kiss them helter-skelter)
GIRL *(leaping on a platform)*. For the duration: Five dollars flat for any man in uniform!
(Soldiers cheer)
(Enter the modest virgins of La Paz, almost naked, in chorus line)

VIRGINS
We are the modest virgins of La Paz,
All daughters of good families (alas).[1]
Our thoughts on holy wedlock used to dwell,
But this is war, let's kiss and go to hell.
So don't forget us, lads, on your next spree:
We daughters of good families come free.

(The soldiers cheer again)
GIRL *(furious)*. Scabs! Amateurs!
NEWSHAWK 1. The women of Bolivia in scenes of personal commitment!
*(The virgins dance away, waving; the soldiers begin to
march after them. A little boy, dressed in a white sheet, appears)*
BOY. Halt!
GENERAL. Halt!
(One soldier keeps marching)

---

1 The "alas" is piped by a solo voice.

GENERAL. Halt, I said!
(The others make him halt)
SOLDIER. He's deaf in the second ear, sir.
GENERAL. At ease! *(To the boy)* Oh sublime vision! Say, what art thou? Whence comest thou? Thou seemest to shine upon our countenances like a phantom out of the deepest time to be!
CROWD. Yea, thou seemest.
BOY. Kneel, soldiers, kneel, general, kneel, oh people of mother Bolivia. I am none other than the vision of the future generations for which you are about to die. Ah, let me take pride in you. Upon you all my watchful gaze is resting: do not fail me in the hour of danger; do not weaken; do not falter, Bolivians! The world knows that you do not raise the standard of liberty for mean and selfish purposes, for petty greed and low private ambitions. The world knows that you are laying down your lives for the future generations. We of the future generations sincerely thank you in advance. If you die for our sakes, we feel that you shall not have died in vain, but rather for the worthiest of all causes: us. *(He vanishes to gentle music)*
GENERAL. Sweet vision, do not go. Remain yet awhile. Alas, it is no more.
SOLDIERS. We see it no more.
CROWD. It is gone for aye.
MAN. But not from our memories.
GENERAL All right, men, get off the bloody gravel and look smart. Form ranks! Shoulder arms! Forward, hup two three four....
(Crowd cheers)

FIRST SOLDIER.
Three square meals each goddam day,
Cabbage, beans and coffee on our tray.
We're cannon fodder like the feller said,
But cannon fodder must be fed.

SECOND SOLDIER.
Our work ain't seasonal, we're always wanted,
We don't go home, not us, just 'cause the flag is planted.
No ma'am, the soldier's job is steady,
When one war's over the next one's getting ready.

THIRD SOLDIER.
The pay ain't much, so what, there's plenty of fresh air.
Fresh air ain't much, but busses is half-fare.
Half-fare ain't much, but who should grouse?

Plenty of women on the house!

FOURTH SOLDIER.
Course if you goof or play it dumb
Or show the foe a trembling bum,
With ten bullets in your belly you're retired,
But man you're in the army and can't be fired!

FIRST SOLDIER *(pointing to second soldier)*.
Thank God, the man what's gonna die ain't me, it's him,
Cause some has got to sink, but *I'm* the boy who'll swim.
That's why don't bug me, man, with no disloyal gripes.
I'm gonna die in bed with sergeant's stripes.

GENERAL. Enough singing! Keep in step, you sons of bitches! Look smart! Rodriguez, blow your nose. In your hanky, goddamit. Hup two three four.... Back to the barracks, men. Hup two three four....

OLD MAN. Hup two three four. Let every able-bodied man enlist! I'm too old to go, but I ain't too old to stir up others to go.

(Major Cucuchabaz appears as the army departs; he leaps on the platform)

VOICE. Viva Major Cucuchabaz, hero of Camarones! *(Cheers)*

NEWSHAWK. The unexpected appearance of Major Cucuchabaz galvanized the patriotic masses.

MAJOR. Our cause is just. Yes, old veteran, I embrace you. Here is my sword, riddled with wounds but gallant yet. Here is my rusty breast, a shield for my country against the enemy. We shall carry peace into the heart of the Chaco with a flaming brand. But citizens, will you renounce your quarrels and reaffirm your Bolivian solidarity with a single voice? You, for instance, you, what party do you vote for? Speak up, don't be afraid.

MAN. I'm a Liberal, major.

MAJOR. And you?

MAN. Radical Liberal.

MAJOR. And you, sweetheart?

WOMAN. Liberal Democrat.

MAJOR. And you, my good fellow?

MAN. Christian Radical.

MAJOR And you, dear?

GIRL. Free Democratic Union Liberal.

MAJOR. And you, dad?

MAN. Vegetarian Technocrat.

MAJOR. Now all of you, hug one another. Again, again! Ah sweet war, that brings neighbor and neighbor together. The enemy looks, and is confounded. United we stand.

NEWSHAWK. Major Cucuchabaz's moving words made an effect upon the people unparalleled in recent Bolivian history. As if caught by a fever of solidarity, they broke spontaneously into the song of Wartime Love.

> CROWD. *(part ensemble, part solo)*
> When peace dwelled in the land
> We were so mean, so low, so bad—
> He played the boss—She bit my hand—
> I caught your cold—And I was glad.
> When peace dwelled in the land
> We cut each other's throats all year.
> He took my job—You said be damned—
> She stole my man—He kicked my rear.
> When war came to the land
> We cried—Shake here—Dear friend—My dove
> United by our war we stand,
> Filled with sweetest wartime love.

(Enter two brawny young men carrying posters: FARMERS FOR THE CHACO: LET'S DIG IN and BOLIVIAN RADISHES SHALL SPROUT IN THE CHACO)

MAJOR. Our farmer lads! Join us, join us! My sword and your plough. Come into the shadow of the flag with me.

GIRL. What do the posters say? I can't read.

MAN. "Farmers for the Chaco: Let's Dig In," and "Bolivian Radishes shall sprout in the Chaco."

WOMAN. Can a girl feel your biceps, farmer-boy?

FARMER. Here. Some potato, hey?

WOMEN. Oooooh!

ANOTHER FARMER. Mine too. Feel them. The left one's better 'cause I'm a lefty. I can pitch twice the load of hay in half the time of any Paraguayan, lemme tell you.

WOMEN. Oooooh!

MAJOR. Young Bolivian manhood.

A YOUNG WOMAN. Young manhood hell! Draft-dodgers is what they are!

A MAN. Thass right.

FARMER. What did you say? Just say that again!

THE YOUNG WOMAN. They took my man away. Why aintchoo in uniform?

HONEST URUBAMBA

MAJOR. Children—solidarity—
FARMER. For half a turnip I'd shovel up your ugly snout.
MAN. Listen to that flour-sack! Are you picking on a girl is it?
FARMER 1. Come on, I'll pick on you and anything else that grows in this here slum.
MAN. Oh yeah? Cowhand. Go rassle a milkmaid in the daisies.
FARMER 2. He's insultin' us that feed the likes of him.
(He tries to hit the man with his placard)
MAJOR. Children! Bolivians!
MAN. You think you're gonna hit a defenseless bystander? Gimme that flag somebody!
THE YOUNG WOMAN. Take it. Go on. Stick it into the draft-dodger.
FARMER 2. He struck me with the sacred emblem—I'm bleedin'!
MAJOR. Our sacred emblem!
FARMER 1. I'm comin' to the rescue!
MAJOR. Keep them apart. Get them reconciled! Give me that flag, you there! *(Swinging his sword, he manages to conquer the flag)* Embrace, my lads, unite against the common enemy.
FARMER 1. My pal's bleeding.
CROWD *(they have been holding the combatants down)*. Go on—have a beer instead—all three of you.
FARMER 2 *(to the girl)*. Did you call me a draft-dodger too?
CROWD. No she didn't. Go on, go on with the others.
VOICE. And take your lousy spuds to the Chaco.
FARMER 2. Who said that?
CROWD. Nobody!
(They are hustled off the stage. The flag is replaced)
NEWSHAWK 1. So great was the popular fervor that here and there a good-natured commotion occurred, quickly dissolved in a renewed outburst of public togetherness.
NEWSHAWK 2. At every moment the spirited crowd was treated to another manifestation of civic enthusiasm.
A GIRL. Look who's coming!
(Enter four men carrying the foreigner on their shoulders)
FOREIGNER. Mon âme pleine d' amour pour la Bolivie....
MAN. A lousy foreigner!
MAJOR. No! He is the Foreign Volunteer!
(Crowd cheers. The foreigner is carried off)
NEWSHAWK 2. In a gesture of spontaneous affection and loyalty to their adopted land, the foreign colony of La Paz contributed a splendid corps of

volunteers to the armed forces.

RADIO. We interrupt our patriotic music to bring you a news bulletin. At dawn today a force of two thousand Paraguayan infantrymen, supported by heavy mortar fire, mounted a surprise attack on the Bolivian fort of Pitiantuta. Our heavily outnumbered garrison is staging a heroic defense against the brutal invader.

RADIO PARAGUAY. It's a lie! This is Radio Paraguay, the Voice of Truth. The Paraguayan military command categorically denies that its forces have launched an attack on Fort Pitiantuta or at any other point in the Gran Chaco. This is yet another in the long series of vindictive, malicious and futile lies spouted by Bolivian provocateurs and warmongers, whose imperialistic designs on the Paraguayan Chaco are known to the entire world.

RADIO BOLIVIA. Another bulletin from Radio Bolivia! The outnumbered Bolivian forces manning Fort Pitiantuta have compelled the enemy to raise his siege, and dramatically reversed the military situation. Our army is once again in full control. Paraguayan casualties are heavy. On our side it is reported that a Bolivian corporal suffered minor scratches in a cactus patch while pursuing the Paraguayan cavalry. According to the latest dispatches, the enemy is falling back in a disorderly rout.

RADIO PARAGUAY. The Bolivian propaganda machine cranks on! But the truth cannot remain concealed for long. Our troops have captured Fort Pitiantuta. We are in undisputed possession. Three hundred exhausted and undernourished Bolivian soldiers have fallen into our hands, and have requested political asylum. The Chaco— *(static, roars, silence)*

MAJOR. Jammed at last. There is no power on this earth so strong as the naked truth. Listen, my friends, to the guilty silence of Radio Paraguay.

RADIO BOLIVIA. We resume our program with a selection of patriotic sambas.

GIRL *(worried)*. Is the war really on?

WOMAN *(to a friend)*. I'm gonna lay in a few pounds of sugar. *(Off)*

CROWD *(waving flags, dubiously)*. Hurrah???

NEWSHAWK 1. Declaration of President Salamanca, extra, extra: "We are determined to make a last effort to secure a peaceful and honorable settlement of the issue which divides our two nations. Our ambassador to the United Nations, Dr. Fortunato Concepcion Urubamba, has instructions to explore every possible avenue of conciliation which does not imperil our national security."

MAJOR. And now, citizens, attend. I give you Fortunato Concepcion Urubamba, the flower of Bolivian diplomacy!

(Enter Urubamba, carrying a briefcase and an umbrella)

MAJOR. Sir: the people of Bolivia and I the hero of Camarones, greet you, and wish you God's speed in the difficult task that awaits you in New York.

(Cheers)

URUBAMBA. Thank you, Major Cucuchabaz. Friends and citizens, I pledge myself to work unremittingly for the good of our country.

A MAN. Tell the Yankees we're buying an atom bomb from the Rooshians.

ANOTHER. Tell the Russians the Americans are promising to lend us the good old hydrogen bomb.

ANOTHER. Bring back grants and corn flakes and weapons and experts and whiskey.

ANOTHER. Tell 'em a passel of lies!

URUBAMBA *(shocked)*. Lies? Lies, my friends?

THE MAN. I meant for the good of the country—not lies, really, but the right kind of lingo, you know—

URUBAMBA. The Holy Virgin defend me. I thank God that our country needs no lies, as some others do. I have studied the old border dispute, my good people. Our cause, I am happy to report, is just. Otherwise I would not represent it. And, given time enough and the efforts of good men and women, right always prevails in the world, along with freedom, democracy, and justice. And now, allow me to get through—I am on my way to the airport. Remember, my conscience is satisfied.

MAJOR *(privately)*. A diplomat with a conscience, Dr. Urubamba? This could be dangerous.

URUBAMBA *(benevolent)*. Tut tut, major. You will not part me from my conscience. I don't go anywhere without it. Well—

MAJOR. Wait. What do you propose to say when the Paraguayan shows his map of 1620?

URUBAMBA. I reject the map of 1620, I annihilate it with my Charter of 1583, which proves that the Gran Chaco lay within the jurisdiction of the Bolivian Court District.

MAJOR. What about that lousy Soler-Pinilla Protocol of 1907?

URUBAMBA. A protocol is a protocol, my friend; it is dignified but it has no legal standing. *(He turns to the crowd)* People of Bolivia, have faith. I intend to bring you back a favorable vote in the World Assembly and major concessions from Paraguay. And now—

CHOCOLATE MAN. Dr. Urubamba, I would like to offer you a chocolate bar as a gift from the common people.

URUBAMBA. Thank you, my good man. But an official is not allowed to accept gifts. Thank you. I really must be on my way. Farewell. *(Cheers; he*

leaves)
A MAN. Urubamba will show those horse thieves who's in the saddle!
MAJOR. A lovely man. And honest as my mother's milk.
(Urubamba returns)
URUBAMBA. One more thing. Don't for God's sake overthrow the government while I'm up there pleading our cause.
MAJOR *(moved)*. We won't, Dr. Urubamba. Not this week. Allow me to assure you— *(He follows Urubamba out)*
(A moment of silence. Then a man leaps to the flag)

A CITIZEN.

From border to border
Joy and disorder!
Rumba, samba,
Urubamba!

(The crowd goes wild. The radio blares, the newshawks shout, the crowd yells and dances, the boy reappears selling flags, the soldiers and farmers re-enter, general enthusiasm and amity)
NEWSHAWKS. War imminent—Final peace efforts—Urubamba confident—Vickers of England pledges to strengthen Bolivian army—Is Paraguay trying to distract its people from home troubles by its imperialistic adventures?—French war profiteers sign contract to beef up Paraguay with fighter planes—Airport statement from Dr. Urubamba: "Decency and honesty shall be my guides at the United Nations."
BOY. Patriotic tunes, fifty cents a sheet! Cut-rate flags! Paraguay dolls with two-weeks supply of pins! Loyalist buttons! Photos of Bolivian generals in three volumes!

CROWD.

Oh happy happy happy we
To quell the Paraguayans' infamy!
And when our might those bastards quells,
We'll go on quelling someone else!

(Crowd leaves. Only the newshawks, dancing arm in arm, remain)

NEWSHAWK 1.

And when our might Bolivia quells,
We'll go on quelling someone else!

Noble words!
NEWSHAWK 2. Say you so, brother newshawk?
NEWSHAWK 1. I do. But as for being your brother newshawk, I'm not so sure.
NEWSHAWK 2. Why aren't you sure?
NEWSHAWK 1 *(tearing off his mustache)*. That's why.
NEWSHAWK 2. Blodgett! The Industrial Magnate! *(Tears off his mustache)*
NEWSHAWK 1. Pimpkin! The Labor Union Leader!
(They fall into each other's arms)
PIMPKIN. Good old war-monger!
BLODGETT. Dear old hate-peddler!
PIMPKIN. Great days, what?
BLODGETT. I'll say. Brace the nerve.
PIMPKIN. Stiffen the bowel.
BLODGETT. Production rates are soaring.
PIMPKIN. Wages are up.
BLODGETT. New plants are being built.
PIMPKIN. Wages are up.
BLODGETT. Stock averages climbed 18 points overnight.
PIMPKIN. Wages are up.
BLODGETT. You old union agitator, where's the class war now?
PIMPKIN. The what war? Let's sing the Song of Industrial Peace.

PIMPKIN.
There's no class war in a first-class war—
Owners, workers pull together.
There's money in the air, so roar roar roar
For bloody thundering weather.
BLODGETT.
Our stock, from bullet to atomic pile,
Is wrapped up for delivery.
We'll quote you with a cheerful smile
The going price of victory.

TOGETHER *(saluting the flag)*.
Drive out the foe, but slowly please,
Don't jostle the production rate.
Give us a hundred costly victories,
Oh generals, to celebrate.

BLODGETT. Which leaves us only with Urubamba to worry about, our peace-loving delegate to the United Nations. Shall I discredit him in the press? There's a picture of him at dinner in the same room with a Paraguayan only nine years ago.
PIMPKIN. Oh I don't know, Blodgett. I think you're unfair to the man. Is Urubamba a thief?
BLODGETT. I didn't say that.
PIMPKIN. Then he won't rob us of our hopes. Is he a killer?
BLODGETT. Oh no.
PIMPKIN. Then he won't stab our war effort. Is he dishonest?
BLODGETT. Dishonest he is not.
PIMPKIN. Then he won't cheat us of our expectations.
BLODGETT. Say you so, brother?
PIMPKIN. Take it from me. Goodbye now, I'm off to inspire the masses.
BLODGETT. And I, to stimulate the business community.
(They shake hands and part. Silence on the empty stage. Then a hideously wounded soldier stumbles in and falls before the flag)
WOUNDED SOLDIER *(ultimate terror)*. Mother, I was the first one—who died!
(Wild cacophony of music and crowds on the radio, in the midst of which…)
RADIO. Latest news! Dr. Fortunato Concepcion Urubamba has landed in New York!

SCENE TWO

(The United Nations. A few delegates, white, yellow, and black, are sitting and half-listening. One plays a surreptitious yo-yo. One emits an occasional snore. A number of empty chairs. Onesto Morales, the Paraguayan delegate, is nearing the end of his speech. The President of the Assembly is in his seat. Sitting among the delegates, Urubamba is listening in very visible discomfort, and frequently mops his brow and nibbles his knuckles)

MORALES. As for their so-called possession of the Chaco, it is an uncontroverted historical fact that the last official Bolivian attempt to penetrate into that territory occurred in the sixteenth century, when Captain Andres Manso, a Bolivian adventurer, was boiled alive by the outraged Indians whom he sought to baptize. Bolivia lost interest, and retreated behind the fortifications of the Andes. The rest is a story of occasional private interlopers, shabby incursions and shabbier setbacks. Until your government, Dr. Urubamba, was ignominiously beaten away from the Pacific Ocean by Chile in 1883, and until your government, Dr. Urubamba, began to suspect the existence of oilfields under the Chaco—until that time your government took less interest in the Chaco than we do in Alaska. I could distribute maps drawn by as many "experts" as my esteemed colleague has been pleased to call upon for his side; I could exhibit Royal Charters, Privileges, Decrees dating back to the days of Pizarro himself! But what are ancient maps against fact? Fact tells us that Paraguay has held the Gran Chaco for three and a half centuries. Held, gentlemen, settled, colonized, ploughed, policed. It is we who impose and collect taxes on the ageless legal principle that he who owns a land taxes it, and he who taxes a land owns it. And to us fell the difficult tasks of converting the Indians to the Christian faith and of wiping them out—both privileges stemming directly from the King of Spain, as stated in the royal decrees of January 23, 1765 and July 15, 1769, of which you have received copies. Come, Dr. Urubamba, do you deny these facts? Or do you claim that we Paraguayans have been squatting illegally upon your land since 1580, without so much as a protest from your side for three hundred years? But my Bolivian colleague is feebly waving his copy of that excellent Charter of 1583, which calls the Chaco a portion of the Bolivian Court District. He has given each one of you a photocopy of this interesting document. I remind you that I never denied its authenticity. The truth will never find a more ardent supporter than the government of Paraguay. But Paraguayan exhibit number 462—and I ask you to glance once more at the photocopies I have distributed of our documents—Dr. Urubamba, will you oblige me with another glance?—this exhibit is, it seems to me, a decisive one. 1581. Observe the date. 1581. The seal of King Philip II, of revered memory. I quote. "Let it be known to our beloved Viceroy in La Paz that whereas the Law Court residing at Sucre and La Paz shall sway under God from the Ocean to the Argentines, the authority of the executive bodies, of the administration, and of the constabulary forces shall be confined to the land lying West of the Chain of the Andes." I read no further. The truth has burst into full view. What Bolivia never held in fact it never held in law. All that remains to me is to call upon Dr. Urubamba, whose integrity is well known to this Assembly—I need only recall his splendidly impartial decisions as arbitrator in Puah-Puah at the time of the Fifilese uprisings—and to call upon the people of Bolivia, whom we embrace as brothers in spite of these differences of ours; to call finally upon the government in La Paz to heed the voice of reason and the claims of justice: join us, I say, join the people of Paraguay in seeking the flower of peace under the jagged stones of controversy. I thank you.

(He regains his seat. Hand-clapping. The President hems, shuffles papers. His aide whispers at him now and then)

PRESIDENT. We have just heard—indeed—the delegate from—from—I believe—Paraguay—ah yes—the forty-first crisis of this season—this session. The issue being debated—the Chaco—we shall put a suitable motion—after preliminary procedural dispositions—the roll call of course—unless a veto—

AIDE *(whispering)*. You must call on the Bolivian delegate, sir. Article 126, as amended.

PRESIDENT. Ah yes—there *is* always another side, isn't there? I daresay that is why God gave us two ears. Where are the documents? *(He confers in a low voice with the aide)*

DELEGATE A *(low)*. Shall we see you at the Japanese Grand Ball tonight, Ossip?

DELEGATE B. You joke! We are launching the fishing boat crisis this afternoon.

DELEGATE A *(appalled)*. Before the Grand Ball? Is that the action of a mature state?

PRESIDENT. I've got it now. Dr. Fortunato Concepcion Urubamba. Please take the floor and let us hear the other just side. Dr. Urubamba? Are you with us?

URUBAMBA. I am, Mr. President, I am. *(He rises painfully and walks slowly to the rostrum, where he remains speechless)*

DELEGATE C *(waking up suddenly)*. Huh. What's the silence? I'm frightened. The United Nations are never silent!

EVERYBODY. Sssh. For shame.

DELEGATE D. Urubamba is about to speak.

DELEGATE C. Oh, the Congo again. Good night. *(Instantly falls asleep again)*

URUBAMBA. Fellow delegates to the United Nations. As the delegate of the Republic of Bolivia, I am called upon to—it is my duty—my instructions—in brief, my instructions are to instruct you in the—to point out the justice—in short, to speak. In the past forty-eight hours, I have had greater leisure to restudy the claims—that is to say to review the Chaco problem once more. I have given the documents presented to the Assembly by my honorable colleague and I may truly say, my friend, Dr. Onesto Morales, the delegate of the Republic of Paraguay, who has been addressing this Assembly, and who, you will recollect, has appealed to our sense of honor, of justice, of reason—claims which touch me personally—deeply—indeed—deeply, for he did not allude in vain to these principles, which govern, I hope, the actions of all our governments, and of their representatives, among whom I have been numbered these three years and two months—not unhonorably, I think, as indeed Dr. Morales was good enough to note when he referred to the difficulties in Puah Puah, and—aaah—as I was saying—

PRESIDENT. Do you need a break, Dr. Urubamba?

URUBAMBA. No thank you—thank you kindly. In short, the evidence is all too clear—the documents—the Royal Charter of 1581—not to mention the facts—in a word— *(He draws a deep breath)* Paraguay is right, we haven't a leg to stand on, and there it is.

(The delegates have sat up. Gasps)

DELEGATE D *(nudging Delegate C in vain)*. Wake up, wake up!

DELEGATE A *(dazed)*. President, a word, a point of order....

PRESIDENT *(who has dropped his gavel)*. Excuse me, Dr. Urubamba, but I think we failed to catch your meaning. May I ask you to repeat?

MORALES *(choking)*. Yes—repeat. I feel faint.

URUBAMBA *(drawing another deep breath)*. My country is in the wrong. Our documents are worthless. I suspect we forged two or three of them. Ah, so did Paraguay—

MORALES. An open insult!

URUBAMBA. But Paraguay was right anyway. *(Crying out)* The Gran Chaco belongs to Paraguay! I must care for my soul!

(General panic)

DELEGATE E. His soul!

PRESIDENT. Shocking! Offensive!

DELEGATES. This is outrageous—A scandal here, here of all places!—Indecent exposure—A maniac!—I refuse to be a witness—Hear hear—Shame! *(The cry is taken up)* Shame! Shame!

DELEGATE F. In view of the circumstances, this delegation boycotts the meeting. Make way please!

DELEGATE A. Us too. Positively shameful. Excuse me.

DELEGATES. With your permission—allow me—excuse me please—may I?

MORALES. Wait—wait—don't go!

(Rush to the exit)

PRESIDENT. The meeting is adjourned and struck from the record! It has not existed!

MORALES. Wait everybody!

DELEGATE C *(waking up in the rush)*. Hey, hey! *(Catching somebody's coattails)* What happened?
DELEGATE B *(pointing to Urubamba)*. Honesty! *Honest* honesty!
DELEGATE C *(suddenly commanding)*. Keep the reporters out! *(He runs away with the others)*
MORALES. Wait everybody! My government utterly rejects and disavows— *(Left alone with Urubamba)*. They're gone. Fortunato my boy, why have you done this? Are you ill? Lean on me. What made you give in?
(A reporter rushes in. Morales jumps away from Urubamba)
REPORTER. Dr. Morales, do you have a statement for United Press?
MORALES *(thundering)*. I do! The Paraguay denounces the Bolivian move as a desperate device which will deceive no one. This maneuver, whose transparent goal is to cause Paraguay to relax its vigilance, will be met with renewed firmness and resolution.
REPORTER. Thank you, sir. *(Rushes off)*
MORALES. Fortunato, speak to me! I'll call the delegates back! There's time yet for a retraction. Denounce me a little, for God's sake!
URUBAMBA. I can't—Onesto—something here *(he points to his heart)*....
MORALES. All right, but listen to me. *(Whispering)* Fortunato, you're finished. Don't return to La Paz. I'll make you comfortable in Asunciòn. You and your family....
URUBAMBA *(embracing Morales)*. No, Onesto, no. Thank you, but no.

SCENE THREE

(Cabinet meeting in La Paz. Members attending: President Salamanca, Ministers of the Exterior, Interior, Defense, Transportation, Commerce, and Information. With them: a couple of aides, and a nurse who is giving pills and glasses of water to the Cabinet. General despondency. Now and then a noise of clamoring multitudes in the distance)

SALAMANCA *(to the nurse)*. What's the idea of giving me only two pills, like the others? Am I the President of this jackass republic or what the hell?
NURSE. I am ever so sorry, President Salamanca. *(She gives him extra pills)* *(A cabinet member sobs)*
COMMERCE. My country, my Bolivia.
DEFENSE. Disgraced.

TRANSPORTATION And the people—outraged—humiliated—listen to them, our heads may fall.
ALL. Ooooh. *(Their hands go out for more pills)*
EXTERIOR. Couldn't you call the army out to defend us, Carrion?
DEFENSE. Don't give the army ideas.
SALAMANCA. It's dangerous to be defended too much.
INFORMATION. Is Urubamba still in the anteroom?
AIDE. Yes, sir.
INFORMATION. Guarded?
INTERIOR. Three policemen are supposed to be sitting on him.
SALAMANCA. Just wait till I bring him to trial. I'll try the pudding out of him, I'll try him from the end of a rope. A man I trusted like a brother....
TRANSPORTATION. He seemed so honest, I can't understand it....
(Silence. Sighs, a sob or two)
INFORMATION. Listen to that mob. Lousy rabble. *(Pulls out a pistol, puts bullets in it)*
COMMERCE. My dear Gomez!
INFORMATION. As Minister of Information, I can tell you this speaks better than me.
EXTERIOR. What do we do, President Salamanca?
SALAMANCA. Until the messenger arrives, we'll stand firm and do nothing.
INTERIOR. I have seen plumbers and charwomen weeping in the streets.
COMMERCE. Bolivia, Bolivia, I shall die of grief and shame.... *(He slumps)*
SALAMANCA. Come on, Alessandro, buck up. A little grief is good for your circulation.
DEFENSE. Ortiz, look here, what's the matter with you? Nurse!
NURSE. Dr. Ortiz! *(Examines him)* He's dead of grief and shame.
SALAMANCA. I'll be damned!
EXTERIOR. A shining example to us.
INTERIOR. Only yesterday I was playing tennis with him.
SALAMANCA. Ayala, as Minister of Transportation—a sad duty—
TRANSPORTATION. Me? Well, I suppose— *(He and the aide carry out the Minister of Commerce)*
SALAMANCA. My heart's near breaking too, and our country shown up for a weakling. When I think of our past—who had the right to sneer at us up to this moment? Every year a hundred forceful declarations, accusations, challenges, denials, protests as good as any country can show—we've been called brutal aggressors as far away as Denmark—and now....
EXTERIOR. All up in smoke—in one evil minute.

(The Minister of Transportation reappears)
TRANSPORTATION. News! The messenger is arriving at last!
SEVERAL. At last! The messenger!
SALAMANCA. Nurse, leave us now. Remove these pills. What will we be hearing? Santa Maria dolorosa, what will it be?
AIDE *(flinging open the door)*. The Messenger!
MESSENGER *(entering to the sound of trumpets)*. Bolivia, I bear tidings of glorious events!
(She is a creature from a fairy tale: a vision of gold and silver, blue and pink resplendance; brocades and sequins, satins and laces, a shimmer of cascading yellow hair, a coruscating train held up by a cherub, and a wand in her right hand)
SALAMANCA. Speak, Messenger; we had almost lost the will to live.
MESSENGER. Bolivians, behold, I bring you comfort, high pride, and sweet replenishment. The honor of our ancient realm is secured: the war has begun.
ALL *(coming to life)*. Ah!
SALAMANCA. I knew it, I sensed it.
EXTERIOR. My spirit never flagged.
INFORMATION. Trust the noble people of Bolivia.
SALAMANCA. Speak on, Lady Messenger, tell us all you know.
MESSENGER. My tale is brief. No sooner had the traitorous Urubamba received his sudden dismissal from the post he darkened with infamy than his successor rose before an expectant Assembly of the potentates of this earth to prove to the world the sacred claims of mother Bolivia to its child the Gran Chaco. Conscious of high and bloody destiny, he cast his indignant challenge at the Paraguayan bosom, and, filling with his voice the shivering silence of the appareled hall, he confirmed our historic determination that the Chaco, which must be ours, by the just heavens shall be ours!
SALAMANCA. A sage.
INTERIOR. A patriot at last.
MESSENGER. The Paraguayan delegate shed tears and perspiration in vain. Suddenly the powers nodded. The ballots were cast. Eighty-seven voices crushing one dissenting vote gave the world's decision, which I am charged with reciting to you: "The Assembly of the United Nations expresses its support for a just settlement of the dispute which has arisen over the Gran Chaco." This decisive vindication of the Bolivian cause compels you to act at once. Give the command! History is watching you!
(The trumpets blow, and the Messenger leaves)
SALAMANCA *(jumping up)*. Manuel, send a wire at once to Colonel Rojos.

He is to attack Fort Masamaklay within the hour of receiving your order. I want the fort recaptured before tomorrow morning. At any cost. Repeat: at any cost.

DEFENSE. Done!

(He dashes away)

SALAMANCA. Gentlemen, to work. What's next on the agenda?

TRANSPORTATION. Urubamba, by God and by Satan.

EXTERIOR. The quicker and quieter the better.

INTERIOR. We give him a fair trial in three minutes and hang him this afternoon.

TRANSPORTATION. I know just the lamppost.

INFORMATION. Gentlemen, gentlemen, what is this? I'm simply shocked.

SALAMANCA. You, Gomez?

INFORMATION. Yes, I. You are planning a gross injustice, a gross, gross injustice, and as Minister of Information I raise my voice against it.

SALAMANCA *(worried)*. What injustice are you talking about? It's a legal hanging.

INFORMATION. If you hang Urubamba, you'll be admitting to the world that we stupidly sent a traitor to represent us at the United Nations. A pretty picture of us! Well, I call this conception of Bolivia a gross injustice to our nation.

EXTERIOR. It's a good point, but how can we help it? It's all been in the open, you know, and the harm's done.

SALAMANCA. He's right Gomez. Your scruples do you honor, but we're stuck with Urubamba.

INFORMATION. Not necessarily. I propose that we redeem him.

(General surprise)

SALAMANCA. But how? The man's plainly a traitor.

INFORMATION. No. The man is plainly—insane. *(Silence. Effect)*

SALAMANCA. A stroke of genius!

TRANSPORTATION. An idea altogether worthy of you, Gomez.

EXTERIOR. By the glorious Virgin, this will wipe the grins off the diplomatic set. We'll be able to hold up our heads at cocktail parties again.

INTERIOR. Bring in the rascal at once.

SALAMANCA *(to an aide)*. Tell the guards to get off Urubamba and have him come in.

(Exit aide)

SALAMANCA. Compose your faces, my friends, into a mask of indignant hostility.

(The Cabinet do so)

INFORMATION. But at the same time, may I suggest a relaxed expression? Give me permission to question him and to humor him into a confession. Relax, gentlemen, look friendly.

(Faces relax)

SALAMANCA. I leave him to you, Gomez.

AIDE *(appearing)*. Dr. Fortunato Concepcion Urubamba.

(Enter Urubamba, his clothes in shreds)

URUBAMBA. President Salamanca, members and friends of the cabinet—

INFORMATION. Your appearance, sir—

URUBAMBA. The people, Alfredo—I mean Dr. Gomez—a strange misunderstanding of my motives.

INFORMATION. Ah, your motives?

URUBAMBA. Yes. The common people failed—I don't know—They are not capable of judging fine moral points—they failed to understand—my honesty—my—they tore my clothes, called me vile names—

SALAMANCA. You don't say.

URUBAMBA. But here—intelligent men, thank heaven—my own peers, so to speak—my colleagues—

SALAMANCA. Ha!

URUBAMBA. President Salamanca, you and I were students together—in Professor Arvieja's law seminar—Fundamentals of Justice—and you—San Martín—in the consular service—in short—

INFORMATION. In short?

URUBAMBA. You understand me.

INFORMATION. And?

URUBAMBA *(suddenly firm)*. You will reinstate me.

INFORMATION. Perhaps. But will you first submit to a brief, though formal, interrogation? Merely for the record.

URUBAMBA. I'll answer anything.

INFORMATION. The questions may seem strange to you. I'll be open with you, Urubamba; you've behaved in an unorthodox manner in New York.

SALAMANCA. The United Nations may never recover.

INFORMATION. And we want to look into— well— frankly —

URUBAMBA. My mental condition.

INFORMATION. Yes.

URUBAMBA. I'll answer all your questions, Alfredo.

INFORMATION. Good. *(He goes to a door, and opens it)* Will you come in, sir?

(Enter the CIA agent, a figure robed in black from head to foot. The cabinet members are startled and frightened. They creep nearer to one another. Urubamba is surprised)

SALAMANCA. Who is that?

INFORMATION. Don't you recognize him, President?
SALAMANCA. Recognize *who?* Come on, Gomez, what's the story?
EXTERIOR *(crosses himself)*. Sweet Jesus....
INFORMATION. I've simply called in a CIA agent to conduct the interrogation.
SALAMANCA. What in holy damnation is the CIA?
CIA MAN. The Committee on Insidious Agitation. Maybe.
INFORMATION. I'm dumbfounded, President Salamanca. The CIA is the highest security branch of the Bolivian administration.
SALAMANCA *(bawling)*. Then why haven't I been told about it?
CIA MAN. We're fabulously secret. The fact is, I am possibly not a CIA man at all.
SALAMANCA. What does *that* mean?
CIA MAN. I might be a woman disguised as a man. Or a man disguised as a woman impersonating a man. I am not supposed to be sure. Or maybe I am.
SALAMANCA *(squealing)*. But I'm the president of this asstail republic!
INTERIOR *(timidly)*. How about us? I'm Minister of the Interior.
INFORMATION. And as such, Prado, you will be so kind as to take notes of the proceedings. That is, President, assuming we are ready to proceed.
SALAMANCA. Yes, I order you to proceed.
CIA MAN. Thank you, President Salamanca. Dr. Urubamba, a simple question: how many ten-centavo coins were situated in your pocket last Tuesday at nine o'clock in the evening?
URUBAMBA. Is this a game, sir? I mean—
INFORMATION. This is deadly serious, Urubamba. It is nothing less than psychology. And remember, we haven't got forever.
EXTERIOR. There's a war going on.
URUBAMBA. A war? Oh God, did the war break out?
CIA MAN. The question, please. How many ten-centavo coins were in your pocket last Tuesday evening?
URUBAMBA. This is absurd. I don't know. How should I know?
CIA MAN. Thank you. Take note, Dr. Prado. Dr. Urubamba has lost his memory for the simplest recent events of his own life.
INTERIOR *(puzzled)*. Yes, of course.
URUBAMBA. This is outrageous. I have *not* lost my memory! What childish game is this?
CIA MAN. Thank you, Dr. Urubamba. We appreciate your cooperation. Next question. How much is 8.37912 minus 6.9716? A few seconds should be ample.

URUBAMBA. I protest. This is a monstrous—
CIA MAN. It is not a monstrous, Dr. Urubamba. Kindly answer the question.
URUBAMBA. How can a man answer that kind of question? Without even a pencil.
CIA MAN *(solicitous)*. Here is pencil and paper.
URUBAMBA. This is a farce. *(He makes the subtraction)* 1.40752.
CIA MAN. Thank you. That is correct *(Signals to Prado)* Dr. Urubamba cannot subtract figures under 10 without a pencil.
URUBAMBA. This is grotesque—a trap—let me go!
INFORMATION. Cristobal, kindly help Dr. Urubamba back to his seat. Thank you.
URUBAMBA. Heaven cries out—
SALAMANCA. Damn it, Fortunato, leave heaven upstairs. What are you complaining about? Are we pulling your nails out? Are we burning you with cigarettes? Are we threatening you? You ought to thank us.
URUBAMBA. I'm sorry....
CIA MAN. It's only a routine check, Dr. Urubamba. Now I want to ask you: last Thursday, while you were going up the escalator of the Buen Gusto department store, what person you are well acquainted with stood in the crowd that was coming down the escalator?
URUBAMBA. How should I know? I was thinking coffee pots!
CIA MAN. Please enter, Dr. Prado. Dr. Urubamba did not recognize his own sister-in-law at less than two meters from himself.
URUBAMBA. Stop this! Stop this right away!
CIA MAN. It cannot be stopped. Now tell me, Dr. Urubamba, simply, on what latitude and longitude does your house stand? Be honest, sir, and give us a fairly accurate answer.
URUBAMBA *(shouts)*. Monster, I don't know! *(Breaks down)*
CIA MAN. Thank you. That will do. Dr. Urubamba does not know the whereabouts of his own domicile. President Salamanca, members of the cabinet, it appears from a confidential routine check that Dr. Urubamba's mental stability is seriously impaired. He has lost his memory, he cannot make under-10 additions and subtractions in his head, he does not recognize persons utterly familiar to him, he cannot tell us the location of his own house. Furthermore, he has admitted that he is subject to fits of madness, as is shown by the minutes of the interrogation. This, however, is as far as the responsibility of the Committee on Insidious Agitation goes. The secular arm must do the rest.
(As he goes, all huddle away from him)
TRANSPORTATION *(crosses himself)*. Mother of God....

SALAMANCA. Hey, you're walking into the wall!
(But the wall opens, the CIA agent vanishes, the wall returns to normal)
URUBAMBA. I protest!
TRANSPORTATION. Did you really know nothing about—about *them*, Salamanca?
SALAMANCA. Oh, I wouldn't say that. You can never tell. I may have made believe....
INTERIOR *(dreamily)*. Maybe I'm one myself.
EXTERIOR. It would be nice....
INFORMATION. Gentlemen, shall we?
SALAMANCA. Right. Back to Urubamba, all of you. Gomez, take over again.
INFORMATION. Will those who favor the motion that Dr. Fortunato Urubamba is insane raise their hands and say aye?
ALL. Aye!
URUBAMBA. Nay!
INFORMATION. As the object of the motion, you are naturally disqualified from voting. President?
SALAMANCA. I hereby declare Urubamba insane.
URUBAMBA. Let me go! You'll murder me next!
EXTERIOR. Delusions of persecution.
URUBAMBA. Oh God, oh God, I am in your hands now.
EXTERIOR. Delusions of grandeur.
SALAMANCA. Fortunato Concepcion Urubamba, stand up! On grounds of legal and illegal insanity, you are stripped of all your posts, dignities, civil rights, and emoluments. Your birth certificate is rescinded. Your labor permit is revoked. Your passport is recalled. You become an individual without legal footing and standing, except for your inalienable right to be taxed.
INFORMATION. As Minister of Information, I shall issue a public release at once. *(He leaves)*
URUBAMBA. And still I say: Bolivia was wrong.
SALAMANCA. The patient has lost touch with reality.

SCENE FOUR

(Family scene at the home of the Urubambas. Urubamba, Mrs. Urubamba, their little son Pepe—with a bandaged head—the father-in-law General Cochón, and Aunt Urubamba. Mrs. Urubamba is holding her son and sniffling. General Cochón is patting her hand)

COCHON. My daughter, this won't do. The Cochóns don't give way.
MRS. URUBAMBA. But how can I bear it? This morning the butcher refused to sell me veal cutlets. And look at Pepe.
PEPE. They knocked my head to pieces in school because daddy betrayed his country they said.
(Groans and weeping)
COCHON. Child, child, this curse will stunt your growth. Better if I strike you down at once and spare you a life of suffering.
MRS. URUBAMBA. Father! Put back your sword!
COCHON. You women have no pride. But for myself, the alternatives were clear. Either I turn in my sword, or, in my old age, I carry it to the field of honor. I didn't turn in my sword.
MRS. URUBAMBA. Father!
AUNT. It's easy for you men. But what about us women: unmarried women especially. To what field of honor are we going to carry ourselves?
COCHON. You're only his aunt, Miss Urubamba.
AUNT. Only his aunt! I was on the Entertainment Committee of the Library and Museum Association, and now they've put me in the back room licking envelopes. Only his aunt! And under a weak bulb, too.
MRS. URUBAMBA. I'm sorry, auntie.
(Urubamba turns away, as if to leave)
COCHON. Stop, sir. You do not leave this house without making reparations. Who owns the property? The automobile? The securities?
MRS. URUBAMBA. I'm too delicate to listen to these horrors. Let me go.
AUNT. So much refinement, and such suffering....
MRS. URUBAMBA. Pepe, come with me.
PEPE. They say that daddy is a scum in the earth.
(They leave)
AUNT. There you are, Fortunato. Look at your handiwork. You're killing your wife, you've ruined your innocent babe, and I don't even talk about *us*.
COCHON. To the point.
(He takes a document out of his wallet and places it on the table. Urubamba signs without

reading it. He removes a ring from his finger)
URUBAMBA. Two diamonds.
(General Cochón places the signed document and the ring in an envelope, seals it, and returns it to his wallet. Aunt Urubamba breaks down)
COCHON. Miss Urubamba, control yourself!
AUNT. If I could only change my name, if I could only go away! Saying on a platform the Paraguayans are right and we are liars! What did we ever do to you, Fortunato? You were always a good boy!
COCHON. Be brave, Miss Urubamba.
AUNT. I refused a dozen offers so I could devote myself to the family, little thinking the day would come I'd do anything to bear another name, even marry a man.
(Martial music outside)
COCHON. The 94th Cavalry. My old outfit. Hearts and hooves beating in unison. Bugles fifes, pennons in the wind. *(Re-enter Mrs. Urubamba and Pepe)* My child! I go to my last battle, my mustache erect to the end. May the blood of a Cochón cover the foul stain on the name of Urubamba. *(Gives her the envelope)* Keep this. The property is yours. And remember your father. He sought the bullet that found him.
MRS. URUBAMBA. Oh father! I'm so proud of you. I'll visit your grave twice a year.
(They kiss. Cochón kisses Pepe)
COCHON. Pepe, be brave. Miss Urubamba, the horses neigh, and I go. I kiss your hand. *(He leaves)*
(Mrs. Urubamba and Pepe run to the window and wave)
PEPE. Granddad! Granddad! Kill a lot of Paraguayans!
(Urubamba leaves through the back door)

SCENE FIVE

(A park, a bench, gray weather. A beggar in a ragged uniform is sitting on the bench, shivering and playing on a ruined guitar)

BEGGAR. It has been a long, long war. We call the Chaco the Green Hell. Hard to believe in this cold and damp, but in the Chaco it's hot, hotter, and hottest. You dig fifty feet into the tough earth for water, and when you get there you don't find any, the flies crawl over you when your hands are busy with your rifle or your mattock, when you die a million white butterflies fall on you to suck you dry, you're just a bloody cocktail lounge as far as the butterflies are concerned, and in the last battle I was at, that was the battle of Zenteno, we lost 80,000 men who croaked of heat and thirst in the retreat, and the Paraguayans who were the winners alack and alas lost 90,000 men in the advance, serves them right for winning, besides the 25,000 who were done for fair and square by gunfire, and the 90,000 who've pooped their guts out in the scrub, I'm rounding the figures, and all the rest of us down to one loaf of bread a month, and the women alone in their beds and getting frantic, I've got six wives in town myself out of sheer patriotism, and although we hanged President Salamanca from a lamppost for allowing General Pfundt to lose the battle of Nanawa, all we got for it was total mobilization, hospitals included, under President Jose Luis Tejada Sorzano, that's when they mobilized me out of my chocolate store, I went to the front where I fought like a tiger until I came down with typhus and they sent me back here because they don't want any weaklings in battle, it looks bad in the photographs, but what's the use, my chocolate store is ruined and nobody can afford to buy chocolate anyway, and if they could, where would I find chocolate to sell? Thank God I still have my guitar. *(He plays and sings)*

BEGGAR
Soldiers march, soldiers sweat,
Soldiers shoot and soldiers die.
Let news be good or news be bad,
The casualties are high.

Above the ragged battlefield
The happy vultures fly.
Above the bloated battlefield
The happy buzzards fly,
Appraising all that human meat
With an impartial eye.

The birds don't ask you
"What's your side,
Where d'you come from, when and why?"
They eat alike Bolivian boys
And lads from Paraguay.

HONEST URUBAMBA

The birds are a tolerant, democratic, liberal bunch.

> They love alike Bolivian boys
> And lads from Paraguay.

Hey! Look who's coming. The Crippled Veteran; and over there Honest Bamba, the shoeshine man. Join me, join me, fellow revelers.
(Enter, from different directions, the ragged war veteran, using a crutch, and Urubamba, unshaven and shabby, with a shoeshine kit)
URUBAMBA *(to the beggar)*. Shine, mister?
BEGGAR. Them shoes aren't worth shining, Bamba, but I'd hire you all the same if I had the money. *(To the crippled veteran)* You wouldn't be interested in a serenade, would you? Ten pesos.
VETERAN. Sure I would, being as I'm a music lover from way back, but first I gotta get the money to pay you with. *(To Urubamba)* You got ten pesos for a wounded war veteran, old pal? Don't hold back on me.
URUBAMBA. I do have ten pesos. Here it is.
VETERAN. Thanks, old pal. Ok, troubadour, shoot the serenade.

> BEGGAR.
> A shepherd by a stream did stray
> And gently breathed his amorous tune,
> The while his sheep did gently play
> And frolic 'pon the grassy dune.
>
> "Aminta," went his piteous moan,
> "O cruel maid, why dost thou flee,
> And leave me with these tears alone
> To bear me humid company?"

VETERAN *(weeping)*. Jesus that was pretty. Sent a goddam shiver through my crutch. Here's ten pesos.
BEGGAR. Thank you, sir. Are you at liberty to give me a shine now, honest Bamba?
URUBAMBA. Certainly, sir.
(He shines the beggar's shoes, with many a flourish of his brush and a professional regard for the torn shoes)
URUBAMBA. I'm afraid it isn't the old shoe polish, sir. They thicken it with ratshit nowadays.
BEGGAR. Well, do your best, Bamba. *(To the veteran)* So how's the leg?

VETERAN. I know it's there, and a man shouldn't be thinking he's got a leg.

BEGGAR. Better than thinking he hasn't got one. Where was it they shot you?

VETERAN. At Boquerón. Only I wasn't shot. Y'see, I was kicking a sick prisoner when I missed him and kicked a rusty nail instead. Serves me right for taking my duty serious.

BEGGAR. Bad.

URUBAMBA. Here you are, sir.

BEGGAR. A bit more on this flap. That's right. Thanks. Here's ten pesos.

URUBAMBA. Thank you, sir. *(Exit)*

VETERAN. There's prosperity in that man. Now that he's got ten pesos, maybe he'll buy me a drink outa this cold. *(Turns up his collar and hobbles out after Urubamba)*

BEGGAR. It all keeps the economy rolling.

(Enter the Ministers of the Exterior and Information, the latter holding an umbrella, both in overcoats)

EXTERIOR. Let's sit down a minute, Gomez. These meetings tire me out. Too many lousy statistics.

INFORMATION. Good idea, though it's going to rain any minute.

(They sit next to the beggar)

INFORMATION *(glaring)*. Hrmph.

BEGGAR. Serenade, gentlemen? Springtime lyric of youthful love, ten pesos.

INFORMATION. No thank you. You'll find an audience over there by the duck-pond. *(Beggar doffs his cap and leaves)*

EXTERIOR. Is your watch still on your wrist, Gomez?

INFORMATION. It is. I had my finger on it.

EXTERIOR. You can't be too careful. It's become totally sickening.

INFORMATION. What do you expect? The country is aswarm with cripples, paupers, bums, orphans; even the widows are becoming dangerous. I don't allow my wife to leave the house anymore, and I'm waiting to have my throat cut any afternoon for saying no I don't want a serenade.

EXTERIOR. Who would have guessed the Paraguayans were going to turn aggressive about that patch of dust? And suppose it doesn't yield any oil after all?

INFORMATION. Somebody lifted the pacifier right out of our baby's mouth while Nanny had her back turned.

EXTERIOR. They'd steal the cracks off the sidewalks.

INFORMATION. Day before yesterday I went to the Café de la Paz to meet Cucuchabaz—remember? Of course, I draped my overcoat over the back of my own chair—you can't hang up a coat anymore. Well, I got up, put

HONEST URUBAMBA

on my coat, and guess what—somebody had made off with all the buttons!

EXTERIOR. The buttons!

INFORMATION. Plastic buttons.

EXTERIOR. Incredible. *(Silence; then confidentially)* Speaking of buttons, Fernando, what about General Pfundt?

INFORMATION. What *about* General Pfundt?

EXTERIOR. Well—is he or isn't he?

INFORMATION. At the front?

EXTERIOR *(impatient)*. At the front! You know what I mean. I mean is he getting the Grand Cross of the Condor of the Andes?

INFORMATION. He is getting it.

EXTERIOR. I thought as much. It's disgusting. Look at what they're saying about him in London. *(Shows Gomez a newspaper)* "General Pfundt, the German military expert imported by the Bolivian government to carry out the war according to the latest scientific methods, has proved to be the most brilliant innovator of the century in the art of surprise retreats. He has indeed been known to organize highly effective evacuations of territories not even threatened by the enemy." And so on. They also know about these blasted fourteenyear-old infants he's been using in the artillery. While you and me sit here day after day doing the dirty work now that Salamanca has left us *(he crosses himself)* and get nothing but stones in our faces.

INFORMATION. You don't understand, San Martín, and you're all steamed up about nothing. If we give Pfundt the Grand Cross, people will suppose he's getting it for winning battles, won't they? It's good for morale.

EXTERIOR. It's not good for mine. I've been working my ass to the bone for two years without a medal.

(Enter Urubamba)

URUBAMBA. Shoeshine?

INFORMATION. How much?

URUBAMBA. Ten pesos.

INFORMATION. It's going to rain in a minute.

URUBAMBA. Only five pesos, in that case. On request of the customer I also enumerate the provinces of Brazil or Argentina, each with its capital.

EXTERIOR. Good heavens, what for?

URUBAMBA. A little entertainment, sir. The effect of competition in the shoeshine enterprises.

INFORMATION. Well, we'll see about the provinces. Start shining anyhow.

URUBAMBA. Yes, sir. *(He shines the shoes)*

EXTERIOR. How is it you're still charging ten pesos, my good man, what with prices going up for everything?

URUBAMBA. Because, to tell you the truth, Dr. San Martín, although everybody is charging twice the price, I feel that our shoe polish is not as good as it used to be.

EXTERIOR. How do you know I am Dr. San Martín?

URUBAMBA *(to Gomez)*. The other shoe, sir. *(To San Martín)* I see your picture in the papers, sir. And that of Dr. Gomez too.

INFORMATION. How about those provinces, my good fellow? Let's have a rundown on Brazil.

URUBAMBA. Yes, sir. Alagoas, capital Maceio. Amazonas, capital Manaos. Bahia, capital San Salvador. Ceara, capital Fortaleza. Espirito Santo, capital Victoria. Goyaz,—

INFORMATION *(laughing)*. Stop, that's enough! I'll take your word for the rest. Clever businessman. Here is your five pesos. Come along, San Martín.

URUBUMBA. Thank you, sir.

EXTERIOR *(as they are going)*. Have you checked for your watch and purse?

INFORMATION. Everything's in place, I've got my finger on them.

(They leave, but Gomez has forgotten his umbrella)

URUBAMBA *(sniffing the shoe polish as he is putting his kit together)*. Pah! How can a man do a decent job with this? Cracks right on the shoe. Well, that's war for you. *(He notices the umbrella)* What now! Gomez left his umbrella behind. Hm, I even remember *it* from the old days. I wish *I* had an umbrella to keep my bones dry. *(Calling)* Dr. Gomez, your umbrella!

INFORMATION *(off stage)*. What's that? Oh! My umbrella. *(Both he and San Martín return)* Yes, that's it. Thank you, my friend.

EXTERIOR. Heart-warming, really heart-warming.

INFORMATION. I don't know where my thoughts are any more. Thanks again, and here—here are the other five pesos, rain or no rain. *(His hand on Urubamba's shoulder)* I wish there were more honest men of your kind in this country.

EXTERIOR. Amen to that.

INFORMATION. Come along, San Martín, it's beginning to drizzle.

(He opens the umbrella and they leave arm in arm)

URUBAMBA. Thank you, sir. *(Alone, he takes out a small bag and places the coins in it)* Almost three-quarters of the way to a loaf of bread. *(He sits on the bench, his collar up. He covers his head with a newspaper, then changes his mind and protects the shoeshine kit instead. Enter the beggar, covering his head with his guitar.)* And now, accompanied by the beggar with the ruined guitar, I am going to sing the song entitled, "The Whole World Loves an Honest Man." Ready?

BEGGAR. Wet but ready.

HONEST URUBAMBA,

(There is a period of complete silence, then the curtain slowly falls)

The End

Notes

Honest Urubamba appeared in the Autumn 1965 issue of *The Literary Review*, and then again in Volume I of my 1970-1972 *Collected Plays*. I have revised it for this final appearance.

The savage Chaco War between Bolivia and Paraguay was fought, and lost by Bolivia, from 1932 to 1935.

Some of the U.N. delegates and members of the Salamanca cabinet can be women. A change of first names will be no trouble.

WATER FROM AN ITALIAN PUMP

CHARACTERS

Peter Mandolino
Delancey Krott
Vittoria Grazzi
Sarah (Angela Danone)
Bill (Dr. Nethergood)

SCENE ONE

(An average college office in New York City. Peter Mandolino, a mild assistant professor who puffs conscientiously on the standard academic pipe, is laboriously calculating grades and entering them on an official form)

MANDOLINO. An eight, a seven, B+ on the final, here we go. *(He enters a grade)* Ay! Here comes Meadow. *(He stares gloomily at his grade book, scratches his cheek, fiddles with his pipe, mutters to himself, and finally picks up the telephone and dials a number)* Registrar's office? Let me talk to Mrs. Perkins, may I? Thank you.... Mrs. Perkins? This is Dr. Mandolino in the Romance Languages Department..... Fine. How about yourself? Oh my God! In the Catskills? How awful! What kind of snake was it? Ha! And where did it bite you?... I see. Lucky it wasn't worse. Still, two weeks in bed. You can't be too careful when you go hiking—ever since the Fall, you know. No no, the fall of Adam and Eve is what I meant—the serpent—that's it, an academic joke! You see, I've made you laugh, I bet it hurts less already.... Hm.... My, my. But what did your laryngitis have to do with a snake bite, Mrs. Perkins?... They *collided!* Incredible. But I'm glad you're on the job again.... No, don't worry, I'm not the tramping type, I'm the swim-in-the-ocean sort, a regular dolphin.... Yes.... Good for you.... Well now, what I'm calling you about is Jim Meadow.... That's right, who else? What am I supposed to do with him? I mean, he's come to class six or seven times all semester, he wobbles in with a weird, glassy stare, barefoot of course, I'm sure he sleeps in his clothes, such as they are, there are congregations of things in his beard, live or dead, I don't know, and—frankly, I've got to open the windows—I do it unobtrusively, but—yes, yes, that's right, no, you're right—he hasn't taken a single exam or handed in a single paper, I know it looks like a clear case, I flunk him and that's it.... What's that?... I agree, but on the other hand, he's bright—very bright—he's read Pirandello on his own.... Pirandello, never mind, what I mean is, he's promising, he'd be somebody if somebody would wean him from those drugs.... Frankly I can never remember their names, the kids inject them—into their arms, isn't it?... Where?... I'll be damned!!... Well, facts are facts, I agree. And the stuff moves *up* into their system?... What do you call it?... Well, I'm not going to try to remember, they seem to change the slang every two weeks.... Right,

right. Still, I'd like to give Meadow another chance. How is he doing in Dr. Nethergood's class? *(Someone knocks at the office door)* Hold it. Come in, come in! *(Enter Vittoria Grazzi)* I'll be right with you. Sit down. *(Into the telephone)* Excuse me, Mrs. Perkins, a student just walked in.... Well then, if it's all right with you and Mr. Simpson, I'll give the boy an Incomplete.... Fine. And keep away from those reptiles! Bye bye! (To Vittoria) Will you excuse me one moment?

VITTORIA. Oh sure!

(She is pleasantly plain and shy. Mandolino enters Meadow's grade and turns amiably to Vittoria while cleaning out his pipe)

MANDOLINO. Now, what can I do for you?

VITTORIA *(shyly)*. I'm one of your students, Dr. Mandolino. I sit in the back row of Italian Five.

MANDOLINO. I know. Your name is Vittoria Grazzi.

VITTORIA *(delighted)*. That's right!

MANDOLINO. And you want to find out your grade.

VITTORIA. Oh no—

MANDOLINO *(looking into the grade book)*. A very commendable A minus, Miss Grazzi. You don't make a lot of noise in class—I mean, you don't much "participate"—but at least you recognize an irregular verb and you nail it down.

VITTORIA. I'm very anxious to improve my Italian.

MANDOLINO. Well, you're improving it. Some special reason?

VITTORIA. Yes. In a few weeks I'm going to have a chance to put it to practice.

MANDOLINO. Fine! You're going to Italy?

VITTORIA. Yes, I'm going to Italy. And that's why I'm here, Dr. Mandolino. I was wondering whether I could talk to you about my trip.

MANDOLINO. Will you be visiting relatives? I'm asking because of your name.

VITTORIA. Yes—most of the time. But—well, my relatives—that's the really important part of my trip. It's a—it's a mission, you might call it. But they live in such a tiny place—

MANDOLINO. Where is it? What's it called?

VITTORIA. I'm sure even you have never heard of it. It's called Acquaviva and it's kind of in the Deep South of Italy, but one of my cousins is going to meet me in a place called Campobasso—I'm afraid it's all rather complicated. Am I taking too much of your time, Dr. Mandolino?

MANDOLINO. Not at all! I'm interested.

VITTORIA. Thank you. As I said before—I didn't come in to inquire about my grade. I knew I'd done pretty well on the exam.

MANDOLINO. Good girl!

VITTORIA. It was a very fair exam, I thought. But I was hoping you might give me a few tips, a few hints about travelling in Italy—you've talked so much about your experiences—you've seen it all!

MANDOLINO. Perhaps I overdo it....

VITTORIA. Oh no! Everybody enjoys hearing your stories. They make a language class come alive. They're *really* helpful.

MANDOLINO. Thank you.

VITTORIA. Oh, I didn't mean—Anyway, I'm going to have a good three weeks, or even a month, to run around the country by myself. I want to see everything that matters—and, to be perfectly honest, I don't think my relatives will be much help—they've never even been to Rome!

MANDOLINO. It's a rough life people lead in those stony villages. I've driven through a number of them, and stopped in a few. The old women in perpetual black—they mourn for thirty years, so of course they're always in mourning for somebody. The mule clomping uphill with a man riding sidesaddle. The old villagers under the trees with their hats on, staring at the outsider in the foreign car. Sure, they read the papers—mostly gory tales of jealous husbands shooting their wives—they watch television—but the world abroad registers deep inside them like legendary material—or daily entertainment. Americans, Russians, China, Arabia, India—it's all real, but a reality so distant that it acquires the charm of fiction. The real truth is those stooped backs and that tough sun over the fields.

VITTORIA. It'll be strange for me.

MANDOLINO. Stranger for them. Suddenly, out of the newspapers, the radios, the television set in the only bar in the village, out of all that quasi-fiction, you manifest yourself in threedimensional glory, carrying your Macy's suitcase, and holding forth about subways, Fifth Avenue, your dates. You'll be using a weird vocabulary for them—"I'm majoring in Italian!" "I have a job in summer camp," "We meet at the Mall"—stuff that seems ever so average to you.

VITTORIA. It'll be wild.

MANDOLINO. And better be tolerant as far as the plumbing is concerned.

VITTORIA. *They're* terribly worried.

MANDOLINO. But what about that mission you were talking about?

VITTORIA *(shyly)*. You didn't read about it in the school paper? There's a copy on your desk.

MANDOLINO *(picking it up)*. I haven't gotten around to it. Why, here's a picture of you! "Vittoria's Mission to Italy." Sounds like the State Department is sending you!

VITTORIA *(laughing)*. Oh no. It's all in the family. I know I talk too much about it. Everybody and his kid brother knows by now. But it's all so important. To me. Not to anybody else. I'm not *that* silly.

MANDOLINO. Tell me all about it. It may help me give you the right sort of advice.

VITTORIA. Well—I'm a kind of emissary. There's a lot more to it than what it says in the paper. It all began long ago, when my father came to this country, long before I was born. He left Acquaviva with his older brother. I guess they were both in their early thirties. It was the usual story. No future for them in Italy.

MANDOLINO. They did well in the States?

VITTORIA. Oh yes! *Pretty* well.

MANDOLINO. And so?

VITTORIA. Well, when they left Italy—my uncle and my dad—they left their parents behind, naturally, but also two little sisters, much much younger, kids. My father loved them, he loved them so much—

MANDOLINO. Are they alive?

VITTORIA. Oh yes. My grandparents are dead, but my aunts are alive. Only, my dad never saw them again. For years and years he and my uncle worked as hard as they could. The idea was for dad to return to Italy, first to see their parents again, if only once, but then they died, two years apart, and there wasn't enough money to go—and then, now I remember, the news came too late both times—I remember seeing my father cry when I was hardly more than a baby, it frightened me terribly.

MANDOLINO. What did your uncle and your father do here?

VITTORIA. Same thing they're doing now—they opened a little restaurant. At first they were waiters, dishwashers, cooks, but they finally managed to open a place of their own a couple of years before I was born, and they've had several places since—one at a time, of course.

MANDOLINO. Which one is it now? Maybe I've eaten there.

VITTORIA. It's called Da Giorgio, on Thirteenth Street, between Seventh and Eighth Avenues.

MANDOLINO. No, I guess not.

VITTORIA. It's not very well known.

MANDOLINO. So your father never made it back to Italy.

VITTORIA. No, he didn't. First he got married, then he had all of us children—two boys and three girls. And then trying to keep the businesses going. All these years, though, he kept putting away a few dollars at a time in a special account. It was his great secret—even mother didn't know about it. Suddenly last Christmas he said: "There it is! Enough for one ticket to Acquaviva!" And then he got drunk for the only time in his life. You don't know what it meant to him. His sisters....

MANDOLINO. I think I understand....

VITTORIA. The one thing he still wanted out of life, he said, was to see the little girls again.

MANDOLINO. Not so little anymore.

VITTORIA. No! They're both married, and they look pretty stout in the pictures, and I've got more cousins than I can keep straight in my head.

MANDOLINO. But now *you're* going. What happened? Nothing to your dad, I hope.

VITTORIA. No. It's hard to explain. He went to the travel agency right after Christmas. When he came back, he sat down at the kitchen table and said nothing for an hour. That was the end of his trip. Too many years had gone by. Thirty years. He couldn't go. And we couldn't get him to explain. He kept shaking his head, and all he ever said was, "next life, next life."

MANDOLINO. And that's how you inherited the ticket to Italy.

VITTORIA. There was a full family reunion. We have them every now and then—both families, wives, children, cousins, everybody. My father said, "The money's in the bank. Who'll go? I'm not going, and I need mother at home, my heart ain't what it used to be; who'll represent me?"

MANDOLINO. Why not your uncle?

VITTORIA. No, Uncle George never cared to go back. "If they wanna see me, let them come here like I did." It's funny. My dad says Uncle George beat the old country off the soles of his shoes the day he left, while dad sort of scraped it lovingly off and kept the bits of earth in a box. A big part of my mission is to bring back a bottle full of water from a pump in the village where he used to wash his face and drink after playing with the other kids.

MANDOLINO. Customs shouldn't object to *that*. Anyway, you were elected.

VITTORIA. I'm the youngest, and the only one going to college. There was a great weighing of "factors"—it's a word dad happens to like—and all "factors" considered, it looked as if I should be the one to go.

MANDOLINO. Were you happy?

VITTORIA. Was I happy! All my life I've dreamed of it! I guess when a person has gone as often as you have—but for me—and I never thought it would happen—not for many years—and then suddenly the secret bank account—and father—I feel as if I were living in a movie. I've been preparing for months.

MANDOLINO. I'll do my best to help.

VITTORIA. I would have asked you before, but at first I didn't even know whether I'd have time away from my mission.

MANDOLINO. I'm glad you're taking it seriously.

VITTORIA. I suppose we're all terribly sentimental. But I'm not hopeless, you see, because here I've gone and made lots of room for "culture" and fun like any other girl.

MANDOLINO. Where do I come in? The culture or the fun?

VITTORIA. Anywhere you like!

MANDOLINO. That's good. You can count on me for guidance; I love to give advice on travelling.

VITTORIA. Wonderful.

MANDOLINO. Frankly, that's one of the great rewards of travelling abroad: badgering others with information, ostensibly for their good, actually to display one's own feathers.

VITTORIA. I'm glad I'm doing you a favor! I was afraid I'd be imposing.

MANDOLINO. Let me get a few items together for you—books, pamphlets and maps—some of the material is at my fiancée's house—and let's make an appointment. When do you leave the country?

VITTORIA. In a month.

MANDOLINO. Good. That gives me all the time I need. Shall we say in exactly two weeks, same time, same place?

VITTORIA *(writing it down)*. That's perfect. And thanks a million!

MANDOLINO. See you in two weeks.

VITTORIA. I'll be here. Bye-bye.

(Mandolino waves to her as she leaves. He goes back to his grades, broods over his pipe, mutters to himself)

MANDOLINO. Carrying home a bottle of water from Acquaviva! A mission! *(His eyes light on the telephone)* Hey, I wonder.... Hm. *(He hesitates, then takes the plunge and dials a number)* Hello? Mrs. Flanagan? This is Peter Mandolino, how are you?... Good. Is Delancey in his room?... Aha.... I see.... Ttttt, that's terrible. But I know Delancey, I'm sure he'll pay within the week. You know how writers are, Mrs. Flanagan, they're not like you and me.... Oh.... Ink on the wall?... Ttttt, that's really—but I think there's a new cleaning fluid on the market.... Oh, of course.... Of course.... I *know*. You're practically a mother to him, Mrs. Flanagan, letting him use the shower and all that. He's terribly fond of you.... OK, I'll wait. *(A pause. To himself)* I hope I'm not making a mistake. Hi, Delancey.... Fine. How about you?... Asleep, at this time of day? I don't believe it!... Thank you, she's fine too.... No, we didn't decide last night, how many times do I have to tell you? Ethel and I will get married the moment we *can* get married, and that's the end of that. Let's change the subject. The reason I'm calling is this. I guess it's crazy, but one of my students was telling me a story five minutes ago—something charming out of her own life—and suddenly I thought of you telling Ethel and me last night that you're desperate for something for a one-act play. Maybe this is it—No, not over the telephone, it would take too long.... Don't rush me! I'm not skipping town with your plot. Anyway, it may be of no use to you, how do I know? You're the playwright. All I know is that it's a wonderful story. Psychological interest? Don't ask *me*. I teach Italian grammar, remember? But listen. I'm meeting Tim Nethergood for lunch down in the cafeteria at one o'clock.... Nethergood. I don't think you know him. The Rise and Fall of Phallic Imperialism.... No, you clown, it's a course he teaches in Women's Studies. Why don't you come over to my office right away, I'll tell you the story and then the three of us will go down for lunch together. I want to talk to Nethergood about a stu—. Don't worry, I'll treat you. Don't I always? Ciao! *(He hangs up, returns to his grades, and scatches his head with his pipe)* I bet I made a mistake.

SCENE TWO

(Mandolino's office. Mandolino sitting at his desk, Krott standing)

KROTT. A bottle full of ancestral water! I'm not going to survive this. You sneaked up to that telephone on purpose to fell me with the bullshittiest story that ever befouled my ears. A bottle full of village water! A virgin on a sacred mission! Tender reunion of sundered families! Where have you been all your life, you suffix, you pleonasm, you expletive! Get out into the cold world, hit the streets, you pipe-puffing, tennis-playing professors!

MANDOLINO. We will, we will. But Nethergood is waiting for us. I'm hungry and I've got a meeting at two-thirty.

KROTT. He's got a meeting at two-thirty! To discuss next year's allocation of paper-clips. Twelve professors, frowning gravely, assemble to make the fatal decision.

MANDOLINO. I told Nethergood—

KROTT. And me what do you tell? He calls me over with urgent syllables, causes me to trip over a fox-terrier and two innocents pushing a soccer ball over the pavement, I arrive at his desk wet with expectation, I know my Redeemer cometh, my play is a wind between his rosy lips, and then crunch, he flattens me with a tale of lollipops and teddy bears, confident that I can never set pen to paper again.

MANDOLINO. I was trying to help.

KNOTT. Penis envy! That's what it is. The green worm scrounging at your entrails ever since we sat together in Bliffin's creative writing class twelve years ago, and while I triumphed with brutal pictures of life in the dank ghettoes of New York, you wrote accounts of "My Afternoon at the Metropolitan Museum." The virile erection of my genius clobbered your subconscious. You fed the green worm under the Poison Tree while conjugating the palest irregular verbs you could find in your listless grammar books, until at last you heard the story of a larmoyant Italian maiden who longed for a bottle of water from her unspeakable village, and the monstrous thought mushroomed in your mind: Delancey Krott needs a story: with this one I shall emasculate him till the day after the Second Coming.

MANDOLINO. Well, you're always spouting theories about Reality, so I thought here's a real story.

KROTT. You pitiful subterfuge for manhood, do you dare mention Reality in my presence? Open your blinkered eyes, Mandolino! This is Reality! *(He opens a huge billfold crammed with clippings, which he pours over Mandolino's desk)* Orphans forced to lick their own excrement by sadistic overseers! Massacred civilians discovered in open graves in the jungle! Young girl stupefied by drugs kills four and jumps to her death! Large pharmaceutical firm indicted for marketing dangerous contraceptives! A thousand animal species a year wiped out by manmade pollutants! Three prominent senators and an ex-vicepresident accused of influence-peddling in favor of an aeronautics firm! Guerrillas mutilate bodies of victims! Outbreak of typhoid fever in famed Swiss resort blamed on criminal silence of local merchants! Three black women beaten to death in tobacco field! Two hundred twenty-nine spectators at football game crushed to death as crowd celebrates victory of home team! National Guard fires on student picnickers! Inflatable plastic genitals on sale in Times Square shops! Sixteen-yearold boy sets fire to his parents after tying them up! Exemplary Rotarian, father of two, goes berserk in beauty parlor and kills eight women under dryers! Innocent black man leaves jail after forty-one years for a crime he didn't commit. So much for reality! And if that's not enough to turn your stomach, you'll oblige me by remembering that any day, any hour, mankind can blow itself into oblivion by pressing a single pimple of a button.

MANDOLINO. Well, I don't understand—

KROTT. What you don't understand would fill an encyclopedia, my ablative boy, but what is it you don't understand this particular time?

MANDOLINO. Well, with all these clippings and all, why do you *worry* about mankind blowing itself up? Why aren't you promoting it?

KROTT. Ha ha ha ha ha! The lad has wit! He dares put together an independent clause! But enough's enough. Give me back my documents. *(He gathers up the clippings)*

MANDOLINO. Here. You dropped the inflated genitals.

KROTT. This, this is what meaningful art is about. The artist is not an entertainer, the artist is a surgeon.

MANDOLINO. Last night when you told Ethel—

KROTT. Ethel! When are you going to marry that girl, you future conditional?

MANDOLINO. I've told you a hundred times. Until I get my promotion—

KROTT. In seventeen years—

MANDOLINO. I won't be able to support Ethel. She's got her parents to take care of. I can't ask her to pack them off to some dingy asylum. I have to think of all three of them.

KROTT *(gives Mandolino a hefty kiss)*. You 're an insufferable saint. As soon as my royalties exceed the price I pay for computer ink, I'll take you all to live with me in Vermont.

MANDOLINO. Meantime let's be off for lunch.

(He gets up from his desk)

KROTT. And thanks for the story.

MANDOLINO. What story?

KROTT. The one about the water from an Italian pump.

MANDOLINO. I thought it was no good!

KROTT. Of course it's no good! But I'll make it good. I'll make it real, God damn it. I've promised a play for the Workshop, one hour running time, five actors maximum, ready a week from today. But I'm as dry as a lizard. My most creative hours are spent dodging Mrs. Overdue Flanagan. What's to be done? I'll listen to your pulpy story over lunch again.

MANDOLINO. It's in the school paper, by the way. Why don't you take it along?

KROTT. "Vittoria's Mission to Italy." I will. Tonight I'll descend like a hailstorm on my keyboard, and tomorrow I'll have the first draft of something that tells it like it is. And that, my misplaced semicolon, is what genius is all about.

SCENE THREE

(An office of the same sort as Mandolino's)

NETHERGOOD *(on the telephone)*. But what's the use, Doris? Everybody else'll be swimming, I'll be the only one holding down the sand, I'll look stupid. I said *I'll* look stupid, Doris. Why don't you go by yourself, they'll be happy to have you.... All right, all right, don't get mad, it's not the end of the world. Everybody knows we're engaged, so it wouldn't look as if nobody wanted you.... I can't help it if I don't know how to swim. Mom never allowed any of us near the water.... There you go again.... I don't care, she raised four kids, not one of whom, as it happens, went bankrupt.... I'm *not* being aggressive, Doris, but if you start in on my mother I can allow myself a remote allusion to a cousin.... But what's the use if I can't swim?... It's not true! Who's self-conscious in his bathing trunks?... My arms are *perfect!* Not too fat and not too thin. *(A knock at the door)* Listen, Doris, there's a student at the door.... I tell you there's a student at the door! The school year isn't over! *(Towards the door)* One moment, please! *(Into the receiver)* OK? I'll call you in an hour.... All right! You call me. Where should I be? Right here.... Good-bye.... Good-bye *honey*.... All right, but somebody's waiting at the door. *(He sends a dozen kisses through the telephone and hangs up)* Come in, come in. *(Enter Angela)*

ANGELA. Hello!

NETHERGOOD. Oh hello, Miss Danone!

ANGELA. You haven't forgotten our appointment, Dr. Nethergood?

NETHERGOOD. Of course not. Come in, sit down, I've got everything ready for you. *(He exhibits a large folder)*

ANGELA. Oh wonderful. I'm so grateful!

NETHERGOOD. Lists of hotels, good inexpensive restaurants where you *really* meet the natives, some wonderful out-of-the-way spots, brochures—I like to go to hotels and ask for their brochures—plans, maps, a few guide books. I'm going to send you to places the tours don't know about—the towers of San Gimignano, the Giottos in Padova, a wonderful Fra Angelico in Cortona, a fantastic pulpit in Salerno—

ANGELA. This is so exciting!

NETHERGOOD. And a few places for sheer relaxation too.

ANGELA. Good! Please tell me where the best swimming is.

NETHERGOOD. Swimming?

ANGELA. Yes, I love to swim, and I want to swim in the Mediterranean once in my life.

NETHERGOOD. Swim with all those brawny and muscled Italian boys, eh?

ANGELA. Why not?

NETHERGOOD. Swim with boys whose arms are not too thin.

ANGELA (*a bit puzzled*). I guess so.

NETHERGOOD. Why don't you look over some of this material, and then we'll talk. We'll talk about swimming.

ANGELA. Wonderful. (*She begins to leaf through the brochures, etc., making little comments, while Nethergood hovers about the office. Suddenly he locks the door and places the key in his pocket. Angela raises her head and turns around, surprised and alarmed by Nethergood's action*)

NETHERGOOD. The door is locked. The ritual can begin. The fake skin, the everyday lie, peels off, and it doesn't even hurt.

ANGELA (*frightened*). What do you mean?

NETHERGOOD. I know you, Angela Danone. I know through you. I know past you. I know beneath and beside and above you. (*He walks over to the desk and with a brutal gesture sweeps all the papers to the floor*) You shouldn't have said swimming. Yet if you hadn't said it, you might just as well have said it, because it is all the same. All differences are the same.

ANGELA. All differences are the same. It's so true, isn't it?

NETHERGOOD (*contemptuously*). Giotto in Padova. Screw Giotto in Padova! Look at me! Into my eyes! Tell me why you came here two weeks ago. You think I don't know who you are, or what you are. (*Almost tenderly*) Slut. Aha! I know too much! I've watched too close! But that was the very thing you wanted all along, wasn't it? You've been too successful, that's all. It started as your game, but I'm taking it over. The key is in *my* pocket. When you were baring your thighs for me in Phallic Imperialism as if inadvertently, when you were fingering the crook of your elbow, where the compassionate needle goes in there! (*He rips her sleeve*) you thought, "Let's see what I can do with him, I'll play my meek-little-sweetie game with him, talk to him about well-behaved journeys abroad to see the cultural monuments, and then, bit by bit, I'll turn him into one of *us*, the damned."

ANGELA. You swine.

NETHERGOOD. There's only one thing you didn't know, sweetie. I was one of you before you became one of us. I liked the little game you were playing. I enjoyed every move. And don't forget the trump card in my hands: I had access to the files. I knew all about you. Where you lived. The police record. I knew about the uncle. I knew about the aunt in the lock-up. And I knew, sweetie, that you had—a *brother*.

ANGELA. You're bluffing.

NETHERGOOD. Sure I'm bluffing. The brother! The brother whose name was scribbled in all your notebooks. Dear Fabrizio, employed as a mechanic, nothing against him, a steady worker. Fabrizio, I said to myself, Fabrizio, what is the connection between an honest citizen like yourself and the open knees in Women's Studies and the marks in the crook of the elbow? Oh, I was enjoying the game. But why was I playing it?

ANGELA. Why does anyone play it?

NETHERGOOD. Why does anyone play it? I'll tell you why *I* play it, sweetheart. It starts out with a kid's bicycle. A kid who lives with his mother in a grimy third-story walk-up. With his mother and the cockroaches and the rats and the weak light bulb hanging from a wire. A family. But I was lucky. I could choose any dad I wanted, because there was a new one around on the average every two months. You didn't get bored up there with the rats and the cockroaches and the changing of the guard every two months. But you learned pretty quick to hang on to anything that came your way, which was on the average nothing a year. Follow me? Don't say you follow me. Above all for God's sake don't tell me you follow me. One day, one of the gentlemen gives this kid a bicycle. Imagine! A fancy new bike, chrome handles, shiny blue frame, gears—the kid was ten years old! I guess the dad of the month had made a pile betting on the horses that day, or maybe he wanted something from the old lady she hadn't granted him yet. Never mind. The kid had a bicycle, the first object he'd ever owned that wasn't fit to be thrown on the junk-pile. His first possession. His first pride. He talked to that bicycle. Why not. They talk to a horse when they groom it. The kid talked to his bicycle when he polished it. A bicycle is no dumber than a horse, when you come right down to it. And you don't get to see a lot of horses where that kid was living. Well, for five days that kid had his bicycle. Five days living like an emperor, looking for excuses to mount that saddle. Like forgetting part of the groceries in the store. Or having to consult another kid on a math problem, what's 2 plus 2. On the sixth day, dad got drunk, clouted my mother's face, broke two of my ribs, cracked a window open and threw my bicycle out of it. Sure I had it on the third floor with me. You don't keep a brand-new bicycle in public places around where I lived. Dad of the month went down to give the bike his personal attention after it had failed to pulverize from its fall. And that, ducky, is where I learned to play the game. And the name of the game is Smash it before you get to like it, smash it, baby, before it smashes you.

ANGELA. I knew it from the first time I saw you.

NETHERGOOD. What did you know, honey?

ANGELA. That you and me were on to the same game. Like you said. Smash it before you get to like it, smash it before it smashes you.

NETHERGOOD. Except I play to win, kid.

ANGELA. So do I.

NETHERGOOD. Don't forget Fabrizio.

ANGELA. What about Fabrizio?

NETHERGOOD. I was going to look for him. Instead, guess what, day before yesterday he shows up here. I sat him here where you're sitting now.

ANGELA. What did he want?

NETHERGOOD. "I'm Fabrizio Danone," he says, "I'm Angela's brother. I want you to talk her out of that trip to Italy. Tell her she'll come down with cholera. Tell her anything." "Why?" says I. "What's the matter?" "She's needed here. Mother and father are both sick (*Angela laughs*) and I've got a full-time job. This is no time for her to go picking daisies in Europe." "You're lying," says I.

ANGELA. You louse.

NETHERGOOD. "I happen to know that your mother and father are in the pink of health. Out with it! Why do you want to keep your sister here, eh? Why do you want to keep your little sister under your thumb?"

ANGELA. You louse.

NETHERGOOD. "Why do you want to keep your sister, eh?" His lips were twitching.

ANGELA. Louse!

NETHERGOOD. "Why do you want to keep your sister? Eh? Eh?"

ANGELA. Louse! Louse! Louse! (*Nethergood grabs her and holds her tight against him*)

NETHERGOOD. Only me, I didn't get upset. On the contrary, I liked it. I liked the idea very much. The more we talked, and we talked plenty, the more I liked it.

ANGELA (*hoarsely*). You don't know about Uncle Pietro yet.

NETHERGOOD. I know all about you and Uncle Pietro. Fabrizio told me. I like that too. Uncle Pietro is trying to get rid of you.

ANGELA (*frantic*). You're lying and Fabrizio *doesn't* know!

NETHERGOOD. You dumb bitch, if he doesn't know, how did I find out? Now I've got you where I want you.

ANGELA. You're hurting me.

NETHERGOOD (*pulling out a switchblade*). It'll hurt more if you don't submit.

ANGELA. What do you want?

NETHERGOOD. What do I want! (*Furious whisper*) Lie down. And say "brother" to me. All the way, from now to climax. Say "brother." Say "brother!"

ANGELA. Brother.
NETHERGOOD. Lie down. On the mat. (*He begins to strip her*) I don't hear you.
ANGELA. Brother!
NETHERGOOD. I'll show you a million stars—*sister*.
ANGELA. Brother!!
NETHERGOOD. I'll make the planets sing for you.
ANGELA. Brother, brother!!!
NETHERGOOD. I'll cram you full of juicy sweets.
ANGELA. Brother, brother, brother!!!! (*The lights go out. A few moments go by. Various noises spread from the floor. Then Angela is heard laughing. As the lights go on again, she is smoothing out her skirt while Nethergood is fumbling at his trousers*)
ANGELA. So much for my *little* brother! (*She laughs*)
NETHERGOOD. You bitch. A man can't always—
ANGELA. Some can, *tiny* brother. (*She laughs*)
NETHERGOOD. Shut up.
ANGELA. Is something *chronically* wrong, mini-brother? (*She laughs*)
NETHERGOOD. Shut up, you bitch.
ANGELA. Don't like what didn't happen, *eenzy-weenzy* brother? (*She laughs*)
NETHERGOOD. Shut up! (*He strikes her violently across the face and she falls back against the desk*)
ANGELA (*complete change of tone*). Oh dear, my sleeve! Hold it, Bill.
NETHERGOOD (*complete change of tone*). What happened?
(*Delancey appears, script in hand*)
KROTT. No fatalities, I hope.
SARAH. There must be a splinter in this desk—my sleeve is torn.
BILL. I'm sorry. Gee.
KROTT. I'll treat you to another blouse, kid, don't worry. (*He embraces her*) You're great, Sarah, great! Bill, you too, absolutely tops, I wish you'd ripped something too so I could replace it for you.
BOTH. Thank you.
BILL. It's a great script, Delancey.
SARAH. I *love* it, I just *love* it.
KROTT. Why don't we take a break and discuss my notes. I've got a couple of beers in the desk drawer. Surprise.
BILL. Resourceful.
SARAH. Just a tiny sip for me, that's all. I've got to watch my calories. Thank you. Can I ask you a question about the script, Delancey?
KROTT. Ask me a million.
SARAH. I'm still a bit puzzled by my motivation. What am I doing in

Nethergood's office anyway? Do I *want* to go to Italy or am I faking it? Have I got something against Nethergood? You've given him a chance to explain himself, but Angela doesn't get her turn.

KROTT. Beautiful! You've seen the heart of the lettuce, Sarah darling. The confusion is exactly what I want. She has no motivation. Motivation is out. She drifts. She is absurd. In fact, she's not unconditioned enough for me. I'm striving toward metaphysical incoherence as an echo of our social anarchy and the death of feeling in our world. What I'm thinking of is introducing myself in this scene.

BOTH (*unenthusiastic*). Oh?

KROTT. Dressed in my underwear, carrying an umbrella in one hand, and a clock in the other. The author enters mysteriously even though the door is locked, you two remain totally unaware of me, and I intone from Beckett—

SARAH. I'm *crazy* about Beckett.

BILL. Me too.

SARAH. Me too.

KROTT. I intone, "Astride of a grave and a difficult birth. Down in the hole, lingeringly, the gravedigger puts on the forceps." Then I depart. Maybe I enter in the other scenes as well, always the vague threatening figure that no one can see, or rather that no one wants to see. Meantime, Nethergood—that's a real name, by the way, I hope the guy doesn't sue me—Nethergood—I'll change the name—Nethergood is laboriously digging into his motivation—

BILL. By way of contrast.

KROTT. Precisely! The utterly unmotivated pitted against the overmotivated.

BILL. I hope the reviewers understand.

KROTT. I urinate on the reviewers.

BILL. What about Doris? I've been meaning to ask you. Isn't there a kind of discrepancy between that conversation of his with Doris over the telephone—about his mother, about the swimming party—between these things and what comes later?

KNOTT. Ah! But—is there a Doris?

BILL. Ah!

SARAH. Ah!

KROTT. Is there an Angela?

SARAH. Oh!

BILL. Oh!

KROTT. Or is it all a dream, a ritual played off in Nethergood's mind, a myth of compulsive self-humiliation?

BILL. That's the question I keep asking myself.

SARAH. Me too.
BILL. Me too.

SCENE FOUR

(Mandolino's office)

KROTT. Then the knife goes into her belly, again, and again. It's the apotheosis.
MANDOLINO. My poor Vittoria.
KROTT. I'm using a different name, of course. But don't pity her. It's the moment of understanding. And it couldn't have come without that knife. For him, you see, the erect knife—obvious symbol, even a cretin can understand it—that knife is the supreme compensation and fulfillment. It turns out to be his only way of communicating. That, I am saying in effect, is what our culture is reduced to; and my anti-hero emerges as a pathetic signifier, raised to the level of myth, groping for some way, available to him, that is to say to our culture, of *reaching* another human being. As for her—what are you doing, you gross misprint?
MANDOLINO. I'm listening! And filling out an interlibrary loan form.
KROTT. Put that form away! World: take note: Mandolino fills out interlibrary loan forms while Krott is speaking. Take note, and weep.
MANDOLINO. Don't get mad, Delancey. Tell me what happens to Vittoria.
KROTT. Ah, Angela. For her, the supreme moment is what I call an *euangelismos*.
MANDOLINO. An *euangelismos*?
KROTT. An Annunciation. The knife blade is in her womb, you see, and in her, too, is begotten the final understanding, the *Logos* which is Love. I'm thinking of doing an article to prove that *euangelismos* is present in every major literary work. I'll show that serious literature is inconceivable without it. A stupendous idea, eh?
MANDOLINO. I—
KROTT. Terrific, I know. Don't steal it from me, you ambitious lower case.
MANDOLINO. But how are you going to convey all this stuff to Vittoria—or Angela? I mean, with the knife in her stomach and all?
KROTT. All I need is a symbolic gesture from her, or a single word. I don't know yet. Something with infinite repercussions, like—

(*Vittoria Grazzi appears through the open door of the office*)

VITTORIA. Hi!

MANDOLINO (*cordially, getting up*). Hello, Miss Grazzi, come on in.

VITTORIA. I don't want to disturb you—I'm in no hurry.

MANDOLINO. You're not disturbing. I was expecting you, and you're absolutely on schedule. Sit down. Do you mind very much my having somebody in the office?

VITTORIA. Oh no!

MANDOLINO. Somebody who wants very much to meet you.

VITTORIA. To meet *me?*

MANDOLINO. Allow me to introduce. This is Delancey Krott. Miss Vittoria Grazzi.

VITTORIA. Glad to meet you.

KROTT (*kissing her hand*). Delighted to meet you, Miss Grazzi. I've been looking forward to this delicious *incontro*.

VITTORIA. Uh—

MANDOLINO. Don't be startled, Miss Grazzi. Mr. Krott is a playwright—a *living* playwright. Maybe you've heard of him? The author of *Dirty Toenails?*

VITTORIA. *Dirty Toenails?* I don't—

MANDOLINO. It played off-off-Broadway about a year ago.

KROTT. You're embarrassing your pupil, Dr. Mandolino. The name of Krott, Miss Grazzi, has failed to reach the sprinkled suburbs so far where the elm trees ruffle their verdant robes, but all the same, unknown to you, your destiny and mine have converged and fused for eternity.

VITTORIA (*having fun*). Is he putting me on, Dr. Mandolino?

MANDOLINO. No, he isn't. You're not annoyed, are you? I'll explain everything to you.

VITTORIA. Annoyed? I'm having a wonderful time.

KROTT. And you are *giving* me a wonderful time, dear Angela—excuse me, dear Vittoria.

MANDOLINO. Here's what happened, Miss Grazzi. Except that now *I* feel embarrassed.

KROTT. Shoot from the hip, my boy.

MANDOLINO. I may have committed an indiscretion.

KROTT. The beginning of Art is impudence.

MANDOLINO. But after you told me your touching story about the circumstances of your trip to Italy, I remembered that my friend here—

KROTT. Delancey Krott, no middle initial, amateur cannibal, gigolo by appointment to her Majesty the Queen Mother, and suicide pilot on the Australian glider team.

VITTORIA. He's so funny!

MANDOLINO. I don't think I'll ever finish my explanation.

KROTT. I'll finish it. Primo, Dr. Mandolino told me your story. Secondo, I turned it into a play.

VITTORIA (*overcome*). Into a play?

KROTT. Terzo, I became anxious to meet my onlie begetter.

VITTORIA. A play of your own?

KROTT. The music of my own sphere. Wherever I go in the history books, you will follow as a beguiling footnote in the shade of my text.

VITTORIA. My story will be on Broadway?

KROTT. Not this year. But I'm going to send you four tickets to the Slaughterhouse Drama Workshop, where we're trying out the play, "previous," as they say, "to a Broadway engagement."

VITTORIA. Nothing like this has ever happened to me. Wait till I tell my family!

MANDOLINO. I want to warn you that our friend has taken a few liberties with the story—

KROTT. In the interest of Reality.

VITTORIA. Oh, that's fine with me.

MANDOLINO. Delancey is not concerned with anecdotes—he reaches for the essentials of life.

KROTT. The luridly dripping gut.

VITTORIA. How exciting! But you didn't leave me out, did you?

KROTT. Paint a shipwreck without a ship?

MANDOLINO (*who has been ferreting among his books*). Look. (*He gives Vittoria a volume*)

VITTORIA (*reading the title*). "American Drama from Fitch to Krott," by Mortimer Zwi, zwi, swi—

KROTT. Zwiegelbein.

VITTORIA. I'm impressed.

MANDOLINO (*leafing through the book still in her hands*). Let me show you.

KROTT. Children, children! I'm crimson with bashful delight. (*He covers his face with a vast red handkerchief*) Go on, don't stop, I can't stand it.

VITTORIA. Isn't he a scream!

MANDOLINO. I've found it. (*He points to a passage*)

VITTORIA (*reads, not without some difficulty*). "The degradation, corruption and ultimately the collapse of the American dream is nowhere better exemplified than in the shorter plays of Delancey Krott, in which the festering sores of an overripe society are exhibited without pretty evasions."

KROTT. *Petty* evasions.

VITTORIA. Isn't it true though. This country is in terrible shape, isn't it?

KROTT (*removing his handkerchief*). Gruesome.

MANDOLINO. "They are not so much short plays as rotten leaves torn directly from a decaying tree."

KROTT. I wish I'd written that sentence.

MANDOLINO. I don't want you to be too amazed when you see the play, Miss Grazzi. I haven't read it yet, but—Hey, you won't see the play! (*He beams*) You'll be in Italy during the whole run—and by the way, I've got all the material I promised to bring you. Why don't we look it over now? Delancey, sit in a corner and polish your ego.

KROTT. Witling! I want to see to what pestilential holes you're driving your lovely *studentessa*.

VITTORIA. I'm afraid I'm not going to Italy.

MANDOLINO and KROTT. What? Why not?

VITTORIA. Something happened the day before yesterday. I tried to call you but I couldn't reach you. And then I thought, by this time he's certainly gone to all the trouble already, so I might as well keep the appointment, especially since Frank may be able to use the material.

MANDOLINO. Who is Frank?

VITTORIA. My next-older brother.

KROTT. Aha!

MANDOLINO. Of course your brother is welcome to everything here, but do you care to tell us what happened, or is it a family secret?

VITTORIA. Oh, I don't suppose it's a secret. But it'll sound awfully silly to sophisticated people like you and especially Mr. Krott.

KROTT. I'll leave the room at once—after hearing the story. Tell us, tell us.

VITTORIA. Well, I was looking for a plain box for my jewelry—I haven't got much, but I'd hate to have it stolen—so I was rummaging in our closets, when I saw exactly what I needed. I opened the box and lo and behold it was full of letters.

KROTT. Sinister.

VITTORIA. Love letters.

MANDOLINO. How nice!

VITTORIA. Love letters between Frank—my brother—and a girl by the name of Luisa Rosso. And now I'd better explain who Luisa Rosso is.

KROTT. I should hope so!

VITTORIA. She's the closest friend of one of my cousins in Acquaviva. We've all been corresponding ever since we were kids—although we've never seen each other—and even some of the neighbors and relatives of relatives have gotten into the game. We write in English and they answer in Italian. It was always a lot of fun. And then we exchanged photographs.

KNOTT. Franco saw Luisa, Luisa saw Franco, a secret correspondence began, and, as we all show to advantage in the haze of distance and foreign languages, the two children inevitably fell in love.

VITTORIA. Frank is twenty-two.

MANDOLINO. What happened after you found the letters?

VITTORIA. I gave Frank an awful scolding. "Why didn't you tell me about this?" I said. "Am I some kind of stranger; are you ashamed before your own sister? *You're* the one who's going to Italy now." The poor boy hadn't opened his mouth when the family chose me because he knew how badly I longed to go. But I went to work fast. Day before yesterday I called the two families together again—we've got our own funny way of calling family meetings—and there I made a long speech about love, and then we all decided that Frank was the one who must be our emissary.

MANDOLINO. After making all your wonderful plans!

VITTORIA. A girl shouldn't be selfish.

KROTT. A splendid Jamesian comment! If I hadn't all but completed my script, I might have taken a cue from your last words to reprogram my brain. The girl who seeks a desperate escape from "America" in quotation marks and all that it represents, and who lives for her one journey to Europe—freedom, civilization, the arts. At the last moment she sacrifices it all to a brother, a worthless brother—

VITTORIA (*protests*). Frank is—

KROTT. The ethical claim asserts itself over the hedonic life—duty triumphs over pleasure — and the girl experiences a victory of sorts, but oh, the price she pays! A life of drab sameness and joyless confinement.

VITTORIA (*cheerfully*). Well, I certainly don't want anything drab to happen to *me*. So I've decided to take a summer job and maybe even work a few evenings a week during the next academic year. My dad promised that if I keep up my grades he'll give me a job himself. I've already got my travel outfits. So it'll only be a year—I won't be an old lady yet!

KROTT. Hopeless!

VITTORIA. Not me! I'm always optimistic.

MANDOLINO. Here, Miss Grazzi, take these to your brother, he can keep them all summer.

VITTORIA. Thank you so much, Dr. Mandolino. Frank is very neat, so I'm sure they'll all be as good as new when you get them back.

MANDOLINO. Let me know when the wedding is!

VITTORIA. Let you know? You're both invited!

MANDOLINO. Till September then, and I expect a full report. I suppose I'll see you in Italian Six.

VITTORIA. Wouldn't miss it for anything. (*To Delancey*) Will you still send me those tickets, in spite of my not going to Italy?

KROTT. Of course! And be sure to bring the family.

VITTORIA. 26 Flower Street, Brooklyn 11211.

KROTT (*writing it down*). Done. Let me know what you think of the play.

VITTORIA. Oh, I will! Thank you so much. Well, I guess I'll say good-bye now.

MANDOLINO and KROTT. Good-bye! Have a nice summer. (*Delancey opens the door for her and she leaves*)

MANDOLINO. Well well well well.

KROTT. Well well well well what?

MANDOLINO. Really a sweet girl. And a wonderful family, obviously.

KROTT. Are you about to suggest that I throw perfume into that bottle of pumped water?

MANDOLINO. Why not? Reality. Now don't get mad at me again. Let's have lunch, I'm starved.

KROTT. You're treating me for a change?

MANDOLINO. I'm treating you for a change. Let me get my things together. (*He gathers papers and books*) Reality, when you come down to it—

KROTT. Reality, you dangling participle, reality is the dung under the ding dong bell. Do you hear the bells of the world tolling? Ding dong dung. No you don't hear the bells of the world tolling. You've got your Vittoria, your Italian pump, your sweet secret in Frankie's bosom. The real Vittoria and Frankie that I am trying to make you see, the slime under these buttercups, you don't want to see. But I, and every honest artist with me, shall pull their smiles wide open and show you down those sickening gullets the corridors to death.

MANDOLINO. All right, all right, but after lunch, Delancey?

KROTT. Tragic muse, poison his apple pie!

The End

Notes

Water From an Italian Pump appeared in *The Mediterranean Review* (a short-lived quarterly whose real home was Long Island) in its Winter 1972 number. I published a corrected version in *The Virgin and the Unicorn: Four Plays* (1993). It is further revised here.

The 1993 version was followed by an "Afterword with a Tinge of Manifesto" which I give here with some modifications:

Vittoria Grazzi's tale as seen by Vittoria herself comes to me as a true story my wife told me at the dinner-table one day concerning a student of hers. Impressed by this piece of the rawest reality, I began to wonder whether a writer boasting of an irreproachable record of publication by the most esoteric quarterlies and the obscurest presses, and productions in the least commercial of all possible theaters—whether, in short, an immaculately *serious* writer of our times could flaunt such a kind, happy, simple and normal character in a fiction without instant expulsion from the brotherhood of Intellectuals.

Let me explain. Victorian England and Fillmore America sentimentalized sanity, happiness, and goodness almost to death. Their grand cultural reluctance, we all know, was bare sex. We, instead, have bared sex almost to death, recording a thousand times over—in our elite stories, poems, novels, plays and films—every imaginable performer, partnership and position. Our grand cultural blushes (to complete the symmetry) are aroused by goodness, sanity, and happiness. Only "commercial hacks," only confectioners of lollipops for the Moral Majority, come forward to affirm that not all men, women and children are either globs of shapeless jelly or pestiferous predators. Hearing this, and hearing it from such quarters, highbrows give each other the wink, and sneer.

There is a touch of exaggeration in what I say, but only a touch. And I feel free to ask, in the next place, like Dr. Mandolino, What about Reality? We have sufficient evidence that sex *was* practiced in the nineteenth century, and that people did not procreate by means of an exchange of fine English words. And we are quick to chide the very best Victorian writers for lowering their eyes before this vast sector of Reality. But by the same token, there *is* sanity, goodness and happiness abroad in our times. They too continue to occupy a vast sector of Reality. Let us leave our "commercial hacks" to one side, and severely quiz our serious writers: Where, ladies and gentlemen, is *your* honesty? Are you not the self-same cowards and hypocrites as Jane Austen, and Charles Dickens, and Henry James? You are; and arbitrary convention trammels you as tightly as it did your craven predecessors. You have not, contrary to your belief, broken free of convention; you have merely enslaved yourselves to a new one.

I might add, as it were in parentheses, that this very nearly universal exclusion of mere goodness from serious literature finds parallels in the widespread absence of the element of beauty from the visual arts and the near-total rejection of melody in serious music. But this needs exploration elsewhere.

As soon as the serious writer gives his assent to the proposition that even in our century of gas chambers and hydrogen bombs the Vittoria Grazzi qualities survive, he ought to claim for his art (be it realistic or dada) the right of access to this lovely material. It *must* be possible to reconcile high Art with a subject even as recalcitrant as human goodness. It is intolerable that *any* sector of Reality be excluded from the best literature.

Though fired by this conviction, I had still to face the problem of how to "imitate" kindness, simplicity of heart, and innocent sanity without dishonoring myself. I came up at last with the hoary trick of the wooden horse concealing the Greeks. I gave myself the proper credentials: invented Krott (the reader whose French has weakened is invited to look up the word *crotte* in his dictionary), wrote an "experimental" comedy, provided sexual antics, injected a dose of psychobiographical cant—everything suitably nasty—and so, flashing my best off-off-Broadway grin, smuggled in my Vittoria—and an amiable satire of avant-garde theatre.

HOW ALOOTOOK CAME TO DANCE A GAVOTTE

CHARACTERS

John Sebastian Talbot
Daisy Talbot, *his wife*
Alice Talbot, *their daughter*
Alootook
Jim Cash
Tennyson Cash, *his son*
Reginald Buckingham
An Angel
A Policeman
An Ambulance Driver
A Doctor
The Black Shadow

SCENE ONE

(A used car lot. Used cars. An office. Bunting. A banner which reads: DON'T BE RASH, DEAL WITH CASH. Reginald Buckingham is polishing up one of the cars. Jim Cash and his son Tennyson are sitting on the office steps. A radio at their side is broadcasting one of Scarlatti's sonatas. Cash is reading aloud from a book.)

CASH. "And Saint Francis goes behind the altar and kneels down in prayer. And as he prayed he was inspired by the divine presence with fervor so exceedingly great that his whole soul was burning with love for holy poverty; in such wise that what with the hue of his face and the strange yawning of his mouth, it seemed as if flames of love were bursting from him. And coming thus aflame towards his companion— "

REGINALD. Here's a customer, Mr. Cash.

CASH. Eh? So there is. Will you take care of him, Mr. Buckingham?

REGINALD. Of course, Mr. Cash.

CASH *(to Tennyson)*. We'll go on reading inside the office, son.

REGINALD. Don't go for *my* sake.

CASH. No, Mr. Buckingham, there's something private, mysterious and tender between a salesman and his customer which no man should intrude upon. Why, I might glance at his left lapel and destroy the vital atmosphere. Come along, Tenny.

TENNYSON. Shall I turn off the radio?

CASH. What do you think, Mr. Buckingham?

REGINALD. Well, sir, he might be fond of Scarlatti, and then again he might prefer something by one of the modern gentlemen with drums and electric guitars. One never knows. Indeed—

CASH. You're right, Mr. Buckingham. Silence Scarlatti, my boy, and let's take Saint Francis into the office. Mr. Buckingham, I wish you success.

REGINALD. Oh, after ten years with you, sir—but thank you anyway.

(Cash and his son disappear into the office. Enter John Sebastian Talbot. He looks at the banner to make sure he is in the right place.)

TALBOT. Mr. Jim Cash?

REGINALD *(giving Talbot his card)*. No, sir. Reginald Buckingham, chief salesman. Can I be of assistance?

TALBOT *(reading the card)*. "Reginald Buckingham. Integrity backed by four centuries of British aristocracy. 97 Myrtle Street." (*Holding out his hand*) My name's Talbot. John Sebastian Talbot.

REGINALD. Pleased to meet you, Mr. Talbot. I hope we can accommodate you this morning. Anything in particular?

TALBOT. I'm not sure. Maybe you can offer a few suggestions. I stopped at Cutright's car lot earlier today—

REGINALD. Our roughest competitor, Mr. Cutright. Dear man. Impeccably in business for twenty-nine years.

TALBOT. I know, but then again he told me he didn't have a single car on hand that he could recommend.

REGINALD. I'm surprised.

TALBOT. He said, for some reason or other all his cars were gargling today.

REGINALD. Gargling?

TALBOT. Or gurgling. They go glg-glg-glg-glg on the road. Mr. Cutright thought it might be due to the southwesterlies we've been having lately. He said they carry sand particles into the differentials.

REGINALD. That's odd. We haven't experienced anything like it. Perhaps the General Motors plant across the way keeps the wind out for us. And so?

TALBOT. And so Mr. Cutright said I could of course take a chance, because in time some of the cars might grow out of their gargle, or gurgle, but for the moment he would take it upon himself to recommend Mr. Cash. I'm quoting.

REGINALD. I see. Of course, this places quite a responsibility on our shoulders. About how new or how old a car were you thinking of? And what sort, speaking in a general way?

TALBOT. I was thinking of something about three years old. Or two, or four, or somewhere in between.

REGINALD. I see.

TALBOT. And the car should be friendly, even a little on the—on the witty side, if you know what I mean. We're a humor-loving family.

REGINALD. Nothing too—compelling—too authoritarian—

TALBOT. Or too solemn.

REGINALD. I have it. I think I know what you need.

TALBOT (*looking around*). Actually, most of your cars look pretty attractive.

REGINALD. Oh, you mustn't let appearances deceive you, Mr. Talbot. We polish them, true; our dignity demands it; but sometimes underneath these shining bodies, shocking blemishes lie concealed.

TALBOT. You don't say. Well, I'm in your hands, Mr. Buckingham. Frankly, I'm a cretin as far as automobiles are concerned. I'm in real estate myself.

REGINALD. A very interesting line, Mr. Talbot. But let me show you a car that may suit you. This one, for instance.

TALBOT. Not bad. It's the color of Daisy's eyes. Daisy is my wife.

REGINALD. A good omen, Mr. Talbot.

(*Reginald lifts the hood*)

TALBOT. Spic and span. Even I can see that.

REGINALD. Well now, not quite, not quite. A used car is a used car, Mr. Talbot; don't entertain too many illusions about it even under the best of circumstances. Here, for instance, the generator is none too efficient.

TALBOT. Still, I'm sure—

REGINALD. Oh, of course, the car *will* do its duty, if you are firm with it. It will move, both forward and backward. The valves and pistons, I might add, are in tip-top shape, the spark plugs are clean and decent, and the oil filter filters the oil. But now and then the crankshaft tries to move sideways.

TALBOT. Don't we all.

REGINALD. Let me turn on the ignition. (*He is inside the car*) Are the headlights delivering? (*He turns on the lights*)

TALBOT. Yes, they're fine.

REGINALD. Here goes. (*He turns on the engine*)

TALBOT. Sounds good. Putt-putt-putt. Sounds normal.

REGINALD. What's that?

TALBOT. I said, "Sounds normal."

(*Reginald reappears*)

REGINALD. Normal, Mr. Talbot! What is normalcy? An open invitation to trouble. (*He listens to the motor*) I suppose the engine will do. Wait—there's a ping. Can you hear it?

TALBOT. No.

REGINALD. Listen carefully. (*He accompanies the rhythm of the motor*) There, there, there, ping - ping - ping -

TALBOT. Oh, I don't know. Nothing is perfect. You've got to make allowances.

(*Reginald plunges in with a wrench*)

TALBOT. You shouldn't get yourself dirty.

REGINALD. There! How is it now? Hush ... I can still detect it. My ear is attuned, you see. It's nothing dangerous; but this is a ping that will have to affect the price of the car. (*He listens again*) Ping ping. Unquestionably.

TALBOT. Really, I can't see why—

REGINALD. What are you saying, Mr. Talbot? I hope you trust me. (*Turns motor off*)

TALBOT. I do.

REGINALD. You admitted that you know next to nothing about automobiles.

HOW ALOOTOOK CAME TO DANCE A GAVOTTE

TALBOT. Still—

REGINALD. This *may* be the car for you, Mr. Talbot, but only if we can agree on a price.

TALBOT. The more I look at it, the better I like it. All right, Mr. Buckingham, cards on the table. How much?

REGINALD. Cards on the table, Mr. Talbot. For you—we'll say a thousand dollars.

TALBOT. That's ridiculous. A thousand dollars! For this car?

REGINALD. A thousand dollars is a reasonable price. Remember the dubious generator.

TALBOT. I remember it; but what about the healthy valves? And the clean spark plugs?

REGINALD. What about the ping ping?

TALBOT. Far-fetched.

REGINALD. Believe me—

TALBOT. No, Mr. Buckingham, I've been in business too long to be fooled with. Let's say twelve-hundred, that's what the car deserves, and we'll call it a deal.

REGINALD. That would be robbery! I don't mean to offend you. But Mr. Cash wouldn't stand for it. It's not an offer I could even show him.

TALBOT. If that's your last word (*he moves away*)—maybe another time.

REGINALD. Wait! You're a hard bargainer, Mr. Talbot. Let's split the difference. The car will need a new clutch within the year, I'm sure; I'm almost sure. Eleven hundred.

TALBOT. I don't like to rob anybody. You people are squeezed from all sides. I know the profit margin is minute.

REGINALD. Minute? We'll live like feudal kings on your eleven hundred, Mr. Talbot.

TALBOT. Pooh.

REGINALD. Like Byzantine emperors!

(*They laugh*)

TALBOT. I'm a pushover for a good sales talk. Here.

(*They shake hands*)

REGINALD. You won't regret it, Mr. Talbot. She's really a healthy little car.

(*A band nearby is heard playing a rousing fanfare*)

TALBOT. Good God, that's more than—

REGINALD. What did you say?

TALBOT (*louder*). I said that's more than I expected! Do you always celebrate a deal with music?

REGINALD. Ha, ha, ha, very good! No, Mr. Talbot, just a coincidence. It's

HOW ALOOTOOK CAME TO DANCE A GAVOTTE

the General Motors band. Wait. They're bound to have somebody out singing too. They always do in warm, sunny weather.

ALOOTOOK (*singing off stage while the band accompanies him; Reginald nudges Mr. Talbot and encourages him to pay attention*)

> Let every voice in industry be raised;
> The mercy of the Lord be praised;
> With meteors dreadful destroy us he might,
> Yet daily he spares us the heavenly blight.
>
> And sing of heaven's mighty grace
> Which orders the moon "Stray not from thy place,"
> Which keeps down the sun to a civilized heat
> When broil us it could with most horrible speed.
>
> Amen

TALBOT. That's what I call a fine baritone. He ought to go far in the automobile industry.

REGINALD. I'm glad you think so. He's a friend of ours.

TALBOT. The baritone?

REGINALD. Yes. His name is Alootook. He's an Inuit.

TALBOT (*impressed*). An Inuit? You don't see many of *them* here in town. I guess the climate's too warm for them.

REGINALD. This one is a black Inuit, he doesn't mind the sun.

TALBOT (*more impressed*). Do tell!

REGINALD (*confidential*). Not only that. His mother was Jewish. Before she passed on.

TALBOT. I'll be damned! What does he do at the plant?

REGINALD. He's a foreman. That's why he gets the solo parts, you know.

TALBOT. You don't say!

(*Enter Cash and Tennyson*)

CASH. Alootook was booming like a happy bull this morning.

REGINALD. Oh, Mr. Talbot, I want you to meet the owner and my employer, Mr. Jim Cash. And this is his son, Tennyson.

CASH. Glad to meet you, Mr. Talbot.

TALBOT. The pleasure's mine. Hello, my boy.

TENNYSON. How do you do.

CASH. Well, Mr. Talbot, has Mr. Buckingham fitted you with a car you can live with?

TALBOT. Yes he has. I'm buying this supersonic job right here. Oh, I forgot! The money. Money-money-money. We said twelve hundred.
REGINALD. Eleven hundred, Mr. Talbot.
TALBOT. Oh yes. (*He counts out the bills*) Here you are. Byzantine dollars.
REGINALD. And here's your certificate of ownership. I do hope you're happy with the car.
CASH. Remember, we stand behind our merchandise.
TENNYSON.
> Impartial censure we request from all,
> Prepared by just decrees to stand or fall.

TALBOT. Aha. So that's how it is. Poetry.
TENNYSON. Yes, sir. William Congreve.
TALBOT. Is your son studying to be a poet, Mr. Cash?
CASH. Yes he is. That's why my wife and I named him Tennyson. We wanted him to do something practical and useful. She alas left me for other horizons. What do *you* do, Mr. Talbot, if I may ask?
TALBOT. I'm in business like yourself, Mr. Cash, except that I scrounge in the real estate line. Work work work. Adam's curse.
CASH, REGINALD and TENNYSON. How true.
TALBOT. Well, I'd better be on my way. I'll drive the car up and down a few hills.
REGINALD. Any time we can be of help. It's been a genuine pleasure.
TALBOT. It has. (*Reginald is about to open the car door for him when he stops*) You know, the more I look at the three of you—
CASH. Yes?
TALBOT. I like your faces, hang it.
CASH. We like yours too, Mr. Talbot. What's on your mind?
TALBOT. I wonder if I could interest you in a deal.
CASH. Why not?
TALBOT. I mentioned that I'm in real estate.
CASH. You did.
TALBOT. All right, here's the story. I've had my eyes on a property in the outskirts—a vacant piece of land crying out to be developed. Mind you, this is inside information. I'm looking for a few partners to raise the necessary funds with me. And beyond that, I'm simmering up a scheme, a scheme, in a word, a scheme, a good scheme, as sound as the first bleat of the newborn lamb. This is sudden, I know, call it a gush of sympathy, anyway I wonder if you gentlemen might be interested.
CASH. We might.
REGINALD. Sounds jolly.

HOW ALOOTOOK CAME TO DANCE A GAVOTTE

TALBOT. A windfall, gentlemen.

CASH. Tell us more.

TALBOT. I've got a better idea. Let's see. It's ten-thirty now—

TENNYSON. Ten-thirty? How about our coffee break, dad?

CASH. In a minute, son. Don't interrupt Mr. Talbot.

TALBOT. That's all right. Coffee breaks must be taken seriously. But here's what I suggest. Come over to my house at three or four this afternoon. Let me give you my card, here's the address. Close shop early; you'll drink coffee again, we'll talk business, and you'll get to meet my wife and daughter. How does that sound?

CASH. I'm willing. How about you, Mr. Buckingham?

REGINALD. Women, coffee, and business: I'll be there, Mr. Talbot.

TALBOT. Well, that is that. Open the door, Mr. Buckingham. I'm driving off.

CASH. Why don't you join us for our coffee break before you go?

TALBOT. Thanks, but I'm overdue for the one at my office.

REGINALD. Here you are, sir. The keys are in the ignition. Go easy on the fuel pump, Mr. Talbot. (*He brushes the car seat*)

TALBOT. Good springs. I feel at home with the beast already. Fine. I'll see you all between three and four.

CASH. We'll be there, ready to deal and dally. Good luck!

TALBOT (*driving off*). I'm off!

ALL (*waving*). So long!

CASH. Watch the fire hydrant!... He made it.

(*Talbot is gone*)

CASH. Well, Mr. Buckingham, you've done it again. Another car sold, another entry in the ledger, another vacancy on the lot, and another commission for you.

REGINALD. Thank you, sir.

CASH. How much did you ask for the car?

REGINALD. A thousand dollars.

CASH. You should have started at nine hundred. I hope you are not endangering your soul.

REGINALD. I hope not, Mr. Cash. I do my best.

CASH. Well, your best, I must admit, is very good indeed.

TENNYSON. Coffee break, dad.

CASH. All right, Tenny, go get the coffee. Here. (*He gives money to Tennyson*) One with and one without. And a lemonade for you.

(*Exit Tennyson*)

CASH. In fact, Mr. Buckingham, I think we should be looking into the question of a promotion for you.

REGINALD. Oh really—

CASH. I mean it. I read in the paper this morning that Fred Spalding is on the road again.

REGINALD. Spalding? The president of Chase National?

CASH. That's right. Left the bank yesterday at three in the afternoon with a satchel over his shoulders and a staff in his hand, and headed for the countryside, patting dogs and children as he went.

REGINALD. Not a week goes by—

CASH. As you know, I keep a walking stick in the garage, and satchels can be bought. At my age, Saint Francis was dead. I'm single; why shouldn't I walk into the woods? I'll take Tenny along; the beauty of the poet's trade is that you can ply it on the road as well as in the office.

REGINALD. I don't know what to say.

CASH. You've been chief salesman for six years, Mr. Buckingham; a faithful disciple, in short. Now I've been studying a proposal, which I happen to have drawn up myself, to create the post of executive manager for my business, and to appoint you to fill the vacancy. You'll send me ten percent of the gross care of General Delivery hither and yonder, wherever the grass is green and the cows look satisfied. This is no mean promotion, Mr. Buckingham.

(*Tennyson has returned with the coffee*)

REGINALD. Thank you, Tenny. I'm overwhelmed, Mr. Cash; and yet, as promotions go, I had hoped—

CASH. Go on, don't be afraid to speak.

REGINALD. What I'd really like is more vacations, Mr. Cash. Two months instead of six weeks.

CASH. You're pushing me against the wall, Mr. Buckingham. May I borrow your spoon? Very well, take the two months. Either I'll close shop while you're gone or I'll delay my pilgrimage.

REGINALD. I wouldn't worry about Saint Francis, sir. You've plenty of time. The medieval life-span was a good deal shorter than ours.

CASH. I don't know. I love my used cars, but I need to be drenched on the open road, and my mouth wide open to the wind.

TENNYSON. Look, here comes Mr. Alootook! Mr. Alootook, come over here, I'll get you your glass of milk.

CASH. Here. (*He gives Tennyson money. Exit Tennyson*)

ALOOTOOK. Morning everybody.

CASH and REGINALD. Good morning, Mr. Alootook.

CASH. Roll up a chair, Alootook. You were in fine voice this morning. I was in the office reading aloud, and the trucks going down Broadway, but I heard you all the same.

REGINALD. A rich throat, Mr. Alootook, mellow thunder.

ALOOTOOK. Nature has been good to me. Do you gentlemen realize, by the way, that 3,466 days have gone by without a detectable meteorite damaging this city? There's not been so much as a bump on a sparrow's head.

CASH. Is that the reason you're strolling about instead of terrorizing the assembly line?

ALOOTOOK. Terrorizing is good, ha, ha, ha! No, seriously. Muffle, you know, the vice-president, he came over to me and said, "Alootook, you were in fine voice today; take the morning off; we're turning out too many damn cars anyway." So here I am. The men have gone bowling.

(*Tennyson returns with the milk*)

ALOOTOOK. Thank you, Tenny.

TENNYSON. Your voice was round as a melon this morning, Mr. Alootook.

ALOOTOOK. Oh, I don't know. How about you, Tenny? Perpetrated any good poems lately?

TENNYSON. I hope so, sir. Would you like to hear my latest?

ALOOTOOK. I certainly would.

TENNYSON. Good! Gather round, everybody.

CASH. Is it a poem I know, Tenny?

TENNYSON. Nope. Hot off my pencil, and I mean hot.

REGINALD. This is going to be a treat.

(*Enter the Angel, dressed as a customer. He has a pair of wings growing out of his back through slits in his shirt. We only catch a glimpse of these wings, however, because he tucks them in and puts his coat on over them*)

ANGEL (*to the audience*). Why am I here? We are everywhere....

TENNYSON (*who has taken a sheet of paper out of his jacket*). The title—

REGINALD. Wait a moment, Tenny. Here's another customer.

TENNYSON. Oh no! This is our coffee break.

ALOOTOOK. The boy is right, Mr. Cash.

CASH. Don't anybody get excited. (*He walks over to the customer*) Sir, my name is Jim Cash. Are you shopping for a car?

ANGEL. I am, but there's no hurry. I'll look around quietly.

CASH. I won't hear of it. Join our little session. My boy Tennyson is about to recite one of his new poems. Here's a comfortable fender. Sit down, and we'll look at cars afterwards.

ANGEL. Thank you.

ALOOTOOK. Go on, Tenny.

TENNYSON (*reading*). "To Glycinta." That's the title, G-l-y-c and so on.

    I am weary, oh Glycinta, of thy raven kisses—

ALOOTOOK. Raven kisses? Excuse me for interrupting.
TENNYSON. That's all right.
ALOOTOOK. Why raven kisses?
CASH. Yes, Tenny, why raven kisses?
TENNYSON. Because a raven is a bird of ill omen and because it is predatory. You'll see; the kisses I'm talking about are of ill omen and they're predatory too. And then, raven reminds you of ravenous, which fits too.
ALOOTOOK (*whistling with admiration*). I'm answered all right.
REGINALD. Isn't the raven a kind of crow, Master Tennyson?
TENNYSON. Yes, they're related. The raven is a poetic crow; or you might think of the crow as a pedestrian raven.
REGINALD. I was thinking that the crow is supposed to be an intelligent bird.
CASH. That's correct.
REGINALD. Perhaps this adds something to raven kisses too.
ALOOTOOK. Ill-omened, predatory, ravenous and intelligent kisses?
TENNYSON. I doubt it.
REGINALD. It was only a thought.
ALOOTOOK. Go on, Tenny.
TENNYSON. I'll start again, otherwise it's like jumping over a ditch without a headstart.

TO GLYCINTA

I am weary, Oh Glycinta, of thy raven kisses,
I have lain between thy pudgy breasts, thy hungry
        thighs, too long,
And having wasted, flame by flame, the holy fires
        of my youth,
And lost my teeth embracing thee, I seek the grave
        where I belong,
My flesh is eager for its worm; and yet I cannot pass away,
For still thy bawdy venom doth sustain my hated breath:
Thy tyrannous beauty beats me with soft hands
        away from death.

(*Applause*)
ALOOTOOK (*enthusiastic*). Did you all catch those paradoxes? Come on, Tennyson, read it again.
(*Tennyson reads the poem again*)
ALOOTOOK. Fantastic! The venom that keeps him alive, the beauty he hates because he loves it, because because he loves it he can't die. Fantastic!
REGINALD. I liked that bawdy venom.

HOW ALOOTOOK CAME TO DANCE A GAVOTTE

TENNYSON. Did you notice the pun?
REGINALD. What pun?
TENNYSON. Bawdy, body.
REGINALD. Oh, very good, very good.
CASH. And "my flesh is eager for its worm"—a shrewd reversal, I thought. But I don't know about "pudgy breasts".
ALOOTOOK. No, "pudgy breasts" is good. I mean, it doesn't really fit, Tenny, not here, your dad is right; but it's nice in itself. Realistic. Nice and homely and squishy.
REGINALD. Sexual and yet friendly.
ALOOTOOK. It stays in the family, so to speak. No, the line I object to is where you lose your teeth embracing the girl.
TENNYSON. I guess that's not right, is it?
CASH. Take it out, Tenny. Makes the girl sound like a piece of leathery steak. Or, come to think of it, like the crow you were just talking about.
TENNYSON. I only meant that the poet has grown old.
CASH. We know what you meant, Tenny, but that's not what you achieved.
TENNYSON. I'll change it, dad. But you liked "my flesh is eager for its worm"?
REGINALD. Magnificent!
ALOOTOOK. And those hungry thighs! (*Whistles*)
TENNYSON. You see, they go with the raven kisses. Everything fits.
CASH (*to the Angel*). What is your opinion, sir?
ANGEL. For a boy of fifteen—
CASH. It shows a lot of experience, don't you agree? The iambics, to mention nothing else.
REGINALD. When did you write this, Master Tenny?
TENNYSON. I finished it yesterday after the ball game. I was lapping up an ice cream soda with Sharon Goldberg when the bawdy venom struck me and I rushed home to put it down. In five minutes it was all over.
ALOOTOOK. Fantastic. Who's the girl, Tenny? Somebody real?
TENNYSON. Oh yes, it's Sharon Goldberg. She's in my Spanish class. She was mad because I don't come right out and mention her name.
ALOOTOOK. Well, I hope you're not *really* all that tired of her.
TENNYSON. No, I'm not. I'm only fifteen, you know. But I'm old and weary for the poem's sake. And I told Sharon, "If the poem is good, to hell with the truth."
ANGEL. Well said, Master Cash. (*To Cash*) I predict your boy will go very far.
TENNYSON. Thank you, sir.
ANGEL. I came to look at used cars, but all I can think of now is love. A

pleasant improvement. No offense meant to your cars, Mr. Cash.

ALOOTOOK. I'm all quivery too. Those hungry thighs! But I've got to go back to work. So long everybody. Thanks for the milk and poem.

CASH. Come again tomorrow, Mr. Alootook.

ALOOTOOK. I will; and I'll bring a few doughnuts.

(Enter Alice Talbot, holding a couple of parcels. Alootook stops)

ALICE. Excuse me—which is Mr. Cash?

CASH. I am he. What can I do for you? A great deal, I hope.

ALICE. My name is Alice Talbot. I'm looking for my father. Mr. Cutright told me I might find him here.

CASH. Delighted to make your acquaintance, Miss Talbot. Your father left a few minutes ago after buying one of our cars. I think you will like it. He also summoned us to a business conference at your house this afternoon. With coffee and what-not.

ALICE. How nice! Well, since he's gone—I was going to invite myself to lunch with him—after gadding about all morning — but I'll go home instead. Thank you so much.

CASH. Are you walking, Miss Talbot?

ALICE. Yes, I am.

CASH. Not anymore. Allow me to give you a lift in one of my many cars. *(Pointing at the Angel)* Mr. Buckingham, take care of this gentleman while I'm gone. *(He opens a car door)* Miss Talbot.

ALICE. Thank you.

(She is standing at some distance from the car. She has already caught a glimpse of Alootook. Reginald hands Alootook a brick; Alootook advances resolutely between Alice and the automobile, and places the brick on the ground. Alice takes a long look at him; she looks at the brick; and then deliberately inadvertently stumbles over it and drops a parcel.)

ALICE. Oh!

ALOOTOOK. Let me help you. Dear me, you might have hurt yourself. *(He picks up the parcel. They hold hands for a longer time than is natural)* I'm afraid you've scuffed your shoe.

ALICE. And I almost fell. But thanks to you I didn't. I'm very grateful, Mr.—

REGINALD. This is Mr. Alootook. A prince among men. Single. Excellent baritone.

TENNYSON. Loves good poetry.

REGINALD. Mad about mechanical engineering. He works for General Motors.

ALICE. It must be very interesting.

ALOOTOOK. Oh yes. Thumping machines, great echoes of metal, hammers and rivets going all day, whistles and wheezes, it's tremendous.

ALICE (*shyly*). They must like you.

REGINALD. Everybody likes him. My name is Reginald Buckingham. Executive manager.

ALICE. I'm glad to know you. (*But she doesn't see him*) Shall I take my parcel again?

ALOOTOOK. I have a better idea.

ALICE. Yes?

ALOOTOOK. Let me hold the other one for the time being. Until you're completely recovered.

ALICE. Actually it's very light. Two lace handkerchiefs.

ALOOTOOK. Still, one never knows. After almost taking a fall.

ALICE. I suppose so. (*She gives him the second parcel*)

ALOOTOOK. Miss Talbot—

ALICE. How do you know my name? Oh yes, I mentioned it.

ALOOTOOK. I even know Alice.

ALICE. Yes.

ALOOTOOK. I have a substantial income; suitable for—for anything.

ALICE. I'm so glad. I mean, it's pleasant for you.

ALOOTOOK. And whoever else. Did you know that baritones are professionally less demanding than tenors?

ALICE. Really?

ALOOTOOK. It's a fact. Domestically too. They tend to help around the house.

ALICE. The baritone's a more restful voice, anyway, like a cello.

ALOOTOOK. Exactly! May I ask, Miss Talbot, do *you* do anything for a living?

ALICE (*laughing*). Oh yes, I breathe regularly.

(*Alootook laughs*)

ALOOTOOK. You're fond of jokes.

ALICE. Only silly ones.

ALOOTOOK. Looking at you—I would like to remark that you are more beautiful than an angel.

ANGEL (*aside*). Gently!

ALOOTOOK. I say to myself, she must be tremendously engaged to somebody.

ALICE. Oh no.

ALOOTOOK. Not even a little?

ALICE. Not even. I had never met the man I wished to marry.

ALOOTOOK. How would you know if you did?

ALICE. How would I know? I'd meet him suddenly, out of nowhere. He'd do

something, and say something, it would taste like fresh water when you're parched, and then suddenly I'd want to be fascinating and irresistible, only it wouldn't matter, because at the same time I know what he'd like to be—
ALOOTOOK. A Greek God shooting about the clouds—for your sake—
ALICE. Well, not in the clouds. But he's not a god, and I'm not fascinating, so it fits together, and then his knowing what I felt and my knowing what he felt would make a circle around us, but it's very difficult to explain.
ALOOTOOK. I suppose I'm asking too many questions.
ALICE. One doesn't mind from a stranger.
ALOOTOOK. Oh, I'd forgotten.
ALICE. Forgotten what?
ALOOTOOK. That I *am* a stranger to you.
ALICE. It's better than—
ALOOTOOK. Than?
ALICE (*very softly*). Not being even that.
CASH. I have a feeling I won't be driving Miss Talbot home.
ALICE. Alootook....
ALOOTOOK. Alice, Alice....
(*She touches his lips with two fingers and brings them to her own*)
ALOOTOOK. And now?
ALICE. My shoe is scuffed, Alootook. Remember?
ALOOTOOK. By the grace of God, I know a shoemaker three blocks away.
ALICE. Please show me where he is.
(*They walk away, hand in hand*)
REGINALD (*cries after them*). Bless you, lovely creatures!
CASH. Now the earth is two, or even three loves richer than it was. There may be a presence haunting the neighborhood.
TENNYSON. I *thought* I smelled feathers.
CASH (*to the Angel*). My dear sir, you must be thinking it's about time we applied our faculties to your used car.
ANGEL. No, no, not at all. I'm somehow no longer in the mood for a car. For the moment, you understand.
REGINALD. I certainly understand. Lovely creatures!
ANGEL. Besides, I have other means of conveyance. But I'll be back.
CASH. If only to hear one of Mr. Buckingham's sales pitches. They are prize-winners. But you're right. Today—I don't know what.
ANGEL. Another day, Mr. Cash. Gentlemen. And Master Tennyson, keep composing; at eighteen, at twenty-one—heaven knows!
(*Tennyson bows; the Angel leaves*)
CASH. Well, Mr. Buckingham, we've heard Scarlatti on the harpsichord,

we have had a poem read to us, we've drunk coffee in peace and good company, we have witnessed the beginnings of a marriage, and I've come close to falling in love myself, but how many cars have we sold?
REGINALD. One, Mr. Cash.
CASH. That's plenty. Let's all go for a walk.

SCENE TWO

(In the Talbot's home. Daisy Talbot is sewing and listening to dance music over the radio.)

DAISY *(humming)*. Alice Alice Alice has done it has done it.
RADIO. We interrupt your afternoon entertainment to bring you a late bulletin. A series of volcanic explosions has rocked the island of Saint Barabbas. Within five minutes of the first explosion, the village of Granitti was engulfed by a flood of lava. Early reports put the toll at twenty-one dead and at least three times as many injured. We are extremely sorry to disturb you with this tragic report. More bulletins as they come in. *(Daisy is crying. Organ music on the radio. There is a honk outside, then John Talbot enters)*
TALBOT. Come out and meet the new car, Daisy! Why—you're crying—what's the matter?
(They kiss)
DAISY. Oh John—it's the radio—
TALBOT. What now?
DAISY. One of those awful volcanoes. Why do they have to exist?
TALBOT. Where did it happen, Daisy?
DAISY. The island of Saint Barabbas. Twenty-one people died. *(She cries again)*
TALBOT. Twenty-one! *(He wipes an eye too)* And here I come with a brand new car, all chipper and all. Poor devils!
DAISY *(trying to carry on)*. Did you find the car you wanted?
TALBOT. Yes, I did. You'll like it, Daisy-maisy. It's the same blue as your eyes. Shall we go look at it? It'll cheer us up a little.
DAISY. First let's say a prayer, John.
TALBOT. That's a wonderful idea.
DAISY. My Lord, take our brothers and sisters of Saint Barabbas under your special mercy, and especially the children.
TALBOT. And extinguish the volcano which revolted against you.

DAISY. And do better next time if you possibly can.

TALBOT. Amen. Give me your hand, Daisy.

(*They go out. The music plays on a while, and then the Black Shadow, in suitable burglarish clothes and a black mask, comes in carrying a full bag over his shoulder. He has entered through a window, calling out "Anybody home?" While he goes about his business, the music stops and the announcer's voice is heard again*)

RADIO. We interrupt this program to bring you another news bulletin. Washington. The War Department discloses that the 17th Infantry Division launched another assault on the rust-covered Potomac Bridge before dawn today. Armed with scrapers and benzene, the division's thirty-eight men succeeded in clearing several more steel girders without meeting with more than token resistance. It is reliably reported, however, that reinforcements will have to be flown in before the main cable tower can be handed over to the painting crew. We asked War Secretary McBoodle to comment on the report. (*Voice of McBoodle*) "We're still appraising the situation, Sam. Our boys are doing a heroic job." (*Announcer*) Is it true, sir, that the Russians have embarked on a major bridge-painting project throughout Siberia? (*McBoodle*) "Uh, all I'm free to say at this point, Sam, is that the Potomac Bridge is damn rusty." (*Announcer*) Now back to our regular program of flimsy music.

(*All this time the Black Shadow has been busy looking about carefully, opening doors and drawers and examining every object he sees. Outside a couple of honks are heard. The Black Shadow finally opens his bag and takes out a silver candlestick. Just as he is about to place it on a credenza, he notices that the Talbots already possess a silver candlestick. He replaces his own in his bag, from which he now extracts a silver teapot, which he sets down on the credenza. Another honk is heard. Hearing the front door open, he finds a hiding place, from which he will follow events with marked interest*)

DAISY. I like it, I really like it. And it hasn't got a vulgar honk, like most cars, but a pretty kind of toot toot.

TALBOT. I'm glad I hit it right. Well, I hope Alice likes it too.

DAISY. Alice! Our daughter Alice!

TALBOT. What's the matter?

DAISY. How could I forget? Where's my brain? Oh, it was that awful earthquake. Alice called an hour ago—

TALBOT. Look! Daisy! (*He points to the teapot*)

(*They look at each other, then huddle in each other's arms*)

BOTH. The Black Shadow!

DAISY. Oh John, he must have been here a minute ago, while we were looking at the car. Maybe he's still in the house. Why do you suppose he left us a teapot? I'm trembling all over.

HOW ALOOTOOK CAME TO DANCE A GAVOTTE

JOHN. Who knows? Do you realize that he has struck our neighborhood three times this month? So now it's become our turn. You always think it only happens to the other people.
DAISY. John, look for him, please, catch him and make him take the teapot away, and call the police.
JOHN. Oh, all right, I'll look for him. How do you talk to a criminal?
DAISY. I don't know. Be polite. Hurry up!
(*Talbot walks out of the room without great hurry, and we hear him rummaging*)
DAISY. See anyone?
TALBOT (*off-stage*). Not a trace.
DAISY. Try the back yard.
(*She examines the teapot, takes her coffee service out of the credenza, notes with approval that the teapot matches. The excited voice of the radio announcer suddenly breaks in on the music. Daisy pays close attention*)
RADIO. Ladies and gentlemen, I have just been handed the following late-breaking story. Boulder, Colorado: Professor Norman Harrington revealed today at 11:06 A.M. that the final effect of Chaucer's "Merchant's Tale" is not comic at all but sardonic, a dark and unsettling view of an aspect of man's experience. Questioned by newsmen who arrived on the scene at the University of Colorado, Professor Harrington asked (*voice of Professor Harrington*) "What about the prologue? What about the prologue? You must not read the "Merchant's Tale" outside the dramatic context of its prologue! We must fight the tendency to ignore the strong, viable presence of the narrator!" As soon as further particulars are available—
(*Daisy turns the radio off*)
DAISY. I'd better go read it again. Always something new.
(*Talbot returns*)
TALBOT. Not a sliver of him anywhere. I guess we'll have to call the police. What a nuisance. Good God, don't tell me he was here again!
DAISY. No, silly, that's our own coffee set. Look, a perfect match.
TALBOT. We're well off, damn it, we don't need his bric-a-brac.
DAISY. I wouldn't call it bric-a-brac. It's Victorian silver, John, let's be fair to the man.
TALBOT. Daisy, look into my eyes! Are you planning to use it? I knew it! What about the police? (*Solemn*) And what about your conscience?
DAISY. Oh, I don't know. You did have to stir it up. Wait! An inspiration! Daisy, you've done it again!
TALBOT. What now?
DAISY. It's divinely simple: we'll give the entire set to Alice for a wedding present.

HOW ALOOTOOK CAME TO DANCE A GAVOTTE

TALBOT. A *wedding* present?

DAISY (*clutching her head*). My head is spinning—I haven't even told you—every second another crisis!

TALBOT. Haven't told me what? Daisy, take hold of yourself.

DAISY. It was that awful Black Shadow, just as I was going to tell you. Alice called—that's it. She's married! Almost married.

TALBOT. To whom? When? What happened? I saw her at breakfast this morning. She was as unengaged as a baby. To the point of saying she'd let me take her out to lunch.

DAISY. Well, between breakfast and now, eight hours have gone by. It takes only thirty seconds to get engaged. Besides, it was you who practically introduced them.

TALBOT. Say that again?

DAISY. Alice went looking for you at the car lot for that famous lunch, but you were gone; instead she ran head-on into your son-in-law, a young man by the name of Alootook.

TALBOT. The General Motors baritone! I'll be pummeled!

DAISY. You've seen him?

TALBOT. No, but I heard him. He was singing two blocks away. Buckingham, the salesman, told me all about him. A splendid voice, Daisy, a *solid* voice.

DAISY. Well they met, and it was love at first sight. They went rowing on the lake—

TALBOT. Fast worker.

DAISY. She fell into the water and he saved her life. Of course—this is not for anybody else to know, John—she leaned over and pushed herself a little. Besides, she swims like a fish.

TALBOT. The minx!

DAISY. Whereupon they decided to get married.

TALBOT. For good?

DAISY. For good? What do you mean? Do you take your daughter for an idiot, John Sebastian? For good!

TALBOT. Young people go wild sometimes. For how long is it then?

DAISY. They decided on a decent five years. And then they'll see.

TALBOT. Five years is sound. It's long enough and yet it's not eternity either.

DAISY. John.

TALBOT. Yes?

DAISY. Are you remembering? That's the way we did it, the first time round?

TALBOT (*fondly*). I remember. And look at us now. (*They kiss. Daisy giggles happily*)

DAISY. He sounds like a very sensible young man.

HOW ALOOTOOK CAME TO DANCE A GAVOTTE

TALBOT (*suddenly grave*). Alootook. Yes. This reminds me, Daisy. I don't know whether Alice told you. Who and what he is.
DAISY. Yes, she did. I wanted to discuss it with you. I *am* a little worried, as a matter of fact.
TALBOT. No clouds on your pretty face, Daisy-maisy.
DAISY. No clouds, darling.
TALBOT. What did Alice tell you exactly?
DAISY. Well—first of all—he's Black.
TALBOT. So they told me.
DAISY. And then—this is really wild—he's an Inuit.
TALBOT. A very unusual combination. But is that all she mentioned?
DAISY. Oh dear, is there more?
TALBOT. Yes. Daisy, he is a Jew. His mother was Hebrew.
DAISY. Oh dear. I guess she forgot to mention *that*.
TALBOT. Let's face it, half of him is Black, half is Inuit, and half is Jewish.
DAISY. Oh dear, oh dear.
TALBOT. I'm sure he doesn't make a *display* of anything, Daisy.
DAISY. Still, look at him, and then look at us. Episcopalians with pink cheeks.
TALBOT. I thought we were Congregationalists.
DAISY. Well, whichever.
TALBOT. Come on, Daisy, cheer up. Alootook's not marrying the Talbots but Alice, and Alice is a charming girl, almost a beauty. You're not giving enough credit to her solo charms, so to speak.
DAISY. She *has* blossomed, hasn't she?
TALBOT. She's past the pigtail stage, anyway.
DAISY. And the freckles! Remember the lemons she used to rub on her cheeks?
TALBOT. Oh God, those lemons! (*They laugh*) Well, well, I've got a hunch that Alootook is open-minded. Besides, we'll see to it that she gets a suntan before the wedding day. Maybe she could read up on Deuteronomy. No—there was something that made me trust him the moment I heard Mr. Buckingham talk about him. And don't forget the voice and the music.
DAISY. Yes, that's a good point.
TALBOT.
>In sweet music is such art,
>Killing care and grief of heart.

(*The doorbell rings*) Who's that? Oh, it must be the gang from the car lot. I asked them over for coffee to discuss the property—you know.
DAISY. Fine! Open the door, I'll put the coffee on. (*She leaves one way, Talbot*

the other)

TALBOT (*off-stage*). Hello there!

REGINALD. How d'you do, Mr. Talbot.

TALBOT. Come in, come in; hang your hat here; follow me.

REGINALD. Thank you. (*Both enter; Reginald is holding a bouquet of flowers*) I had to come alone, Mr. Talbot. The chief was detained at a special knapsack sale. He sends his regards, and hopes you'll allow him to call on you another day. Meantime, I have full powers to negotiate in both our names.

TALBOT. Good good good. Daisy! Coffee and cake for a single guest! Mr. Cash couldn't come!

DAISY (*off-stage*). All right. I'll be with you in a minute.

TALBOT. Sit down, Mr. Buckingham. Wait—I'll take these. (*He relieves Reginald of the flowers*) Not necessary, you know.

REGINALD. Oh....

TALBOT. But Daisy will be delighted. (*He places the flowers in a vase as Reginald sits down*)

REGINALD. Before anything else, Mr. Talbot, I want to ask you whether you're satisfied with the automobile so far. I saw it snugly parked in the driveway.

TALBOT. No trouble so far, Mr. Buckingham. An unblemished record from your lot to my driveway, by way of my office.

REGINALD. If there's any indecency in the engine, you *will* let us know, I trust.

TALBOT. Certainly.

(*Enter Daisy with coffee, cakes, etc.*)

DAISY. Coffee everybody?

TALBOT. You bet. Daisy, this is Reginald Buckingham. Mr. B., my wife.

REGINALD (*very much impressed*). Delighted! (*He kisses Daisy's hand*) More than I can say!

DAISY (*also favorably impressed*). How do you do, Mr. Buckingham. I do like the car.

REGINALD. I'm so happy.

TALBOT. Daisy—look. (*He points to the flowers*)

DAISY. Oh, they're beautiful! But you shouldn't have, really! A silly cup of coffee!

REGINALD. Please don't mention it.

TALBOT. Do you want me to pour, my dear?

DAISY. Oh no, let me take care of everything. One thing at a time. Sugar and cream, Mr. Buckingham?

REGINALD (*who can't take his eyes off Daisy; at first forgets to answer*) Oh! Black, if you please, and no sugar. Thank you.

DAISY (*not unresponsive to his attention*). A tiny slice of chocolate cake?

REGINALD. Tiny. Oh, this is too much.

TALBOT. Nonsense. You can afford to put on a bit of flesh. A big one for me.

DAISY. Piggy! (*Jollity*)

TALBOT. I must notify you, Mr. Buckingham, that romance has blossomed in your car lot. (*Reginald, who is still staring at Daisy, is a little startled*) My daughter and Mr. Alootook—

REGINALD (*enthusiastic*). I know what you're going to say! I knew it! We all guessed it, even Tenny. I offer you my congratulations, your daughter is a lovely person. And now, I might add, I know why. (*He plunges his eyes into Daisy's*)

DAISY (*lowering hers*). Do you think they'll be happy, Mr. Buckingham?

REGINALD. I know they will. And I can vouch for Mr. Alootook. A prince. We've all known him for years; benevolence and peace in every vein. Also in every artery.

DAISY. I'm so glad. (*Blushingly*) I do believe in love at first sight.

REGINALD (*meaningfully*). I swear by it!

TALBOT. Pour some more stimulant for Mr. Buckingham.

REGINALD. Thank you. Yes, love at first sight is the most reliable of all—and also the most thrilling—of course. The most reliable, because it flares up naturally, you see, without calculations. Let's say that a maybug is walking on your arm. It tickles you. Instantaneously, you see, without your interfering with reasons and suppositions and evaluations. It touches, it tickles. Utterly reliable, utterly true and real. That's how it is with love at first sight.

TALBOT. Like a bug crawling over you, eh?

REGINALD (*protesting*). Oh no!

DAISY (*modestly*). I understand you, Mr. Buckingham.

REGINALD (*pregnantly*). I was sure you would.

DAISY. Do you think that Mr. Alootook feels as you do?

REGINALD. I know he does; we have had many conversations about these wonderful feelings. Besides, remember that he is a working man. Did Mr. Talbot tell you?

DAISY. My daughter did.

REGINALD. He works with his hands, he builds cars, he handles wrenches and drills. Such a man is, how shall I put it? palpable; you trust him; he is concrete.

TALBOT. Well, I'm glad Alice showed so much sense the very first time.

REGINALD (*amazed*). The very first time?

DAISY. Yes.

REGINALD. Even more exciting! Historical! And with a man of Alootook's tremendous experience and, hm, vitality. Splendid!

TALBOT. That's Alice for you. Always practical.

DAISY. And yet always a dreamer too, like her mother, always looking, looking....

REGINALD. Are you a dreamer, Mrs. Talbot?

DAISY. A little.... I'm afraid so.

TALBOT (*patting her hand*). And the softest heart in the world besides, like a newborn robin.

REGINALD. I hoped—I thought as much.

DAISY. Let's not talk about me. I keep thinking about my little girl. It all happened so suddenly.

REGINALD. Suddenly and yet, I'm sure, with every step in place. Even an avalanche is well-ordered, if you think of it sympathetically. I feel as though I could reconstruct in my mind the decisive scene between Alootook and your charming daughter. I see them walking hand in hand through the streets, oblivious to the world, interpenetrating each other's beings like two confluent rivers.

DAISY. Beautiful....

TALBOT. I'll have another slice.

REGINALD. They sit down in the park under a flowering chestnut tree. Alootook is the first to speak: "Our love is sudden, but it is as true as a fire ignited by lightning."

TALBOT (*his mouth full*). Longer-lasting, I hope. But I'm glad you brought up the subject of parks, Mr. Buckingham, because, if you'll remember, that was precisely—

DAISY. Oh John, can't you let your park wait five minutes? I want to hear what happened, or what might have happened, between Alice and Alootook. "Our love is true," he says ...

REGINALD. "As true as the river is portly under a summer rain." And she replies ecstatically—

DAISY. "As fine as the flower's start when an unrepentant bee pecks it for honey."

TALBOT. Good little Alice, always ready with an answer! Would you reach me the cream, Mr. Buckingham?

REGINALD (*absent-mindedly giving Talbot the cream, his eyes fixed on Daisy*). And he comes back with: "As splendid as a landscape alighting out of the fog."

DAISY. And she: "As delicate as the sun at dawn, removing its grey scarf and brushing every field awake."

TALBOT (*eating more cake*). Umblgffrmf. (*Aside*) Daisy's right, I'm making a pig of myself.

REGINALD. "I feel," he says, "like Adam waking upon Eve, there she stood, and his lips envied his eyes because his look outsped his kiss."

DAISY. "And I," she said, "I am Eve, newborn, child, and wife together."

REGINALD. He must have wanted to fall on his knees before her.

TALBOT. In the park? On the gravel?

DAISY. She must have wanted him to ask her, to dare, to wait no longer—

REGINALD. "Shall we flee? Shall we escape?"

DAISY. "Yes, my beloved"—she answered—"at once, anywhere, I will kiss your mouth as many times as there are galaxies in heaven."

TALBOT. Why should they flee and escape? They have our blessing, don't forget, and I intend to pay for their honeymoon, the best hotels.

REGINALD. "My happiness is like a storm of all the elements"—he says—"my body is a feather—I could leap over this table—I mean these trees—"

TALBOT. Daisy, this was one of your better cakes; but take it away before I devastate it.

REGINALD. *You* baked this cake, Mrs. Talbot? This delicious cake?

DAISY. I did. You see, I have my practical side too.

REGINALD (*enthusiastic*). I do see! (*He snatches another piece, and eats it devoutly*)

TALBOT. All right, now, down with the dishes. Let's talk business with Mr. Buckingham.

TALBOT. Cigar?

REGINALD. Thanks.

TALBOT. I'll be brief and blunt; all my cards are on the table.

REGINALD. Good; mine too.

TALBOT. There's a piece of undeveloped land going up for sale on the outskirts of town. A death in the family—land has to be unloaded—and I can get my hands on two hundred acres provided I scrape together fifteen thousand dollars in cash. I've got half the money myself, and I'm looking for the other half, and another five hundred a month thereafter.

REGINALD. Sounds interesting. But what will you do with the property? And do I smell a plot?

TALBOT (*chuckling*). This is confidential, old man.

REGINALD. Padlock on my lips.

TALBOT. A park, Mr. Buckingham. Daisy and I plan to convert the land into a park. Flowers, grasses, trees—the works. All the way. Let the fur fly and the windows rattle. A duckpond. Lawn chairs.

REGINALD. Like London.

DAISY. Puppet-shows.

REGINALD. Like Paris.
TALBOT. Open-air cafés—
REGINALD. With wicker chairs?
TALBOT. With wicker chairs, and waiters in black tie. Playgrounds. Fountains designed by mad sculptors. Statues.
REGINALD. Of naked goddesses!
TALBOT. Woodsy paths for lovers. Bicycle paths for children. Peacocks. Wasps in the yoghurt. You get the idea?
REGINALD. I do.
(*The Black Shadow, who has been visible to the audience all this time, becomes particularly attentive*)
TALBOT. So far so good. Then—say in five years—
DAISY. We strike.
REGINALD. We strike. How?
TALBOT. Donate the park to the city. Bang! Every competitor left gasping. Overnight we're civic benefactors. Overnight, Mr. Buckingham. Civic.
REGINALD (*whistling*). Civic. Deep.
TALBOT. Everything foreseen. Practically no risk. All we need is money to get started.
REGINALD. Very deep.
TALBOT. Brain at work twenty-four hours a day.
DAISY. Files available for inspection.
REGINALD. Oh, hardly necessary.
TALBOT. Interested?
REGINALD. Indeed.
TALBOT. What about Mr. Cash? What do you anticipate?
REGINALD. Don't worry about him. The best nose in town for a fragrant opportunity.
TALBOT (*rubbing his hands*). Good good good. Next question: how much have you personally got?
REGINALD. Oh, about three thousand, if I sell this and that.
TALBOT. Not bad. How about Mr. Cash?
REGINALD. Plenty.
TALBOT. But I don't want either of you to come to any sudden decision. Talk to Mr. Cash. Think it over. And we'll all get together again in a few days, visit the property, look at the papers, and all the rest.
DAISY. What do you think of it, Mr. Buckingham?
REGINALD. If it helps to bring me nearer—
TALBOT. Hold on, hold on, friend; I don't want you to participate for sentimental reasons. You're one of us anyway, we've adopted you, park or no

HOW ALOOTOOK CAME TO DANCE A GAVOTTE

park. The rest is strictly business.

REGINALD. It is. And it looks fabulous. Off-hand, of course. Mr. Cash and I *will* study the documents by and by. I'll come here to study them.

DAISY. I hear the door. It's Alice at last. Oh dear, I'm so excited!

(*Enter Alice and Alootook*)

ALICE. Mother! (*She flings herself in her mother's arms*)

ALOOTOOK. Sir. My name is Alootook.

TALBOT (*embracing him*). Son.

ALICE. This is Alootook, mother. We're married. We got married an hour ago.

ALOOTOOK. Baruchim hanimtzaim.

TALBOT. That is to say?

ALOOTOOK. Blessed are you who are here.

DAISY (*half-crying*). I don't know what to say. I guess I'll kiss the groom. Blessings on you both. Be happy.

ALOOTOOK. I'll be a good husband to your daughter, Mrs. Talbot.

TALBOT. Mrs. Talbot! She's your mother now, Alootook!

ALOOTOOK. I know, but it feels odd. You're too young. I'm thirty myself, you see.

DAISY. All the same, call me Daisy. Sit down, sit down. This is all so sudden, so wonderful. An hour ago?

ALOOTOOK. Yes. We decided not to wait.

REGINALD. Bravo!

ALOOTOOK. Mr. Buckingham! I didn't even see you!

REGINALD. Don't mind me. I'm really one too many in this family scene.

(*Protests*)

ALOOTOOK. I'm glad to find you here. (*To the Talbots*) We've known each other for years. (*Patting Reginald's back*) A prince!

ALICE. But *I* haven't really met Mr. Buckingham.

TALBOT. That's right!

ALOOTOOK. Sorry! Mr. Reginald Buckingham, Mrs. Alice Alootook, born Talbot.

REGINALD. We did meet briefly this morning.

ALICE. Yes, of course.

REGINALD. That lucky purchase of yours, Mr. Talbot! My abundant felicitations to both of you.

ALOOTOOK and ALICE. Thank you.

DAISY. May I ask you, Mr. Alootook—Alootook—is this your first and your last name?

ALOOTOOK. Yes, it is, Mrs. Talbot.

TALBOT. Daisy.
ALOOTOOK. Daisy. It'll be a little difficult at first. But enjoyable.
DAISY. I think Alootook is very nice. Sweet, short, and simple. Alootook. It has authority too.
TALBOT. Well, children, let's deflower a bottle of champagne, and when you're reeling we'll meditate on a wedding gift. (*He leaves, we hear a bottle popping, and then he returns with champagne and glasses*)
DAISY (*meantime*). Don't worry about a wedding present, Alice. I've got one here all ready for you. (*She shows the silver teapot*)
ALOOTOOK. Pretty!
ALICE. I've never seen this teapot before. When did you buy it?
DAISY. I didn't buy it. The Black Shadow was here while we were out, and this is what he left behind.
REGINALD. The Black Shadow! When will that fiend be caught at last? Why, the teapot matches the rest of your set!
ALOOTOOK. That's the way he works.
DAISY. Now that the set is complete, it will be lovely for the children.
TALBOT. Good idea. Illegal, though. Well, here's to a full five years of relentless bliss, and maybe a renewal or two!
EVERYBODY. Amen. (*Bride and groom embrace*)
ALICE. Oh, if you all knew how I love him! I wish I could run out into the street and hug everybody and cry "I married Alootook!"
ALOOTOOK. Alice! (*He kisses her again*)
TALBOT. Does this awaken something in you, Mr. Buckingham?
REGINALD (*ardently*). Oh, it does, it does. Oh, it does. Aaah.
TALBOT. Is anything the matter? Your glass is shaking.
REGINALD. No, nothing—*everything!*
ALICE. You are pale all of a sudden, Mr. Buckingham.
ALOOTOOK. Tell us what's the matter.
REGINALD (*to Daisy*). Shall I? Now? (*She nods demurely*)
TALBOT. Shall you what? Speak up, Mr. Buckingham! Has love bitten you too?
ALOOTOOK. That must be it. He has the same delirious look as mine.
REGINALD. This is—I propose—I am about to make a significant statement.
(*Daisy mutely encourages him*)
TALBOT. Steady now.
ALICE. I know it's going to be exciting! (*She kisses Alootook*)
REGINALD. Mr. Talbot, your wife and I wish to spend four weeks in Acapulco.
(*General surprise. Even Daisy is a little surprised*)

HOW ALOOTOOK CAME TO DANCE A GAVOTTE

ALICE. Mother!
ALOOTOOK. Fantastic!
TALBOT. Daisy! Is this true?
ALICE. In Acapulco?
TALBOT. I'm dumbfounded.
DAISY. Isn't that in Mexico, Mr. Buckingham?
REGINALD (*ardently*). In tropical Mexico. (*Daisy and Alice embrace*)
TALBOT. Daisy, you're taking me by surprise! When did all this develop?
DAISY. Now—somehow—with magnetic waves and things.
ALICE. You're wonderful, mother, every day another trick.
DAISY (*modestly*). I'm a little surprised myself.
ALOOTOOK. So much fire! And you, Mr. Buckingham, a volcano!
TALBOT. One moment, everybody! All these events in a single day. Alice—Alootook—our new car—the Black Shadow—and now Daisy—(Reginald pours him a glass of champagne) Thank you, old man. Reginald—Daisy—you are splendidly mature human beings—I hope you know what you're doing.
DAISY. It's only for four weeks, John. And only if it's not too too inconvenient for you. If it is, we can postpone it.
REGINALD. Quite.
TALBOT. Oh no, no inconvenience worth mentioning.
DAISY. My only worry is your being in the house by yourself for a month now that Alice is married.
TALBOT. Wait, wait! There's a solution for everything. When are you two leaving for your honeymoon?
ALICE. We were going to start tomorrow, and do the Grand Canyon.
TALBOT. What about General Motors?
ALOOTOOK. The usual three weeks honeymoon leave. No difficulty. Warm personal note from Muffle, our vice president.
ALICE. But we could postpone our trip, couldn't we?
TALBOT. You're a dear girl, Alice. But now that I've had a moment to think about it, I see the way clear for everybody. I've had a few—talks—as you know, my dear—with—
DAISY. Mrs. Glimmer, that's right! Her husband's the famous skindiver.
TALBOT. This might be a good time—four weeks—yes, my lovely people, I don't foresee any trouble. Glimmer's been wanting to skindive Rhode Island. It's all settled. Mr. Buckingham, your hand.
REGINALD. And yours, Mr. Talbot.
TALBOT. A magnificent final idea! As I'll be home for the next four weeks—or a few blocks away, to be precise—take the new car, drive to the Grand

Canyon with it, I'm paying all the bills, and when you're at the bottom of the canyon, Alootook, sing "John Talbot's a jolly good fellow," but loud, make my name, John Sebastian Talbot, bounce from wall to wall, let the sound print itself into the granite.
ALOOTOOK. Champagne! To John Talbot, may he thrive!
ALL. To John Talbot!
(From his hiding place, the Black Shadow mimicks the toast)

SCENE THREE

(A country road. At one end of the stage we see Alootook lying on the ground, Alice bent over him, and the wreckage of Talbot's car. The Angel appears in all his glory)

ANGEL. Alootook is dead. How did he die? It was raining. The wet highway curved while Alootook was telling Alice about the new synagogue in the Yukon. The car rolled off the road. It broke into many pieces. What can angels do? Alootook is dead. And you, my dears, are going to die too. So it goes. You know, of course, that for you too heaven is waiting with open arms and that your nostrils shall be filled with perfume. But still, it is a wrench. In spite of heaven, you die reluctantly. You are attached to the beautiful earth which we made for you in its nest of time. Believe me, we are flattered. I ask you, however, to consider our Creator's quandary. He longs for every conceivable human being, for every human being who can be conceived, to partake of his creation. Therefore fresh babies leap day and night into the world, bright new guests of life. But your globe is small. Most of it is water, because that is what the fish need. How can we house God's innumerable children? Where shall we move the old so that the young can breathe? God pondered and puzzled, until one day he smiled and invented death. "This is clever of me," he said; "but," he added, "it is not perfect." Fortunately, heaven is not lazy. We think, we brood, we fence with problems, we engineer little improvements. Why, friends, are we flinging you into outer space with roars of metal and fire? A bright display of high spirits, you think? Not entirely. We are working, my dears, on the suppression of death. Find a few temperate planets under distant suns, settle on their surprising meadows, build new cities, and to these the overflow from earth will journey instead of dying, and men and women shall live as long as they choose. We mend our faults, you see, but not overnight, there is no hurry in God. And meantime Alice is offended with us. Although I am about to tell her that Alootook has preceded her to a better world of spirits, where she will be reunited with him, she will refuse this consolation at first. However, we look on our speech as a seed, it does take root and with time it bears flowers.

(*The Angel now approaches Alice*)

ANGEL. Alice, I have come to take his soul away.

ALICE. I know. I felt your coming. I am angry with you. Where, tell me, is the beautiful world your master is supposed to have made?

ANGEL. All around you. He made it as beautiful as he could. It is still vexed by accidents.

ALICE. Blunders! Your blunders!

ANGEL. Alas.

ALICE. Do you say alas? Then let me go with Alootook. Look, I'm injured too.

ANGEL. No. Not now. Time must be satisfied. But on time's other side you will meet Alootook in a world still better than this one, and there you will hold him again, him and the others.

ALICE. Angel of God, don't speak to me of better worlds. I knew him for only twenty little days. What evil game are you playing with me? You drove me to love him, and a moment later you stole him from me. This is stupidity.

ANGEL. One day you will be reconciled.

ALICE. Never! I hate you!

ANGEL. We love you.

(*The Angel now plants a tall hyacinth near the body, and, making a summoning gesture toward Alootook, leaves. Shortly afterward we hear the siren of an ambulance, and then the ambulance driver enters with a helper*)

ALICE. Leave him alone! He's mine!

AMBULANCE DRIVER. No use, lady. The hyacinth, you see. Excuse me. Bad luck, dumb luck. (*They pick up Alootook's body and take it out*)

ALICE. Alootook, Alootook........

(The ambulance driver returns)

AMBULANCE DRIVER. Now you come along. You're injured too. I'm taking you to a hospital, though it don't look serious to me. Hopsa! You know, five thousand million trillion zillion people have died ahead of your mate. What bothers me is how they've all managed to find room, considering the earth ain't bigger than it is. Lean on me some more, lady, I'm only trying to distract you with outlandish stories. (*He takes her out. We hear him say, "Wrap a blanket around her, Tom." Then he returns once again, and plants a headstone behind the hyacinth. He reads off the epitaph*) "Here died Alootook of an automobile

accident. Great singer. Great lover. In Heaven he sings and loves."
(*Exit. We hear the ambulance driving off. Silence. A gentle wind is blowing. After a while, at the other end of the stage, enter Jim and Tennyson Cash as pilgrims—cloaks, satchels, staves, sandals*)

TENNYSON. Dad, I'm tired, my feet are still wet from that awful downpour, and one of my toes is swollen.

CASH. Don't say "awful downpour," Tenny. Think of the strawberries and the barley growing because of it.

TENNYSON. Well it was awful for me. I also feel the sniffles coming on. And one of my toes is swollen.

CASH. To be sure, Saint Francis never had a swollen toe that I know of.

TENNYSON. He was more experienced than me. Can I sit down for a few minutes?

CASH. Sure. Here's a milestone you can sit on—the grass is still wet. But don't forget it's a long way to the next motel.

TENNYSON. Whew! I don't know that I'm the type to become a pilgrim, dad. My socks are drenched.

CASH. Take off both sandals, Tenny. And here's a change of socks.

TENNYSON. We've gained a solid ten pounds a piece ever since we started being impoverished mendicants. Everybody has got his hands stretched out with chickens and potatoes and cherry pies. We can't ever walk off all those calories.

CASH. Not to mention my knapsack and pockets full of money. I don't know how to refuse without offending people. Well, cheer up, Tenny, and breathe in this lovely wind.

TENNYSON. Wind or no wind, I'd like to be in the ball park or the ice cream parlor. I mean nature is sublime, but not with swollen toes. I bet Wordsworth never had swollen toes.

CASH. I bet he did, wandering over hill and dale. Do you realize what the rain is like in England? You say a word—wham, the rain falls on you. You keep still—wham, the rain falls on you again. If you ask me, Wordsworth must have had dripping socks weeks at a time.

TENNYSON. Maybe that's when he wrote his bad poems.

CASH. Ready to move on, my boy?

TENNYSON. I guess.

(*They do so and see the wreckage*)

TENNYSON. Look dad! Look!

CASH. A smashed car! Still warm and the oil dripping! Rubble! Everything gone! I hope nobody was hurt.

TENNYSON. What should we do, dad?

HOW ALOOTOOK CAME TO DANCE A GAVOTTE

CASH (*holding up a piece of car*). Devils in hell! This is the car I sold John Talbot! I recognize it! My God, what happened? Where's Talbot?

TENNYSON. Don't you remember? He lent the car to Alootook and what's her name, his daughter.

CASH (*thunderstruck*). Alice! Alice!

TENNYSON. Dad! Here's a headstone!

CASH. Let me see, let me see! "Here died Alootook of an automobile accident. Great singer. Great lover. In Heaven he sings and loves." But what about Alice?

TENNYSON. She must be safe, dad. It doesn't mention her.

CASH. My knees are giving way. Here he died—here! where we stand.

TENNYSON. I'm frightened, dad. Oh, I feel sick.

CASH. Come here, my boy. Here's some brandy. Alootook gone! What could have happened? He must have been too happy, and that made him careless. And Alice? She's angry. I feel it, Tenny. She's angry. This morning I was thinking of them. And then I stepped on a caterpillar.

TENNYSON. Let's turn back, dad, let's go home. You ought to say a few right words to the Talbots.

CASH. And our pilgrimage?

TENNYSON. It was never a real pilgrimage, since we weren't heading for anywhere in particular.

CASH. It was the going that mattered, Tenny, not the getting anywhere.

TENNYSON. They must have brought Alice home after the accident.

CASH. Do you think so?

TENNYSON. I'm sure. We ought to return, dad.

CASH. Yes. Say a few words over the headstone before we go, Tenny. Give him your best.

TENNYSON. I will. Let's bow our heads, father.

> Alootook was a singer bold and strong;
> When he died, he died too young.
> He would have died too young at ninety-seven.
> Therefore receive him, angels, into heaven.

CASH. That was nice, Tenny. Poor happy fellow. Heaven is heaven, but he couldn't have wanted to rise so soon.

(*They stand silent over the headstone*)

TENNYSON. Dad, you know what?

CASH. What?

TENNYSON. I wouldn't object to having a mother. Even if she wasn't all

that much older than me.
CASH. Let's turn back, Tenny, my boy. I want to say a few right words to the Talbots.

SCENE FOUR

(The Talbot residence, as in Act Two. On the table a tall potted hyacinth. John Talbot, Daisy, and Reginald Buckingham are sitting and nervously looking at the door leading to the next room. For a while no one says anything.)

TALBOT *(he has obviously said this before)*. Am I glad I finally located you between Acapulco and Whatsitepec or wherever it was.
DAISY. Hush, my dear.
(Reginald squeezes Talbot's hand)
TALBOT. Why is it taking so long?
DAISY. It hasn't been long at all, John.
REGINALD. It always seems that way. Anyway, I'm sure he knows his business.
DAISY. Of course he does.
TALBOT. I didn't mean to imply that he doesn't.
(Another silence)
REGINALD. Peppermint?
TALBOT. No, thank you.
REGINALD. Daisy?
DAISY. Thank you, dear; later.
(Another silence)
TALBOT. They were difficult days. She didn't smile once from breakfast to midnight snack. After three unsmiling days I had to stop pretending and face the brutal fact: Alice was sulking. That's when I called you.
(Daisy begins to cry)
DAISY. I never saw Alice sulk since that fox-terrier ran off with her doll when she was seven years old. And then it only lasted an hour.
REGINALD. Don't, Daisy. Now we'll all have something else to think about.
TALBOT. He's right, Daisy. Do you remember? It was the Glimmer's fox-terrier. That's how we became acquainted.
DAISY. Here he is!
(The door opens, all three jump up, and the doctor comes out, followed by Alice)
DOCTOR *(peacefully)*. A child will be born.

HOW ALOOTOOK CAME TO DANCE A GAVOTTE

ALICE (*unsmiling*). Alootook has a child.
(*General excitement*)
DAISY. Alice, come here.
TALBOT. My girl.
REGINALD (*shaking the doctor's hand*). I knew we could rely on you, doctor.
DOCTOR. I did my best.
DAISY (*to Alice*). Sit here; I want you to relax from now on.
REGINALD. Wait; this one is more comfortable.
DOCTOR. Don't overcoddle her now! Let her exercise! Tennis, roller skating, shopping in the best stores. We don't want a weakling born into the family, do we?
TALBOT. We'll make her exercise, doctor. But today she'll be coddled. We'll be the three Magi, and bring her gifts. Let the incense fly!
DOCTOR. I recommend the incense of roast beef, medium rare. But right now I'd like her to lie down for an hour.
DAISY. I'll put her to bed. Thank you, doctor.
ALICE. Thank you for everything.
DOCTOR. No more moping.
ALICE. I'll try.
(*Daisy takes Alice out of the room*)
DOCTOR. Have her come to my office once a week, will you?
TALBOT. I'll see to it.
DOCTOR. Well, I'll be on my way. Don't move, I know where the door is. Mr. Buckingham, a bit plump.
TALBOT. Doctor, before you go....
DOCTOR. Yes?
TALBOT. You noticed the moping yourself, didn't you?
DOCTOR. Sure.
TALBOT. She hasn't unmoped once, so to speak, since the accident happened. Don't you think it's unnatural?
DOCTOR. Oh, I don't know. To have her husband dispatched so soon—it's irritating.
TALBOT. How did she respond when you told her she was going to have a baby?
DOCTOR. Nicely.
TALBOT. But—
DOCTOR. No smile. Not yet.
REGINALD. She was having such a wonderful time.
DOCTOR. That's what you have to understand, John. I examined Alootook once for General Motors, and I know he was no slouch. Suddenly bang,

he's in a better world. Very nice for him, but damned inconvenient for Alice.

TALBOT. What do you suggest we do?

DOCTOR. Come on now, you're not children!

TALBOT and REGINALD (*looking at each other*). Another man!

DOCTOR. Two intellects.

TALBOT. I don't know. Alice is fussy.

DOCTOR. The world's aswarm with lovable candidates.

REGINALD. The doctor is right, Mr. Talbot.

TALBOT. I suppose he is. But we'd better be tactful with Alice. She's fragile.

REGINALD. I agree, but tact will do it. I remember, when my mother left us, the last words she whispered to my dad were: "Algernon, the boy loves haggis, and I want him to eat it twice a week." I was standing by her bedside at the time.

TALBOT. What's that got to do with Alice?

REGINALD. Tact, that's all. My father couldn't boil an egg, the dear man, and where do you go for haggis in this town? He took the hint and married again two weeks later. She managed it, you see, by not seeming to push.

TALBOT. A nice woman.

REGINALD. Oh, a saint.

DOCTOR. Well, you know what to do. Be tactful and grab the first good man who rings the bell.

(*The doorbell rings*)

CASH (*off-stage*). Anybody home?

TALBOT and REGINALD. Ha!

DOCTOR. Providence strikes again.

TALBOT. Coming!

DOCTOR. I'll slip in for another look at Alice and leave the back way. So long.

TALBOT. Thanks for the wisdom and bill me for it!

DOCTOR. I will.

(*He leaves while Talbot goes to the front door*)

CASH (*off-stage*). Greetings from the road!

TALBOT (*off-stage*). Shake off your dust, old bachelor!

(*Enter Jim Cash, still as pilgrim, and carrying a satchel fuller than ever*)

REGINALD. Good to see you again, Mr. Cash, very good indeed.

CASH. The feeling is mutual. You should have tramped with us, Mr. Buckingham. Getting a bit stocky, you know.

TALBOT. Daisy! Jim Cash is here!

DAISY (*off-stage*). I'm coming!

HOW ALOOTOOK CAME TO DANCE A GAVOTTE

CASH (*to Reginald*). So glad you two came back.
TALBOT. Alice is resting.
CASH. I understand. How is she?
(*Enter Daisy*)
DAISY. Dear Mr. Cash! Welcome! When did you arrive in town?
CASH. This very moment, Mrs. Talbot. I know I'm unpresentable. I'll dirty your carpet. But I wanted to inquire.... I was anxious....
DAISY. Who's worried about carpets? Alice is welL Mr. Cash. She's resting a little. John, pull up a comfortable chair for our guest. Where is Tennyson?
CASH. He's gone ahead to open the house. May I? (*He places the satchel on a table*)
DAISY. You must be exhausted.
CASH. Not at all. Only eleven miles today.
TALBOT. Why not take a bath upstairs? We want you to feel like one of the family. (*He nudges Reginald*)
REGINALD. I should say so. After eleven miles!
CASH. Not a bad idea.
DAISY. Fresh warm towels.
CASH. Wonderful. But as for the eleven miles, and it might have been twelve, don't forget, Mr. Buckingham, that I've got the habit by now, my legs move up and down like a pair of steamship pistons.
DAISY. I wish my men would take a lesson from you.
(*Enter Alice*)
THE TALBOTS. Alice!
CASH (*rising*). Mrs. Alootook.
DAISY. You should have slept a little.
ALICE. I heard your voice.
CASH. Forgive me. But I needed to come here before going home. He was our friend. Never a cloudy word. Children followed him about.
ALICE. You knew him better than I did.
CASH. It was unfeeling of them to take him from you.
ALICE. To *steal* him from me.
DAISY. Alice!... Sit down again, Mr. Cash.
TALBOT (*to Alice*). And you, sit here. (*He places her next to Cash*)
REGINALD. Mr. Cash, I'd like to report that the car lot's in tip-top shape.
CASH. Good, good.
REGINALD. I reopened and sold three or four cars. I do think there was more fuel in them than when we left, but nothing alarming.
CASH. I don't suppose they've caught the Black Shadow yet, have they?
TALBOT. No, they haven't.

CASH. I've come as a sort of Black Shadow myself.
TALBOT. Oh?
CASH. Look at this satchel. A little unsightly, you've probably been saying to yourselves. Mr. Cash ought to have set it down in the hallway instead of parading it on the table like a trophy.
DAISY. I never noticed it, I swear.
CASH. Feel it. As hard and tough as a football. And yet, my friends, this bag is filled with soft paper money, bills and checks in high denominations.
REGINALD. You haven't sold the car lot, have you, Mr. Cash?
CASH. No, sir. This is what comes of being a neo-Franciscan mendicant. People fill your cup so fast, you all but need a bank clerk in tow. But, said I to myself, where shall I bestow these holy alms? And then I remembered the Talbot Park. And I stretched out my hand in the name of the park. Why not a corner for the animals Saint Francis was fond of? A good thought, said I to myself. Subject to your approval, of course, because it's the Talbot Park and none other.
TALBOT. This is an important idea, Mr. Cash, a special contribution, exactly the detail that was missing from our plan.
DAISY. Animals, Alice; aren't you glad?
ALICE (*quietly*). I think it's a lovely idea.
TALBOT. Mr. Buckingham?
REGINALD. Oh, you know me. Always in agreement with everybody.
CASH. I'll feed the animals myself, and talk to them, if I may.
ALICE. Mr. Cash....
CASH. Yes?
ALICE. I don't know whether Saint Francis mentions them, but would you allow one or two seals?
CASH. A flock of them! I assure you that he would have blessed them if he'd known they exist.
ALICE. Thank you so much.
DAISY. Now that I think of it, we haven't told Mr. Cash—
REGINALD. Our good news!
ALICE. Oh mother....
CASH. What is it?
DAISY. There is going to be a child.
CASH. Heaven be thanked! (*To Alice*) I was looking into your eyes, and I thought, yes, here is something blissful, in spite of everything, like a candle behind a smoky pane of glass. I am immensely happy.
TALBOT. Good man.
ALICE (*almost in tears*). Thank you, thank you.

HOW ALOOTOOK CAME TO DANCE A GAVOTTE

TALBOT. Children, I think we should be going to the garden now.
DAISY. Yes, this is a good time. Mr. Cash—Jim I will allow myself to say—we are planting this hyacinth in our garden in memory—
CASH. I understand. Alice, may I carry it?
ALICE. Do.
CASH. Then on to the garden. I'll follow you all. And since I'm covered with dust already, I'll do the spading.
TALBOT (*to Alice*). Take my arm.
REGINALD (*to Daisy*). Take mine, Daisy.
(*All leave. After a brief interval, the Black Shadow reappears. But this time he is secretly followed by a policeman. The Black Shadow surveys the room. He notices the money-bag on the table. He opens it, finds much money, chuckles, and then deposits a money-bag of his own next to it. He is about to leave when the policeman pounces*)
POLICEMAN (*throttling the culprit*). Got you at last!
BLACK SHADOW. Aaaah!
POLICEMAN. Your career is over and done with, Black Shadow! You'll take everything back now, Gol darn it, down to the last toothpick. Malefactor! Recidivist!
BLACK SHADOW. You're squeezing my windpipe, officer.
POLICEMAN. Oh, excuse me. But this is it, Black Shadow. What's your name, who are you, don't lie, and off with your mask!
BLACK SHADOW. Let me remain anonymous! I'll take everything back, I swear it on my mother's head, I'll rot in jail but don't ask who I am.
POLICEMAN. Okay, I won't ask; I'll find out without asking. (*He rips off the Black Shadow's mask*)
BLACK SHADOW. Mercy!
POLICEMAN (*dumbfounded*). Willifred P. Rockefeller! The plastic flower tycoon!
BLACK SHADOW (*meekly*). Maybe I only resemble him.
POLICEMAN. Mr. Rockefeller—(*he doffs his helmet*)—I don't know what to say—but it ain't my fault that I happened to be the man on duty here. How can I apologize? But why? Why?
(*Reenter the Talbots et al. from the garden. General exclamations. The Policeman blows his whistle*)
POLICEMAN. Ladies and gentlemen, the Police Department regrets this unforementioned intrusion, but is pleased to announce the apprehension of the Black Shadow, alias Willifred P. Rockefeller—I am terrible sorry, Mr. Rockefeller—in the act of depositing a money bag in your domicile.
ALICE. Oh! (*She sits down, faint from the excitement*)
CASH. Water, Mrs. Talbot—Daisy—water, Reginald!

ALICE. It's nothing, Mr. Cash—Jim—too many things happening, that's all.
DAISY. Here, here, my love. You'll be all right.
(*Rockefeller tries to slink away*)
POLICEMAN. No, Mr. Rockefeller, I don't know how to put it, but you're so to speak under arrest.
ROCKEFELLER. I'll be good.
TALBOT (*stepping forward*). Now, Mr. Rockefeller, what in God's name is the meaning of this? A man like you, who teaches Sunday school two days a week, should know better than to break into people's houses.
REGINALD (*whispering*). Perhaps the poor man—
ROCKEFELLER. Oh no, sir, I'm rational, I'm only too rational, oh the shame, the torment!
TALBOT (*to Daisy*). Give him a drink, Daisy. Sit down, Mr. Rockefeller.
ROCKEFELLER. Thank you, Mr. Talbot. You're awfully kind.
TALBOT. Now tell us all about it.
POLICEMAN. I ought to be handcuffing him, Mr. Talbot.
CASH. Have a drink too.
POLICEMAN. Not possible, sir. I'm on duty.
TALBOT. Take a ten-minute break.
POLICEMAN. Good idea. Thanks. (*He drinks*)
TALBOT. Proceed, my poor misguided friend. Unload your guilty conscience.
ROCKEFELLER (*groaning*). I hope you enjoyed the teapot, Mrs. Talbot.
TALBOT (*severely*). Don't change the subject, sir. The teapot goes back to Mrs. Rockefeller. But why the money? Why your fearful effractions in the city? What ails you?
ALICE. Dad, don't be too hard on him.
ROCKEFELLER. Oh thank you, Miss Talbot. If you only knew!
REGINALD. Knew what?
POLICEMAN (*stage whisper to the ladies*). The confession!
ROCKEFELLER. If you knew what it means to be the plastic flower tycoon. Plastic flowers! I notice your look of repugnance. And plastic rubber plants—a profitable sideline—plastic soil—another source of miserable lucre—and now, on our drawing boards (*he suffocates*)—
TALBOT. What—what have you got on your drawing boards?
DAISY. What can it be? Make an effort, Mr. Rockefeller.
ROCKEFELLER (*in a hoarse whisper*). Plastic snails. Genuine realistic effect.
DAISY. Tut, tut, Mr. Rockefeller, that really isn't nice.
POLICEMAN. Oh I don't know. My wife's got plastic pots of plastic flowers all over our bedroom—I'm speakin' off duty now—all kinds and all colors.
ROCKEFELLER (*groaning*). And does she spray them with our imitation

perfumes? (*Miserable*) Another thriving subsidiary.

POLICEMAN. Sure, a different perfume for each kind. She says the real kind asphyxicates you at night, while the plastic ones is harmless and they last a lot longer. We send them to the laundry once a month.

ROCKEFELLER. You see, you see. Millions of them, orchids, roses—floribundas and grandifloras—camellias, tulips, lilies, irises, with beards and without, all fakes, phonies and fiddlesticks, and masses of money rushing into my vaults. But I try to make up for my filthy millions in a small humble way. I skulk from one house to the other, I unload, you see, it makes me feel better, and besides—it's fun. (*He breaks down and sobs*)

POLICEMAN. None of that, Mr. Rockefeller. Conduct unbecoming a criminal.

ROCKEFELLER. I'm sorry.

TALBOT. Is this believable?

CASH. As much as all the rest!

ROCKEFELLER. I swear it's the truth! And then, Mr. Talbot, I heard about your park. I overheard, hiding.... (*he points*)

TALBOT. Say no more! You thought, "Here's my chance."

REGINALD. A park without a single artificial flower in it.

ROCKEFELLER. Or snail.

DAISY. A chance to redeem yourself.

ROCKEFELLER. And to undermine the plastic flower market.

ALICE. He's a dear man. I like him.

POLICEMAN. Mrs. Alootook! I don't know if pre-trial sympathy is legal.

TALBOT. I'll keep an eye on her, officer.

CASH. Officer!

POLICEMAN. Sir?

CASH. Just now—didn't the party convey a smile to the culprit too?

POLICEMAN. Yes. She aggravated with a smile.

CASH. There!

TALBOT. Did you smile, Alice?

DAISY. Did you?

ALICE. Did I? Yes, I did!

DAISY. I knew she would! (*She embraces Alice*) She's back in the world!

TALBOT. Mr. Rockefeller, we owe our daughter's renovation to you. The Talbots offer you their thanks: all three of us, or all four, or all five, depending on developments. Logic dictates the next step. The Talbot Park goes into a quadripartite partnership. You sign on the dotted line, the bag of money becomes your original investment, and we drop all charges. Agreed?

CASH and REGINALD. Agreed.

ROCKEFELLER (*on his knees*). Gentlemen, let me kiss the cuffs of your pantaloons.

TALBOT. Stand up, Willifred, we're all equal partners now, and the officer gets another drink—but in the tavern across the street, where he'll toast our healths. (*He puts money in the policeman's hand*)

CASH. With a special health for the ladies. (*He puts more money in the policeman's hand*)

REGINALD. Another for the unborn child. (*More money*)

ROCKEFELLER (*the tycoon again*). And one for Talbot Park, my good man.

POLICEMAN (*saluting*). Sorry once more for the intrusion, ladies and gentlemen. You know where to find me in case law and order breaks down again. And remember the Police Department's motto: "Every thief has a silver lining." (*He leaves*)

DAISY. Sit next to me, Mr. Rockefeller. You'll stay for dinner. And so will all of you, of course.

ROCKEFELLER (*kissing her hand*). You're too kind. You too, Mrs. Alootook. My congratulations on the little one to come. As for me, I'll water the flowers in the park and teach their names to the baby.

REGINALD. Well, I'm glad that everything is somehow falling into place.

CASH. Not everything. Not yet. Alice....

ALICE. Yes, Jim?

CASH. My friends, I would like to ask a question, or make a statement—we'll see which.

TALBOT. It's about time.

DAISY. You look perturbed. What's the matter?

CASH. Is everything really falling into place? Does everyone have his—or her—appointed task? Daisy and Reginald are going back to Acapulco for a week, the rest of us will busy ourselves with used cars, poetry, real estate, and parks, but you, Alice, dear Alice, what are you going to do? There is the summer to spend, the fall, part of the winter.... Tell us.

ALICE. I'll be with my family. I'll sit in the garden, near the hyacinth and the goldfish, and I'll do nothing much of anything until my time comes.

CASH. Suppose I had a better idea? Suppose I said, marry me, Alice.

(*To his amazement, no one seems surprised*)

CASH (*resolutely*). I'm not a *very* young man, I admit, but I'm as sturdy as a sapling, my pulse is strong, I'm not bad to look at, my principles are high, I'm well-read, musical, a good businessman; above all, I've a warm disposition, turn on the light and I melt; I've got a boy of fifteen in training to be an immortal poet who wants you in the family; and before the beginning and after the end of everything, I've yearned for you ever since you appeared in my lot that first day looking for your father. Not that it spoiled my appetite, and by the way I'm not fussy about food, I eat anything, nor that it blurred my vision, I'm not an idiot; on the contrary, it made a happy, fresh stir inside me; sharpened all my pleasures; something fine to think about, you see; and not jealous of anybody, God forbid; the best man took you, Alice, Alootook, a prince, many a time we've broken bread together and soaked our noses in the foam of a mug of beer, and he'd burst into a song that stopped the trucks on the asphalt—

TALBOT. You're weaving off course, Jim.

CASH. No I'm not. I know where I'm going. Alice, we'll be living and working on the spot where it all began. We'll raise the child, Tenny will have a brother or a sister, and then everything will have fallen into place.

DAISY. Alice, dearest, what do you say?

TALBOT. I accept! You can't become a spinster, Alice. Alootook liked you ripe and rich. If you let yourself shrivel for his sake, you'll be exactly the opposite of what he liked.

ALICE. I don't intend to shrivel, father.

TALBOT. Splendid. Cash, she's yours.

CASH. Does this mean yes, Alice?

ALICE (*low*). It does.

CASH. Ah!

ALICE. A year from now.

CASH. Oh!

DAISY. A year from now?

TALBOT. Fiddlesticks! Why a year from now?

ALICE. For Alootook's sake.

TALBOT. Stuff! I'm a man of action. If later's good, sooner's better.

ROCKEFELLER. Leap before you look.

REGINALD. A girl without lover is a form without content.

DAISY. Reggie!

TALBOT. Talk to her, Jim! Don't run out of words now of all times!

CASH. What can I say? If that's the way Alootook would want it.

TALBOT. How do you know that's the way Alootook would want it?

REGINALD. He was always a sensible fellow.

ROCKEFELLER. If we could only talk to his ghost!

(*Whereupon an uncanny music is heard and the room darkens*)

ROCKEFELLER. What did I do?

DAISY. A manifestation!

REGINALD. Be still, everyone!

ALICE. Mother, hold me!

HOW ALOOTOOK CAME TO DANCE A GAVOTTE

(*The ghost of Alootook appears, and as it does, the eerie music resolves itself into a Telemann gavotte—or the like—to which the ghost performs a charming dance*)

GHOST (*as the music concludes*). Marry merry! Merry marry!

ALICE. Alootook! Do you mean it?

(*The ghost vanishes. The lights come on again*)

REGINALD (*timidly*). What did he say?

TALBOT. Marry-merry is what he said. Though he seemed a bit out of breath. Funny for a ghost.

DAISY. I heard it too: It was quite distinct, wasn't it, Reggie?

REGINALD. No doubt about it; marry and be merry.

TALBOT. Fate has opened its mouth, mortals must obey.

DAISY. Alice, you're not saying anything. You understood Alootook, didn't you?

ALICE. Of course I understood him. I love him unspeakably.

TALBOT. Well?

CASH. Alice?

(*Alice goes to him, puts her hand in his, and lets him lead her out through the door*)

EVERYBODY. Hurrah!

ROCKEFELLER. The wedding's on me!

DAISY. Alice has done it, Alice has done it again!

TALBOT. God, this has been an exhausting day. (*He plumps down on the sofa*) Sit down, children.

REGINALD. Not now, amigo. (*He produces a pair of airplane tickets*) Off to Acapulco!

DAISY. Efficient!

TALBOT. Inexhaustible!

ROCKEFELLER. Send us a postcard!

TALBOT. And don't forget to come back!

(*Daisy and Reginald dance off, singing a Mexican song*)

TALBOT. Well, Willifred, that leaves only the two of us behind. I'm too tired to move. Hoo! Getting on, I guess.

ROCKEFELLER. What about Mrs. Glimmer?

TALBOT (*leaping up*). I knew the day wasn't finished yet! How did you know about Mrs. Glimmer?

ROCKEFELLER. The Black Shadow....

TALBOT. That does it. I'm off for the week too. (*He puts a flower in his buttonhole*) Willifred, can I leave you in charge till my return?

ROCKEFELLER. Yes, sir.

TALBOT. One. Call the nursery and tell them to start shipping the rhododendrons. Two. Modify the blueprints to make room for a flock of seals.

Three. Summon the bulldozers and have them sharpen their fangs, because next Wednesday we churn.
ROCKEFELLER. Rhododendrons. Seals. Bulldozers. It'll be done; you can sleep easy.
TALBOT. Not with Mrs. Glimmer. So long, Willifred.
ROCKEFELLER. Wait! I'm coming with you—home to my mansion.
(They leave. The Angel enters, closes a window, switches off a lamp, sets a chair right)
ANGEL. So ends another heavenly day.

EPILOGUE

(Spoken by one, several or all the actors in turn)

Before we part, friends and mankind,
We actors, fearing we may be maligned,
Ask to be — in part — dissociated
From the play our talent has created —
A play which — no one can deny —
Is merry, sweet, and spry —
Deserves a kindly thought or two
(Especially from the acting point of view),
But which exhibits, here and there, a shocking unawareness of
                                                                                    fact—
Unlikely episodes—to be quite frank—in almost every act.
We Thespians, famous for our zeal
In acting drama that is up-to-date and real
Whether in the mode Absurd or Psychological
Socialprotestiferous or Scatological,
Believe that every play ought to convey uncompromising lessons
Concerning man's deepest existential essence.
And while our playwright, I suppose,
Has tried his best to paint the world he knows,
He is regrettably short on information
And somewhat immature about the world's true situation.
Yet I myself have met him, up and down,
Peeking, pecking, poking through the town,
Busy with his facts and taking busy notes

HOW ALOOTOOK CAME TO DANCE A GAVOTTE

In taverns, car lots, banks and ferryboats,
Trying, it would seem, to make his judgment ripe
Before sitting down to type.
And for this reason, when he lapses from the truth,
I personally blame it on his youth.
He's only fifty-four, you see,
And taking writing courses at the local university.
Our next play, though, will strike you like a violent gale.
You shall see a young tough and his husband in the county jail,
Spitting love and snarling hate, both in the relentless nude,
Racked by anguish, condemned, like all of us, to solitude.
The heroin they crave for and to which they cling
Does not, you understand, come with a wedding ring.
A bloodstained Black excites them wildly on the drum
While tortured by a drunken white cop swilling rum.
We actors feel that, come what may, we must not shirk
From challenging the smug with this tormented work,
Written at white heat by a sensitive killer on Death Row
Whose genius seems with every new reprieve to grow.
Meantime—I speak in confidence—we're much relieved, each time
            we finish here,
To drop back down to earth out of the stratosphere;
We're happy, when the house lights shine again, to see before us—
            you know who—
Discriminating, sensitive and thoughtful YOU.

The End

Notes

How Alootook Came to Dance a Gavotte started life in 1967 under the title *Of Angels and Eskimos* (the plural made no sense) and as such it stands as the last of my texts in Volume II of my Collected Plays (1970-1972). The present, final version is retitled and revised. The word "Eskimo", which, I am told, has become offensive, is expunged, as is the word "Negro". I have no doubt that "Black" will also become offensive in the near future, at which point the reader, critic, and producer are invited to replace it as well.

Specifics like dollar amounts and objects can be adjusted and updated *ad libitum*.

I have not reproduced the usable score for Alootook's "Let every voice in industry be raised" which I appended to the *Collected Plays* version. It was based on a hymn by William Croft (1678-1727).

A SPLITTING HEADACHE

CHARACTERS

Hans Gropius
Theobald Griggs
Mrs. Griggs
Freddy Griggs
The Sign Painter
Mr. Wikkle
Martha Wikkle
Jim Wikkle
Stanley Clover
Philip O'Toole
General Culpepper
Senator Floogle
Senator Sallow
Corporal Bletterman
Private Dupont
Private Griggs
Private Stein
A Captain

A SPLITTING HEADACHE

SCENE ONE

(A miserable room in a miserable dwelling. Mr. Theobald Griggs is lying sick on a cot. His wife is darning a sock. A clock is ticking. Mr. Griggs wheezes and coughs painfully)

MR. GRIGGS. I don't feel my right leg no more.
MRS. GRIGGS. Sure you do.
(Silence)
MR. GRIGGS. What time is it?
MRS. GRIGGS *(patiently)*. Same time it always is this time of day.
MR. GRIGGS *(angry)*. What time is it?
MRS. GRIGGS. Four o'clock and some. Does that make you feel better?
MR. GRIGGS *(after another coughing spell)*. Where's Freddy?
MRS. GRIGGS. Drink some more water. Maybe Mr. Gropius will be coming soon. Today's Tuesday I think. Sure. Sunday was day before yesterday. I don't know why you can't be more careful with your socks.
MR. GRIGGS (angry). Where's Freddy?
MRS. GRIGGS. You know where he is.
MR. GRIGGS. I mean why ain't he home yet.
MRS. GRIGGS. Drink some more water. Here. You know it's an hour's walk to town. Then to the haberdasher's, another fifteen minutes. And then to the pharmacy, another fifteen minutes, maybe more. And then back home, another hour. Unless somebody gives him a ride, a truck maybe, or Mr. Gropius if he happens to catch sight of him.
MR. GRIGGS. The haberdasher! Ain't we high and glorious today!
MRS. GRIGGS. The boy needs a sweater, Tib. The boy needs a sweater, that's all. He ain't strong and this is October already.
MR. GRIGGS. He'll outlive us both.
MRS. GRIGGS. He needs a sweater.
MR. GRIGGS. I need them pills! I'm the support of this family!
MRS. GRIGGS. Freddy's buying the pills too.
MR. GRIGGS. Yeah, but it's the haberdasher first, the haberdasher first, I heard you.
MRS. GRIGGS. Maybe it'll be the pharmacy first. I was only talking. This first or that first. It don't matter none that I can see.

A SPLITTING HEADACHE

MR. GRIGGS. It matters to me. It's my twelve dollars. I dug trenches for it for the goddam army.

MRS. GRIGGS. And look where it's got you.

MR. GRIGGS. Gimme a cup of coffee.

MRS. GRIGGS. Wait till Freddy comes back with the pills, then you can take the pills with your coffee. We're down to the last of the sugar, too.

MR. GRIGGS. I can't hardly feel my right leg anymore. Here, touch it.

MRS. GRIGGS. Sure you can.

(*A knock at the door*)

MR. GRIGGS. Somebody at the door.

MRS. GRIGGS. Who is it?

HANS (*outside*). It's Hans Gropius!

MRS. GRIGGS. Come in, come in! (*She opens the door*) Welcome to you, Mr. Gropius, God bless you, I was just saying it's Tuesday today.

HANS. How are you, Mrs. Griggs. Close the door quickly, it's getting awfully chilly. Here, take this. (*He gives her a large paper sack*)

MRS. GRIGGS. Thank you, Mr. Gropius. Thank you. (*She takes various edibles out of the sack*) Look, Tib, fresh tomatoes, Mr. Gropius remembered! And here's a can of condensed milk!

MR. GRIGGS. We appreciate your help, Mr. Gropius, even if I can't swallow a morsel the way I'm sick.

HANS. Not feeling any better, Mr. Griggs?

MR. GRIGGS. Worse. I won't be around much longer, though I'm only forty-two.

MRS. GRIGGS. Go on!

MR. GRIGGS (*half rises*). Forty-two, and look at me! Worn out at forty-two! But I'm only a working man, so who cares? God damn it, I remember the day the members of the Board come walking down the factory aisle on their inspection tour. Yeah. I remember their white hands, same as yours. One of 'em had a carnation in his lapel. Closer and closer they come. I was holding a heavy wrench in my hand, and it made my palm itch, I tell you. "Lemme take a crack at one of them rich bastards," I kept telling myself. "Lemme present one of 'em with a widow and a couple orphans." Course I didn't. They was born to drink champagne, right? and I was born to be laid off and to die my stinking death.

MRS. GRIGGS. Oh shut your mouth, Tib.

HANS. You should try to keep calm, Mr. Griggs. Getting angry only makes you worse.

MRS. GRIGGS. He was always like that, violent.

MR. GRIGGS. And if there ain't enough pheasant to go round for everybody, let everybody take turns, God damn it, let everybody take turns. (*He coughs furiously*)

HANS (*sadly*). I agree with you, Mr. Griggs. I wish I could really really help. I wish I could start from zero and build something decent.

MRS. GRIGGS. How can you talk like that, Mr. Gropius? You're an angel sent from heaven.

MR. GRIGGS. You're ok, Mr. Gropius. I didn't mean you. You're ok.

MRS. GRIGGS. Look at all that meat, Tib.

HANS. Don't mention it, Mrs. Griggs. People like me—we're like paper towels trying to soak up a flood. Has your boy gone for the medicine?

MRS. GRIGGS. Yes, he has. He should be right back.

HANS (*aside to her*). And the sweater too, I hope.

MRS. GRIGGS. Oh yes. (*Taking a few coins out of her pocket*) Look, there's even forty-five cents left.

HANS. When is the government check coming?

MRS. GRIGGS. Early next week, I hope. (*She sees Freddy through the window*) Here's my boy now. And he's got a package under his arm! (*She opens the door*)

MR. GRIGGS. Sure, it's Christmas.

MRS. GRIGGS. Look at him! Look at that grimy face! Let me wipe it.

HANS. Hello, my boy.

FREDDY (*looking glum*). Hello, Mr. Gropius.

MRS. GRIGGS. What's the matter with you? You got your sweater, didn't you?

FREDDY. Yes, mom.

MRS. GRIGGS. Lemme see. (*She opens the package*)

HANS. Very nice.

MRS. GRIGGS. Isn't it? We saw it a month ago, didn't we, Freddy? And we figured brown's the best color, being that dirt don't show on it so bad. Try it on, Freddy, come on, try it on. The poor boy's tired, look at him, he's been perspiring in spite of the cold.

MR. GRIGGS. What about my pills?

MRS. GRIGGS. Give him the pills, Freddy, your dad needs 'em.

HANS. I'll make him take a couple while you're trying on the sweater.

FREDDY. I haven't got the pills.

MR. GRIGGS. What?

MRS. GRIGGS. They was out of pills?

FREDDY. No, they wasn't out.

HANS. Come on, my boy, don't be afraid to tell us.

MR. GRIGGS. He forgot! He plumb forgot! I'll kill you!

FREDDY. I didn't forget.
MRS. GRIGGS. Don't just stand there! What happened? I'll give you a hiding you won't forget if you don't tell us the truth.
(*Freddy hands Mrs. Griggs some money*)
MR. GRIGGS. He forgot! I told you! He don't care if I die on this cot tonight!
MRS. GRIGGS. That's only a dollar sixty-five, Freddy. The sweater was six dollars. I gave you twelve.
HANS. What happened, Freddy? Did you really forget?
MR. GRIGGS. Belt him for me! That'll make him talk.
(*Freddy starts to cry*)
HANS. Come on, come on, sit down, fella, give the boy a chance, Mr. Griggs. Did you stop to buy something else, Freddy, some candy?
MRS. GRIGGS. Did you, Freddy?
FREDDY. No, I didn't. The sweater was ten twenty-five, mom, we musta made a mistake. I went in—
MR. GRIGGS. Ten twenty-five! You're outa your mind! Take it back! I'll beat the daylights out of you before I let you keep a sweater that costs eleven dollars.
MRS. GRIGGS. Shut up! Shut up! Let the boy tell his story.
MR. GRIGGS. I don't want to hear it!
MRS. GRIGGS. Shut up!!!
HANS. Go on, Freddy. What store was it anyway?
FREDDY. Mr. Wikkle's haberdashery.
HANS. All right. Then what? You went in.
FREDDY. He said to me—
MRS. GRIGGS. Who said?
FREDDY. I don't know. I guess it was Mr. Wikkle himself. He said the sweater cost ten twenty-five.
MR. GRIGGS. And all you could say was fine, great, is that all, and you handed him the money.
MRS. GRIGGS. Let the boy finish!
MR. GRIGGS. I'm a sick man! What you both gonna do when I'm in the grave? Tell me that! Live on air? You gonna marry Mr. Gropius?
FREDDY. I was all set to go for the pills, dad. But when the man said the sweater was ten twenty-five I thought maybe *we'd* made a mistake.
MRS. GRIGGS. No we didn't. I didn't, Mr. Gropius. The price tag was on it as clear as daylight. They took advantage of the boy.
HANS. That's what it looks like. I'm going to take care of this right away.
FREDDY. There wasn't enough money left over for the pills.
MR. GRIGGS. Don't come near me! I'm through with all of you.

HANS. I'm going to drive into town this minute, Mr. Griggs. Leave it to me. I'll make that shopkeeper whoever he is return the difference to you.

MRS. GRIGGS. Give Mr. Gropius the sweater, Freddy.

HANS. The rascal must have thought, "Here's a child, I can make a large extra profit. His parents must be poor. They won't know what to do." I've seen it too often, Mrs. Griggs. They call it charging what the traffic will bear. All right, Freddy, you're coming with me.

FREDDY. Are you gonna return it to him, Mr. Gropius?

HANS. No, my boy, that sweater is yours no matter what.

MR. GRIGGS. What about my pills?

HANS. You'll have them by tonight. Leave everything to me.

MR. GRIGGS. Be sure to tell that bum your father was a senator.

MRS. GRIGGS. Won't the store be closed by now, Mr. Gropius?

HANS. I'll kick it open.

(*He and Freddy leave*)

SCENE TWO

(*Street and shop. A signpainter is standing on a ladder finishing a large sign which reads GOOD LUCK! Enter Hans, holding the sweater, and Freddy*)

HANS. Excuse me up there.

SIGN PAINTER. Yes?

HANS. I'm looking for Wikkle's Habersdashery.

SIGN PAINTER. You mean old Cash-on-the-line Wikkle?

HANS. Is that what they call him?

SIGN PAINTER. Who is they?

HANS. Well—people.

SIGN PAINTER. Some does and some doesn't. I do. What's in your package?

HANS. A sweater I'm returning.

SIGN PAINTER. Overcharged you? A rip in the sleeve? Color come off in the wash?

HANS. He overcharged us.

SIGN PAINTER. Well, don't be hard on Mr. Wikkle. He's got to pay off the mortgage, you know. On the ten-room villa up the hill. That's his shop over there.

HANS. Thank you.

A SPLITTING HEADACHE

FREDDY. Why does that sign say GOOD LUCK!, mister?
SIGN PAINTER. Because it's always up to date, sonny.
HANS. Come along, Freddy.
(*As Hans reaches the shop, the sign painter comes down the ladder and follows out of curiosity. Hans tries the door but finds it locked. He looks at his watch, decides he has arrived after business hours, and knocks. He has to knock several times before an answer is heard*)
WIKKLE (*inside*). Who is it?
HANS. You don't know me. Open the door.
WIKKLE. It's after five o'clock. I'm closed for the day.
HANS. Open the door or I'll call the police!
(*Wikkle opens the door. He is dressed as a Boy Scout leader*)
WIKKLE. What do you mean, call the police? What is this, anyway? Who are you?
HANS. I'll tell you who I am in a minute, Mr. Wikkle. But first, do you recognize this?
WIKKLE. Looks like the sweater I sold this boy today. What's going on?
HANS. My name is Hans Gropius.
WIKKLE. *The* Gropius? The senator's son?
HANS. That's right.
WIKKLE. Come in, sir. Surely this isn't—
HANS. No, this belongs to one of the families I try to look after. I don't know you, Mr. Wikkle, but I'm going to be blunt with you. Here's a six-dollar sweater you sold for ten dollars and twenty-five cents today. Is this correct, or did the boy lie to me?
WIKKLE. He lied to you.
HANS. Oh?
FREDDY. I didn't, I didn't lie!
WIKKLE. This is a ten twenty-five sweater which I sold for ten dollars and twenty-five cents. It *was* a six-dollar sweater. Once upon a time.
HANS. Once upon what time? This morning?
WIKKLE. No, Mr. Gropius. Two weeks ago. If you'd like to return it—
HANS. How did this wonderful leap come about, Mr. Wikkle? Seventy-five percent! Simply because there's a war on?
WIKKLE. Speaking with due respect, I don't owe anybody an explanation. I don't care whose son you are, Mr. Gropius.
BOY'S VOICE. Mr. Wikkle! We're waiting for you!
WIKKLE. I'll be out again in a minute, boys! Do the half-hitch a few more times, let Jim show you how!
BOY'S VOICE. Ok, Mr. Wikkle!

WIKKLE. We're learning how to tie knots. Like I said, Mr. Gropius, I don't mean to be disrespectful, but I've been serving our community for wellnigh thirty-five years. There's not a speck of dust on my reputation. I'm a Boy Scout leader. I love children. But—

HANS. If you love children, you might have noticed that here was a child in bitter need. (*He puts his finger on Freddy's worn clothes*)

WIKKLE. There's a war on, Mr. Gropius. Maybe there won't be any woollen goods at all to be had in another two months, and then where will I be? People are buying up everything in sight, pins, buttons. I could have sold that boy's sweater three times over this afternoon for fifteen dollars. And what about the prices *I* have to pay to keep going? What about the relatives I need to feed that fled from the border?

HANS. Sure, sure.

WIKKLE. Martha! Martha!

MARTHA (*off*). Yes?

WIKKLE. Come here a minute!

(*Enter Martha Wikkle from the store, wiping a cup*)

MARTHA. What's the matter, honey?

WIKKLE. Who is living with us up on the hill these days? The gentleman would like to know.

MARTHA. You mean Ben, the children, and everybody?

WIKKLE. Yes. Tell him why they're here.

MARTHA. The war, of course. We're giving them shelter, sir. Is anything wrong? Something wrong with their papers?

WIKKLE. No, no, everything is all right. You can go back to the kitchen, don't worry. (*He shoos Martha out*)

HANS. Fine. You've convinced me that you're kind to your relatives. But not that you aren't cruel to strangers. There's a shortage of woollens. Granted. So you double the price. Economic law. But when a ragged boy stands before you, and you're a Boy Scout leader, why don't you duck economic law for five minutes?

(*The sign painter barges in*)

SIGN PAINTER. Because he's a greedy pig, that's why!

WIKKLE. Who are *you?* Get out of here! I'm closed!

SIGN PAINTER (*waving his brush*). I'm nobody but I ain't leaving. I been listenin' to your crud and I've had all I can take. Greed, nothin' but lousy greed. The house on the hill, that's who he loves. (*To Hans*) You and your boy! Are you kidding? He'll let that boy starve in the gutter before he'll clip a dime off of his price. Boy Scout leader! He makes me sick! But I'll let you in on a little secret, Mr. Wikkle. We've got your name. The name of

Wikkle will be remembered when the day of reckoning comes, and that'll be sooner than you think, the way your rotten war is going.
WIKKLE (*tremulous*). Get out of here! I'll call the police! Get out! Martha, call the police!
HANS. You'd better leave.
SIGN PAINTER. Ok, ok, as long as we know who the bloodsuckers are. Just remember, Wikkle, there's eyes watching this place day and night. (*He leaves*)
(*Martha has re-entered meantime; she and Wikkle hold each other*)
BOY'S VOICE. Grampa!
(*Wikkle does not hear it*)
MARTHA. Who was that? What's going on? Somebody tell me.
WIKKLE (*pale*). I don't know.
HANS. I don't either.
FREDDY. It was the sign painter who told you where the shop was, Mr. Gropius.
HANS. Whoever it was, I hope he's given you something to think about, Mr. Wikkle. Exploitation can go too far, and then the smashing begins.
WIKKLE. I don't exploit nobody. That's political talk. I work day and night, six days a week.
HANS. Let's go, Freddy. You see, Mr. Wikkle was right to charge you whatever he could get away with. He was only obeying the law of supply and demand, which says that some people have a right to villas on the hill and others have the right to be cold in winter.
WIKKLE. You're unfair to me, Mr. Gropius.
MARTHA. What did he mean about eyes watching this place day and night?
WIKKLE. They're giving me a bad name. Why don't you take on the textile people? Who am I, anyway? Small fry. When the pressure comes from the top, I've got to raise my prices same as everybody else.
HANS. Blaming somebody else is too easy, Mr. Wikkle.
MARTHA. Why don't you show him the letter? You still have in your pocket.
WIKKLE. I didn't want to.
MARTHA. Don't be proud. Everybody can be caught short, it's no crime.
WIKKLE. All right.
(*He takes a letter from his pocket and gives it to Hans*)
WIKKLE. It's from my supplier, Ultra Textiles.
HANS (*reading*). "Dear Mr. Wikkle: May we draw your attention to the fact that your payment for Shipment No. 44 is now one month overdue. Wartime circumstances beyond our control compel us to depart from our peacetime policy and to require prompt and full remittances in order to insure future

A SPLITTING HEADACHE

deliveries. With regard to your current order, we are obliged to charge a late-payment penalty of 25% of the full amount before said order can be shipped. We sincerely regret" etc. etc. etc. Signed Ultra Textiles.

(*He returns the letter to Wikkle*)

WIKKLE. Am I supposed to sell my house? Every merchant in town was hit by this. Everybody rushed to the bank, and the bank says, all right, we'll have to charge you 12% interest for this loan, you people are working without a safe cash margin, you're charging unrealistic pre-war prices for your merchandise.

MARTHA. It's not in our interest to overcharge. But how else can we raise the cash? And keep our own heads above water?

HANS (*softly*). You could sell your house.

WIKKLE (*staring*). Am I supposed to become a poor man so as to help strangers? Where is it written I'm supposed to be a saint?

MARTHA. We didn't make the world.

WIKKLE. We're plain people who worked hard, seldom took a holiday, and finally made it. This is a crime?

(*Jim Wikkle comes running into the shop from the backyard*)

JIM. Grandma!

MARTHA. What's the matter, sweetie?

JIM. Dave splashed some juice on my sleeve, look, we tried to wash it off but we couldn't.

MARTHA (*kissing him*). It's just a tiny nothing of a spot. Come to the kitchen, I'll get you spanking clean in a jiffy.

JIM (*noticing Freddy*). Who's this, grandma?

MARTHA. A little boy who bought something from us.

JIM (*whispering to Martha*). He's awful dirty.

MARTHA. Hush! Come along! (*They leave*)

WIKKLE. Isn't he cute? (*To Freddy*) Here, my boy, here's something for you, buy yourself some candy on the way home.

FREDDY. Thank you, sir.

WIKKLE. Why don't you go and complain to Ultra Textiles, Mr. Gropius? They're the ones you should blame, believe me.

HANS. I'll go to Ultra Textiles.

BOY'S VOICE. Mr. Wikkle! We can't do nothin' without you!

WIKKLE. Coming! Coming!

(*He leaves*)

HANS. Let's go buy your dad's medicine, Freddy.

FREDDY. Can I buy a chocolate bar with this on the way, Mr. Gropius?

HANS. Sure.

FREDDY. He was a nice man.
(*Hans' hand has gone to his skull*)
FREDDY. Something the matter, Mr. Gropius?
HANS. A headache....
(*They shuffle out*)

SCENE THREE

(*The office of Stanley Clover, vice-president of Ultra Textiles*)
STANLEY. That sweater story of yours is very touching, but you know, your do-goodery from one end of the country to the other is going to conduct you from headaches to outright ruin.
HANS. Maybe.
STANLEY. Of course, when I say from one end of the country to the other, I mean what's left of it.
HANS. I've still got 10,000 shares in your lousy company.
STANLEY. Ultra Textiles is no lousy company, old pal. And don't forget that your dad was one of the founding fathers. Memory certified on brass plaque. Besides, we're keeping our boys warm, including my own brother by the way, while they're up there fighting in the mountains.
HANS. At huge profits to yourselves.
STANLEY. Are you starting *that* again?
HANS (*jumping up*). Somebody has to be guilty!
STANLEY. I suppose. (*The buzzer sounds*) Who is it? Oh fine. Ask him to come in. (*To Hans*) It's Phil O'Toole, the union representative. He's coming in to get my signature on the settlement.
(*Enter Philip O'Toole*)
O'TOOLE. Hi. I'm not disturbing, I hope.
STANLEY. Not at all. Phil, I want you to meet Hans Gropius, college chum and noble soul.
O'TOOLE. The senator's son.
STANLEY. Right.
O'TOOLE. So glad to make your acquaintance, sir. Your father was as a true friend of working men and women.
HANS. How do you do.
STANLEY. Got that piece of parchment, Phil?
O'TOOLE Sure thing. (*To Hans*) Look at him now. Grinning from ear to ear.

A SPLITTING HEADACHE

Two weeks ago at the bargaining table you should have heard him bark and fume that another raise was going to break Ultra Textiles. How come I don't see anything broken around here, Stan? Matter of fact, I saluted your Lamborghini Amphibian parked in the lot, so I see you haven't had to sell it to support any of your mothers and grandmothers.

STANLEY (*laughing*). Gimme that historical document, you bastard. (*He signs it*) If you guys hadn't kept that last meeting going till past my beddy-bye time—on top of which the coffee machine broke down—hey, I don't suppose one of your boys sabotaged that coffee machine?

O'TOOLE (*laughing*). Sure!

STANLEY (*holding up the contract*). Look at this. Dental insurance!

O'TOOLE. Shocking, isn't it? A working class without cavities! Dental. Medical. Old age. Unemployment insurance. Right to strike. The works. A civilized country. All right, Stan, hand it over. Nice to meet you, Mr. Gropius. So long, Stan.

STANLEY. So long, Phil. Don't forget our golf date.

(*Exit O'Toole*)

STANLEY. Phil is a man we can work with. But that settlement has really put the squeeze on us; no fooling, Hans. It's their fault, believe me, if that sweater of yours went up to ten twenty-five.

HANS. They're not driving Lamborghini Amphibians. You are.

STANLEY. You want me to donate my car and my salary and stock options to Freddy Griggs?

HANS. They should be forced from you.

STANLEY. Remedy more fatal than disease. Poverty is ugly, but a gun is uglier.

HANS. Cut your prices then! Cut your profits!

STANLEY. The stockholders own this company, Hans! Lots of *us*, I admit, but a gaggle of mothers and orphans too. You've read about those mothers and orphans. They really exist. And don't forget your ten thousand shares.

HANS. Or your fifty thousand.

STANLEY. If I'm deprived of my fifty thousand shares, I'll quit, and your downtrodden friend Mr. Griggs will have to replace me. If he botches the job, the business will sink, the workers will be laid off, and a new Freddy Griggs will be sweaterless. If he doesn't botch the job, the fifty thousand shares will go to him—they'll call it something else, of course—and we'll be back where we started, only with new personnel. (*A siren sounds*) Here goes again. Come on, Hans, maybe today the bombs will do the job for you. Ultra Textiles will be blown to the skies and justice will have been done.

A SPLITTING HEADACHE

HANS. By the unjust.
STANLEY. To do justice requires force. Force is violent. Violence is unjust. Hence it is unjust to do justice. As all revolutions prove.
HANS. Aren't we taking shelter?
STANLEY. Only if you want to. But as a man with a certain responsibility, I like to set an example. Besides, who'd want to blow up a textile plant? First come the refineries. (*The siren has stopped*)
HANS. Why couldn't you have extended credit to Mr. Wikkle, so he wouldn't have had to raise his prices?
STANLEY. I *told* you.
HANS. I know, I know. But I'm not an economist, I'm a man who suffers. The strike, wages, lost output, the government, the war....
STANLEY. Let's try again. We're hit by a strike, the payroll shoots up ten percent, retroactive to sixty days ago. Last month our army lost Gorinia when it was supposed to hold the town till the morning after doomsday. Now we suddenly have to go overseas for our raw wool, at three times the cost, provided the ships aren't sunk. Meantime we're contracted to the government—
HANS. At prices set half a year ago....
STANLEY. In the merry merry springtime.
HANS. Give up your salaries! You, the directors, the vice-presidents!
STANLEY. A drop in the bucket. No, my lad, nothing can save us. Grim reaper besets large textile firm. One alternative remains. We duck under the tidal wave by collecting on all outstanding debts without playing favorites; which seems fair enough.
HANS. And a boy who can't afford ten dollars for a sweater pays ten dollars for a sweater.
(*Explosions in the distance*)
STANLEY. Why blame us? Blame the unions. Blame the war. Prices are going up like kites on the beach. If it weren't for the silly war and the strikes, that sweater would still be costing six dollars.
(*Silence*)
HANS. I must find where the chain begins. Is General Culpepper still in town?
STANLEY. No. I was on the plane with him about a week ago. He told me he was leaving for the front almost immediately. If he could find it.
HANS. I'll go look for him.
STANLEY. Why?
HANS. To go up the chain, link by link, till I find....
(*His hand goes to his head*)
STANLEY. What's the matter?

A SPLITTING HEADACHE

HANS. Give me a glass of water, will you? Thanks. My head....
(He takes a couple of aspirins)
(More explosions)

SCENE FOUR

(The front. The artillery is going full blast. In a protected position, General Culpepper is entertaining Senators Floogle and Swallow. Corporal Bletterman is pouring coffee)

CULPEPPER. I always take my Rosenthal set to the front. It gives me a feeling of continuity and reminds me of my wife.
FLOOGLE. It's quite a thrill for us to be so close to the action, General Culpepper. Your men are performing miracles of valor.
SALLOW. What are you shelling just now, general?
CULPEPPER. Everything in sight.
(A shell burst almost knocks the cup out of Sallow's hand)
SALLOW. Oops!
CULPEPPER. This is not the Senate floor, my friends. You've got to expect a few rough moments.
FLOOGLE. War is war.
CULPEPPER. Especially with the enemy coming on as strong as he is. But I'm counting on the artillery to put them to flight.
FLOOGLE. Good! But this reminds me of the question some of us in the Senate have been wanting to raise with you, General.
SALLOW. Exactly.
CULPEPPER. Before you go on—Corporal Bletterman!
CORPORAL. Yes, sir.
CULPEPPER. Tell Lieutenant Williams to silence the guns for half an hour, will you?
CORPORAL. Yes, sir.
FLOOGLE. That's mighty considerate of you, general.
CULPEPPER. Well, it's hard to carry on a conversation.
CORPORAL. What about the soldiers' deputation, sir? Should I tell the men on my way that you can see them now?
CULPEPPER. How long have they been waiting?
CORPORAL. A couple of hours, sir.
CULPEPPER. And how many are they?

CORPORAL. Three, sir.
CULPEPPER. Tell them from me that's six man-hours lost to the army. They could have been stacking shells instead of sitting on their asses. That's all, Corporal. I'm busy with the senators.
CORPORAL. Yes, sir.
CULPEPPER. On the other hand, the moment Mr. Gropius arrives, have him join us and bring some fresh coffee. Make sure it's piping hot.
CORPORAL. Yes, sir. (*He leaves*)
SALLOW. Is that Hans Gropius you're expecting?
CULPEPPER. Yes. His dad and me were army buddies.
FLOOGLE. That was one of the best men we ever had in the Senate. A warm friend to commerce and industry.
SALLOW. And of the army.
CULPEPPER. True. It was his vote for the S-4 tank that carried the appropriation, when was it, two years ago, just before he passed on.
FLOOGLE. Don't you think, general—and by the way, I've been talking—informally, of course—with General Stillitoe and General Bancroft.
(*The cannons have gone quiet*)
CULPEPPER. I respect their opinions, Senator Floogle.
FLOOGLE. They seem to feel that front-line reports have become a shade too optimistic recently.
CULPEPPER. Say, that's interesting.
FLOOGLE. I don't know if you've been keeping an eye on the legislature.
CULPEPPER. I'm pretty busy here, you know. Every day another advance, another retreat. The layman thinks that in a retreat you just pack up and leave. But the fact is that retreats take more brainwork on the part of commanding officers than advances. On top of that, the men are griping and whining like a flock of bloody Girl Scouts. Excuse me. You were saying.
FLOOGLE. Only that last Thursday Senator McAllister stood up on the Senate floor with a bulletin issued from this very sector.
CULPEPPER. He did, did he?
FLOOGLE. And he said—I don't recall his exact words—but he said, in effect, that on the basis of your reports we might as well slow down on the TSF-111 fighter plane program.
CULPEPPER. Oh?
FLOOGLE. It was your opinion, apparently, that under present conditions the artillery was better able to cope with the enemy than the Air Force.
CULPEPPER. Did I really say that? Son of a gun! Well, what was the reaction?
FLOOGLE. I raised the question that since we're being forced to retreat at this point in time, what was meant by "coping with the enemy"?

CULPEPPER. You've got a valid point there, Senator Floogle. But on the other hand, for us military men coping may mean clobbering the enemy, coping may mean standing still, or coping may mean retreating a wee bit. It depends on the overall strategy.
SALLOW. Overall strategy—that's the key to the problem.
FLOOGLE. But the nub of the matter is that we're retreating. Are we or aren't we, General? I'm asking as a friend.
CULPEPPER. As a friend, just now we are retreating a little. Remember, we weren't as ready as we should have been when they started the war.
FLOOGLE. So I pointed out in the Senate. I suggested that what we needed was more TSF-111's, not fewer.
CULPEPPER. Good idea. I'm all in favor. How did they react to you, Senator?
FLOOGLE. Hard to judge. But it didn't help—I'm being frank with you, General—as open as a child—you don't mind, do you?
CULPEPPER. Mind? I appreciate it, believe me.
FLOOGLE. Because I'm under heavy pressure in my constituency. A lot of fine people out there are interested in the TSF-111. Billions are at stake. And I don't get elected to stop billions from coming in, if you know what I mean.
CULPEPPER. I do.
FLOOGLE. So that when you report that the TSF's are being shot down at a "dramatic" rate over enemy lines—
CULPEPPER. You have a point, Senator, but you're doing me an injustice.
FLOOGLE. Oh?
CULPEPPER. Honestly, I thought to myself, "If I report how many TSF's are lost every week, what the hell, they'll have to step up production to replace 'em and Floogle and Sallow will be happy." But I guess that was a booboo.
FLOOGLE. I appreciate the idea, even if it miscarried. The Senate is volatile. There are contrary winds, if you know what I mean.
SALLOW. And meantime there's an election coming up.
CULPEPPER. I'd forgotten about that. Thank God, we don't go in for elections in the Army.
(*Enter Corporal Bletterman*)
CORPORAL. Sir, the soldiers' deputation is asking—
CULPEPPER. Can't you see I'm still busy? Clear out.
CORPORAL. Yes, sir. (*He leaves*)
CULPEPPER. Sassier every day.
SALLOW. What do they want, General?

CULPEPPER. Who knows? Maybe they want elections too!
SALLOW and FLOOGLE. Ha, ha, ha.
CULPEPPER. Or their coffee in Rosenthal cups. Anyway, to get back—those bulletins of mine. I guess I'd better rethink them. Tone down these reports of mine a bit.
FLOOGLE. A little less brisk, in the national interest.
CULPEPPER. Maybe I've been overrating the artillery. Yes, more planes....
FLOOGLE. Now that the artillery is quiet, one can smell the field-flowers from here. By the way, is your aunt Ursula still active in the Nature Club, General Culpepper?
CULPEPPER. Active? She *is* the Nature Club, Senator!
FLOOGLE. That's wonderful.
SALLOW. Just wonderful. Nature is wonderful.
FLOOGLE. When I think of what she's done to keep our country beautiful, the times she's gone to jail for tearing billboards down—
CULPEPPER. She's beautified the jails too.
FLOOGLE. And so many indifferent people, so much inertia to overcome, so much downright cynicism, not to mention the scarcity of funds.
SALLOW. The scarcity of funds is terrible.
CULPEPPER. Who wants to support nature clubs in a time of war?
FLOOGLE. Some of us want to, General, and some of us do.
CULPEPPER. Everybody knows you're a giver, Senator Floogle.
SALLOW. Oh, he is.
FLOOGLE. I'd like to prove it now, General. Perhaps this isn't the ideal time or place for a donation to the Nature Club—
CULPEPPER. Oh, I don't know.
FLOOGLE. Then you wouldn't actually object if I asked you to remit a small sum to your aunt? A personal heartfelt contribution. We all know the club is non-political.
CULPEPPER. I don't see why Aunt Ursula would object.
FLOOGLE. We won't bother you with a check here at the front, General.
CULPEPPER. It's not exactly the place to open an account, is it?
FLOOGLE. Ha, ha, ha. That unfailing sense of humor! (*He gives Culpepper a pile of bills, which the General promptly places in a briefcase*) You'll give Miss Ursula my very personal and confidential regards.
CULPEPPER. Leave it to me. She'll be delighted, the dear old body.
(*Enter Corporal Bletterman*)
CORPORAL. Sir, Mr. Gropius arrived a few minutes ago. Shall I tell him to wait till the deputation has met with you, sir?
CULPEPPER. You'll do no such thing. Tell Gropius to join us here. And have

the shelling resume at 17:04.
CORPORAL. Yes, sir.
(*He leaves*)
FLOOGLE. The Senator's son? I wonder what he wants here.
CULPEPPER. I don't rightly know.
(*Enter Hans, carrying a tattered sweater*)
HANS. Peace, General, peace. I want peace. The country wants peace.
CULPEPPER. Hans! You look like some kind of apparition! You're not sick, are you, boy? Peace is exactly what we've been talking about here. Hans Gropius. Senators Floogle and Sallow. Inspecting the front lines.
FLOOGLE. We both knew your father well, Gropius. A genuine patriot.
SALLOW. A friend of the farmers.
CULPEPPER. What brings you down here, my boy? Are you trying to enlist? And what are you doing with that frazzled sweater?
HANS. This is a bribe for you.
ALL THREE (*horrified*). A bribe!
HANS. Take it, and in exchange for it—you're an influential man, Culpepper—I want you to tell the civilians to make peace, so we can begin from the beginning, down to zero, you understand, down to zero and then up again, but something decent this time, food and shelter for every human being at a decent price.
CULPEPPER. What's he saying? Hans, you're not well. I ought to call our medic. I don't want your sweater. What's it all about?
HANS. I found it in the last village coming here. A dead boy was holding it lying in a shell-hole in the street. I've brought it to you. The clues have led me here. This is where it begins. We demand peace. I am here to cry out against abomination.
FLOOGLE. Mr. Gropius, I happen to be here on the same mission as yours. These gentlemen will bear witness. You may not have met Senator Sallow. May I —
HANS. Isn't there enough and plenty on this earth? Enough and plenty of meat, enough bread, enough fruit for every man, woman and child? Basically?
SALLOW. Basically, yes. Science—
HANS. And enough and plenty for a roof over mankind? And enough for a sweater when a child is cold? And medicines when a man is sick? Basically?
SALLOW. I agree. Science—
HANS. Then why are they cold? Sick? Hungry? Somebody is guilty! And it's you, Culpepper, you! I have found you.
CULPEPPER. Hey! My uniform! Easy!

HANS. Silence the artillery!
CULPEPPER. I did! Don't you hear the silence?
HANS. Ground the planes! Send the men home! Bury the guns! Begin from the beginning!
CULPEPPER. Hans, remember where you are! This isn't a college campus! I'm conducting a serious war here. Grow up, kid. I thought you wanted some favor or other. Always ready to oblige in memory of your dad. But I've got no time for games.
FLOOGLE. You seem to be forgetting that the Isphians attacked *us*, young man.
SALLOW. An unprovoked attack.
FLOOGLE. And that they've occupied 35 percent of our land.
CULPEPPER. And that was yesterday, God damn it. Was it my fault they started a war? I was headed for retirement, God blast it, and then bang they dropped a load of bombs on Tailana when nobody was looking, killed two hundred people—
FLOOGLE. And ruined the Gothic cathedral, Byzantine mosaics and all.
HANS. But you're making money in it! All of you!
SALLOW. Not me.
HANS. You too. I smell money around here. Victory or defeat, it's all the same. Deals. Profits.
CULPEPPER (*hand on briefcase*). What about yourself?
HANS (*producing a bundle of papers*). Ten thousand shares of Ultra Textiles. Here. Here. Here. (*Tears them up. Exclamations*)
CULPEPPER. The boy's gone mad. Bletterman! Corporal Bletterman!
(*Enter the corporal*)
HANS. I'm sane! That's why I'm crazy! Stop the war!
CULPEPPER (*bellowing*). We're losing it! We're running! Tell Isphia to stop the war! They started it! Go to the bloody Isphians!
HANS (*beside himself*). I will! I will! (*He starts to climb over the earthworks*) Somebody is guilty! *Somebody* is guilty!
CULPEPPER. Stop him, Corporal, he'll get killed!
HANS. I don't care! Hands off!
CORPORAL. I couldn't, sir.
(*Hans is out of sight. Shots in the distance*)
CULPEPPER. Stop, you fool! Listen! Turn back! Oh well. (*To the senators*) The boy forgets that if we hadn't got the better of them with the Treaty of Klagenfurt nine years ago they wouldn't have started this war. And what made us impose the treaty? I forget.
(*Hans reappears*)

HANS. I didn't want to get killed yet.

CULPEPPER. Sit down, Hans, you're overwrought. Have a cigarette.

HANS. Thanks. Give me a glass of water, somebody.

CULPEPPER (*to the corporal*). A glass of water. (*to Gropius*) What are those?

HANS. Aspirins.

FLOOGLE. We'll take him away with us, General.

SALLOW. Maybe a cup of coffee....

HANS. Let me go. (*He tries to get up, but falters*) I'll sit down five minutes. Go ahead. I interrupted your deals. Go on with the war. It's not your fault. It's them. It's always them.

CULPEPPER. Rest a little. Bletterman, why don't you tell that deputation I'll see them now.

CORPORAL. Yes, sir. (*He leaves*)

FLOOGLE. We ought to be on our way, General.

CULPEPPER. Don't hurry. (*Aside to them*) A couple of witnesses might come in handy.

(*Enter the three privates, accompanied by Corporal Bletterman. They salute and stand at attention. All three are armed.*)

CULPEPPER. At ease, men. Glad to see you, and always ready to hear any legitimate complaints in my division. Your names?

FIRST PRIVATE. Dupont.

SECOND PRIVATE. Griggs.

HANS. Griggs?

GRIGGS. Yes, sir.

HANS. You're not related to Theobald Griggs, are you?

GRIGGS (*surprised*). Yes, sir. He's my cousin. How would you know the likes of him, sir? He's a loser if there ever was one.

HANS. My name is Gropius. Hans Gropius.

GRIGGS. Oh, Mr. Gropius. I should have known. The way they carry on about you, you're the raft in a shipwreck to them. (*He shakes Hans' hand*)

HANS (*moved*). Thank you, thank you.

CULPEPPER. All right, Private Griggs. (*To the third man*). Your name?

THIRD PRIVATE. Stein.

CULPEPPER. Ok, Griggs, Stein and Dupont. On with it. The shelling resumes at 17:04.

DUPONT. Sir, we've been elected by the men to petition you. Military Code, Article 68, paragraph C.

CULPEPPER. Ok. Go on.

DUPONT. Number one, sir, considering as it's almost winter, the men would like to be issued winter boots. (*He shows one of his heels*) You see what happens

A SPLITTING HEADACHE

to these, sir. They're not made for this here climate where it's wet most of the time. The men are suffering real bad and morale is low.

CULPEPPER. Number two?

DUPONT. Number two is the food.

CULPEPPER. I thought so.

DUPONT. The officers—

CULPEPPER. Leave the officers alone! If the officers eat steak, that's *their* lookout. What's the point of being an officer if you can't eat steak?

STEIN. But it doesn't seem fair—

CULPEPPER. You're not in the Boy Scouts, Private Stein.

GRIGGS. Well, sir, the men are sick of dry biscuits, that's all. You can't fight forever on dry biscuits.

CULPEPPER. What about the beans?

GRIGGS. Dry biscuits and beans. There's a lot of dysentery too because the water is dirty.

CULPEPPER. So you don't like the food! You're unhappy because the Ritz doesn't operate a restaurant at the front! You ought to blush your three heads off. And in front of the senators. Every word you say is going to be repeated on the Senate floor. With your names attached. To tell you the truth, Griggs, I thought you men were going to petition for more ammunition. Now *that's* a grievance I sympathize with. The supply convoys have been slow and unreliable. And it wouldn't have surprised me if this had caused a raised eyebrow or two in the ranks. Instead you come to me chattering about boots and biscuits like we were sent here for a Sunday picnic. But I'm willing to listen. I'm not like some others who'd have you up for mutiny the moment you let out a squawk. I don't even use the word mutiny. Did you hear me say mutiny? Not General Culpepper! All right then, let's get on with number three.

DUPONT. Well, sir, last week Captain Baxter took out a patrol at night, and then he decided for us to take a look at an Isphian gun emplacement at close quarters.

CULPEPPER. Yes, I know the story; only two men came back. Tough, but didn't the captain get killed too? You can't say he didn't do his bit. What's your point?

DUPONT. The men feel that they should vote on missions.

(*Culpepper looks speechlessly at the senators and Hans*)

GRIGGS. Not emergency missions, sir; but routine missions.

CULPEPPER. You're insane. Everybody's going berserk today! Vote? You've got the cheek to stand here and use the word "vote" before an Army man?

STEIN. It's our lives.

A SPLITTING HEADACHE

CULPEPPER. What else? Don't stop now! Abolish ranks? Elect your officers? Stop saluting?
DUPONT. Yes, sir.
(*Culpepper nearly suffocates*)
CULPEPPER. They're under arrest! Bletterman, call the Military Police! Five years in the stockade!
DUPONT (*yelling*). We're through with this war!
(*Hans rises excitedly; but at that moment a captain comes running*)
CAPTAIN. The Isphians are all over the place! Who's the moron who shut down the artillery? They took advantage of the lull, they're overrunning our positions!
(*Shooting is heard*)
FLOOGLE. Where do we go?
CULPEPPER. Everybody stop! I'm in command!
SALLOW. What do we do?
STEIN. Raise the blue flag! Stop the war!
DUPONT. Nobody's fighting!
GRIGGS. Alert the 7th and the 13th! On the telephones!
CAPTAIN (*to Culpepper*). Stop them, for God's sake! (*Aside*) It's the subversives, I know them, make concessions, you numbskull, it's only words.
VOICES OFF-STAGE. Fire! Fire!
CAPTAIN (*towards the wings*). Don't give an inch! General Culpepper is taking personal command!
(*The three privates are in a corner consulting*)
VOICES OFF-STAGE. Raise the blue flag! Fraternize!
CULPEPPER. Men! Your demands are granted! No more saluting! Election of officers! I'll sign! Winter boots! Steaks! Now go back there and fight!
DUPONT. Like hell.
(*The three privates point their weapons at all present. The corporal follows suit*)
CULPEPPER. You too, Bletterman?
CORPORAL. Hands in the air, all of you.
(*He catches hold of the captain and pins him down. Culpepper has whipped out his pistol*)
CAPTAIN (*to Culpepper*). Shoot, you cretin!
CULPEPPER. I'm a general, I've forgotten how to shoot.
(*He throws his pistol to the ground*)
DUPONT. I'll go spread the word. Don't let the pigs escape.
STEIN. Get Jones in the 7th and Stevens in the 13th!
DUPONT. I know what to do. (*He leaves*)
HANS. Raise the blue flag! Hallelujah!
CULPEPPER. Traitor! He's insane!

GRIGGS. He's one of us, fellas.
CORPORAL. I know. Pick up that pistol, Mr. Gropius, and join the gang. (*Hans does so*) The rest of you don't move.
HANS (embracing Griggs and Stein). I'm one of you. We'll start from zero.
(*While the men embrace, Culpepper, Floogle and Sallow dash away*)
CULPEPPER. Run! Run!
CORPORAL (*who is holding on to the captain*). Get them!
(*General outcry ad libitum. The captain tries to free himself, and Bletterman knocks him down. Stein and Griggs start shooting. The two senators escape. But Culpepper has made a small detour to pick up his briefcase, and as a result Hans brings him down with a single shot. Roar of satisfaction*)
STEIN. Culpepper is down!
CULPEPPER. Bastard! (*He dies*)
GRIGGS. Culpepper is dead!
CORPORAL. Long live the revolution! Summon the Soldiers' Council!
STEIN. Raise the blue flag! Culpepper is dead! The war is over! (*Bletterman and Stein leave*)
(*Griggs is disarming the captain, who is lying unconscious on the ground. Now he examines Culpepper's body*)
GRIGGS. Cripes, that was a clean kill, Mr. Gropius. Keep an eye on the captain till I come back, will you? You're going to be needed here. (*He leaves. Hans opens the briefcase and sees the money. He drops all the bills over Culpepper like a shower of leaves. The captain groans. Hans helps him*)
CAPTAIN. Thanks. What happened? (*He sees the body*) Jesus! Who shot the general?
HANS. I did.
CAPTAIN. Jesus Christ! (*He kneels beside the body, clears the paper money from it, puts his head to Culpepper's chest*) He's gone all right. Killing out of uniform is murder, my friend. What are you after? His money?
HANS. Fool. I shot him for mankind.
CAPTAIN (*stupefied, looks up into Hans' face*). For who?
HANS (*shouting*). For mankind!
CAPTAIN (*as one who sees the light*). Oh. That's different. (*He leaves*)
HANS (*alone*). Start from zero....
(*He begins to leave; stops; his hand goes to his head; he groans; he swallows two aspirins*)

SCENE FIVE

(A room as miseerable as the one in the opening scene. Mr. Wikkle is lying on a cot and coughing, while Martha darns a sock)

MARTHA. Don't be so bitter, dear. What's the use? A revolution is bound to be nice for *some* people.

WIKKLE. But this is too much—the Griggs Brothers, Haberdashers for the New Society! (*Laughs bitterly*) In neon!

MARTHA. I wish you'd never gone to look.

WIKKLE. Never gone to look! After ten months in jail, and my lungs in shreds, God knows how much longer I've got—

MARTHA. Don't say such things.

WIKKLE. And working in the sewers, me, Wikkles, at my age (*he coughs*). I'm not long for this filthy earth. So I went on a pilgrimage. I wasn't going to miss it. The Griggs Brothers! And you never told me.

MARTHA. Take a little more tea, dear.

WIKKLE (*violently*). I hate tea! I want my coffee!

MARTHA. There isn't any, love. Since the civil war in Guatemala, or was it the drought, or the new craze for coffee in China, I don't know, but since then it's been ever so scarce and expensive. Please drink a little more tea, do it for my sake.

WIKKLE (*drinking*). Ha, ha, ha, Haberdashers for the New Society!

MARTHA. Hush! Don't take it to heart. Hush baby, go to sleep now. (*She sings softly*)

WIKKLE (*relaxing*). Why don't you read to me again?

MARTHA. I will. What would you like me to read?

WIKKLE. The book Mrs. Appelbaum lent you. I like it.

MARTHA. I'll begin where I left off last time, all right?

WIKKLE. All right.

MARTHA (*she has a little trouble with the French and the hard words*). "Don't overlook the restaurant La Tour d'Argent, where a most particular kind of duck is served, called Pressed Duck. The duck is squeezed until it quacks Uncle—"

WIKKLE. Ha, ha, ha! That's good.

MARTHA. "And cooked before your eyes in a super-rich sauce flavored mainly with its own blood: a grand manner, if you have the stomach that can take dissection, dismemberment, and hearty squeezing by a heavy Iron Maiden."

WIKKLE. What's an Iron Maiden?
MARTHA. I don't know, dear.
WIKKLE. Turn my pillow around, would you? There's a rip on this side.
MARTHA. All right like that?
WIKKLE. Ah-hah.
MARTHA. "You may not like duck; you may detest duck; but if you visit Paris and fail to try the pressed duck at the Tour d' Argent, for the rest of your life, I warn you, you will have to explain to friends who will infallibly ask you if you have tasted pressed duck at the Tour d'Argent." Oh dear. Are you awake?
WIKKLE. Mmmm ...
(Martha sees that Wikkle has fallen asleep. She takes the teacup away to wash in the sink. The doorbell rings. She opens)
MARTHA. Oh, Mr. Gropius! How nice!
(Enter Hans, carrying a bag of groceries)
HANS. Hello, Mrs. Wikkle. It's a fine day.
MARTHA. Yes, isn't it? The birds are all singing today. Let me take this from you.
HANS. I'll set it down on the table. Mr. Wikkle's asleep?
MARTHA. Yes, he dozed off. A can of pineapple chunks! Isn't that nice!
HANS. I thought I heard you say you liked pineapple.
MARTHA. You're an angel, Mr. Gropius. I don't know how we'd survive without you. *(She is removing the items from the bag)* Just when we were running out of sugar. And look at this! "Heavenly Chocolate Cookies." That's a treat.
HANS *(smiling)*. Since I'm an angel—but how is Mr. Wikkle? I pay you a visit and you don't even tell me.
MARTHA. He's so-so. I think he's better. God wouldn't let him down now, after ten months in jail. But he never used to do much physical work, poor thing, so now, digging in the sewers, at his age, it makes his cough worse.
HANS. Here are some pills. They should help. What else can I bring to help him? Please tell me.
MARTHA. Maybe—I don't know....
HANS. Tell me, Mrs. Wikkle.
MARTHA. Maybe you could bring him a sweater. It's cold in the sewers.
HANS: Of course. I'll bring you one the very next time.
WIKKLE *(in his sleep)*. The Griggs Brothers!
HANS. What did he say?
MARTHA. Nothing.
HANS. I thought he said "the Griggs Brothers."

A SPLITTING HEADACHE

MARTHA. Well, what happened—when we took him from jail last month, maybe you remember, I asked you to drive the long way around the park.

HANS. I remember.

MARTHA. It was so as we wouldn't pass in front of our old store.

HANS. Oh, I didn't realize.

MARTHA. But today he took a walk that way after work, and he saw the new sign. It bothers him a lot.

WIKKLE (*waking*). Is that you, senator?

HANS. Yes, it's me. You're looking much better today, Mr. Wikkle. In another week you'll be used to the work, while I try to get you something more suitable.

WIKKLE. You think so?

HANS. No doubt about it. Come on, let's have a cup of tea together.

WIKKLE. You didn't maybe bring us some coffee?

MARTHA. You know the price is out of reach!

WIKKLE. I want my three cups of coffee every day like I've always had them since the time I was eighteen years old!

HANS (*low*). I'll try to find some coffee next time, Mr. Wikkle.

WIKKLE. Will you, senator? It sounds silly, but after two years of drinking slop, you don't know how I long for it, it's as if it was the last thing I ever wanted on this filthy earth.

MARTHA. Why has it become so expensive, senator? Is it the civil war in Guatemala? Mrs. Appelbaum next door and me were asking ourselves. And soap too. Not to mention clothes. Why? Whose fault is it?

HANS. Whose fault?

MARTHA. Who is to blame?

HANS. Who is to blame?

MARTHA. Yes.

(*Hans stares at her*)

HANS. When Adam and Eve—

WIKKLE (*sitting up*). What did you say?

HANS. When Adam and Eve—

MARTHA. What's wrong, Mr. Gropius? Why are you crying?

HANS. It's my splitting headache....

The End

A SPLITTING HEADACHE

Notes

A Splitting Headache was printed in the second volume of my *Collected Plays* (1970-1972). It is here substantially revised.

THE FATAL FRENCH DENTIST

CHARACTERS

Bill Foot
Mary Foot
Bill Nethergood
Mary Nethergood
Bill Tuttle
Mary Tuttle

SCENE ONE

(A nice American living-room. Mr. Foot is examining a quiz in his newspaper. Mrs. Foot is doing nothing)

MR. FOOT. Newspapers are becoming more educational all the time. This quiz is called "Are You Socially Acceptable?"

MRS. FOOT. It seems a little insulting for them to doubt it, considering we're subscribers.

MR. FOOT. Nonsense. It's scientific. You get points and then they add up the points for you and you find out how socially acceptable you are. The best and second best and third best and the worst answers are printed upside down so you're not tempted to cheat. Ok, here goes. Question one: When you leave a party, how do your hosts react? (a) They sob; (b) They faint; (c) They grin; (d) They guffaw. *(He makes a mark)*

MRS. FOOT. What are you answering?

MR. FOOT. This quiz is confidential, but so far I'm satisfied with myself. Two: How do you behave when an unwelcome guest rings your doorbell just as you are settling down for a quiet evening with your wife and/or video-game? (a) You shoot him.

MRS. FOOT. And be thrown in jail?

MR. FOOT. (b) You slam the door in his face; (c) You tell him to come in if he must, but to keep his mouth shut; (d) You make him feel he is the nicest thing that could have happened to you that evening. *(He makes a mark)*

MRS. FOOT. I would not answer the doorbell at all and pretend I wasn't home. It's the best solution, because it keeps you happy and doesn't offend your guest. I think shooting him is simply too awfully overdone.

MR. FOOT. You do go on, don't you, my dear. Question three: What do you do when your hostess serves you a dish you do not like?

MRS. FOOT. I eat everything.

MR. FOOT. (a) You throw it on the floor; (b) You tell her you'll eat it but you wouldn't feed it to your hogs.

MRS. FOOT. Oh, that's a terrible thing to say.

MR. FOOT. Why?

MRS. FOOT. Well, I mean, throwing something on the floor isn't so bad;

nobody need notice, especially if there's a low-hanging tablecloth, and maybe a cat or a dog under the table. But to say "I wouldn't feed it to my hogs" is awfully rude.

MR. FOOT. I suppose so, and yet when you look at it sympathetically it really isn't. Let's say the husband overhears me. "I wouldn't feed these asparagus to my hogs," says I. He rises from the table, he's furious, "You've got a nerve telling my wife you wouldn't feed these asparagus to your hogs!" "What," says I, "would you feed them to your hogs?" "Of course not," he hollers. "Well, that's precisely what I said," I reply, and he crumples.

MRS. FOOT. Well, fortunately there aren't any hogs in Queens, so why trouble our heads about them?

MR. FOOT. The hogs are meant as a for-instance, my dear. Let me see, where was I? (c) You eat it but you sulk for the rest of the evening; (d) You wrench your mouth into a wonderful smile and you say—

(*The doorbell rings*)

MRS. FOOT. Oh, maybe it's somebody exciting at last!

MR. FOOT. Hope springs eternal.

(*Mrs. Foot opens the door. Enter Mr. and Mrs. Nethergood*)

MR. and MRS. NETHERGOOD. Hello hello hello hello!

MR. and MRS. FOOT. Hello hello hello hello hello!

MRS. FOOT. Wonderful to see you people! Those dear Nethergoods!

MRS. NETHERGOOD. So good to see you two again, plump and ruddy and all.

MR. NETHERGOOD. How are you, Bill?

MR. FOOT. How are you, Bill?

MRS. FOOT. Bill, get the Nethergoods a drink. Sit down, children, sit down, Mary.

MRS. NETHERGOOD. We absolutely can't, Mary dear. You stop those drinks, Bill Foot.

MRS. FOOT. Why? What's the matter?

MRS. NETHERGOOD. We're on our way to a wedding. Bill Lumley and Mary Finkelberg. Do you know them?

MRS. FOOT. I don't think so. Come on, tell us all about it, do sit down, both of you—five minutes, that's all, we'll set the alarm if you insist; I want to hear all about the wedding.

MRS. NETHERGOOD. All right, five minutes, but no drinks, not a thing. Sit down, Bill.

MR. FOOT. All right, but what's the rush? Just another wedding. And what's a wedding these days? A legal requirement for a divorce.

MRS. NETHERGOOD. This is not just another wedding, my dear man. I'll tell you all about it if you swear to take the secret to the grave with you. Bill, you naughty, that goes for you too, you mustn't tell anybody.

MR. FOOT. I don't gossip about people I don't know.

MRS. NETHERGOOD. Well, it's a dreadful story.

MRS. FOOT. Wonderful. Go on!

MRS. NETHERGOOD. The Lumleys and the Finkelbergs had agreed not to invite anybody on either side beyond uncles and aunts. Parents, grandparents, brothers, sisters, authentic uncles and genuine aunts, and that was to be all for the dinner. No cousins.

MR. NETHERGOOD. Mark this. No cousins.

MRS. NETHERGOOD. And that's where the roof caved in. It seems that Bill Lumley's cousin just came back from three years of mission work in darkest Boola-Boola. He's alone in the world, the natives ate his wife, he arrives in America penniless, all yellow with malaria and something shot off, an arm or leg, I don't know which—

MRS. FOOT. So?

MRS. NETHERGOOD. So, Bill Lumley decides to make an exception for the one cousin, in view of the special circumstances. Well! The Finkelbergs go wild. They've got a cousin who almost drowned while trying to leave a submarine before it reached the surface. A tragic case, half a lung taken out, a few medals on the sound side of the chest—so why the Boola-Boola cousin but not the submarine cousin? I assure you the marriage just about broke up. Mary's mother said that without the submarine cousin the marriage was off. Bill's folks answered that one exception was enough, because once you started adding exceptions you'd soon have the hall full of them.

MRS. FOOT. So?

MRS. NETHERGOOD. So, Mary said she surely wasn't going to give up Bill because of a cousin who wasn't smart enough to keep the door of a submarine closed when it was under water. And then she asked Bill to give up his missionary cousin. So Bill blew up and then Mary blew up and it was a mess.

MR. FOOT. But they patched it up?

MRS. NETHERGOOD. They did; they decided to invite everybody, including us. But nobody is talking to anybody. Even the bride and groom aren't on speaking terms.

MR. FOOT. A quiet wedding, in short.

MRS. NETHERGOOD. Aren't people just too horribly horrible?

MR. FOOT. The trouble is, they're not socially acceptable.

MRS. FOOT. I always tell Bill if only people were reasonable and did what's right, the world would be a better place.

THE FATAL FRENCH DENTIST

MR. NETHERGOOD. Bless you, those are almost exactly my words, aren't they, Mary?

MRS. NETHERGOOD. Be quiet, dear, and let me speak. What was I saying? Oh, yes, we absolutely must go. We only stopped in to bid you to a homely feast chez nous.

MR. NETHERGOOD. At Nethergood Manor.

MRS. NETHERGOOD. Next Saturday, dinner at seven. We want you to meet an exciting dentist visiting from Paris. He's looking into photodontic equipment in the States.

MR. NETHERGOOD. Dental surgery, actually. Top man in his field.

MR. FOOT. How drilling. (*He and Mr. Nethergood enjoy themselves*)

MRS. FOOT. You're an angel to ask us, Mary, and we'll be delighted to come. I simply adore Parisians. France wouldn't be the same without them.

MRS. NETHERGOOD. That's why we're asking only the two of you. We didn't want to scare him with too many strange people. Well—(*she embraces Mrs. Foot*) we've got to run.

MR. NETHERGOOD. Sorry we can't stay, old Billberry, but I'll hold you to a double scotch next time.

MR. FOOT. Great. Say, do you know the difference between a double scotch on the rocks and Siamese twins on gravel?

MRS. FOOT. Do stop, my dear, you're unbearable.

MRS. NETHERGOOD. Never mind, I think he's a love. Well, bye bye now.

MR. NETHERGOOD. Bye bye.

MRS. FOOT. Bye bye.

MR. FOOT. Bye bye.

(*The Nethergoods leave*)

MRS. FOOT. So here we are again. The excitement's over.

MR. FOOT. I hope they serve broccoli.

(*He goes back to his newspaper*)

MRS. FOOT (*to herself*). Me, my husband, and the question why. Maybe something interesting will happen again before I pass on.

MR. FOOT. It says in the paper that according to the best thought of the day, people like you and I live the desperate lives of meaningless automata in a consumer-driven society which has lost touch with the inner springs of a rich and fruitful existence.

MRS. FOOT. Well, the newspapers always make things sound more exciting than they are. It's true that you have your position in the company and we have our friends and our home and our birch tree in the backyard, but I don't think that the paper is right to point to people like us as models of anything.

THE FATAL FRENCH DENTIST

MR. FOOT. I'd better get back to the quiz.
(*The doorbell rings*)
MRS. FOOT. More excitement I bet!
MR. FOOT. With this infernal doorbell going all day I'll never find out how socially acceptable I am.
(*Mrs. Foot opens the door. Enter Mr. and Mrs. Tuttle*)
MR. and MRS. TUTTLE. Hello hello hello hello!
MR. and MRS. FOOT. Hello hello hello hello!
MRS. FOOT. Mary! How lovely to see you again! And dear old Bill with you for a change!
MR. FOOT. Dear old Bill and Mary.
MR. TUTTLE. Dear old Billberry and good old Mary.
MRS. FOOT. Come in and sit down. Fix the drinks, Bill.
MRS. TUTTLE. Don't make a move, either one of you. We're on our way to a funeral and we can't stay but a minute.
MRS. FOOT. What funeral? You scare me.
MRS. TUTTLE. Mary Spiffin's husband—don't you remember Mary Spiffin, at the Happy Orphanage Circle?
MRS. FOOT. Of course I do.
MR. FOOT. You mean Bill Spiffin who was in gaskets?
MR. TUTTLE. That's right. Gaskets and washers.
MRS. TUTTLE. Anyway, this is one funeral we don't want to miss.
MRS. FOOT. And yet you talk about running away without even telling us. No, I'll really be unhappy if you don't sit down for at least five minutes. We'll set the alarm if you insist.
MR. FOOT. Come on, be friendly with the natives.
MRS. TUTTLE. All right, but five minutes is all, I swear.
MRS. FOOT (*to Mr. Tuttle*). Here, put this pillow behind your back.
MR. TUTTLE. Thanks. Go on, Mary, open the old valves and tell her about the funeral.
MRS. FOOT. Yes! You were saying?
MRS. TUTTLE. Well. About a year ago Mary Bartlett's husband died.
MR. TUTTLE. You knew Bill Bartlett, the piston man.
MR. FOOT. Sure I remember him. I wrote a policy for his outfit.
MRS. FOOT. So?
MRS. TUTTLE. So—the funeral that Mary Bartlett gave her husband positively sickened Mary Spiffin. She was so jealous it was all she could do to bring out a decent condolence. There was Bill Bartlett lying on an adjustable mattress, satin and velvet and Venetian lace on the sides of the coffin, looking ten years younger than what he'd been, and holding his

THE FATAL FRENCH DENTIST

pipe in his hand! And when I say coffin, I should say triple casket: one of mahogany, the next of bronze, and the third a genuine Roman sarcophagus, flown over especially by an antique dealer in Italy. As for the guests, half of General Motors was there—with a floral piece by the Chairman of the Board himself—"For Bill Bartlett, whose pistons shall not be forgot." The eulogy was spoken by the archbishop, and while the organ played they had birds twittering I don't know where, it was deep and inspirational and we all cried. I counted fifteen boys in white standing around the caskets like so many Cupids, you never saw anything so cute in your life. And in the midst of all, there was Mary Bartlett sobbing her heart out and blubbering "If only Bill were alive, he'd be so proud!" Well, you should have beheld Mary Spiffin. She was sitting there with her lips pressed together taking it all in, and swearing to herself (so I could tell) she'd show that Mary Bartlett a funeral when the time came. But of course you can't just ask your husband to up and die so you can throw a big funeral—I don't think Spiffin would have gone in for that at all because he wasn't the kind of man who approves of making a show, if you know what I mean, he was really a quiet sort of man. So all she could do was stare at him a great deal. And then suddenly he popped off after all—three days ago it was—

MR. TUTTLE. Keeled over while he was having a drink with the boys at the convention of the Gasket Association of America.

MRS. TUTTLE. Aren't men unpredictable? And that was that.

MRS. FOOT. What an opening for Mrs. Spiffin!

MRS. TUTTLE. Exactly. Naturally Mary Bartlett is at the top of her guest list, and I'm dying to see what she's rigged up. Well, we're sitting here chattering with you. Come on, Bill, we'd better be off.

MR. TUTTLE. My dear, you've forgotten what you came here for.

MRS. TUTTLE. Didn't I ask you over for Saturday?

MR. TUTTLE. No, you didn't ask them over for Saturday.

MRS. TUTTLE. I'm in a daze.

MRS. FOOT. Actually—

MRS. TUTTLE. You must join us next Saturday night—two bridge tables, the Simpsons, the Hardys....

MR. TUTTLE. Bridge at the Tuttle Estates.

MRS. FOOT. We'd love to come, it sounds delightful, but I'm afraid we're taken next Saturday.

MR. FOOT. Broccoli and all the rest.

MRS. TUTTLE. What a pity!

MR. TUTTLE. A blow to the solar plexus, old Billberry.

MRS. TUTTLE. Well, I'll ask the Nethergoods.

THE FATAL FRENCH DENTIST

MRS. FOOT. Oh, but it's the Nethergoods we're going to! (*Mr. Foot coughs*)
MRS. TUTTLE (*miffed*). Oh, I see. That's odd.
MR. TUTTLE. Yes, that's odd. What's odd about it, dear?
MRS. TUTTLE. Nothing. Are the Nethergoods throwing a party?
MRS. FOOT. Oh no, nothing like that.
MRS. TUTTLE. They usually ask us.
MR. TUTTLE. How about our funeral, Mary?
MRS. FOOT. Couldn't you go a little later, and have a cup of coffee with us?
MRS. TUTTLE (*cold*). No, we can't. Well, good bye, you all. Bye bye.
MR. TUTTLE. Bye bye.
MRS. FOOT. Bye bye.
MR. FOOT. Bye bye. We'll see you, Billberry old man.
(*The Tuttles leave*)
MR. FOOT. Well, you've did it.
MRS. FOOT. Don't be funny. What was I to do?
MR. FOOT. Why did you have to tell the Tuttles we were going to be at the Nethergoods? Wasn't it enough to say we weren't available on Saturday?
MRS. FOOT. I just saw a little deeper into the situation than you, that's all, my dear. Mary Tuttle was going to call the Nethergoods to ask them over. And what would have happened? Mary Nethergood would have answered that they couldn't because we—oh no, I guess she wouldn't have—(*She gasps*)
MR. FOOT. You guess! You see a little deeper into the situation than me! A nice puddle you've made of it. You didn't think the Nethergoods would have had enough sense just to say, "Thank you but we're engaged"? What a woman! A social misfit.
MRS. FOOT. I made a mistake.
MR. FOOT. A whammer.
MRS. FOOT. I made a big mistake.
MR. FOOT. You've just caused an international incident between the Tuttles and the Nethergoods. And they the best friends in the world. Adored each other, that's all. But the Tuttles don't like to be left out.
MRS. FOOT. But why do you suppose the Nethergoods asked us without asking them?
MR. FOOT. Don't you remember anything? She didn't want to scare the French dentist with too many strange people. Very delicate, I think. Besides, do they have to ask everybody they know? The only trouble is that a famous French dentist would be a nice morsel for the Tuttles, and they'd better not find out about him.
MRS. FOOT. Dear oh dear, what am I to do? How can I clean up this horrible

mess? Wait. What time is it?

MR. FOOT. Let me check. (*He goes up to a clock and moves the minute hand*) It's eight o'clock.

MRS. FOOT. The funeral must be over by now. I've got an idea.

MR. FOOT. Tell me.

MRS. FOOT. Just let me do what I have to do. (*She picks up the telephone*)

MR. FOOT. Hadn't you better tell me first?

MRS. FOOT. Quiet. (*Into the telephone*) Hello! Mary? This is Mary Foot. How are you, dear? How was the funeral? A hit? The Governor! And the Vienna Choir Boys! How simply lovely! Yes ... yes ... (*She gasps*) Bill! You have to hear this! Yes! ... yes ... Bill! Listen to this! They had a mausoleum ready for Spiffin, and they rolled him in sitting inside his Hudson Super Six—worth millions—they wheeled the Hudson Super Six right into the mausoleum. Yes ... yes ... All they took out was the air conditioning....

MR. FOOT. This will kill Bill Bartlett a second time.

MRS. FOOT. Yes? No! Well, why not? It's a thing you can do only once. That's right. That's right. You're so right. Listen, Mary, the reason I called—we got to thinking, after you left, Bill and me, it sounded a little funny, I mean about the Nethergoods—Yes! No! I mean—of course! I understand perfectly! Of course!—Yes, yes, by all means!—I didn't—I wouldn't—anyway the point is that the Nethergoods are having a life insurance man over from India—

MR. FOOT. What's that?

MRS. FOOT. Yes, that's right—exactly—Hong Kong—ha ha ha, cosmopolitan is the word. Anyway, since my Bill is in life insurance himself, they thought—that's it—naturally—right—awfully technical—indemnity tables and so on, frankly it's going to be a bore for me personally—but I thought—that's right—you're so right—of course—I'm so glad I talked it over with you. Are you lunching at Peewee's tomorrow? Wonderful. About twelve-thirty. Bye bye! (*She hangs up*) Satisfied? I'm a genius.

MR. FOOT. You're playing a dangerous game. You should have consulted me first.

MRS. FOOT. What would you have advised me to do?

MR. FOOT. Book the first flight to Siberia.

MRS. FOOT. Very funny.

MR. FOOT. You'd better call the Nethergoods right away.

MRS. FOOT. What on earth for?

MR. FOOT. Don't you want to tell Mary Nethergood that you told Mary Tuttle that she, that is to say Mary Nethergood, was having a life insurance man from Hong Kong over for the soiree to which she didn't invite her, that is to say, Mary Tuttle? I mean, they see a lot of each other. You'll be feeling pretty sick if Mary Tuttle shakes her curls at Mary Nethergood at the beauty parlor next week and asks "How was your soiree with the life insurance man from Hong Kong?" "What life insurance man from Hong Kong?" "Why, the life insurance man from Hong Kong that Mary Foot told me about!" Bang!

MRS. FOOT. I'm going to have to take a chance on that.

MR. FOOT. Why?

MRS. FOOT. Very simple. You want me to call Mary Nethergood.

MR. FOOT. Right.

MRS. FOOT. But if I do, I'll have to admit to Mary Nethergood that I told Mary Tuttle that she, that is to say Mary Nethergood, invited us for next Saturday. Insurance man or dentist, what's the difference? The point is that I'll be miserably exposed, and the Nethergoods will know that the Tuttles know that they, that is to say the Nethergoods, did not invite them, and that it was me who told the Tuttles. They'll never talk to us again.

MR. FOOT. Who?

MRS. FOOT. The Nethergoods, silly.

MR. FOOT. And if you don't call her?

MRS. FOOT. There's at least a chance. Mary Nethergood naturally won't tell Mary Tuttle about the party. And maybe Mary Tuttle will be tactful and proud enough not to let on she knows there was a party. And it will all blow over.

MR. FOOT. Something is bound to blow over. Oh well, hand me the paper, will you?

MRS. FOOT. I'll sit down and do nothing for a while. It's the most restful thing when all is said and done.

MR. FOOT. Where did I leave off? Ah, here it is. "Why, in your personal opinion, is it incorrect to wear a necktie on the beach over your swim trunks? (a) Because this is too conservative for our day and age. (b) Because it shows an exaggerated concern with your personal appearance. (*As the lights go down*) (c) Because the necktie would leave a white streak on your sun-bronzed chest. (d) Because you wish to avoid political and religious controversy.

SCENE TWO

(Mr. and Mrs. Tuttle are sitting on a bench in a park)

MR. TUTTLE. Look at the birds looping all over the air. Look at the grass cuddling the flowers. Look at the wind nibbling the leaves. Look at the innocent youngsters with sailboats and bicycles. Look at the romping butterflies. Come here, pretty pigeons, here are crumbs for you.

MRS. TUTTLE. If the Nethergoods want to invite a life insurance man from India especially to meet Bill Foot because Bill Foot is also a life insurance man, even though he is not from Hong Kong, why make a secret of it? What is wrong with doing what they did? Was Mary Nethergood afraid I'd be offended just because she didn't invite *us?* Why *should* she invite us? You're not in life insurance, you're in preformed cardboard and you don't export to Hong Kong. Why should we be offended? She must take us for a pair of fools if she thought we'd be small enough to resent her not asking us. Do I ask her over every time I have a guest, especially if he is in preformed cardboard? How stupid can a person be? Why didn't she talk to me honestly and say, "Mary, we're having a life insurance man from Hong Kong over next Saturday. I'm asking the Foots, because Bill Foot is in life insurance too. You don't mind, do you?" Instead she had to keep it a secret as though she'd been guilty of something, and when I met her on Thursday and asked her over to our house for Saturday, just to test her, mind you, just to test her, because I knew damn well that she was having her own party with the Hong Kong man and the Foots, she just played innocent and pretended they were going out. I'm glad Mary Foot happened to tell me the truth. I like to know what goes on.

MR. TUTTLE. That pigeon sure was hungry.

MRS. TUTTLE *(rising from the bench)*. Hello hello hello hello!

MR. TUTTLE. Who's coming?

MRS. TUTTLE. It's the Nethergoods!

MR. TUTTLE. Well, I want you to be nice to them. Let's everybody be nice to everybody and everything will be nice.

MRS. TUTTLE. Be quiet. You talk as if I was a hyena. *(Enter the Nethergoods)* Hello hello!

MRS. NETHERGOOD. Hello hello!

THE FATAL FRENCH DENTIST

MR. NETHERGOOD. Hello Billberry old man!

MR. TUTTLE. Good to see you again!

MRS. NETHERGOOD. What an adorable purse, Mary! Perfect for a spring day in the park. Is it new?

MRS. TUTTLE. Bill gave it to me for my birthday ten years ago, thank you. By the way, we ran into the Foots the other day.

MRS. NETHERGOOD. Oh, how are they? Have you noticed how the park has become full of dirty pigeons?

MRS. TUTTLE. They said they had a lovely time at your place last Saturday.

MRS. NETHERGOOD. I'm so glad.

MRS. TUTTLE. And they enjoyed meeting the life insurance man from Hong Kong.

MR. NETHERGOOD. Life insurance man from Hong Kong? There was only a French dentist.

MR. TUTTLE. A French dentist in life insurance in Hong Kong?

MR. NETHERGOOD. What life insurance? Is everybody going crazy? He's a French dentist, I tell you, or a dental surgeon to be precise. Of course, Bill Foot talked to him a lot, and maybe he has a life insurance practice on the side, but that's more than I know.

MR. TUTTLE. Maybe he needs two jobs to make ends meet. Life in Hong Kong is awfully expensive, you know.

MR. NETHERGOOD. That's true. Or he might be divorced, and paying alimony.

MR. TUTTLE. Or he could be supporting an old mother or two.

MR. NETHERGOOD. Anyway, what with the rate of industrial growth having slowed down to 0.6% per annum in France, I wouldn't be surprised if a Frenchman actually needed two jobs.

MR. TUTTLE. Well, that explains our little confusion.

MRS. TUTTLE. When are you two males going to stop chattering? Who cares how many jobs the man had? The main point is that the Foots had a very pleasant time.

MRS. NETHERGOOD. Well, I don't know where the life insurance story started, I'm sure he is a dentist and nothing else. We had a casual spur-of-the-moment thing at the house. He was going to show pictures of French teeth and I remembered how your Bill came down last month was it? with a headache watching our World Tour pictures. By the way, will you be free next Sunday afternoon? Could you stop by for cocktails? The Willoughbys will be there.

MR. TUTTLE. Old Bill Willoughby of the Security Federal Union Security Universal Trust Bank?

MR. NETHERGOOD. That's the one.
MR. TUTTLE. Great. We'll be there.
MRS. TUTTLE (*frosty*). You're forgetting we're engaged, my dear.
MR. TUTTLE. We are?
MRS. TUTTLE (*frosty*). I'm sorry, Mary, but we can't this time. Our schedule is full. Come along, Bill. It's getting chilly. Goodbye all.
MR. and MRS. NETHERGOOD. Goodbye.
MRS. NETHERGOOD. I'll call you!
MRS. TUTTLE. You do that. (*On the way out, soft-loud to Mr. Tuttle*) The liars, the simpering liars.
(*They leave*)
MRS. NETHERGOOD. We goofed.
MR. NETHERGOOD. *You* goofed.
MRS. NETHERGOOD. *You* goofed.
MR. NETHERGOOD. We goofed.
MRS. NETHERGOOD. Why didn't you keep your mouth shut when she rattled on about the life insurance man from Hong Kong? Why did you have to stick your stupid facts into the conversation?
MR. NETHERGOOD. What's the difference? She was mad already, that was as obvious as a pimple on an egg. "I hear the Foots had a lovely time at your house," she says with a snaky smile that would have poisoned you at fifty paces if you hadn't smiled right back. I told you that you should have asked them to the house.
MRS. NETHERGOOD. Don't start on *that* again. It so happened that I didn't feel like asking them that time. Do I have to ask the Tuttles every time I have anybody at the house? And I tell you that she wouldn't have objected if it hadn't looked suddenly as though we'd tried to keep the French dentist hidden from her for some evil reason or other.
MR. NETHERGOOD. Or if you hadn't told her last Thursday that we were engaged on Saturday when later she found out that we were engaged because we were having friends at our place.
MRS. NETHERGOOD. Found out! But where in sweet heaven did she find out that we had asked the Foots, and where in all that's holy did she hear about the life insurance man from Hong Kong. I can't figure it out.
MR. NETHERGOOD. Maybe somebody heard about the Foots meeting a life insurance man from Hong Kong at another party.
MRS. NETHERGOOD. That's very odd. Mary Foot has never mentioned it to me. Why should Mary Foot make a secret of a life insurance man from Hong Kong?
MR. NETHERGOOD. Well, then, suppose the Foots had this life insurance

THE FATAL FRENCH DENTIST

man from Hong Kong at their own house along with some other people who happen to know the Tuttles, and suppose they hadn't invited us. That would explain their not telling us about him.

MRS. NETHERGOOD. I suppose so. But behind our backs?

(*Enter the Foots*)

MRS. FOOT. Mary dear, oh, hello, Bill. There's something I'd better tell you.

MRS. NETHERGOOD. Oh, hello, Mary, hello, Bill.

MR. NETHERGOOD. Hello both!

MR. FOOT. Hello, Bill and Mary. Nice day, pretty birds.

MRS. FOOT. There's something I want to tell you, Mary.

MRS. NETHERGOOD. As a matter of fact, there's something I want to ask *you*.

MRS. FOOT (*apprehensive*). Oh. Why don't you ask first?

MRS. NETHERGOOD. No, you tell me first.

MRS. FOOT. Well, I couldn't get out of it, Mary. I won't go into details, but I had to tell the Tuttles *something*, so I told them you had invited—

MR. and MRS. NETHERGOOD. A life insurance man from Hong Kong.

MR. and MRS. FOOT. How did you know?

MRS. NETHERGOOD (*frigid*). We talked to the Tuttles.

MRS. FOOT. Oh no!

MRS. NETHERGOOD. We ran into them just now, and Mary said to me, "We heard you had a life insurance man from Hong Kong over at your house last Saturday to meet the Foots," she said to me, and naturally Bill said, "What life insurance man? He was a dentist," and then it all came out. Now what I'd like to know, just for curiosity's sake, is why you made up that story about the life insurance man from Hong Kong.

MR. FOOT (*to Mrs. Foot*). I told you.

MRS. FOOT. Oh, shut up. Mary, listen to me.

MRS. NETHERGOOD. You know how sensitive the Tuttles are; you know one can't take a step without treading on one of their hundred toes. And yet you have to blab to them, and tell them a cock-and-bull story about a life insurance man from Hong Kong. Excuse me for saying so, but it's plain stupid, that's all.

MRS. FOOT. Mary—!

MRS. NETHERGOOD. I'm sure you had your reasons for inventing this idiotic figure, but you might have given a moment's thought to the impossible hole you were digging for me. You made me look like a liar, a plotter. Mary Tuttle left here convinced I had told you to make up that story of the life insurance man from Hong Kong. They gave us a frosty goodbye. Two of our dearest friends down the drain. Thank you very much.

MR. NETHERGOOD (*weeping*). Bill Tuttle, who was my buddy in the army, my chum at the Bowling League, my pal at the Lodge.

MR. FOOT (*to Mrs. Foot*). I told you.

MRS. FOOT. May I put a word in sideways one of these years? Is anybody going to listen to me? Thank you. I wish you'd realize, my dear, that I invented the life insurance man from Hong Kong exclusively to save your face.

MRS. NETHERGOOD. Well, I never!

MRS. FOOT. I repeat: to save your face. I told the Tuttles it was a kind of business affair—insurance shoptalk between the men—so that she wouldn't be offended at being left out.

MRS. NETHERGOOD. And how did she come to know I hadn't asked her in the first place? Answer that one, if you please.

MRS. FOOT. Well, why didn't you?

MRS. NETHERGOOD. I've heard too much.

MR. NETHERGOOD. Me too.

MRS. FOOT. And why were you fool enough to tell her "Oh no, it wasn't a life insurance man from Hong Kong, it was a French dentist?" How naive can you get? A child would have guessed something and would have confirmed my story.

MR. FOOT. My wife has a point there, you know.

MR. NETHERGOOD. I protest.

MRS. NETHERGOOD. Don't bother protesting. You can't argue with boors. Let's—

MRS. FOOT. Boors? Did you say boors?

MRS. NETHERGOOD. Boors. Without an ounce of etiquette. You're a pair of public hazards, if you want an unbiased opinion. Come along, Bill, let the Foots enjoy the park by themselves.

MR. FOOT. We will, damn it. Good riddance to the windbag.

MR. NETHERGOOD and MRS. NETHERGOOD. Boors!

(*They leave*)

MR. FOOT. I guess they don't like us any more.

(*Enter the Tuttles from the other side*)

MRS. TUTTLE. There you are.

MR. and MRS. FOOT. Oh my God.

MRS. TUTTLE. We heard all about your phony life insurance man from Hong Kong.

MR. TUTTLE. Our eyes are unplugged and the scales have fallen from our ears.

MRS. TUTTLE. All of a sudden he's a dentist.

THE FATAL FRENCH DENTIST

MR. TUTTLE. A French dentist. Ha!

MRS. TUTTLE. Next time, you and your friends had better get together on the fables you're going to tell your stupid acquaintances. Come along, Bill. I just wanted to let her know we're wise to all of them.

MRS. FOOT. Won't you—

MRS. TUTTLE. Don't worry. I'll put your copy of *Love in the Suburbs* in the mail for you.

MRS. FOOT (*weakly*). You can finish it first.

MRS. TUTTLE. Come on, Bill. Let's leave the Foots and the Nethergoods to enjoy a good laugh at our expense.

(*They leave*)

MR. FOOT. So here we are.

MRS. FOOT (*sniffling*). I'm sure I did my best. If you hadn't—

MR. FOOT. If I hadn't! I like that! If I hadn't! That takes the prize! I told you a thousand times—

MRS. FOOT. You told me! You're always telling me! You think you're Einstein, don't you? You're always telling me what I found out three weeks before.

MR. FOOT. Keep talking, and if it makes you happy to unload your guilt on me, go right ahead, it's cheaper than analysis, you can tear me to bits to relieve your subconscious frustrations. But in the meantime, don't forget you've ruined six beautiful friendships.

MRS. FOOT. So it's all my fault. You take their side. Everybody else's wife is a pure spotless angel, only your own is a monster. I should have known. (*Tears and moans*)

MR. FOOT. Oh, well, it's not as bad as all that.

MRS. FOOT. Nobody understands me, not even my husband.

MR. FOOT. Sure I understand you. God knows I understand you. Come on, Mary, don't cry in the middle of the park. People are staring. There, there.

MRS. FOOT. Do you love me? (*He wipes her eyes with his handkerchief*)

MR. FOOT. Of course I love you. Who else should I love? Forget those Tuttles and Nethergoods.

MRS. FOOT. We've got plenty of other friends, don't we?

MR. FOOT. I should say so. We've got so many wonderful friends that when we lose a few we don't even notice. Look, Mary, we're in luck, look who's coming our way!

MRS. FOOT. Oh, it's Bill and Mary McGrue!

MR. FOOT. All right, make yourself presentable. We'll ask them over for drinks. Ready?

MRS. FOOT. Ready.

THE FATAL FRENCH DENTIST

MR. FOOT. Forward!
(*They advance into the wings, smiling, arms stretched out*)
MR. and MRS. FOOT. Hello hello hello hello!

The End

Note

The Fatal French Dentist was printed in 1965 in *First Stage: a Quarterly of New Drama*, a magazine founded and edited at Purdue University (Indiana) by Professor Henry F. Salerno. Two years later it was brought out by the firm of Samuel French, dispenser of plays for both the amateur and the professional theatre. It reappeared in Volume II of my *Collected Plays* of 1970-1971, and then again in my *Last Pages* (2019). Revisions have been made at every stage of this journey.

PROFESSOR SNAFFLE'S POLYPON

an extravaganza

CHARACTERS

Professor Lancelot Snaffle
Hepsa Snaffle, *his wife*
Percy Loop, *his assistant, going on sixty*
Joshua Pappendeck, *a graduate student of physics*
General Winston Culpepper, *a notable military figure, though later reduced*
Mrs. Culpepper, *his wife*, later Mrs. Molassis
"Crusher" McBoodle, *Secretary of Defensive Expansion*
Mr. Nose, *a reporter*
A SPY, *whose actual name cannot be disclosed for security reasons*
An Interpreter
The Duke of Ostersund, *Chairman of the Dynamite Peace Prize Selection Board*
Dr. P. P. Folpap, *a distinguished colleague of Professor Snaffle*
Mr. Smith, *a Demonstrator*
Mr. Jones, *another Demonstrator*
Nameless people
The Author

The tots:
Mistress Molecule
Master Atom
Master Proton
Miss Electron
Master Alpha Ray
Mrs. Beta Ray
Mrs Isotope

SCENE ONE

(The left side of the stage is occupied by a large, many-sided, colorful, odd-roofed structure: the Polypon. It is equipped with certain apertures in the roof, several vents or crannies along the sides, and a substantial sliding door facing the audience. As the curtain rises, the sliding door opens wide, we hear a heavenly tinkling music, and we discover the Tots dancing gracefully about, all except Miss Isotope, who, being on the unstable side, has a little difficulty keeping up. The interior is a rich garden. As the Tots dance, they sing both in chorus and separately)

CHORUS. We jiggle and rattle
And scamper and prattle
And wiggle and prance
And retreat and advance.
We are the dancers, and we dance.

ATOM. We are the midgets
With the fidgets.

PROTON. We attract and we repel,
In orbit and in parallel.

ELECTRON. A snappy, happy phalanx,

ISOTOPE. Sometimes in, and sometimes out of balance.

ALPHA RAY. We burst, we fuse, we bump, we split,
Because we glow, the world is lit.

BETA RAY. What are the sounds that tinkle in your ears?
They are the music of the spheres!

CHORUS. The music of the spheres!

MOLECULE. Zigzags, circles, dashes, spots,
Holes and angles, hooks and dots,

> Crackles, thunders, motion, flight
> From zone to zone and light to light,
> Vast nothings between which we are
> Now the dust, and now a star,
> Oh, world of all that can forever be,
> We are the law, the number and the harmony.

CHORUS. Oh world of all that can forever be,
We are the law, the number and eternity.

(*The dance continues for awhile, and as it does, the Tots detach themselves one by one, introduce themselves, and then rejoin the dance*)

MOLECULE. I'm Mistress Molecule, I'm big and basic, and I'm boss around here.
ATOM. I'm Master Atom, and confidentially, I'm even basicker than she, but of course I'm smaller as you can tell, and so I cooperate.
PROTON. And I'm Proton. Wherever Brother Atom goes, me too. Positively.
ELECTRON. As for me, I'm Miss Electron. I'm fast and charged and I can run circles around anybody. Take care!
ALPHA RAY. My name is Master Alpha Ray. I'm a big shot and I'm tough. I run out of breath easy but I do a lot of knocking down on the way.
BETA RAY. And I'm Beta Ray. I'm tiny, swift, and penetrating, and I'm unattached.
ISOTOPE. And I's little Isotope. I's unstable, you know, but it's a nice dopey life and I gets a lot of attention.
MOLECULE. Come back here, you!
ATOM. Dance!
CHORUS. Dance!
ALPHA RAY. Forward and forward!
ELECTRON. Round and round!
ISOTOPE. Stumble crumble!
MOLECULE. Organized, particles, always organized!
PROTON. Sanity and courtesy!
BETA RAY. Tra la la la tra la la!
ATOM. Always cool.
BETA RAY. Even when we sizzle!
MOLECULE. We are the law,
ALPHA RAY. The number,
ISOTOPE (*quavering*). And eternity!

(*The Polypon now closes, the order of the universe vanishes out of sight, and the music is gone. Enter Professor Snaffle and Mr. Loop, engrossed in shop-talk which the profane are compelled to admire without understanding*)

SNAFFLE. We bring about, in due course, a hyperactive fusion of heavy hydrogen and liquid plutonium—

LOOP. Converting it to thorium 227.

SNAFFLE. We raise the temperature in obverse disrelation to the motion of rp over t, observing, of course, the rising deceleration and increasingly diminished reaction in the reinforced tank.

LOOP. At 50,000 atmospheres, Professor Snaffle?

SNAFFLE. At 50,000 atmospheres, Mr. Loop. The heated mixture concentrates, advances toward the critical point, velocity multiplies as frequency jumps, the radon particles are absorbed in the beryllium rods, quanta of energy enrage the nuclei, the critical point is reached, and—

LOOP (*modestly*). Pop!

SNAFFLE. Precisely.

LOOP. The earth splits—

SNAFFLE. Mountains disintegrate—

LOOP. Rivers boil—

SNAFFLE. The animal world diffuses into space—

LOOP. Mankind dissolves—

SNAFFLE. And I prove, beyond the vestige of a doubt, that the center of the earth is a drum of compressed cooking gas extremely useful to the average American household.

LOOP. The only possible objection—

SNAFFLE (*dangerous*). An objection, Mr. Loop, before you have completed your thesis for me?

LOOP. No, nothing—only a thought—nothing at all.

SNAFFLE (*still more dangerous*). Speak up, Loop, my good man. We scientists thrive on free discussion.

LOOP. Well—I was only going to ask—a detail—namely, who will use the cooking gas?

SNAFFLE. Who will use the cooking gas? What kind of eccentric question is that?

LOOP. Well, sir, what with the annihilation of cooks—

SNAFFLE. I'm amazed to find you dabbling in sociology, Mr. Loop.

LOOP. Goodness! Is that what I—

SNAFFLE. Furthermore, the scientist solves one problem at a time, Mr. Loop.

LOOP. Of course, Professor Snaffle, and yet—

SNAFFLE. He isolates the irrelevant and the variable—

LOOP. Of course, Professor Snaffle, but—
SNAFFLE. But nothing. I state my hypothesis: cooking gas. And those who love me agree with me, Mr. Loop.
LOOP. I hope, sir, you have always found in me an ardent supporter of that hypothesis. Cooking gas—with, possibly, a few traces of iron.
SNAFFLE. Oh? Really? What makes you say iron?
LOOP. I was reading P. P. Folpap's analysis—
SNAFFLE (*terrible*). Percy Loop!
LOOP (*frightened*). Yes, Professor Snaffle?
SNAFFLE. Folpap is a clyster.
LOOP. Sir—I didn't know—I—
SNAFFLE. I do not require his analyses!
LOOP. Indeed not, Professor Snaffle, indeed not. I—may I say, sir, that I, for one, in the thesis I will be presenting for your approval—in due time—I will attempt—
SNAFFLE. Oh?
LOOP. In a modest way —
SNAFFLE. Very good.
LOOP. To show that the presence of iron posited by—hm—posited elsewhere is not capable of experimental verification through any known method of—of—verification.
SNAFFLE. Which Folpap tried to deny.
LOOP. Overlooking the fact, I remember now, that the thiocyamate test yielded not a speck of iron.
SNAFFLE. And what about his amateurish attempt to precipitate it by using ammonium chloride?
LOOP. When did he do *that?*
SNAFFLE. The time he brought up his so-called sample.
LOOP. And he used ammonium chloride? Oh no! (*He laughs*)
SNAFFLE. Before even getting his filtrate! (*He laughs louder*)
LOOP. Before getting his filtrate? Oh no no no!
(*Here Loop laughs so hard that he loses his equilibrium, collides with the Polypon and thereby discovers it, although this fact will not be known to posterity*)
LOOP. Ouch!
SNAFFLE. What's that?
LOOP. An object in experience. It struck my nose.
SNAFFLE. Measure it! Calibrate it! Tabulate it!
LOOP. Calm yourself, sir.
SNAFFLE. Here's something I may have been looking for all my life without knowing it. And now I've found it. It's all mine, mine, mine! Pappendeck,

my equipment!

(*Enter young Pappendeck, carrying a couple of long poles, a hammer and a computer which he sets up and which Snaffle plugs into the Polypon*)

SNAFFLE. Come, gentlemen, let us address ourselves single mindedly to our problem. Hand me a research tool.

LOOP. I suggest this kinetic thrust agent. (*He offers the hammer*)

(*The Polypon's door opens. The tots, unseen by the men of science, are squatting on the floor looking uneasy. While they speak, Snaffle cautiously examines the Polypon, tapping with the hammer and poking with the pole*)

BETA RAY. I still say something's wrong. There was a collision.

PROTON. The cosmos is full of collisions, Beta Ray.

ATOM. But the music stopped for this one.

ELECTRON. I think we made a mistake when we left Interstellar D Major to come here.

ALPHA RAY. We came by accident, remember? Laws of probability and all that.

ATOM. I smell amino acids.

ISOTOPE (*timidly*). Why don't we try dancing again?

ATOM. I don't know....

SNAFFLE. Let's take a sample.

(*He gives the Polypon a great blow and a piece falls off. The tots cry out and scurry. Snaffle, Loop and Pappendeck surround the chunk at a respectful distance*)

MOLECULE. Stop, stop! It's only a jostle!

ELECTRON. No, it's something more. I feel it, I know it!

ATOM. Maybe it's anti-matter. Puff, we're gone.

MOLECULE. Silence. Let's wait and listen.

BETA RAY. If it's an enemy, I'll flash.

ISOTOPE. What's a enemy? I's scared.

(The door of the Polypon closes. Snaffle, after trying in vain to get Loop or Pappendeck to pick up the chunk of matter, picks it up himself)

SNAFFLE (*tossing the chunk from one hand to another*). It sizzles! Ergs and joules! What's going on? It's burning a hole through my hand. Catch it!

(*He tosses it to Loop*)

LOOP. Fascinating, sir. (*Hastily tosses it to Pappendeck*)

PAPPENDECK. Sensational. (*Tosses it back to Snaffle, who has put on a pair of gloves*)

SNAFFLE. It sizzles, and yet it was cold! (*Sniffs it*) There are things imbedded here—some devil of a new element. I can smell the pi-mesons frying in it. Loop, man the computer. Pappendeck, to work! (*The two, seizing the poles, manage to poke into the Polypon in various places*) Is the data coming in, Loop?

LOOP. A torrent of data, sir!
PAPPENDECK. From my side too?
LOOP. A flood of data, my boy!
SNAFFLE. And now?
LOOP. More data!
PAPPENDECK. And now?
LOOP. More data! I've just done a myriad calculations in half a nano-second!
SNAFFLE. That will do, Pappendeck. Let me look at the computer results. (*He takes Loop's place at the computer and taps it about. Exclamation. He rises*)
LOOP. You look pale, sir. What have you found? Tell us for God's sake!
SNAFFLE (*awed*) Holy Galileo. Holy Newton. Holy Einstein. A revolutionary contradiction to received notions of radiation. In short: spontaneous frigoradiant emissions!
LOOP and PAPPENDECK. Spontaneous frigoradiant emissions!
SNAFFLE. One millimicrosecond ago, gentlemen, we lived in the simple, cozy world of string theory, and the next: frigoradiant emissions.
LOOP (*confidentially*). Sir, may I—a word on the side?
SNAFFLE. What is it?
LOOP. Only a thought sir. Hm. The unusual nature of the—hm.
SNAFFLE. Yes; go on, Loop.
LOOP. Perhaps a word to the press—a newsleak so to speak.
SNAFFLE (*whisper*). Good idea. (*Loud*) No, my loyal colleague, science works without publicity. Above all no fanfares! (*To Pappendeck*) You, my boy, don't snoop, or I'll ionize and discharge you.
PAPPENDECK. Yes, sir. No, sir. (*Leaves*)
SNAFFLE. And you, attend to what you know. I'll mention you.
LOOP. Thank you, sir. I leave on the wings of duty. (*Exit*)
SNAFFLE. All mine! All mine! Folpap will burst. I shall control this object. It will yield. For me, a fallout of riches and renown. Ah, the future comes to me in a vision! I accept decorations, honors and contracts. I take the Dynamite Peace Prize. No! I turn it down. Better yet! I accept it so I can publicly bestow the money on the Interracial Institute for Unwed Orphans. And when I am dead—if I can die—a building at the California Institute of Technology is named after me. If necessary I pay for it myself. Students in days to come will report for lectures not to Physics 207, but to 207 Snaffle Hall.
(*Enter Loop with Mr. Nose, the journalist*)
LOOP. Professor Snaffle, I happened to run into Mr. Nose, a star reporter for the *Washington Post*. I couldn't forbear—
NOSE. Professor Snaffle, let me shake your hand. My nose for news and my

hunger for scoops has led me straight to you; and sure enough Mr. Loop tells me you've dug something up that's going to remake the future before it's even happened. Will you tell the world what it is?

SNAFFLE. Only if silence becomes impossible. It's a new structure in space and time, to mention only these.

NOSE. A structure?

SNAFFLE. Yes. We predicted its appearance, and it appeared according to our calculations. It is too early to announce practical bearings, and please, Mr. Nose, let your publication be cautious with its claims. However, I am free to report that my laboratory, directed by myself (with a few assistants), is conducting a series of experiments—under my direction—which may revolutionize our concepts of the universe, explain the beginning and the end, and leave the Chinese and the Russians far behind. My purpose is to open new vistas to mankind, and to share the fruits of our research with one and all, the enemy always excepted.

NOSE (*who has been taking furious notes*). Have you given your discovery a name, Professor Snaffle?

SNAFFLE. I have. It is provisionally called the Snaffle Polypon, one l.

NOSE. "The Snaffle Polypon." And now, if I may ask—

SNAFFLE. Of course, of course! I am a happily married ex-bachelor, the father of two children, a boy of 14 and a girl of, needless to say, 9. We live in a pleasant and unostentatious house on El Molino Avenue, near the Institute, and my greatest pleasure is to help my children with their homework in mathematics. Our little joke is to call it "math." In spite of my international reputation, I am shy. My attractive wife is devoted to gardening and grows the best begonias in the neighborhood. She is also an active non-sectarian church member who bakes chocolate cakes for the indigent. I am myself a familiar figure on the tennis courts. Popular with my students, who call me Old Snaffle-bags—unbeknownst to me—I take a personal interest in their intellectual development. My only ambition is to continue, as long as health permits, in my unswerving and selfless devotion to the Spirit of Science.

NOSE. "Spirit of Science." I'll capitalize these, of course. Thank you, Professor Snaffle, for taking this forthright stand. Sir! (*He shakes Snaffle's hand*) I'm on my way. My deadline is at hand.

(*Exit*)

LOOP. Thank you for including me, Professor Snaffle. But it's awfully late, sir. Shall I bring you a sandwich before I go, Professor Snaffle?

SNAFFLE. No, my boy, I need a clear stomach tonight.

LOOP. Then I'll be going home to mother.

SNAFFLE. Regards to her, my lad.
LOOP. Thank you, sir.
(*Exit. Snaffle is alone*)
SNAFFLE. Folpap will burst. This is my king of days; let every alley-cat dine on broiled fish tonight. After the mule came steam, after steam, petroleum, after petroleum, electricity, after electricity, atomic energy, after atomic energy, my polyponal impulses. Benefits to mankind. Benefits to Snaffle. But of course Another series of experiments is called for. Grants from the government. A vacation in Thailand what with the grants. Naked girls. Here comes my wife.
(*Enter Mrs. Snaffle*)
MRS. SNAFFLE. Lancelot, dear. it's way past dinner time! The lamb chops are waiting. The children already ate theirs.
SNAFFLE. In an hour, Duckypuddle, in an hour.
MRS. SNAFFLE. All right, but our Timmy—that's our son, Goosypie—our Timmy has been fretting about his math assignment, and he's going to the movies with friends, and he'd like you to help him.
SNAFFLE. Let's hear the problem.
MRS. SNAFFLE (*taking out a piece of paper*). 3 men are digging a hole in a garden, while 12 faucets are filling $8¼$ bathtubs at the rate of 15 gallons of water every 60 seconds. The faucets are set at 2.6 mile intervals from New York City and the hole is speeding at 54 miles per hour toward the oncoming bus. How fast was the bus going?
SNAFFLE. 42.6 miles per hour.
MRS. SNAFFLE. 42.6?
SNAFFLE. Obviously.
MRS. SNAFFLE. I'll tell Timmy right away. I'll send him an e-mail so he can have it before the movies. (*She sits down at the computer and taps it open*) I don't believe it!
SNAFFLE. What is it?
MRS. SNAFFLE. "ELIMINATE INTERFERENCE". All caps, 24 point Times Roman font!
SNAFFLE. "Eliminate Interference" is technical talk, Duckypuddle.
MRS. SNAFFLE. I don't believe it. It's a message. So that's what I've earned scrubbing dishes and underwear and forks and children and then having to pretend I'm some beautiful ravishing mistress on top of the laundry basket?
SNAFFLE. Pretend? What pretend? Admired by every man!
MRS. SNAFFLE (*comes out under the sobs*). What do you mean by that?
SNAFFLE. Why, wasn't it last week you picked me up at the Institute?

MRS. SNAFFLE. Yes.

SNAFFLE. That was when Loop looked out of the window and called everybody from the electroscope when he saw you. "Look at that virginal beauty!" he cried out, and the rest were open-mouthed! And then Wimbelheim, the vacuum-tube washer, turned around and said, "That's not a virginal beauty! You're myopic. That's Mrs. Snaffle!" And so it was.

MRS. SNAFFLE. You didn't tell me.

SNAFFLE. I forgot. Come here. (*He kisses her*)

MRS. SNAFFLE. Oh Lancelot, I shouldn't forgive you. But will you take me to Tahiti this winter?

SNAFFLE. I will, I promise. Or to Thailand.

MRS. SNAFFLE. All right then. Here's a peck for you. I have to run now. Don't be too late, do you hear?

SNAFFLE. I won't, my love.

(*Exit Mrs. Snaffle*)

SNAFFLE (*calling after her*). Don't over-broil the lamb-chops! (*Alone*) Impeccable woman. Back to work. (*He sits down at the computer and goes to work on it*) Very interesting. The Polypon is no slouch. Dispersing energy 1.85 Mev.... Graph at 150 centimeters.... Infra-green waves at 0.594 times 10^{-9} seconds.... Steady stream of photons.... Naked girls.... Detector bias 800 kev, 10,000,000,000 negative pions per millisteradian in the forward direction for a 6% momentum interval at 2.80% Bev per c.... Apply Thompson's formula to the equations....

(*The Polypon opens again. The tots are dancing to the tinkling music*)

CHORUS.   Zigzags, circles, dashes, spots,
           Holes and angles, hooks and dots,
           Crackles, thunders, motion, flight
           From zone to zone and light to light,
           Vast nothings between which we are
           Now the dust, and now a star,
           Oh, world of all that can forever be,
           We are the law, the number and eternity.

SCENE TWO

(The Polypon has now been moved to the far side of the stage, so that only a fragment of it can be seen, thus making room for a social space, furnished with chairs, in which appear Mr. Nose, the much decorated General and Mrs. Culpepper, Mrs. Snaffle, and Secretary McBoodle, chatting. Enter Loop)

LOOP. It's four o'clock, ladies and gentlemen. Professor Snaffle will be joining us very soon.
NOSE. A truly historic occasion.
CULPEPPER. All of us in the military entertain the highest hopes for Professor Snaffle's Polypon. As a military man I speak bluntly.
MCBOODLE. A mysterious frigonuclear reaction! Another breakthrough for America. And once more we are on the right side of the gap, so to speak. Let the enemy take note. I won't name him or them because I'm here in my official capacity as Secretary of Defensive Expansion. Let the informed read between my lines.
NOSE. May I quote you, Secretary McBoodle?
MCBOODLE. Go right ahead, Mr. Nose. I feel that Professor Snaffle's investigations will stiffen our defensive posture. Another defensive punch, in short. Perhaps the Polypon will encourage other nations to eliminate their costly military burdens and to entrust these burdens exclusively to us.
NOSE. What are *your* feelings, General Culpepper?
CULPEPPER. To speak bluntly, I agree.
LOOP. Professor Snaffle!
(Snaffle briskly steps forward, followed by Pappendeck carrying the computer. General greetings)
SNAFFLE. Excuse me for being late, ladies and gentlemen. Last-minute calculations. Pappendeck, plug her in.
(Pappendeck plugs the computer into the Polypon and, as they say, boots it up. He and Loop both work at it, one sitting, the other standing)
SNAFFLE. For your information, ladies and gentlemen, I have verified the amazing new potentialities of the Polypon through an elaborate series of experiments, and relying of course on my infinite-capacity computer to work out the optimum military applications for the Frigoradiant Polyponal Impulses I have captured from it. My esteemed colleague, Dr. P. P. Folpap, has speculated that the Polyponal Impulses cannot be adapted to warfare. His opinion must be weighed with the greatest respect, and for myself, I refuse to regard Dr. Folpap's successive failures with the directional system

of our Goliath missile as casting any doubt on his judgment. Fortunately, scientific hypotheses are capable of verification, and I am at this moment in a position to perform before you an experiment, the results of which are likely to revolutionize our concepts of warfare. What I am contributing, ladies and gentlemen, is a foolproof means of neutralizing any hostile attempts to infiltrate our country with agents, spies, or saboteurs, plus a means of paralyzing their combat troops in the heat of action.

(*Applause and exclamations*)

CULPEPPER. Bravo, Snaffle. I speak bluntly, but I say: Bravo!

MCBOODLE. We're ready, Professor Snaffle. Show us your miracle of science.

PAPPENDECK (*at the computer*). Not quite ready, sir.

LOOP. A few more minutes, sir.

SNAFFLE. The instructions are complicated, ladies and gentlemen. While my brilliant associates are sending the correct signals to my demonstrator of the Frigoradiant Polyponal Impulses waiting in the hallway, allow me to elaborate briefly on my friend's affecting remark concerning "miracles of science"—if Mr. McBoodle will allow me to repeat his elegant phrase. Miracles of science! Let us look about us, my friends, and what do we see? Our mighty factories adorning our countrysides, our power lines arching their graceful nets over our metropolitan streets, the melodious roar of jets in the skies and of trucks and automobiles in our neighborhoods, our infinite means of instantly communicating our noblest thoughts and images, from "I am busy scrambling eggs" to "I think therefore I think I am," how can I speak without choking when I allow my fancy to range from the lowliest electric can-opener to our explorations of the delightful beauties of the moon! But let me return to the subject of military applications. Let me point with ill-concealed emotion to our magnificent arsenal of supersonic fighters, our flame-throwers, machine guns, cannons, aircraft carriers, submarines, hydrogen bombs, poison gases, mortars, radar equipment, missiles and anti-missiles, and even—you will smile—the homely rifle with its everyday bullet—these too are making their patriotic contributions! What, you will ask, these dangerous weapons? Is it possible, dear Professor Snaffle? Yes, my friends. These weapons, which on first appearance seem almost unfriendly, keep the enemy's teeth out of our sirloin steaks; these weapons mean butter on the bread of our working men, civic duties for our public servants, maneuvers for our generals, golf courses for our industrialists, grants, Secretary McBoodle, for our men of science, excitement for our radicals, publications for our intellectuals, sermons for our clergymen, and hope for our undertakers. To these weapons, ladies and gentlemen, my Frigoradiant will make a significant and even indispensable addition. Oh my contemporaries, compare yourselves with your wretched ancestors, compare your smiles, your good health, your high spirits with their gruesome medieval dejections and their dark age bank accounts, and you will join me, I know, in praising and repeating the story of Human Progress, the story of a spreading springtime of blossoms over the created land, to which, if I may conclude on a personal note, I hope I will have contributed a daisy of my own.

(*A ghastly electronic music begins, and everybody except Loop and Pappendeck, who are busy with the computer, dance to it in a ring. Each one steps out of the ring to speak his/her stanza, then rejoins the dance*)

>Stone Age life, in one blunt word, was crude,
>The men were mostly in a filthy mood.
>They glared and growled and took great whacks
>With club and hatchet, spear and axe.
>
>In ancient Egypt who could life endure?
>For some were rich, but most were poor.
>The poor ate grass, the rich sipped honey,
>And holidays abroad cost money.
>
>And who can talk of Periclean Greece
>Without a shudder in her knees?
>Girl liked boy, but boy liked boy,
>Even when a girl was far from coy.
>
>The Roman Age was never long at peace.
>Nations, in those days, had enemies.
>Between diplomacy and slaughter
>They impolitely robbed each other.
>
>In Chaucer's England, horrible to tell,
>Marriage was, from time to time, sheer hell.
>A drunken husband and a nagging wife
>Were not uncommon in pre-modern life.
>
>Rule who ruled, Cromwell or Pope Gregory,
>Ivan, Plantagenet, or Medici,
>Existence was no ring of posies

But a sack of hardships and neuroses.
People coughed, and cursed, and cried,
And somehow everybody died.

ALL
The past is dead, our tale ends cheerfully
With science, progress, and democracy.

LOOP and PAPPENDECK. The system is go!
NOSE. "A subdued excitement could be plainly felt."
SNAFFLE. Thank you, lads. Now: let me explain the operation of the Frigoradiant Polyponal Impulses. Briefly: when the FPI, loaded in capsules, are trained by certain taps on the coeliac ganglion of the adult enemy male or female, they trigger the sympathetic trunk nerve, the superior laryngeal nerve, and the entire glossopharyngeal system. This in turn sets up vibrations in the *plica vocalis*, known to the vulgar as the vocal cord, and these vibrations emerge as involuntary sound, to wit, the strains of *God Bless America*, in high-fidelity at less than ¼% harmonic distortion. For the moment, I admit, we are able to direct these emissions only at individual subjects; but I want to paint for you a picture of what will be possible when full use is made of the Polyponal Impulses, and a whole division of the enemy is stopped in its tracks, singing *God Bless America*, while we mow them down. But these are future benefits. Let us return to the present, and begin our experiment. This is where we are obligated once more to our Secretary of Defensive Expansion, who—but will you take it from here, Secretary McBoodle?
MCBOODLE. Well, all we've done is to contribute a live Russian spy we happened to catch the other day. Come on, let's bring him in.
(McBoodle claps his hands, and the Interpreter brings in the Spy by a rope affixed to a thick collar. The Spy is extremely bearded, and his hands are tied)
MRS. SNAFFLE. I just *adore* dangerous spies.
MRS. CULPEPPER. And I am attracted to beards. Yes, even enemy beards.
MCBOODLE. The man's name is Tipoff. Step forward, Tipoff, and stop muttering. Mr. Interpreter, untie the fellow. Curious case. He was betrayed to the Secret Service by his own gang, who felt he'd become a liability to them. Double-crossed by his own comrades, in short.
NOSE. Why didn't they want him anymore, Secretary McBoodle?
MCBOODLE. The poor chump made the kind of blunder the Russians don't forgive. Stole one of our top-secret designs for a retrojet unit. Passed it on to his contact. Contact passed it on to his. Bang! The design was a Russian

design to begin with! *We'd* stolen it from *them*, and now Tipoff had stolen it back from us! (*General guffawing*) Come on, Tipoff, is that the truth or isn't it? He's blushing into his beard. What's the good of being faithful to your bosses now?

SPY. Vernosts kak syr; chem starshe, tsem silneye!

MRS. CULPEPPER. Good heavens, what was that? It sounded so foreign.

INTERPRETER. He says in the dialect of the Malozemelskaya Tundra: "Loyalty is like cheese. The older, the stronger."

CULPEPPER. He must be a military man. On with the experiment, Professor Snaffle. We're all anxious to see this.

SNAFFLE. Roger, general, roger. Mr. Loop, enter the code, if you please. Tipoff, press the switch on your wrist.

SPY (*With a thick Russian accent*). Stop the experiment or I swear you'll be sorry!

CULPEPPER. Silence, dog! Or ten extra years behind bars.

SPY. You'll be sorry!

CULPEPPER. Shut your snout! (*To the ladies*) I apologize, dear ladies, but sometimes a soldier must talk rough. On with the experiment, Snaffle. (*The spy tries to speak again*) Boo!

NOSE. "An air of expectancy hung in the air."

SNAFFLE. Press the switch, Tipoff!

(*The Polypon crackles and glows*)

MRS. CULPEPPER. Oh, I think I'm going to faint.

(*Sounds begin to come out of the spy*)

MCBOODLE. Listen! He's beginning to sing. And look, he's as rigid as a flagpole!

CULPEPPER. Good work, Snaffle!

SPY (*suddenly bawls out*).

> Russia—our sacred state,
> Russia—our beloved nation.
> A mighty will, a great glory
> Are your patrimony for all time!

SEVERAL (*at the same time*). What's he singing, Professor Snaffle?—What has Russia got to do with *God Bless America!*—We should call the police!—Devil's work!

SNAFFLE. Mr. Loop!

LOOP. Yes, sir?

SNAFFLE. What was the man singing? I am holding you personally responsible.

LOOP. I don't know what he was singing, sir.

INTERPRETER (*gloomily*). He was singing the Russian national anthem, in translation.

(*Sensation*)

CULPEPPER. An insult to my uniform!

MCBOODLE. Snaffle! We've poured twelve million into this! You've got a winter home in Florida and an expense account!

SPY. I told you you'd be sorry. Better send me back to jail.

SNAFFLE (*flings himself at the Spy with a cry of rage*). You're a fraud! (*He tears at the spy's beard, not without meeting with strong protest. The beard comes off, revealing a nice Midwestern face. Another sensation. The ladies scream. Snaffle is as surprised as the others*) Ergs and joules!

CULPEPPER (*thunderously*). Agent PX-91767!

SPY. Reporting, sir.

CULPEPPER. What are you doing here?

INTERPRETER. Shall I untie him, sir?

SNAFFLE. Do so! I knew it! I knew it! The Frigoradiant Polyponal Impulses do not lie. The man was forced to sing. Let me shake your hand, sir. You are a fine American. The experiment has been a complete success.

MRS. SNAFFLE. My husband is a genius.

MCBOODLE. You mean he's one of *your* boys, Culpepper?

CULPEPPER. Well—to speak bluntly—I—

SPY. The pipe is leaking, General. Drip drip.

CULPEPPER. Isn't he one of yours, too, McBoodle?

MCBOODLE (*indignant*). Certainly not! The PX spy series is yours, General. I wash my hands.

NOSE (*who has been busy taking notes*). "Thunderclap Breaks Up Experiment." What's the story, General Culpepper? Where's the slip-up?

CULPEPPER. Well—I'd have to refer to my files—I can't be expected—but the gist of it is that PX 97616 here—

SPY. 97617, General. I don't like my name mispronounced.

CULPEPPER. Agent PX 97617, as I was saying, was assigned to investigate— eh—to obtain—in short, he was on a secret mission. Right, Chuck?

SPY. How about a cigarette?

CULPEPPER. Oh, of course.

(*Culpepper complies, gives him a light. The Spy bows to the group and makes himself comfortable on a chair*)

MRS. CULPEPPER. He seems like a gentleman.

SNAFFLE. The main point is that the Polypon doesn't lie.

MCBOODLE. Let me take over. Stand aside, Culpepper. All right, PX 9 whatever, out with it. How did you land into this mess, and how the hell did you manage to drop into our own jails disguised as a Russian?

SPY. I don't think you want to know, man.

MCBOODLE (*exploding*). You're not asked to think! You're in government service! Just talk, and talk good if you don't want to live on dry bread for the next twenty years.

SPY. Ok. You asked for it. I was a double agent.

SNAFFLE. The Polypon sensed it. (*To Loop and Pappendeck*) Didn't it?

BOTH. It did, sir.

MCBOODLE. The details.

SPY. Don't rush me, Mac. Ok. I'm one of your boys. That's the basic fact. Ok. The Russians think I'm one of theirs, name of Tipoff. They arrange to turn me over to you. A fake double-cross. Plan is for me to give out to you like I'm sick of the Russians and I'll spy on them for you. Ok. You fall for this gag, they think, and you let me make a break out of the clink so I can slip back into Russia. Ok. I'm in Russia. I send you phony information to gum up the military peace effort in the U.S. Mission for the Russians accomplished. Ok. But all the time I'm not really Tipoff, I'm Agent PX 97617. You people know the whole set-up—

CULPEPPER. Now I remember! I can see the file in question where you sit.

SPY. OK. You play along. You give me the trick trial and you let me off because of the phony deal to spy for you, when I'm *really* gonna spy for you! and then you sneak me off to Russia, but let on you feel sick and crappy about it. And sure enough I send you a lot of fake secrets to please the Russians, but I mark it fake with a secret signal and send you the 24-carat stuff on the side. And that's the ticket. Pretty neat, too. But now you let that silly-ass professor experiment on me, Culpepper, the champagne is down the drain and bubbles to you.

SNAFFLE. He called me a nasty name.

MRS. SNAFFLE. Poke him, dear.

MRS. CULPEPPER. I didn't understand a word of his story, not a word, and he looked so nice in his beard.

NOSE. I wish he could repeat it. I got lost.

MCBOODLE. It was clear as crystal to *me*. Well, General, what have you got to say for yourself?

CULPEPPER. Well now, I just didn't—I couldn't—God frizzle it, McBoodle, am I supposed to carry my gigabytes of data all in my head, and with the budgetary squeeze we're in—only 46 bleeding percent of the national revenue? The hell with it! Question the colonels. Besides, I'm a paratrooper, not a bureaucrat.

MCBOODLE (*voice of thunder*). General Culpepper!
CULPEPPER. Yes, sir.
MCBOODLE. Come here.
CULPEPPER. Yes, sir.
(*McBoodle tears off the General's stars and decorations*)
MCBOODLE. There. There. There. I demote you to the rank of corporal and assign you to kitchen police in the Pentagon.
MRS. CULPEPPER. But that's unjust, Secretary McBoodle! Winston and I are invited to a garden party at the General Trollopes' next Sunday!
MCBOODLE. Your husband will serve drinks with a towel over his arm.
CULPEPPER. I'm bearing it like a soldier. I've broken the dishes and I've got to pay for the damage.
MCBOODLE. Fine. You're adapting to your new station in life, Corporal Culpepper. You are excused.
INTERPRETER. I could tell there was something wrong by the way he pronounced the s in "silneye".
MCBOODLE. You are excused too. (*The Interpreter leaves, dangling the rope and collar*)
MRS. SNAFFLE (*very kind*). I will let you do my sewing, dearie.
MRS. CULPEPPER (*grateful*). Thank you, Mrs. Snaffle, thank you in the name of our five or six little ones. Come, Winston, I will undoubtedly stand by you. Remember the Culpepper motto!
CULPEPPER. Yes, dear. "Our Wives Fight With Us Forever."
(*The Culpeppers leave*)
NOSE. A gripping scene. (*Aside to the Spy*) *The Morning Pest* will offer you 20,000 for exclusive confessions.
SPY. 50,000.
NOSE. Sorry.
MCBOODLE (*to the Spy*). As for you, my boy, none of this may be your fault, but your usefulness to the nation is at an end and we'll have to place you on half-pay with a good character.
SPY. Excuse me, sir. I am bound to be a nuisance to my country and a burden to the taxpayer. A secret agent, and especially a double one, knows his duty when his mission fails.
NOSE. What do you plan to do?
SPY. This.
(*He produces a pistol and shoots himself*)
MRS. SNAFFLE. How tragic, and yet how inspiring.
MCBOODLE. One of our most popular spies.
NOSE (*aside*). Oh remorses! I wouldn't give him the 50,000 and he blew his

brains out!

(*Leaves, clutching his brow*)

SNAFFLE. Nothing Slavic about the man. The Polyponal Impulses are infallible, and so am I. (*To Loop and Pappendeck, indicating the body*) Would you mind?

LOOP. Not at all.

PAPPENDECK. A pleasure, sir.

SNAFFLE. Besides, I want a few words in private with the Secretary.

(*Loop and Pappendeck carry out the Spy. As they do so, the Spy hoists a small American flag*)

MCBOODLE. A patriot even beyond the verge of life.

MRS. SNAFFLE. His mother will be so pleased.

SNAFFLE. Now then, McBoodle, I'm glad everything turned out so well. Nothing stands in the way of a contract. Six or seven million will do for the first fiscal year, plus the usual complement of assistants, equipment, office help, nightclubs, official automobiles, and a per diem for inci—

MCBOODLE (*voice of retribution*). Professor Snaffle!

SNAFFLE. Yes?

MCBOODLE. Your Polypon pooped.

MRS. SNAFFLE. Secretary!

MCBOODLE. Pooped I said, and pooped I mean. What, Professor Snaffle, do you propose we do with a secret weapon which causes our own mothers' boys to break out singing the Russian national anthem (in translation) at the moment of crisis? Your Polypon, sir, is not worth a rotten banana. Work on it, tinker as much as you like and come to us with results; but use your own funds! Your own funds, Snaffle!

(*He leaves*)

SNAFFLE (*destroyed*). My own funds!

MRS. SNAFFLE (*weeping*). What's to become of us?

SNAFFLE. Hepsa Snaffle! Run full-steam after McBoodle, throw yourself against his shins! Remind him of our affection for him with madness in your eyes and delirium in your voice! Run!

MRS. SNAFFLE. I'll try, dear.

(*She runs after the Secretary, her arm pathetically stretched out, and crying "McBoodle!"*)

SNAFFLE. What can have gone wrong? Where did I miscalculate? (*He seats himself at the computer*) And you, Apple, beloved computer, do you want to see Folpap grinning over my grave? (*He does some calculations, then rises*) Hail Computer, full of transistors; the Datum is with thee; blessed art thou among devices, and blessed are thy computations. Holy Computer, Mother of Data, work for us physicists, now and at the hour of our miscalculations. Amen.

(*Enter the Spy, hidden from Snaffle by a screen he is carrying*)

SPY. Now that I'm legally dead, I can continue to serve what has always been my true and only fatherland: Paraguay! Yes! I am a *triple* agent! (*As the curtain falls*) Viva Paraguay! Muerte a los extranjeros! Bonitas mujeres ! Visit Asunción! (*The lights are out, the Spy is gone, but he reappears*) It's a tough life, I tell you, but the work is steady.

SCENE THREE

(*Snaffle has fallen asleep over his computer and is snoring away. Now and then we hear from him "My own funds!" Enter Loop. He dusts off the Polypon, pulls his tongue at Snaffle, arranges the chairs, sneezes. Snaffle wakes up with a start*)

SNAFFLE. Oh, it's you, Loop.
LOOP. Yes, sir. I thought I'd better clean up a bit, after these fearful events.
SNAFFLE. I'd better set sail again too.
LOOP. I lament the disgrace that has fallen on you, Professor Snaffle.
SNAFFLE. Thank you, Loop.
LOOP. And I am very sorry that Mrs. Snaffle was not admitted to see Secretary McBoodle, and that his receptionist chased her down the stairs.
SNAFFLE. Very good of you, Loop.
LOOP. I deplore, too, that you will be cut off without a penny, sir. I feel it deeply.
SNAFFLE. I appreciate your sympathy, Loop.
LOOP. And I fervently hope that Dr. Folpap can be kept ignorant—
SNAFFLE. Blast your tongue, Loop, another kind word from you and I'll slap five more years on your thesis. Get out of here, I've got work to do.
LOOP. Yes, sir. (*He leaves*)
SNAFFLE. The impudence of these assistants. You use them day in and day out for sixteen years and they're not even grateful. Grateful! And who, I ask you, *is* grateful these years? The nation maybe? Ha! "Use your own funds!" Monday, as you are sharpening a pencil, an official stands before you. "Snaffle, teach us a trick to lay a dozen enemy cities flat." So we do. Tuesday, same official, "Snaffle, what's the best way to pull those cities up again? They've become our allies." We tell them the way, and never a grumble, mind you; selfless. Wednesday, another official; the last one's in jail for giving his wife a high-paying fake job in his office. "Look here,

Snaffle, can you make beer bottles grow on trees?" "Full or empty, sir?" "Don't waste our money with gags, Snaffle. The natives of Gumbaba want beer bottles on trees and if we don't do it for them the Chinese will. I scratch my head and say, "It's an unusual request; give me an hour or two for an experiment." "An hour or two? Take five years! But there's twenty like yourself in line for this juicy contract that aren't asking for an hour or two. Good-bye and use your own funds!" And that, in a word, is official gratitude. All right, gentlemen, have it your way. Secretary McBoodle, I propose to devote my efforts henceforth—or henceforward, sounds even nastier—exclusively to the non-military uses of my Polyponal Emissions. That'll show them. Peaceful applications. They'll crawl to me for a way to pulverize a population and I'll shout, "Nothing but peaceful applications, you imperialists!" I'll apply peaceful applications to their behinds and send them flying out of my office. But first—after that Russian anthem incident—I need to redo my calculations. Bless my equations, what is that? Ergs and joules, the Polypon is discharging!

(*And, in fact, Miss Isotope is squeezing herself out of the Polypon through the rooflight. She manages to climb down and to wobble about, looking hopefully for a moment of stability, or the equilibrium to which all matter aspires, including mankind. Snaffle is hiding and watching*)

ISOTOPE. I's scared of funny things going on in this planet and I's going to break down.

(*Snaffle makes a mighty pounce, catches Isotope, and waves her aloft, practically throttling her*)

SNAFFLE. Ha!

ISOTOPE. Eek!

SNAFFLE. I've got you, imp! The greatest discoveries are made by accident. Talk! Unzip the facts! Where do you come from? And don't deny it!

ISOTOPE (*choking*). Ggggg.

SNAFFLE (*relaxing his grip a little*). What's your name and what's your atomic weight? Out with it!

ISOTOPE. My name is Isotope.

SNAFFLE. U-238?

ISOTOPE. No, I's only seven and a half. I decay awful fast.

SNAFFLE. Listen to me, you particle. You're about to tell me precisely what's going on in the Polypon.

ISOTOPE. The whatsipon?

SNAFFLE. The Polypon—that's the scientific name of the place you've just come from, but then I don't suppose you particles know anything about science. You're going to tell me what it looks like and how it ticks.

ISOTOPE. What if I don't?

SNAFFLE. I'll convert your bloody mass into bloody energy until there isn't any you left.

ISOTOPE. Don't do that, lord and master. I gets dizzy when I's a burst of energy. That's why I slowed down enough to be me in the first place.

SNAFFLE. Well, since you're you, get on with it. What's it look like in there? What are the laws?

ISOTOPE. I got a few snapshots. Here they be.

SNAFFLE. I'll keep them.

ISOTOPE. Will you maybe put me down?

SNAFFLE. All right, but I'm holding on to your arm. What gives in the Polypon?

ISOTOPE. We dance. The bunch of us we dance all the time.

SNAFFLE. All right. Show me and don't try to escape.

(*He releases her. Isotope dances and sings the tinkling tune of the Polypon as best she can. Snaffle takes notes and makes diagrams, with an occasional "oho," "I thought so," and "the pieces fit." Suddenly Isotope stops*)

ISOTOPE. That's the music of the spheres sort of, but I don't carry a tune too good.

SNAFFLE. Keep vibrating and don't change the frequency.

(*Isotope resumes, but after awhile she stops again*)

ISOTOPE. It just ain't right, sir lord. I mean, without the trillions of us. You don't get the—what d'you calls it?

SNAFFLE. The configuration?

ISOTOPE. Thass right.

SNAFFLE. I'll tell you what. You volunteer to show me the way inside the Polypon so I can take in the scenery myself. That's an order.

ISOTOPE. Zu befehl (we speak everything). Back to the Polypon.

(*She clambers up the Polypon, with Snaffle puffing after her*)

SNAFFLE. Give me a hand. I'm slipping.

(*They get to the top*)

ISOTOPE. I's got to slip through here again but it's too tight for you.

SNAFFLE. I'll look through the hole.

ISOTOPE. You won't see much from that there angle, lord and master, but here's a place with a cork.

SNAFFLE. Sure enough. Eureka. Fancy my not noticing before. The ingenuity of Nature! (*He pulls the enormous cork and peers inside*) There they are! Kind of battered, sure enough. All right you. In you go.

ISOTOPE. Down I goes. (*She vanishes*)

SNAFFLE. I can see them all together. (*We hear faintly the music of the spheres*)

The little bastards are dancing! So ... Hmm ... So that's it.
(He vanishes into the Polypon, which is seen to glow. Loop appears on stage carrying a large clock-dial, on which he turns the hands to indicate time going by. He leaves, and soon after Snaffle emerges from the Polypon in a sweat, and rushes to the computer, which is still plugged into the Polypon. He works furiously at the computer)
SNAFFLE. Tremendous! There it is, the waves don't lie! And now I enter: "Open the Polypon!" Tremendous!
(Indeed, the Polypon now opens, and we see the Tots standing at attention, facing outward)
SNAFFLE. I am Professor Lancelot Snaffle, I am Man and master of Nature. Without me your existence has no purpose. Submit to me at once
(Mistress Molecule waves a white flag)
TOTS. Enter, lord and master and take possession!
(Snaffle enters, trumpets sound)
SNAFFLE *(royally)*. How beautiful! My children! My children! I am here for peaceful applications only. Folpap will burst.
(But the Spy has tiptoed in and filmed the scene)
SPY. No he won't. If he agrees to work for Paraguay, the information is his.
(Diabolical chuckle)

SCENE FOUR

(A sumptuous room or hall. Chandeliers, plush chairs, ample buffet. A placard descends from the flies. It bears the words "This is Sweden," and vanishes. Standing about and chatting vivaciously amidst a crowd of guests: Mr. Nose, Mr. McBoodle, Mrs. Snaffle, Mr. Loop, the young Pappendeck, Mrs. Molassis—formerly Mrs. Culpepper—and the former General Culpepper, now a waiter with a moustache and a French accent who is handing cocktails and digestible dainties all around)

MRS. MOLASSIS *(to Mrs. Snaffle)*. Ten minutes after I met my dear Molassis on his yacht, he declared he simply could not exist without me. I am told he dropped three mistresses on the spot. This made quite a noise, of course. One of them was a world-famous soprano. Nothing could quench his desire for me. It was caviar and pheasant all the way. But I told him, "Reveling in Chateau Lafite is very well for your sopranos and your Spanish duchesses, but I am a simple American girl and with me you'll have to come by our raptures legally."

MRS. SNAFFLE. Bravo! And what did he say to that?

MRS. MOLASSIS. He was ever so understanding. And I could see that I had won his respect. What a high C could not accomplish, a moral Yankee stand did.

MRS. SNAFFLE. But what happened next, dear Mrs. Molassis?

MRS. MOLASSIS. I divorced Culpepper on grounds of extreme cruelty, namely his reduced income, and I married dear, dear Triandaphilos—that's his little name—on board his yacht between one Cyclad and another. It was marvelously thrilling. The Princess of Monaco was with us, of course. She plays such a divine roulette!

MRS. SNAFFLE. I'm so sorry dear Mr. Molassis couldn't be among us this afternoon, when my husband is being honored.

MRS. MOLASSIS. He simply can't stir from our yacht, my dear. He becomes landsick.

CULPEPPER (*with a tray*). Un verre de vin, mesdame?

MRS. MOLASSIS. Mercee. French waiters have such—such Savor Fair! Ah, there's our dear McBoodle!

MCBOODLE (*kissing hands*). Delighted, delighted.

MRS. MOLASSIS. Naughty! He only kisses a lady's hand when he is abroad. Are you in Sweden just for the ceremony, Mr. McBoodle?

MCBOODLE. That and the usual small-talk about rocket bases, Mrs. Molassis. But where is dear Mr. Molassis? Whipping the galley-slaves, eh?

MRS. MOLASSIS. Oh—such an idea, Mr. McBoodle! These are wicked, wicked rumors. Molassis is ever so democratic. He calls the crew "his boys" and he dunks his bread in the gravy. Oh, Dr. Loop, delighted!

LOOP. Alas, still old Mr. Loop, dear Mrs. Molassis, but at your service as always.

MRS. MOLASSIS. Dear me, what Europe does to people! (*She takes Loop by the arm*) I am simply fascinated by thermodynamics, and you and I are going to gossip about retarded potentials. (*They walk away*)

MCBOODLE. My dear Mrs. Snaffle, this must be the greatest moment of your life. And such an honor to our country! Ever since Dr. Folpap settled in Paraguay, we have been afraid of losing our keenest brains.

MRS. SNAFFLE. Dr. Folpap is not a keen brain, Mr. McBoodle. And my husband is far too attached to our month in Palm Beach every winter to think of settling anywhere else.

MCBOODLE. A great man, Mrs. Snaffle. When I see a person of his calibre getting the Dynamite Peace Prize, the most coveted award in Christendom, I realize there is Justice in the world, an Eye that watches us all.

MRS. SNAFFLE. The dear works hard enough, I'll say that for him.

MCBOODLE. His Polyponal Pedilift has brought relief and comfort to untold millions. At last a substitute for walking!
NOSE (*joining in*). "Untold millions" is newspaper talk, Secretary McBoodle, and I take this pretext by the horns to butt in.
MRS. SNAFFLE. Do, dear Mr. Nose.
NOSE. My ravishing lady, I covered your husband for my paper from the moment he laid hands on the Polypon. But how I wish that I could cover *you!*
MRS. SNAFFLE. What *does* Europe do to people?!
NOSE. Waiter!
CULPEPPER. Monsieur? Rouge ou blanc?
NOSE. Mix the two, will you?
CULPEPPER. Certainement.
(*Mrs. Molassis, Loop and Pappendeck are now in the foreground*)
LOOP. You have met my young assistant, Joshua Pappendeck.
MRS. MOLASSIS. Yes. And here you are, the two of you who have labored at the side of the great Lancelot Snaffle, the disciples who followed with him the shining star of knowledge. It's simply thrilling.
PAPPENDECK. I am more thrilled to be standing so close to you at last, Mrs. Molassis.
MRS. MOLASSIS. Your young man is a graduate in compliments as well, Dr. Loop. Charming!
LOOP. Europe....
PAPPENDECK (*pressingly*). I have always longed for a middle-aged woman to teach me the wild caresses she knows so well.
MRS. MOLASSIS. Middle-aged! Excuse me, but—
PAPPENDECK (*languorously*). Let me place my monograph on "Excitation of Magnetic Susceptibility" at your feet. I broke through every equation to reach a solution that might find favor in your eyes.
MRS. MOLASSIS. A proposition! Already! Excuse me, but the ceremony is about to start and I *must* do my hair. (*She leaves*)
LOOP. You've done it, Pappendeck, you frightened her with the wild caresses and all that. Now she's gone off to comb her hair.
PAPPENDECK. No, I could see that my youthful fires troubled and aroused her. Disheveled is not her hair but her soul.
MCBOODLE (*joining them*). Your assistant has a long antenna out for Mrs. Molassis, if I'm not mistaken.
LOOP. The lab is such a poor outlet for a young man's tempestuous cravings, Secretary McBoodle.
MCBOODLE. If he wants to visit a broad that bad, let him join the Navy and

travel. (*Roars with laughter*)

CULPEPPER. Un cocktelle, messieurs?

MCBOODLE. Sure. Say, I'm sure I've seen you somewhere before.

CULPEPPER. Ce n'est pas impossible, monsieur.

MCBOODLE (*takes him aside*). Fact is, you're as like General Culpepper as two jiggers of scotch, except for the moustache and the voulezvous stuff.

CULPEPPER (*dropping the accent*). I *was* General Culpepper, McBoodle.

MCBOODLE. I never forget a man, especially when I've done him in. But I bear no grudge against you, Culpepper. How's life been treating you?

CULPEPPER. You assigned me to kitchen police in the Pentagon.

MCBOODLE. I remember.

CULPEPPER. They made me wait on tables, and I got to enjoy the life. So I decided to quit the army and go professional. Nobody can take orders like an ex-general.

MCBOODLE. Leave it to McBoodle. He knows where a man belongs.

CULPEPPER (*French accent again*). *Pardon*, here is Madame Molassis who enters without a drink. (*To Mrs. Molassis*) Un petit verre, madame? (*Confidentially*) I am your humble adorateur, Madame Molassis.

MRS. MOLASSIS. What? (*Culpepper is gone again*) I'm positively persecuted today! A boy who shaved for the first time a week ago, and a faded French waiter, not to mention the knuckle-smooching of McBoodle. Well, it does prove I appeal to all kinds.

MRS. SNAFFLE. Dear Mrs. Molassis, do join our little circle. Ah, here comes my husband at last!

(*Enter the Duke of Ostersund, followed by Snaffle, both of course in formal dress. Applause. The Duke directs Snaffle to one of the chairs by the speaker's stand. Snaffle is holding a small box, which he carefully nurtures, and which he will be stroking amiably now and then. The Duke kisses Mrs. Snaffle's hand*)

DUKE. Dear Mrs. Snaffle!

MRS. SNAFFLE. Dear your Grace!

DUKE. My friends, please possess your places. The ceremony is about to incipiate and I must be delivering of my speech. (*He mounts the platform and takes the speaker's stand*) Ladies and gentlemen, as Chairman of the Selection Board of the Dynamite Peace Prize, I am deeply afflicted to give the prize this year to the renownable American physicist and mathematician, Professor Lancelot Snaffle. (*Ovation*) The Dynamite Peace Prize, I am glad to reminisce you, was funded by Sigurd Loftung, who did give the world so much explosive without he kept it from any nation that wished to have it, he was so generous. How happy Sigurd Loftung would be if he is with us today, when we honor and do give money to Professor Snaffle for the Polyponal Pedilift! Let me bepaint the human's condition before the Pedilift exploded in the scene. The humans had maked missiles who fly to the Moon and to Mars. Good. They fabricate airplanes who fly from one ending of the globe to the other ending. Good. They invent steamships who run over the ocean and submarines who are giggling under the water. Good. They make railroads and autobuses and scooters. It is the miracle! The human man makes more and more effort to make less and less effort. And this, ladies and gentlemen, is the aiming of science and technology, is to make the life easy. Relax, as you Americans say.

MCBOODLE. Such a brilliant diplomat.

DUKE. But evermore and yet, the man and the woman must use and articulate his muscles of the leg: the *sartorius*, the *quadriceps femoris*, the *biceps femoris*, the *adductor magnus*, and much others, all in Latin. Because not all the distances are formidably enormious. Professor Snaffle has magnificently calculated that 65% of humane trajections is of the order of 2 km or under. Imaginate! The terrible sap of energy, the attrition of lymph, the unendless output of heat, the debilitating of the heart, the decay of the tissue—all this, and it is a malicious picture—means that our life is extremely shorter as it has the necessary to be. We relax when we do travel from New York to Stockholm, but we do not relax when we do walk to the grocery storage to purchase a bottle of milk, if I may be let loose a filthy image. 65% of our trajections are using non-necessary animal energies. And also it is using non-necessary spiritual attentions, because we see a dog in the way and we say "excuse me," and we notify a piddle in the street and we are worried not to bestep it. In one word, we are watching our muscles when we can be thinking over noble and great thinkings. And that is why the Pedilift is a liberator! It releases to the liberty new energies hitherbefore by mankind expended into the mechanical ambulating locomotion. One day it is perhaps that walking can be annihilated completely. Not perhaps! I beforecast certainly! Man shall be conquering the painful walking! But until that glorible day, we shall proudly step into the earth with Professor Lancelot Snaffle's Pedilift. (*Ovation*) And now, I present Professor Lancelot Snaffle himself!

(*Snaffle acknowledges the applause, shakes the Duke's hand, and takes the speaker's stand, blowing his nose and wiping a tear*)

SNAFFLE. I am overcome.... So many friendly faces.... The tear must fall. My friends, pardon this weakness. Your Grace, Duke of Ostersund, before I accept the modest yet nutritious check awarded to me for my peaceful application, I want to offer you all a little surprise: the Pedilift itself!

(*Applause*)

DUKE. Delicious!

(*Snaffle blows a whistle, whereupon Mr. Smith the demonstrator enters equipped with the Pedilift. The Pedilift, speaking roughly, consists of an extremely heavy kind of metal knapsack, containing the machinery. From this piece, which burdens the demonstrator to a perspiration, emerges a system of rods, shafts, cams and gears which culminate in a pair of braces for the legs and feet. The Pedilift also has a conspicuous opening for the insertion of the Frigoradiant Capsule, and levers for starting, stopping, speed, direction, etc. The demonstrator walks like a very noisy robot*)

SNAFFLE. The demonstrator is still using his own energy, ladies and gentlemen; energy which, as his Grace pointed out a moment ago, should be put to higher uses than getting from one place to another. I am not the first Benefactor of Mankind to have attempted to relieve man of the primitive need of using his own feet; but I *am* the first to have given the problem its definitive solution. This solution, ladies and gentlemen, is due to my Polypon, whose Frigoradiant Emissions I have succeeded in concentrating in capsule form. Here is a typical pellet. It will be sold in attractive packages at every supermarket in the country. Mr. Smith, will you kindly introduce it into the Injector? Observe, ladies and gentlemen, that this tiny capsule, which I am holding in my ungloved hand, has such a lengthy halflife that it hardly needs a full life. It will last Mr. Smith 300,000 years! (*Murmur of amazement among the public*) Remains only the project of making Mr. Smith last 300,000 years, one that other scientists will have to address. Here, Mr. Smith. (*He gives Smith the capsule*) Watch him if you can. He sets the Directional Pointer and the Path Computer. Now he sets the required speed, which he can change midcourse at will, or pre-change through the built-in electronic brain. Now he switches on the Angular Release, which enables him to ascend or descend steps, and to kick impediments away. Are you ready, Mr. Smith? Have you chosen your destination?

SMITH. Yes sir.

SNAFFLE. Contact!

(*The demonstrator walks with a great noise. Exclamations of admiration. He walks up and down the steps of the platform and around the hall*)

DUKE (*beaming and applauding*). Disgraceful!

MCBOODLE. Ouch! My foot!

SMITH (*passing by*). Sorry, Mr. McBoodle.

SNAFFLE. Please observe, all his energies are now available to him for intellectual functions.

NOSE. Where is he going?

(*Mr. Smith walks straight to Mrs. Molassis, kisses her passionately, and picks her up under his arm*)

MRS. MOLASSIS. How unusual!
SNAFFLE. Mr. Smith!
PAPPENDECK. Mrs. Molassis!
NOSE. "The Romance of Science!"
MRS. MOLASSIS (*as she is carried away*). My worst enemy is my beauty, thank God. (*Smith vanishes with her*)
DUKE. Most disgraceful and delightsome!
PAPPENDECK. What a wink she gave me as she left!
MCBOODLE (*to Culpepper*). Aren't you going to stop them?
CULPEPPER. Why? Madame left her glass behind, didn't she?
SNAFFLE. Well! This ought to remove any doubt as to the efficiency of my Pedilift. Your Grace, I am ready to be honored.
DUKE. An expiring spectacle, Professor Snaffle. Another applause? To the Pedilift, and the happiness of Mrs. Molassis. And now, in the name of the King, the Cabinetry, and the Dynamite Peace Prize Selection Board, I present to you, Lancelot Snaffle, the Sigurd Loftung Award of the year. (*He produces a large shopping bag and extracts from it a large tin box whose label, "Laurel Crowns, imported from Greece," he reads aloud. He opens the box, extracts the crown, remarking that it is very fresh, and places it on Snaffle's head. Applause. Then he produces a check from a wallet*) In Swedish kronor, Professor Snaffle, at 5.18 to the dollar.
(*Snaffle has his hand out for it, when Dr. P. P. Folpap makes a dramatic entrance*)
FOLPAP. Stop! The award is mine!
SNAFFLE. Folpap!
(*Sensation*)
DUKE. Dr. Folpap, the great Paraguayan theoretician!
MCBOODLE. Deserter!
FOLPAP. Silence! I come forward to challenge Lancelot Snaffle! He has forfeited his right to the Dynamite Peace Prize!
ALL. Why?
FOLPAP. Because he stole *my* idea!
SNAFFLE. Stole? Stole your idea?
MRS. SNAFFLE. Your Grace—
DUKE. Stole, Dr. Folpap? That is an illegitimate word.
FOLPAP. I withdraw it. But I contend that Professor Snaffle has been less than original in his invention, for his Pedilift shows an unmistakable debt to my own Footomat, a debt which candor would have compelled him to admit in public.
DUKE. That is better language.
SNAFFLE. Better, your Grace, you call this better? I'm dreaming! Who

discovered the Polypon? Who created Frigoradiant Emissions? Who published the results in the *Engineering Quarterly?*

FOLPAP. And who miscarried in his experiments so wretchedly that he caused an American spy to intone the Russian national anthem?

SNAFFLE. And who flubbed the Goliath missile five times?

FOLPAP. And who lost his government contract?

SNAFFLE. It's a lie!

FOLPAP. A lie? A lie? You say this to a member of the Paraguay Institute for Advanced Brooding?

DUKE. A lie, Professor Snaffle....

MCBOODLE. No international incidents, Snaffle. Paraguay is working on the Bomb.

SNAFFLE. I apologize. But I affirm under oath that my esteemed colleague has drawn a hasty inference, and that his conclusions are not, perhaps, convincingly buttressed by the available evidence, nor marked by the forthrightness we have come to expect of him.

MCBOODLE. Very satisfactory.

NOSE. "Scholarly Debate Enlivens Peace Prize Giveaway."

PAPPENDECK. We're with you all the way, Professor Snaffle.

CULPEPPER. I shall refuse to serve the Paraguayan, Monsieur le Professeur.

MRS. SNAFFLE. Oh, thank you, thank you. This is such a trial for me. (*She breaks down*)

DUKE. Is it peaceful among us again? Sigurd Loftung—

FOLPAP. Your Grace! It is *not* peaceful! I am indignant! But I intend to maintain my case by visible fact. Allow me.

(*He too blows a whistle, and Mr. Jones, the second demonstrator, comes in, wearing a hat. He is carrying pretty much the same apparatus as Mr. Smith—though in a different color—but his has an additional contraption, namely an articulated claw which clasps his hat*)

NOSE. Another Pedilift!

FOLPAP. Not a Pedilift, sir. A Footomat.

DUKE. This is a real disturbement.

SNAFFLE. A miserable copy of the Pedilift.

FOLPAP. I scorn to reply. Your Grace, if you will kindly stay where you are, I will ask Mr. Jones to walk in front of you while reading a newspaper, namely the Ogallalla Daily Gazette, from deepest Nebraska. Mr. Jones? (*He hands him the newspaper*)

JONES. I am reading and paying no attention to anything.

(*He starts the levers and walks with his nose in the newspaper. As he passes before the Duke the respectful machinery lifts his hat and sets it back on his head*)

MCBOODLE. Jesus!
NOSE. It lifted the hat!
CULPEPPER. C'est très français.
LOOP (*rushing to his doom*). Excellent! Excellent! Excellent! (*He claps*)
SNAFFLE. Loop!
LOOP. Bravo, I repeat. It lifts the hat. Dr. Folpap, I wish to congratulate you on this brilliant invention.
FOLPAP. Thank you, *Dr.* Loop. I hire you herewith.
SNAFFLE. Loop, you cockroach, you scumbum, he doctors you, but you just wait.
LOOP. Piffle.
FOLPAP. Please observe, your Grace, that my Footomat affords its user an amazing new convenience; to wit, it allows a mechanism to take over the burdensome and distracting duties of everyday courtesy. The benefits which will accrue to mankind through the automation of politeness can hardly be overestimated. And note that my Footomat will doff the hat of the most backward jungle native as easily as yours and mine, thus promoting the cause of world understanding. It will also shake hands through an elaborate system of cranks and shafts at a small additional cost.
NOSE. "Jet Age Comes to Good Manners."
DUKE. Professor Snaffle, what do you please to say to this more refined achievement?
SNAFFLE. Very impressive, of course.
DUKE. Aha. Excuse me. (*He removes Snaffle's crown*) Dr. Folpap—
FOLPAP. Thank you. The money too.
SNAFFLE. One moment, my lord. May we see the demonstration again, my dear Folpap?
FOLPAP. Gladly, good Snaffle. Mr. Jones, the Gazette. Go!
(*Snaffle pretends to come in for a close observation, but instead he places a chair in Jones' path while everybody is exclaiming over the hat. Jones falls over the chair with an homeric clatter*)
FOLPAP. Jones!
ALL. Oh!
JONES. Who's the idiot? Help me up, you fools. Goddam shaft in my rib.
SNAFFLE. Poor man. Take my hand.
MRS. SNAFFLE. Serves him right.
FOLPAP. I suggest that this chair did not travel fortuitously to the locus of intersection with Mr. Jones!
JONES. Stuffed hokum! Somebody put the chair in my way and I'm gonna make him eat it!

DUKE. But this is beyond belief, Dr. Folpap.
SNAFFLE (*nobly*). No. Dr. Folpap is right. It was I who placed the chair in Mr. Jones' way.
FOLPAP. He admits it!
JONES. Why you—wait till I get rid of this junk!
MCBOODLE. Snaffle! The State Department—
SNAFFLE. One moment! Mr. Jones, I apologize to you and Mrs. Snaffle will tip you at the exit. For the rest, my friends, I only intended to show you the shortcomings of my brilliant colleague's imitation of the original Pedilift. No, Dr. Folpap, *I* am speaking now.
(*He blows his whistle again. Smith reappears, still carrying Mrs. Molassis, though she is now in a state of minor disarray*)
MCBOODLE. Welcome back!
PAPPENDECK. She found me again!
MRS. MOLASSIS. Do set me down in a chair, Jimmy sweet. (*She tousles Mr. Smith's hair*) Dear friends, have I been missed?
CULPEPPER. Un autre verre, madame?
MRS. MOLASSIS. Thank you. Mrs. Snaffle! (*They embrace*)
MRS. SNAFFLE. Dear Mrs. Molassis! I have gone through so much!
SNAFFLE. Delighted, Mrs. Molassis.
DUKE (*to Mrs. Molassis*). I will tend over you in the tingling of an eye. (*He kisses her hand*) What are you doing, Professor Snaffle?
(*Snaffle brandishes the box he has been nurturing since the start, and plugs a little black device into the Pedilift*)
SNAFFLE. I am loading the Searcher into my Pedilift.
FOLPAP (*aside*). Lost!
LOOP (*aside*). I'm a dead cockroach!
MRS. MOLASSIS. Jimmy, do be careful!
SMITH. No danger, lassie. I've been vaccinated.
SNAFFLE. Gather round, ladies and gentlemen, gather round and watch. The Frigoradiant Capsule, Smith?
SMITH. Active, sir.
SNAFFLE. Let me inspect....
MRS. MOLASSIS (*to Mrs. Snaffle*). Isn't he darling? My own Tirian—Tridalph—Trinian—oh dear, these foreign names! But what's in a name, as Desdemona says? I mean my own Molassis; he is rich but practically an Ancient Greek.
PAPPENDECK (*who has nuzzled in*). And I am poor but young, Mrs. Molassis.
MRS. MOLASSIS. Naughty! (*To Mrs. Snaffle, in strict confidence*) Between you and I, these capsules have a marvelous effect on—in short, a marvelous

side-effect.

MRS. SNAFFLE. I must tell my husband! Another application!

SNAFFLE. Ready! Dr. Folpap, may I trouble you for the Ogallalla Gazette? Now, Mr. Smith, leave the room for a moment while I allow the audience to scatter in a random dispersion. (*Smith leaves with the Gazette*) All right, everybody, take up any position you like, sitting or standing. Dr. Folpap, will you monitor the experiment? And my excellent Mr. Loop, and Mr. Jones, may we have your cooperation as well, in the interest of science?

JONES. I'm game.

LOOP. Delighted, Dr. Snaffle. A brilliant experiment.

PAPPENDECK (*to Mrs. Molassis*). I will disperse myself at random beside you.

MRS. MOLASSIS (*coquette*). I really don't think I should allow you, Mr. Pappendeck.

MCBOODLE. I'll take up a chance position near the martinis.

SNAFFLE. Everybody ready?

EVERYBODY. Ready!

(*Snaffle blows his whistle. Enter Smith, arduously reading the Gazette*)

SNAFFLE. Not a word, not a whisper from anybody. Take a casual walk, my boy.

(*Smith circulates with a ghastly clanking among the spectators in the room, neatly avoiding them all. Whenever he comes near a person, there is a toot from a horn, and he veers away. Gurgles of amazement. Folpap tries in vain to make him collide with himself; Smith avoids him every time*)

SNAFFLE. Test him, test him, worthy colleague. Still plunged in the Gazette, mind you. As though fascinated by Nebraska.

(*Smith finally arrives before Mrs. Molassis, who prepares herself for another abduction. But the horn toots, Smith clanks on and vanishes from the scene*)

MRS. MOLASSIS. Jimmy!

(*The others applaud and cry Bravo*)

MRS. SNAFFLE. My hero! (*Embraces Snaffle*)

DUKE. Professor Snaffle, the prize is yours! Not another word!

CULPEPPER. Champagne!

(*General enthusiasm*)

MRS. MOLASSIS. Jimmy....

FOLPAP (*in a corner*). I am disgraced forever. History books will caricature me as a spiteful failure. (*He flees*)

JONES. Hey, my wages! (*He clanks after Folpap as best he can*) Damn this contraption! (*Exit*)

(*Everybody except Pappendeck and Mrs. Molassis is crowding around Snaffle*)

DUKE. The laurel crown.

SNAFFLE. And the check.
(*Much hand-shaking, compliment-making, champagne-bibbing*)
PAPPENDECK. Mrs. Molassis, I am still here.
MRS. MOLASSIS. Hush, handsome young man.
LOOP. Professor Snaffle, it is with a feeling as deep as the abyss—
SNAFFLE. Sir, you are dust.
LOOP. Yes, Professor Snaffle.
SNAFFLE. You will take your dingy person and your unfinished doctoral degree with the Folpap fellow.
LOOP. I deserved this. Let oblivion snuff me out. (*Stumbles off*)
DUKE. Morality has winned, as always.
NOSE. "Traitor Meets With Just Deserts."
MRS. SNAFFLE. The ungrateful man! After twenty years my husband bestowed on him.
CULPEPPER. More champagne!
DUKE. Music! Let the fanfares jubilate!
(*Music. Procession. Clanking of Pedilift and tooting of horn. Brandishing of champagne glasses. General hilarity*)
SNAFFLE (*drinking*). Next step: a reactor in every backyard!
EVERYBODY. Hurrah!
(*The procession is on its way out*)
PAPPENDECK (*to Mrs. Molassis*). Dearest Ursula, tonight, in my private cloud chamber....
MRS. MOLASSIS. Josh, my good name!
DUKE. Let the trombones festivate!
(*Pappendeck roots a passionate kiss on Mrs. Molassis' hand as the procession leaves the stage*)

SCENE FIVE

(*Snaffle's office. The Tots, dressed as factory workers, stand in the background, each one holding a tool. Snaffle is sitting at the desk, the Spy is sitting beside him. The Spy is now dressed as a British agent—mackintosh and all—and speaks accordingly*)

SPY. It's true. I sold you to Folpap, and then I sold Folpap to you. Might have shuttled two or three times more—sold your secret information about Folpap's secret information about you back to Folpap, and then forward again to you—but I'm not getting any younger, so where's the 3,000 quid?

SNAFFLE. It wasn't easy, Fitz-Gordon. I borrowed—

SPY. Borrowed my mother's navel! You're making millions with your bloody capsules. Come on, Snaffle, pop out the three thousand.

SNAFFLE. All right, all right. (*He counts out a bundle of banknotes to the spy*)

SPY. Right. Well, good luck to you, Yank. (*Leaves*)

SNAFFLE. Good riddance. Well well well. I have bestowed the Pedilift on humanity and given bunions their death-blow. I leased the Pedilift patent for an outrageously businesslike sum of money, while I retained full and exclusive rights over the capsules which make it move. I am so important that I will not relieve myself without my lawyer's advice. I have also become modest, and why not? The world sees through my modesty. I am written about in the papers for my secret charities. I get urgent calls from Paris, from Abu Dhabi.... But right now it's break time for my Tots. Let's hear you, good workers!

TOTS.
>We love the company we're working for,
>It's been our dad and mom and nurse!
>That's why we're pushing it from shore to shore,
>And putting dollars in its purse!

(*Snaffle blows a whistle. The Tots lay down their tools, advance in regimental order, and salute. Molecule steps forward*)

MOLECULE. Molecule reporting, sir. Tots meeting your schedule. Machinery at 35% capacity to prevent overproduction and buttress prices. Quota for today 76% filled.

SNAFFLE. Let me see today's orders and the mail.

MOLECULE. Here you are, sir.

SNAFFLE (*to Atom*) You.

ATOM. Yes, sir.

SNAFFLE. Take a few capsules out of your pocket and give them to me. (*To Isotope*) And you. Light me a cigar and make an ashtray. (*Atom and Isotope obey. While Atom returns to the group, Isotope stands by the desk holding her hand open for ashes. Snaffle examines a few capsules*) Not bad. Not bad. Good quality control. The petroleum interests are yelling guff and murder. Wells closing down from Oklahoma to Kuwait. (*To Atom*) All right, you. Put these capsules back in your pocket.

ATOM. Yes, sir.

SNAFFLE. Let's look at the orders. Hm. Manchester wants 22,300 capsules, delivery in three months. Liège: 20,000. Düsseldorf: 14,500. What's this?

Five! Oh, Lichtenstein. The usual from Smolensk: 30,000 for this month, but must be labelled Made in Smolensk. (*To Isotope, as he flicks an ash*) Are you staring at me?

ISOTOPE. No, lord and master of albumen.

SNAFFLE. I know you're as willing to work for the enemy as for us. Get rid of these ashes and scratch behind my left ear. A little lower. A little higher. Enough. All right, everybody, back to the production line! (*The Tots march off*) Now for the personal mail.... Pink envelope and rose-blossom perfume. Another one! Let me see. "Dear Professor Snaffle. I adore you." A good beginning. "Oh, do not be frightened. My love is pure and spiritual, being only a silent admirer of yours, beheld from afar. I am nineteen years old and they say I am beautiful. But what is beauty to me? Beauty is such a transitory thing. It dies as the flower dies. I long for a deeper beauty of the soul which does not drown like the common dust. I hate the mediocrity of life! But something mystical that has flowed from your spirit to mine tells me you have felt this thing too, for you have sacrificed your comfort to enthrone a ray of hope in the hearts of mankind which is so unhappy. I know that you are a man who would understand the poetry that is so ready to blossom within me. To you I can write,

> I lifted up mine eye that is aye mortal,
> And lo, an angel smiléd from his portal!

But you will shake your head and take umbrage with my boldness. Oh do not scold your Stradella ! You see, I already call myself *your* Stradella. Oh, do with your slave whatsoever you please. What care I for conventions? Let the world talk! I fling my throbbing heart at your foot which longs for love and understanding and the ideal. Do, do respond, for otherwise I shall not, will not, live." Signed, "Your Stradella Nussbaum, 2136 Olive Street, the Bronx, New York." (*He places the letter in a folder*) Number four. If I hadn't my hands full with Rosie Molassis..... But I'd better answer my Stradella. (*He is about to write a letter, when the intercom buzzes*) Miss Crowley? Yes? So what? I know he's been waiting for two hours and eleven minutes. Muttering is he? Who does he think he is? I'm busy. What's that? Oh, all right, let him come in but tell him I'm very busy. (*Aside*) That'll show him.

(*Enter McBoodle*)

SNAFFLE. So, it's you, McBoodle.

MCBOODLE (*meekly*). Yes, Professor Snaffle. I hope I haven't disturbed you by waiting in your reception room a tiny half-hour.

SNAFFLE. No, that's all right. Sit down if you want to and tell me what's on your mind. I'm in a hurry.

MCBOODLE. Thank you; I'm most grateful. I hope that Mrs. Snaffle—

SNAFFLE. To the point, man, this is a business office, not a lounge.

MCBOODLE. Amazing efficiency. Admiration of the world. I'm here, Professor Snaffle, on behalf of the government—specifically, of course, the Department of Defensive Expansion.

SNAFFLE. Which awarded me a handsome kick in the rear not long ago.

MCBOODLE. Most regrettable. All the same, we are interested in renewing contact with your enterprise. We believe that the Pedilift can be adapted to jungle and mountain warfare—places where the conventional foot-soldier is still needed. You see the picture, Professor Snaffle.

SNAFFLE. I do. But I'm dedicated to peaceful applications, thank you.

MCBOODLE. I might secure a contract for you—may I lean forward? (*He whispers into Snaffle's ear*) This is an approximate figure....

SNAFFLE. I see. Of course, jungle and mountain warfare are a kind of peaceful application too. Peace of mind for the Army.

MCBOODLE. Exactly.

SNAFFLE. I hope nobody has ever questioned my patriotism, in spite of my devotion to peace.

MCBOODLE. Questioned your patriotism! Professor Snaffle, the very thought is shocking.

SNAFFLE. The contract you were talking about—

MCBOODLE. Is only a beginning. That's understood. A period of extensive testing.... Of course, certain members of congress must be sold on the idea.

SNAFFLE. Sold....

MCBOODLE. And I'm prepared to use my influence.

SNAFFLE. Sit over here, McBoodle, you'll be more comfortable. Put your feet up; here, that's better. Wait. I've got a bottle of something choice in the cabinet. (*He pours drinks*)

MCBOODLE. Here's to you, Snaffle old man.

SNAFFLE. And to you. Hey! It's good to see an old friend again. How's Mrs. McBoodle these days?

MCBOODLE. I'm not married, but I bet she'd be fine if I were.

SNAFFLE. Let me fill you up again.

MCBOODLE. Thanks.

SNAFFLE. What's the deal, old man? You know me; cards on the table.

MCBOODLE. Snaffle, this is the time to strike. The sky's the limit. But you need an inside man, and that's where I come in. If there's one guy in town who can tell you where the switches are located, it's Crusher McBoodle.

SNAFFLE. Cards on the table, McBoodle. What's in this for you?

MCBOODLE. Nothing at all, Snaffle.
SNAFFLE. That's going to be more than I can afford. But if you're willing to be reasonable, I'll listen to your proposition.
MCBOODLE. All I want you to do is take on a lady—I'll name her—a business genius—take her on as—I don't care what—vice-president in charge of procurement—or something—and put her on a ten-year contract at a three hundred thousand a year.
SNAFFLE. Two hundred
MCBOODLE. Two hundred seventy-five.
SNAFFLE. Two hundred fifty.
MCBOODLE. So be it. Shake.
SNAFFLE. Shake.
MCBOODLE. We're in business, pal.
SNAFFLE. There's only one more thing I want from you, McBoodle, to compensate me for the aforementioned kick.
MCBOODLE. What's that?
SNAFFLE. I wonder if you could use your influence to obtain for me—
MCBOODLE. Obtain what?
SNAFFLE. I'm blushing.
MCBOODLE. Go on, you rascal.
SNAFFLE. I hesitate, I'm bashful....
MCBOODLE. Go on, have another drink, good, now tell all to old Crusher.
SNAFFLE. Well, I'd like—I truly would like—it's not important, actually—
MCBOODLE. Out with it!
SNAFFLE. A statue to Lancelot Snaffle in Central Park. There! I've said it.
MCBOODLE. You've got a sensational idea there. Snaffle, you're one of the finest promotion men in the country. What a stunt! A statue for a great public servant! I'll get it done. Trumpley is a friend.
SNAFFLE. Trumpley?
MCBOODLE. Secretary of American Culture. Ok, Snaffle, I'm off. Remember I came here to talk to my old pal about tennis and golf.
SNAFFLE. Right. So long, old friend.
MCBOODLE. Nice to see you again, and my best to dear Mrs. Snaffle.
(*Exit*)
SNAFFLE (*beginning to write*). My dear Miss Nussbaum....

SCENE SIX

(Central Park. Autumn leaves on the ground, but it's a sunny day. A large statue of Snaffle in Roman garb and benevolent gesture, a Polypon capsule in his right palm. Enter Snaffle, disguised in a large beard. He walks up to the statue)

SNAFFLE *(to the audience)*. I come here when time permits incognito in order to bask a little. *(He turns to the statue)* An excellent likeness, no? Such humility in my chiselled countenance! And I like the inscription. "Lancelot Snaffle: *Amplificator lmperii Humani*," that is to say, "Enlarger of the Human Empire". It was my idea; I paid Dr. Gladwin, assistant professor of Latin and Greek at City College $100. *(He walks around the statue)* A little piece chipped off my behind. How come? And another inscription: *"Homo Fronte Creationis Stat."* Dr. Gladwin again. "Man Stands at the Forefront of Creation". Another chip. Oh well. *(He sits down on a park bench)* What dignity! What benevolence! Ah! Here come two visitors. I don't believe it! Folpap and Loop! Become park custodians! Lucky I'm wearing the false beard.

(Enter Folpap and Loop, reduced indeed to the honest and yet unenvied rank of park custodians, with rake, broom, pick and bag. They push the leaves around without eroding the park)

FOLPAP. Here's a corner of Central Park I cordially dislike.

LOOP. It fills me with thoughts of blood-baths.

FOLPAP. Have you got the hammer?

LOOP. Here it is.

FOLPAP. Is anybody looking?

LOOP. I see a man with a beard, but he's asleep and snoring.

FOLPAP. Good. *(He chips a little material from the statue)*

SNAFFLE *(one eye open)*. Pimple-bottomed louse.

FOLPAP. What did you say?

LOOP. Nothing. I'm just raking away.

FOLPAP. Well, so much for today. Bit by bit. One chip at a time.

LOOP. Oh Dr. Folpap, private action is so useless. Why don't you join our cell? Mother is a wonderful organizer. As well-organized Anarchists, we can overthrow the state, secure justice for all men, shoot our enemies, and liquidate Snaffle.

SNAFFLE. Grrr.

FOLPAP. I don't know that I can afford the membership, but I'll give it some thought. Meantime I chip away.

LOOP *(plaintively)*. If only I were in my old lab again. This fresh air is bad for

my yellow complexion.
(*Snaffle saunters up to the statue*)
SNAFFLE. Admirable statue. The famous Professor Snaffle!
(*Folpap and Loop exchange a significant wink*)
FOLPAP. We'd be glad to give you the official tour, sir. We are both—ahem—licensed guides as well as official gardeners.
SNAFFLE. Tell me, tell me.
LOOP (*voice of the official guide*). The statue of Lancelot Snaffle is made in its entirety of red porphyry, a 20-ton block of which was hand carried from Karelia to New York. Its style is late flamboyant Gothic, although obvious traces of the neo-Byzantine workshops of Siena appear in it as well, particularly in the superb arching of the upper lip.
FOLPAP (*same*). The noble figure of the physicist, clad in an ample robe symbolizing Purity, has been called by one critic "the last breath of the Hellenic spirit in a world of welded steel."
LOOP (*same*). The statue adorns a popular corner of Central Park. Guided tours are a dollar per person.
(*Loop stretches out a hand*)
SNAFFLE. Oh, a pleasure. (*He pays Loop*) It might interest you, my friends, that I am personally acquainted with the man Snaffle, though the statue was new to me.
LOOP. Really, sir? A noble figure.
SNAFFLE. Densest mass of vices this side of the bubonic plague. I should know. I'm his accountant.
FOLPAP (*changes his tone*). Well! Confidentially, we've heard the same judgment from many experts.
SNAFFLE. You have, have you? Tell me more.
FOLPAP. We hear that he stole the Pedilift from a brother scientist. I don't know if you ever heard the name. Folpap, I think it was.
SNAFFLE. Yes, I *have* heard something about that episode. And didn't he also sack a faithful old assistant of his?
LOOP. He did, and for no reason at all. He drove the poor gentleman to a premature end.
SNAFFLE. Oh, he's dead, is he?
LOOP. To peace and comfort.
FOLPAP. So we're told.
LOOP. Yes, so we're told.
SNAFFLE. Well, he's a tough old customer. He'd steal the crutch from under his grandmother's armpit.
FOLPAP. Both crutches; and make her pay him to get them back.

SNAFFLE. A grim beast of a man.
LOOP. Bribed the mayor to have this statue put here. We know it for a lugubrious fact.
FOLPAP. And stole the idea for the Pedilift, don't forget that. It's his only really unforgivable crime.
LOOP. Along with the sacking of the assistant.
FOLPAP. Who deserved the statue? Dr. Folpap, I tell you. This Folpap was worth ten Snaffles.
SNAFFLE. Twenty! I told him so myself.
FOLPAP. Let me shake your hand! You really know that barrel of dung.
SNAFFLE (*holding Folpap's hand*). Know that barrel of dung? That's nothing! Shall I tell you something more?
FOLPAP and LOOP (*eagerly*). Yes!
SNAFFLE. I *am* that barrel of dung! (*Tears off his beard*) What now!
FOLPAP. Snaffle!
LOOP. Misery!
SNAFFLE. You wait, you lapses of nature! Malformations! Dead-ends! (*He grabs a rake*) Out of my sight, or I'll have you arrested for vandalism and anarchism!
(*Folpap and Loop run away, pursued by Snaffle. Snaffle returns, wiping off his sweat, puts on his beard and sits again on the bench. Enter various Central Park strollers, some of them equipped with the Pedilift. They admire the statue, take pictures etc. and then move off*)
SNAFFLE. Very gratifying. Hey, I'm in the shade! (*He moves a little and basks*) The sun shines on me, and always will. (*He sings*)
> We love the company we're working for,
> It's been our dad and mom and nurse!
> That's why we're pushing it from shore to shore,
> And putting dollars in its purse!

(*Enter the Author, woebegone. He stands over Snaffle*)
SNAFFLE. Who are you?
AUTHOR. I am the author of this drama.
SNAFFLE. Congratulations. Then why so woebegone?
AUTHOR. Because I found no way of punishing you to end it.
(*He shuffles off. Snaffle calls after him*)
SNAFFLE. Punishing me? For what?

The End

PROFESSOR SNAFFLE'S POLYPON

Note

Professor Snaffle's Polypon, written in 1962, appeared in the Summer 1966 issue of *First Stage* (see my Note to *The Fatal French Dentist*). This second and final version has been extensively revised.

A BEAUTIFUL INVESTMENT

A script for stage and film

CHARACTERS ON STAGE

Mel Broxton
Sol Krakowitz
George O'Malley
Charlie Figmueller
Louella Broxton, *Broxton's mother*
Ralph Peckam
Mary-Ann, *secretary to Broxton and Krakowitz*
Mary-Lou, *secretary to Charlie*
Mary-Belle, *Louella's maid*

CHARACTERS ON SCREEN

Mr. Elkins
Mrs. Elkins
Their secretary
The foreman
A truck-driver
A buyer
Antonio, *a lad*
The work force

A BEAUTIFUL INVESTMENT

ON SCREEN 1

(The camera approaches a perfectly ordinary one-story industrial building standing to one side of a large fenced-in parking area. A sign: DESIGNS UNLIMITED with ORLANDO, FLORIDA underneath, has been stuck unglamorously over the entranceway, in keeping with the plain look of the brick establishment itself. The camera circles the building and arrives at the back, where a truck is unloading bolts of fabric. We then move just inside the plant, catching our first overall view by lingering over the unloading, which is performed by the truck-driver and the foreman. As the bolts are being stacked on the floor, the foreman carefully checks them against a purchase order. From the background come the typical mixed noises of machinery, voices trying to rise about the hubbub, several radios blaring away, and the ring of telephones from several cubicles serving as offices. Much of the dialogue will be created ad hoc at the time of production. It must remain routine and unremarkable, and in the spirit of the samples provided in these notations)

FOREMAN. Three months we been waiting for this one.
TRUCK-DRIVER. Wait a minute! There's a bolt left back of the truck.
FOREMAN. What is it?
TRUCK-DRIVER. Looks like more of that Waldorf Brown.
FOREMAN. That'll make Mr. Elkins happy for sure.
(As they finish unloading, Mr. Elkins walks over from his office. He is an affable and sturdy lover of the pipe who conscientiously empties it and turns its bowl downward whenever he leaves his office)
FOREMAN. Lots of Waldorf Brown, M. Elkins.
ELKINS. Three months we've been waiting for it.
(He counts and examines the goods and shouts toward the offices)
ELKINS. Madge! Four pieces of Waldorf Brown arrived in the truck!
(Mrs. Elkins appears at her office door)
MRS. ELKINS. It's about time. Three and a half months!
ELKINS. You can now go ahead and schedule it.
MRS. ELKINS. Sure, but don't forget we need two pieces more now that Speck and Speck want—
ELKINS. I'm not forgetting. Send Antonio over to ticket these, will you?
MRS. ELKINS. Right.
FOREMAN. I don't understand. There's an extra bolt of the Dragon Orange

we didn't order.
ELKINS. Be sure to send it back, and pin a note to it, will you?
FOREMAN. Will do.
(*Under this, we've heard Mrs. Elkins shouting for Antonio, who is now seen affixing tickets to the bolts identifying them*)
TRUCK-DRIVER. All set, Mr. Elkins? I'm running half an hour late.
(*The secretary appears at the door of her office*)
SECRETARY. Mr. Elkins! It's Mr. O'Malley calling from New York!
ELKINS. Who?
SECRETARY. Mr. O'Malley. George O'Malley. He owns this place, remember?
ELKINS. Right. Tell him I'll be with him in a second. (*Unhurriedly to the truck-driver*) Make sure that Dragon Orange goes back to Summermill, ok?
TRUCK-DRIVER. Don't worry. I'm used to mistakes. Did you sign?
ELKINS. Here you are.
(*As we watch Mr. Elkins sauntering towards his office, we get a general view of the plant and a glimpse of Mr. Elkins on the telephone*)
ELKINS. Hi, Mr. O'Malley, what can I do for you?

ON SCREEN 2

(*The offices at Designs Unlimited. They consist of cubicles, one for Mr. Elkins, another for Mrs. Elkins, the third for the secretary. The furniture and equipment are strictly hand-me-down; fabric samples are everywhere; the walls are covered with paperwork, calendars and a few faded posters and picture-postcards suggestive of brief and forgotten holidays; file cabinets overflow with more paperwork. Mrs. Elkins is answering the telephone over the noises of the shop. We catch only snatches, like:*)

MRS. ELKINS. I tell you we can't before April 20! (*To the secretary*) Barbara! Get me the Singleton file! (*Back to the phone*) Let me look it up again. Hold on a minute!
(*We move on to Mr. Elkins, in conference with the foreman*)
ELKINS. Let's reschedule the Leeds chair so we can make up another Langdale order. They've been after us for a dozen more of the Monicas.
FOREMAN. Either that new salesman of yours is a whiz-kid—what's his name again?
ELKINS. Collins.

A BEAUTIFUL INVESTMENT

FOREMAN. Right. Andy Collins. Or else we're doing something right.

ELKINS. For good old Arizona anyway. Make sure that new girl, you know the one I mean, make sure she puts a ticket on her work plus her initial. She's already forgotten once.

FOREMAN. I'll keep an eye on her, but I've got a hunch she'll be okay.

(The camera takes us towards seven or eight upholsterers working at their benches. Each upholsterer works on a single chair-frame. Several are carefully molding foam onto the wooden elements, others are attaching the sewn fabric over the foam, others are already fastening the material by means of air-staplers. Close-ups of hands and tools concerned in this skilled work. In the background a girl's voice)

GIRL. Who took my scissors?

(Thereupon the camera switches to half a dozen seamstresses, and we discover Mrs. Elkins talking to one of them)

MRS. ELKINS. These welts for instance. You see. The nap isn't going the same way on them. You can see the difference in the color. It wasn't held properly. Make sure the nap goes down all the time you're sewing on it. Feel it. Check your welts when you're finished. Don't put them on anything if the nap isn't going in the same direction all the time. Ok?

SEAMSTRESS. Ok, Mrs. Elkins. Was the boxing I did all right?

MRS. ELKINS. It was fine, Maria.

FOREMAN. Ladies, are you checking your dye-lots? Be sure they're marked, otherwise there'll be a helluva mixup at the end of the line and you know who's gonna catch it from Mrs. Elkins!

MRS. ELKINS. You heard him, ladies. Over here, Antonio.

(Antonio, rolling a dolly, picks up bundles of sewn fabric from a holding bin in the seamstresses' area)

ANTONIO *(to one of the women)*. I don't see nothin' from you here.

SEAMSTRESS. Get out of here, you twerp!

(Laughing, Antonio rolls the dolly to a shelving area, from which one of the upholsterers is just about to pick up a bundle of sewn-up fabric for his work)

WORKER. How's it going, kid?

FOREMAN *(off-camera)*. Dye-lot 64!

ON STAGE 2

(BROXTON and KRAKOWITZ in their office)

KRAKOWITZ. When did the check to O'Malley go out?
BROXTON. It was supposed to go out this morning. Wait. *(Into the intercom)* Mary-Ann? Did you mail out the O'Malley check to New York like I told you? *(We hear Mary-Ann's response, "by Federal Express")* Fine, thank you.
KRAKOWITZ. You didn't forget those $10,000 for the appraisal fee, did you?
BROXTON. No, I didn't.
KRAKOWITZ. Ok. Let's go over these notes. I sat up half the night with them.
BROXTON. You look it! *(They laugh)* I'd better pour you a cup of coffee.
KRAKOWITZ. Good idea. Hey, what happened to the powdered stuff, the Cremora or what d'you call it?
BROXTON. It seems to have wound up in my drawer. Here you are.
KRAKOWITZ. Thanks. You too?
BROXTON. Right.
KRAKOWITZ. So, how does Rosy like this particular deal?
BROXTON. She's tickled pink.
KRAKOWITZ. Pink. Rosy. *(They laugh)* You shoulda been a nightclub comedian.
BROXTON. Well, let's face it, it's a beauty. Still, explaining that O'Malley owned the place, that Datatronics was leasing it from him, that Designs Unlimited had a sublease from Datatronics, and that we were trying to move Datatronics out of the picture wasn't all that easy.
KRAKOWITZ. Well, as long as she likes the bottom line.... Let's see now. The way I figure it, between payments to O'Malley and Tustin, and assuming the boat don't rock too much in the next three years, we're headed into a shortfall of $176,500. That's interest only to George and interest and principal to Tustin, with 5% thrown in for contingencies. Those are the big parameters. We'll do better if the interest rates keep level or go down, but that's up to Washington and I'm not counting on it.
BROXTON *(writing on a pad)*. Got it.
KRAKOWITZ. Accounting and legal expenses, $8,250.
BROXTON. You being the accounting and me the legal expenses.
KRAKOWITZ. Right. Travel, I estimated $11,800 to inspect the property as needed.

BROXTON. Fair enough. I'll send you, you're not married anymore.

KRAKOWITZ. Insurance—

BROXTON. I thought Datatronics carried full insurance.

KRAKOWITZ. What's full insurance? They carry insurance, but I studied the policy and it ain't enough. Besides, I insured us for rent loss too. You know my motto, Mel: Extra-careful is just careful enough. So I asked Dave—

BROXTON. Which Dave? Your cousin Dave Epstein?

KRAKOWITZ. Yeah. I asked him to cover us for—

BROXTON. Forget the details; I trust you.

KRAKOWITZ. Of course you can't get decent coverage for earthquakes, floods, you know, the catastrophes.

BROXTON. Is Florida earthquake country?

KRAKOWITZ. Oh no. I don't think so. I never heard of an earthquake in Florida. Have you?

BROXTON. I haven't paid attention. Anyway, how much for Dave?

KRAKOWITZ. $7,000.

BROXTON. Well, Dave is a nice guy. What about our management fee? You didn't overdo it, did you? Don't forget I'm putting my mother and my in-laws into this deal.

KRAKOWITZ. And what about my sister and her husband? What a guy! I put us down for ten thou. Over three years, I figure that's more than fair.

BROXTON. That it is. I feel good about that. I mean, ten thousand for managing, for both of us, over three years—

KRAKOWITZ. Should I have—?

BROXTON. No no, I like it that way. Looks good. I feel good about it.

KRAKOWITZ. Of course I put in $26,000 for consulting, I mean with reference to the partnership, the tax planning, the whole goddam structure, thousands of hours, let's face it.

BROXTON. We still owe Bill Kievers $4,000 for his consultation fee.

KRAKOWITZ. I've got $4,200 here in my notes.

BROXTON. Right. The point is, I mean for the additional partners, that the tax set-up is half the beauty of this deal, and you don't create a tax situation of this magnitude for nothing. Next?

KRAKOWITZ. Reserves, a hundred thousand, which God willing we'll never need, and the $120,000 of immediate distribution to the Initial Partners.

BROXTON. Total?

KRAKOWITZ. $460,000.

BROXTON. This means we break it up into ten units of $46,000 each, nice and easy. What's $46,000? We should try to sell two units at a time. It doesn't matter, but I figure the fewer partners the less trouble.

KRAKOWITZ. Myra will want two units for sure, and I've had feelers already from her neighbors. You remember the Blooms, don't you?

BROXTON. Weren't they at her wedding?

KRAKOWITZ. That's right. He was the guy who balanced the empty champagne bottle on his nose.

BROXTON. How could I forget.

KRAKOWITZ. They were real good to me while I was going through the divorce. Had me over for dinner twice, set me up with a few dates....

BROXTON. How many units do you think they'll want?

KRAKOWITZ. Two for sure. I want them to get in on this.

BROXTON. Well, mom is good for two. No more, because I want her to diversify. Rosy's folks will take another two, and tomorrow I'll call the Mandel.

KRAKOWITZ. Who are they?

BROXTON. Friends of the family. The wives especially. Adrienne and Rosy do fancy lunches at the Bel Air and places like that while I munch on a lousy sandwich here in the office.

KRAKOWITZ. My heart bleeds for you.

BROXTON. Not that they can basically afford a deal like this, if you know what I mean, but they're on salaries and they're looking for a decent tax-shelter plus eventual appreciation.

KRAKOWITZ. Fine with me. That pretty much sews it up, don't it?

BROXTON. Right. Let me see that pile of papers again, will you? How many projections did you run through the computer?

KRAKOWITZ. Five, with three different resale prices five years from closing of escrow.

BROXTON. Looks good. I'll take the figures home.

KRAKOWITZ. Good idea. You know something?

BROXTON. What?

KRAKOWITZ. This deal has gone almost too smooth. It worries me. Remember the Pacoima property?

BROXTON. Don't remind me. I still get nightmares.

ON SCREEN 3

(The camera inspects the cutter at his long cutting table, in conference with Mr. Elkins)

CUTTER. What do you think? There must be 15 to 18 yards of this stuff fu—mucked up, I'd say.
ELKINS. Let's see how bad it really is.
CUTTER. I could cut around it, but—
ELKINS. Yeah, and waste I don't know, $500 worth of material, not to mention your time.
CUTTER. You in a rush for this?
ELKINS. Well, yes and no. I like to be ahead. Look at this! Geez, talk about quality control.
CUTTER. Usually they're ok.
ELKINS. Roll it up and I'll send it back. I figure we'll get it replaced in a couple of weeks, and I can live with that. Did you finish cutting the Paradise Magenta?
CUTTER. I finished that one yesterday. Maybe you need a couple extra girls at the sewing machines. These layers just seem to melt ever since we got our knife fixed.
(The secretary emerges from her office)
SECRETARY. Mr. Elkins, there's a guy on the phone who wants to talk to you about Italian frames.
ELKINS. Did you tell him we already import from Italy?
SECRETARY. I did; he says he knows but he has another line he thinks you'll like.
ELKINS. Ok, I'm coming!
(As he saunters toward the office, the camera sweeps toward the foreman, who is testing nearly finished chairs—their backs are not made up—by sitting in them, checking the straightness and smoothness of the fabric, etc. Past the foreman, the camera focuses in on the springer, who, taking chair and sofa frames from stacks, busily attaches the springs to them. Near him several sprung frames are waiting to be upholstered, and behind him we see a large storage area for fabrics)
VOICE. Gimme a hand, will you?
VOICE. Antonio!
(Several toots from a horn)
VOICES. Lunch-wagon!
VOICE. Pick that up, you wonkhead! You ate breakfast, didn't you?
(We follow the general rush towards the lunch-wagon parked at the loading dock. In Elkins'

office, Mrs. Elkins is unwrapping some sandwiches)
MR. ELKINS. I need a rest! And so do you, sweetie.
(*He lights his pipe*)
MRS. ELKINS. How about selling out and retiring to the Bahamas?
MR. ELKINS (*laughing*). Sure!
(*A worker is stapling flounces to nearly finished chairs. The foreman passes by and checks for straightness and even pleats. He gives the worker a friendly pat on the back. Elsewhere, standing up at a boxing machine—a box is the lateral strip of fabric going on a cushion—a seamstress is feeding her material attentively into the machine so that the welts will be sewn on straight. Close-up of the basket into which the welted boxing falls. The camera cuts to Mr. Elkins on the telephone, puffing at his pipe*)
ELKINS. I appreciate your calling. Most buyers don't bother: I know we're all right if I just don't hear nothing from them. Fine. I'm glad. Well, you know, these people, most of 'em, they've been with the firm gosh I don't even know how many years. Exactly. You want repeat orders, we tell 'em, do the work right and do it right the first time. Sure, we check for pitch, each unit.
(*In Mrs. Elkins' office, a well-dressed buyer is looking over a catalogue*)
MRS. ELKINS. We've been manufacturing this couch for five years; it's one of our best sellers.
BUYER. Can you make it up in all three sizes?
MRS. ELKINS. Any size you want.
BUYER. Is the Executive model on page 24 the one Speck and Speck bought from you a couple of years ago?
MRS. ELKINS. A couple of years and ever since. As a matter of fact, you can look at some on the floor right now. But there's a slightly modified type you might like. Wait, let me show you.
(*The camera looks in on the secretary, who is typing a letter and muttering to herself*)
SECRETARY. Yours very untruly if you really want to know my mind.
(*Her telephone rings*)
SECRETARY. Designs Unlimited of Orlando, hello. Oh, hi there; everything's fine, thank you; sure; I'll page him, he must be somewhere on the floor. Hold the phone.
(*She rises and goes to her door*)
SECRETARY. Mr. Elkins!
(*Over her shoulders, at some distance, we see Mr. Elkins arguing a point with the foreman over some documents on a clipboard*)
ELKINS. What now?
SECRETARY. It's Mr. Broxton on the phone in L.A.!
ELKINS. Who?
SECRETARY. Mr. Broxton. Mel Broxton. God.

ELKINS. God? In that case tell him I'll be with him in a minute.
SECRETARY. Ok.
(*Elkins pursues his argument with the foreman*)
SECRETARY. He'll be right over, Mr. Broxton.
(*She goes on typing her letter. As Elkins saunters into his office to pick up the telephone, the camera proceeds outward onto the floor for an overview, including the foreman now arguing with the cutter over the same documents, as we hear Elkins' voice behind us*)
ELKINS. Good to hear from you, Mr. Broxton. What can I do for you? ... No doubt about it.... Right.... Well, it's a nuisance all right; who likes holes in his parking lot? So? Aha.... Say that again? ... I see.... I see.... A third?... Sure we'll think it over.

ON STAGE 4

(*In Louella Broxton's upper-class condominium. Louella is lying comfortably on a couch wrapped in a blanket and reading a giant art book. Friendly knock at the door*)

VOICE OF BROXTON. Anybody home?
LOUELLA. Only your mother. (*Enter Broxton*)
BROXTON. Hi mom. Have I got great news! (*Kisses her*) But first I want my usual.
LOUELLA. I think it's ready. Mary-Belle!
VOICE OF MARY-BELLE. Yes, Mrs. Broxton!
LOUELLA. My son is here.
DITTO. Everything's sitting on the tray; I'll be there in a jiffy.
BROXTON. I can't wait to tell you the news!
LOUELLA (*always placid*). And I can't wait to hear it. But you said after the coffee. Have you called Rosy about it whatever it is?
BROXTON. Of course. We're dining at the La Vrai Bistro to celebrate.
LOUELLA. The one in le vrai Beverly Hills?
BROXTON. Right. Well—and how are you? Did you just come back from the museum?
LOUELLA. About an hour ago. The Giacometti exhibit is opening on June 24, so we're required to bone up before we start showing the Mels and Rosys around.
BROXTON. Let's see. (*Whistling*) Now I know what skinny means! This guy never lived in Southern California.

A BEAUTIFUL INVESTMENT

BROXTON. Hi old chum.
MARY-BELLE. Hi Mr. Broxton. How are Mrs. Broxton and the kids?
BROXTON. Everybody's fab, and Bimsy is learning to surf. How's the arthritis in the left index?
MARY-BELLE. The arthritis is ruining my life, Mr. Broxton, but otherwise I'm getting on ok.
BROXTON. Well, that's what counts.
MARY-BELLE. Anything else, Mrs. Broxton? Here's your real cream, and the powder for Mr. Broxton.
LOUELLA. Thank you, Mary-Belle.
MARY-BELLE. See you all later.
(*Exit*)
BROXTON (*after her*). Try aerobics! (*To Louella*) Shall I pour? See how I can draw things out too? (*He pours*)
LOUELLA. Thank you, dear, and help yourself to the cookies.
BROXTON. I'd better not. Well!
LOUELLA. Well?
BROXTON. We have—hold your breath—an offer on the Orlando property!
LOUELLA. How sweet.
BROXTON. How sweet! I am toiling night and day to make you rich.
LOUELLA. I'm rich already.
BROXTON. Twice as rich, and you hardly pay attention.
LOUELLA. I delegate my attention to you, dear. Too many attentions spoil the broth. I hope the offer was a good one.
BROXTON. Two million five! And from Equitable, so it's not some hot air balloon.
LOUELLA. Is that a lot more than we paid for it?
BROXTON. Almost 20% over! Just as I predicted at the start!
LOUELLA. Very nice. They must really like Orlando.
BROXTON. They got to like it real well after they heard through the grapevine that Datatronics wasn't exercising their option to renew.
LOUELLA. To renew what?
BROXTON. Oh my God, you've forgotten again. Not to renew their lease. We're the landlords now, we'll be collecting rent and calling the shots, the partners, that's you, won't have to put up the final capital installment on the partnership, and D. U. which doesn't have an option to renew, will either bleed a little or else look for other quarters.
LOUELLA. Is that nice of us?
BROXTON. They can afford it, believe me; they're paying a solid 10% under market right now.

LOUELLA. Poor D.U.... What does D.U. stand for?
BROXTON. Designs Unlimited.
LOUELLA. How interesting. And what does Designs Unlimited do for the happiness of mankind?
BROXTON. They build museums full of Giacomettis.
LOUELLA. No, really, Mel. I want to know who I'm evicting or whom.
BROXTON. You're not evicting a soul, because they're sure to pay the reasonable rent you're going to ask for; and they make furniture.
LOUELLA. Well, mankind does need furniture. I'm glad. Maybe Rosy and I should buy some of it. Do they make tables and chairs, marble and glass things, upholstered pieces?
BROXTON. Who cares? They're reliable, that much I can tell you. I seem to remember they make upholstered furniture.
LOUELLA. Traditional? Contemporary? Nice? Vulgar?
BROXTON. What kind of questions are those?
LOUELLA. I don't know. Simple questions, I guess.
BROXTON. And what has all this got to do with what we're doing?
LOUELLA. Nothing; I'm quite sure of that. Hand me a cookie. I don't know whether Giacometti would have approved.
BROXTON. The point I hope you won't forget is that our investment is flourishing. D.U.'s only a phase, for us or for the next buyer, Equitable or whoever. Because that chunk of land is hot, and I'm not sure we shouldn't build on it ourselves in a year or two.
LOUELLA (*still placid*). A year or two? Why not five? I haven't seen a penny so far, and God only knows how many months have gone by.
BROXTON. Are you serious or are you putting on an act?
LOUELLA. I won't know until I've introspected.
BROXTON (*pulling out papers*). Look, mom. In the first year you put in $42,000.
LOUELLA. I remember. It was a wrench.
BROXTON. That year the paper loss amounted—for you, for the Mandels, for Rosy's folks, for everybody—to about $34,000 a piece. Since you're in the 50% bracket, you saved about $17,000 in taxes. The following year you paid in $13,200 and you saved over $18,000 in taxes. The year after that—
LOUELLA. Et cetera, et cetera. Oscar told me the other night that we're a gang of parasites battening on honest work. I had the Mandels over for dinner with the Dudleys, remember?
BROXTON (*good-humored*). The son of a bitch! I'm pouring money into his beggar's cap and he insults me! Do you think I would have let him take his two units if Rosy hadn't begged me to invest their scroungy savings? If Adrienne wasn't a good-looking girl—

LOUELLA. He said he was sorry he wasn't a playwright.

BROXTON. A playwright? Why?

LOUELLA. Because he'd write a comedy about us. It sounded ever so funny. The Dudleys were in stitches. You know how brilliant he is.

BROXTON. I do? How come I never noticed before? On what he makes as a schoolteacher!

LOUELLA. He said he'd write a series of scenes showing how all of us are pocketing gobs of money wheeling and dealing, and in between—I mean in between the scenes—you know, the scenes of wheeling and dealing—he'd have a screen come down in front or in back of the stage or some place and show a movie of the really productive goings on at the factory, workers at work, trucks loading and unloading, "virtuous capitalism" he called it.

BROXTON. The guy is crazy.

LOUELLA. Not minding our shenanigans a bit, just producing, producing the goods and making the decent profit they deserve.

BROXTON (*still good-humored*). The son of a bitch. And doesn't he object to being a parasite himself?

LOUELLA. That's what Peggy Dudley asked him, and he said he does, but he doesn't enough.

BROXTON. Ha ha ha ha! I like that! And what was he going to call his brilliant play?

LOUELLA. "The Fabulous Transaction" or some such. But now you know why I asked you what they make at the factory or warehouse or whatever. He didn't know, and I didn't know. And of course our not knowing, and your not knowing, was going to be part of the comedy. I can call him up now and tell him about the upholstered furniture.

BROXTON. In other words, you'd be willing to feed the jackal who wants to tear your son to pieces.

LOUELLA. That's right. Reach me one more cookie, will you? What with the cookies and the tax write-offs, you're nourishing the mother who would feed the jackal who wants to tear her son to pieces.

BROXTON. Good thing for him he's not a playwright. I'd sue the little bastard for every dime he's making off of me. Seriously, mom, now that Datatronics is out of the picture, I can practically promise the partners that, besides not having to put up the last ten thousand, they can be pretty sure of a cash distribution within the year. That's not a promise, it's not a guarantee, but it's practically a certainty.

LOUELLA. That's my Mel. I wish your dad could have seen the day.

BROXTON. Well, I'd better be on my way. Any message for Rosy?

LOUELLA. Tell her I love her. And thank you, dear, for stopping by with the news.

BROXTON. It was a pleasure. (*He kisses Louella and goes*) So long, Mary-Belle! Thanks for the coffee!

VOICE OF MARY-BELLE. Good-bye, Mr. Broxton! Regards to the family and specially to Bimsy! I hope he enjoys his surfing!

ON SCREEN 5

(*Mr. Elkins is talking to the springer*)

ELKINS. I've been on the phone with the customs broker. We're picking up those frames around 10 A.M. tomorrow, so you can schedule them for right after lunch.

SPRINGER. I look forward to that batch, Mr. Elkins. They're made solid. It's a pleasure.

(*The camera moves on to the cutter, whose electric knife is slicing through layers of fabric. Antonio is picking up bundles of ticketed fabric and dollying them to the seamstresses. Mrs. Elkins is checking flouncing as the foreman did before. Mr. Elkins joins her*)

ELKINS. Those two dye lots from Burlingame came out so different

MRS. ELKINS. You mean that Bristol linen again?

ELKINS. No, those were pretty even. I mean that green celadon what-you-call-it they sent over. One of the lots looks pink to me if you really want to know.

MRS. ELKINS. I guess I noticed it too. Well, the girls will have to be extra careful. We ought to put up a big sign for them: ONE BUNDLE, ONE DYE LOT. I hate it when—

(*The foreman approaches*)

FOREMAN. Those couches came out perfect. Not a flaw in the lot of them.

ELKINS. Good. One less wrinkle in my face.

(*The camera wanders in a leisurely manner towards the secretary, who is again typing a letter and muttering to herself*)

SECRETARY. One t or two t's? Two looks nicer. (*Close up on rapid typing*)

ON STAGE 5

(In Broxton's office. Broxton, Krakowitz and Ralph Peckam)

PECKAM. You got some of that powdered polyester cream?
BROXTON. Here it is.
PECKAM. Doctor's orders, you know. Besides, it tastes better than dairy cream.
BROXTON. I think so too. But shouldn't we celebrate this with a bottle of bourbon? Mary-Ann keeps one in her cupboard for special occasions.
PECKAM. Not at 11 A.M., Mel, but thanks anyway.
BROXTON. You know, you could have knocked me over with a feather when Sol greeted me with the news
KRAKOWITZ. Yeah, you should have seen his face. He came in maybe ten minutes after I'd hung up. I says to him, "Guess what, Mel?" And he says, "You're engaged to a girl from Yemen," and I say "Better than that, Ralph Peckam wants to buy Orlando." "What," he says, "Ralph Peckam, Rosy's cousin?"
BROXTON. I never expected—
PECKAM. Sure, but sooner or later it was bound to happen. The residential market has just about caved in. I've been flopping around like a fish outa water. So I say to myself, "Broxton is in industrial, why shouldn't Peckam be in industrial too?" Besides, dealing with you, well, you know, I guess I feel you'll be straight with a cousin of Rosy's on the Indiana side.
BROXTON. We'll be straight with you all right, provided you don't expect any special favors. Business is business.
PECKAM. I'm not asking for special favors. But here's an example of what I mean. I didn't want to ask you on the telephone, but it's an important question.
BROXTON. Shoot.
PECKAM. Have any of them internal revenuers come snooping around this deal over the years? It's only fair you should tell me now and give me an out.
BROXTON. Would I conceal that kind of a booby trap from you or from any buyer for that matter? Come on, Ralph, give me a little credit, will you?
PECKAM. Sorry, but—
BROXTON. Anyway, you can relax. The tax picture is spotless. Krakowitz and I structured this deal 100% legitimate; there hasn't been an audit within twenty miles of it.

KRAKOWITZ. There might have been one, you know, if Congress hadn't killed the Bradley-Martinez bill—because of that 277% write off in the third year, you know. But once that was squashed in committee—good thing the Republicans were in charge.

PECKAM. Fine, I won't give it another worry. Now, as I was saying before, I'm not asking for any favors. Just lemme hear the facts again.

BROXTON. The main fact, my friend, is that we turned down a bid for two million eight hundred thousand, which gives you a five-minute opening to get your hands on this gorgeous investment.

PECKAM. I know, I know.

BROXTON. But the Tustin balance is coming due—

PECKAM. How much is left of that again?

BROXTON. Over four hundred thousand, and coming due in eight months. We have to move fast, either sell or refinance, and remember, we can refinance any moment and make a handsome distribution to the partnership.

PECKAM. Well, I'm not gonna beat around the bush. I trust you. And I've got cash sitting in my lap, more than I know what to do with right now. I'll give you the two million nine, provided you fix the roof and pay the insurance premiums for two years like I agreed with Sol.

KRAKOWITZ. We can live with that. And you'll get the property in A-1 ship-shape hotsy-totsy condition.

PECKAM. Fine. We're talking about $800,000 down, I take over your first which is—damn, I forgot again.

BROXTON. A million and a half. Keep in mind we've been paying interest only on this note. Parker has okayed your assuming the debt at 6% plus a point.

PECKAM (*using his pocket calculator*). Eight hundred thousand down, a million five makes two million three, which leaves six hundred thou in paper for you, amortized over ten years.

KRAKOWITZ (*consulting a document*) Quote, at 4% over the monthly Weighted Average Cost of Funds for Eleventh District Savings Insti tutions, as published by the Federal Home Loan Bank, and to be adjusted monthly, unquote.

PECKAM. Tough, fellas, tough.

BROXTON. Maybe so. But more than manageable. Designers Unlimited is good for another 5% rent hike in January, and I don't have to tell you about Orlando. The place is going crazy. In another five years they'll want to knock down that dumb factory for an insurance skyscraper or a shopping mall. Send us a box of chocolates when that happens, will you?

PECKAM. Well, the deal looks ok. Besides, I like the fact that we've cut out the brokerage commissions et cetera, and that Rosy's folks are gonna be ahead too.

BROXTON. We're all glad for them, after that stroke he suffered.

PECKAM. I guess the papers are drawn up, aren't they?

KRAKOWITZ. They'll be ready tomorrow morning. I think we should unglue that bottle of bourbon at this point.

PECKAM (*looking at his watch*). At this point, why not? A quick one before lunch.

BROXTON (*into the intercom*). Mary-Ann, bring in the bourbon, will you, and a pitcher of water, ice, and three glasses, ok? Thanks. I've made reservations for the three of us at Yamato. It's close by and I remember you like Japanese food.

PECKAM. What I like best in Japanese restaurants is taking off my shoes!

(*Mary-Ann enters with the drinks*)

MARY-ANN. This all right, Mr. Broxton?

BROXTON. Perfect. Thank you. Lock up if you want to and take your lunch break; we'll be going out shortly ourselves, but Wendy will take calls.

MARY-ANN. Ok then. I'll be on my way.

(*She leaves*)

PECKAM. I don't know. I take 'em a lot younger.

BROXTON. Bad for concentration.

PECKAM. What was I gonna say? Oh yeah—remember I gotta run down to Palms to talk to my manager before lunch.

BROXTON. I didn't forget. I made our reservation for twelve-thirty.

KRAKOWITZ. Is that the 42 units you own down there?

PECKAM. Yeah. Now and then I take a look around, though I trust the old guy. Ok boys, fill up. No water, thank you.

BROXTON. Sol?

KRAKOWITZ. Half and half.

BROXTON. Well, here's to us, and to a beautiful investment all around.

KRAKOWITZ and PECKAM. To a beautiful investment.

BROXTON. Another round?

PECKAM. No, thanks. That was great. Ok fellas, see you later.

BROXTON. Tell you what. We'll wait for you down in the lobby at twelve fifteen.

PECKAM. Fine, I'll be there. So long.

BROXTON and KRAKOWITZ. See you.

(*Exit. A pause*)

BROXTON. Well.

KRAKOWITZ. Well.

BROXTON. I'm sort of proud of us.
KRAKOWITZ. Just what I was thinking.
BROXTON. I did well, you did well, Peckam is doing well, the partners will be doing well, what more does anybody want?
KRAKOWITZ. And you know something else?
BROXTON. What?
KRAKOWITZ. You're gonna laugh at me.
BROXTON. No, I'm not, I swear. What else?
KRAKOWITZ. It's a great country.
BROXTON. Is that what?
KRAKOWITZ. Yeah. It's a great country!
BROXTON. Sure.
KRAKOWITZ. Everybody contributing and getting their reward. My granpa was a tailor in Poland. Can you imagine?
BROXTON. Mine was a solicitor in Liverpool.
KRAKOWITZ. See what I mean? Soliciting. From nothin. That's why I think this Reno Nevada package is worth looking into. We might lose our shirts, but we could wind up making a killing.
BROXTON. I'll study it some more tonight.
KRAKOWITZ. Two twenty-eight per square foot in an area that's worth a good two ninety, and that's net, net, net.
BROXTON. Net, net, net?
KRAKOWITZ. Yeah. Net, net, net.
BROXTON. Hm. Net, net, net. (*They dream*)

ON SCREEN 6

(*Crates are being loaded onto the truck. Mr. Elkins is talking to the truck-driver*)

ELKINS. You stick to your route no matter what.
TRUCK-DRIVER. But suppose they haven't opened up the exit ramp from the 607? Shouldn't I make my drop at Ozick Limited first?
ELKINS. No way. That's just what I'm trying to explain to you. Major emergency? Ok. Call me, but don't change the route on your own.
TRUCK-DRIVER. I hear you.
(*The secretary appears*)
SECRETARY. Mr. Elkins!

A BEAUTIFUL INVESTMENT

ELKINS. What now?
SECRETARY. It's Mr. Peckam long distance.
ELKINS. Who?
SECRETARY. Mr. Peckam. Ralph Peckam. The landlord.
ELKINS. Tell him to hold his horses; I'm coming.
(*A worker has approached Mr. Elkins*)
WORKER. Do I load that damaged chair that's been sitting here a week, Mr. Elkins?
ELKINS. Geez, I'd forgotten all about that chair. Ask Mike whether it's ok with him. He's in the cab, I think.
WORKER. Will do.
(*The camera is now high above the shop floor, though we see Elkins sauntering toward his office. We catch sight of Mrs. Elkins gesticulating with one of the upholsterers over a couch in the works, we fly past the busy seamstresses, then, still from on high, and at a distance, we see and hear Mr. Elkins*)
ELKINS. Mr. Peckam, Elkins speaking, what can I do for you?... Oh, not bad. We've seen better days, but then who hasn't, and we've seen worse. What's on your mind? (*To Mrs. Elkins, who has just come in*) As if I didn't know.
(*The camera sweeps on, and returns to the loading dock just in time to show the back panel being noisily shut. The truck departs. It diminishes in the distance, passes through the perimeter gate, and exits onto the highway beyond*)

The End

Note

This is a slightly revised version of the comedy as is appeared in my 1993 *The Virgin and the Unicorn: Four Plays*. I quote from the Preface: "I am thankfully indebted for all its manufacturing lore to Mrs. Eve Heyman, who, together with her late husband, owned the business I describe...and had the kindness to expend several of her crowded hours teaching me how it works." As for the real estate matter, my easy guess is that my information was mostly due to the technical know-how of my long-dead partners in a few ventures, Rudy Cordova and Al Werner. Today, ages later, I no longer understand my own words in these passages. My readers need not understand them either.

In years to come the dollar figures in the play may be raised in production in order to remain realistic.

THE ONE WHO DIDN'T DIE

On a bien le droit d'avoir une opinion sur sa propre mort.

CÉLINE

CHARACTERS

Pierre Dupont
Robert Tavrac
Stella Tavrac
Boris Selvin
Underground fighters

Captain Ollendorf
Private Kalk
Private Lembo
Colonel Frank

The Jailer
The General
The Prefect

SCENE ONE

(An abandoned barn. Captain Ollendorff is sitting behind a small table set up for the occasion. The two prisoners, Robert Tavrac and Pierre Dupont, their wrists tied, are standing in front of the table, guarded by Private Kalk. After the lights go on, there is a period of immobile silence, followed by a shot outside. Tavrac does not wince. Dupont moans)

CAPTAIN. Number two. (*He crosses a name off a sheet before him, and affects to rummage through a few documents*) Next. Monsieur—let me see—Tavrac—Robert Tavrac. Tavrac?

TAVRAC. Yes.

CAPTAIN. I repeat my questions. Where is Boris Selvin? Where are his accomplices? Where did they go after leaving the Center Garage?

TAVRAC. I don't know. I demand to know why I was pulled out of my bed at three o'clock in the morning.

CAPTAIN. *You* were pulled out, Tavrac, make a note of that. We left your wife on the mattress. I hope you won't force us—to go further?

TAVRAC. I can't tell you what I don't know. I heard the explosion like everybody else. I didn't know what it was. Next thing I was arrested.

CAPTAIN. Not exactly next thing. In between, Selvin and his men found their way to your garage, and were conveyed out of it again to a destination known to you. Why deny it? We have our friends in town, and they report to us.

TAVRAC. I've never seen Selvin. He's just a name, a name I respect, I respect him, but I've never set eyes on him. You're trying to get speech out of stones, Captain.

CAPTAIN. Our political officers have ways of making even stones talkative, my friend. Consider yourself lucky you are in the hands of a regular soldier like me. I am reluctant to turn you over—sheer humanity! Come now, let's start again. Four of you knew where he and his accomplices are at this moment. Now only two of you know. Are we agreed so far?

TAVRAC. No.

CAPTAIN. What do you mean? I see only *two* of you left.

TAVRAC. None of us knows a thing.

CAPTAIN. Us? None of *us?* You *know* that the two corpses outside knew nothing? You *know* that your friend here knows nothing?

TAVRAC. I know *I* know nothing.

CAPTAIN. You're the peaceful manager of a garage, Robert Tavrac. You hate us, but quietly. Your record is downright virginal, not a blot on it. Yet in three minutes you will be dead in a ditch. In an hour or two your Stella will be informed, but she will not receive your body. Your body belongs to us. It will vanish. And Boris Selvin will be downing his apéritif ten years, twenty years from now with *his* Stella—or even yours, why not? A widow, after all. He will wipe a tear off a corner of his eye and say: "Those fine comrades who died for me!" And you will be delicately decomposed in the sour ditch. Unrecognizable! Bones with a few shreds of flesh, while the world is having dinner! Look at me, Tavrac. I'll make peace with you. With both of you. You tell me where to dig out Selvin, quietly, nothing in writing, and I'll let it be known that it was, number two out there— what was her name? Anna Tommasini—who talked. She talked, and we removed her, sent her to prison in Germany. And number one, well, he was shot. Reprisals. Forgotten already. There are so many human beings in the world, gentlemen. I take an oath, as an officer of the German army, Ollendorf by name, nobody will know. I'll send you both home, you'll go back to bed and sleep it all off. Your friend, now, I can see he realizes I'm talking sense.

TAVRAC (*grim, to Dupont*). Don't let Ollenshit wheedle you. A mess of words.

CAPTAIN (*suddenly shouts*). Where is Selvin?

TAVRAC (*shouts back*). Go to hell!

CAPTAIN (*to Kalk*). Hit him!

(*Tavrac falls*)

TAVRAC. Go to hell!

CAPTAIN. Hit him! Where is Selvin?

TAVRAC. Go to hell! Go to hell!

CAPTAIN. Hit him!

DUPONT. Stop—stop—

CAPTAIN. Where is Selvin?

(*Tavrac is almost unconscious*)

TAVRAC (*weakly*).

DUPONT. We don't know. We don't know nothing.

DUPONT. Have pity.

CAPTAIN. I'm through with him. (*To Kalk*) Call Lembo and take him out.

KALK. Excuse me, sir. Same as the other two?

CAPTAIN. Yes. Go on.

KALK. All right, you. Get up.
DUPONT (*to Ollendorff*). He doesn't know; I see him every day, and I swear he doesn't know!
CAPTAIN. Kalk! Don't just stand there.
KALK. No, sir. Come on. Out. (*Calling*) Lembo! (*Private Lembo enters the barn*) Same as the others. (*Lembo grabs Tavrac*)
TAVRAC. Let me write to my wife!
CAPTAIN. Take him away.
TAVRAC (*struggling*). Pierre, Pierre— tell her—
DUPONT. He doesn't know! Don't kill him!
(*Tavrac is dragged out. The barn door is banged shut. Kalk returns to Dupont. Another frozen silence. Then the voice of Tavrac:* "Swine! Dirty butchers! Long live—" *stopped by a shot*)
CAPTAIN. Number three. (*Dupont moans. Ollendorf crosses out a name*) One moment a man. Next moment, a nothing. Horrible. Now you: Pierre Dupont.
DUPONT. I don't know anything—I've got nothing to say—believe me—
CAPTAIN (*soothingly*). Come, come. We are alone now. The witnesses are gone, eh? (*He winks*) Kalk, move along to the door and stay there. You are safe, Dupont. There is no shame when you are not watched by somebody. And I'm nobody; a nameless foreign officer who'll flit out of your life as though he'd never existed. Do you understand me, Dupont?
DUPONT. Yes.
CAPTAIN. Nobody will ever know who talked. We'll send you to a camp deep in Germany. It will not be pleasant. It will be far from pleasant. But I sense that you wouldn't want it to be pleasant. Call it your penance. When the war is over, you can return clean to your people. Just a word, Dupont, the name of a street, a house, a village; one word, and all's over.
DUPONT (*low*). I don't know anything. What's the use of killing me?
CAPTAIN. A train blew up. We lost eighteen men, and an enormous amount of petroleum. We have to shoot hostages anyway.
DUPONT. But why me? Suppose I did know—
CAPTAIN. Ah.
DUPONT. Suppose it—that's all I said—then if you killed me, you'd never find out. But if you don't, there's always a chance that I'll—don't you see? Do you follow my reasoning? There's always a chance for you—
CAPTAIN (*still mild*). A reasoner! But if you reason with me, I'll have to reason right back with you. Reason tells me to turn you over to our political officer. Shall I tell you about our Captain Neihart?
DUPONT (*low*). I already know.

CAPTAIN. Sometimes one doesn't know whether to cringe or laugh. This pumping air into you with a bicycle pump, or making you swallow gallons of water, or ripping your nails out, or burning out an eye. Sometimes it isn't funny anymore.

DUPONT (*almost inaudibly*). Be human, I am a human being.

CAPTAIN. What did you say? But after all, that is what you yourself were asking. To be kept alive just in case. Whereas my way is more civilized. Kalk, come here. Take Mr. Dupont to the window. Allow him to see his three friends, so undignified in a heap.

(*Kalk pushes Dupont to the window*)

KALK. Come along. Open your eyes. (*Slaps him*) I said open your eyes!

CAPTAIN (*changing his tone*). No what?

KALK. Answer!

DUPONT. You are not bluffing.

CAPTAIN. You are not bluffing—who?

DUPONT. I don't understand.

CAPTAIN. You're talking to an officer, you scum!

DUPONT. Sir.

CAPTAIN. You are not bluffing, sir!

KALK. Repeat, damn you.

DUPONT. You are not bluffing, sir.

CAPTAIN. That's better. And now I am going to ask you my question for the last time. Where is Boris Selvin?

(*Silence*)

CAPTAIN. Call Private Lembo.

DUPONT. No—wait—

CAPTAIN. For what? If you don't know, I don't need you. Call Lembo.

KALK (*at the door*). Lembo! Come in. Number four.

(*Enter Lembo*)

CAPTAIN. Relish your last seconds, Pierre.

CAPTAIN. Carry out the execution.

LEMBO. Yes, sir. All right, you.

DUPONT. Wait—not yet—

LEMBO. Get going.

DUPONT. Wait! Wait! I'll talk, I'll talk!

CAPTAIN. All right. Talk!

DUPONT. The farm! Les Pins! Route 31—

CAPTAIN. Is it the whole gang?

DUPONT. I don't know. I think so. Oh God, oh God. (*He is near collapse*)

CAPTAIN (*to Kalk*). Give the information to Captain Jahmann. On the double.

(*Exit Kalk, running*) All right, Lembo, take him to the infirmary—keep him there—and give him a bowl of soup.

DUPONT. Oh God, what did I do?

LEMBO. On the level, sir?

CAPTAIN. Sure. Cheer up the little man. You can untie him, too.

LEMBO. Yes, sir. Let's go, you lucky dog!

(*He drags Dupont away, sobbing. Ollendorf wipes his brow, gathers up the papers. Enter Colonel Frank*)

CAPTAIN. Sir.

FRANK. At ease, Ollendorf. Sit down. Cigarette? (*He sits on the table*)

CAPTAIN. Thank you, sir. This is one I'm going to enjoy.

FRANK. Ollendorf, you're a magician. I was really skeptical this time. All that psychological bunk. I kept asking myself why didn't we turn the whole damn mess over to Neihart and have done with it.

CAPTAIN. I'm glad we kept him as a last resort, sir.

FRANK (*lifting an imaginary glass*). "Cried the German troopers"—

CAPTAIN (*falling in*). "Hang the Party snoopers!" (*They laugh*)

FRANK. All the same, when you began to shoot your witnesses, my gut was in my mouth. All that information down the bloody drain.

CAPTAIN. Four informants were too many, sir. They kept glaring at each other. I felt I must narrow down to one.

FRANK. Which one was it, by the way? The fellow with the children and grandchildren?

CAPTAIN. No, sir. The one who is all alone in the world.

FRANK (*extremely surprised*). You don't say so! You gambled on a man who's got nothing to live for?

CAPTAIN. I gambled on the man who's got everything to live for.

FRANK. Ollendorf, I'll be sending out a report on this that will make your mother happy. If my voice carries at headquarters—this is between us, Ollendorf—but I've got you down for a citation.

CAPTAIN. I appreciate this, sir.

FRANK. Never mind. One Hessian to another. I hope I can still tell a good man when I've got one. You're a professional, Ollendorf, long live the professionals!

CAPTAIN. Amen. (*Sings*)

> Shine your buckle and your boot,
> Share the lasses and the loot,
> Give Von Kluck a smart salute
> And the French a bloody snoot.

FRANK (*laughing*). Von Kluck? What a name!

CAPTAIN. Yes, Von Kluck. First World War.

FRANK. Write that song down for me. I'll recite it to our Major Baron von Eben dash Eckenbach when he comes back.

CAPTAIN. Where has the major gone, sir, if I may ask?

FRANK. Oh, to the railroad station. Suddenly it became necessary to hop-hop and oversee the unloading of small weapons.

CAPTAIN. I'm sorry. I'm sorry about the whole affair. It shouldn't have happened.

FRANK. It's a mucky situation all right.

CAPTAIN (*offering Frank a cigarette*). Will you try one of mine, sir?

FRANK. Thanks.

CAPTAIN (*lighting the cigarette*). And yet I think I can understand Major von Eben-Eckenbach's—eh—reluctance. I beg your pardon, it's really none of my business.

FRANK. Well I'm making it your business, damn it. Fact is, I need my staff's advice. Goddamned insubordination. (*Ollendorf makes a gesture of protest*) I mean it, Ollendorf. Make no mistake. And I'm gagging over it.

CAPTAIN. Baron von Eben-Eckenbach is a splendid man, though. The best connections in Berlin. And an old name, which he didn't want to besmirch.

FRANK. But you and me without the best connections or the stinking old name can besmirch and beshit our names all we want—is that what you're trying to say?

CAPTAIN. Not that strongly!

FRANK. I'll tell you this much, an order's an order and I'll make him eat his hyphen for disobeying it. Do you know what our nobleman said to me? "Colonel Frank," says he politely. You know? He ought to wear a monocle. "If I decline to obtain information from our hostages by any method not stipulated in the Geneva Convention, will you or will you not have me shot?" (*Ollendorf whistles*) "No," says I, just as polite as him, "no, I will not have you shot; but I won't answer for anything else." "That's all I want to know," says he. "I cannot undertake the interrogation." And if that isn't disobeying an order, I'm a Polish Jew.

CAPTAIN. "Stipulated in the Geneva Convention." I don't know what to say, sir, except that you were damn patient.

FRANK. Listen, join me about ten tonight, will you? Informally, over a cognac. As I said, I've got to sound out the staff.

CAPTAIN. I'll be there, sir.

FRANK. Well, let's move along. Better set up a reception committee for the Selvin gang—in case Jahmann brings 'em back alive.

THE ONE WHO DIDN'T DIE

CAPTAIN. In case.
FRANK. What did you do with the informer?
CAPTAIN. Sent him to the infirmary. I told Lembo to feed him before we send him back to town.
FRANK. All right. What condition is he in, Ollendorf?
CAPTAIN. Alive, sir, alive.

SCENE TWO

(A cage-like cell is partly seen on one side of the stage. Dupont is in it clutching two of its bars and staring at the spectacle which occupies most of the stage: the interior of a farmhouse, occupied by Selvin and his armed co-fighters)

MAN (*loud whisper*). Boris, I see them. Curse God.
MAN. Over there! I told you! There! There! Boris!
SELVIN. Keep away from the windows.
VOICE OUTSIDE (*through megaphone*). Selvin! The farmhouse is surrounded! We know you're in there! Come on out, all of you, the whole gang, hands high, one by one, through the front door. We're giving you five minutes!
MAN. You, get out of the light!
MAN (*at the same time*). Get out of the light, damn you!
SELVIN. Steady, all of you.
VOICE OUTSIDE. Selvin! Come on out, one by one, hands in the sky. You're surrounded! Four minutes and we'll make a bonfire of the lot of you!
MAN. The bastards, oh God oh God.
MAN. I can just make him out. If I could get a crack at him—
MAN. What about the kitchen door?
MAN. Too late.
MAN. Selvin, why don't you say something?
MAN. Another spotlight!
DUPONT (*wailing*). Get out of the light....
MAN. Selvin's given up. Me too. I've done my job, to hell with it and good-bye, sweet universe.
MAN. Shut up, shut up!
VOICE OUTSIDE. Three minutes, Selvin! Get moving. We'll fry you alive, we'll make torches of you. I'm not bluffing, Selvin. Come on out the front door, one by one.

THE ONE WHO DIDN'T DIE

MAN (*hysterical*). What do we do, Boris? Why don't you think of something again?
DUPONT (*moaning*). Please! Think of something....
MAN. Will they shoot if we come out?
SELVIN. They will, my boy.
VOICE OUTSIDE. Two minutes!
MAN. Maybe they won't.
MAN. We've got to take a chance! Somebody yell we're coming out. Boris! You.
MAN. I'm for getting out too—but drilling their guts till we drop—finished.
MAN. Sure—with four toy pistols between us. Lemme out of here right now—
MAN. Hold him!
MAN. Get down—you'll do like the rest of us.
VOICE OUTSIDE. One minute, Selvin! Your last minute. We're ready to go!
MAN. Curse God.
MAN. Tell 'em to wait! Another minute!
DUPONT. Selvin—beg them to wait....
MAN (*hysterical*). Tell 'em we're thinking it over—we're deliberating!
SELVIN. Friends, it doesn't matter anymore.
(*Orders are shouted outside*)
MAN (*hysterical*). This is it. Aaah! They're throwing something! We'll burn alive! Open the door!
DUPONT. Don't go out the door!...
MAN (*in terror*). Selvin!
SELVIN. All right. (*Shouting*) We surrender! You out there! Do you hear me?
VOICE OUTSIDE. We hear you. Keep talking.
SELVIN. We've got enough ammunition to blast you to hell, fire or no fire. Do you guarantee our safety if we pledge to throw away our weapons?
VOICE OUTSIDE. Right you are. We do.
DUPONT. Don't go out....
MAN. Lord, be with us in the agony of death....
VOICE OUTSIDE. You've got sixty seconds, Selvin! Come on out, one by one, hands up!
SELVIN. We are coming out! Repeat that you guarantee our safety!
VOICE OUTSIDE. Don't play with us, Selvin! We guarantee your safety.
MAN. Be with us in the agony of death....
DUPONT. Take them alive! Why not? Why not?
VOICE OUTSIDE. Thirty seconds!
(*A door is thrown open*)
SELVIN. I'll go first. You people follow, one by one. Heads high, do you hear,

heads high! Adieu.
DUPONT (*stretching his arms through the bars*). Must it happen?
(*The fighters walk out the door and vanish from sight*)
VOICE OUTSIDE. Open up!
(*Fusillade and cries. Dupont collapses with a cry*)

SCENE THREE

(*The jail. A gallery, adorned with French flags and a large photograph of Charles de Gaulle. Dupont's cage, fully in view now. Dupont is eating his dinner. Enter the Jailer*)

JAILER. Put down your tray, pal. This is a busy day, and I have something for you. Here.
(*He gives Dupont a piece of paper through the bars*)
DUPONT (*astonished*). Stella Tavrac? Madame Tavrac? She wants to see me?
JAILER. So she says.
DUPONT (*tremulous*). Of course....
JAILER. I asked her to wait until the Prefect and the General are done. In fact, I can hear them. Look nice.
(*Enter the Prefect and the General*)
JAILER. Gentlemen, coffee will be ready for you whenever.
PREFECT. Thanks, Pradelle.
(*Exit the Jailer*)
GENERAL. Every prefecture I visit seems to have its own system, more or less.
PREFECT. So it will be until Paris has settled down and the directives go out to all of us.
GENERAL. Let's recapitulate.
PREFECT. With pleasure. We began in our First Tier where you met with the lowest. More of them than we could wish. Those who collaborated with the Nazis because they were believers. Burn the books. Exterminate the Jews. The thousand-year Reich. The Master Race. We don't starve them, but we do the minimum. And we investigate. Those who went and denounced, and those who have direct blood on their hands are shot.
GENERAL. Be careful about private grudges, private revenges.
PREFECT. Of course. Next you saw those of the Second Tier. Those who

had no love for the Boches but concluded that Hitler was winning the war, the swastika was going to wave over the word, and to make money and advance careers one had better become one of them.

GENERAL. And what if, without being, as you called it, believers, they have blood on their hands too? (*The Prefect discharges an imaginary pistol*) Good. But again—be careful.

PREFECT. To show you how careful we are, general, we've released about a dozen since your men retook the prefecture. And now (*turning toward the cell*), our Third Tier prisoners. I should say "prisoner", because there's only one left. The others have been let go, and our Pierre Dupont is due out in forty-three days.

GENERAL. Let's look at you, Dupont. I am acquainted with your case.

DUPONT. Sir.

GENERAL. So then, the Third Tier—

PREFECT. Is for the forgivable weaklings. Those who collaborated with the enemy under torture, the threat of torture, and the threat of death. If you'll peer inside, general, you'll see that they are comfortable.

GENERAL. I see. My Lieutenant Griffes was beaten by the Gestapo till his skull was fractured. He was tied to the ceiling by his thumbs, his body was burnt with cigarettes, his limbs were crushed with clamps, and still he didn't talk.

DUPONT. I am a swine, sir.

GENERAL. Let *us* be the judges of that. Good day, sir, and be thankful to our country. On our way, Fontanel. I'll do some writing in the jailer's office.

(*They leave. We hear greetings between the two men and Stella. Then enter the Jailer with Stella Tavrac*)

JAILER. This way, Madame. I am honored. Visits are fifteen minutes. But for you, Madame Tavrac—you understand—

STELLA. Thank you. Would you be so kind as to bring me something to sit on?

JAILER. Of course!

(*He leaves and returns with a chair. Stella and Dupont stare at each other*)

DUPONT. Madame....

STELLA. It's been a long time. I wanted to see you.

DUPONT. To call me again—

STELLA. No, no, no! That was then.... How are they treating you, Dupont?

DUPONT. Better than I deserve. How are *you* managing, madame? Is the business doing all right?

STELLA. I sold it, I sold it well. And I have a pension. The widow of a hero, you see.

DUPONT. I am glad.
STELLA. They are going to release you in a month or so, Dupont.
DUPONT. Yes.
STELLA. What are your plans? What will you do? You have no family that I know of.
DUPONT. Yes I do; a cousin in Metz. But now.... Now he hates me.
STELLA. Do you have any money?
DUPONT. A little; enough for a few weeks to live on before I find a job. There's always work for a good mechanic.
STELLA. Not in this town, Dupont, not in this town anymore.
DUPONT. I know. I'll go somewhere else. France is a big country.
STELLA. How old are you, Dupont, if I may ask?
DUPONT. Thirty-six. Why....?
STELLA. I am fifty-three. Not quite old enough to be your mother! But almost. You are wondering what this is all about. Yes?
DUPONT (*humbly*). Yes. Who am I to question....?
STELLA. Where will you live when you come out, before you go elsewhere?
DUPONT. I asked.... I still have my room in the rue du Pavé. It is kind of you to ask.
STELLA. You will come to my house.
DUPONT (*dumbfounded*). Come to your house?
STELLA. You will come to my house. You will live in my house as long as you wish. You will go back to work in *this* town as a friend of Madame Tavrac, widow of a hero, who has become a Somebody. No one will turn his back on Madame Tavrac's friend.
DUPONT. Is it Pierre Dupont you're speaking to? A year ago—
STELLA. A year ago was a life ago. After selling the shop I've had time to think. Let none of us alive be required to die for others.
DUPONT. "Let none of us...." Excuse me. Did you read this somewhere, madame?
STELLA. You're smiling, Dupont.
DUPONT. For the first time since....
STELLA. Since the days and months when I would gladly have torn you to pieces. But now the hero's wife tells you that life gave you the right to life. The town won't put up a monument to you, my poor Dupont, as they have for Selvin—
DUPONT. Pradelle showed me the picture.
STELLA. Pradelle?
DUPONT. The jailer.
STELLA. Speak of the devil—

(*Enter the Jailer*)
JAILER. Madame—
STELLA. Of course. Au revoir, Pierre. In how many days?
DUPONT. Forty-three.
JAILER. Allow me to accompany you to your automobile, Madame Tavrac.
(*They leave. Silence. Dupont returns to his dinner but doesn't eat*)
DUPONT. What did she say? "Life gave you...." something about life. (*He begins to eat*) I'll make myself useful in her house, even if she has servants. A good mechanic is always useful. (*He stops again*) Maybe I'll ask her to explain....

The End

Notes

The One Who Didn't Die was published in the *Minnesota Review* in 1964 under the title *The Cage Opened, and Out Flew a Coward*. Dissatisfied with the title, I rebaptized the play as *Adam Adamson* for inclusion in Volume Two of my 1970-1972 *Collected Plays*. Now, rereading it after almost fifty years, I peremptorily threw out half the text, wrote a new scene, and reworked everything else; all this, however, without altering the idea which was from the start and which remains the soul of the play.

A producer may wish—and is invited—to make women part of Selvin's group, even though I have kept the tag MAN for all the speakers.

II

THE REBELS OF NANTUCKET

a romantic comedy of the American Revolution

CHARACTERS

Colonel Elias Mayhew, *in his fifties*
Nicholas Mayhew, his nephew, *in his thirties*
The Marquise de Tourville, *in her forties*
Madeleine, *her daughter*
Thomas Weamish, *loyalist Judge of the Peace, in his forties*
Henry Wallace, *confidential agent to the Starbucks*
Sergeant Alexander Cuff, *in command of a British detachment*
Enoch Swain, *proprietor of a tavern*
Joshua Mamack, *an Indian man of all trades*
Obed Coffin, *a seaman*
Jenny, *maid to the Weamish*
Ruth, *maid to the Mayhew family*

The action takes place in and around Sherburne, as the county seat of Nantucket was called, from Tuesday, June 20 to Saturday, June 24, 1775.

SCENE ONE

(Tuesday, June 20, 1775. Late morning. The residence of Judge Thomas Weamish. We are in the cheerful second-story sitting room. The only blemish in the room is that one windowpane is broken. Weamish, a portly gentleman, is sitting at an elegant writing-table and concluding a letter to his mother)

WEAMISH. "For the rest, my dear mamma, the weather today is but middling fair and somewhat blustery, as if the (*he hesitates*) united?—conjoined? (*He writes*) conjoined elements deplored the absence of one whom not a few among the natives of the island call the queen-mother of Nantucket. Speed, speed to these shores again, for our human storms require a hand such as yours that knoweth how to chide the weak and chastise the guilty. Ever your devoted son, Thomas. Mailed at Sherburne, Nantucket. Tuesday, the 20th of June, 1775." (*He dries the letter and rings a bell. Enter Jenny*)
JENNY. Yes, Mr. Weamish?
WEAMISH. When the post boy comes, tell him I have a letter for him.
JENNY. I will, Mr. Weamish. I saw Josh Mamack coming up the street, sir.
WEAMISH. It's about time! Catch him and send him up at once.
JENNY. Yes, sir.
(She leaves. Weamish re-reads his letter with complacent satisfaction)
WEAMISH. "Dearest mamma. God grant that this letter find you in the full enjoyment of your customary health and cheerful spirits. Need l tell you how sorely you are missed by all your friends in town? To fly to an ailing sister, a despondent and helpless brother-in-law, in the midst of an embattled Boston, within hearing of cannon fire, insulted daily by a rabble of treacherous (*he pauses, then inserts*) 'and unprincipled' villains, who, like froward children, dare to question the mild authority of a monarch beloved of all his rational subjects; to rush, I say, to a sister and brother (*he makes another insert*) 'cruelly expelled from their ancestral home at Cambridge'; to nurse them in their affliction; to comfort them for the loss of property, familiar grounds and acquaintances; all this proves you a Saltonstall, the proud daughter of a governor, and sister-in-law to a royal Councillor of Massachusetts. But let me descend from these heights, and commend myself to Dr. Brattle and to your dear sister, my aunt. Pray tell them they acted wisely in taking shelter in Boston under the victorious

wings of his Excellency our governor and general, who, if reports tell true, hath recently beaten the impudent rebels out of Charlestown, and will now drum them handily out of the entire province. Alas, how I wish that I myself could wield a sword in these stirring times, rise to defend my king, and scourge the contumacious mob! But the robe enjoins its own duties, the law hath its own heroes. My sphere, at the moment, is our dear county of Nantucket, and here I mean to sustain his Majesty's mild rule and enforce his just decrees. What if you and I, my dear mamma, permit ourselves, in the intimacy of our household, to nurse the virtuous hope that Governor Gage will see fit some day soon to call me to his side, perhaps into his Council, to serve my king in a wider and nobler field of activity? I make no secret of my feelings. I do not care if a hint should come to the governor's ear that Thomas Weamish, who suffered for his king in the time of the Stamp Act, and who now once again beholds his windows shattered as the reward of his loyalty, that this same Thomas Weamish burns with a noble ambition to sacrifice his repose on the altar of our cherished colony. But you, my dear mamma, will know better than anyone how to convey these not unworthy sentiments to General Gage. Speak to him apart at the next assembly, when music hath made him cheerful. For is it fitting that a son of yours should pine away in a rude colonial outpost, among uncouth fishermen and Quakers, distant from elegant society—"

(*Enter Jenny and Joshua Mamack carrying tools*)

JENNY. Here's Josh, Mr. Weamish; and here is a letter for you.

MAMACK. Good day to you sir.

WEAMISH (*taking the letter*). Well well, Mr. Mamack; very good of you to call on us, I'm sure. (*Mamack scratches his head*) I'll attend to you in a moment. Is the post boy downstairs, Jenny?

JENNY. Yes, Mr. Weamish. The mail packet will be sailing a bit early this afternoon on account of the storm that's brewing.

WEAMISH (*seals the letter to his mother*). Give him this, and pay him, will you?

JENNY. Yes, sir.

(*She leaves*)

WEAMISH (*showing the broken windowpane*). Here, Mr. Mamack.

MAMACK. Yah. I seed it. Same one they break nine years ago. Mamack good memory. Trouble trouble.

WEAMISH. Why, Mr. Mamack, has it taken you four days to find your way here?

MAMACK (*puzzled*). Find my way?

WEAMISH. To answer my summons, Mamack. Am I to sit in this room for an entire week while the wind whistles through a broken window?

MAMACK. I mean to come right away quickly, Judge—

WEAMISH. But?

MAMACK. Well—

WEAMISH. Well well well! Well what?

MAMACK. Well—I got a large family to support, I got a position in the community—

WEAMISH. A position in the—! A carpenter—a glazer—a jack Indian with a position in the community! So this is the new spirit blowing over the land! And what has your precious position in the community to do with my broken window, Mr. Mamack?

MAMACK. Ah, I was only talking, Judge. I fix that window fast.

WEAMISH. I insist that you tell me!

MAMACK. Well—

WEAMISH. Well?

MAMACK. Well, the folks around here see you comfy cozy with Sergeant Cuff and Mr. Applegate—

WEAMISH. Aha.

MAMACK. There's a heap of bad feeling on the island, Judge, like a wind, speak East, speak West, a cold wicked wind. But I don't meddle none in white man's business. I don't sit down into no committees.

WEAMISH. Committees, eh? I assure you I know all about their rebel committees.

MAMACK (*grinning*). They know all about you that you know all about them. They say you and Mr. Applegate hush hush at night, in the dark, only one candle, you write names with ink in a book.

WEAMISH. Rubbish!

MAMACK. But maybe they write names too, eh?

WEAMISH. Vicious agitators!

MAMACK. I better fix that window. Big storm stepping out of sky.

WEAMISH. And so these patriotic gentlemen have tried to keep you from mending my window.

MAMACK. They call a small meeting about it.

WEAMISH. A meeting! A meeting about my window!

MAMACK. Small meeting, Judge. A bowl of cider and a pipe in Swain's tap room. I said to them, I said, "Gentlemen, who am I? Josh Mamack, Pokanoket tribe, honest worker, no rum hardly ever, I must mend the Judge's window, not decent to keep the Judge in draft." And they said, "Go, friend, go in peace."

WEAMISH. So now it's the rebel committee that runs Nantucket! The magistrates and the selectmen no longer count. Tell me, Mr. Mamack, while you gentlemen were guzzling cider and puffing on your pipes, was not the vandal's name mentioned by chance?

MAMACK. Who?

WEAMISH. The window breaker's name!

MAMACK. The window breaker? O Lord—I don't know—

WEAMISH. Mr. Mamack, I am the chief magistrate of this county.

MAMACK. I know, sir. We're awful proud of you.

WEAMISH. I order you to speak. Who broke that window? One of the Coffins? Young Macy? Coleman? Hussey's children?

MAMACK. How would I know? How would anybody know? But I have an idea, Judge.

WEAMISH. Aha!

MAMACK. Because it's the same window what break when you was stamp distributor—

WEAMISH. What of it?

MAMACK. I better fix that pane. I talk too much.

WEAMISH. Don't go near that window! Finish what you were about to say!

MAMACK. Yes, sir. I figure the moment I come in, I says to myself, by cod, Mamack, it must be the same spirit which done it in sixty-six. Spirit, he smashed like he was trying to tell you, "Watch out, Judge Weamish, the people don't have forgotten!"

WEAMISH (*tremulous*). Spirit be damned! Rogues and rascals! They will not forgive a man for carrying out British law. Thank God for Sergeant Cuff! Fifty redcoats should suffice to curb these Sons of Liberty.

MAMACK. Oh, they don't like the redcoats, Judge Weamish. They don't like the redcoats none whatsomever.

WEAMISH. I wonder why not!

MAMACK. We don't see so many soldiers since the French War. (*Casually*) How long they purposing to stay, Judge?

WEAMISH. Forever, damn it! Go mend that window!

MAMACK. Yes, Judge.

(*He begins to work. Weamish paces up and down in some agitation*)

WEAMISH (*to himself*). Impudent heathens!

(*Drums and fifes are heard outside*)

MAMACK. Here come the soldiers now.

(*Weamish goes to another window, opens it, and waves*)

WEAMISH. Proud looking lads!

MAMACK. Good boys. Good for Nantucket, I say to everybody. Keep the peace. Mind, I don't meddle, white folks know best.

(*The detachment is drilling below*)

MAMACK. Listen to them! Rat tat tat!

WEAMISH. Sturdy lads! One, two, one, two, shoulder arms!

MAMACK. What's your opinion, Judge? They going to hold down the harbor? Put a few fellows in jail? Take our ships away from us?

WEAMISH (*smug*). We'll see. Sergeant Cuff has orders from General Gage to make no move without my consent.

MAMACK (*whistling*). One day, spirit tell me and tell me sure, one day you going to be Royal Duke in London. Mark Mamack's words, your mummy, she be the proudest lady from here to Boston.

WEAMISH (*inspecting Mamack's work*). Good work, Mr. Mamack.

MAMACK Thank you, sir, it's close to finished.

(*The detachment is moving off. Weamish waves again*)

WEAMISH. Ah, there's Colonel Mayhew. Colonel Mayhew!

VOICE OF MAYHEW. Good morning, Judge!

WEAMISH. Were you watching the drill all this time?

VOICE. Indeed I was!

WEAMISH. I defer to your military experience, Colonel. But to my civilian eyes these lads performed like a sturdy and reliable lot.

VOICE. A splendid set of young men, Judge Weamish; England's best, I'm sure.

WEAMISH. What a comfort to have them in our midst, is it not?

VOICE. A sturdy lot. Well, Judge, I'm on my way to the wharves. We're unloading a consignment of seasoned timber. It may be our last for many a day.

WEAMISH. I shan't detain you, Colonel. Isn't that Mr. Applegate approaching?

VOICE. I believe it is. Good day to you, Judge.

WEAMISH. Good day, Colonel. Commend me to your sparkish nephew. Greetings, Mr. Applegate!

VOICE OF MR. APPLEGATE. Good morning, Judge! Nippy day for June, isn't it?

WEAMISH. Ah, you don't know our Nantucket as yet, Mr. Applegate. At Concord you were snugly sheltered in your trees, if I may say so. Here the wind blows, the clouds scour the land....

VOICE. Still, better the anger of the elements than the fury of disloyal men.

WEAMISH. True and affecting words, Mr. Applegate. A pity you missed the bracing spectacle just now. One of Sergeant Cuff's sergeants parading his men. Such a comforting sight.

VOICE. Good boys! There'll be brisk work for them on this island presently, if my presentiment don't lie.

WEAMISH. I shall tell Jenny to open the door.
VOICE. No, thank you kindly. I'm meeting with Sergeant Cuff. Besides, I've no wish to intrude upon your elegant visitors.
WEAMISH. What elegant visitors, Mr. Applegate? This is Joshua Mamack, a plain laborer.
MAMACK. At your service, Mr. Applegate.
VOICE. I'm astonished! The two ladies who debarked from the New York packet—
WEAMISH. When? Who? I know nothing about the matter! Two ladies?
VOICE. Well then, I am the bringer of good tidings, or so I hope. Two foreign ladies. They came ashore this morning, drove to Swain's, and will undoubtedly be calling on you before noon. So I was told by the ship's master, Sergeant Frobish by name.
WEAMISH. I'm speechless! Allow me to take my leave of you, Mr. Applegate. I must prepare—two foreign ladies—of dear, oh dear—
VOICE. I'll stop by this evening for news.
WEAMISH. Jenny! Jenny!
MAMACK. Sounds like a treat. Two ladies. Too bad Mrs. Weamish had to be in Boston. *(Jenny appears)*
WEAMISH. Jenny, two guests will be arriving any moment!
JENNY. What are you talking about, Mr. Weamish?
WEAMISH. Two foreign ladies are coming! Don't stare at me, for goodness' sake. Mr. Applegate told me the news through the window. Hurry, tidy the house—perhaps they speak no English.
JENNY. The house is always tidy, Mr. Weamish.
WEAMISH. Dust the vestibule again. And prepare a collation. Use the silver. Hurry, while I brush— *(The doorbell rings)*
JENNY. Too late.
WEAMISH. They must have rounded the street corner! Dear me—I'm totally unfit—but I'll have to make do. Go, Jenny, and let me not hear any milkmaid familiarities—
JENNY *(peeved)*. I don't know what you mean, Mr. Weamish.
(She leaves)
WEAMISH. Mamack—
MAMACK. Just a bit more putty, your honor.
WEAMISH. All right, but leave quietly. I shall settle with you another time.
MAMACK. Oh, don't you worry 'bout settling.
WEAMISH. Try not to bang anything.
(Weamish attempts to preen himself under Mamack's stare. Enter Jenny, too overwhelmed to say much of anything, Madame de Tourville, and Madeleine. Both ladies speak

impeccable English, but Madame de Tourville has kept a slight French accent)

JENNY. This is—

AIMEE. I am Aimée de Tourville. This is my daughter Madeleine. Am I addressing Judge Thomas Weamish?

WEAMISH. You are. Allow me to welcome you—and forgive my unpresentable—Jenny! Chairs! Such an unexpected honor—

AIMEE. In what sense unexpected, Mr. Weamish? Did I not pronounce my name clearly?

WEAMISH. Beautifully—pray sit— (*to Madeleine*) I beg you—Jenny, you know what to do.

JENNY. Yes, sir.

(*She hastily withdraws. Mamack is gawking*)

AIMEE. I see an unopened letter on your escritoire, Judge Weamish. Its contents might have relieved you of your astonishment.

WEAMISH. Letter? (*He flings himself on the letter Jenny has given him*) The press of business—night and day—may I?

AIMEE. You may and you must.

WEAMISH (*sits down and opens the letter*). Governor Gage! (*He leaps up again*) "My dear Weamish—"

AIMEE. Who is this man?

WEAMISH. Who—? Oh—nobody, madam, a common laborer mending my—Mamack, come back this afternoon.

MAMACK. Yes, your honor.

(*He puts on his cap, bows and leaves*)

AIMEE. The colonies are at war, Judge Weamish. A poodle could be a spy.

WEAMISH. I assure you—every measure has been taken—

AIMEE. Pray read the letter. Don't fidget, Madeleine.

WEAMISH. "My dear Weamish, do not under any circumstances allow any man of rank to leave your island until further advice reaches you."

(*Aimée has stood up and walks casually about the room. She suddenly flings open the door, revealing the stupefied figure of Josh Mamack. Weamish stops reading. Everybody stares at everybody. Mamack doffs his cap*)

WEAMISH (*thundering*). What were you doing behind that door?

MAMACK. I forgot my chisel.

(*Aimée walks to the window, picks up the chisel between two fingers, and hands it over to Mamack*)

MAMACK. Thank you, ma'am.

(*He vanishes and Aimée closes the door*)

AIMEE. War, Judge Weamish, war.

WEAMISH. To be sure, but—an untutored Indian—

AIMEE. Pray continue your letter.

WEAMISH. Ah yes. Let me see. "Similar instructions have been sent to Sergeant Cuff. On the same day as you receive this, or shortly thereafter, the Marquise de Tourville—" (*he gapes*)

AIMEE. Come, my dear Judge, we are two-legged animals all the same. Read on.

WEAMISH. "The Marquise de Tourville— (*he bows to Aimée*) accompanied by her daughter— (*he bows to Madeleine*) will arrive at Sherburne with verbal orders that you are to obey implicitly. Madame de Tourville— (*another bow*) is well known to me and to their Excellencies the Governor and Lieutenant-Governor of New York. She will name the gentlemen who are the objects of our present concern, and inform you of the high importance we attach to her mission."

(*Enter Jenny*)

JENNY. Chocolate and buttered buns.

WEAMISH. Get out! Not now!

AIMEE. Tut tut. Why not now? Madeleine, you haven't said a word all morning. Do you fancy a little refreshment?

MADELEINE. I should love a cup of chocolate.

WEAMISH. Delightful! (*To Jenny*) Serve the ladies, if you please. Ah, Marquise, your visit gives me unspeakable pleasure. Nantucket will never be the same— I hope! (*To Madeleine*) Did you enjoy a fair crossing from New York?

MADELEINE. Very—

AIMEE (*loud*). Not fair at all. The weather proved unseasonably rough, and for Madeleine's sake we decided to rest a few days before resuming our journey to Canada. (*To Jenny*) That will do, my good woman.

(*Weamish grimaces at Jenny, who leaves in a daze*)

AIMEE. This is the story we shall allow to be spread, my dear Judge. Delicious chocolate.

WEAMISH. You are too kind.

AIMEE. It is no lie, however, that we are proceeding north. Now that the rebels have taken Fort Ticonderoga, I am informed that they will attempt to secure Canada.

WEAMISH. Secure Canada! Ha! That's a bone on which the dogs will choke at last.

AIMEE. Your confidence is heartening. But General Carleton, who commands in Canada, is far from easy in his mind. I am going there to animate our French people against the rebels. That, however, is neither here nor there. My daughter and I have been sent to Sherburne to investigate Colonel Elias Mayhew and his nephew Nicholas. You look surprised, Judge Weamish.

WEAMISH. I do?

AIMEE. Can it be that you entertain no suspicions in that quarter?

WEAMISH. I do entertain suspicions. Yes! I suspect everybody! This island is a hatchery of rebels!

AIMEE. That is more than I can say. My instructions are limited to the two Mayhews. Are they presently on the island?

WEAMISH. Of course, I would never—I spoke with Colonel Mayhew a few minutes ago. From this window. Ha! He was watching a British sergeant drilling his men. Tell me, Marquise, what are they guilty of? I'll proceed with every severity known to the law.

AIMEE. Who said they were guilty of anything? I spoke of suspicions. You know of course that Colonel Mayhew fought side by side with Colonel Washington in fifty-nine.

WEAMISH. I had heard—

AIMEE. And with General Amherst at Montreal in 1760.

WEAMISH. With General Amherst was it? Hm. Allow me to advise you, Marquise, that Colonel Mayhew has a brother serving at this very moment in the congress of traitors at Philadelphia.

AIMEE. A cousin, I believe.

WEAMISH. Though he himself laughs at the matter, babbles about his loyal relations in Boston, and tells the world he has been a peaceful merchant for fourteen years.

AIMEE. Perhaps he is. In the meantime, it appears that Colonel Washington is to be appointed by the rebels to a particularly brilliant post of command. This cannot have reached you as yet.

WEAMISH. I assure you, Marquise, that we receive prompt and accurate intelligence here.

AIMEE. Then you know that the rebels who now besiege Boston are anxious to enlist capable officers to lead their miserable bands.

WEAMISH. They'll never find them.

AIMEE. Perhaps you will put two and two together. Or, if inconvenient, one and one.

WEAMISH. Of course. A terrifying plot—

AIMEE. What terrifying plot?

WEAMISH (*to Madeleine*). May I pour again? Ah, such a winning smile. You were saying, Marquise?

AIMEE (*with a sigh*). We believe—that is to say, Governor Gage believes—that Colonel Mayhew has been approached to play a considerable part in the siege of Boston.

WEAMISH. The Mayhews are indeed considerable men in Nantucket.

AIMEE. That is precisely why I am ordered to proceed with caution. Before risking a popular uprising, I must have proof, proof, proof that they are plotting to escape from the island. Of course we hope that the rumors are false. My mission here is to take accurate soundings and to instruct you accordingly. Fortunately, as Frenchwomen we are thought to be the Yankees' natural allies and Britain's natural enemies. I'll see to it that my calling on you is dismissed as a frigid courtesy.

WEAMISH. A clever game, Marquise.

AIMEE. Now. We have taken rooms at your only inn—whatever you call it.

MADELEINE. Swain's Tavern, maman.

AIMEE. Thank you, my dear. There we shall find occasion to chat with the natives, place a few questions, distribute a trifle of coins, and meet the Mayhews themselves. As the old one's a widower, and the young one a bachelor, both are sure to be found in a tap room. I expect to have all the facts within three days.

WEAMISH. This is a disappointment to me.

AIMEE. Why?

WEAMISH. You land on this poor island of ours—diffusing the radiance of Versailles—music in the park—ridottos—rank and fashion—and now you dash all my hopes by telling me we must be enemies and you will perhaps depart in three days.

AIMEE. I have not been at Versailles since 1757, my dear Judge, the year my husband, may God have mercy on his soul, took his regiment to Canada.

WEAMISH. You followed him.

AIMEE. Of course. I am a Fapignac!

WEAMISH. Ah! (*To Madeleine*) Poor child!

AIMEE. Madeleine was born in France. At the age of three she was fatherless in Canada.

WEAMISH. The horrors of war.

AIMEE. The Marquis was carried off by the smallpox.

WEAMISH. Bitter, bitter. What can I possibly do to comfort you during your stay? Needless to say, I offer you my house.

AIMEE. True American courtesy, Judge Weamish. But you have understood the reasons which compel us to endure your tavern.

MADELEINE. It seems like a pretty place, maman, with a view upon the ocean.

WEAMISH. Pretty enough for our islanders, I daresay. But, my dear ladies, you cannot conceive what it is for a man of breeding to live among fishermen, Quakers, Indians, farmers—with never a ball, a concert, or a play to relieve the tedium. I am—if I may take the liberty of mentioning it—the grandson of a governor.

AIMEE. Governor Saltonstall, is it not?

WEAMISH. Yes.

AIMEE. Your mother, Mrs. Wearnish, is presently in Boston?

WEAMISH. To my sorrow, she is. Nursing her sister and her brother-in-law, both refugees from Cambridge, and sadly come down since their flight.

AIMEE. What is the news from Boston? We have been on board our wretched vessel since Saturday.

WEAMISH. Ah Marquise, why didn't you remind me before? I am in a position to give you news of capital importance.

AIMEE. Oh?

WEAMISH. A magnificent victory at Charlestown.

AIMEE (*happily*). Under Gage's command?

WEAMISH. Indirectly, madam. He dispatched General Howe across the bay to give chase to the villains who had occupied the hills overlooking Boston. Their leader, a firebrand named Joseph Warren, was left dead on the field, and the Whiggish dogs were driven from the peninsula licking their desperate wounds.

MADELEINE. I pray they can still be reconciled. Your country is so beautiful —so plentiful—I feel that God has meant it for peace.

WEAMISH. They shall have peace shortly, mademoiselle. Our generals are making ready to sweep the province clear of rebels. They are a loose collection of shallow rascals, all brave enough behind their fences, but routed by the first volley of our muskets. They cannot enlist respectable officers—ah, you said so yourself, Marquise. This is June. We shall have peace before winter, I assure you.

AIMEE. In the meantime, you and Sergeant Cuff—

WEAMISH. Have you met the Sergeant, madam'?

AIMEE. Not yet. But you and he will see that no personage of any consequence shall leave the island. This must be gone about discreetly, of course.

WEAMISH. I have heard of no one who has declared a wish to leave.

AIMEE. Good. Madeleine and I will repair to our inn—

WEAMISH. May I put my mother's calash at your disposal?

AIMEE. By no means. I have hired what appears to be the only chaise in Nantucket.

WEAMISH. I am mortified.

AIMEE. I had hoped for a phaeton, but this is not New York.

WEAMISH. Alas.

AIMEE. Still, I have worked under worse conditions. Madeleine!

(*Jenny rushes in*)

JENNY. Begging your pardon. (*She curtseys*) Mr. Weamish, there's Mr. Mayhew, the young one, storming below and wanting to see you at once.
WEAMISH. What shall I do? Young Mayhew of all people! You didn't tell him these ladies are here, did you?
JENNY. How else could I keep him from rushing upstairs?
AIMEE. The girl is right. Come now, show Mr. Mayhew upstairs. No harm at all.
JENNY. Yes, ma'am.
(*She hurries out*)
AIMEE. We'll turn this to our advantage. It's a piece of luck that we should meet one of the Mayhews so soon.
(*Enter Nicholas Mayhew*)
NICHOLAS. Judge Weamish, where is our mail? I know you are entertaining distinguished visitors; pray accept my sincerest apologies. (*He bows to the Ladies*) I am Nicholas Mayhew, gentle ladies, my bad temper was given me by the gods, I was not consulted. Sir: myself and my uncle are expecting important commercial letters from the mainland. Three weeks have gone by without a single message. Today the New York packet arrives. (*Again to the Ladies*) And by the way, allow me to report that I happened to see your trunks safely delivered at Swain's Tavern. (*Back to Weamish*) Today, I repeat, the packet from New York puts in. Several sacks of mail emerge from the Sergeant's cabin. Your constable George Hackbutt removes them. Now sir: I make no accusations, but I demand of you, as chief magistrate of this island, whether orders have been issued to seize, withhold, or destroy our mail.
WEAMISH. My dear Mr. Mayhew, calm yourself—
NICHOLAS. I am enraged, but in full control of myself.
WEAMISH (*to Aimée*). May I introduce'?
AIMEE. Of course.
WEAMISH. Mr. Mayhew, this is the Marquise de Tourville, and this is Mademoiselle de Tourville.
NICHOLAS. Honored.
AIMEE. Charmed. I sympathize with your anger, Mr. Mayhew.
WEAMISH. And so do I. Nothing is being withheld *here*, Mr. Mayhew. What is confiscated in New York, or intercepted on the way, I cannot tell. My orbit is limited to these few islands.
AIMEE. We were not intercepted, were we, Madeleine?
MADELEINE. No.
AIMEE. But why, Mr. Mayhew, should you in particular be harassed? Do the authorities have reasons—?

NICHOLAS. No reasons whatever. Thank you for your concern, Marquise; my remarks are addressed to the Judge.
AIMEE (*laughing*). Forgive a meddlesome old woman, Mr. Mayhew; I'm rather too accustomed to ordering people about. Friends? (*She reaches out her hand*)
NICHOLAS (*kissing it*). Friends.
WEAMISH. Come, sir, sit down with us. I predict that you shall have your letters before the week is over. Let me propose something a shade stronger than warm chocolate before we all dine together.
NICHOLAS. Judge Weamish, if I'm not mistaken, this is a product of contraband.
WEAMISH (*laughing*). Justice is blindfolded.
AIMEE. A little concession to the good life, eh?
WEAMISH. Ah, how else can a gentleman survive? Nothing but sperm oil, tar, pitch....
NICHOLAS. All the same, old Mr. Weamish made a pretty thing out of your low-born sperm oil. (*To the Ladies*) Manufactured sperm candles. (*Mock aside*) A fortune!
WEAMISH. To be sure. We colonials must be content to derive from trade and industry.
AIMEE. Don't apologize, sir. I have lived on your continent long enough to value the spirit of commerce.
WEAMISH. This is true elevation of mind! Ah, how I feel the absence of my mother. She is worthy of your acquaintance, Marquise.
AIMEE. Let us drink to her prompt return, shall we?
NICHOLAS. With pleasure.
(*They all drink*)
WEAMISH. Thank you. And now, I propose a toast to His Excellency, Governor Gage. Will you join us, Mr. Mayhew?
NICHOLAS. Of course. To the health of Tom Gage!
WEAMISH. And to his brilliant victory at Bunker Hill!
NICHOLAS. What brilliant victory?
WEAMISH. He doesn't know! Come, come, you're jesting.
NICHOLAS. No, I protest. No jest intended. What brilliant victory?
WEAMISH. At Charlestown, Mr. Mayhew, on Saturday, three days ago! Nonsense! You do know! Here's the account in the *Gazette and Post-Boy*.
NICHOLAS (*looking at the paper*). So that's the battle, is it? Upon my word, the engagement is so differently described in *The Spy* (*he pulls out a gazette of his own*) that I became confused.
WEAMISH. Rubbish! *The Spy!* A well-deserved name. How came you by it, Mr. Mayhew?

NICHOLAS. I found it crumpled on the floor of the custom collector's office.

AIMEE. You pique my curiosity, Mr. Mayhew. Tell us more. What *really* happened at Charlestown?

NICHOLAS. Perhaps this rebel sheet is lying, Marquise. It reports that over a thousand redcoats were killed or maimed.

MADELEINE. How dreadful!

WEAMISH. Stuff and nonsense! The rebels were driven from the peninsula!

NICHOLAS. The writer manfully confesses it: an admission which throws some flickers of likelihood upon the rest of his account. And if the rest be true, the British are broken at Boston.

WEAMISH. Pah! Your gazette cannot impose on a rational observer. Trust me, my kindhearted mademoiselle. The rabble is not born that can slaughter the king's army in fair battle. However, this glee of yours, Mr. Mayhew, hardly accords with your recent vows of loyalty at the meeting house.

NICHOLAS. Glee? What glee? Long live King George, third of the name! My father left me a fine house in Boston, for which an officer of his Majesty's 47th, Major Sutcliffe, is paying me good rent. I am no rebel against my property!

AIMEE. I perceive that my daughter and I must keep our opinions to ourselves while residing in Sherburne. Before you came in, Mr. Mayhew, and before I knew, indeed, where the Judge's allegiance lay, I spoke rather too freely in favor of liberty.

WEAMISH. They being French, you see. But oh, had ever England a sweeter enemy?

AIMEE. You are a charmer, sir. Who would have expected such elegant manners on this windy island?

WEAMISH. You will all remain for dinner, I hope. I shall give Jenny orders at once.

NICHOLAS. Not I, thank you. I've accounts to settle with Hugh Catchcart— that's my cooper, Marquise, if I may use the low word.

AIMEE. And we had better unpack and dine quietly in our rooms today. Another time, Judge.

(*Enter Jenny*)

JENNY. Excuse me, but it's Colonel Mayhew downstairs, who doesn't want to intrude but who'd like a word with you, Mr. Weamish.

NICHOLAS (*to the ladies*). My uncle.

WEAMISH. Ask him up.

(*Exit Jenny*)

WEAMISH (*significantly*). This is fortunate, Marquise. Colonel Mayhew is one of our leading citizens. The Mayhews are among the founders of

Sherburne.

(*Enter Mayhew*)

WEAMISH. Come in, sir. Your nephew is here.

MAYHEW. I apologize. Egad, I see you are evenly paired without me. Well met, Nicholas.

WEAMISH. May I introduce? Marquise, Mademoiselle, this is Colonel Elias Mayhew; Colonel Mayhew, I have the honor to present you to the Marquise de Tourville and her fair daughter.

AIMEE. My Madeleine.

MAYHEW. Welcome to Nantucket, Marquise, Mademoiselle. I hope you will spend the summer with us.

AIMEE. Oh no, Colonel. We are traveling to my property near Montreal. But Madeleine found the crossing from New York excessively fatiguing. She's a delicate child, unlike her mother, who's as sturdy as a jailer's wife. I decided to break the journey, and to wait here for the next packet.

MAYHEW. That will give us the pleasure of keeping you for a whole week.

WEAMISH. You wanted a word with me, Colonel?

MAYHEW. In my capacity of selectman, my dear Judge. Tom Arthur happened, for some reason I know nothing of, to be rummaging in the attic of Timothy Morton's store. There he discovered a stock of tea hidden under several bushels of flour. He ran down with it in a rage and threw it all into the pond nearby. Morton raised a clamor; one of Sergeant Cuff's men came running, knocked Arthur to the ground, and dragged him off to jail.

WEAMISH. Heavenly mercies! My dear ladies—this is a grave incident—

AIMEE. Attend to it, sir, attend to it at once.

NICHOLAS. Since when is Sergeant Cuff the constable here? This must be stopped immediately.

MAYHEW. The question of jurisdiction is critical. I am deeply concerned.

WEAMISH. And I am all a-quiver. The rebels are showing their claws. To dump private property into a pond! Colonel, I beg you to step into my cabinet for a signed deposition.

MAYHEW. Gladly.

WEAMISH (*to the ladies*). I humbly beg your permission—

AIMEE. Proceed, proceed.

(*The two men leave*)

MADELEINE. How dreadful—on such a tranquil island—here at least one might have hoped—

NICHOLAS. I must disillusion you, sweet lady; we are the same beasts here as they are in New York or London.

AIMEE. But why so much excitement over a sack of tea?

MADELEINE. You've forgotten, mother.
AIMEE. What have I forgotten? I'm an alien, I know so little about your politics—Nicholas. May I call you Nicholas?
NICHOLAS. No—unless you allow me to call your daughter Madeleine.
AIMEE. Shall we petition her directly? Well, my child?
MADELEINE (*shyly*). You may.
NICHOLAS. This is a high privilege.
AIMEE. Now Nicholas, tell me about this wearisome tea.
NICHOLAS. A symbol, Marquise, nothing more. Our brothers in Britain granted themselves a monopoly of the tea trade in the colonies—
AIMEE. Ah, now I remember.
NICHOLAS. And the colonies object.
AIMEE. You men! If you cannot make war over the gold mines of Peru, you will do it over a tea leaf.
NICHOLAS. Tea leaf is unjust, Marquise. Our Whigs speak of Liberty.
AIMEE. Are you a Whig, Mr. Mayhew?
NICHOLAS. Like yourself, Marquise, I forget. I attend to my business affairs.
AIMEE. You disappoint me. Or rather, I hope you are using discretion in front of two strangers. I confess my heart pounds to the drums of liberty. But I pray you do not mention this to Judge Weamish, who, between you and me, appears to be an ultra on the Tory side.
NICHOLAS. I promise to say nothing.
AIMEE. Were I a man, I would swim away from this island if need be and make for the hottest sector of the battlefield!
NICHOLAS. You too, Madeleine?
MADELEINE. Perhaps....
AIMEE. This reminds me; now that we have done our duty to your magistrate—Madeleine, let's be on our way. Mr. Mayhew, may we expect you for tea—I should say coffee—or cider—I shall allow you to choose—but do call on us—your uncle and yourself—at Swain's Tavern, shall we say at four?
NICHOLAS. At four? I believe I can answer for my uncle. We'll be most happy. Today's a blustery day— (*Weamish and Mayhew reenter*) but on the next clear evening I engage to show you a sunset from the *eastern* part of this island that you will never forget.
WEAMISH. Our famous dusk at Sconset.
AIMEE. I look forward to it. Judge Weamish, you have entertained two helpless female travelers beyond their deserts. We shall ask for our *revanche* before long.
WEAMISH. Use me as you will, Marquise. But allow me to escort you to your

chaise.

AIMEE. You are too kind.

MAYHEW. We follow in a moment.

AIMEE. Colonel, Mr. Mayhew.

(*The two bow, and the ladies, followed by Weamish, leave*)

MAYHEW (*hurriedly and in a whisper*). A word with you, Nicholas.

NICHOLAS. Yes?

MAYHEW. A message from the first mate of the New York packet: the *Enterprise* is anchoring off the Bluffs this afternoon or tonight.

NICHOLAS (*excited*). Wallace is landing in person! And here I came storming after the mail.

MAYHEW. Be careful, don't do any storming, do you hear? Wallace will bring important letters for both of us.

NICHOLAS. Uncle! They want you in command before Boston.

MAYHEW. Hush. I'll be a common private if necessary.

NICHOLAS. You don't fear that the *Enterprise* will make for the harbor, do you?

MAYHEW. Not if they see our signals. I have dispatched Mamack to Trot's Hills with instructions.

NICHOLAS. Good. Listen—quickly. This will help, by Jove! The French ladies have asked us for a collation at the tavern at four o'clock.

MAYHEW. Splendid. It's the best lookout we could hope for. Come along. We've tarried too long.

WEAMISH (*outside*). Colonel! Mr. Mayhew!

NICHOLAS. We're coming! I struck my knee against your confounded table, Judge, and have been rubbing the wound till I can walk again!

WEAMISH (*same*). So sorry!

NICHOLAS (*to his uncle*). Come along!

MAYHEW (*grinning*). Young devil!

(*They leave, Nicholas affecting a limp*)

SCENE TWO

(Tuesday, June 20. Late afternoon. The tap room of Swain's Tavern. Sergeant Cuff is drinking grog. Enoch Swain is behind the counter)

CUFF. Take another peek into the parlor, Mr. Swain, will you?
SWAIN. I'd rather not, Sergeant. The parlor door is closed, and I don't like—
CUFF. Hell's fires! You're a dainty fellow, Mr. Swain. Come, fill my bowl again. I'll moisten my melancholy while our two Mayhews nibble cakes with their French trollops.
SWAIN. Sergeant!
CUFF. Do I hear cups clinking?
SWAIN. Very likely, Sergeant.
CUFF *(contemptuously)*. French gentlefolk!
SWAIN. Are they not to your liking, Sergeant?
CUFF. Why—look you, Mr. Swain—I exchanged twenty words with them today—and when 'twas over, what with putting a ribbon upon every word I spoke, I felt as weary as if I'd hauled a cannon up a mountainside. This flimsy-whimsy is not for me. I'm a man of the earth, God strike me.
SWAIN. Well—I'm almost with you, Sergeant, on this particular point. The devil's in all that luxury, for sure. You should have seen the uncommon quantity of luggage.
CUFF. I saw it this morning. Let them enjoy it. Though they may own a hundred gowns a piece, they can't do anything with what's under them that your tinker's wife can't do as well, or better.
SWAIN. Sergeant!
(Cuff looks out the window)
CUFF. Wretched weather. As if this scurvy island of yours wasn't bleak enough in the sunshine. I shall drivel of nothing but herring, cod and whaleblubber when they fetter me down in Bedlam. Stranded on Nantucket like with two-score men. Islanders plotting treason. Not three friendly words to be got in a week's time. The women as sour as milk a year old. God's bleeding body! More rum, Mr. Swain.
SWAIN. I must ask you in all humility, Sergeant Cuff, not to swear in this house. We are Quakers—
CUFF *(simultaneously)*. We are Quakers—I know it, God damn your pokey faces! Y'are too virtuous to grin while you ram your women, but y'are willing enough to plot against your God-given King!
SWAIN. Sergeant Cuff—we are simple folk, fearful of the law, trembling

before divine wrath—ah, here they are at last.
(*The parlor door opens, and the Mayhews enter the tap room*)
CUFF. Well met, gentlemen, I've been waiting for you. Let me have a word with you afore you go.
(*They shake hands*)
MAYHEW. Good afternoon, Sergeant Cuff.
NICHOLAS. What cheer, Sergeant?
CUFF. Cheer be hanged! I'm soaking my gloom in Mr. Swain's rum. And your ladies? Awash in coffee?
MAYHEW. The ladies are a delight. Nick, I believe you have reason to agree with me. If the rogue knew how to blush, I swear you might toast bread on his cheeks. Come now, is not Madelin a pretty name?
NICHOLAS. Ma-de-leine, uncle, you must say it after the French manner. The name is pretty, but 'tis the least pretty thing its owner has to show.
CUFF. Now that's spoken like a villain in a penny romance! Drink a bowl with me, gentlemen.
MAYHEW. Gladly. Mr. Swain, my nephew and I desire something a bit stronger than our genteel refreshment in the parlor.
CUFF. At last a sensible word. Sit down, my buccaneers.
(*Nicholas has been looking anxiously out the window*)
NICHOLAS. It's beginning to rain. The wind is whipping it in.
MAYHEW. Well, we'll make ourselves comfortable here for a while. Let's sit nearer the window, Sergeant. The light's growing dim.
SWAIN. Would you like a candle, Colonel?
MAYHEW. Oh no, not yet.
(*During what follows, Mayhew and Nicholas will be stealing looks out the window*)
CUFF. Colonel, you and young Nick must help a fellow soldier. I know y'are kith and kin with the natives here, but then again y'ave travelled, y'ave fought for your King, y'ave killed your share of Frenchmen from the Carolinas to Quebec. Now comes the time again to show whether there's blood or muck in your veins.
NICHOLAS. That's a mighty diplomatic speech, Sergeant Cuff.
CUFF. True by God's gut—I'm brushing your fur a bit, but I've heard about you, Nick, you was an ensign at Montreal afore you shaved, and you fought the savages near Niagara Falls when General Amherst was commanding. It's no lie; I can name you the officers of every regiment that's been raised since the French wars began in the year fifty-four.
NICHOLAS. That's all water long ago under the bridge. What's on your mind, Sergeant?
CUFF. Mr. Swain, kindly look after my horse, now that the rain is falling.

SWAIN. Yes, sir. (*He leaves*)

CUFF (*leaning forward confidentially*). Look you, friends: sure as my mother bore me, I know there's powder, flints and bullets stowed away in a dozen holes up and down the island. And they're not meant for shooting whales, says Sergeant Cuff.

NICHOLAS. Whoever gave you this information is a fool. Why should anyone be hiding ammunition? Our island is defenceless. Three of your frigates could level every house upon it, and never a man living on the mainland would lift a finger to help us.

CUFF. You tell this to your whaling crews, young Nick—do—they need to hear it. Because all the same they're making cartridges, and there's many a cache under a windmill or a meeting-house that could tell a tale on my side. I'm not willing—yet!—to send my troops out digging and delving—forty men is too few, God blast it, and if tempers flare we'll finish as manure for your cornfields. But you two—you can do the work quietly for me. God's nails, are you loyal men or not?

NICHOLAS. Are we loyal men?

MAYHEW (*interrupts with a gesture*). You're in the right, Sergeant. Nick and I, why, we meddle so little, it startled us to hear that the situation is as grave as you portray it.

CUFF. I tell you it is.

MAYHEW. Leave the matter in our hands. We know where to ask a discreet question or two. If your reports are correct, trust me—

(*Voices outside*)

VOICES. Man overboard! Man overboard!

(*The men leap up and open the windows. Swain comes running in*)

SWAIN. Trouble again!

VOICES. He's lost! Where is he now? He's gone for sure! There he bobs again! (*Etc. ad libitum*)

MAYHEW (*in a whisper, seizing Nicholas' arm*). Wallace!

CUFF (*shouting out the window*). Don't stand there, you ninnies! Dive in!

SWAIN (*moaning*). It's raining into the room!

(*Aimée and Madeleine rush in*)

AIMEE. A man is drowning!

VOICES. The breakers are too rough—we can't launch her!

MADELEINE (*piteously, to Nicholas*). Won't anyone save him?

CUFF. Cowards one and all!

NICHOLAS (*to Mayhew*). Let's go!

(*The Mayhews rush out, followed by Cuff. Swain tries to shut the windows, dry his property, pick up fallen objects, etc., but Madeleine tears open a window again and the two women*

peer outside, where the shouting continues)
MADELEINE. I saw him! Nicholas! I'm sure I saw his head!
SWAIN (*still sweeping up*). Oh, madam, how many of these I've witnessed in my lifetime.
AIMEE (*astonished*). What's the young man doing?
MADELEINE. Nicholas! He's diving into the water! Stop him! Stop him! He'll drown!
(*She wants to rush out, but Aimée holds her back*)
AIMEE. Where are you going, silly girl?
MADELEINE. He'll die! Nobody else dared!
VOICES. Where is he?
VOICE OF MAYHEW. Nicholas! He's to your left!
SWAIN. It's a murderous squall.
(*Enter Cuff*)
CUFF. God blast it! What an island! I'm soaked for nothing!
MADELEINE. Sergeant, is he safe? Is Mr. Mayhew safe?
CUFF. Who knows? I can't swim, at any rate. But I trust the young fellow. They say he's scalped a brace of Indians with his bare teeth!
MADELEINE. I'm crying.
AIMEE (*In a whisper, handing Madeleine a glass of water*). Bravo! I'm proud—
VOICES. There they are! Hurrah! Heads up! (*Etc. ad lib.*)
SWAIN. You see! God is merciful.
AIMEE. Quite a young man!
MADELEINE. He almost drowned....
CUFF (*still drying himself*). Spare your tears, young miss; your laddy's a proper dolphin.
AIMEE. He's not our laddy, Sergeant Cuff. My daughter happens to be tender-hearted; she makes no distinction between strangers and relations. There, there, Madelon, all's well. (*In a whisper*) Good work, young lady.
(*Enter the men, carrying Henry Wallace*)
MAYHEW (*to the outside*). Keep everybody away, Mamack! Tell them to go home! (*Inside*) Make room! Make room! Over there, on the table!
MADELEINE. Yes—it's the best place!
NICHOLAS. Gently, gently. His head on the cushion.
(*The four men stretch Wallace on the couch*)
CUFF. Go fetch a doctor, Swain; don't dawdle!
AIMEE. And have a bed made ready for the poor man.
SWAIN. Here? In my place?
MAYHEW. Never mind the bed. Go call the doctor. On your way!
(*Exit Swain*)

MAYHEW. We live a stone's throw from here, Marquise; he'll be more comfortable with us. Don't press too close upon him, all of you.
AIMEE (*to Nicholas*). Young hero! I must embrace you, wet or dry! Ah, so much emotion! But you must change into dry clothes at once. And you, Madeleine? Are you indifferent to this splendid action?
NICHOLAS. You've cried!
MADELEINE. It was beautiful. Beautiful and selfless.
NICHOLAS. Who wouldn't try to save a drowning man? But let's attend to the poor fellow.
MAYHEW. He's breathing regularly. But we must find dry clothes for him too, and quickly.
AIMEE. What's this?
MAYHEW. Nothing. A pouch around his neck.
(*He gently lifts Wallace's head to take it*)
AIMEE. Let me see.
MAYHEW. It's nothing; a woman's picture—
AIMEE. How exciting—may I see?
MAYHEW. Keep it safe for him, Nick.
(*Nicholas casually snuggles the pouch away and creates a diversion*)
NICHOLAS. Look, he opened his left eye! Marquise, will you help me undo these buttons?
CUFF. You're wrong. He's still out.
AIMEE. Perhaps we should lift his feet to make him give up the water he must have swallowed.
CUFF. That would really finish him off.
WALLACE (*coming to*). What happened? Am I safe?
(*Exclamations ad lib*)
MAYHEW. Among strangers but safe—*strangers* but safe—do you hear me?
WALLACE. Yes. I understand. Thanks be to God Almighty.
AIMEE. Who are you, my good man?
MAYHEW. Let's not question him now.
WALLACE. Steward on the—on the—
MAYHEW. It doesn't matter.
AIMEE. Steward?
WALLACE. I was rowing ashore—for a barrel of oil—and some candles.... Where's my pouch?
NICHOLAS. In my pocket, my good fellow. The *portrait* survived. Happy now? Well, the man's alive and conscious. Ready, uncle?
MADELEINE. Why not carry him up to our rooms?
AIMEE. A good thought. Colonel, take your brave nephew home and dry

him off. Sergeant Cuff and I shall help the poor steward to my bed; he has travelled enough for one day; and bid one of your servants bring a suit of dry clothes for him. Don't forget, if you please, that the doctor will be coming here to examine him.

MAYHEW. Kindly tell him to call at my house.

(*He and Nicholas start to take Wallace up. Aimée pushes him down*)

AIMÉE. What do you think, Sergeant? Is not mine the better plan?

CUFF. I don't care. Take him away, Colonel; I think our host Mr. Swain will be grateful to you.

MAYHEW. Help me, Nick. Oops! Can you walk, my friend?

WALLACE. If I put my arm over your shoulder.

NICHOLAS (*to the ladies*). As soon as I've changed into something respectable — (*he sneezes*)

MADELEINE. I knew it! You will die of a congestion. Hurry home!

NICHOLAS. But may I hurry back?

MADELEINE. Why?

MAYHEW (*impatient*). Nicholas!

NICHOLAS. To give you news of our castaway.

MADELEINE. Yes, do.

MAYHEW. Come along, Nicholas.

NICHOLAS. Marquise, Sergeant.

CUFF (*shaking his hand*). Well done, Mr. Mayhew. We need bully lads like you.

(*Exeunt, Cuff holding the door open for them*)

CUFF. The rain has stopped at any rate.

AIMÉE. I wish, Sergeant, that you had seconded my request to keep the steward here.

CUFF. Why, Marquise? He'll be better cared for by the Mayhews than here, for I doubt that the fellow brought enough money to satisfy Mr. Swain. This Mr. Swain, I assure you—

AIMÉE. Let it pass, Sergeant.

CUFF. My homages to you, noble ladies; you may command me day—or night.

AIMÉE. Thank you, Sergeant Cuff.

(*He bows and leaves. Aimée is in deep thought*)

AIMÉE. A strange affair.

MADELEINE. Why strange?

AIMÉE. Look at you! Dieu me damne! You've fallen in love with that American Leander.

MADELEINE (*playfully*). Why do you say that, mother? Didn't you order me to be friendly with the suspects?

AIMEE. Pooh! I've never yet seen you so keen to do your duty.

MADELEINE. Don't scold me, mamma! You must admire him too. How brave he was! For the sake of an absolute stranger—no one else so much as removed his coat—and he plunges in—swims like a Neptune—

AIMEE. Swims like a Neptune! A duck can swim as well. Now we're in love with a fellow because he swims.

MADELEINE. Have it your way.

AIMEE. As for being selfless—

MADELEINE. To be sure. This steward is a pasha in disguise who will leave his millions to Nicholas.

AIMEE. He may leave him something more important. Steward be hanged! You must be blind, my girl! Thank goodness I'm an expert, I snap at details.

MADELEINE. What details?

AIMEE. You weren't struck by that sealskin pouch? How worried he was about it?

MADELEINE. It was lovely of him to think of his wife the moment he came to.

AIMEE. The girl's determined to be an idiot! To think that I raised you on Plutarch and Tacitus! I don't suppose you noticed how anxious the Colonel was to keep that pouch out of my hands.

MADELEINE. You're right; I didn't notice.

AIMEE. And you didn't think it was odd that a common cook should be wearing a silk shirt, ruffled wrist bands, and gold buttons; mind you, got up like a man of condition when he was out rowing a dinghy to take on a barrel of whale oil. Silly details, of course.

MADELEINE. He was a steward.

AIMEE. If he was a steward, a seaman should have been rowing his boat.

MADELEINE. Another detail.

AIMEE. Details, my dear girl, make all the difference between a professional and a dilettante. Without details we'd still be selling keys in Montreal. I suppose you've forgotten that dreadful winter in 1760 when we nearly died of the cold.

MADELEINE. In Montreal? I was five years old!

AIMEE. I remember my life from the day I was weaned. Another tell-tale difference between us. I can only say it again: your father must have been that clod of a bailiff, I wish I could remember his name, the one with the heavy jowls and the slow aa ôô aa.... I've noticed the same slowness in you.

MADELEINE (*sadly*). I'd rather hear about the winter in Montreal.

AIMEE. Why not? Now that I may be able to use you at last, why not take a lesson from your mother? A lesson about details, for instance. How a sharp eye raised me high in the world.

MADELEINE. I thought you didn't like me to know too much about the past.

AIMEE. True. But when I see you not quick enough to step around a puddle, I wonder did I overdo your ignorance. I didn't escape out of that key shop, or make friends with Tom Gage, by singing ballads in moonlight. It never occurs to a child that her parents had to arrive where she found them when she was born.

MADELEINE. I'll try to learn from you, mother.

AIMEE. A cold, cold winter it was, the first under English rule. I was struggling to survive on that miserable shop. All my Number Two had left me was a dented sword and a tunic with braids, out of which, by the way, I made you the prettiest skirt. But food was scarce, and you were no Amazon, God knows; more than once I thought I'd lose you. Gage was a fair man, however, as Englishmen go. He gave an order—in French, to show you how fair he was—that beef was to sell at no more than ten sous the pound. I hadn't been in Montreal long enough to deserve special favors from the butchers. To keep you alive, I'd run from one to the other, an ounce here, a slice there, sometimes as far as the Arsenal, knee-deep in snow or falling on the ice. Beef at ten sous, mutton twelve. You see what a memory I have. But somehow I was always dealt the worst cuts, meat that stank in spite of the cold, never a smidgeon more than my ration, and my pittance handed over the counter with sour distrustful faces. I was a newcomer, that was all. Pretty soon, though, I noticed a detail. Every butcher displayed an alms box no eye could miss for the hospital or the Ursulines. Nothing unusual about that, you would have said. Or rather, *you* wouldn't have noticed. I, instead, I was struck, the same as when I saw that business of the pouch and those frills on Mr. Steward. I thought, "How wonderfully generous we all are! Everybody's freezing and starving, but never a trip to the butcher's without a few pious coins into those boxes." And one day—another detail—I saw one of our good ladies of Montreal drop a coin and throw the butcher a wink. And that, my dear girl, is how I ceased to be Madame Pichot and became the Marquise de Tourville.

MADELEINE. You informed, mother?

AIMEE. I obeyed the law, my love; I always walk on the sunny side of the law. If I hadn't married a jail warden in Lyon on the sunny side of the law, I wouldn't have met the Vicomtesse de Brion in a cell—

MADELEINE. A vile poisoner; I wish you weren't always talking about her.

AIMEE. She was a brave woman; instead of crying over her brute of a husband, she poisoned him. When she came out to be hanged, my first husband cried like a baby and insisted on kissing her hand. I owe her everything I am. In the year we had her with us she taught me how to speak, dress and comport myself like a lady; accomplishments I've tried to pass on to an ungrateful daughter.

MADELEINE. I would have been glad to remain plain Mademoiselle Pichot, and run your key shop for you.

AIMEE. You have a low mind. I, instead, wrote to Monsieur Maturin, who was Gage's secretary, named myself, poor widow of Gustave Pichot, late sergeant in the light infantry, the butcher got twenty lashes, the alms boxes disappeared, and I quietly entered the Governor's service.

MADELEINE. In more ways than one.

AIMEE. I was attractive and Tom Gage was lonely.

MADELEINE. Well, now I know how it happened.

AIMEE. And I hope the knowledge will help you in life. Chin up, curls in place, tidy drawers, and an eye that can pick out a flea in the fur of a dog at fifty paces: that's how a woman makes her way in the world.

MADELEINE. I wish I had your fire—but I can't manage it.

AIMEE. Well, you're a goose, or a kitten by somebody's fireplace. But not Nicholas Mayhew's fireplace—not if he is what I think he is.

MADELEINE. What is that?

AIMEE. A firebrand Whiggish rebel—he and his uncle both. So they are in their souls, I'll wager, but I need to catch them in the act. Pah! Our luck amazes me. Heaven will punish us if we don't make the most of it. Here's Tom Gage, who I thought I'd never see again—commander in Boston—and willing to pay three-hundred pounds a head for a pair of Yankee rebels. Almost baronet's income in England! Well, dreaming never filled a purse. I must see that fool Weamish, and you must go on flirting violently with Mr. Nicholas. That's not too painful a task, is it?

MADELEINE. Now it is.

AIMEE. Twaddle! You're to tickle the truth out of him, d'you hear, whether by godly means—or otherwise. Six-hundred pounds! Your mother forgives you in advance.

SCENE THREE

(The morning of Wednesday, June 21. The Weamish residence, as in the first scene. Judge Weamish and Sergeant Cuff in conference.)

CUFF. How many windmills d'you have on the island?
WEAMISH. Oh, quite a few—
CUFF. Quite a few is a slovenly answer, Judge. I've but forty men under me. Everywhere we go we're surrounded by swarms of urchins. The urchins run ahead to warn their elders and by the time we reach a spot it's been swept clear of weapons and ammunition. But Sergeant Cuff can play the fox too. You wait and see.
WEAMISH. Most of the islanders are loyal, sir. Need I remind you that a dozen of our vessels are secretly supplying General Gage and Admiral Graves, at great risk to themselves?
CUFF. What of it? You're giving me tuppence with one hand and picking my pocket with the other.
WEAMISH. Didn't the Mayhews promise to help?
CUFF. They did. But we was interrupted by that sea rescue you heard of. Brave lad, young Mayhew; once a soldier always a soldier—it's the bloody merchants I can't abide—
WEAMISH. Well—
CUFF. Now here's what I expect you to do, Judge—
(Enter Jenny)
JENNY. Excuse me, sir. The French lady is here again, Mr. Weamish.
(Enter Aimée)
AIMEE. No ceremony, please. Good morning, Judge. Ah, Sergeant Cuff—
CUFF. Madam—
WEAMISH. Marquise, what a pleasure to see you this morning. I hope you spent a restful night at Swain's.
AIMEE. So so, thank you. The wind, the sea, and the seagulls kept us company.
WEAMISH. Pray sit. Jenny—
AIMEE. Thank you. No refreshments. That will be all, Jenny.
JENNY. Yes ma'am.
(She hurries out)
WEAMISH. And how is your daughter this sunny morning, Marquise?
AIMEE. My daughter is strolling by the seashore, thank you. But I didn't—
WEAMISH. I have been apprised of the dreadful and thrilling event to which you were a helpless witness yesterday.

AIMEE. Precisely what—

WEAMISH. On your first day in Sherburne! Our life, you see, is a rough one. Not a month goes by without a tragic loss at sea—weeping widows and orphans—valuable freights of blubber lost—

AIMEE. Life is a series of tempests, Judge. I—

WEAMISH. How true! And how sad! I feel you are divining the thoughts I nurtured during the night.

AIMEE. Thoughts, Mr. Weamish?

WEAMISH. To distract us all from the very tempests you have named, I have decided to offer a ball in your honor this Saturday. If you would condescend—you and Mademoiselle Madeleine—to grace this soiree, it would, I assure you—

AIMEE. Let me cut you short, my dear Judge. Not to be rude—I am utterly grateful for your delicate attentions—but I came to Nantucket with an important charge. Let us talk about dancing another time.

WEAMISH. I defer to you, Marquise.

AIMEE. Sergeant, yesterday, very briefly, I had the pleasure of meeting you and of presenting my credentials. (*Cuff bows*) When that supposed steward was rescued from the sea, I tried as effectively as I could to show you my interest in this dubious figure.

CUFF. I don't follow these subtleties, madam. Supposed steward? Dubious figure? What the deuce do you mean?

AIMEE. It's simple enough. Between this castaway and the Mayhews I sensed a connection that needs to be probed.

CUFF. Between the Mayhews—

AIMEE. Do keep repeating my words after me, Sergeant; it can do you no harm.

WEAMISH. Extraordinary woman!

CUFF. Devils in hell! Explain yourself, Marquise; I'm a plain Briton; I'm not the man for your Frenchified mysteries.

WEAMISH. You don't know as yet, Captain Cuff, what Madame and I happen to have learned: the Mayhews are suspected.

CUFF. Suspected! God's guts! I'm down to repeating everybody's words this morning! The Mayhews suspected! The drowning steward a spy! And what am I? The buffoon in a Punch and Judy show? Weamish—damn your legal mincing—you let me rattle on about the Mayhews five minutes ago without saying a word.

WEAMISH. Not without the Marquise's—

CUFF. I'll arrest the lot of you! Everybody's suspected here!

AIMEE. Calm yourself, Sergeant. If you'd taken notice of my signs, this pretended steward with his silk shirt and his gold buttons would have been in our custody by now instead of resting quietly at the Mayhew's house.

WEAMISH. More acuity and less shouting, Sergeant.

CUFF. Y'are right, damn my tongue. I'm lessoned. Explain to me, Marquise.

AIMEE. I'm not sure of anything yet. But we know that the rebel Congress is desperate for experienced military leaders. We know that Colonels Mayhew and Washington are acquainted. We believe that young Nicholas was implicated in a Bostonian affair in '65—

CUFF. What affair?

WEAMISH. What is this, Marquise?

AIMEE. We *think* he was one of your so-called Sons of Liberty.

WEAMISH. Impossible!

AIMEE. One of a gang that smashed the Stamp Distributor's furniture in Boston.

WEAMISH. I'm speechless! Mr. Oliver it was—and they threw mud against my door that very same week! Heaven cries out—

CUFF. I'll cut his throat!

AIMEE. Gently, Sergeant Cuff—

CUFF. I'll cut it gently, by Lucifer's pike, but I'll cut it!

AIMEE. We also know that he shot and wounded a British officer in Long Island two years ago—an officer who was trying to impress a couple of Mr. Mayhew's seamen.

WEAMISH. *That*, Marquise, is known to all of us.

CUFF. Not to me, devils in hell, not to me!

WEAMISH. What can we do? Young Nick has braved the oceans from New Guinea to Labrador; he has a prompt temper. When two of his men were being forced away from him—well, Marquise, I must own—reluctantly—that the Nantucket people regard this action of Mr. Mayhew's as—how shall I put it—

AIMEE. A businesslike move?

WEAMISH. Very nearly.

CUFF. Shooting an officer of His Majesty is a businesslike move?

AIMEE. Gently, Sergeant, gently. I too don't choose to lay heavy stress on that transaction. It might have been the impulse of a loyal subject, am I right?

WEAMISH. A loyal subject of our peculiar Nantucket—yes, Marquise. Reluctantly, yes.

CUFF. I have three arrests to make. Good day!

AIMEE. You are not arresting anyone, Sergeant. Not until I'm vastly more confident than I am now. The past, as they say, is past. I need proof that they are plotting *now* to join the rebels on the mainland.

CUFF. I'm to twiddle my thumbs, am I, while your rebels bubble the King of England? The house is burning, says Sergeant Cuff; don't wait for the fire engine, man the buckets and pour!
WEAMISH. What house is burning? You say this after our glorious victory at Charlestown?
CUFF. Judge Weamish: with all due respect, you civilians are dreamers. We got trounced on the confounded hill, what d'you call it? Y'are a fool, let a soldier tell you.
WEAMISH. Sir!
CUFF. A fool! Hang the pussyfooters!
AIMEE. Sergeant Cuff, gently gently will do it. Did we or did we not rout the Yankee mob?
CUFF. First of all, my dear Marquise, with due respect once more, y'are a fool to talk about a mob. Don't credit the gossip you heard in your New York mansions. That mob bled us white afore they took leave of the peninsula. Y'are a friend of General Gage's are you? Then tell him from Sergeant Cuff, he knows me well enough, the fine gentleman, tell him he'd be wise to clear out of Boston altogether, for he'll never set foot on another inch of Massachusetts soil. The fop hasn't so much as a good map of the country. He pinches actresses at the playhouse while the enemy is mustering. He waits for reinforcements from England instead of peppering the rebels from cock-crow till curfew. When he does fight them, what does he do? Climbs up the confounded hill in a frontal attack, because, don't you see, the enemy is nothing but a cowardly mob, show 'em your teeth and they'll run. Well, they forgot to run. They chopped us into little pieces and strolled away at their own sweet leisure.
AIMEE (*to Weamish*). Is this true? Is it then as Mr. Mayhew suggested yesterday?
CUFF. Aha; Mr. Mayhew suggested, did he? He'll suggest from the jailhouse as of today. Without further ceremony—
AIMEE. No, Seergeant, I forbid it all the same.
CUFF. A Frenchwoman forbids an Englishman? Ha ha ha!
AIMEE (*rising*). In the name of Governor Gage. The Mayhews have committed no illegal act, and arresting them without grounds would turn a thousand loyalists into as many rebels.
WEAMISH. The colonel is one of our selectmen this year. An old, highly regarded family, with numberless influential relations, here and in Boston.
CUFF. When these courtesies are over, Judge, your colonies will have whistled off the King for good.
AIMEE. Are not several of the Mayhews' merchantmen tied up in Sherburne now?

WEAMISH. I daresay they are.
CUFF. Wrong. The Colonel's *Queen Bess* put in a week ago, but his other three sail are on the seas, and so, worse luck, are two sloops belonging to the nephew.
AIMEE. That still gives us a respectable hostage. Keep a discreet eye upon the *Queen Bess*, Captain. Let there be no suspicions. I engage to discover the facts within twenty-four hours. My daughter is working on young Nick; I shall attack the uncle. Never fear.
CUFF. I take my leave.
AIMEE. Don't violate your instructions, Sergeant; or the Governor shall hear of it.
CUFF. I shan't touch either of the Mayhews. Good day to you both.
WEAMISH. Good day, Captain. Always a— .
(*Cuff is gone, slamming the door*)
WEAMISH. Bear in mind, Marquise, that our Sergeant has reached an age when, had he been a man of any consequence, he would have commanded a regiment. Thoughts such as these cloud his perceptions.
AIMEE. His perceptions look pretty clear to me.
WEAMISH. Now, however, that our political affairs are running their course, I beg of you, dearest lady, to take pity upon our ball this Saturday. Make history on our island, madam!
AIMEE. That is what I propose to do.
(*Weamish kisses her hand*)

SCENE FOUR

(*The morning of Wednesday, June 21. The Mayhew house. Henry Wallace is sleeping on a couch. Beside him sits Nicholas, watching him, and obviously happy and excited. Enter Ruth, the maid, carrying a large tray with breakfast and coffee*)

NICHOLAS. Hush. Don't wake him. Put the things down quietly. Is there a cup for me? Ah. Thanks, Ruthie.
(*Exit Ruth. Nicholas walks about the room, looks out of a window by edging open a shutter—the shutters have been closed for Wallace's benefit—then pulls out a letter he has clearly read several times already*)
NICHOLAS (*kissing the letter*). Did ever mistress speak more sweetly? (*He reads*) "You, Nicholas Mayhew, may, by force of arms, attack, subdue, and take

all ships and other vessels belonging to the inhabitants of Great Britain. You shall—"

WALLACE. The pouch!

NICHOLAS. Wallace, are you awake?

WALLACE. Ah, Mr. Mayhew, it's you.

NICHOLAS (*taking his hand*). You haven't forgotten that we spoke for a few minutes before you fell asleep again?

WALLACE. When?

NICHOLAS. Last night.

WALLACE. Yes....Yes! I remember! Mr. Mayhew—you saved my life—I don't know whether I thanked you—or thanked you enough—

NICHOLAS. You did, you did—more than enough.

WALLACE. Without you—

NICHOLAS. And where would *I* be without *you?*

WALLACE. Is the pouch safe?

NICHOLAS. You *have* forgotten!

WALLACE. Forgive me.

NICHOLAS. You were clutching it, half drowned you were holding on to it. My uncle and I took it away from you. He has his letter, and I have both of mine.

WALLACE. Thank God! Where is your uncle?

NICHOLAS. In his study, meditating upon the letter. Shall I open the shutters?

WALLACE. Oh—it's daytime, is it?

NICHOLAS. As glorious a morning as I ever hope to see.

WALLACE. And I'm alive!

NICHOLAS. Brave Wallace. Raise yourself up; come, I'll help you. Set your face boldly toward the table. What do you see there?

WALLACE (*laughing*). Breakfast!

NICHOLAS. Shall I bring it to you?

WALLACE. No, I'll try to get up. Thank you for the clothes.

NICHOLAS. Try to stand, Harry.

WALLACE. Not bad. Not bad. Wait—I'll do it alone.

NICHOLAS. Good man.

WALLACE. Your floor's a bit unsteady, Mr. Mayhew.

NICHOLAS. But navigable, eh?

WALLACE. Navigable. Ah, the sun! the sun! But the news I carry for you—I haven't forgotten, God be praised.

NICHOLAS. Sit down. Eat. Drink.

WALLACE. Yes. I want to. Forgive me, but I'll discard manners and fling myself.

NICHOLAS. Cautiously, Wallace.

WALLACE. Yes. Good. Oh, this is a blessed day. (*Nicholas pours the coffee*) Thank you, thank you. There were two items in writing for you, Mr. Mayhew, and General Washington's letter for your uncle. You have all three?

NICHOLAS. All three. Eat, Wallace, eat. But did you say *General* Washington?

WALLACE. He was promoted the day before he wrote that letter. But he had premonitions and intimations, you understand. A Mr. Reed is his secretary. Most capable. Some of the letters were written in advance. There will be lively actions, Mr. Mayhew, sudden decisions and prompt executions.

NICHOLAS. And we must be sudden and prompt enough, by God, to keep ahead of them. Eat, Wallace, eat and drink. What else?

WALLACE. Your cousin Mr. Pigeon.

NICHOLAS. Yes! What does he say? Did he reach Philadelphia in time?

WALLACE. In good time; Mr. Pigeon is now commissary general for Massachusetts—

NICHOLAS. And will purchase—?

WALLACE. And will purchase whatever you choose to capture, sir. No questions asked. He'll purchase doilies for the Army if doilies is what you take at sea. We were sitting in a private room at the City—that's the tavern of our true-hearted Whigs when the speechifying has made them thirsty—and he was laughing till the tears rolled from his eyes and his belly bobbed like a lifebuoy. Doilies and diapers, he kept repeating, Cousin Pigeon will buy for Massachusetts! You can't miss, Mr. Mayhew.

NICHOLAS. He gave you nothing in writing?

WALLACE. Pigeon don't put anything in writing except birthday wishes to his mother.

NICHOLAS. But is Fillmore going to believe this in Salem? Verbal promises reported at second hand?

WALLACE. The question occurred to me. Pigeon agreed to send a trusted messenger to Salem; the man will tell Fillmore what I have told you. Nothing in writing.

NICHOLAS. That will have to do. And Pigeon himself—what are his terms?

WALLACE. Ten percent; plus an eighth share in Mr. Davis' chocolate mill.

NICHOLAS. An eighth? You didn't agree, did you? A full eighth?

WALLACE. I argued; ordered more rum; but Mr. Pigeon is quite above rum. It was an eighth or nothing. "Young Nick ain't the only cannon in the Atlantic," says he. I must report honestly, Mr. Mayhew.

NICHOLAS. You must indeed. An eighth it shall be. I need him more than he needs me, damn his bloated belly!

WALLACE. There you are.

NICHOLAS. And a wise man knows how to give in order to take. The pieces are falling into place, Wallace! Christ—if we'd lost you yesterday! One missing nail will bring an empire down. (*He takes out another letter from a pocket*) Do you know what's written in this?

WALLACE. I know it's from Mr. Davis, of course, and I know it concerns Mrs. Applegate—that's all.

NICHOLAS. I'll tell you. Wait. (*He goes to the door, looks into the next room, and comes back. Then he pulls close to Wallace*) Davis writes that Mrs. Applegate does have the power to sell. To sell every blessed acre they own at Concord.

WALLACE. That's good. Is her husband still in Nantucket?

NICHOLAS. More than ever; very thick with Judge Weamish and Sergeant Cuff; and offers snuff to the redcoats on Duke Street.

WALLACE. What redcoats?

NICHOLAS. Right—you don't know that we are entertaining the British army. Now. Davis tells me that dear Mrs. Applegate is suffering many vexations alone at Concord as the wife of an escaped Tory. One or two more frights and she'll sell for ten shillings in the pound. Davis has her confidence and is willing to buy for me when the time is ripe. You, Wallace, shall make it ripe.

WALLACE. How?

NICHOLAS. You'll go to Concord and spread the word that Mr. Applegate is compiling secret lists of Whigs for Gage's benefit and acting as go-between to supply the British from Nantucket. The fact is, they are being supplied, no one can deny it.

WALLACE. I'll do my best. And after Concord—on to Salem to see Mr. Fillmore?

NICHOLAS. Right. I'll give you a letter.

WALLACE. When will *you* be crossing to the mainland, Mr. Mayhew?

NICHOLAS. That's for my uncle to decide. For the moment no one's allowed to leave the island. But if the *Enterprise* is returning for you this Saturday—

WALLACE. It is without fail.

NICHOLAS. I *think* we'll go with you, Wallace. A little voice tells me so. And if we do—once we get to the mainland—Henry, how would you like the command of a brig?

WALLACE. Very much!

NICHOLAS. Trust me. You see but a part of my machine, you can't see it all.

WALLACE. I don't ask—

NICHOLAS. You don't need to. I'll tell you this much, however: Ben Fillmore is going to launch me with a dozen brigs on the strength of cousin Pigeon's promise; and you shall command one of them. (*Wallace grasps Nicholas' hand*)

Hush—I think I hear my uncle stirring. Not a word, Wallace.

WALLACE. Not in my dreams!

(*Enter Mayhew, grave*)

MAYHEW (*stretching out his hand*). Happy to see you up and well again, Mr. Wallace.

WALLACE. Happy to be alive, Colonel, thanks to Mr. Nicholas.

NICHOLAS. Enough of that.

MAYHEW. We're deeply in debt to you, Henry. Impossible to think of you as our "agent." As anything except a most precious friend.

WALLACE. I don't know what to say. Mine is a family of humble sailors—

NICHOLAS. Uncle—are you free to tell us what was in that letter of yours? I can't help being miserably curious about it.

MAYHEW. Before we talk about letters—no one recognized you last night, Henry—*I* wouldn't have recognized you! But now we'd best be careful. Stay within as much as possible, until we all take wing from Nantucket.

NICHOLAS. Take wing; music to my ears! The letter, uncle!

WALLACE. Perhaps I should withdraw.

MAYHEW. By no means. You told us last night that the *Enterprise* will return three days from now.

WALLACE. Yes, Colonel. Captain Fleming will bring her round the island on Saturday and drop anchor off the south coast between Weweeder and Nobadeer Pond. He'll look for signals from us all day.

NICHOLAS. So we're off!

MAYHEW. We're off, come what may. Saturday at sunset.

NICHOLAS. At last!

MAYHEW. Obed Coffin will row us aboard. He's a man I trust like a brother. We have orders to be at Cambridge before Washington's own arrival.

NICHOLAS. Washington at Cambridge? Come, sir the news; I'll enlist with the redcoats if you keep your secrets another minute!

MAYHEW. That would be ungrateful of you, seeing he mentions you in his letter.

NICHOLAS. How does he know me?

MAYHEW. By reputation, you dog! He personally approved your privateering commission.

NICHOLAS. And you, uncle, what about you?

MAYHEW (*takes out the letter*). Let me find the place. Here it is. "Your bold nephew"—

NICHOLAS. Uncle! To the point!

MAYHEW (*laughing*). Can't I interest you in my bold nephew? Very well. Your uncle Mayhew is to accompany General Schuyler into Canada.

NICHOLAS. Canada again!
MAYHEW. Yes. We took it away from France, and now we must take it away from England. Wait. 'Tis a longish letter. "Your bold nephew"—no, that's not the part. Here it is. "Our capture of Fort Ticonderoga on the 26th of May has encouraged the Congress to strike boldly into Canada. General Schuyler has been appointed to lead the northern expedition. He will not pause until Montreal and Quebec have fallen into our hands and our Canadian brethren are embraced into the common cause. Your task, my dear friend, will be to assist General Schuyler as his brigadier."
NICHOLAS. Wallace! Did you hear that?
WALLACE. I had an inkling—
MAYHEW. "I entreat you to meet me at Cambridge in the first days of July, for I may as well make known to you here and now what you shall undoubtedly be reading in the gazettes, to wit that the Congress has seen fit to entrust me, for the time being, with the defense of our sacred interests. I am proceeding immediately to Cambridge to take command of the army surrounding Boston."
NICHOLAS. This should be sung by a choir, d'you hear?
WALLACE. May I offer my congratulations, sir?
MAYHEW. Thank you, Henry. Think of it, young Nick—you at sea, I on land, God in heaven, and Washington before Boston!
NICHOLAS (*laughing*). Blow, ye trumpets!
MAYHEW. For the eighth day of Creation. Oh my friends, a nation made with our hands!
WALLACE (*who has been facing one of the windows*). Somebody's coming!
(*Mayhew and Nicholas turn quickly to the window*)
MAYHEW. The Marquise's daughter!
NICHOLAS. Madeleine!
MAYHEW. She stopped. She's hesitating. Why so shy? I shouldn't be surprised—by Jove, she's anxious about you—modesty at grips with—
NICHOLAS. Rubbish! But she *is* coming towards the house. Isn't she beautiful?
MAYHEW. We sail on Saturday, Nick.
NICHOLAS. That's three times twenty-four hours! Gentlemen, you've business to discuss in my uncle's study—if you haven't, invent it—and tell Ruthie I shall open the door myself.
MAYHEW. Come on, Henry; I'll explain who this beauty is.
WALLACE. Have I not seen her before?
NICHOLAS. Away, away! (*The two leave, laughing. Nicholas gazes out the window*) Is this for me? Daughter of a marchioness. Nicholas, "bold nephew"....

(*There is a knock at the door; Nicholas vanishes; the stage is empty; then he reappears, escorting Madeleine into the room; she is manifestly agitated*)

MADELEINE. Might someone have seen me from one of the houses?

NICHOLAS. Pray calm yourself. What if someone has?

MADELEINE. No, they mustn't. Mr. Mayhew—

NICHOLAS. Nicholas.

MADELEINE. Nicholas—what will you think of me? But—your action yesterday—it was so beautiful—terrifying and beautiful—and I needed to know—are you well? But I see now that you are!

NICHOLAS. The swim braced me. I sneezed a little only to alarm you—and to give me the pretext I wanted to allay your fears in person this afternoon. You forestalled me.

MADELEINE. I'm shameless!

NICHOLAS. You're lovely.

MADELEINE. And the steward—?

NICHOLAS. Slept as if never to wake again. But here you see the ruins of his breakfast.

MADELEINE. Is he grateful? Does he know?

NICHOLAS. Oh yes—but, my dear—(*softly*) my dearest Madeleine, what I did yesterday is an everyday occurrence among us. We live from the sea, and alas we are apt to die in the sea. These rescues are like helping someone from an overturned coach in Paris.

MADELEINE. And yet, who else threw himself into these monstrous waves—and for a stranger? Don't say any more; I shall believe in you, Nicholas.

NICHOLAS. Forever?

MADELEINE. Forever? What do you mean?

NICHOLAS. Madeleine—I cannot be near so much beauty—such grace—so much tender regard—without saying "Forever." (*He takes her in his arms. She half resists*)

MADELEINE. This is not why I came—believe me—do believe me. (*He kisses her*) Nicholas.... (*She kisses him*)

NICHOLAS. Madeleine—we have met only three times—

MADELEINE (*recoiling*). You see, you despise me!

NICHOLAS. Angel of heaven! My presumption is what makes me tremble. You will think me rash—brutal—to ask you—after so brief an acquaintance—but war is impatient. Would you be a sailor's bride—take your share of my hardships and rewards—sail with me to the end of the world—

MADELEINE. I would, Nicholas, and I say it because it can never be. I came here only to warn you—please don't misunderstand!

NICHOLAS. Sit beside me. You're trembling, my angel.

MADELEINE. I don't know what you are, Nicholas, you and your uncle—Tories or Whigs—

NICHOLAS (*surprised*). Oh?

MADELEINE. But I trust you utterly, my instinct tells me you are better men than your stupid judge and that nasty Sergeant—

NICHOLAS (*smiling*). I hope so.

MADELEINE. If you are a Tory, I'm alarmed about nothing at all—and then you must forgive a silly girl, a stranger, for meddling to no purpose. But if you are Whigs, Nicholas, I mean active Whigs, beware, I beg you, beware.

NICHOLAS. How is it you know so much, Madeleine?

MADELEINE. I have been hearing rumors, tales....

NICHOLAS. Our tavern's a fine place for that! But rest assured. I know all about these suspicions. Loyalists are not exempt. Everybody is watched and everybody is watching.

MADELEINE. True. But with you—there is a difference.

NICHOLAS. Why? (*Madeleine hesitates*) Why is there a difference?

MADELEINE (*whispering*). Don't speak—you and your uncle—don't speak of.... ideas, projects.... before my mother. She she is quite wonderful, and discreet, but—not always discreet. (*She rises and tries to run away, but Nicholas stops her*) Let me leave—

NICHOLAS. Not with tears in your eyes. Don't go yet—come back to me—gently—calm yourself. (*He makes her sit down; she is crying a little, he puts his hands on her cheeks*) Calm yourself, lovely, kind Madeleine.

MADELEINE. Did you understand me?

NICHOLAS. Of course I did. I'll not babble in front of your mother, I promise. She's fond of company, lively conversation, and a bit of gossip out of turn. I understand. I shall speak to her only about us, Madeleine and Nicholas. (*He pronounces his own name in the French manner*) Is not my French pretty? Nicholas et Madeleine. Or will you become simple Madelyn in our homely English?

MADELEINE. It can never be, Nicholas, never never never—

NICHOLAS. Because of your rank?

MADELEINE. No no no....

NICHOLAS. How little you know about this America of ours! Between you and me I recognize neither moat nor wall. Here we begin fresh, as in a new Garden of Eden.

MADELEINE. I know. But—

NICHOLAS. Wait! Don't answer yet. Will you listen to me a little while longer?

MADELEINE. Of course.

NICHOLAS. You land among us for a few days of rest. You discover our unpolished seamen and farmers, so different from the elegance you have known. No fine carriages, no jewels—

MADELEINE. How wrong you are—

NICHOLAS. But you haven't probed beneath the surface. Let me tell you my story. When I'm done, you shall lead me proudly to the fearsome Marquise, and she shall give us her blessing.

MADELEINE. Never, my dear, never.

NICHOLAS. We are Whigs, Madeleine.

MADELEINE (*joyful*). It couldn't be otherwise.

NICHOLAS. The man I rescued yesterday was our agent.

MADELEINE. And you knew it?

NICHOLAS. Of course. We were expecting him—with important messages from Philadelphia. They proved even more important than we thought. I love you, Madeleine. I will tell you my deepest secrets.

MADELEINE. No....

NICHOLAS. We have been summoned, my uncle and I, to meet the new commander-in-chief at Cambridge.

MADELEINE. To do God's work, Nicholas!

NICHOLAS. I knew that a Frenchwoman would think so. I am nothing now, Madeleine; I own a mere two ships, but the doors are opening to me. Look. This is a precious document. By virtue of it your Nicholas is now a privateer.

MADELEINE. What is a privateer?

NICHOLAS. A pirate!

MADELEINE. I understand—a *corsaire*—for your people's sake.

NICHOLAS. Yes. But this is only the first link. At Salem a great man is waiting for me. He wants to equip the fleet which is to sail under my command. My private share of the booty is an entire fifth, Madeleine, nothing to be sneered at. But now comes my second man. A gentleman in a high place in the army, who undertakes to purchase whatever I capture, sight unseen, lock, stock, and barrel. Do you follow me?

MADELEINE. I think so.

NICHOLAS. My third man is a banker in Philadelphia. The moment I have got my first two winnings in my pocket, he will advance me, what shall I call it? a majestic sum of money. And then—

MADELEINE. You will be a nabob.

NICHOLAS. We shall see! A year ago, when the Parliament ruined our sea trade, I joined in an expedition against the Shawnees, deep in the West—

MADELEINE. Did you kill many Indians, Nicholas?
NICHOLAS. I have killed better men than Indians.
MADELEINE. Yes, you are brave.
NICHOLAS. Though they have nearly killed me more than once! At Niagara Falls—but that's another story. In Virginia I met a fascinating person—a Judge Henderson—I can't tell you all the particulars now, Madeleine, but they're magnificent! Henderson bought land from the savages for next to nothing—a few pound sterling—a sack of trinkets—plenty of rum, too! More land than your French king possesses. Tell me, how well do you know our country?
MADELEINE. I'm very ignorant.
NICHOLAS. Have you heard of the Kentucky, the Ohio, the Cumberland?
MADELEINE. Yes. They are mountains and provinces.
NICHOLAS. They are also rivers. With land in between. A country unto itself. We've given it a noble name—Transylvania—and in that country Henderson is holding a splendid tract for me. No one knows about this, Madeleine, except you.
MADELEINE. Not even your uncle?
NICHOLAS. I should say not! Not about this nor about anything else I have told you. He has more important concerns. General Mayhew is going to lead an army. You needn't be ashamed of us, you see. But where was I?
MADELEINE. Your land—and the savages—
NICHOLAS. I am entrusting you with my secrets, Madeleine.
MADELEINE. They will die with me.
NICHOLAS. Land! And more land! We'll be lords! Your princes of the blood will come and kiss our hands. But Henderson wants hard cash on the table. And that is why I forged that long beautiful chain.
MADELEINE. You're extraordinary.
NICHOLAS. With special beauties in it—an estate at Concord—a chocolate mill.... But we'll not live in Massachusetts, you and I. Virginia is the place for us.
MADELEINE. Why?
NICHOLAS. You'll feel at home there. They will treat you as you deserve. You'll be waited upon by a retinue of glistening blacks! Oh Madeleine, I've been prating like a fool this half hour—sordid mercantile affairs, but how else could you learn that we are not unworthy of you? I love you. You are as beautiful—
MADELEINE. As the chain you forged?
NICHOLAS (*tenderly*). The chain is to bind you with.
MADELEINE. Nicholas—I'm a little dizzy—

NICHOLAS. And I'm a boor I haven't even offered you—
MADELEINE. Only a glass of water, please
NICHOLAS. Here.
MADELEINE. Thank you. Such marvelous stories—only in America can one hear such stories. I feel so old. Let me go back now to my little inn.
NICHOLAS. I've babbled and babbled.
MADELEINE. No—it was good to hear....
NICHOLAS. Was it? Was it truly? Madeleine, I loved you the mo—
MADELEINE. Will you remember the one important thing I said?
NICHOLAS. Which one, Madeleine?
MADELEINE. Not to speak—
NICHOLAS. Before—
MADELEINE. Anyone. My mother. Anyone....

(*She leaves. Nicholas watches her from the window*)

NICHOLAS. Was I too hasty? No, that was love in her blue eyes, and love on her thirsty lips, as sure as fish can swim. A wife worthy of me. Uncle! Wallace! Let's resume!

SCENE FIVE

(*The morning of Thursday, June 22. A lane in Sherburne. Sunny day. Madeleine is sitting on a bench. She is deep in thought. Mayhew enters. He is walking slowly, reading a book with great attention. He stops, struck by a passage, and, lifting his head to reflect upon it, he sees Madeleine. For a few moments he looks at her—she has not seen him—with evident admiration. He hesitates to intrude on her, but finally decides he will*)

MAYHEW. Mademoiselle.
MADELEINE. Colonel Mayhew! Forgive me, I didn't see you. (*She gives him her hand*)
MAYHEW. I was loth to disturb you in the very good company of your thoughts.
MADELEINE. My thoughts today are like unpleasant guests in the house.
MAYHEW. I'm sorry to hear you say so, on such a fine morning.
MADELEINE. It is a fine morning, isn't it. Will you sit by me? No—you are undoubtedly a busy man.
MAYHEW. Not just now. I was reading—strolling—raising my hat to my.... I

accept your invitation.

(She smiles; he sits down)

MADELEINE. What is your book, Colonel? I know! A treatise on fortifying exposed harbors.

MAYHEW. No. Guess again.

MADELEINE. The poems of some refined and ailing gentlewoman of Connecticut.

MAYHEW. No.

MADELEINE. I give up.

MAYHEW. It's a manifesto.

MADELEINE. Ah, that's dangerous.

MAYHEW. More than you think. It came in the same bottom that brought you to Nantucket two days ago.

MADELEINE. Come, tell me what it is.

MAYHEW. Are you not afraid of seditious literature?

MADELEINE. As a Frenchwoman I am immune.

MAYHEW. You are lucky to be the citizen of an old, stable nation. I believe the French have not engaged in civic broils since—let me see—when Louis XIV was a boy—and then the tumult was quickly settled. We must be a singularly restless people.

MADELEINE. Because you don't know how to be slaves.

MAYHEW. So writes my author, Mr. Jefferson.

MADELEINE. Read to me, Colonel. It will go no further than myself.

MAYHEW. Still, remember that a man needn't subscribe to what he reads. A man may read the words of an enemy in order to better foil him.

MADELEINE *(smiling)*. I understand.

MAYHEW *(leafing through the book)*. Here's some passable rhetoric. "The common feelings of human nature must be surrendered up before his Majesty's subjects here can be persuaded to believe that they hold their political existence at the will of a British Parliament. Shall these governments be dissolved, their property annihilated, and their people reduced to a state of nature, at the imperious breath of a body of men whom they never saw, in whom they never confided, and over whom they have no powers of punishment or removal, let their crimes against the American public be ever so great? Can any one reason be assigned why one hundred and sixty thousand electors in the island of Great Britain should give law to four millions in the States of America, every individual of whom is equal to every individual of them in virtue, in understanding, and in bodily strength? Were this to be admitted, instead of being a free people, as we have hitherto supposed and mean to continue ourselves, we should suddenly be found the slaves not of one but of one hundred and sixty thousand tyrants."

MADELEINE. I like that! Who is this flaming orator? Will you confess that he is a friend of yours? Why not? An enemy of the state might have been one's friend in the days of innocence.

MAYHEW. It is God's truth that I don't know the man.

MADELEINE. Do you think he is in jail?

MAYHEW. No; for I've been told that he is presently a delegate in Philadelphia. And were I a rebel of his complexion, *were* I, I would embrace him for these words.

MADELEINE. You show a fine sense, Colonel, in the estimate of your opponents. What else does your interesting firebrand say?

MAYHEW. Many wicked things—oh, if I were George the Third, I should not sleep easy until I did see Mr. Jefferson in fetters. For example: "By an act passed in the fifth year of the reign of his late Majesty, King George the Second, an American subject is forbidden to make a hat for himself of the fur which he has taken, perhaps, on his own soil—an instance of despotism to which no parallel can be produced in the most arbitrary ages of British history."

MADELEINE. Stop! Here I think your Mr. Henderson begins to foam at the mouth! What? Not to be allowed to make your own hat is a piece of brutality without parallel?

MAYHEW. I shouldn't have read you this passage. It is followed by a weightier one on the manufacture of iron.

MADELEINE. No, no more. Your hero must be permitted at once to sew his own beaver hat, whereupon he will turn into as good a Tory as—yourself.

MAYHEW. Well, he does allow himself to be carried away now and then. However, I beg you, Mademoiselle, to listen to one more passage.

MADELEINE. Very well.

MAYHEW. "The abolition of domestic slavery is the great object of desire in those colonies where it was, unhappily, introduced in their infant state. But previous to the enfranchisement of the slaves we have, it is necessary to exclude all further importations from Africa. Yet our repeated attempts to effect this, by prohibitions and by imposing duties which might amount to a prohibition, have been hitherto defeated by his Majesty's negative, thus preferring the immediate advantages of a few British corsairs to the lasting interests of the American States and the rights of human nature, deeply wounded by this infamous practice." Does this not touch you? "This infamous practice." Such words are quite beyond faction—we'll say no more about the beaver hats.

MADELEINE. Had you the opportunity, wouldn't you engage in the slave trade yourself, Colonel Mayhew?

MAYHEW. I—in the slave trade? I would die—no—I would kill—before I would allow a man to be handled like a bale of merchandise.

MADELEINE. But what of the pleasure of being waited on by a band of glistening blacks?

MAYHEW (*deeply grieved*). Is this you speaking, Mademoiselle?

(*Madeleine places a reassuring hand on Mayhew's arm*)

MADELEINE. God forbid. (*She pauses*) I was quoting your nephew.

MAYHEW (*smiling*). So *that* was the subject of your conversation yesterday—the slave trade!

MADELEINE. Or rather, trade in general. Nicholas is very gifted that way.

MAYHEW. Indeed he is. But give me leave to assure you that, like myself, Nicholas would raise his tent in Muscovy or turn heathen before he would engage in the buying and selling of slaves.

MADELEINE (*she is close to tears and replies in a whisper*). I am not so sure.

(*They sit silent for a while. Then, impulsively, Madeleine takes a pencil and a scrap of paper out of her purse, and writes a few words*)

MADELEINE. Please give him this for me. Oh, you may read it!

MAYHEW (*after reading the note*). Is that all?

MADELEINE (*low*). Yes.

MAYHEW. Nicholas is one of best, Madeleine. A plain dealer and a gallant fighter. He lost father and mother when he was a boy. Perhaps he wants the softer counsels of a woman to complete him as a man. But he is generous, quick-witted, exuberant in imagination. We shall need men like him. They will be our especial glory.

MADELEINE. Or your particular downfall.

MAYHEW (*downcast*). No. It must not be. You don't know him, Madeleine. He needs someone like you.

(*He tries to return the scrap of paper to her; she refuses with a gesture, and moves quickly away.*)

SCENE SIX

(Thursday, June 22. Late afternoon. Aimée's bedroom in Swain's Tavern. Aimée and Madeleine are alone)

AIMEE. I don't know how long I can keep that brute of a Sergeant from arresting them.
MADELEINE. Wouldn't the islanders riot if he tried?
AIMEE. That's what I and Weamish told him. But he may want to take the chance. What a blow if he catches them before I do! Sacré nom de Dieu, I'll not have an English bully get the better of Aimée Pichot. Not while I've got a set of teeth in my mouth. More or less.
MADELEINE. What have you found out so far, mother? Are they rebels or loyalists?
AIMEE. Rebels at heart I say. But Gage is not interested in hearts. What I need is palpable proof they are plotting to join the Whig army. Or else a plot to seize Nantucket. Or smuggle arms to the mainland. Palpable mischief. I have an idea. Why don't you bewitch the uncle while I bring down the nephew?
MADELEINE. Why?
AIMEE. Older men are more susceptible. It'll turn his head when he sees a pretty young girl fluttering about him.
MADELEINE. You're better looking than I am, mother.
AIMEE. I was. God what a girl I was when I kept jail in Lyon! But I've lost my looks—some of my looks. What I've kept, though, is blood and guts, and that's more important with a man, when all's said and done. You're too mousy, Madeleine. You've had two days, and what have you accomplished? Nothing.
MADELEINE. Oh, I don't know. Nicholas Mayhew proposed to me.
AIMEE. Very amusing. Yes, I think I'll unleash myself at him, and have you nibble at the uncle.
MADELEINE. I'm not joking, mother.
(Aimée stares at her)
AIMEE. God strike me! Nick Mayhew—*proposed* to you? That's all? When? What happened? Where? Why?
MADELEINE. I suppose he likes me. I think he likes my noble lineage too.
AIMEE. A miracle has happened! Suddenly the girl's an expert! Come here, Madelon! *(She hugs Madeleine)* You'll make your fortune after all. I take back the mousy. Tell me all about it, and don't leave out the erotic details, you

naughty baggage!

MADELEINE. Well, he wants to marry me.

AIMEE. When did he propose? Where?

MADELEINE. What does it matter? We talked for a long time—he was very wild—very eloquent—but of course my rank made him keep his distance—most of the time.

AIMEE. What did you discover about him? Can we deliver him to Gage?

MADELEINE. We didn't discuss the political situation, mother, but I can tell you that Mr. Mayhew is a man with a very large future.

AIMEE. A firing squad is not a future.

MADELEINE. I'm not so sure about the firing squad. He has a very keen mind for business, mother. I wish you'd been there to listen to his projects. A fleet under his command; an estate at Concord; huge tracts of land in the West; a chocolate mill; shiny slaves; bankers urging loans and credits upon him—I tell you my head was spinning. And I kept thinking how much you'd have enjoyed it.

AIMEE. Why was he giving you this inventory?

MADELEINE. To convince the daughter of Madame de Tourville that she wouldn't be taking a dreadful tumble down the social ladder.

AIMEE. He may have been bragging.

MADELEINE. Such details, such confirmations! No, he wasn't bragging.

AIMEE. Madeleine, this is serious. Stupendously serious. A fleet under his command. And then that cock-and-bull steward of theirs. You'd better tell me the rest. Out with it, hussy. What passed between you and Nicholas?

MADELEINE. I allowed him to kiss me once.

AIMEE. Nothing about soldiering? Good only for trading and kissing?

MADELEINE. If they are good for anything else, that's for you to discover.

AIMEE. By putting *you* to the question, miss. Or better yet, by striking at once. The longer I look at you, the more I'm tempted to take the risk.

MADELEINE. Don't be rash, mother. Your guess might be dreadfully wrong. Why should prosperous men like the Mayhews fight the king? Mother— (*with unexpected force*) leave—them—alone.

AIMEE. Aha, the little spitfire is in love! You accepted him, did you?

MADELEINE. No.

AIMEE. You refused him?

MADELEINE. Yes.

AIMEE. Why?

MADELEINE. A rebel, mother, whom you intend to deliver to a firing squad?

AIMEE. A rebel with a fleet, and land in the West, and chocolate mills, and bankers, is no rebel until I've decided he is. I shall strike at once, that's settled, but which way? Here's an ambitious dog proposing to you; a man the government fears like the plague; a fleet at his command; a wizard in business. What shall we tell him when he proposes a second time?

MADELEINE. You're a whirlwind, mother! One moment we're arresting Nicholas and the next we're marrying him. *I* say let's leave the island. No plots, no machinations this time. Please, mother. You'll make up in Canada for the few wretched pounds you sacrificed here.

AIMEE. So anxious! You really must know a great deal! I ought to ship the Mayhews to Boston at dawn tomorrow and produce you there as a witness. I assure you there's nothing wretched about six-hundred pounds. A baronet can live a year on six-hundred pounds. And I'll thank you not to threaten your own mother. On the other hand, aren't we missing the larger landscape? To hear Sergeant Cuff talk, the Yankees are not the sheep we've been told they are. And the Mayhews prove him right. There must be thousands of these sturdy rogues arming up and down the continent. Providence may have placed the uncle and nephew in our path to show us we were about to commit a terrible sin.

MADELEINE. But what about your former lover?

AIMEE. Who's that?

MADELEINE. General Gage.

AIMEE. What about him?

MADELEINE. Would it be quite correct to betray him?

AIMEE. Quite correct. Tom Gage is a man of the world. And I need to provide for you.

MADELEINE. Thank you, mother. Yet I don't want to marry Mr. Mayhew.

AIMEE. Because he loves King George?

MADELEINE. Because.

AIMEE. He's brave and handsome, and he's a revolutionary. Don't tell me that's against him. I hope I can read my own daughter. You're a rebel yourself, you've never fooled me, fear of your mother is all that's kept you in line.

MADELEINE. And yet I will not marry him.

AIMEE. I haven't yet decided that you should. I need time to think. Thank God we can live without Montreal, where I must be dull Madame Pichot again. We're free, Madeleine. Let's look at this Nicholas together.

MADELEINE. I'm not marrying him, mother.

AIMEE. Why not? What happened? What's wrong with him?

MADELEINE. He's too pretty for me.

AIMEE. The girl's a lunatic! One minute you talk like a woman of sense and experience; the next, you babble gibberish that would shame an infant!

MADELEINE. I don't care.
AIMEE. Madeleine my child, I love you dearly, and I forgive you your dubious origins, but gold turns to clay in your hands. You'll become a bad influence on me when I'm older and weaker and can't put up a fight. Mr. Swain!
SWAIN (*appearing*). Madam desires?
AIMEE. A bowl of grog, if you please! (*Swain vanishes*) Young Mayhew proposes to you; you refuse him; but you'll throttle your mother to protect him. He needs protecting, does he? I wonder why! (*Swain reappears with the order*) Thank you, Mr. Swain. (*He leaves*) Yes.... I must have a talk of my own with Mr. Mayhew. I find that I'm partial to fleets and Concord estates.

SCENE SEVEN

(The evening of Thursday, June 22. A beach on the south shore of Nantucket. In the back, we see a so-called "stage"—that is to say a small house used by the cod fishermen of Nantucket. The sound of the ocean surf nearby. Enter the Mayhews and Obed Coffin)

MAYHEW. This is the place I have chosen. Saturday at sunset we'll flash our signal to the *Enterprise* from here. Let's hope the weather holds.
OBED. I've got a feeling it will, Colonel. My bones usually tell me three days in advance if there's a storm stirring up.
NICHOLAS. Two days of your bones is all we need, Obed, so don't let them fool us.
MAYHEW. With God's help we shall reach our destination on Sunday, in time to kneel in church.
NICHOLAS (*laughing*). Uncle, for once I'll kneel with you. I expect we'll have something to be thankful for.
MAYHEW. When shall we see our island again, Nick?
NICHOLAS. When indeed?
MAYHEW. This particular sea-wind and this especial odor of the heather that grows nowhere else in America. I know by anticipation the ache I shall feel when we are gone.
NICHOLAS (*to Obed*). Bring plenty of pitch for our signal.
OBED. I've got a barrel of it in the house, sir.
NICHOLAS. Good.
OBED. I forgot to ask. Will you be taking a heap of baggage? Because if you

are, I'll ask my brother Tim to help row us out.
MAYHEW. We'll have next to nothing. Better to arrive on the mainland naked than to be met by the Sergeant's men carrying out a couple of trunks.
OBED. We'll guard your house when you're gone, Colonel. Let them try to touch it!
MAYHEW. Thanks, Obed. But don't allow violence and bloodshed, God forbid, on account of our house. If the war goes against us, it will be lost anyhow.
OBED. We'll haul my boat to the water's edge on Saturday afternoon. You'll not waste a minute.
NICHOLAS. It's getting chilly. Hey—who's this?
OBED. Somebody running our way. What shall we do?
MAYHEW. Somebody who knows we're here. (*He pulls out a pistol*) Stand still and leave him to me.
VOICE. Colonel! Mr. Mayhew!
MAYHEW. It's Mamack!
(*Enter Mamack*)
MAMACK. They've arrested Mr. Wallace!
(*He falls on the sand out of breath*)
NICHOLAS. Damn!
MAYHEW. Catch your breath, Mamack, and tell us what happened.
MAMACK. I'll try—in a minute—I been lookin' for you high and low—left my horse half a mile away! They arrested Mr. Wallace right outside your house, Colonel, I guess he was taking the air. I hear that four redcoats come up to him and drug him away.
OBED. They'll pay for this!
MAMACK. There's worse to come. The Sergeant got three or four men to say who is Mr. Wallace.
NICHOLAS. Tupper, Folger, Rotch—I'll take my oath they were the first to play Judas.
MAMACK. You say right, Mr. Mayhew; and Abe Myrick too.
NICHOLAS. We'll pickle them to our taste before this war is over.
OBED. Amen.
MAYHEW. What else, Mamack?
MAMACK. As soon as word go out that somebody was arrested off o' your doorstep, Colonel, people start comin' out into the streets. There's a crowd in front of the jail, another one in front of the Judge's house, and another one by your house to see nobody touches you.
NICHOLAS. What next, uncle?
MAYHEW. Well, they've got Wallace. And who is Wallace? Our business

agent. Where's the crime in that?

NICHOLAS. Yes—but why did we conceal him? Why, when I pulled him out of the sea, why didn't I cry "Wallace, dear old business agent"?

MAYHEW. Because our business affairs are private. I hope we've a right to keep our affairs to ourselves.

OBED. Sounds reasonable to me. They're bound to release Wallace tomorrow.

NICHOLAS. Unless they whip or beat the truth out of him.

MAYHEW. I don't think the Sergeant feels safe enough to misuse a prisoner. Back to town, men. We must pay the Judge a visit.

NICHOLAS. Right! Cuff wouldn't have struck without Weamish's connivance. We'll make our fop of a judge sweat a little.

MAMACK. I hear hoof beats. Wait.

(*He hurries out*)

NICHOLAS. What now?

MAYHEW. Perhaps the Sergeant has come to arrest us too.

(*He draws his pistol again. Obed brings out his knife*)

NICHOLAS. I'll twist his head about his neck if he tries.

(*Mamack returns*)

MAMACK. It's the lady in the chaise! Coming from 'Sconset way!

MAYHEW. What lady?

MAMACK. The French one, the older one—old Moses is driving her!

NICHOLAS. Christ! Madeleine warned me her mother's a babbler. Snuff the light, Obed! A pox on her! Wallace arrested—all of us confabulating at the seashore at night—

MAYHEW. Steady, steady. Leave this to me. (*He advances*) Who goes there? Stand and answer ere you take another step.

AIMEE (*entering*). Don't shoot, whoever you are—this is the foreign lady. Ah, Colonel Mayhew! What a heavenly surprise!

MAYHEW. The surprise is all ours, Madame. What brings you so far from Sherburne?

AIMEE. Obedience to your nephew, Colonel. Good evening, Nicholas.

NICHOLAS. Good evening, Marquise. Pray tell us in what particular you obeyed poor Nicholas.

AIMEE. Well, it was you who bade me look at the sunset from the eastern part of the island. What do you call it?

MAYHEW. 'Sconset, Marquise?

AIMEE. No, we drove a little beyond.

MAYHEW. Ah, to Sancoty Head it was.

AIMEE. That's it.

NICHOLAS. You weren't disappointed, I hope.

AIMEE. Most certainly not. Sunsets are my passion—and this one took me back to my childhood. My family, the Fapignac, owned a small property on the Breton coast where the sunsets resemble yours. The rugged land, you know, the wild sea, the steeples. I was enchanted.

MAYHEW. It is a romantic evening, is it not?

AIMEE. Yes. And I expect a splendid moon. But you gentlemen—I seem to have stumbled upon a band of conspirators! I find you miles from Sherburne—

NICHOLAS. A mere five miles, Madame.

AIMEE. It seems farther because of the wildness. I am quite sure I have found you out in some wickedness. How delightful. Your men are staring at me.

NICHOLAS. They are amazed to see this fairy-tale apparition by a fisherman's hut.

AIMEE. Who knows what is concealed in that hut? I am determined to enjoy something extraordinary and positively forbidden.

MAYHEW. Where is your charming daughter, Marquise?

AIMEE. No, you cannot fob me off, Colonel. There's mischief in the air. Would that it were directed against England and its minions! So speaks a Frenchwoman.

NICHOLAS. It grieves me to—

MAYHEW. No, no, Madame has discovered us, Nick; I think we had better confess.

(*Nicholas stares at him*)

OBED. Colonel—

MAYHEW. But do you swear not to give us away, Marquise?

AIMEE. I swear! This is wonderfully exciting.

MAYHEW. Still, I tremble.

AIMEE. I swear on the bones of Bertrand de Fapignac, the founder of our house. Does that satisfy you?

MAYHEW. You are irresistible. Well then—I am afraid you surprised us bargaining for ten barrels of rum to be delivered on this spot a week from today. But you'll give us away, Marquise.

AIMEE. Trust me, Colonel. However, your ten barrels of rum are a disappointment. What barrels? Where from? And why this night-time huddle?

MAYHEW. These barrels—as a man of honor I detest the word, Marquise, but they are being *smuggled* into the island.

NICHOLAS. Dreadful times.

OBED. Terrible times.

MAYHEW. I am deeply embarrassed at being found out a common smuggler.

AIMEE. Nonsense. My grandfather on my mother's side, the Comte d'Epervisse, took smuggled tobacco all his life. But why are you smuggling rum? Isn't your rum distilled, or whatever you do with rum, here in your own Massachusetts?

MAYHEW. We have it from Rhode Island, Madame. We are landing it secretly. But I shouldn't tell you, for you are a friend of Sergeant Cuff's.

AIMEE. That bulldog? You know better, Colonel.

MAYHEW. Then I can speak freely. Sergeant Cuff would seize the rum and ship it to General Gage at Boston. Now, we are peace-loving and law-abiding citizens, we hate rebellion, but is it our duty to drink water for King George? We say, let Boston find its own rum. Besides, the loss of their customary supply would cause our people to grumble against the king.

AIMEE. Enjoy your rum, Colonel. You didn't leave *all* my romantic needs unsatisfied, though I was hoping for something—oh, I don't know—a trifle more dashing—a plot to seize Sergeant Cuff—to smuggle in a cannon or two—to make an escape from the island—who knows?

NICHOLAS. Only rebels would do such naughty things. No, Marquise, this is a prosaic island. Nothing but whales and cod.

AIMEE. And a few sheep, mules and asses grazing in the fields.

NICHOLAS. There you have it.

AIMEE. Well, it's growing darker by the minute. Madeleine will fret if I don't return presently, and besides I'm to make the fourth at Judge Weamish's card table tonight. Those wearisome Tories! Dear me! I could wish that the road were less destroyed with ruts, and that Mr. Moses had keener eyesight!

MAYHEW. God forbid your chaise should overturn in the dark. Nicholas!

NICHOLAS. I shall take the reins in my own hands, Madame, never fear!

AIMEE. I hesitate to trouble you in the midst—

NICHOLAS. No trouble at all, I assure you! It will be a pleasure.

MAYHEW. Trust my nephew, Marquise. You need only oblige us by walking to your chaise while I say a few last words to him about our trifling business here.

AIMEE. Do, do. You have a mother's heartfelt thanks.

(*She leaves*)

NICHOLAS (*low and hurriedly*). Will she keep quiet, uncle? I know she means no harm, but—

MAYHEW (*likewise*). Let her tattle. I lack time to tell you, but I know what to do. Your only task is to deploy your charm, detain her, amuse her, and keep her away from the card table until *I* see Weamish.

NICHOLAS. You can depend on me. I'll do—

VOICE OF AIMEE. Are you coming, sir?

NICHOLAS. Yes, Marquise! J'arrive. (*To MAYHEW*) She'll be in good hands,

I promise you. And besides, it may *really* be a pleasure!
MAYHEW. Go, go!
(*Nicholas leaves*)
OBED. And now, colonel, if I may ask?
MAYHEW. Now? Back to town, where I'll call on Mr. Weamish before he sits down to cards, raise a storm about Wallace, and be the first to tell him about our beach and our rum.
OBED (*astonished*). Am I hearing you right, colonel?
MAYHEW. You are. Didn't we promise Sergeant Cuff to look for secret stores of weapons? And come to think of it, our good deed will bolster our demand that Wallace be set free at once.
OBED (*laughing*). Hats off to you, colonel, as usual!
MAYHEW. Away! The lady might be in a hurry to win the kitty tonight.
(*Exeunt*)

SCENE EIGHT

(*Friday, June 23. One o'clock in the morning. Aimée's bedroom on the second story of Swain's Tavern. We also see a portion of the landing, and a couple of doors leading to other rooms. The bed is of the alcove type, surrounded by curtains*)

(*Nicholas is putting on his clothes*)
NICHOLAS. You're not falling asleep, Amy?
AIMEE'S VOICE (*from the bed*). *Aimée*, you puppy, *Aimée*. I insist.
NICHOLAS. Not while you're in my country, and never again for me. Not for me, d'you hear?
AIMEE. Yes for you. And you, sir, are Nicolas—Nee-ko-lah (*she pronounces the name in French*) when we're alone. Not Nick, young Nick, Nicky, or any other vulgar middle-class nick-names. Give me another kiss, you villain, you seducer of elderly ladies.
NICHOLAS. No, Marquise.
AIMEE. Why not?
NICHOLAS. Twenty kisses or nothing.
AIMEE. So be it. Twenty kisses.
(*Nicholas flings himself onto the bed and vanishes from sight*)
AIMEE. Not so hard, darling.
NICHOLAS. Witch—mermaid—sorceress—so much pleasure no man ever

tasted before—and survived to remember it.

AIMEE. The pleasure was mine, sir.

NICHOLAS. No, no, it couldn't—it wasn't—

AIMEE. It will improve with time, and is keen already. My pretty boy. What sweet silky lips you have, and what a lovely little nose! Mmmmrn. Ah if I were twenty years younger!

NICHOLAS. I refuse to listen! You are a masterpiece of nature. Don't grow a day younger or I shall cut my throat. Let us enjoy, enjoy, enjoy. I wish I could, once more—if I remained till dawn—

AIMEE. What are you thinking of? Silly Yankee! There will be other times, I hope—or will you toss me aside, like the rind of an orange you've devoured?

NICHOLAS. You are my inexhaustible orange tree! Permit me, Marquise, to nibble again.

AIMEE. Pray do. Mmrnmm. A little more....

NICHOLAS. Your loyal servant....

AIMEE. Ah!

NICHOLAS. Pleased?

AIMEE. Delighted.

NICHOLAS. I must be gone, mustn't I? Still, let us have a tiny conversation before you send me away.

AIMEE (*lazily*). Very well.

(*They reappear*)

NICHOLAS. May I? (*He helps her with a scanty robe*) Oh how yielding and warm you feel through this gauze!

AIMEE. I thought we were going to converse?

NICHOLAS. By all means. (*They sit on an upholstered bench by the window*) You're not chilly?

AIMEE. I will be if you take your arm away.

NICHOLAS. Amy—what next? Tell me.

AIMEE. Anything you wish, my darling rebel.

NICHOLAS. Rebel? Who is a rebel?

AIMEE. My daughter's suitor.

NICHOLAS (*takes this in*). Madeleine told you, of course—before I could.

AIMEE. She made such a serious point of *not* telling me that I understood at once.

NICHOLAS. You must think me an infinite scoundrel.

AIMEE. That's why I love you, my daredevil.

NICHOLAS. Are you a daredevil too?

AIMEE. In a modest way.

NICHOLAS. Do you dare—marry me?

AIMEE. Even though I am my daughter's mother?

NICHOLAS. It was an error. It seemed romantic. But it was too pale, too prim, too strait-laced. It would have been a disaster after six months. You, instead—you shall romp audaciously with me through life.

AIMEE. And yet, there on the beach, were you not setting out to romp across the water without me?

NICHOLAS. Amy! What has Madeleine told you about us?

AIMEE. She tells her mother very little. But when I saw you all tonight huddled together, I suddenly knew it all. I teased you because I was so glad.

NICHOLAS. What a relief for me! Now I needn't preach the good cause before you marry me.

AIMEE. Did I say I'll marry you, sir?

NICHOLAS. Do, my love, do. I'll devote my life to turning your regrets into as many gratitudes. I'll not buckle my shoe without consulting your happiness. What say you, Amy?

AIMEE. Let me taste again. (*She kisses him*) Yes.... I'd be sorry to lose this. But my name, Nicolas, my name. I know your family is respectable—very fair for America. And you are a person of some means—

NICHOLAS. More than some, Amy. Perhaps Madeleine didn't tell you. I have a privateering commission in my pocket, commitments for a fleet out of Salem, the guarantee of a prodigious—

AIMEE (*stopping her ears*). Ta ta ta ta! Spare me these horrors! I hope you'll not oblige me to do your ledgers for you. But the difference in age—

NICHOLAS. Amy, does Venus obey a calendar? Your skin is all cream and roses—

AIMEE. Tempter! Your words intoxicate me. Hold me close to you. I'll do anything you ask. I'll renounce my title for your sake.

NICHOLAS. Oh no! Though I intend to be a king myself, in Virginia or in the Carolinas. You and I will hold court in a plantation. You'll walk on my arm as my consort. And when we Americans come to make titles of our own—need I say more? This is the new world, the new life—trust your passionate buccaneer!

AIMEE. I will. I do.

NICHOLAS. Amy, Amy, my wife! (*They kiss*) Who would have thought, when I ran to help you—?

AIMEE. It was ever so sweet of you, my love.

NICHOLAS. There was more than sweetness in it, I can now confess. We fancied that you might be tattling to the judge while playing cards, in all innocence of course. I decided to escort you, plead for discretion, and—to tell you the truth—make love to you if necessary.

AIMEE. And I—to tell you the truth—decided to let you.

NICHOLAS. Oh the hussy!

AIMEE. Oh the scamp!

(*They kiss*)

NICHOLAS. Shall we go back—there (*he points to the bed*)—or make projects for our lives?

AIMEE. My wifely voice says, we had better make projects for our lives.

NICHOLAS. And begin soberly at the beginning. We were struck a nasty blow earlier this evening, Amy.

AIMEE. What blow, my pretty lad?

NICHOLAS. Our so-called steward, the one who almost drowned—

AIMEE. Why so-called, my dear?

NICHOLAS. He was in fact our agent, Henry Wallace by name.

AIMEE. The tricks you men play!

NICHOLAS. They don't always suffice. Several townspeople recognized him, and Sergeant Cuff arrested him tonight.

(*Aimée jumps up. Her tone is very different now*)

AIMEE. While I was—! Hang the ruffian!

NICHOLAS. If Wallace confesses that he came ashore to plot our escape from Nantucket, we'll be in jail with him tomorrow.

AIMEE. We must fight this Sergeant, Nicholas.

NICHOLAS. We will, my darling. What a comfort to see you so indignant! And my plan's already formed. My uncle will certainly not leave the island without Wallace—though in my opinion the fool ought to fend for himself for allowing the redcoats to catch him. Myself, my uncle and ten armed men will overcome our booby of a judge, use him for a hostage, pluck Wallace from his cell, and force our way to the sloop that's waiting to take us aboard. You and Madeleine will join us at Cambridge in your own good time.

AIMEE. No, no, no! I hate your scheme. Your hostage won't stop the Sergeant. And he has ten times your ten men.

NICHOLAS. We have most of Sherburne!

AIMEE. Worse still! You're too young, you believe you're indestructible! But I know better; I've seen too many indestructible youngsters bleeding to death in the snow! Leave it all to me instead.

NICHOLAS. To you! What in the world can you do?

AIMEE. I can denounce you.

NICHOLAS. What do you mean?

AIMEE. I'll play the spy. I'll inform against you. You'll see. To save you I'll become clever. I'll stop that bully of a Sergeant. Tomorrow—I mean later today—I'll send out dinner invitations to you, your uncle, the Sergeant, and the judge. I'll serve them an unforgettable meal, I promise you. Before dessert is on the table, your enemies will be in your hands, bound and gagged; you shall walk to your beach in triumph. And meet me there.

NICHOLAS. You leave me speechless! Is this my tender Marquise?

AIMEE. I know—you thought me nothing but a gossip, a dainty plaything for a night—

NICHOLAS. Amy!

AIMEE. Instead I'll show you a tigress.

NICHOLAS. More and more marvelous! But what will you prepare for these gentlemen? A sleeping potion? A brew to make them mad? A Borgia poison?

AIMEE. Tat, tat, curiosity killed the cat. Hurry to your uncle now. He must think you're in jail.

NICHOLAS. By God, you're right. But when shall I hear the rest?

AIMEE. Before noon. And kiss me before you go.

NICHOLAS. Must I leave you?

AIMEE. I wish I could say no. But you must. Wait, I'll see you out.

(*Aimée lights a taper and they walk out together. On the landing they embrace again. One of the doors opens, and Madeleine appears in her nightdress, also holding a taper*)

AIMEE. Madeleine! What are you doing here stark naked?

MADELEINE. Why, I'm as decorously dressed as you, mamma.

NICHOLAS. My dear Madeleine, embarrassment is useless, concealment impossible: I am your new father. I aspired at one time to another, more intimate connection, but you gave me my freedom, which I hastened to surrender to this precious lady, your mother, who is, indeed, more precious to me for being your mother.

MADELEINE. My dear new father, and mother dear, I offer you my tenderest congratulations. But permit me to withdraw at this time.

NICHOLAS. By no means! I am the intruder here, the thief in the night who has snatched away a priceless pearl. (*He kisses Aimée's hand*) I wish you both a restful night, though little remains of it. My dearest Marquise, will you convey all the necessary intelligence to our Madeleine?

AIMEE. I will, my prince.

NICHOLAS. Good night, then.

(*Nicholas goes down the stairs and disappears. The two women stand without speaking until they hear the door downstairs open and close*)

AIMEE (*very excited*). Come with me, Madeleine. (*She takes Madeleine by the hand back into her room*) Put down your candle. Madelon! We've jumped to the other side!

MADELEINE. I thought as much from the noises I heard.

AIMEE. Isn't it exciting? All my political opinions are turned upside down. I'm as hot a revolutionary now as you've been all along, Miss Twoface. And I'm going to commit a ghastly misalliance by marrying Nicholas Mayhew.

MADELEINE. What will our relations say when they get wind of this tragic degradation?

AIMEE. Ah, I'm so glad you're taking it lightly. I was terrified—I thought you'd make a great moral scene on the landing. Madelon, my little canary, you're not jealous of your old mother, are you? I didn't take him away from you—you practically bequeathed him to me.

MADELEINE. I don't want to bequeath him to you, mother, because of what will happen when he learns the truth.

AIMEE. Why should he learn anything so unpleasant?

MADELEINE. Because your former friends will see to it.

AIMEE. No, my girl. I know too many of their secrets. However, I'll secure myself on Nicholas' side as well. You'll see.

MADELEINE. I don't think I'll see. I'll go back to Lyon.

AIMEE. What do you mean, "back"? You're a stranger in France.

MADELEINE. What of it? Tante Marie has asked me often enough; she has a small room for me; and I'll help her mind the shop.

AIMEE. You've always wanted fire. But I intend to fight your destiny, which, if I don't, is to marry a tailor—and be faithful to him.

MADELEINE. I'm sorry I disappoint you, mother.

AIMEE. Nonsense. Come here. (*She kisses her*) Won't we look fine, you and I, strolling arm in arm on one of young Nick's plantations!

MADELEINE. And so we leave the island with the Mayhews?

AIMEE. Yes; but not without a fight. The Sergeant has arrested their agent— the very man I knew at once to be no steward.

MADELEINE. I see. And then?

AIMEE. I have in mind a charming dinner for the two factions, where I shall serve the one as a main course to the other.

MADELEINE. Charming! And what if somebody is killed?

AIMEE. If anybody is killed, he'll have only himself to blame. I'll give the blackguards every chance to surrender meekly.

MADELEINE. Mother, mother! How much longer shall we live by these dangerous schemes?

AIMEE. This will be our last, Madelon; one more—and then —God forgive me —I'll miss them.

SCENE NINE

(The morning of Friday, June 25 in the Weamish residence. Weamish, in morning undress, is feverishly finishing another letter)

WEAMISH. "Therefore hasten your return, dearest mamma; the kingdom's fate is being decided here; all is lost without you. Your devoted and beleaguered son —" *(calling)* Jenny!
(Instead of Jenny it is Aimée who enters. The Weamish jumps up)
AIMEE. Urgent matters, Judge; I could not wait to be announced.
WEAMISH. Welcome, Marquise, welcome! Oh the storms that have swept this island while you were innocently asleep in your bed! Last night—it must have happened after you fell in with the Mayhews on the beach—for I have heard all about your sunset-gazing—sunsets at a time like this!—still, let that be—last night, I repeat, the colonel berated me like a—but first, I daresay it is news to you that the man who almost drowned *incognito* the other day, you saw him, well! that man proves to be no man at all but the Mayhews' agent! Whereupon the Sergeant swoops in, arrests him and clamps him in fetters. Night falls. In strides the Sergeant—I mean the colonel. Standing upon the very spot where you are standing now, he berates me like a schoolboy, me! and why? because, says he, the agent's secret is nothing but commerce and trade and business. So now the population is up in arms, I utterly tremble for my life, and I am near believing that the world is coming to an end.
AIMEE. Calm yourself, my friend. Come, sit down. I am here to help you. I drove to the seashore last night for reasons higher than sunsets, believe me, and of course I am fully aware that Henry Wallace is under arrest.
WEAMISH. Oh, what comfort you bring me, Madame. You even know his name.
AIMEE. Let us sit down. You may recollect that I became suspicious at once when the man was rescued, and made strenuous attempts to have our mulish Sergeant convey the fellow to our own quarters. Sergeant Cuff understands only blunderbusses and twenty-pounders.
WEAMISH. Thank God for your presence here, Marquise. With you at my side, I shall smite to the left and right. I shall spare no one.
(Enter Jenny)
JENNY. It's Sergeant Cuff to see you.
AIMEE. Good!
WEAMISH. Have him come up at once.

JENNY. Yes, sir. But here he is.

(*She leaves as Sergeant Cuff enters*)

CUFF. Good morning all.

AIMEE. Good—

CUFF. Y'are here to give me a dressing down by leave of General Gage. Consider it done. I arrested that rascal of an agent on my own initiative.

WEAMISH. Let me inform you, Sergeant, that the colonel burst into this room last night and vented his rage upon my person.

CUFF. Let him vent upon mine. I'll teach 'em to rage, the scurvy rebels.

WEAMISH. You call them rebels. But does Mr. Wallace confess he came here on a political mission?

CUFF. He hasn't confessed yet, but leave him to me until Sunday, and after church I'll serve you a confession on a platter.

AIMEE. By Sunday the Mayhews will be in Cambridge.

WEAMISH and CUFF. What?

AIMEE. I repeat. By Sunday the two Mayhews will be in Cambridge. Wallace came here to take them off the island. And off they'll go, with him or without. (*Imitating the Sergeant*) Y'are too slow, Sergeant Cuff.

CUFF. Od's guts, who told you all this?

WEAMISH. Marquise—?

AIMEE. I never reveal the sources of my intelligence, gentlemen. But I hope you credit me. If you do not, the event will speak for me soon enough.

CUFF. I credit you so thoroughly that I'm off to arrest them both. I should have done it the day you arrived. It was you that kept me. Od's liver, I smell a vile rebel a league away. Judge, write me out a warrant. We'll do it by the book this time.

WEAMISH. Sign a warrant against the Mayhews? Who settled here in the year 1659? I'll be stoned to death.

AIMEE. Judge Weamish is right. He is interested in avoiding bloodshed.

CUFF. I'm not.

AIMEE. To each his profession. But a soldier's first duty, as I understand—

CUFF. Is to destroy the enemy.

AIMEE. Is not to be destroyed by the enemy. That's a *sine qua non* for the other.

CUFF. The devil of a sinecure it is! Madam, with all due—

AIMEE. Sergeant, with all due, arresting the Mayhews in the open is not advisable. Twenty-five armed patriots are standing guard over their house; twenty-five others are milling about your quarters; more are gathering in the street below.

WEAMISH. Merciful gods!

AIMEE. Your life is not safe, Judge; and yours even less, Sergeant. Granted, these yokels are untrained, but they come in large crowds, they shoot in all directions, and they are philosophical enough to hide behind fences and trees. Must a woman teach you these nursery-school facts?

WEAMISH. I am taught, Marquise; consider me your devoted pupil.

AIMEE. Sergeant?

CUFF. The women are in command here. I see we must go by ruses and devices.

AIMEE. Be patient, Sergeant. I am reserving a capital role for brawn and firepower. Will you both kindly dine with me tomorrow in Mr. Swain's private dining room? Shall we say at one in the afternoon? This will be a modest repayment for the many delicate attentions I have received at Sherburne since my arrival.

WEAMISH. This is handsome, Madame. But what of the entertainment I had designed?

AIMEE. Another time. May I count on your company, my dear Judge? (*Weamish kisses her hand*) And yours, Sergeant?

CUFF (*fuming*). Hang good manners, this flummery has gone too far!

AIMEE. My other guests will be Colonel and young Mr. Mayhew.

(*Effect*)

CUFF. I'll be there.

AIMEE. As a French neutral, I wish to bring the two sides in the Wallace affair together for explanation, negotiation, and conciliation. I suggest, Sergeant, that you also invite two of your trusted men, and place them within earshot in the cellar. When the meat is served, the Judge will propose a toast to His Majesty King George the Third. The moment the glasses are raised, you, my dear Sergeant, will produce a pistol in the intimacy of our dining room and summon your two warriors.

CUFF. Marquise, I apologize for my sour words.

AIMEE. I have forgotten them.

WEAMISH (*pale*). What if—

AIMEE. Yes?

WEAMISH. What if the Mayhews are armed?

CUFF. I hope they are. We'll cut 'em down on the spot. It will save Tom Gage a trial.

WEAMISH. Shoot them? At the table? Before two ladies?

CUFF. Before or behind. It's all the same to me.

AIMEE. I hope they will display enough courtesy to offer no resistance. The fact is, they will be disarmed before we sit down to dinner.

CUFF. How will you manage that?

AIMEE. Easily. Give me your pistol, Sergeant. Yes, your weapon. Thank you.

I shall place it on a footstool under the table and cover it with a cushion. At your entrance, you'll offer to be searched, and demand to do likewise upon the Mayhews. Are you right-handed? I shall sit to your right, and while Mr. Weamish is offering the toast I will be slipping the weapon into your hand.

WEAMISH. What if the Mayhews will not dine without their firearms?

AIMEE. Our nakedness will lull them all the same, and Sergeant Cuff will be prompt enough to amaze them as soon as I hand him the pistol and he calls for his men.

CUFF. I'll amaze them out of their scalp, I will.

WEAMISH. Permit me, Marquise. Why not try gentler means?

CUFF. With a man like Nicholas Mayhew?

WEAMISH. The Mayhews are all persons of birth and consequence, Sergeant; they are not Trinidad pirates.

AIMEE. What is your proposal, Judge?

WEAMISH. Suppose that when the fruit is brought in after dinner, I turn to the colonel, and inform him with my severest demeanor that important disclosures have come to my attention. "Colonel Mayhew," I shall say, "unimpeachable revelations have reached my ears; discoveries of the gravest character, conveyed by private informants whom, needless to say, I am not at liberty to name—"

CUFF. By the time y'are done with that parliament sentence, the rascals will have cut our throats with your fruit knives!

WEAMISH. No, Sergeant, I believe they will be mute. But to oblige you I will be more direct. "In short," I shall say, "I know that you and your lively nephew are harboring a secret purpose injurious to the peace of this nation and contrary to that cheerful subordination which has hitherto made the happiness of these colonies—an attempt, I am told, to escape from Nantucket with the object of joining—"

CUFF. Et caetera, et caetera, et caetera.

WEAMISH. Just so. "But now," I shall continue, "your avenues are barred, for Sergeant Cuff has surrounded these premises." At this terrifying news I shall rise to my feet—no, I believe I am on my feet already—and call upon the Mayhews to renounce their wicked purpose. "As you hope for eternal salvation in the world hereafter, and ease, honor, and comfort in your present existence, you now solemnly swear that you shall cease to be the treacherous ministers of satanic rebellion, and that you shall uphold his Majesty George the Third, defend the British Constitution, and lend the support of your arms to his Majesty's forces."

CUFF. Ha, ha, ha, ha!

WEAMISH. Why are you laughing, Sergeant?

CUFF. Because my bedtime will have come before y'ave run through that monstrous oath!

WEAMISH. I—

CUFF. No, Judge, excuse me. I'm a raw fellow, I know, I ran from school when I was nine, but this will never do. If we let the Mayhews slip out of our hands tomorrow, we deserve to be hanged without benefit of clergy.

AIMEE. Your plan has distinct merit, Judge; but what if the Mayhews, besides refusing to dine unarmed, bring along a detachment of their own? I foresee a general massacre.

WEAMISH. Oh.

AIMEE. My own contrivance seems a little less boisterous, on the whole.

CUFF. If y'are afraid for your life, Judge, you can pretend to faint the moment I aim my pistol at the Mayhews.

WEAMISH. I am not afraid for my life, Sergeant, though I know full well—and better than you, if I may say so—that to deprive Nantucket of its royal magistrate at this juncture would be to invite mere chaos. But I bow to the majority. You'll not see me flinch.

CUFF. That's settled then. We tie up and gag our two Mayhews, take them to the harbor, and ship them to Boston.

WEAMISH. Under the eyes of our people?

AIMEE. The people will be helpless to prevent us, since the Mayhews will be at the same time our prisoners and our hostages.

CUFF. Good point.

WEAMISH. What if they decline your invitation in the first place, Marquise? Have you thought of that?

AIMEE. They cannot decline. They must keep up the pretense that Wallace is their business agent, and they are mortally afraid that if he is not released, he'll betray them.

WEAMISH. If you say so.

CUFF. Well, that concludes our palaver. I'll see to my side of the plan; the men to be posted in the cellar—

AIMEE. No more than two—one might suffice.

CUFF. No, we'll stick to two. They'll bring a couple of halyards along to tie up our rebels. If we're obliged to open fire, let the ladies dive under the table and you, Judge, pacify the rabble that's sure to come running. Are you staying, Marquise?

AIMEE. No, Sergeant, I'm coming with you. Don't forget the toast, Judge; loud and clear, so the soldiers can hear you—our lives may depend on it.

WEAMISH. Yes, Marquise.

AIMEE. Till tomorrow, then. At one.

WEAMISH. Yes, Marquise.
CUFF. Good day, Judge.
WEAMISH. Good day, Sergeant.
(*Aimée and Cuff leave*)
WEAMISH (*alone*). Death and damnation! Why did I allow these firebrands to overrule me? I'm the chief magistrate, by all that's holy! He'll amaze them, will he? Suppose they refuse to be amazed and yell for help instead? A swarm of Nantucket hotheads will come rushing in firing muskets and pistols, the Sergeant's men will be shooting back left and right, and I sprawled on the floor with a bullet through my heart. That rustic of a Sergeant has little enough to live for, but I'm in line for a seat in the Council, confound it! Let the ruffians fight it out among themselves. I shall bid Jenny rush in to call me away—"At once, sir, at once, Constable Hackbutt caught a fellow who tried to break our windows again!" And when I'm gone let Mistress Spy pledge the king in my place. Loud and clear, so the soldiers in the cellar can arrest whomever they want. Jenny! Jenny!
JENNY'S VOICE. Yes, sir?
WEAMISH. Come here! I must give you particular commands!
JENNY'S VOICE. I can't. I'm busy folding linen in the kitchen.
WEAMISH (*furious*). Damn the kitchen! Come up at once, or I'll bloody your nose! (*To himself*) Pshaw! We'll see who is in command here!

SCENE TEN

(*The afternoon of Friday, June 23. The same lane and bench as in Scene Five. This time Mayhew is sitting and reading a book, and Madeleine approaches, halts, and looks at him. Signs of inward struggle in her face. Mayhew senses her presence and turns around*)

MAYHEW. Oh, Mademoiselle de Tourville! Good afternoon.
MADELEINE. Good afternoon....
MAYHEW. Are you hurrying somewhere?
MADELEINE. No.
MAYHEW. I'm so glad. May I make a confession?
MADELEINE. A confession?
MAYHEW. I was hoping to meet you here—and to have you share the sunshine with me for half an hour.

MADELEINE. Gladly.
(*She sits down next to him*)
MADELEINE. Are you still reading Mr. Stevenson's book?
MAYHEW. Mr. Jefferson's pamphlet?
MADELEINE. Yes.
MAYHEW. I finished it somehow between one urgent matter and another. I believe I would read to the end of a book even though I were called into battle and obliged to read on horseback. I have no peace until I conclude.
MADELEINE. This new one is slender enough to finish by tomorrow, I suppose.
MAYHEW. Yes—by tomorrow.
MADELEINE. May I ask what it is?
MAYHEW. If you do not, I shall tell you without being asked, for I took it down from my shelf thinking of you. (*He gives her the little book*)
MADELEINE. "Elihu Coleman, of Nantucket. 'A Testimony Against That Anti-Christian Practice of MAKING SLAVES OF MEN'." In very large letters!
MAYHEW. The date is here.
MADELEINE. 1729.
MAYHEW. Aye; I was eight years old then; but I remember Mr. Coleman. He was a Quaker minister and, for this modest island of ours, a learned man. We Mayhews prayed in the Episcopal church. Still do, of course. We felt something of a superiority over these prim Quakers. But now I am proud of old Mr. Coleman. Few men before him, if any, had spoken out against slavery. All Christianity was content to emulate the pagans in their vilest practice. But not old Mr. Coleman of Nantucket, bless him.
MADELEINE. This is pretty: "Now although the Turks make slaves of those they catch that are not of their religion, yet (as history relates) as soon as any embraces the Mahometan religion, they are no longer kept slaves, but are quickly set free, and for the most part put to some place of preferment; so zealous are they for proselytes and their own religion. Now if many among those called Christians would but consider, how far they fall short of the Turks in this particular, it would be well; for they tell the Negroes, that they must believe in Christ, and receive the Christian faith, and that they must receive the sacrament, and be baptized, and so they do; but still they keep them slaves for all this."
MAYHEW. Yes, it is pretty, as you say. Mr. Coleman did not stray far beyond the obvious, but far beyond the obvious is often an artificial and useless place. Read; let me not interrupt you.
(*There is a silence, while Madeleine reads a little. Then she returns the book to Mayhew*)

MADELEINE (*softly*). You will struggle to make this America of yours stainless?

MAYHEW. Without oppressors and without victims at any rate.

MADELEINE. Can this ever be?

MAYHEW. I must believe it. My own happiness will be hobbled as long as I know that somewhere black men are being abused, Indians robbed, other white men persecuted. Oh, this reminds me. Look, here is an old Indian stone pipe. It's one of the very few left on the island.

MADELEINE. It has such a contented look! Is it very old?

MAYHEW. Perhaps a century; perhaps more. They smoked these long before we Englishmen came. An Indian told me they used a weed they called *poke*. It no longer grows here.

MADELEINE. I want to puff on it!

MAYHEW. Please do. (*They both laugh*) It's not really a stone pipe, you know, though they call it that. It's made of a mixture of blue clay and mussel shells, pounded, mixed, and burnt.

MADELEINE. Thank you for showing it to me.

MAYHEW. May I leave it for you at Swain's, in recollection of your days in Nantucket?

(*There is a silence*)

MADELEINE. I'll never part with it. (*Another pause*) Have you heard—what has taken place—between your nephew—and—

MAYHEW. Yes, I've heard. We are going to be relations!

MADELEINE. Yes.

MAYHEW. Does it disturb you very much that—I mean—the difference in their age—

MADELEINE. Not at all. Not that. And you?

MAYHEW. Then it's something else. I am afraid you feel the blemish on your name—

MADELEINE. Oh God, never say such a thing again! Never never—

MAYHEW. What is it, then? Are you wondering what's to become of you—where to turn?

MADELEINE. No, no. Everything is decently arranged. I have an aunt in France who has often begged me to come. I will see my country for the first time.

MAYHEW. True; you have never set foot in France.

MADELEINE. I was a baby when we left.

MAYHEW. How far away.... But surely you will return one day to your mother—she holding court, no doubt, wherever young Nick decides to fix. You and I shall visit the happy couple together.

MADELEINE. I will never return.

MAYHEW. You do feel the disgrace after all.

MADELEINE (*getting up*). Again! I must go—

MAYHEW. Wait! And forgive me. I ought to know you better. Don't go before I make a request of you. (*He takes her hand and pulls her down again*) It is a matter of extreme importance.

MADELEINE. Anything.

MAYHEW. We have said nothing about tomorrow's dinner.

MADELEINE. The less said, the better.

MAYHEW. Madeleine: I demand that you stay away. Demand it.

MADELEINE. My mother—

MAYHEW (*suddenly angry, standing up*). I don't care! I intend to tell the Marquise that if you appear at table, exposed to violence, I will quit the game at once, happen what may.

MADELEINE. I have as much courage—

MAYHEW. Useless courage. Do you promise me, Madeleine? Do I have your solemn promise?

MADELEINE (*almost inaudibly*). I promise.

MAYHEW. You will receive an invitation from my cousin Mrs. Jones to share a noontime meal with her tomorrow.

(*Madeleine nods, they shake hands, she rises and leaves. Mayhew watches her for a while, then pensively fingers through his book and tries to read*)

MAYHEW. "This practice of making slaves of Negroes, to see whether pride and idleness was not the first rise of it," (*he pauses, dreams, looks where Madeleine went, resumes*) "that they might go with white hands, and that their wives might, like Jezebel, paint and adorn themselves...." (*He stops, and grows pensive again*)

(*Reenter Madeleine. She sits down without a word, while Mayhew looks at her with anxious surprise*)

MADELEINE (*low*). My name is Madeleine Pichot.

MAYHEW (*bewildered*). Pichot? Pichot de Tourville?

MADELEINE (*she is forced to smile*). No. Plain Pichot. It's a name that makes people grin in my country.

MAYHEW. Then you are not the Marquise's daughter?

MADELEINE. Indeed I am.

MAYHEW. Ah!

MADELEINE (*in a trembling voice*). Her name is Aimée Pichot. We are both in the pay of General Gage. Vulgar spies. Mother and daughter. Our destination is Canada, but we paused here for an important special mission, namely to discover whether you are plotting to join the mainland rebels, and to have you arrested if it is so.

MAYHEW. That is to say tomorrow, at table?

MADELEINE. No. My mother has changed sides. Madame de Tourville intends to become the noble wife of an immensely rich Yankee.

MAYHEW. And you?

MADELEINE. I do have an aunt in Lyon. She is a milliner. The hat shop will be my plantation.

MAYHEW. Is your father living?

MADELEINE. I don't know.

MAYHEW. How is that?

MADELEINE. Because I don't know who he is, and neither does my mother. She was married once to a turnkey in Lyon; but he was not my father. When he died, a nobleman took her for his mistress; but he was not my father either. My father may be the baron's bailiff whose name she has forgotten, or else the sergeant who once slapped the baron's face and ran off with mother to Canada. I was two years old when he died. My mother has also been—

MAYHEW. Tell me, don't be afraid.

MADELEINE. Gage's mistress.

MAYHEW. And you?

MADELEINE. Why should you believe anything I say about myself?

MAYHEW (*softly*). Let *me* decide.

MADELEINE. There was a boy in New York—it was quickly over—

MAYHEW. And now—have you "changed sides" too?

MADELEINE. No.

MAYHEW (*smiling*). Do you mean you're still a stubborn Tory?

MADELEINE. I never was.

(*A pause*)

MAYHEW. Why did you come to me with this confession? Why now? Why at all? Was it so urgent to save Nicholas?

MADELEINE (*low*). That was not the reason.

MAYHEW. Surely you don't simply wish to spoil your mother's luck!

MADELEINE. My mother? Who brought me up, gave me teachers, groomed me to be something like a lady, shared her thoughts with me, loved me?

MAYHEW. Yet now you—

MADELEINE. Betray her to you. I couldn't bear to keep you in the dark one moment longer. Come what may.

(*They exchange a long look*)

MAYHEW. You make me inexpressibly happy.

MADELEINE. Then—may I—may I plead for my mother?

MAYHEW. Do.
MADELEINE. I beg you! Do not leave her on the island when all this is over.
MAYHEW. Leave her to be shot by the other side? Surely you know us better, and have no worry on *that* account!
MADELEINE. None anymore. But—I am not yet done pleading.
MAYHEW. Go on.
MADELEINE. Once you are safe on the mainland, could you bring yourself to *whisper* the truth to Nicholas, turn your backs on us without saying a word to anyone else, and allow her to keep—?
MAYHEW. Her noble name.
MADELEINE. I know that silence is also a lie. I asked too much.
MAYHEW. Harmless lies don't frighten me. This one will be a favor to my nephew, since he can hardly wish to have it proclaimed from the rooftops that he was duped. Yes, matters can be quietly disposed of, except for something you have forgotten.
MADELEINE. Namely?
MAYHEW. That your jilted mother cannot fail to understand who—
MADELEINE. Because I shall tell her.
(*Mayhew takes this in*)
MAYHEW. Fatherless and motherless girl, adrift in the world.
MADELEINE (*bowing her head*). That is as it should be.
MAYHEW. That is as it shall never be. Mind you, if we come to grief tomorrow, our worries will take on a darker shade of dark. Madeleine?
MADELEINE. Yes?
MAYHEW. Remember your promise. Does it hold?
MADELEINE. It does.

SCENE ELEVEN

(*Saturday, June 24. Mid-day. The dining room at Swain's Tavern. Seated at the large round table, clockwise from Aimée: Cuff, Nicholas, Weamish and Mayhew. Thus Aimée is sittting between Mayhew and Cuff*)

AIMEE (*roguish*). Someone's staring out the window! (*To Weamish*) Yes—you, sir. You are not doing justice to this excellent potage.
WEAMISH (*nervous*). I *am* a little preoccupied, perhaps. Several urgent cases have turned up—they fret my mind—indeed, at any moment I expect—but

I deserve to be chid, for Mr. Swain keeps a pretty fair cook, old Mrs. Finney.
CUFF. Bless Mrs. Finney. This is better fare than I've tasted since I left England. Colonel, I'll trouble you for the tureen.
MAYHEW. No trouble; but hand me your plate, Sergeant. The Marquise will not object. A retired colonel may pour a ladle of soup into an active Sergeant's bowl without breach of discipline.
CUFF. Ha, ha, y'are a humorous man, Colonel Mayhew. Thank you. The salt, please. A little pepper, too.
NICHOLAS. My uncle tells me that Mademoiselle de Tourville has gone this morning to call on our relation in town. An honor for dear Mrs. Jones.
AIMEE. My daughter was looking forward to a view of the furnishings and a warm cup of—oh dear!
NICHOLAS. The fatal word! Come, we're among friends. If Mrs. Jones keeps a few ounces of tea in case one of her neighbor's children should be indisposed, I believe that even our most frenetic patriots will wink and let pass.
CUFF. Strike me dumb, but this Yankee commotion over tea is the strangest piece of foolishness that was ever heard of. For a tax of threepence on a pound of tea y'are ready to overturn the world. It makes a man mad. (*He pours an enormous quantity of salt and pepper into his soup*) Besides, don't I know, and don't the King, Lord North, Lord Germain and don't everybody know that you smuggle in your tea from Holland anyhow? Your merchants, sir, your invoice-scribbling, bill-of-lading tradesmen can't abide to let a halfpence of profit go without raising an insurrection, bawling tyranny, ringing all the church-bells, and setting the whole continent adrift. Pah! (*He pours more salt and pepper into his soup*) A sensible man must find solace in drink these days. And by God, I find I have a huge thirst in my throat. Judge: give us a toast to a meeting of bullets and troublemakers.
(*Weamish spills his glass of wine*)
WEAMISH. Goodness!
AIMEE. Oh dear!
WEAMISH. I spoiled the tablecloth!
CUFF. Fiddlesticks.
MAYHEW. Nothing of importance.
AIMEE. Is your sleeve wet, Judge?
WEAMISH. A tiny bit.
NICHOLAS. And here's another napkin. We'll spread it neatly over the scene of the crime.
WEAMISH. Thank you.... Forgive my clumsiness....
CUFF. I'll fill your glass again. Almost time for a toast.

WEAMISH *(feebly)*. Thank you....
(Cuff rises to pour, then returns to his seat)
CUFF. A full glass will do wonders. *(He winks at Aimée)*
MAYHEW. Another slice of this rustic bread, Marquise?
AIMEE. Thank you. How delightful it is to dine *en petit comité* without being beset by a flock of fish-eyed servants! Shall I have the tureen taken away, Sergeant?
CUFF. Yes, ma'am. I'm done.
(Aimée rings a bell)
CUFF. Well, gentlemen, do I talk sense or nonsense?
MAYHEW. What about, Sergeant?
CUFF. That commotion over tea.
MAYHEW. Well, this is a proud nation....
CUFF. Nation? Y'are not a nation, says Sergeant Cuff, y'are a British colony, a child, a dependent, you breathe by your sovereign's grace! Too kind a rule has spoiled you, y'are lunatics of freedom, we've given you a leash three thousand miles long and it's time we pulled it in a foot or two.
(Enter Swain)
AIMEE. Excellent *potage*, Mr. Swain. My compliments to Mrs. Finney. I'm tempted to steal her from you.
SWAIN. Thank you, Madam. I hope our joint of mutton answers your expectations as well.
AIMEE. I'm—Are you looking for anything, Judge?
(Weamish has continued to peer anxiously through a window)
WEAMISH. I? No, Marquise, not I.
(Exit Swain with tureen and plates on a tray)
AIMEE. I am not acquainted with every particular of this unhappy dispute between father and child, yet I see so much well-being in your land that I puzzle over its rebellion.
CUFF. Spoken like a woman of sense, though French. What do you answer to that, gentlemen?
NICHOLAS. We wholeheartedly agree with Madame de Tourville. Remember that few Nantucket men have meddled in this uprising. Hence our indignation at your detaining Mr. Wallace. Let's not forget the purpose of this meeting.
CUFF. If Mr. Wallace is nothing more than a business agent, we'll return him ipso pronto to your counting house.
MAYHEW. If the man is using us to screen any reprehensible action, let him take the consequences.
CUFF. Provided, sir, it's us that determine what is and what ain't reprehensible.

AIMEE. His Majesty is fortunate in having soldiers like yourself in his service, Sergeant.
CUFF. There's thousands like me.
WEAMISH. Ha! There's Jenny!
AIMEE. I beg your pardon?
WEAMISH. Outside. What can this signify? I believe she's looking for me. These urgent cases—
CUFF. What's all this?
(*Enter Jenny*)
JENNY (*trying to sound convincing*). Oh, your honor! Come quickly! We need you at home!
(*She curtseys to everybody*)
WEAMISH. What is it, Jenny? Why do you disturb us at dinner?
AIMEE (*into Cuff's ear*). It's a trick—stop him!
(*The Mayhews are enjoying the scene*)
JENNY. It's Mr. Hackbutt, oh dear, oh dear—
WEAMISH (*for the gallery*). The constable.
JENNY. He says he must see your honor right away—it's about a low fellow who has been trying to break our windows—
WEAMISH. Aha! The window-breaker! Caught at last! I'm coming at once! Friends—
CUFF (*rising*). No, your honor, y'are not coming at once, stab my gizzard! Our business with these gentlemen will suffer no delay. What's your name again, woman?
JENNY. Jenny, sir.
CUFF. Jenny, go home, or I'll send ten raping villains to your kitchen to break your china. (*He stamps his feet*) Home! Home! Home!
(*She runs away, terrified*)
WEAMISH. But the constable!
CUFF. Can go hang himself, sir! And if he doesn't, I'll do it for him. From a Yankee Liberty Tree. (*He drinks and sits*) Sit down!
NICHOLAS. Thank you for staying, sir. Sergeant Cuff is right. We must clear up the matter of Mr. Wallace' arrest. Think of the poor man pent in a damp prison cell.
CUFF. Where's the mutton? We'll toast the king over the mutton. Good. Here it comes.
(*Swain has entered; he sets the meat down*)
SWAIN. Done to perfection, I promise.
AIMEE. I trust you like mutton, Judge Weamish?
CUFF. A glass of water will help your voice. Here.

WEAMISH. Oh, my voice is—thank you. (*He drinks*) I—I am fond of mutton.
CUFF. That's all, Mr. Swain; I'll do the carving.
SWAIN. Very good, Sergeant.
CUFF. Keep the door open when you go out, will you? This madeira has warmed my blood. Smuggled, I suppose.
SWAIN. Yes, sir. I mean—I'll keep the door open.
(*He leaves. Cuff carves, and places meat on everybody's plate*)
CUFF. Looks appetizing enough for a last supper.
MAYHEW. Not too generous, Sergeant; I've a bit of rough work ahead of me today, and I shouldn't like to get sleepy.
CUFF. Still, one never knows what the future holds; dine while you can is my motto. Your plate, Judge?
WEAMISH. Very little. I feel—
NICHOLAS. These window panes have affected you, Judge Weamish; but eat and be merry; the Sergeant is right.
CUFF. Thank you, Mr. Mayhew. Judge, let's hear that toast before we fall to our meat.
(*He fills all the glasses*)
WEAMISH. A toast? Now?
CUFF. Aye, a toast.
WEAMISH. This wine is not quality enough for a toast. Mr. Swain keeps a few choice bottles in his cellar. Let me see to it—(*he tries to rise*)
CUFF. Rubbish. This is excellent stuff. A toast! At once!
WEAMISH (*standing up*). I propose—
CUFF. What? I can't hear you, devils in hell!
WEAMISH (*shouting*). I drink to King George—
MAYHEW (*standing up too, together with Nicholas*). And I to the United Provinces of America!
NICHOLAS. Long may they live!
CUFF. I arrest you both in the king's name! Ludley! Harrington!
(*Aimée dips under the table and hands Cuff his pistol*)
MAYHEW. And we arrest you in the name of the Congress.
(*Nicholas and Mayhew approach Cuff from two sides. Cuff retreats, aiming his pistol at both alternately*)
CUFF. Stand back! Ludley! Harrington! Hands over your heads! Stand still! Or die! (*He pulls the trigger, aiming at Nicholas. Nothing happens*) Who unloaded my pistol?
AIMEE. I did.
(*She produces a second pistol from under the table and hands it to Mayhew*)
CUFF (*stupefied*). The French baggage is a rebel too!

AIMEE. Your servant, Sergeant Bully.
CUFF. Ludley! Harrington!
MAYHEW. This one is loaded.
(*He fires in the air. Weamish cries out and faints. Nicholas grabs Cuff and forces him down*)
NICHOLAS. Sit down, Sergeant.
(*Enter Wallace, Coffin and Mamack, all armed. They aim their pistols at Cuff*)
MAYHEW. Welcome, Henry, welcome boys!
WALLACE. Well met again, Colonel, Mr. Mayhew.
COFFIN. Greetings one and all!
MAMACK. How d'ye do!
(*These greetings are rapid and simultaneous*)
CUFF (*gaping*). Where are my men?
MAYHEW. Where are the Sergeant's men?
COFFIN. In the cellar, with more rope around them than a windlass.
WALLACE. And here's some left over for the Sergeant and the judge. Good heavens, is the judge dead?
NICHOLAS. No; he is momentarily absent.
(*Wallace ties Cuff to his chair. Mayhew closes the shutters of the room*)
CUFF. Damn your hide, Mayhew; I knew from the first you were no better than a Turk.
NICHOLAS. Not so much noise, Sergeant. This is a respectable inn.
CUFF. Enjoy yourselves, confounded rebels, but we'll see who laughs last when my men get wind of this.
MAYHEW. Did you carry out my orders, Obed?
COFFIN. Yes, Colonel. We found the corporal in a bathtub.
CUFF. Blast you to hell!
COFFIN. He was a little disturbed at first, but when we started to hang him naked he became friendly. He called off the villains standing guard over the jailhouse, and that's how we freed Mr. Wallace. By that time there was nearly a hundred of us besides the corporal with a rope around his neck, seeing which, the redcoats turned their muskets over to us and wrapped their corporal in a cloak.
NICHOLAS. Done with true British decency. But now, my friends, let us offer a round of thanks to Madame de Tourville, the future Mrs. Nicholas Mayhew, and the sole authoress of this victory.
CUFF. Good. She'll sell your scalp to the Indians. Mr. Mayhew, with her as your wife, I'm well avenged already.
MAMACK. Let him talk, Mr. Mayhew. I cry Hip, Hip, Hooray.
WEAMISH. Ooooh....
AIMEE. You've awakened the judge. (*She moistens the Judge's face*) Come to, your

honor.

COFFIN. In time to take Mr. Wallace' place in jail.

WEAMISH. Pity, my friends, intercede for me, Marquise!

CUFF. You're sending your plea to the wrong address, Weamish. The Marquise is one of *them*.

WEAMISH. Oh dear....

AIMEE. Join us, Judge. If you do, I shall see to it that you remain as free as a sparrow. We're charming people here, and, *entre nous*, the Revolution is likely to become the fashion.

WEAMISH. Oh, Marquise, I am dizzy. You? You who were—?

AIMEE. Tut, tut.

CUFF. You didn't give much help, Judge, but I'm glad to find you're not a bloody rebel like the rest.

NICHOLAS. We could remove you at once, Sergeant.

CUFF. If you do, you'll be left in rotten company.

NICHOLAS. So much for that. Now for the toast that was so interestingly interrupted. I propose, with my uncle, the United Provinces of America, and request that Judge Weamish and Sergeant Cuff join their voices to ours. To America!

ALL EXCEPT CUFF, *but* WEAMISH (*feebly*). To America!

CUFF. God save the King!

COFFIN. God save the people!

CUFF. They'll need more saving than you think, you blockhead! You'll miss the king some day, all you raggle-taggle levellers—when high and low are topsy-turvy—when your haberdashers write your laws—and when y'are ruled by ambitious comedians. God save the King!

NICHOLAS. Carry him into the cellar, Mamack, let him confer below with his two henchmen.

MAMACK. A pleasure.

COFFIN. I'll help. And from the cellar to the jailhouse.

CUFF. Remove me from this kennel, dogs. I'm grateful to you.

(*They carry Cuff out in his chair*)

WEAMISH. Ah, Marquise, was it all deceit? Were you never—

AIMEE. You are still faint, my friend. Let a glass of Madeira soothe your nerves.

WEAMISH. You are right. The nerves are what matters. (*He drinks*)

MAYHEW. Farewell, Mr. Weamish. We shall not meet again for many a stormy day. Will you give me your hand? (*They shake hands*) We are not saints. God knows I have told my share of lies and gone by crooked ways. But all in all, Tom, I am your elder—and a wiser head than you: we are the better men, believe me, and the future is with us. Join us.

WEAMISH. I promise to think it over.... favorably.

NICHOLAS. Do so; and bear in mind that some of your friends will be in jail before we leave the island.

AIMEE. As for myself, I'll not forget your kind welcome, Judge. I shall always keep a set of rooms ready for you—here in America, or at my chateau in the Gascogne.

(*Coffin has reappeared*)

WEAMISH. Will you have me, Marquise?

AIMEE. As long as I live.

(*She gives him her hand; he kisses it*)

WEAMISH. Blood always tells.

MAYHEW. Obed, will you be so kind as to walk out with Judge Weamish and see him safely home?

COFFIN. Of course!

(*He takes Weamish's arm and they leave*)

MAYHEW. Henry, you are to remain on the island long enough to see that Cuff and his troopers are safely transferred to the mainland and delivered to the Congress. The ladies, young Nick and myself will cross on the Enterprise tonight, as arranged, since there will be messages awaiting me on board.

(*Wallace shakes hands with the Mayhews and leaves*)

NICHOLAS. Well, uncle, are you pleased?

MAYHEW. I am. My dear lady, I ought now to display a power of eloquence to thank you, but I believe my nephew is willing to express our obligation for both of us.

AIMEE. I want no thanks. I am now a member of your family, Colonel, and owe you the poor talents and resources that I command. Instead of idle ceremony, let us wait for my daughter's return; we must try to dissuade her from her gloomy purpose to return to a land she has never known. Will you assist me, husband? And you, dear sir?

MAYHEW. Gladly. Come, we have work to do. Dinner must wait.

NICHOLAS. Your arm, Marquise.

(*They leave. Enter Swain, surveying the scene, his two hands holding his head*)

SWAIN. The turmoil! The wreckage! (*Looking at the uneaten mutton*) What will Mrs. Finney say? Let them take their Revolution to another inn!

SCENE TWELVE

(Saturday, June 24, before dark, at the seaside as in Scene Seven. Coffin is sitting by the fishing-stage, whittling, and singing)

COFFIN.
    You must make me a fine Holland shirt,
    Blow, blow, blow, ye winds, blow
    And not have in it a stitch of needlework
    Blow, ye winds that arise, blow, blow.
    You must wash it in yonder spring,
    Blow, blow, blow, ye winds, blow,
    Where there's never a drop of water in,
    Blow, ye winds that arise, blow, blow.

(Enter Mayhew and Nicholas carrying small travel cases)
COFFIN. Greetings.
(They shake hands)
MAYHEW. Ready for us, Obed?
COFFIN. All ready. And the ladies?
MAYHEW. Following us with baggage. *(Looking toward the sea)* She's waiting for us, is she?
COFFIN. She dropped anchor about an hour ago and signaled.
MAYHEW. Well, daylight is waning, so let's set off as soon as possible.
NICHOLAS. I think I hear the chaise with our women.
(He exits)
COFFIN. We're mighty proud of you, General Mayhew. We'll guard your property here like what's his name, the dog in Hades. When you come back, you'll find every speck of it same as you left it, or never trust me again.
MAYHEW. When I come back. Who knows? I fear that streams of blood will be shed before heaven decides who will stand and who must fall.
COFFIN. I hear there's talk of conciliation yet. Perhaps you'll be back sooner than we all expect.
MAYHEW. I wish I could believe it. But who ever in history has given up power without a fight?
COFFIN. Here they come!
(Enter the two ladies and Nicholas)
MAYHEW. Welcome, welcome!

MADELEINE. Thank you.

AIMEE. How pleasant to see this spot again! Eh, you rascal?

NICHOLAS (*kissing her fingers*). Obed, you must lend me a hand.

COFFIN. Yes, sir.

(*They leave*)

AIMEE. What, General Mayhew, no farewell committee? No band of musicians? No flowers?

MAYHEW. No, no, nothing of the sort. We leave quietly. There's too much bad blood in Nantucket as it is. My heart aches when I think I am in part guilty of it.

AIMEE. You are a lamb, General, believe me; I know mankind, if anyone does, and I say unto you, you are a lamb of God.

MADELEINE. Mother!

AIMEE. My cousin on my mother's side, the Chevalier de Cassefer, once tore a Prussian's left arm from the shoulder with his bare two hands.

MAYHEW. I shall try to deal more humanely with our enemy—who, when all is said and done, remains our brother.

AIMEE. The Chevalier behaved worse to his brother.

MADELEINE. Mother, mother....

AIMEE. The poor girl is sensitive for our reputation. Ah, here come our helpers. Gently, my friends, there's porcelain in my trunk.

(*Nicholas and Coffin are carrying a huge trunk*)

COFFIN. Let's take it directly to the boat, Mr. Mayhew.

NICHOLAS. Let's indeed.

AIMEE. That's a bit harder than rescuing a man from the sea, I'll wager.

NICHOLAS. It is, and I hope for a sweeter reward accordingly.

AIMEE. Ogre!

(*Nicholas and Coffin pass off the stage*)

AIMEE. Shall we have a tranquil passage, Elias? I may call you Elias, I hope.

MAYHEW. Of course. I believe we shall. And a brief one, too.

AIMEE. You will call me Aimée, will you not?

MAYHEW. With pleasure, Aimée.

(*Reenter Nicholas and Coffin*)

NICHOLAS. Now for Madeleine's.

(*They leave again*)

MAYHEW. Did you find time to take leave of the judge, my dear niece?

AIMEE. I did. But I found him very low, lying on a sofa, complaining of dizzy spells, and inhaling salts.

MAYHEW. Poor fellow. But I have seen to it that he remains Nantucket's magistrate.

(*Reenter Nicholas and Coffin, carrying a very small portmanteau—Madeleine's*)
COFFIN. I'll take it to the boat myself, Mr. Mayhew.
NICHOLAS. How is it that our Madeleine is carrying so much less than you, angel?
AIMEE. Immaturity, dear. Idealism travels light; but when ideals wear thin, property become a comfort.
NICHOLAS. And what am I, your ideal or your property?
AIMEE. You are—my ideal property.
(*Reenter Coffin*)
COFFIN. I'm afraid we'll have to make two trips. My boat cannot hold five and a trunk.
NICHOLAS. No matter. Uncle, you go first with Madeleine. We'll follow.
MAYHEW. No; I'll follow you. Let me linger here another hour and gently loosen my last roots. Madeleine will keep me company.
NICHOLAS. As you wish. Ready, angel?
AIMEE. Ready. (*She kisses Madeleine*) I'll see you presently, dearest. If the water is choppy, close your eyes and think of babies in cradles.
MADELEINE. Yes, Mother.
NICHOLAS. Stop!
AIMEE. What is it?
(*Nicholas sweeps her up into his arms*)
AIMEE. Rape!
NICHOLAS. My prize! My glorious prize!
(*He carries her off, followed by Coffin shaking his head. Mayhew and Madeleine are left alone. He sits down by the fishing-stage, closes his eyes, and breathes deeply. She begins to move quietly away. Mayhew opens his eyes*)
MAYHEW. Where are you going, Madeleine?
MADELEINE. Only a little farther off.
MAYHEW. Why?
MADELEINE. I—I wanted to leave you to yourself.
MAYHEW. Stay. Because, though I try to dream of meadows and sunsets, my mind reverts to Nicholas and his prize.
MADELEINE. You have been so kind, pretending to know nothing and saying nothing. How long can this last?
MAYHEW. Who knows? A poem is tugging at my brain. It begins:
>Let me not to the marriage of true minds
>Admit impediment.

MADELEINE (*naively*). Is it yours?
MAYHEW (*smiling*). I wish! No it is not, but it speaks to me if I alter it ever so slightly. "Let me not to the marriage of *like* minds admit impediment."

Who am I, who are you to play God? Seeing them so snug together, I feel I will never rise to the high moral plane from which I can pulverize them. And cause a mother to hate her daughter. No. Let Nicholas enjoy his Marquise for many years to come! She'll be "the star to his wandering bark."

MADELEINE. I marvel at you.

MAYHEW. More likely you are a little shocked by my levity—relieved but shocked. What can I say? I discover that I keep my fund of rage for large occasions.

MADELEINE. I wish I could learn from you!

MAYHEW. Do you really?

MADELEINE. Of course. Can you doubt it?

MAYHEW. Beware! I am an old man, fifty-four years old. This means that I have amassed a huge store of useful knowledge. Even Madame Pichot's trunk couldn't hold it all. It would take me years to unload it, sort it out, and bequeath it to you.

MADELEINE. If only it could be done in an hour, before the boat returns. I shall sorely need it.

MAYHEW. Impossible. A lifetime is necessary. (*She turns her head away*) What is it, Madeleine?

MADELEINE. Nothing. You wanted to say farewell to your island, Colonel. General.

MAYHEW. What will you do with your lifetime instead?

MADELEINE. Is this not a cruel question?

MAYHEW. Presently I will give you a chance to be cruel with me in return.

MADELEINE. I never seem to understand you!

MAYHEW. My wisdom I can impart to you in much less than an hour, Madeleine. It is my love it would take me a lifetime to unfold. (*Silence*) You see, now you can be cruel with me.

MADELEINE (*low*). My mother is a swindler, a spy, a libertine. I am her bastard, a pauper, a nobody, a daughter who rewarded her mother's care by betraying her. How would you deal with me if I had not almost a pretty face?

MAYHEW. I would love, admire, and defend you, above all against yourself. Your beauty, I confess, has unhinged me to the point of asking you to be my wife as if I were a catch for a girl of twenty. But I fancy that your good sense will keep you at a safe distance from me.

MADELEINE. Because I would not disgrace you.

MAYHEW. Madeleine is always gentle.

MADELEINE. Because I would not disgrace you.

MAYHEW. Look at these miserable wrinkles. Think of what they foretell!
MADELEINE (*weeping*). Don't abandon me....
MAYHEW. Could you bear me as a husband?
(*She flings herself into his arms*)
MADELEINE. Care for me! I'll please you, you'll see! I shall try so bravely that you'll be proud of your foundling!
MAYHEW. Such wild words! I'll care for you like an old hound standing guard over a treasure. But why take me as a husband? Your friend Elias Mayhew will do it as well, I swear, and he'll slink off the moment you appoint a more tasteful husband.
MADELEINE (*holding him*). Are you turning me away already? So soon?
MAYHEW. Mine then. Mine to the end of my blessed time.
MADELEINE. Yours for as long as my heart will beat.
(*They kiss*)
MADELEINE (*touching his cheeks, eyes, and forehead with her fingers*). So fine, so strong, so merry, so wise....
MAYHEW. Wise indeed, to have bewitched you into my arms and condemned you—
MADELEINE. To be a lifelong burden to you!
MAYHEW. Yes, the way a flower burdens the earth.
MADELEINE. Hold me. Your flower is shivering.
MAYHEW. The sun is setting and the wind is beginning to blow. Is this better?
MADELEINE. Much better.
MAYHEW. Look!
MADELEINE. Must I?
MAYHEW. Look who reappeared beyond that spit of land. To remind us that we are not in heaven. But what is Nicholas doing? I believe he is singing, on my word.
MADELEINE. Mother is pointing at us.
MAYHEW. They're waving! (*Both wave back*) Romantic couple!
MADELEINE. Elias, tell me something.
MAYHEW. What, Madeleine?
MADELEINE. Surely, in spite of us, Nicholas will discover sooner or later that he married Madame Pichot. What will happen then?
MAYHEW. Why, he'll fume for a while, but his interest will be the same as hers: to bury the truth.
MADELEINE. My mother was less confident. She took precautions.
(*She produces a letter and gives it to him*)
MAYHEW. What's this? A letter to Nicholas! From Ezekiel Davis! How did this come into your hands?

MADELEINE. Mother filched it from Nick's case this afternoon, and gave it to me for safekeeping. I couldn't refuse to take it, though I knew I would be betraying her again.

MAYHEW (*reading*). "Our Mrs. Applegate grows desperate; she has indeed every power to sell the Concord estate. Give us some useful intelligence, true or false, concerning the Tory doings of Mr. Applegate in Nantucket, and our Sons of Liberty shall rattle Mrs. A., I assure you, till she will sell to yours truly, and gratefully too, for ten shillings in the pound." (*With deep bitterness*) Ten shillings in the pound is handsome! Good Work, nephew. No wonder you're singing. Oh God! (*His head sinks*)

MADELEINE (*frightened*). What have I done? I'm a fool!

MAYHEW. No, no; you did well; I must try to save this woman....

MADELEINE. I've given you pain—already!

MAYHEW (*vehemently*). Salutary pain. Don't I know that this letter is only a single leaf out of an evil book? Haven't I known it for a long time in some remote corner of my soul that I dared not visit? Thank you for pulling me by the hand and forcing the door open and saying to me in your deeper wisdom than mine, Look look look! Tomorrow on the Sabbath, while you and I kneel in thanksgiving, young Nick—but what am I saying? Every Tom, Nick and Harry will be busy buying cheap and selling dear, abusing the ignorant, hoarding scarce goods, making hyena profits from our war, and sucking the sap out of the land. There's the truth at last. But now what? Where shall I find the strength?

MADELEINE. How I want to comfort you...

MAYHEW. Should we even begin?

MADELEINE. Tomorrow we will be on the mainland.

(*He walks to the water's edge and stares outward*)

MAYHEW. Should we even begin?

(*She joins him, takes his hand, and kisses it. In his other hand, Mayhew clutches the letter*)

MADELEINE. Not, at any rate, with your eyes closed.

MAYHEW. With our eyes open then. So be it.

The End

Notes

This play first appeared in 1976 under the title *The Patriots of Nantucket: a Romantic Comedy of the American Revolution*. With "Patriots" changed to "Rebels", and revised and corrected, I republished it in 1996 in *Two Romantic Plays: The Spaniards in Denmark by Prosper Mérimée and The Rebels of Nantucket by Oscar Mandel*. Mérimée's delightful comedy of 1825 is in fact the begetter of my Nantucket play.

The present version is lightly ameliorated from the 1996 text.

No Redcoats were stationed on the island of Nantucket during the Revolution; no Marquise, fake or real, visited the island, no great officers were recruited thence. All the same, the island is present in my romance in its more or less true character of the time; the lighthouse, the street-names, the wharves, these and other features truly existed. I owe my knowledge of them to a flurry of books and the help of the Nantucket Historical Association, to which I herewith offer my heartfelt thanks. As for the names of my characters, many of them belong in fact to the islanders, often going back to the seventeenth century, and some are still alive in Nantucket families today. And here it is important to declare that I have distributed these names quite arbitrarily. They are real names attached to fictive characters.

Real without qualifications are the words of Thomas Jefferson quoted in Scene 5; they are taken from his 1774 tract, *A Summary View of the Rights of British America*. Alike real are those of Elihu Coleman of Nantucket in Scene 10. And the Nantucket ditty in Scene 12 is perfectly authentic too.

SIGISMUND, PRINCE OF POLAND

*Yo, acudiendo a mis estudios,
en ellos y en todo miro
que Segismundo sería
el hombre más atrevido,
el príncipe más cruel
y el monarca más impío,
por quien su reino vendría
a ser parcial, y diviso,
escuela de las traiciones
y academia de los vicios.*

CALDERÓN, *LA VIDA ES SUEÑO*, I, 708-

CHARACTERS

King Casimir of Poland
Prince Sigismund, *his son (played by two actors)*
Prince Astolof of Muscovy *(played by two actors)*
Princess Estrella Jagiello
Count Bogdan Opalinski
Szymon Klotalski, *castellan of Zakopane*
Zbigniew of Bialistok, *royal astrologer*
Florian Radziwill, *Crown Chancellor (played by two actors)*
Vladimir, *master of the royal household*
Ladislaw Szopen, *court musician*
Father Radim
Agafya Matveyevna Kulkova, *a Muscovite farmgirl*
Layla, *a mute Turkish slave*
Convicts, soldiers, corpses, servants and attendants

SCENE ONE

(Night. A cabinet in the royal palace on Wawel Hill in Cracow. King Casimir is alone)

KING. As many calamities swarm over the land as worms crawling in a carcass. All over Poland the peasants are rioting in the villages instead of harvesting the fields. They pretend they're poor and hungry. But if they're so hungry, where do they get the muscle to pitch rocks at their masters and overturn the haycarts? A good fifty of my best gentlemen have been murdered so far trying to put down the insolent clowns—trained warriors all of them, men I needed to face the infidel Turks in Hungary who, besides rebaptizing the Hungarians into Mohammedans, are keeping me out of the gold mines I was counting on to buy off the Swedish army of Lutheran heathens that's pouring out of Livonia. To save my country I've thought more than once of converting to Islam in order to yoke up with the Turks against the Swedes, or turning Lutheran in order to go partners with the Swedes against the Turks. And my soul be damned for the greater good of my people. Oh, the chroniclers will shudder when they come to me. But all these troubles are like appetizers to the real horror. After twenty-two years of trying, my Basilea finally produces a baby, and dies on me in childbirth in spite of a gang of physicians, surgeons, astrologers, midwives and the Bishop of Gniezno attending her. No sooner has my Sigismund let out his first yell than the sky breaks out in unheard-of depredations and conflagrations. Poland is shaken by dreadful earthquakes, steeples cave in on worshippers, rivers reverse their course, the flowers wilt in unison, donkeys beget calves and fish are seen walking on the roads, and I myself will probably go insane before I hear the next piece of bad news. However, in order to leave no stone unturned, I've summoned my chief astrologer—and here he comes, looking grim.

(Enter Zbigniew)

KING. Welcome Zbigniew. Report to me. Spare me no horror. I'm a military man.

ZBIGNIEW. Learned King Casimir, protector of Poland and mankind, the steeple of the cathedral of Tarnow has just caved in on a crowd of worshippers who were mourning the caving in of the steeple of the cathedral of Lwow, and young Sigismund, God bless him, bit off a nipple belonging to the Countess Matilda, his wet-nurse.

KING. And only twelve days old! I'm petrified. Something ghastly that I haven't yet enumerated is advancing on our land. What do your conjunctions and disjunctions say?

ZBIGNIEW. I tremble, your majesty.

KING. I'm ready for the worst. Poland is sinking into the Baltic or sliding under the Carpathians.

ZBIGNIEW. O anguish!

KING. I am going to be deposed.

ZBIGNIEW. Woe, woe!

KING. Murdered.

ZBIGNIEW. Horrid! Fiery comets crisscross the welkin, blood drips from Saturn, a new constellation appears in the shape of a dragon—

KING. Nothing but allegories! Tell me in plain Polish!

ZBIGNIEW. Your majesty, fearful portents clamor in the sky, I descry an alphabet of poisonous planets, and all that remains is for me, Zbigniew of Bialistok, to interpret the tragic text, though doing so may cost me my head.

KING. I think I'll sit down first.

ZBIGNIEW. "Rising Sigismund shall torment Poland with justified plunder, virtuous rapine and noble massacre. Moles shall grow wings. Eagles shall burrow in ditches. And Sigismund will force the King of Poland to his knees."

KING. What? What's that? What's this gibberish?

ZBIGNIEW. No gibberish, your majesty, but a true quotation of the stars, which are as legible to me as a page of the Gospel is to our bishop.

KING. Repeat before I start tearing up the tapestries.

ZBIGNIEW. Reluctantly, your highness. "Rising Sigismund shall torment Poland with justified plunder, virtuous rapine and noble massacre. Moles shall grow wings. Eagles shall burrow in ditches. And Sigismund will force the King of Poland to his knees." Forgive me, my lord, but these are the very—

KING. Shut your mouth! This has to refer to some Sigismund two thousand years from now. It's nothing to me.

ZBIGNIEW. And the earthquakes? And the steeples? And the murderous peasants? And the infidels on all sides? No, my lord, shun illusion, I implore you, shun illusion.

KING. You're right. I'll rebaptize the little monkey. Who needs a Sigismund? It was my wife's choice of names. My last words to my poor Basilea, before she slipped away, were "Damn it, my best, every second prince of Europe seems to be called Sigismund nowadays!" I must have had a premonition. So be it. I'll call him Jesus if necessary!

ZBIGNIEW. Oh my lord, shun illusion! Heaven dislikes equivocation. God does not stand upon names.

KING. You're right again. I'm deluding myself. I must act neat and direct. I'll do away with the wicked child. I'm sorry, but that is clearly what heaven is asking of me. "Rising Sigismund." In other words, do not let him rise. And then let him try to force me to my knees with his just massacres! Call Captain Teczinski.

ZBIGNIEW (*throwing himself at the king's feet*). God forbid, your highness! And God forbids. Heaven cannot want a crime. It would unheaven itself if it did. Already—allow me the liberty, my lord—already the Pope excommunicated you for—for what you did to your predecessor on the throne. You emptied the treasury for the benefit of the Pontiff's nieces and nephews till he retracted and you were able to hear mass again, thank God! But now will you infuriate him again?

KING. Is it kind of you to remind me? Oh my sins, my sins! I've endowed more than my share of churches, abbeys, convents, hospitals, but my sins still give me nightmares. My soul is a cesspool.

ZBIGNIEW. Imagine killing the helpless baby.

KING (*weeping*). My beautiful little Sigismund! What shall I do?

ZBIGNIEW. Think of your immortal soul.

KING. Yes, but I must think of Poland too. Virtuous plunder, justified massacre—isn't that what you said? I don't even understand what it means. I hate enigmas.

ZBIGNIEW. I too read without quite understanding.

KING. What shall I do? What shall I do? (*Thunder and lightning*) What now? Mary, Mother of God, pray for us sinners.... Kneel, Zbigniew.... (*Both sink to their knees. More thunder and lightning*) It's coming from the mountains.... It's looking for me.... Mary, Mother of God.... (*They pray. More thunder*).... Wait! The mountains!... The wild mountains.... Zbigniew, listen to me....

(*More thunder*)

SCENE TWO

(Twenty one years later. Early evening, which will gradually darken. A cleared area in front of a mountain cave, surrounded by forest. A rustic table and benches. Books piled on the table. A crucifix nailed to a tree. Also visible is the cabin—or part of it—housing Layla. After a while, we hear a clanking noise, and then Sigismund appears, one end of a long chain clamped to one of his ankles. He blinks through the trees at the setting sun)

SIGISMUND. Wretched Sigismund! Unhappy creature! Tell me, heaven, what crime have I committed to be so harshly treated? Some learned men assert that to be born is crime enough for any punishment, but if this be true, it is a crime of which all living men and women are guilty, and yet I am punished far worse than any of them. What other offense is on my head? Why are others happy while I am shackled to this cave? The graceful bird, no sooner is it born than it cuts through the air in a flower of feathers, leaving the nest's peaceful security. Yet I, whose soul is so much greater, enjoy less liberty. The four legged beast, no sooner is it born than it leaves its lair and ranges cruelly in the wild to feed itself. Yet I, whose instincts are more virtuous, enjoy less liberty. The silvery fish, spawned by ooze and weeds, no sooner is it born than it navigates the cold stream like a skiff lovely in the waves. Yet I, whose will is free, enjoy less liberty. That stream itself, no sooner is it born on the snowy peak than it uncoils itself to snake across the meadows, rushing merrily among the poppies of the field. Yet I, possessed of much more life, enjoy less liberty! Thoughts such as these are scorching lava, and I their volcano of anger. Sometimes I want to die. Often I want to kill. Where is justice? Why should a man suffer when bird, beast, fish and river rejoice?

So much for my twilight clamor. Damned chain. Next week Klotalski will be shifting it to my other ankle. But right now I'm hungry. Layla! Where are you? Layla! *(He does gymnastic exercises and calls out in rhythm)* Dinner! Layla! Dinner! Layla! Dinner! Of course she's mute and can't answer, but this way I exercise my lungs too. Some day, somehow I will be shouting commands to multitudes somehow. *(More gymnastics)* Layla! Lovely! Layla! Lovely Layla! And that's no joke. O crucified Jesus forgive me for dwelling on things of the flesh more than a Christian should, but is she ever lively on my miserable cot, and does she ever cook a luscious meal! Layla! Ah—it's about time.

(*Enter the generously endowed Layla, carrying Sigismund's dinner. She will, of course, be responding with sounds and gestures throughout the action*)

SIGISMUND. Show me what you've brought. Good.... Good.... And what is this? Layla! You wade into the woods picking God knows what and trying new edibles on me. One of these days, you slave, Turk and enemy of Christ, you'll despatch me to heaven with some leaf or root of yours. I'm joking, my girl! You're no Medea, thank God, and I like *everything* you do. Give Sigismund a kiss. Have you eaten? Not going hungry? Good. (*A fanfare in the distance*) Here comes Klotalski. Go in and prepare something for him. (*Layla returns to her cabin*) As I hope to be saved, I'll have her baptized and marry her the day after I've rid myself of this accursed chain. (*He eats his dinner*)

(*Enter Klotalski*)

KLOTALSKI. Good evening, young man! And how are we today?

SIGISMUND. Ask me *what* are we today. We are a prisoner, Klotalski, a wretch worse off than a caged bear and you know it.

KLOTALSKI. Nonsense! You're in the pink—what am I saying?—in the purple of health, your muscles bulging like two of our Polish potatoes, and I hope you've studied your Hecataeus.

SIGISMUND. I like ancient history, Klotalski, but live history is more exciting. What's the news at court, eh? Did the crown assessor stop at Zakopane? Did you see him? Tell me all.

KLOTALSKI. Gently! He did stop on his way as promised, and he did call on me with late news, or gossip. It appears that Prince Astolof has arrived at Cracow from Muscovy in order to endear himself to Princess Estrella and offer a Muscovite army to help us. It seems that the court is impressed by his elegance.

SIGISMUND. A toyshop prince! Will she marry him? Didn't she once run away with Bogdan Opalinski? An idyil in the woods?

KLOTALSKI. Gossip. According to the assessor, everyone hopes they marry. Better to have Muscovy on our side than see them helping the Tatars and Turks against us.

SIGISMUND. I could bash Tatars and Turks better than any Astolof if the king would only unchain me.

KLOTALSKI. Let me hear you repeat your lesson instead.

SIGISMUND. Wait. Is Opalinski still murdering landowners left and right?

KLOTALSKI (*sullen*). I don't know. Mind your studies.

SIGISMUND. Good for him! Good for the bandit! Away with oppressors! Oppressors like yourself, Klotalski. No more chains!

KLOTALSKI. I think you're asking for the whip, my son. You know that my men are not far.

SIGISMUND. Who am I, Klotalski? Surely a prince too? I stare for hours at the king's portrait you hung in my cave and tell it aloud I'm his son, the gypsies stole me from the cradle, or maybe you did in order to betray the king, old ruffian, and I'll twist your head off the day I find out.

KLOTALSKI. Hothead! The whip is too good for you. I don't know who you are, but I'm guessing that you're the bastard of some Hebrew ragpicker. That is why I placed the king's portrait where it is, between Saint Stanislas and the Holy Virgin, for you to abase yourself before him and them, not for impudent observations. Enough of that! I'm ordered to keep you alive and I do my duty without asking questions. Did you study your Hecataeus today, yes or no?

SIGISMUND. What else is there for me to do? Marry Princess Estrella? (*Klotalski makes a menacing gesture*) Peace. I'll recite. Book Fourteen. "The night King Mycerinus received the Ethiopian ambassadors, he gave a banquet unmatched for splendor since the days of King Sesostris. A thousand dancing-girls"—

(*Enter Layla with another dish*)

KLOTALSKI. Good evening, resplendent Layla! Ah, our fresh Carpathian berries in cream! What a treat! Continue, my dear Sigismund. And some music from you, Layla.

(*Exit Layla; she returns holding a lute, on which she plucks a Turkish folk tune as best she can*)

SIGISMUND (*eating*). "A thousand dancing girls, an orchestra consisting of innumerable harps, trumpets, oboes, and percussion instruments, and a feast which lasted from evening to dawn, with a different wine brought in for each course, and a mouthwash of Karkemish brandy for every guest. When the ambassadors expressed their amazement as the sun was rising—for they had eaten and drunk with the utmost care and kept their heads clear—"

KLOTALSKI. Make a particular note of that, Sigismund. Kept their heads clear. Incorruptible statesmen.

SIGISMUND. Do you believe it?

KLOTALSKI. I don't know that I do, but the idea of it is wonderful, the moral idea in the historian's mind, and that is what finally matters. Go on.

SIGISMUND. Let me see. "When the ambassadors and so forth, King Mycerinus spoke as follows: 'All this luxury, my lords, this pomp, this magnificence, all this is but gloss. When you return to the emperor of Ethiopia report only, I beg you, that in this fair Egypt of mine all men are equal'—"

KLOTALSKI. What's that?

SIGISMUND. What do you mean, what's that?

KLOTALSKI. Is that in Hecataeus?
SIGISMUND. Where else, for God's sake? Do I have it from Layla?
KLOTALSKI. Layla, go away! (*Exit Layla*) Let me hear the rest.
SIGISMUND. "'No one is richer than his neighbor, we wage no wars, no man lords it over another, our kings are elected by universal suffrage male and female, and I myself, as soon as my successor is chosen, intend to return to the company of dancers in which I toured Egypt every winter before I was crowned pharaoh.' When the ambassadors, having returned to Ethiopia, recounted to the emperor the wonders they had seen and heard in Egypt, he said to them 'Gentlemen, you must have been cleverly drugged with some vicious powder in your wine at that banquet of yours, and then you dreamed all these wonders and extravagances.' But they loudly denied it and affirmed it had all happened as they reported." That's as far as I memorized, because Father Radim came up for confession, my Latin lesson and a bit of cold chicken. But, says he, Hecataeus is even grander than Isaiah, his favorite, and you're no fool for making me study him. Good man! If I were king, I'd make him come true in Poland. No more chains!
KLOTALSKI. Let me see the book. I must be going senile.
SIGISMUND. Here. I kept a chicken bone where I left off.
(*Klotalski examines the passage*)
KLOTALSKI. Hm. You really memorized it. The truth is that it's ages since I read Hecataeus at the university, and read him, of course, in the original Greek. There's some treason in this Polish translation. As for Father Radim, never mind; I'll have a chat with him before next Sunday. But kindly remember that Hecataeus is reporting an extravagant dream, and besides, the Egyptians were infidel barbarians. A king is a king, don't ever forget it, the poor are poor, nobody elected God and nobody except the aristocracy is going to elect the King of Poland and nobody is about to fill a peasant's pocket with zlotys so he can drink himself into a stupor when he should be busy in the fields.
SIGISMUND. Why are we getting all hot under the collar, old man? What are Egypt or Poland to me? I'm chained, remember. Damn damn damn.
KLOTALSKI. Well, that doesn't prevent you from being as smart as any bachelor of arts I've ever met. Bless my soul—the way you memorize!
SIGISMUND. Klotalski!
KLOTALSKI. Yes my boy?
SIGISMUND. I'm sure you are a man of tremendous consequence in the kingdom. A governor, a senator—maybe you're my father.
KLOTALSKI. God forbid! I was never married.
SIGISMUND. Tell me tell me who I am, tell me!

KLOTALSKI. Again! I can't! I don't know! I'm the Castellan of Zakopane, a penniless noble in a leaking castle who was never told a thing other than to obey orders.

SIGISMUND. It's a lie! I'll murder you!

KLOTALSKI. And then what? My soldiers will throw you into a vat of boiling oil.

SIGISMUND. Let them try! But why am I chained for life, I only, only I, worse than a bird, a beast, a fish, a river?

KLOTALSKI. I have told you a million times! A divine voice was heard at your birth, prophesying that, whoever you were, a peasant's brat or whatever, I don't know, you would inflict torrents of tears, unspeakable terror and merciless carnage on the land. Even—I shudder as I speak the words—even trample the king to the ground. Many wanted to snuff your life out in the cradle, but pity prevailed and you were carried to these mountains, chained to the rock, and placed under my care. The end.

SIGISMUND. Vile oppression! I was innocent! A baby! But not a peasant's brat! I know what I am, Klotalski. And because of you I've become the monster you were afraid I'd be.

KLOTALSKI. So you see, they were right.

SIGISMUND. No! They were wrong! That voice was not divine, it came from hell, it tempted you and you fell! Hack this chain off my ankle!

(*Trumpet sound nearby*)

SOLDIER (*off stage*). Lord Klotalski!

KLOTALSKI. Sounds like ensign Kristof. I'm here! What is it?

(*Enter a soldier pushing Agafya, bound, ahead of him. She is coarsely dressed and limps a little. Layla enters, looks on in astonishment, but after a while begins to light torches for the night*)

SIGISMUND. A woman!

KLOTALSKI. Who is this? What happened?

AGAFYA. This ruffian—

SOLDIER. I'll do the talking, miss! (*To Klotaslki*) Here's her dagger.

KLOTALSKI (*to Sigismund*). Back to the cave! At once!

SIGISMUND. I refuse.

KLOTALSKI. You refuse and I'll have you whipped.

SIGISMUND. And I'll break your neck before I let you.

SOLDIER (*aside to Klotalski*). Don't worry, sir; she don't know a thing.

SIGISMUND (*to Agafya*). Lady, if you are a victim too, like myself—

AGAFYA. I am! And now twice!

SIGISMUND. Good. Be patient. One of these days—

KLOTALSKI. Silence, *convict!* I am interrogating the girl.

SIGISMUND. Interrogate but don't harm her! (*To Agafya*) Do you see these chains?

AGAFYA. I see and I am amazed. Are you under a magic spell? Where am I?

KLOTALSKI. In your grave if you say a single wrong word. Who are you, woman? You sound and look foreign. What brings you snooping into these parts?

AGAFYA. What snooping? I fell from my horse!

SOLDIER. That she did, sir. We witnessed it.

AGAFYA. Coming down a rough slope. Bialik which is my mare went flying over a rock like one of them winged horses in story books. I almost died. And then half a dozen armed roughnecks grabbed me and tied my wrists instead helping a lady saddle up again. I protest!

KLOTALSKI. To the point. Who and what are you?

AGAFYA. I'm no spy at any rate. My name is Agafya Matveyevna Kulkova and I'm a Russian farmgirl. I've got manners, I can read, and I'm travelling from the Kingdom of Muscovy to Cracow on pure unadulterated private business, nothing to do with spying nor convicts nor state secrets. So please my lord, let me find my Bialik again and be on my way. I'm not putting no questions to you about what I seen here, I always say there's a reason for everything no matter how weird, and since I can tell that you're some fancy diplomat who doesn't like strangers meddling with his business, and I don't blame you a bit for *that*, you can count on me to keep my thoughts locked up in the barn up here if you tell your brutes to untie me and let me go my way.

SIGISMUND. Have you never heard anything about me, Agafya? About poor Sigismund?

AGAFYA. No sir, but I can see that we're both oppressed victims. You're chained and I'm bound. That's clear enough.

KLOTALSKI. You talk a great deal, my girl. Instead of gabbing about matters that don't concern you, tell me more about your pure unadulterated private business.

AGAFYA. It's about my maidenly honor, sir. Somebody went and besmirched it. I realize I ain't the first girl it ever happened to, but all the same I want restitution and compensation and I'm out to get it with my dad's consent.

KLOTALSKI. All the way to Cracow?

AGAFYA. All the way to Cracow. And for good reason.

KLOTALSKI. For *very* good reason, I'd guess—to come riding this far. I take it that your honor was whatever it was by some fine gentleman.

AGAFYA (*laughing*). Bull's eye! They don't come no finer!

KLOTALSKI. I'm going to take another guess. A fine gentleman in the retinue of Prince Astolof.

AGAFYA (*laughing harder*). Retinue! Oh, I like that! Retinue!

SIGISMUND. Maybe she doesn't know what the word means.

AGAFYA. I do know what the word means, I'm nobody's village idiot. Hang me if I'm not itching to tell you about Lord Retinue! Maybe you could even help me—so as to pay up for scaring me. Fair is fair.

KLOTALSKI. I wonder if the girl is a little crazy.

AGAFYA (*suddenly serious*). Yes, she is. Crazy about Prince Astolof. And him about me. Ha! That gave you a jolt, I see.

SIGISMUND. I believe her!

KLOTALSKI. Silence! Girl, how dare you make such an accusation?

AGAFYA. He did it and I'm going after him. I don't care what you think about it provided you give me back my horse and let me go on to Cracow.

SIGISMUND. Make him marry you!

AGAFYA (*laughing*). Good idea! Or else give me to some fine boyar at least! Lord, my blood boils when I think of it—not so much as a ring, not so much as a flower, nothin'! "How dare you?" says he next day when I catched hold of him riding through the barley field. "It was a dream," he says with a fat laugh; "your sweetheart mixed powders into your drink afore doing it to you and made you dream he was a prince or a king." Well, let's see who he thinks is dreaming this time when I surprise him in his Cracow palace!

SIGISMUND. Jump out at him while he's courting the princess!

KLOTALSKI (*who has been in a deep study*). Silence I say.... Listen, Agafya; your story does sound true to me. At least it sounds *possibly* true. True enough for me to take you to Cracow in my own retinue this very week, and I'll even see if I can't get you presented to King Casimir.

AGAFYA. Will you, will you really?

SIGISMUND. Congratulations, Klotalski, congratulations for once!

AGAFYA. I'll be the most grateful girl in the world. I'll serve you as long as I live and I won't blab about nothing.

KLOTALSKI. I like you so much that I don't even care if you do blab! We Poles like spirited girls. (*To the soldier*) Untie her.

SOLDIER. Stand still, girl.

KLOTALSKI. Here's your dagger. And is that a purse hanging from your belt?

AGAFYA. Yes, my lord.

KLOTALSKI. Full of gold?

AGAFYA. Ha, ha, ha! I wish! But mind you—copper enough for a square meal when I'm hungry, which ain't often, we're tough in our village.

KLOTALSKI. Still, here's a gold piece for you. Tuck it in. It will help you get lodgings fit for a prince's love, and buy diapers for his heir if necessary.

AGAFYA. Don't worry; I can take a joke. And as I see you're giving me the gold piece with an honest heart, with an honest heart I'll accept it.

KLOTALSKI (*to the soldier*). Take her to the encampment, give her a bath, have Tadeusz dress her foot, feed her and her horse, give her a bunk, and treat her like a princess of Muscovy.

SOLDIER. You mean we're not allowed our turn to besmirch her honor?

AGAFYA. You try and I'll cut off your—

KLOTALSKI. Enough! Get out of here both of you.

AGAFYA (*kneeling*). I kiss your feet, my lord.

KLOTALSKI. Brave girl. Behave and I'll take good care of you.

AGAFYA. I promise. Back in the village—

KLOTALSKI. Blab, blab, blab! Get out!

AGAFYA. Yes, sir.

SOLDIER. Come along, spitfire.

(*They leave*)

SIGISMUND. Poor girl! And she must be famished. Look at her and then look at Layla. Will you really take her to the king, Klotalski?

KLOTALSKI. I think I will.

SIGISMUND. Why so noble all of a sudden? What are you hiding from me? And are you that close to the king?

KLOTALSKI. Again! I don't know him and he doesn't know me, except by reputation. But it came to me while the girl was rattling away that I might as well combine your quarterly business, a little lawsuit of my own, and her grievance, all in one expedition. The king is known as a tiger for justice. If the girl isn't lying, he will do something exceptional for her, if only to keep the prince from being embarrassed; and she—well, what can I say? She will be grateful to me....

SIGISMUND. I don't recognize you, Klotalski! Where's Hecataeus now?

KLOTALSKI. I'm a man, Sigismund—old, but still a man. You have your Layla, I have no one.

(*Layla is cleaning up, and will be returning to her cabin during the following speech*)

SIGISMUND. Ha, ha, ha, ha! Forward march! Enjoy the skinny thing! Look at my Layla grinning! Get along, you nauseous Turk. God only knows who was first to besmirch *your* honor! Ha, ha, ha! (*Suddenly serious*) Klotalski, you're lying to me, and don't imagine for a moment that I'm too stupid to understand there's a strange game being played with me—with me and around me. My ankle may be chained but my brain isn't. Godspeed to Cracow, old schemer. I'm going to bed.

(*He drags himself and his chain into the cave*)

KLOTALSKI. Let him believe in the strange game. He is pregnant with high fancies that suit me all of a sudden. To Cracow! The idea struck me so hard while the girl was talking that I almost staggered. Such an idea, round and succulent, must be squeezed of all its sap before it withers. This month Sigismund comes of age. Shall he die here sixty years hence and still in chains? I love the boy I was ordered to guard, but I love my worthy self too. What if I can exalt both Sigismund and myself? The rumors that he is alive have never been silenced. How could it be otherwise? True, the Household Guard is supremely loyal; but now and then a retired guardsman will take one drink too many and slurp out a hint. The opposition is ready to cry tyranny and infanticide. And what an opposition! Twenty years ago we had only a formless rabble of disgruntled peasants inspired by their German brothers. Today it's the peasants and the city riff raff banded together, storing arms, clamoring for privileges and charters and representation and distribution, parading about in finery my own grandparents couldn't afford—well! Just listen to that Muscovy peasant girl! They've caught the fever on the steppes as well! Her *honor* has been besmirched, if you please! I didn't know whether I should laugh or weep. Tomorrow we'll have to address them as Mister and Madam. But I'm wandering off the track. These Muscovites must not be allowed to be our saviors. That is a worse danger than the Swedes! Let the girl raise a hue and cry in Cracow against Astolof, and at the same time advertise at every street corner what a wonder she saw in the mountains. Our Poles will know how to put two and two together. With Astolof looking either guilty or ridiculous, and discredited in any case, I'll beg the king to allow me to convey Sigismund to the palace as our acknowledged heir to the crown. And why not? Twenty one years ago we were all terrified; I myself argued that the infant should be put to death; but those were the dark ages. Omens and prodigies have gone out of fashion. What omens? We have our brilliant Kopernik, bless us, the Bohemians over the mountains boast of their Klepper or Pekler, everybody is making himself cozy with the stars what with peering at them through those newfangled lenses—omens be damned, and the church never liked them anyway. "Your majesty," I'll say, "we need a young man of our very own at the head of our levies, a young, strong, handsome prince of our own blood, reborn from the dead, a legend!—in short, a hero who can command enthusiasm—bully bodies we have plenty of, it's enthusiasm we lack—against Turks, Swedes, the mob and above all against that traitor to his kind, Bogdan Opalinski, who philosophizes by the book and kills by the pistol. Your place, sir, is in the palace, holding all the kingdom's strings in your fingers, while Sigismund, our awakened Polish eagle, proudly hunts down Bogdan the wolf." Leave it to me! I can always count on my eloquence! And I thank myself for having adorned the boy's mind with images of high policy and historic destiny even as I kept him dutifully humbled. So now for another turn of the wheel. Suddenly I appear as the country's liberator and benefactor. And what follows? Whatever God intends. Old I may be, but I have vigor to spare for—we shall see what. Half words are sometimes wisest even to oneself. Godspeed to Cracow! And you, my lad, sleep in your cave and dream of the splendor you shall owe your Klotalski.... Layla! (*Layla appears*) Light a torch and walk me to my horse.

SCENE THREE

(*In a corner of the stage the light falls on Sigismund restlessly asleep in his simple bed. He moans, laughs, gives indistinct commands, and suddenly cries out "Astolof! Puppy!" Thereupon the stage lights reveal a room in the royal palace of Cracow and the foppish Prince Astolof standing before the seated beautiful Princess Estrella. Throughout this scene, in a dimmed light, the sleeping Sigismund will be moving and making gestures*)[2]

ASTOLOF. Princess Estrella, well named in that sweet Tuscan idiom which all men adore—for in that language estrella signifies star—or rather ill named because only half named, forasmuch as your eyes are twins and therefore well might you be called Estrellas or double star—Princess Estrella, then, or Estrellas, at your approach the trumpets and drums pummel and blow, likewise the birds and fountains greet you with amazement, the ones becoming fountains of joyful feathers, the others birds of soaring water. All welcome you: the drum because you banish night, the trumpet because you broadcast wisdom, the birds because you soar above all women, the fountains to signify the flow of your wit. But above all these, with ever renewed worship, a prince kneels before you; I mean myself, so recently arrived from the bleaknesses of remote Muscovy to the jeweled enchantments of mighty Poland.

ESTRELLA. Prince Astolof, I humbly thank you. Rise. The elegance of your discourse suggests that Muscovy, far from being as bleak and remote as you

---

[2] In later scenes, another actor will have to play the role of sleeping Sigismund.

indicate—I have not enjoyed the good fortune of journeying in an easterly direction—for, as perhaps you know, I descend on my mother's side from a *Spanish* line—

ASTOLOF. Of the purest Christian blood!

ESTRELLA. And therefore have travelled only thither—nevertheless, as I was saying, your delicate speech suggests a court deeply penetrated by the humanities, and alive to all the refinements of cultivated feeling. I shall never again credit the reports that your father the Tsar boils his prisoners alive.

ASTOLOF. Ah princess, every word you utter is a happy augury, namely for myself and you, and for our two nations. The great King Casimir is childless, rumors to the contrary notwithstanding. You are his undisputed heiress. I, on the other hand, rejoice in the title of young Caesar of Muscovy. Our union will secure eternal blessings to our twinned kingdoms, together we will pulverize the Turks and Swedes and alarm the Habsburgs; and I would turn into an estrella in the heavens at this very moment were I not preoccupied, I mournfully confess, by the portrait of a man which hangs about your swannish neck and which I asked you in vain last night to unfold to me. Is it, as I hope, the resemblance of a deceased brother or a lamented cousin? Imagine, I implore you, a lover's chagrined jealousy—his tremulous apprehension!

ESTRELLA. Tsarevich, I have nothing to hide, and if the archbishop had not interrupted us last night — but here comes a yet nobler diversion, for I perceive that my uncle approaches.

(*Servants usher in King Casimir, now white-haired and white bearded*)

ASTOLOF. Glorious monarch—

ESTRELLA. Dearest uncle—

ASTOLOF. Terror of the infidels—

ESTRELLA. Protector of orphans—

KING. Children and future rulers of united Poland, Lithuania and Muscovy—

ASTOLOF. Heavenly words!

KING. Let me embrace you both. Give me your hands. There. And now allow me to join them together. So.

ASTOLOF. I place my fervent lips on this angelic hand as though it were the wafer of the Holy Eucharist.

KING. Sit, my children, sit. This is a sweet moment after a troubled meeting with my councillors.

(*He claps his hands and servants bring refreshments*)

ESTRELLA. Will you confide in us, uncle, or must you keep your burden to yourself?

KING. Of course I will confide in you—you two who must be carrying that burden after I am gone.
ASTOLOF. God grant you a hundred more young years!
KING. God forbid.
ESTRELLA. Your burden, my dear?
KING. Alas, the heaviest part of it is due to that gentleman who hangs about your neck.
ASTOLOF. At last! Who is this rival of mine?
ESTRELLA. A penniless exile, prince, whom you need not fear. His name is Baron Bogdan Opalinksi.
ASTOLOF. The great rebel! What are you telling me?
KING. The regrettable truth.
ASTOLOF. My mind totters.
ESTRELLA. I pledged myself to him, and he swore eternal love to me, on my innocent sixteenth birthday.
ASTOLOF. A glass of water!
KING. Compose yourself, prince. All will be well. The path is rocky where it begins but levels out at the end. Continue, my dear. Your honesty touches me.
ESTRELLA. Briefly, my lord: after reminding us that King Piast, the founder of our nation, was born a peasant, Bogdan renounced his birthright, freed eighty thousand serfs, gave them his lands, forsook the court and myself, and became—but this you already know—the leader of the voiceless, the oppressed—
KING. The lawless.
ESTRELLA. Lawless indeed, since no law was ever made for them. However, Bogdan Opalinski is gone. The portrait is a vestige of my childhood. The woman, prince, will marry you.
KING. You see?
ASTOLOF. Dazed but unbowed, I take up the gauntlet. Destiny will not be undone by a miniature. Furthermore, I hope and trust that my ardent kisses and caresses—
ESTRELLA. Prince!
ASTOLOF. I insist: my ardent kisses and caresses—following the pomp of Christian sacrament, I hasten to add, for I am punctilious in all religious observances. As I was saying—what was I saying?
KING. Your pressing attentions to the princess—
ASTOLOF. Ah yes. They will blot that other from your memory. One day soon you will freely and meekly undo the clasp and—

(*Enter a servant*)

SIGISMUND, PRINCE OF POLAND

SERVANT. Your majesty, dinner will be served in one hour. (*Exit*)
ASTOLOF. One hour! Is that all? I beg your permission to withdraw, your highness, and yours, divine princess, in order to let my valet and coiffeur recompose me for the royal table.
KING. Our time is yours to command, prince.
(*More ceremony, then Astolof leaves. A pause, after which the king and Estrella heave a great sigh together*)
ESTRELLA. I agree, dear uncle, but what is to be done?
KING. The Tsar forgot to mention in his letter that his son is a nitwit.
ESTRELLA. Pampered privilege.
KING. My dear, you are pampered privilege too, and yet you are wise and good—except for your attachment to that traitor.
ESTRELLA. Your heart is not in that word.
KING. Only because I dandled little Bogdan on my knees. Only because I spun tops with him and got upon all fours so he could ride on my back. Only because I wished him to replace my Sigismund, oh God!
ESTRELLA. Uncle—
KING. And then he takes to the hills to become a messiah. Talk about pampered privilege! Do you know how much blood is soaking his conscience already? Landlords hacked to pieces, innocent bystanders massacred, peasants looted for supplies, Jews murdered for serving the gentry.
ESTRELLA. As ye sow, so shall ye reap.
ESTRELLA. It may happen.
KING. I ought to stop caring. I dream of the cell my good Cistercians are keeping for me in Oliwa, overlooking the Baltic; I dream of the silver sound of church-bells... the organ booming.... I ought to end my days in remorseful prayers.... Elegant Astolof would ride up and down Poland on his proud stallion, purging our country of Swedes and Turks for the Tsar's benefit, and you... you would slip unnoticed into the forest, find your Bogdan, and make such love to him that he'd forget his peasants.
ESTRELLA. Bogdan is no longer interested in love.
KING. Another nitwit.
ESTRELLA. I think we should dress for dinner too.
(*A pause*)
KING. Estrella, what if I made a colossal mistake twenty one years ago? I think about it day and night.
ESTRELLA. What's done is done, uncle.
KING. What's done might yet be undone. The boy lives and God forgives. Shouldn't I prove that a good deed will always defeat the wicked stars? Klotalski tells me that Sigismund is strong and fierce. Why not put him

in command and send Astolof home? No more chains! Shall I dare it, Estrella?

ESTRELLA. You are consulting me for the best way to ruin my Bogdan! I wish you had never taken me into your confidence.

KING. I needed someone dear to me to hear me sigh out my heart.

ESTRELLA. He is destined to trample you into the ground.

KING. Let him....

(*Enter a servant*)

SERVANT. Your majesty: my lord Klotalski and a young lady.

KING. Klotalski here? With a young lady? What can this mean? I shall see them at once.

(*The servant exits and then opens the door to Klotalski and Agafya. With a motion of the hand, Klotalski bids Agafya wait at a distance*)

KING. Klotalski, what news?

(*Klotalski kneels and kisses the king's hand. Agafya kneels too and then rises but remains where she is. Next, Klotalski kisses Estrella's hand*)

ESTRELLA. Welcome, dear friend.

KLOTALSKI. Sire, Princess, I have come to Cracow sooner than expected in order to attend to certain affairs—a certain lawsuit; but primarily because of this young person who was apprehended—trespassing—you best know where. I would have had her executed at once—

AGAFYA (*still at a distance*). I didn't do nothin'!

KLOTALSKI. Be silent, girl! I should have ordered her executed at once—but the girl's simplicity and youthfulness—an aging man's compassion—the involuntariness of her trespass—

KING. How was that ascertained?

KLOTALSKI. Oh, as for that, she is an ignorant farmgirl from Muscovy, loquacious and bold enough, to be sure—but merely riding horseback into Poland (*low to the king and Estrella*) in order to settle accounts with a jilting swain. The usual story....

ESTRELLA. Poor girl!

(*Agafya curtseys at a distance*)

KLOTALSKI. Crossing the Tatras, she fell off her nag—I believe there are no mountains in Muscovy—almost broke her neck—stumbled about—and was, as I said, duly apprehended. I hope I have not offended your majesty. If I have, she can still—

KING. If she knows nothing, send her packing with a stiff warning.

KLOTALSKI. Precisely my idea. Come here, girl, and thank his majesty for—

(*Enter Astolof, dressed to kill. Agafya lets out a shriek. Astolof shrieks in return*)

AGAFYA. It's him!

ASTOLOF. Agafya!

AGAFYA. Yes, Agafya Matveyevna Kulkova, come to get what's hers!

ASTOLOF. How—I can't believe it!—how did you—all the way—?

AGAFYA. You'll know soon enough, seducer!

KLOTALSKI (*low to the king*). Is this the Prince of Muscovy?

KING. It is.

ASTOLOF. Get away from me!

KING. What does all this mean?

ESTRELLA. Wonderful!

KLOTALSKI. Your highness, if I had known—

ASTOLOF. Keep her away from me! This is a ghastly misunderstanding! I don't know the girl!

ESTRELLA. You named her, prince!

AGAFYA. Liar! I looked for you and I found you. This kind old nobleman eased the way for me, but don't worry, I'd have found you if you'd galloped off to the moon.

ESTRELLA. Delightful! Go on, my girl. What is your name again?

AGAFYA. Agafya, my lady, to serve you.

ESTRELLA. A good, honest Russian name. Tell us your story, and don't be shy.

ASTOLOF. Princess, for goodness' sake! These trashy stories are not fit for your ears. Sordid attempts by peasant girls to rise out of their class—persons who allege God knows what injuries—utterly nauseating!

ESTRELLA. Indeed, I am sickened already. Speak up, Agafya, nauseate us a little more.

KING. Never mind. Let's send the girl down to servants' quarters while we go in to dinner. Later on—

ASTOLOF. Yes, later on—

KLOTALSKI. I will—

ESTRELLA. No, uncle dear, no, Lord Klotalski, I insist on her story before dinner.

AGAFYA. It's a short one, your ladyship. This rascal of a tsarevich seduced me, not that he was much good, and then he said he was off to Cracow for a grand marriage, but first he'd find me a sweet young noble boyar for a husband. And that was the last of it. I never saw no boyar, and when I heard the traitor had gone to Poland, I saddled dad's best horse—we've got three of them on the farm—we're not trash, madam, we're well off paupers as paupers go—and I went after him with dad's and grandad's blessings and a few coppers in my satchel and the Virgin Mary round my neck. I'm a sinner, I know, I did say yes when the gentleman came 'round in all his ribbons and sweet talk in the barn and smelling so good, and I've went to confession to get absolved, but treason and lies is treason and lies and I'm here to get what's coming to me.

KING. I'm speechless. A boyar! What did the girl say? A sweet young noble boyar! And why not the prince himself?

KLOTALSKI (*feigning anger*). Shameless hussy! The dungeon is what's coming to you!

ASTOLOF. And chained to a cave to cool her off!

AGAFYA. I'll murder you first!

(*Guards stop her*)

KLOTALSKI. The world is coming to an end! (*Aside*) She's adorable.

KING. Remove the little devil!

(*Agafya screams*)

ESTRELLA. One moment! Uncle, if I promise to keep the girl a little bit muzzled and leashed, may I have her for a milkmaid on my make believe farm? I can use a sturdy lass.

KING. Have it your way....

ASTOLOF. I protest, with your permission.

ESTRELLA. Listen to me, Agafya. Your wages here will be more to your liking than life with some fop of a nobleman; and after a year or so, you may, if you wish, return to Muscovy with an attractive dowry saved up, and marry a really useful person.

AGAFYA. Thank you, kind lady. I ain't saying yes and I ain't saying no; but while I'm thinking over how to punish that manikin, I'm willing to show your folk how we milk our cows at home. But please don't allow him to inveigle *you*, madam. You're worlds too good for him. However, you look like you're wide awake, and no man—

KLOTALSKI. Enough, chatterbox!

ESTRELLA. She's a dear, *I* say. (*To a servant*) Jan, take the girl below. Tell Barbara to find a sweet little room for her and to await my orders.

AGAFYA. Thank you, madam. (*To Klotalski*) My lord, I kiss your feet for being kind to me except for your rough words—but I'm a rough one myself, so—

KLOTALSKI. All right all right all right! Take her away before I do something rash! (*Exeunt Agafya and the servant*) Like taking her home myself! I have no one, you understand.

KING. Fie on you, old fellow!

ESTRELLA (*laughing*). Bravo for you, Klotalski, and for recognizing merit where others don't.

KLOTALSKI. And yet I cannot forgive myself for causing—

KING. I forgive you, my friend; I forgive your kind heart.

ASTOLOF. As for myself, I assure you all around that it is certainly not the custom *chez nous* in Muscovy for cowgirls and the like to complain of a gentleman's courtesies. I am deeply mortified.

KING. Think nothing of it, my dear prince. And Estrella grants you a full pardon, I'm sure.

ESTRELLA. Heartily. I was afraid you might be a virgin, dear Astolof—and worse—and thus of my having the advantage of you. The cowgirl episode reassures me.

ASTOLOF. You are pleased to jest, my divine star, or stars. I am in fact a man of the most violent libidinous propulsions and appetites.

KING. Appetites! My chef must be desperate by now. Will you, my two children, walk into the dining room before us? I need to exchange a few words with Klotalski before joining you.

ASTOLOF. If Estrella will take my arm.

ESTRELLA. She will, dear Astolof.

(*Exeunt Estrella and Astolof*)

KING. Poland needs a young hero.

KLOTALSKI. It does, my lord.

KING. I must free Sigismund and place him on the throne at once. And if that fails, why then let this impossible Muscovite take the crown. I will have done what I could. A king is but a man. Listen carefully, Klotalski. You are to hurry back to Zakopane tomorrow at dawn and set out with Sigismund for Cracow the next day. Speak to him of soaring eagles, read him that passage in the Iliad where Achilles slays Hector but is kind to old Priam. The hour has struck for challenging the horrid omens. God predestines; but what he predestines no living creature can tell. Twenty one years ago I was sure I could hear God speak. Today I ask in anguish, was the voice I heard divine, or was it from hell, it tempted me and I fell? So now I act again, I undo the wrong, if wrong I did.

KLOTALSKI. God has inspired you, my king, I say God has inspired you. I am your absolute servant.

KING. Thanks, Klotalski. This very evening we shall acquaint the young ones with our design, and bid the Muscovite suspend his ambitions. Tomorrow, a grand proclamation to the Senate even as you are riding toward your mountain. Give me your hand, Klotalski. God prosper our adventure!

(*The stage darkens, but Sigismund in his bed remains visible as he speaks*)

SIGISMUND. God prosper our adventure!

SCENE FOUR

(The lights come up on a great hall in the palace. Festive decorations. A harpsichord in the background. Enter a richly arrayed but open-mouthed Sigismund, escorted by the Crown Chancellor and attendants. The sleeping, agitated Sigismund—played, obviously, by another actor—remains visible in the corner of the stage)

SIGISMUND *(dazed)*. And this?
CROWN CHANCELLOR. This, my lord, is the banqueting hall, built by your ancestor, Casimir the Great.
SIGISMUND *(dazed)*. And these?
CROWN CHANCELLOR. Banners captured from enemy regiments over the centuries; a collection to which we expect you, my lord, to make noteworthy contributions in the coming years.
(Sigismund wanders about the room, gaping, and looks out one of the windows)
SIGISMUND *(dazed)*. And that?
CROWN CHANCELLOR. Our matchless cathedral, my lord, conceived by your ancestor Boleslaw the Brave. *(Significantly)* Our coronations have taken place there since the year 1363.
SIGISMUND *(looking around the hall)*. And this?
CROWN CHANCELLOR. A magnificent tapestry, woven for us at Brussels. It shows young Jupiter emerging from the cave of Mount Ida, ready to strike down his father Cronus with the thunderbolt you perceive in his right hand.
SIGISMUND *(dazed)*. And this?
CROWN CHANCELLOR. One of the six thrones in the palace. Our kings can manifest their authority almost anywhere they happen to bestow themselves.
SIGISMUND *(dazed)*. And this?
CROWN CHANCELLOR. A Flemish harpsichord, presented to your late mother by the Elector of Brandenburg.
SIGISMUND *(dazed)*. And this?
CROWN CHANCELLOR. A priceless Italian mantelpiece, carved by Antonio Lombardo and similar, my lord, to the one you were pleased to inquire about in your bedchamber.
SIGISMUND *(dazed)*. Oh yes.... Where I woke up after, after.... Is that where I will be sleeping from now on?
CROWN CHANCELLOR. Yes, my lord; it is the crown prince's bedchamber.
SIGISMUND *(dazed)*. It has windows....

CROWN CHANCELLOR. Overlooking the royal gardens, my lord.
SIGISMUND (*dazed*). Straight walls....
CROWN CHANCELLOR. Poland boasts of impeccable architects.
SIGISMUND (*dazed*). Pillows upon pillows....
CROWN CHANCELLOR. Goose down from Cathay.
(*Sigismund discovers a full length mirror*)
SIGISMUND. Ah!...
CROWN CHANCELLOR. A mirror, my lord.
(*Sigismund, overcome, stares at himself, touches his garments, his face, the mirror itself*)
CROWN CHANCELLOR. Described in so many books....
SIGISMUND. Hush! (*Tears run down his cheeks*) Sigismund.... Sigismund.... Layla has one.... So tiny.... The size of my hand.... Can you understand?
CROWN CHANCELLOR. Can anyone but you?
SIGISMUND. No.... No one.... I am this.... And I am... wonderful!
CROWN CHANCELLOR. Regal. As you always surmised.
(*Sigismund turns away at last and looks once more around the hall*)
SIGISMUND. My friend, something is twitching at me.
CROWN CHANCELLOR. What can it be, my lord?
SIGISMUND. I know! My regal self is hungry!
CROWN CHANCELLOR. Is it any wonder, after such high emotions? But this was anticipated by our good Vladimir, who is master of your father's household. A modest repast is about to be served. Sit, my lord.
SIGISMUND. Sit? Where?
CROWN CHANCELLOR. Here, Prince Sigismund; where else?
SIGISMUND. This bench?
CROWN CHANCELLOR (*laughing*). Not a bench, my lord; an elegant *fauteuil*.
SIGISMUND. I don't like laughing.
CROWN CHANCELLOR. I apologize, my lord. Will you be so good as to sit?
(*Sigismund sits down and examines the crystal, silverware, porcelain, and so on. He drops a glass on the floor and it breaks. A lackey cleans up*)
SIGISMUND. It broke....
CROWN CHANCELLOR. Do not give it another thought, my lord. You own hundreds of these.
SIGISMUND. What are they made of?
CROWN CHANCELLOR. Crystal, if you please.
SIGISMUND. Crystal.... So this is crystal.... And this must be silver.... So much shinier than in the books.... The dishes, ah! Shepherds and shepherdesses.....
CROWN CHANCELLOR. Purest Saxon porcelain, my lord, and the salt

cellar was carved for us by a pupil of Cellini. But here at last comes your *consommé*.

(*The consommé arrives to a fanfare like the one heard in Scene Two. Sigismund is puzzled*)

SIGISMUND. Will there always be music, no matter what I do?

CROWN CHANCELLOR. We fervently hope so, my lord.

(*Sigismund begins to eat. A dark hued dancing girl enters, performs to the sound of a tambourine and bows*)

SIGISMUND. An Egyptian dancing-girl! Hecataeus was right! And how she danced!

CROWN CHANCELLOR. A thousand dancing girls are yours, my lord; and at a nod from you, this one will also—but here come more pleasures for your palate.

(*He signals to the dancing girl, who leaves. Led by Vladimir, servants appear carrying numerous dishes and flagons*)

VLADIMIR. Your highness, allow me to present: pheasant; bear; calf; lamb; oxen; hares; salmon; perch; truffles; mangoes; persimmon; and an assortment of greens. Our youngest wines are a century old.

SIGISMUND. I'll amaze Layla! (*He eats and drinks*) I think I'm tremendously happy. (*To the Crown Chancellor*) Here, taste the wine.

CROWN CHANCELLOR. Thank you, my lord. Superb!

SIGISMUND. I forget who you are.

CROWN CHANCELLOR. My name is Florian, Duke of Radziwill, my lord, and I am the nation's crown Crown Chancellor.

SIGISMUND. My head feels heavy since waking up.

CROWN CHANCELLOR. You will feel better as the day wears on and your glories multiply.

SIGISMUND. Were you one of the people who dressed me?

CROWN CHANCELLOR. Certainly not, my lord. You were dressed by four subalterns of the wardrobe.

SIGISMUND. And will I always be dressed by others?

CROWN CHANCELLOR. Always, my lord, even on the battlefield.

SIGISMUND. And is the sword mine to keep? It is a finer one than what I exercised with in... in the past.

CROWN CHANCELLOR. It is your sword, my lord, and was given you before your birth by Prince Gabor of Transylvania.

SIGISMUND. I am going to amaze the world with this sword. For I begin to understand that I am the man I dreamed I am.

CROWN CHANCELLOR. You are, and may God bless you.

(*Servants bring dessert. Enter Ladislaw Szopen*)

VLADIMIR. Your highness, may I introduce, along with this Persian sorbet, our chief musician, Ladislaw Szopen, who will now play a sarabande composed for this unforgettable occasion.

(*Szopen soulfully performs, but what emerges is the folk tune we have heard before, still played on a lute, though faultlessly this time. As Szopen plays, Sigismund rises from the table, sorbet in hand, and sobbing*)

SIGISMUND. I never heard it so beautiful before.... I wish Layla could.... I feel all strange....

SZOPEN. It is the power of music, your highness; music hath the power to soothe the savage breast.

SIGISMUND. It does, it does. I am becoming a better man. Kindness, justice, ideals of every kind animate me, thanks to you. No more chains.... (*He returns to the table*) Here... take this, and this, and this.

(*He gives Szopen a great quantity of silverware and porcelain. The Crown Chancellor and Vladimir look uneasy*)

SZOPEN. Prince! Such bounty! I proudly accept. I accept in the name of Art, which flourishes only when kings and princes patronize it.

(*He kneels as best he can with the objects he is holding*)

SIGISMUND. Oh, I like that! At last! (*He walks all around Szopen, patting him on the head*) Rise, artist, go in peace, and soothe as many breasts in Poland as there are notes lurking in your fingers.

SZOPEN. Prince, I humbly take my leave.

(*Exit Szopen with his gifts, picking up one or two that fall on the floor*)

SIGISMUND (*to Vladimir and the servants*). Now you, my friends, all of you gather round and do like the musician, kneel a little too.

VLADIMIR (*kneeling*). Hail, Prince Sigismund!

THE SERVANTS (*likewise*). Hail, Prince Sigismund!

SIGISMUND. God bless you. Now you, Radziwill.

CROWN CHANCELLOR. My lord?

SIGISMUND. You. Your turn. Join these good people and kneel piously to me.

CROWN CHANCELLOR. My lord, the peers of Poland are exempt from kneeling, except to the pope. An inclination of twenty degrees from the waist is all—

SIGISMUND. I don't understand. What peers? Is a prince better than a peer, yes or no?

CROWN CHANCELLOR. Perhaps, my lord; but both custom and law circumscribe—

SIGISMUND. Do a somersault!

CROWN CHANCELLOR. What?

SIGISMUND. Jump out the window!

CROWN CHANCELLOR. This mockery is inadmissible. I am—
SIGISMUND. You are nothing! *They're* kneeling! You kneel with them!
(*He draws his sword*)
CROWN CHANCELLOR. Never!
(*He draws too. The others rise in disarray. But suddenly another fanfare is sounded, and enter the king, wearing a crown, and after him Klotalski, Estrella, Astolof, and soldiers*)
KING. What do I see? Put up your swords, both of you! (*Sigismund gapes*) Radziwill, explain to me! Your sword raised against my son?
CROWN CHANCELLOR. Never, your majesty! In the course of introducing our beloved prince to his new métier, I was demonstrating a new thrust recommended by Carranza.
KING. I breathe again. Yes, Sigismund, here I am, King Casimir, your father. Sheathe your mighty sword. Come to my arms. Kiss your most unfortunate parent.
(*Sigismund allows himself to be embraced but quickly jumps back*)
SIGISMUND (*low, full of hatred*). You kept me chained twenty-one years, like a bear.
KING. Forgive me, my son! Twenty one years ago, at your birth, the most horrid omens ever seen in Poland revealed that you, my son, were destined to inflict merciless carnage upon our land. Many argued that you be put to death instantly. But, horrified by the thought, I decided to secrete you to a distant cave, where you were lovingly raised by the faithful castellan of Zakopane, my beloved Lord Klotalski. To the nation I announced that you had died in your cradle. I raised your fair cousin Estrella so as to fit her for the succession. But my remorse never drew back the claw it had plunged into my heart from the beginning. Had these awesome omens stamped out a decision of almighty God? Or had they been nothing more than a test of my Christian charity, and had I not wretchedly failed that test by cowering before mere signs? I have no answer, O Sigismund, but I have brought you home, and I implore you to defy the portents and to show yourself magnanimous to your land and a scourge only to its rapacious enemies. Estrella, give me your hand. My son, this is your dear cousin, who gladly renounces the throne for you.
ESTRELLA (*kneeling*). Welcome, cousin! I humbly kiss your hand.
KING. Astolof, greet your fellow prince.
ASTOLOF. Greetings, Prince Sigismund, from the tsarevich of Muscovy. May Poland and Muscovy be allied forever!
KING. Klotalski!
KLOTALSKI (*embracing Sigismund*). My prince, my pupil, my child. Yes, I am your Klotalski! I have been your loving master for twenty-one years. Now

you are mine for the rest of my days.
KING. And now, let us cry Long live Prince Sigismund, defender of the Crown, rampart against the Turks, lion to the Swedes!
ALL. Long live Prince Sigismund!
KING. And let us have triumphant music!
(*Another fanfare*)
SIGISMUND (*howling*). Stop the noise!
(*Abrupt silence*)
SIGISMUND. Your omens came from hell!
(*He walks up to the king, and with his two hands on the latter's shoulders, firmly presses him to a kneeling position. He then removes Casimir's crown, places it on his own head, and stands powerfully in front of the throne*)
SIGISMUND. I am the king of Poland!
THE SOLDIERS. Hurrah! Hurrah! Long live King Sigismund!
(*The others are stunned*)
KING (*prostrate*). Oh my son...

SCENE FIVE

(*The bed and Sigismund in the corner of the stage are gone. In a darkened small room, the King, the Crown Chancellor—looking nothing like the dreamed one—and Klotaslki are huddled, speaking in low voices*)

KING. Inviting himself to Cracow! Aspiring to my niece's hand! Offering to lead 10,000 men against our enemies! But how could I refuse? Enemies everywhere....
CROWN CHANCELLOR. You need not refuse outright, my lord. Klotalski's arrival has been providential. For he is right, your majesty. Sigismund must be unchained and brought to Cracow at once.
KLOTASLKI. The Muscovite can be amused while we launch Sigismund into the world.
KING. Amused? This is no toyshop prince, my friends. The man is a rugged warrior.
CROWN CHANCELLOR. We'll amuse him militarily with exercises, parades, inspections, strategic projects, what have you.
KLOTALSKI. And the people are ready for Sigismund. My babbling Agafya has babbled up half of Cracow already. But the chief point is that the boy

is strong, keen-witted, ambitious, well-read, half-believes already he is of royal blood, a born leader.
KING. What you say, Klotaslki, makes me both rejoice and tremble. The omens, don't forget the omens. The words stick in my head. "Virtuous massacres!" They sound like Bogdan mouthing his orations. I fear the worst. I fear a scourge.
CROWN CHANCELLOR. At the first sign, my men will bring him down, and we return him to his cave to the end of his days.
KLOTASLKI. You will not need to, believe me. I am the one who knows the lad.
(Silence)
KING. The die is cast. Come what may. God will do His will.

SCENE SIX

(The sleeping Sigismund reappears in the corner. He will be "participating" in high agitation in everything that follows. The lights come up again on the palace hall. A servant is cleaning up. Startled by the approaching noise, he hurries out. Enter Astolof, pursued by Agafya)

ASTOLOF. Get away from me, you hussy! Go back to your cows! I've troubles enough without your snarling at me all day long.
AGAFYA. I'll go back to my cows after I've had justice done to me.
ASTOLOF. Back to Muscovy on your nag!
AGAFYA. As soon as you've given me the husband you promised me.
ASTOLOF (*stopping*). Dear little Agafya, I *am* giving you a husband. My own assistant groom of the wardrobe. He agrees. He's honored. A fine strapping lad, all sinews and hair on his chest. I have promised him five hundred silver crowns if you'll take him, and double that to you.
AGAFYA. How dare you! Just wait—I'll assistant groom you!
ASTOLOF. You're tearing my sleeve!
AGAFYA. You promised to marry me!
ASTOLOF. Ha! The girl is mad!
AGAFYA. Or find me a real boyar!
ASTOLOF. The assistant groom or nothing!
AGAFYA. I'll show you nothing!
(*She attacks him with her nails*)

ASTOLOF. Help! My cheek is bleeding! Help! Guards!
(He tears himself away and flees)
AGAFYA *(pursuing him)*. Yes, run for your life, you Muscovy doll! *(Exits)*
(Enter the king and Klotalski, in hushed conversation)
KING. Visiting the kitchens and fraternizing with pots and pans I can wink at—after twenty-one years in a cave—God forgive me my sins. And making hot speeches to street sweepers I can try to swallow. But how can I ever forget that humiliating scene—with my own soldiers applauding and yelling hurrah. They ought to be court martialed—but I haven't the courage.
KLOTALSKI. Don't dwell on that terrible image. Let it be a dream.
KING. A nightmare. He did return my crown, but then he stares and stares at me as though I were a picture on a wall and says nothing for minutes on end. What do our informers in town report?
KLOTALSKI. Excitement.
KING. Of what kind?
KLOTALSKI. They love having a native prince, a man of Poland, and curse the Muscovy alliance.
KING. And blame me for chaining him up?
KLOTALSKI. —
KING. You needn't answer. Listen, Klotalski, there are millions of brutal serfs and drunken townspeople in this country, and only thousands of us. Worse yet, they have that traitor Bogdan to goad them. We *must* find a way of enraging Sigismund against Opalinski instead of us.
KLOTALSKI. Your majesty...
KING. What? What now?
KLOTALSKI *(hesitating)*. He has sent for Opalinski.
(The king stares)
KLOTALSKI. Radziwill heard it less than an hour ago but didn't have the heart to bring you the news himself.
KING. Back to the cave. I hesitated, my father's heart pleaded, but this satanic blaze must be quenched before it consumes us all. The omens didn't lie. Back to the cave. We still have the Muscovites. Or I'll lead the troops myself. I may be old but I can still mount my horse and fire a pistol. Here is the powder, Klotalski. It never fails. Give it to Vladimir. He will do what's needed when the wine goes round the table. Are you ready to do your duty, *Duke* of Zakopane?
KLOTALSKI *(kissing the king's hand)*. Your majesty will be obeyed to the last dot in your command. *(Exits)*
KING *(alone)*. Oh my son, my only child, I would so gladly have abdicated in your favor quite without that mountain weight of your strong hands on my

shoulders which I shall feel to my dying day! But in your eyes I see gruesome spectacles of civic destruction.... Dear God, grant me my peaceful monastery by the sea, mild church-bells, steady predictable sea-waves, and no more burdens.... Let me pray....

(*Enter Klotalski and the Crown Chancellor*)

KLOTALSKI (*in a low voice*). Your majesty....

KING. Yes?

KLOTALSKI. Radziwill has more news.

KING. How bad?

CROWN CHANCELLOR. Prince Sigismund is coming up the hill.

KING. What of it?

CROWN CHANCELLOR. I hurried ahead of him to warn you.

KING. Has he come to murder his father?

CROWN CHANCELLOR. No. But he marched into the jail, freed the convicts, and is leading them to the castle. And there is more. Bogdan Opalinski has been observed lurking in the forest of Dulova an hour's horseback ride from Cracow.

KING (*strangled voice*). What is the Palace Guard doing?

CROWN CHANCELLOR. They daren't move against the prince without your express command.

(*Enter servants carrying refreshments which they place on a table*)

KLOTALSKI (*discreetly*). The goblet with the Polish eagle.

KING (*distracted*). What? What?

CROWN CHANCELLOR. The goblet with the Polish eagle. For your son.

KING. Good.

(*Sound of marching and clanging chains outside*)

KING (*to the Crown Chancellor*). Call the Guard!

(*Exit the Crown Chancellor one way as Sigismund enters from another, at the head of a band of armed ruffians, their chains still dangling from neck, arm or ankle*)

SIGISMUND. Hail father, hail tutor, hail Hecataeus, hail dream of freedom, hail all the chained wretches of the world, my brothers in fetters, hail, hail!

CONVICTS. Long live our beloved liberator!

A CONVICT. Ain't this a grand place!

SIGISMUND. Welcome to my palace! It is your house now! Kiss me, father. I have done hard work and I'm thirsty.

CONVICTS. So are we!

KING. Welcome my son! Welcome citizens!

KLOTALSKI (*taking the hint*). Welcome citizens!

KING. Men of Poland, Fortune smiles on you today. Behold! The table is set as if it had guessed that you were coming. Your servants are pouring the ale. Help yourselves, and here, my son, allow me, your father and your king, to serve you.

(*He hands him the eagle-goblet*)

CONVICTS. Long live King Casimir! Long live Poland and Saint Bacchus!

SIGISMUND. I drink to a new age! But wait. (*He puts down the goblet*) Klotalski my friend, I haven't forgotten the books you made me read. Listen everybody!

A CONVICT. Shut up you apes and listen to our savior!

SIGISMUND. "Care for us? They ne'er cared for us yet." *They*, my friends, are the nobles, the patricians, the tutors, the kings, the chain makers, and *us* is the poor. Listen to the poet! "Yea, suffer us to famish, and their storehouses crammed with grain."

A CONVICT. That's the Bible truth.

A CONVICT. Long live poetry!

SIGISMUND. Listen to the poet! "Repeal daily any wholesome act established against the rich, and provide more piercing statutes daily to chain up—chain up!—and restrain the poor. If the Swedish wars eat us not up, they will; and there's all the love they bear us."

CONVICTS (*sobbing and drinking*). Ain't it the truth? Rich bastards! Christ have mercy on the poor.

A CONVICT. And me in jail for stealing a loaf of bread for my children!

SIGISMUND. Drink, my friends, drink!

KLOTALSKI. Dear, dear Sigismund, my pupil, I can't help applauding your generosity, and I'm proud of you. Here is your goblet. Let me drink to you.

SIGISMUND. I'll drink with you, you old slave driver, because I'm in command now. No more lashes for the wayward boy!

KLOTALSKI. No indeed! Hail to—

(*A man comes dashing in, and whispers urgently into Sigismund's ear*)

SIGISMUND. Tell him to come up at once! (*He puts down the goblet*) Ah my friends, I am about to show you something wilder than Egyptian dancing girls! (*To a servant*) Summon Prince Astolof, Princess Estrella, and all the senators you can find in the castle, and also that girl, that Agafya I conversed with in the kitchen. Yes father, I shall overcome the auguries, I shall be a blessing not a curse on Poland. The eyes of the blind shall be opened, and the ears of the deaf shall be unstopped, and the tongues of the dumb, yea the tongues of the dumb shall sing!

KING. If you can be and do so much, my beloved son, what happiness for me! But (*handing him the eagle goblet*) drink, drink, make merry with the rest of us. Oh my God! Bogdan!

(*Enter Bogdan Opalinski, dressed with romantic Robin Hood elegance. Sigismund puts down the goblet. Bogdan advances toward the king, briefly kneels before him, then turns toward Sigismund*)

BOGDAN. Prince Sigismund, for I guess you must be he, I have answered your summons, and I come to make my obeisance.

(*He kneels before Sigismund and kisses his hand*)

CONVICTS. Hurrah for Opalinski!

SIGISMUND. Rise, Baron Opalinski. You are my man—and theirs. (*To the convicts*) Gentlemen! Eat and drink quietly while I confer with our hero.

(*He embraces Bogdan and speaks with him aside. Enter the Crown Chancellor*)

CROWN CHANCELLOR (*into the king's ear*). Opalinski's bandits have overpowered the Guard.

KING. Where's Colonel Lubomirski?

CROWN CHANCELLOR. Fled.

SIGISMUND (*to the convicts*). Men! Baron Opalinski has agreed to enlist you into his army of liberation. Fortune does indeed smile on all of you today. Come! Swear allegiance to him at once.

CONVICTS. Wait a moment!

SIGISMUND. Why?

A CONVICT. Because—what will you do for us if we fight at your side, Bogdan Opalinski?

BOGDAN. What is it you demand, brave lads?

A CONVICT. Land!

ANOTHER. Honest paid work!

ANOTHER. Free money!

ANOTHER. Cheap women!

ANOTHER. Turkish slaves!

ANOTHER. Drive out the Jews!

ANOTHER. Schools and hospitals!

ANOTHER. No more aristocrats!

ANOTHER. No taxes on liquor!

BOGDAN (*laughing*). Aren't they wonderful?

SIGISMUND. The salt of the earth! Unchained convicts, men of Poland, now that you have heard him, you are his soldiers. Swear allegiance!

A CONVICT. We swear to follow Baron Opalinski and Prince Sigismund through fire and flood!

THE OTHERS. We swear!

BOGDAN. Welcome all! I shall give you God's work to do and make you lords of Poland. (*He turns to the king*) My king and almost my father—for I have not forgotten that you cared for me as a child—I have taken the liberty of subduing your Palace Guard as surety for our safe egress from the city.

For myself, King Casimir, the whole world knows that I have emancipated the Opalinski serfs. The peasants are now my free tenants, my lands are prospering, my people are happy. I beg you, I urge you to follow suit on all crown properties in Poland and Lithuania. This will set an example unheard of in the sad annals of mankind: an example, I say, for our stubborn magnates, an inspiration for them to turn Poland from the hell it is now to the paradise it could become.

SIGISMUND. Amen.

CONVICTS. Hurrah!

KING. Irresistible Bogdan! My own child! I shall do what you say. Tears dazzle my old eyes!

BOGDAN. And mine, your majesty. O happiness!

KING. Let us drink to our reconciliation. Klotalski, a goblet for Bogdan, and here is yours, my son. (*He hands him the eagle-goblet*)

SIGISMUND. This is a glorious day! Here is to paradise!

(*A servant appears in the doorway*)

SERVANT. Prince Astolof and Princess Estrella!

(*Sigismund puts down the goblet. Enter Astolof and Estrella, attended, with Agafya behind them. Estrella screams and rushes into Bogdan's arms*)

ESTRELLA. Bogdan! My Bogdan!

BOGDAN. Faithful to me, Estrella?

ESTRELLA. To my dying breath! O my beloved!

ASTOLOF. Look here!

BOGDAN. My joy, my bride! (*To Sigismund*) Prince, I entered Cracow by your leave in order to kneel before you, bind myself to your service forever and receive your commands; but also, I can joyfully confess it now, in order to claim my bride.

ASTOLOF. Look here!

SIGISMUND. Take her. I bless you both. Look at them! A fairy tale of the New Age! What is life without love? Well! I look contentedly around, and if this is not a dream I am dreaming, I will be sending presently for my plump Layla, and by the Holy Trinity I'll have the archbishop marry us. However, Baron Opalinski, let not romantic love blind you like another Marc Antony. Take your men, along with your new recruits, to the Senate. Have them scoop up the lords who haven't fled to their estates. Demand freedom for their serfs and distribution of their lands. And if they refuse—do whatever God demands and your conscience requires.

BOGDAN. Men! Follow me!

CONVICTS. Hurrah!

BOGDAN. My angel, hand in hand with me into my dangerous world?

ESTRELLA. Yes, my hero, yes, yes!

ASTOLOF. Look here!

BOGDAN (*to Sigismund*). Prince, I shall bring you remarkable tidings within the hour. (*To the convicts*) Line up, men! Two by two! Hold the chains in your hands and march. Forward! March! Chests out! My love, make your farewells.

(*The convicts leave in a great clatter of chains. Estrella hugs the king*)

ESTRELLA. I love you, dearest uncle, but this is Fate, isn't it? I'll be praying every day that you come to no harm.

KING. I love you too. Be careful in the cold....

ESTRELLA. Will you have a few things sent after me? But only my roughest dresses.

KING. I will, my poor child....

ESTRELLA (*to Sigismund*). Prince! May you reign for a century over happy Poland!

SIGISMUND. And may your courage and high principles inspire the women of Poland!

ESTRELLA (*bowing to Astolof*). Prince, happy return journey to Muscovy and my respects to the Tsar.

ASTOLOF. One moment!

(*She bows to the others. Bogdan does the same, and elegantly leads her out*)

SIGISMUND (*raising the eagle goblet*). And now—I'm hoarse and parched—

(*Agafya, who has been half hidden in the background, rushes up to Sigismund. He puts down the goblet*)

AGAFYA. Prince Sigismund! A boon!

SIGISMUND. Greetings, Agafya. Anything you wish. I hadn't seen you.

ASTOLOF. Look here! These women are all lunatics.

KLOTALSKI. Later, Agafya dear; I will personally—

SIGISMUND. Silence, all you gaudy oppressors! I have not forgotten the tale of injury you told me, Agafya, when I was still enslaved in my cave; nor have I forgotten who was the author of that injury. Let me hear the boon you ask of me.

AGAFYA. Oh my lord, you are the god of all of us victims. Look at him trying to hide!

ASTOLOF. Fiddlesticks! Who is this farmgirl to bewitch the whole Polish court with her twaddle?

AGAFYA. Force him to make restitution to me, my lord! I haven't told you yet that my dad and my two brothers we work his land four days out of seven for nothing, zero, not even a sack of flour. And for me, after he'd got his pleasure of me, not so much as a letter or a sprig of flowers. Five copper coins thrown into my apron, that's all.

SIGISMUND. Astolof, hands off that door; and a word with you nose to nose. (*To the servants*) Guard all the doors, you people! Come here, Muscovite.

ASTOLOF (*blustering*). How dare you! I tell you I've had enough! Instead of wedding feasts I predict war between our two countries, and I warn you all that for every Pole who carries a sword we can muster ten Muscovites and Tatars, regular savages each one of them.

SIGISMUND. Not half as savage as Sigismund. Take Agafya's hand in yours and marry her as consolation for Estrella.

ASTOLOF. Ha! You cave man! Marry her yourself and set up housekeeping among the bears where you belong.

SIGISMUND. I must be dreaming after all. Is this fluff of ribbons threatening me?

KING. Patience, my son.

CROWN CHANCELLOR (*at the same time*). Allow me to interpose.

KLOTALSKI (*at the same time*). Nothing in the heat of passion, my dear boy.

SIGISMUND. Lackeys—you—run to the cathedral and fetch me a priest!

A SERVANT. At once, your highness. (*A servant opens a door for him and he runs off*)

KING. By your mother's soul—

ASTOLOF (*drawing his word*). Open the door! I declare war on Poland and demand punctilious protection for me and mine, with full safe conduct to the border.

KING. Granted!

(*Astolof tries to leave*)

AGAFYA. Stop him, my lord!

SIGISMUND (*drawing*). Trust me. I counter declare war, you Muscovite flea!

(*A brief skirmish. Sigismund easily knocks Astolof's sword out of his hand, sheathes his own, seizes Astolof by the waist and lifts him*)

ASTOLOF. Help! My retinue! Help!

SIGISMUND (*to a lackey*). Open that window!

SERVANT. At once, your highness.

KING. Sigismund! Stop, for God's sake, stop!

KLOTALSKI. My lord, let me talk to you first!

CROWN CHANCELLOR. Think of the law of nations, think of our honor!

ASTOLOF (*at the same time*). Help! Help!

(*Sigismund throws him out the window*)

ASTOLOF (*his voice receding*). Aaaaaaah.....

(*Agafya screams and rushes out through the still open door*)

SIGISMUND (*leaning out*). A mess of spangles and flesh. And there comes the priest—good, it's Father Radim—just in time for an unexpected sacrament.

KING (*more dead than alive*). The Muscovites will march against us from the east. Bogdan and his ruffians are scorching the land in the center. The Swedes are invading from the north, and the Turks threaten from the south. Are you satisfied, Sigismund?

SIGISMUND. I am a giant. God is with me. Millions of liberated serfs will rise like a single Titan to shatter feeble tyrants and their hirelings east, south and north. Look happy, father, Klotalski—Klotalski, what's the matter with you?

KLOTALSKI. Nothing, my lord, a moment of dizziness....

SIGISMUND. It will pass. Rejoice, I say again, father, Klotalski, Radziwill, and you, dear faithful servants. The blood I shed will irrigate—

(*Re-enter Agafya, a changed woman; with her, Father Radim. She stops at the threshhold*)

AGAFYA (*in a solemn voice*). After laying his royal curse on Poland, Prince Astolof espoused me and expired. Father Radim was kind enough to perform both sacraments *in extremis*, and to place the royal ring on my finger.

FATHER RADIM. Confirmatus est.

AGAFYA. The brief wedding ceremony was witnessed by the prince's groom of the wardrobe and his assistant, who appeared when they heard their master's cry of distress. I am now Princess Agafya of Muscovy, and as such I shall give orders to my people to prepare for departure the moment I have changed into something suitably black. My beloved husband's cadaver will, of course, travel with us. As for the consequences of the treacherous act of regicide committed today in this palace, I shall only say that they will be violent. I have already despatched a trusted officer to our capital with instructions to give an unbiased report of the crime. Our next message will come to you from the mouth of a cannon. Adieu. Father Radim, I shall want your prayerful support in my bereavement during our journey home.

(*Both leave*)

SIGISMUND. Look here!

KLOTALSKI (*to the king*). Poland is dead if he doesn't drink up soon, your majesty.

KING (*in a daze*). You're right. (*Handing Sigismund the eagle-goblet*) Son, this is a blow. Sit down, drink up, and let us ponder—

SIGISMUND. Ponder fire and blood! Did you hear that female talking to me? A low-born farmgirl? I'm speechless! Your books didn't prepare me for this scene, Klotalski! The little upstart! Shouldn't I stop her?

CROWN CHANCELLOR. That would be useless, prince. The officer is despatched and will certainly ride his horse like a demon. We must draw up a new set of urgent plans and mobilize—

SIGISMUND. Mobilize! Magic word! Three million serfs will leap—What this noise? If it's Agafya again, I'll throttle her!
(*Szopen rushes in*)
SZOPEN. The Revolution has begun, and I hail it thus!
(*He flings himself on the harpsichord and plays with wild flourishes. This time the sounds that emerge are those of a triumphant trumpet. Enter Bogdan and his convicts, two by two, each pair carrying a dead man on a litter*)
BOGDAN (*kneeling before Sigismund*). Prince, your commands have been punctually obeyed.
(*The king, Klotalski and the Crown Chancellor hold each other up. The bodies, dripping blood, parade in a circle before Sigismund. Szopen stops playing as all the church-bells of Cracow toll. They will continue to the end of the scene. Bogdan calls the roll*)
BOGDAN. The tyrant Baron Tarnowski, 4,000 serfs and 80 villages. The tyrant Duke of Pultusk, 17,000 serfs and 166 villages. The tyrant Count Poniatowski, 85,000 serfs and 3,000 villages. Ladislaw Popnik, serf. The tyrant Baron Jablonowski, 46,000 serfs and 3,700 villages. The tyrant Count Potocki, crown treasurer.
SIGISMUND. Why Popnik the serf?
BOGDAN. For attempting to defend his master, the tyrant Count Poniatowski.
CROWN CHANCELLOR (*sobbing*). My friends, my friends....
SIGISMUND (*imbruing his hand*). He hath stretched forth his hand against them, and hath smitten them. But fear not! This bloody earth shall be plowed under. A garden shall rise from it. Man, woman and child shall sing aloud—
(*A tremendous howl of lamentation off stage interrupts him*)
KING. Christ have mercy on our souls.
SIGISMUND. What is that?
BOGDAN. Wives, children, fathers and mothers of the criminals.
SZOPEN. I shall weep for them in music!
(*The howl ceases and is replaced by a great noise of splashing water*)
SIGISMUND. Now what?
BOGDAN. Criminal blood washed from stairways and courtyard.
SIGISMUND. Let there be cascades!
KLOTALSKI (*to the king*). My liege, save us, save us!
(*The king recomposes himself*)
KING. Cascades, my son, and you so miserably thirsty?
(*He hands him the eagle-goblet*)
SIGISMUND. Thank you, father. Why is your hand trembling so? Mine is red but firm. Are you with or against me?
KING (*weeping*). How can I be against justice?

(*Sigismund raises the goblet*)
SIGISMUND. Well done, Bogdan Opalinski! I hereby create and ordain you first Grand Master of the Holy Order of Saint Peter Unchained, and grant you and your descendants eternal freehold in the domains of the barons, dukes, counts and prelates you have executed so far or will hereafter execute. Long live the Revolution!
BOGDAN. Long live Sigismund!
THE CONVICTS. Sigismund and Bogdan forever!
SIGISMUND. You the artist, celebrate! And father, Klotalski, Radziwill: raise your voices too!
ALL THREE (*weeping*). Sigismund forever!
(*Sigismund drinks, Szopen plays, and again the sound is that of a trumpet. The church-bells ring. The king, the Crown Chancellor and Klotalski clasp each other. Finally the stage grows dark*)

SCENE SEVEN

(*When the lights return, we are in front of the cave again. The sleeping figure of Sigismund reappears in the corner. It is late afternoon. The dreamed Sigismund is chained once more. Books on the table. Layla is peeling and cutting a large assortment of vegetables and herbs and tossing everything into a pot. Sigismund, book in hand, is staring at her work. Evening will come slowly on as in Scene One. After a little while, Layla becomes aware of Sigismund's attention and gives him a questioning look. Now and then the sleeping figure half rises, looks on, gestures*)

SIGISMUND (*pointing*). This may be why.... You subtle Turk.... You wade into the woods picking God knows what and trying new edibles on me.... I'm glad you love me because if you didn't, I might take you for some murderous Medea.... But the meat and stews are always delicious, and so are the soups, and so is all your cookery.... But they often do taste... I don't know.... experimental. Delicious but experimental.... And one of your hellish innovations must have made me dream so vividly.... Enormous, rich, bloody, ravaging, thrilling dream....
(*Layla motions to him impatiently to continue reading*)
SIGISMUND. I know, I know.... But I don't concentrate as well as I did before I.... Day after day I inspect it.... I can't leave it alone....
(*Layla makes impatient noises*)

SIGISMUND (*sighing*). You're right. And so is dear old Klotalski. Besides, the poets know best. (*He reads*)

> Farewell ye gilded follies, pleasing troubles,
> Farewell ye honored rags, ye glorious bubbles;
> Fame's but a hollow echo, gold mere clay,
> Glory the darling but of one short day.
> Welcome pure thoughts, welcome you silent groves,
> These leafy shades my soul most dearly loves.

(*He looks around and shakes his head half dubiously*)
> A prayer book now shall be my looking glass—

(*He stops*)
My looking-glass.... I'd forgotten! Give me your mirror, Layla. (*She obeys with a show of petulance. He gazes at himself*) Poor me.... Imagine a mirror taller than myself, and Sigismund in it, wonderful and regal.... And now, rags in a broken glass.... Take it back. The poets know best.

(*He picks up the book again*)

> A prayer book now shall be my looking glass,
> Wherein I will adore sweet Virtue's face.
> Here dwell no hateful looks, no palace cares,
> No lurking crimes beget pale fears.
> Here will I shun ambition's folly,
> And learn to prize a holy melancholy.
> And if contentment prove a stranger still,
> I'll seek it nowhere but in Heaven's will.

(*He sighs*)
There speaks a wise Pole.... (Long pause) Did I tell you that I threw a man out of a window? Yes I did tell you. Ten times, I guess! What a scream he let out! And then I dreamed of the girl who'd fallen from her horse.... You saw her.... The little viper....

> Farewell, ye gilded follies....

(*Layla has been lighting a few torches as night approaches. Sigismund turns the page*)
Here's another wise fellow. (*He reads in silence at first*) Ha! If they're so wise, these inspired poets, how is it they give opposite advice?
(*He reads aloud with a martial voice*)

'Tis time to leave the books in dust
And oil the unused armor's rust
And like the falcon high
Dive furious from the sky.

So restless Caesar would not cease
In the inglorious arts of peace,
But through adventurous war
Urged his active star....

(*He pauses, then suddenly rises*) Hail Prince Sigismund! Savior of Poland! You—down on your knees!... Oh, it felt glorious, glorious! (*He sits down again*) But what were all those corpses doing in my dream? To be sure, they were dead rascals. On the other hand, who'd be left, Layla—Layla! What are you doing? Come here and sit down. The question I'm asking you is, who'd be left if all the rascals had to go?... Just you. Certainly not myself. Oh no, not I.... I think too much, damn it. Opalinski didn't look left nor right before he.... I gave the order, though.... I think I did....

Welcome pure thoughts....

I was cruel to the king of Poland my dream father, Layla, looking just as he does in the picture over there, only older.... And to Klotalski.... In that riot of mine I made the omens come true.... I was a superb beast!... The dream may have meant: Sigismund, know once and for all why thou art fettered to thy cave! Or it may have meant: Sigismund, thou art not a peasant's son, thou art the son of a king; seize the thunderbolt; save thy country!
(*Bugles sound in the distance*)
Listen! As if somebody had heard me!... Glorious armies on the road! Our men marching against the Turks.... Or the Turks marching against us.... Glorious, terrible bloodshed.... The books always talk about bloodshed—bloodshed! bloodshed!—but when you really see puddles of red liquid on the stairways and in the courtyard—and the sticky red on your own hand—believe me, Layla.... And Astolof spread out on the cobble stones with his eyes open....

I will adore sweet Virtue's face....

Those trumpets again!... Gone.... No, I think the dream was God's warning to me. I think I think so.... Did I tell you that in my dream there was a girl dancing.... But that was after.... No, it was before.... Or did I read it?... I forget.... Dancing like that.

(*Night has fallen. Sigismund sings and dances. The chain dins horribly. Layla enjoys and applauds*)

I'm a giant! The Revolution has come! You dance to it too, Layla! Dance! Dance! Dance!

(*He sings, dances, the chain rattles, and Layla joins him. Suddenly Bogdan appears with three of the convicts. All are heavily armed and carry axes and other tools*)

BOGDAN. Prince Sigismund! Chained like a galley slave! Horrible sight!

(*Sigismund is thunderstruck. Layla retreats towards her cabin. Bogdan kneels*)

BOGDAN. You are amazed to see me here, my liege, and no wonder! But well met again! Well met and happily!

SIGISMUND (*in a strangled voice throughout*). Bogdan? Bogdan Opalinski? Oh my God my God!

BOGDAN (*rising*). Your Bogdan indeed; though dressed rather more shabbily than I was when you last saw me! Dressed as a fugitive.

SIGISMUND. But it was a dream!

BOGDAN. It was and is and will be until we the soldiers of that dream realize it on earth. And, by God, realize it we shall now that we have found you gloriously alive. Look at these men, my lord, these soldiers. Do they look disheartened? Even though so many of their comrades have fallen?

ONE CONVICT. We're alive and full of fight, my lord.

ANOTHER. And happy as lords that we found you, your highness!

ANOTHER. You what opened the prison gates for us!

SIGISMUND. But what happened to me? How did I—

BOGDAN. You don't know? They told you nothing here?

SIGISMUND. Nothing....

BOGDAN. The savages! I'll make it brief, my prince. After your bold defenestration of the tyrant Astolof, and after they banished you again, the Muscovites came roaring into Poland, massacring your father's men and mine without distinction. We were obliged to regroup in the hills. Now I stand back while the two oppressors of the people slaughter each other. When the historic hour strikes, I will take to the field again and fight on— fight till doomsday if need be.

SIGISMUND. And... Estrella?

BOGDAN. Alive and well. A ministering angel founding hospitals and orphanages wherever we go.

SIGISMUND. How... how did you find me?

BOGDAN. We captured one of Klotalski's men, and after an hour of friendly torture he decided to tell us where they were hiding you.

SIGISMUND. Where is Klotalski?
BOGDAN. The devil knows. All I know is that the man is alive and hatching more plots against us.
SIGISMUND. And I?
BOGDAN. And you, my lord?
SIGISMUND. I was banished?
BOGDAN. Drugged, paralyzed, and cruelly banished. Why do you ask? Has your sleep made you forget?
SIGISMUND. And I must be again and have again and do again what I was almost glad I dreamed?
BOGDAN. O my prince, our sudden appearance has shaken you. But *that* will not last once you are free again. Soldiers! Hack off our commander's chain! We'll preserve it as our holy relic!
(*The convicts go to work on the chain. Layla rushes forward and tries indignantly to push them away*)
ONE OF THE CONVICTS. Out of our way, slave!
ANOTHER. Or I'll split your heathen skull!
SIGISMUND. Don't hurt her or I'll murder you!
BOGDAN. Gently, men, gently.
THE THIRD. I'll hold the Turk while you two split the chain.
SIGISMUND. Don't struggle, Layla.
BOGDAN. At it, men, at it! O my prince! I am wildly elated! Allow me to kiss your hand!
(*As he grasps Sigismund's hand, one of the convicts gasps, points wildly, and before he can speak a volley of musket shots rings out. Crying out, Bogdan, the convicts, and Layla fall dead around Sigismund, who is still holding Bogdan's hand. Sigismund, petrified, is soaked in blood. Presently the king and Klotalski appear at the head of a band of soldiers*)
KING. Hand in hand with the traitor!
KLOTALSKI. And the chain nearly hacked off.
A SOLDIER. We got them all!
SIGISMUND (*dropping Bogdan's hand, with a cry of despair*). Layla! You killed Layla!
KING. *You* killed her, monster unleashed by Heaven against our unhappy land!
KLOTALSKI. Hold him, you two! And the rest of you—remove the bodies!
(*Sigismund struggles and sobs as the bodies, including that of Layla, are carried off to the rear*)
SIGISMUND. Murderers!
KING. Murderers? You murderer dare say "Murderers"? Oh my son, my

son! Listen to me. With tears in my eyes I tell you that you are to remain lifelong in this cave chained to its wall, and sundered forever from the land you wanted to destroy. My father's heart breaks in two as I pronounce the sentence, but the heart of Poland's king beats high. My son, my prince, dear, last hope of my life, we shall not meet again until we both stand naked before the Supreme Judge to render our final account. May He have mercy that day on us both.
(*He goes to Sigismund and embraces him. Exeunt omnes except Sigismund*)
SIGISMUND (*weeping*). You killed her, you killed her....
(*He staggers into the cave and vanishes from sight. The stage darkens*)

SCENE EIGHT

(*The bed in the corner of the stage has disappeared. We are now in Prince Astolof's sumptuous bedroom in Cracow's royal palace. In a corner, the canopied bed. Candlelight. Astolof, of course, looks nothing like his dreamed image. When he stands up, we will see that he is quite as powerfully built as Sigismund. Wrapped in a robe, he is sitting in an armchair, looking at maps. A clock strikes 11 times. A door opens, and a servant enters and speaks to the Prince in a low voice*)

SERVANT. They are coming, my lord.
(*Astolof puts away the maps and rises. Enter the King, the Crown Chancellor and Klotalski. Appropriate greetings ad libitum*)
KING. Is my son-in-law or very nearly son-in-low still content with life in our palace?
ASTOLOF. Three days and nights of content, your majesty. A betrothal not to be forgotten. Sit, sir, sit, my lords. (*They sit around a low table, on which lie the maps Astolof had been studying. He now pats them*) And our terms remain agreeable to all of us, I believe.
ALL THREE. Indeed. They are.
CROWN CHANCELLOR. We want to express once more our gratitude for the kindness you showed when the matter of, the matter of—
ASTOLOF. Prince Sigismund.
CROWN CHANCELLOR. Was made known to you.
ASTOLOF (*tapping the maps again*). The kindness was equal on your side. Poland and Muscovy are one. And thanks to the experience I obtained fighting in the Crimea, I trust that I shall be of practical use standing side

by side in the field with the young prince.
CROWN CHANCELLOR. He will be grateful, my lord.
ASTOLOF. And now, what next?
CROWN CHANCELLOR. As you see, my lord, we are working at this momentous event in the deepest secrecy. Only we four will ride to the Tatras escorted by ten or twelve soldiers. We will hail our prince with solemn simplicity. Proper garb will be brought along. A white horse. In the meantime my son Colonel Janusz Radziwill will have prepared the proper entry into the capital and the procession to the palace, which the prince will enter arm in arm with his majesty.
ASTOLOF. And I? (*Silence. Astolof laughs*) One step behind, gentlemen, one step behind! I am but Poland's guest.
KING. You are magnificent, tsarevich.
CROWN CHANCELLOR. Only then will the cathedral bells ring, ring, ring in exultation, the people will assemble in the square, and from the balcony our Sigismund will be presented to Poland as its next king.
ASTOLOF. Amen. I will inform the Tsar, whose blessing I have.
(*The King rises, followed by the others. He embraces Astolof. The visitors leave. Astolof motions to his servant to remove the maps from the table*)
ASTOLOF. Is she waiting? (*The servant nods*) Brandy-wine on the table and two glasses. (*The servant obeys*) Now go.
(*Exit the servant, but he has ushered in Agafya as he leaves. Astolof gestures to her to sit on a tabouret next to his armchair, into which he now seats himself*)
ASTOLOF. Have you counted the gold pieces, my dear Agafya?
AGAFYA. Yes.
ASTOLOF. Counted them carefully?
AGAFYA. Yes.
ASTOLOF. Have I been miserly?
AGAFYA. No.
ASTOLOF. Do you forgive me?
AGAFYA. I don't know.
ASTOLOF. Let's drink to happiness. Here is something like you've never tasted before. (*He pours, both drink*). Good? You don't answer, so let's both try again. To happiness!
AGAFYA (*sullen*) Are you happy with your Princess Estrella?
ASTOLOF (*laughing*). Princess Estrella with her thick nose, lips as thin as strings, chinless chin and bony body?
AGAFYA. She's like a broom, ain't she?
ASTOLOF. Not like a young Muscovite I know. I miss you.
AGAFYA. Stories!

ASTOLOF. When are you riding back to Pochinok?
AGAFYA. They want me to clean the scullery, but after that I'm gone.
ASTOLOF. I will find you there; yes I will. Be careful with the gold.
AGAFYA. Hmm.
ASTOLOF. You're as beautiful as ever. I'm going to cry. A kiss before I let you go?
(*Both rise; they kiss*)
AGAFYA. You're a devil, you are.
ASTOLOF. Come, come with me, I need you, life isn't worth living without you.
(*He pulls her toward the bed*)

SCENE NINE

(*As in Scene One. Layla is seated at the table mending clothes. Sigismund, book in hand, stares at her instead of reading*)

SIGISMUND. Day after day, it won't leave me: you lying dead in a lake of blood. (*Layla shows impatience*). I see now that the dream was sent to me with a purpose. It had not done what it was trying to do until they murdered you. No more blood! The good poet was right. (*He reads*)

> Welcome pure thoughts, welcome you silent groves,
> These leafy shades my soul most dearly loves.

It's as if the man had lived here, with us.
(*Sound of a trumpet*)
SIGISMUND. Klotaslki? I thought he was in Cracow!
(*Klotalski appears, two soldiers stand behind him. For a moment, as if overcome by the gravity of the moment, he says nothing*)
SIGISMUND. What's the matter, Klotalski? I thought you were in Cracow! Why are you staring at me?
(*Klotalski advances toward Sigismund*)
KLOTALSKI. Hail Prince Sigismund, heir to the throne of Poland! Hail son of King Casimir!
(*Sigismund leaps to his feet; Layla, terrified, retreats to her cabin. One of the soldiers hands Klotaslki an iron box from which he takes a large key. He advances toward Sigismund,*

SIGISMUND, PRINCE OF POLAND

kneels before him, takes and kisses his hand, and unlocks the chain, which the two soldiers then throw wide of Sigismund)

KLOTALSKI. At last! Sigismund is free! Free to ascend the throne! Free to be Poland's shield and sword! Sigismund: greet your king and father!

(The king appears, with Astolof in full military regalia and the Crown Chancellor flanking him but slightly bending him. A few soldiers in the backgound)

KING. My son, my son.... Look at me.... Sigismund.... I am your father.... Your old father, the king.... I love you.... I have come to take you home.... Have pity on me.... I made mistakes.... but.... but I meant well for our poor country.... Your mother died giving you birth.... We were frightened.... Terrible omens appeared.... But everything will be explained.... You will forgive us.... It's I who made Baron Klotalski care for you.... And now you are free forever.... The throne is waiting for you.... My strong, handsome boy!... Look, here to welcome you is our ally, the Tsarevich Astolof. You and he together—Poland is calling you and crying "Draw your swords! Fall on our enemies!" Their blood, their evil blood—

SIGISMUND *(with a violent gesture and a howl)*. No more blood! No more blood!
(He rushes into the forest and mountain)

KING. Sigismund! What are you doing? Come back!

ASTOLOF. What—?

CROWN CHANCELLOR. Soldiers, after him!

A SOLDIER. Yes, sir. Men! Let's go!

KING. Stop! I am leading you!

CROWN CHANCELLOR. What are you thinking of, sire!

ASTOLOF. The soldiers will find him, my lord.

KING. Release me! What's dignity to me? That child is mine! Soldiers, after me!

(He rushes away with the soldiers)

ASTOLOF. What a strange scene! The prince seemed utterly terrified. Of what, Radziwill?

CROWN CHANCELLOR. Klotalski, you know the boy. Explain.

KLOTALSKI. I'm dumbfounded, gentlemen. Come here, Layla. She's mute, Tsarevich. Layla, tell me, what happened? I can usually understand her.

(Layla makes noises of bewilderment and grief)

KLOTALSKI. She doesn't know.

ASTOLOF. I presume that she has been the prince's servant here.

KLOTALSKI. For many years. Calm yourself, woman. Your master was a little startled, that's all, as who wouldn't have been in his place. But we'll find him for you. Go on, make the place fit for your sovereigns.

(Layla takes up her broom disconsolately)

ASTOLOF. As for being startled, I don't know. I have been startled in my time. I was startled now, Klotalski. But I long to hold him in my arms. Estrella my honored wife, Sigismund my companion, neighbors in Europe, he a giant, I no weakling—who could stand up to us? Not the Turks, not the Swedes, nor that bandit Opalinski whom we'll bleed like a Christmas pig when we catch him.

(*A clamor off-stage. Astolof grasps Radziwill*)

ASTOLOF. What do you think?

KLOTALSKI. They've caught him of course!

CROWN CHANCELLOR. Didn't I tell you, Prince?

ASTOLOF. Well, I am breathing a little easier. Shall we go meet them?

CROWN CHANCELLOR. No. Let us wait here; here, on this spot, this place to which pilgrimages will be made. Mark my prophetic words! For our Polish people this grot, this womb, this birth-place will become a shrine.

ASTOLOF. I hope so. I truly hope so. And I shall be distinctly sorry if he refuses.

CROWN CHANCELLOR and KLOTALSKI. Refuses what, my lord?

ASTOLOF. Refuses.

(*At first the two men fail to understand*)

KLOTALSKI. Never! Never on earth! Believe me, Prince, I raised him to be a conqueror, a lion!

CROWN CHANCELLOR. Who knows...?

ASTOLOF. Calm yourselves, friends. *I* am here, and I stand by Poland, no matter what happens. Let me teach you this lesson, gentlemen: History does not stop. It never wants for capable hands. If not Sigismund, then Astolof. If not Astolof, then the next man.

(*Enter a soldier, running*)

SOLDIER. Here they come! Holding the prince between them!

KLOTALSKI. My heart pounds against my ribs.... Sigismund, O Sigismund, think of your country!

(*Sigismund appears, haggard, held between the king and an officer. Layla falls to her knees. Sigismund and Astolof stare at each other across the space*)

ASTOLOF (*in a ringing voice*). One man or another!

(*Kettledrum rising to a violent climax, and blackout*)

The End

Notes

In 1988 a publishing house of dubious honesty called, misleadingly, the University Press of America (it had no connection with any university) published my *Sigismund, Prince of Poland: a Baroque Entertainment*. The Press was not a "vanity" publisher, for all it asked of its authors was that they purchase a reasonable number of their own book. It must be admitted that mine was impeccably produced. Alas, as far as I know, no one ever heard of it or ever saw it. A copy or two must exist somewhere, I suppose, as extreme rarities, and its happy owner or two can read in it an afterword of mine fourteen pages long in which, among other subjects, I speak of Calderón, Grillparzer, von Hoffmannsthal, and my notions of worthy drama.

In 2002 I published what was the first real public appearance of the play in my set of *Reinventions*. I have now greatly revised it for its final existence. Indeed, it now boasts of several entirely new scenes.

Pedro Calderón de la Barca's *La Vida es sueño* (1635) is the obvious source of my utterly different play. Utterly different; but I borrowed the Spaniard's words in several places as a playful tribute. More mindful of Polish history than Calderón was, I made free and fanciful use of Norman Davies' excellent *God's Playground: a History of Poland*. The name of Bogdan Opalinksi combines those of Bogdan Chmielnicki, the ferocious warlord, Cossack leader and scourge of Poland, and Krzysztof Opalinksi, the liberal and enlightened author of certain admired *Satires and Warnings* which I have not read.

Hecataeus, whose works are conveniently lost, is mentioned by Herodotus in his Book Two.

Late in the play, I called on *Coriolanus*, on an anonymous seventeenth-century English lyric, and on Andrew Marvell's Horatian Ode on Cromwell to provide Sigismund with some fine Polish texts.

Szopen is Polish for Chopin, but no slur upon the great pianist was intended.

After many years I turned my play into a short novel, which I called simply *The History of Sigismund, Prince of Poland*. It became one of the three works printed in my *Otherwise Fables* (2014). An interesting technical detail of this metamorphosis is that in the prose narration I was able to indicate easily and discreetly the turns between reality and dream by expressing the former in the past tense and the latter in the present tense, a trick not possible in drama. Here, instead, I have introduced, in a corner of what would need to be a very large stage, the sleeping and dreaming Sigismund, an element that disappears when reality resumes. A director might think of a different way of marking the transition between reality and dream. It is, at any rate, essential that readers and spectators alike be made sharply aware of the one as against the other. Confusion can only harm the beauty of the play.

GENERAL AUDAX

A play in seven scenes

concerning the Roman invasions of Spain

Ser, nada más. Y basta.

JORGE GUILLÉN

For to him that is joined to all the living there is hope; for a living dog is better than a dead lion.

ECCLESIASTES, 9.4

CHARACTERS

The Numantians:

Retogenes, *Governor of Numantia.*
Caravino, *Vice Governor.*
Audax, *General of the Numantian Army.*
Connoba, *his son.*
Marandro, *a merchant.*
Julia, *sister in law of Audax.*
Lira, *a friend of the family.*
Marcius, *a citizen.*
Prisoners, soldiers, citizens, gravediggers.

The Romans:

Publius Cornelius Scipio Aemilianus, *Consul and General of the Army.*
Maximus, *his brother.*
Buteo, *his nephew.*
Polybius, *historian and officer attached to Scipio.*
Minucius, *in command of Scipio's private guard.*
Mummius, *a slave on an Italian estate.*
Officers and soldiers.

GENERAL AUDAX

SCENE ONE: A ROMAN ESTATE

(A villa in the Italian countryside. Night-time and moonlight. A portico, a garden, a fountain, a few trees, shrubbery and flowers. Marandro, an old man, is sitting quietly at a table under the portico, lit by a single candle. He is examining a ledger and other documents, occasionally picking at a grape from a bowl which has been placed on the table. A deeply peaceful scene. A slave, Mummius, enters quietly from within the house. He sets another bowl of fruit on the table)

MUMMIUS. Excuse me, sir.
MARANDRO. Mummius.
MUMMIUS. Yes, sir.
MARANDRO. It's so dark where you stand, I can only see your voice.
(*He chuckles*)
MUMMIUS. Shall I set another light on the table, sir?
MARANDRO. No no.
MUMMIUS. My master has asked me to bring you more refreshments and to inquire whether you have any other wishes.
MARANDRO. I don't wish anything else. I've t-t-told you, you can all go to sleep. I know the way to my rooms. But why hasn't old Audax come yet?
MUMMIUS. He's our only night watchman, sir, and also he's a bit slow on his legs these days.
MARANDRO. But he's sure to come?
MUMMIUS. Absolutely sure, sir. You'll hear the jingling of the keys and him I'll bet humming one of his Spanish ditties.
MARANDRO. Spanish ditties.... Who'd believe it?... And you're sure it's Audax the Numantian?
MUMMIUS. Oh yes, sir. We're very good friends, so of course I know. He tells us stories about his glorious days in Numantia, wherever that is.
MARANDRO. In Spain, my good man.
MUMMIUS. Oh yes. Sometimes we don't believe a word of it. A ragged night watchman in Italy that was a general sitting at table with governors and ladies—prove it, we say, and he goes all red in the face.
MARANDRO. It fits.
MUMMIUS. Excuse me for asking, sir, but is that where you're from,

Numantia?

MARANDRO. Yes, that's where I was when the Romans t-t-took it. And I wasn't eating grapes that day, let me t-t-t-tell you.

MUMMIUS. So it's really true, sir?

MARANDRO. What's really true?

MUMMIUS. His having been the commander and all?

MARANDRO. I don't know, my boy. All I know is that Audax was the name of our commander in chief.

MUMMIUS. Excuse me for asking.

MARANDRO. Well, that's all, Mummius. Go to bed, and t-t-tell your master I'll be t-t-t-talking to him after I t-t-tour the estate in the morning.

MUMMIUS. Very good, sir. Good night, sir. (*He leaves*)

(*Marandro sits back again, dreaming. Then he looks at the ledger. His finger marks the place*)

MARANDRO. "Audax. Place of origin: Numantia, in Hispania. Age: approximately fifty five." And that was seven years ago. "Purchased in fair health from the t-t-tribune Pomponius at Capua" and so on. It t-t-tallies.... Ah—there he must be.

(*We hear the keys and the humming, as promised, and then Audax appears, old but hale, lit by the lantern he is carrying. He vanishes for a moment, and we hear him securing a door. Then he is seen again*)

MARANDRO. General Audax.

AUDAX. Mummius? Never mind the general. I won that jug, and you'll pay up, young puppy.

(*Marandro rises and shows himself. Audax is surprised*)

AUDAX. Beg your pardon, sir. I didn't know there were guests in the house. Wait—was it you?—did you call me Audax? General Audax?

MARANDRO. I did. You don't know me, but I know you. Or do you recognize me? Numantia, eighteen years ago.

AUDAX (*with extreme astonishment*). Numantia! (*He lifts the lantern to look at Marandro, whom he inspects close and long*) Were you in the troops? Yes, one of my officers....

MARANDRO. No no no! I was a merchant. Of course, I only knew you from a distance.

AUDAX. A merchant. And you survived.

MARANDRO. Like you.

AUDAX. Like me?

MARANDRO. Well, not exactly. But I survived.

AUDAX. How did you know I was here?

MARANDRO. I didn't know. I happened to see your name in the ledger of slaves. And I decided to wait for you and see for myself. Hey! To think I'm t-t-talking to our commander!

AUDAX. A commander who locks up stables.

MARANDRO. Sit down, old man, sit down. There's a chair.

AUDAX (*hesitant*). On a chair?

MARANDRO. That's right. Everybody's asleep in the house. And I don't fuss about etiquette. I'm a businessman.

AUDAX. All right. But I can't stay long. I'm the night watchman here.

MARANDRO. I know.

AUDAX. What's your name again?

MARANDRO. Marandro.

AUDAX. Marandro. No, I don't think I knew you. How did you manage to save your skin, Marandro?

MARANDRO. Well—to t-t-tell you the truth—on the day we found out about you—you know—

AUDAX. Speak up, merchant: on the day I defected, say it and don't quibble.

MARANDRO. Well, on the day you went over, I said to myself, I said, "Marandro, you're not going to die either." So I moved myself to an abandoned shack in a lot, and when people began to kill themselves like it was the end of the world, and the Romans came in, I kept quiet and waited.

AUDAX. And here you are, eighteen years later, a guest on the noble if crumbling estate of Quintus Pompeius Aulus. Look at that silk! My congratulations.

MARANDRO. Come on, old fellow, don't blame me for my luck. When you're lucky, it means that the gods love you.

AUDAX. Guzzle your luck in peace! I'll kiss the rim of your goblet, I will.

MARANDRO. That's more like it.

AUDAX. You've come here on business? Wait a minute. You're not buying the estate, are you?

MARANDRO. I might be doing just that.

AUDAX (*whistling*). And I'll be your man! (*Confidentially*) Listen, old merchant, don't bid too high on the property. The soil is fair enough, but you can barely see it under the pile of debts.

MARANDRO. The debts are mostly to me.

AUDAX. Triple gods! To you! Marandro, if you buy—what will you do with me?

MARANDRO. Don't worry. You can have your freedom.

AUDAX. Let me kiss your hand. But—instead of freedom—look, why lose a good man like me? The master allows me to live in an old cabin at the edge of the wheat field. Give it to me outright, Marandro, and I'll serve you well. Give it to me in writing—cut my night duty a bit—and also—damn it, I might as well come out with it—don't scatter my family.

MARANDRO. Your family?

AUDAX. Try to understand, Marandro. I'm an old man. The past is past, oh God, the dead are dead.... A man needs a warm place.

MARANDRO. Sure.

AUDAX. So there's a woman under my roof; who do I harm? and two children—not mine—but I don't care. Let me keep them together.

MARANDRO. Don't worry, they're all yours.

AUDAX. May the gods keep prospering you, sir.

MARANDRO. And you too, Audax.

AUDAX. Sure; me too.

MARANDRO. Why not? To each his turn. The way I see it, you've paid heavily enough for your—(*he stops short*)

AUDAX. Treason, Marandro, treason.

MARANDRO. Who said t-t-t-reason?

AUDAX. Nobody.

MARANDRO. I'm a plain businessman. You didn't rob me, did you? So I don't judge.

AUDAX (*heftily, leaping up*). But I do. I judge. Audax has sat for eighteen years over Audax: who led an army; who twice defeated the Roman legions; who dared to say No in the end; who accepted the name of coward; who became a slave, and suffered, and wouldn't die. Judge all you like, my friend. There is a courage for which trumpets do not blow.

(*Darkness now covers the scene. Silence, then, very faintly, in the far distance of many years before, a sound of trumpets. The sound gradually increases and turns into a shattering fanfare as the next scene opens*)

SCENE TWO: SCIPIO

(*Trumpets. Heralds off stage shout "Scipio Africanus!" Preceded by lictors and flanked by officers, Scipio enters and quickly ascends a wooden tribune*)

SCIPIO. Soldiers, I salute you! Some of you know me. Some of you stood at my side under the walls of Carthage. And some of you broke into Carthage behind me and lived to remember the day. I greet you in the name of Rome, and call you friends. But to the others among you I am only the next general sent down from Rome to roll with you in the Spanish dust. That is why I have come to greet you in particular. Lift up your heads and look at me: Scipio himself is here to take command. Soldiers, in the name of Rome, I salute you!

(*Trumpets*)

Men, how long, how bitterly long have you been serving before Numantia? Ten years, many of you! Ten years of fighting or dawdling. Defeats. Stagnation. Though I've just arrived, believe me I know, and what I don't know, I smell. I've been here before. I was fighting in Spain when some of you were in diapers. And now, as I look at a few of you slouching instead of standing smart, I keep those ten years in mind. Also when I see a few dozen whores, and fortune tellers, and lunatic priests, and when I see card games, drinking and dicing—some of you are grinning, I notice—well, I keep those ten years in mind too. (*He suddenly slams the railing with his fist*) But the games are finished. Off with the cooks, the flute players, the priests and the actors! From now on, you'll work the fat off your bellies! You'll stand square in the ranks! Every man here, beginning with myself, every officer that's got two legs with two feet and ten toes, every twitching body will be assigned his job until the job is done. What job? Numantia taken. Taken and occupied. Occupied and colonized. By Roman farmers. You. Your families. Numantia a safe civilized Roman city, and the country a safe civilized Roman country. But for this I need hard bodies and clear minds. Myself, I've come to this camp naked: no servants, no pillows, no ivory tables and no Persian candy; not so much as a bed. I'll be sleeping on a cot and so will you. Away with the wagons of clothes, the jolly stuffed beds, the beads and trinkets! Instead of pins for your girls you'll play with picks, axes, mattocks and spades. Away with the harlots and the gypsies! Away with glassware and dishes! To each man—officer and plain soldier alike, me and you—a pewter cup, a dish and a spoon: period. At nine the camp is asleep. Guards caught napping: off with the left hand. Scipio will snoop and Scipio will poke anywhere anytime. He's not proud. At five, up. Half of you training. The other half digging and building. Yes, digging and building. A trench clean around Numantia except where the river is. Next: a palisade around Numantia. And last: behind the palisade, a stone wall around Numantia: thick, tough and high. Parapets. Towers. Stairs. Architecture! Numantia will starve inside a hoop! Not a drop of Roman or allied blood will be lost! Provided we keep a Roman discipline. Alert twenty four hours a day. Steady work. Patience. One solid front. Your reward will come when Numantia is in our hands. Yours, I should say: its money, its shops, its cellars: yours. And triple pay in the month of victory! A week of dancing and the rest of it! Let Hades pay the bill! Numantia is yours. And there will be no favorites then, as you will see none now. Where Scipio commands, the great get no favors and the humble suffer no wrongs. You'll not be riding chariots to and from work; but neither will I. You'll have no Lusitanian slaves to wash your bodies; but neither will Scipio. And you'll be spading the dry soil from light to dark; but so will your general: spade in hand you'll see me beside you and puffing with the best of you. Romans and allies! My grandfather fought and died in this country. My father campaigned in this country. Myself, I served in it eighteen years ago as prefect to Licinius Lucullus now dead. I have been elsewhere since, you know where. The man who comes from Carthage does not tolerate defeat! In a year Numantia will be ours. Today we outnumber them three to one. Tomorrow more are coming! Four thousand fresh troops—my nephew in charge—another Scipio! Volunteers from every part of our dominions—sent to me Scipio by kings and princes who remember Carthage. Romans and allies, hold onto Discipline, Work and Patience. Under these three hammers Numantia will splinter and break. The gods, I say, the gods are with us!

(*He abruptly descends as the trumpets sound once more. Off stage cries of "Dismiss!"*)

SCENE THREE: THE WAR COUNCIL

(*Numantia. Meeting of the Military Council. Retogenes, Caravino, and Audax around a table. Behind them, a few officers, including Connoba. Maps on the table. Off stage, the tolling of the death bell, gradually receding. Caravino has been speaking. His finger is jabbing a map*)

CARAVINO. Here. Is it or isn't it a fact that he has sent half of his seventh legion away to Termantia?

AUDAX. He has, Caravino. And it is also a fact that half of it remains.

CARAVINO. I have made that calculation too, General Audax. What of it? Are they supermen? They're men like our own, just as tired, just as hot under the sun.

RETOGENES. So then.

CARAVINO. So then. My plan is simple enough. We send a squad out on the first moonless night, that is to say a week from today. The men swim across at this point here. They scale the cliff. They surprise the enemy on his flank. Meantime we open the Minervan Gate wide—something the enemy never expects.

AUDAX. Because he thinks better of us, perhaps.

CARAVINO. Something the enemy never expects, and we launch a frontal assault smack against him with our fourth, fifth and eighth.

RETOGENES. The casualties would be high.

CARAVINO. They will be high, Retogenes. But twenty five percent will come back.

RETOGENES. Can we afford it?

CARAVINO. Can we afford anything else? We need to shake up Pallantia; prove to them we're alive and capable of putting meat into an alliance; what they need to convince them is a show like this one.

AUDAX. A show like this one will bleed us dry.

CARAVINO. I expected nothing else from you, Audax.

RETOGENES. Gentlemen....

AUDAX. It's not blustering over a map will get you through the Roman lines. Retogenes, we are being asked to engineer an idle massacre of our own best men. I want no part of it. Let this be understood.

RETOGENES. You mean there's no chance for the plan to succeed?

AUDAX. Of course there's a chance. But the chance must be weighed against mischance. You take one in two, one in five, but not one in ten, in twenty! To count on surprising Scipio—that, for example, is lunacy.

CARAVINO. Scipio again!

AUDAX. Yes, Scipio again. This is no amateur you're fighting, my friend. Whether or not he expects us to march out at the great gate to tweak his nose, the point I am making is that one does not surprise Scipio Africanus. One may defeat him in pitched battle, one might buy him off, but one does not plan a campaign which depends on surprising him.

CARAVINO. The invulnerable Scipio! There we have him again. Take it from me, I know where Scipio succeeds. Not in starving our bodies. Good, he has starved our bodies too—you needn't prove it to me, I hear the death bell and I can smell bodies too; but that's not it. Scipio is starving our wills. Our wills are sick. One against a hundred we used to crack the Roman lines. Now we let them huddle us into the city, we sit down and starve, we grumble and we die, we send peace delegations, we allow, damn it! we allow a Peace Party in our midst: we don't move. One good blow! That's what I demand. Not only to smash through the Roman lines, not only to wake up our spineless allies, but to get our own blood circulating again.

AUDAX. Circulating? You mean flooding the land. Gentlemen, you are both respected administrators, but you are not soldiers. This is not the rostrum, you are not making speeches to our good citizens. The squad you want to send up the cliff will be picked off and killed. Fine. It's their business to die: signed, Audax. But what next? Scipio knows better than to be taken in by a feint. Our men throw their bodies against the wall he's built, or into his trenches. Scipio butchers us with his left hand and laughs at us besides. Now I understand Caravino's intentions: they are good, but they are political. Not good enough to justify a military catastrophe. I'm ordering no frontal attack.

CARAVINO. Here you have it, this is the very flabbiness I spoke about. I allowed the general to have his say.

AUDAX. We'll not be saving Numantia with insults.

CARAVINO. If only Scipio were defending this city instead of attacking it!... This hopelessness, this unwillingness to make sacrifices: there's the true enemy. Audax, I'll say freely that I reject your policy of inaction.

AUDAX. And I reject your policy of reckless action. It makes me mad—ten years of fighting, lives and more lives—the waste—the ruin — the fanatics —and now all I hear is more more more—"no sacrifice is too great," and I see you ready to depopulate the city for the sake of a "policy of action." If you want victory, Caravino, leave us a few people alive to know we've won.

CARAVINO. Are you suggesting that the war is lost, Audax?

AUDAX. Not lost and yet lost, and if not lost, lost anyway.

RETOGENES. *That* is a conundrum you must kindly explain to our lesser minds, general.

AUDAX. I mean, Retogenes, that we might yet win in the legal sense, especially if we are able to suck in Pallantia, Malia, and Lutia. But we cannot win back those ten years. Those are ten defeated years. The dead are dead, the waste is wasted.

RETOGENES. Perhaps you have taken certain personal losses too much to heart.

AUDAX. Your own have been as great as mine, Retogenes; that's not to the purpose.

RETOGENES. Well, you're an elusive sort. You think well, Audax, no man better in this city, but undoubtedly you think too much. However, let's come to some kind of agreement. What do you propose, Audax? Specifically now.

AUDAX. My proposal is far from heroic—or new, for that matter. Scipio still likes money. We've bribed him before. Let's bribe him again. Or accommodate him with a loan, in civil language.

CARAVINO. To make him lift the siege? What?

AUDAX. No such foolishness. But we might be allowed to buy a little food again. Last time he sold us his own—stolen from his men, some say. That's risky for him; so let's propose that he give safe passage to a single one of our men. Let him allow the man to reach Pallantia, ostensibly to buy food in secret. The supplies can trickle in at night by way of the river, provided the Romans look the other way again. And then, while our man is in Pallantia, let him demand a full commitment at last. Three thousand men within four weeks.

CARAVINO. Extravagance. Until we prove to Pallantia that we've got muscles—enough to give *them* a few knocks when the day comes—they won't show their anxious faces to the Romans.

AUDAX. Possibly. And yet many of them are saying, like us, that the cities are only waiting to be picked off one by one. We must propose a coordinated attack, rear and front. If the move is carefully prepared, we can open the gate at last and try Caravino's plan. But not without safeguards.

CARAVINO. Safeguards! Safeguards! That's all I hear in the council nowadays. The chimney sweeps have more courage than some of us.

AUDAX. Then make the chimney sweeps your generals.

CARAVINO. There are those who think too much of safety, sir.

AUDAX. And others who have reasons of their own perhaps for not caring any more. Let the world collapse with them!

CARAVINO. The meaning of this?

AUDAX. Gladly!

RETOGENES. Gentlemen!

CARAVINO. I'm proud to be on Scipio's blacklist, Audax, and on that honor roll second only to Retogenes, and shame on you, and something more, who knows, for not standing in it.

AUDAX. Call me traitor, say traitor to my face, miserable politician.

RETOGENES. Enough! Silence! Both of you. Now look why Scipio picked one to die and another to escape alive. Here is the fruit. Numantia will tear itself to shreds while Scipio rubs his hands and laughs. Caravino, you have gone too far. I must ask you—

CARAVINO. Yes yes—I apologize.

RETOGENES. And you.

AUDAX. Sweep it under. Peace.

RETOGENES. Let's consider your plan, general. I don't see any reason for not trying it out. If it fails, there's still time for other ideas. We'll risk one man—and try to blind Scipio with golden coins over his eyes. Caravino?

CARAVINO. Very well. Try it. I agree.

RETOGENES. Remains the choice of a man to undertake the cold swim in the river at night, the dart through the Roman patrols, the scratchy climb along the face of the cliff, and the long gallop to Pallantia after demanding a farmer's horse; and I can't think of anyone more suitable than our prefect of the second cohort. What do you think, gentlemen? (*He is addressing the officers*)

OFFICER. An excellent choice.

CARAVINO. First rate.

RETOGENES. General? I can't better express my confidence—

AUDAX. My son is ready. I can speak for him; but let him speak for himself.

CONNOBA. Name the time and give me precise instructions. I'll do the rest.

RETOGENES. Good. We'll reach Scipio through the usual muddy channels, and find out whether he'll dance if we fiddle. Anything else, my friends? If not, I bid you good night. Let me shake your hand, Connoba; and yours, Audax. Remember, all of you: our strength lies in our unity. (*He leaves*)

CARAVINO (*as he is leaving with the other men*). In short, we need a Scipio of our own. Buying artichokes in Pallantia, ha ha-ha! (*They are gone*)

(*Audax and Connoba are left alone*)

AUDAX. God be with you, my boy, God be with you. They took my breath away. How was I to guess?

CONNOBA. I think we can count on Scipio.

AUDAX. I suppose so. Did you see Caravino grin and pretend to hide it?

CONNOBA. Father—

AUDAX. Yes?

CONNOBA. Don't worry about me.

AUDAX. Who else shall I worry about? Your mother died in the first epidemic, your brother was killed three days later....

CONNOBA. Worry about yourself. Your gloomy talk.

AUDAX. Gloomy talk?

CONNOBA. They don't like it. I don't like it.

AUDAX. I understand.

CONNOBA. Well, I'm overdue at the barracks. Equipment to check, orders to give, and all the rest before I go.

AUDAX. Maro will replace you for the few days.

CONNOBA. He'll do.

AUDAX. I'll see you again tonight.

CONNOBA. If you wish. I'm off now.

AUDAX. Connoba.... One reason is what you know. I swore to your mother I would pester you into safety....

CONNOBA. I'm not a child any more. I have duties. Excuse me—

AUDAX. Go.

(*Connoba leaves. Audax sits down and looks at the maps, his forehead in his hand*)

AUDAX. Twenty years old.... Not even....

GENERAL AUDAX

SCENE FOUR: THE PRISONER

(Scipio's tent. Two bunks, a table, a chest: the minimum. In the darkness before dawn, Scipio, his brother Maximus and Polybius are seated round the table, lit by a small lamp)

MAXIMUS. We've had them in a vise for eight months and thirteen days, you know. Fourteen counting today.
POLYBIUS. No doubt about it. They are down to licking hides, eating straw, and even boiling limbs of the dead. They chuck people into mass graves. And according to reports, they also talk with extremely noble words about Saguntum.
MAXIMUS. Saguntum?
POLYBIUS. Another Spanish town. Your brother knows. Hannibal besieged it. He too put a ditch and a wall around it, like Publius Scipio.
SCIPIO *(laughing)*. My good Polybius, I'm not a "great originator of strategic maneuvers" and so forth! But it takes something, doesn't it, to choose what to imitate?
POLYBIUS. My respected general, Carthage swallowed Saguntum, but you swallowed Hannibal. That speaks for itself.
MAXIMUS. Tell me what happened at Saguntum.
POLYBIUS. When the fatal hour drew near, the men burned their own city, melted down all valuables, destroyed every sitting and standing object in town, murdered the prisoners, dispatched their own women and children, and then disemboweled themselves.
MAXIMUS. And that's what the Numantians are talking about?
POLYBIUS. So I hear.
SCIPIO. I don't like it. The senate won't like it. I could storm the city right now, but if I do, those fanatics may leave nothing for me to show. Make a strong effort at the next parley, Polybius.
POLYBIUS. I've been making a strong effort for six months, Scipio! What else can I do? Do you have new ideas? Concessions?
SCIPIO. Yes, concessions. I'll guarantee the safety of every man, woman and child in Numantia, except those on the list. And I'll find new land for them.
POLYBIUS. But that's nothing new. You're talking to Polybius, my dear general, not to your enemies. Come, what *new* proposals have you got?
SCIPIO. I'll reduce the tribute, God blast it!
MAXIMUS. What?
SCIPIO *(red-faced)*. You all think I'm a robber, a squeezer, a purse-snatcher!

They kick my name about in Rome as though I were a pawnbroker. They send accountants to sniff into my "practices"! And you too, Polybius.

POLYBIUS. I didn't say a thing!

SCIPIO. But you smiled. Well, I say reduce the tribute. Take a twentieth off and let's have peace, by all the thunder in heaven! Rome won't let me do more for them. Talk to them.

POLYBIUS. I'll try, Scipio. You know my feelings.

(*Enter Buteo in haste*)

BUTEO. Uncle!

SCIPIO. What?

BUTEO. A squad of men sent out by Fulvius Flaccus caught someone down by the river.

SCIPIO. Damnation! Polybius—more ideas later this morning—

POLYBIUS. Yes, yes, all in good time. (*Exit*)

SCIPIO. Sit down. Take a breath. Here, drink. Now tell me what happened. (*To Maximus*) Hand me my belt.

BUTEO. Pure luck for us. I was on duty. I noticed a patrol by the river. Recognized them in the dark. Fulvius Flaccus' men, of course.

MAXIMUS. Snooping.

BUTEO. They noticed somebody landing from a skiff on our side of the river.

SCIPIO. Whereabout?

BUTEO. Near Tower Six.

MAXIMUS. Ay!

BUTEO. Their leader cries out "What's this? What's this? Isn't the river supposed to be triple watched? Stop that man!" And three of them dive quietly into the brushwork down the embankment. The man fights back, but they disarm and pinion him in a second. That's when I shot away to tell you.

SCIPIO. Go meet them, Buteo. Tell them Scipio's been informed—don't say how—and say I want to see the prisoner at once. Bring him to me yourself before Fulvius himself gets to him. Quick, quick.

(*Buteo leaves the tent*)

SCIPIO. A nasty turn of the wheel.

MAXIMUS. But are you sure it's the man?

SCIPIO. Tonight was the night, Tower Six was the spot. Who else was it? The ghost of Achilles? And where else would that louse Fulvius have his men except where there's trouble against me?

MAXIMUS. Maybe it was somebody else. Maybe!

SCIPIO. Shut up.

MAXIMUS. All right, it isn't. What are you going to do?

SCIPIO. We took the money and yet he was captured. He'll be shouting this dirty fact every step of the way.

MAXIMUS. Think, brother.

SCIPIO. Fulvius! A snivelling dandy whose only speech in the Senate has been "Gentlemen, I propose we decorate the vestibule with a painting of Justice and Virtue." Does he think he'll get the better of Scipio?

MAXIMUS. Not likely! Quiet.

(*Enter Buteo and Connoba. Connoba's hands are tied. Buteo throws Connoba's dagger on a table*)

CONNOBA. Which one of you is Scipio?

SCIPIO. One minute. (*Aside to Buteo*) Where's Fulvius?

BUTEO. Still in his tent, but certainly informed by now.

SCIPIO. Of course.

CONNOBA. One of you two is Scipio. Which one is it?

MAXIMUS. Silence! You'll find out soon enough.

SCIPIO (*still to Buteo*). Go to his tent and tell him I'm questioning the prisoner.

BUTEO. Good. (*Exit*)

SCIPIO. I am Scipio.

CONNOBA. Why am I here? Answer me.

SCIPIO. Your name and rank?

CONNOBA (*draws himself up*). Connoba. Prefect of the second cohort of Numantia.

SCIPIO. Son of?

CONNOBA. A citizen and no concern of yours. Now let me question *you*.

MAXIMUS. Hold your temper, Numantian; remember who it is you're addressing.

CONNOBA. I'm remembering it, Roman; I'll be remembering it as long as I live. Scipio, you've put our money in your pockets. Deny it.

SCIPIO. I don't deny it.

CONNOBA. Why do these Roman hyenas live? Their generals pickpockets. For this miserable money you were letting me reach Pallantia, God curse you! to beg a few loaves of bread for our children. Didn't you swear? Deny it!

SCIPIO. I don't deny it, Connoba. Calm down. I had my own people down by Tower Six—

CONNOBA. Three of them knocked me to the ground. What's this drivel?

SCIPIO. That was another patrol. One I didn't know about. I have enemies here, Connoba. I'm not almighty.

MAXIMUS. That's the whole story and God's truth.

SCIPIO. We're as shocked as you are, believe me. But don't worry. I'll have you on the road to Pallantia within a day or two.

CONNOBA. Here, untie me for a start.

SCIPIO. Gladly, but in a little while, because I'd better not seem too friendly in the open. Tell me what you said to the men who caught you—what you cried out, or deliberately spoke, or let fall before you could think. Think hard. I truly need to know before I can plan your escape.

CONNOBA. I said nothing, and I didn't "let fall" anything, I'm not a fool. I said and repeated one thing only, loud and clear: "Take me to Scipio."

SCIPIO. Ah, very good.

CONNOBA. Look, Scipio, I'll swallow your story. You just carry out your side of the bargain. Nobody denies your word's always been good—until now.

SCIPIO. Thanks.

(*Enter Buteo, holding a letter*)

SCIPIO. Sit down, my friend, while I talk to this man.

(*He goes to one side with Buteo*)

SCIPIO. Back so soon?

BUTEO. I ran into his messenger. He's written to you.

(*Scipio takes the letter, sits down facing Connoba again, and reads it to himself*)

SCIPIO. This concerns you, my boy. Fulvius Flaccus, our senatorial legate from Rome, will be interrogating you tomorrow morning. He can't today, luckily he's committed to a tour of inspection all day long. (*Confidentially*) Better for both of us if he never makes your acquaintance. I'll post a couple of my own men over your cell—with instructions—and you can handle the rest during the night. The prisoner escaped; sorry! More luck for us, the stockade is on the Pallantia side of our camp.

CONNOBA. Let me warn you, though. You try foul play on me and I won't die I promise without every man in this camp hearing the facts.

SCIPIO. I understand. You have my word, Connoba. Here's a token of my confidence.

(*Scipio slips the dagger into Connoba's clothing, and makes a hush sign on his lips*)

CONNOBA. Thanks. In exchange, I'll keep my mouth shut—as long as it's good for Numantia.

SCIPIO. I like that! Buteo, kindly call in an escort for our guest.

(*Exit Buteo and reentrance with two soldiers*)

SCIPIO (*aside to Connoba*). Get some sleep, and keep your promise as I'll keep mine. My enemies are yours. (*To the soldiers*) Make the prisoner comfortable in his cell. Cut him free as soon as you arrive, and see to it that he is given dry clothes, a good meal and decent bedding.

SOLDIERS. Yes, sir.

(*The soldiers lead Connoba out. Scipio watches at the tent opening and then returns, somber*)

MAXIMUS. What will you do with him, brother?

SCIPIO. Why ask? Give me that quill. The senator must be informed that I have taken cognizance of his plan, and that I have already locked up the prisoner. (*He writes hastily and hands the note to Buteo*) Take it to him, then find Minucius and send him to me.

BUTEO (*troubled*). Minucius?

SCIPIO. Go.

(*Exit Buteo. A long silence*)

SCIPIO. The sun is up.

MAXIMUS. Looks like another warm day. Summer is coming.

(*Another silence*)

SCIPIO. Strutting about the camp with his "mantle of office"! Rome sets a spy on me! On me! I took Carthage for them! They're sitting in their villas lapping their wines while I kill myself in this desert. And they send me a spy; a prig who never saw a spear before except in a museum!

MAXIMUS. I don't recognize you, brother. What's the use of crying? But why don't you let the boy escape tonight just as you told him? I think you should.

SCIPIO. By all the gods in heaven and hell, I wish I could! Listen to this. (*He picks up the letter*) "To allay any fears you may have, or any inconvenience you may suffer, I shall post two trusted sentinels in six-hour shifts alongside yours to keep watch over the stockade from dawn to dawn."

MAXIMUS. Well then, trust the boy to keep his mouth shut.

SCIPIO. Why should he keep his mouth shut? I made him a promise, and I can't keep it. Why would the boy want to protect me?

MAXIMUS. Damn damn damn.

(*Minucius appears*)

MAXIMUS. Maybe I'd better look for my breakfast. I'll return in awhile.

(*Maximus, glad to leave, makes his way out. Minucius salutes him, then stands in front of Scipio*)

SCIPIO. Trouble at dawn, Minucius.

MINUCIUS. I know, sir. We saw it all.

SCIPIO. Oh.

MINUCIUS. I couldn't see nothing we could do about it, sir. We had no orders. Sure, we could have jumped that patrol of theirs. But I said to myself it wasn't what you'd be wanting us to do, out in the open.

SCIPIO. Right. Tell me what happened exactly.

MINUCIUS. Not much to tell, sir. Me and the other five was on duty at Tower Six. I took my turn about two in the morning, on account of the man you said was supposed to show up about three. About four o'clock sure enough I hear a quiet kind of splash in the river, and the man comes rowing up to the bank. He looks around, and I'm looking at him from the tower—of course he can't see me—and then him and me see the others at the same simultaneous time. A squad of our own men. He tries to get away—

SCIPIO. Fine. I know the rest.

MINUCIUS. I hope we did right, sir.

SCIPIO. You did. You're not to blame for a thing. But now we've got the prisoner on our hands, and there's a nasty job for you.

MINUCIUS. Anything, sir. You know me.

SCIPIO. I do. That's why I called you. But you'll need helpers.

MINUCIUS. Anyone in mind, sir?

SCIPIO. I was thinking of our two Numidians.

MINUCIUS. Mago and Gulussa. Good idea.

SCIPIO. Listen carefully. The prisoner is in the stockade. I'll see to it that the three of you are on duty to guard him from sundown to midnight. You'll bring him his supper, with plenty of wine. Your supper too. You'll all sit down at the same table. Eat, drink, taunt him, insult Numantia, accuse him and them of cowardice, tell him these Hispanic tribes are savages, say—

MINUCIUS. Leave it to me, sir.

SCIPIO. He's got a dagger. Pretend you want to take it away from him. Anyway, a brawl. All of you in a rage. Don't forget he's only a boy, and I had a taste of his temper a few minutes ago. Killed in a brawl. Three weeks in the lockup for you and the Numidians. *This* should make it bearable.

(*He opens the chest, takes out a locked box, opens it with a key, and retrieves a bag, which he fills with pieces of gold and gives to Minucius*)

MINUCIUS. Thank you, sir. I don't see no impediment. What next?

SCIPIO. Several of Fulvius Flaccus' men will be on duty nearby. They will overhear the brawling. You'll open the door, all bloody and besmirched, and yell for assistance. An officer will be called who will arrest you and report the disaster to me.

MINUCIUS. Will be done, sir.

SCIPIO. If nobody blabs, you'll share a second one of these. But God help all three of you if anything leaks out—

MINUCIUS. Trust us, sir; we know what's smart and what's dumb.

(*He picks up the bag, hides it in his cloak, salutes and leaves. Scipio remains in deep gloom. Enter Maximus*)

SCIPIO. Are you fed?

MAXIMUS. Not hungry. Well?

SCIPIO. Well? Do you want a speech from me? Fine. Some live, some die, and some die that some may live. Sit down. (*Low*) You know where I keep what we took from the Numantians.

MAXIMUS. Sure.

SCIPIO. Have it returned to them.

SCENE FIVE: HUNGER

(A market square in Numantia, bordered by houses and porticos, and backed by a parapet overlooking the country beyond and below. Benches, stalls, a drinking trough for horses, perhaps a monument. The death bell is heard for a little while. Audax, his back to the audience, gazes out over the ramparts. To one side, by one of the houses, a ragged man sits weakly, head down, on a doorstep. There is a long silence. A second and third man enter and aimlessly join the sitting man. They are pale, ragged, and long haired)

SECOND. Still watching his dead soldier lad, as if it was yesterday.

FIRST. Who?

SECOND. The general. Look.

FIRST. I don't know.

SECOND. Did your boy find anything?

FIRST. A dead dog. With flies.

SECOND. You can die eating it, in my opinion.

FIRST. Why?

SECOND. What do you mean—why?

FIRST. Why should I die eating it? The flies don't die.

(The third man laughs)

SECOND. Flies don't die so easily.

FIRST. That's what I said.

(Silence. In the distance, the death-bell)

SECOND. It's hot again.

THIRD. Day after day. And the smell....

SECOND. The Romans won't be able to take it much longer.

THIRD. Who said?

SECOND. I heard it. Now I think of it, it's what Retogenes said on Sunday.

FIRST. What did he say?

SECOND. "We must persevere, stand firm, and fight on, because the Romans are wilting in the sun." I always like the way he puts things.

FIRST. I wish I could stand up.
SECOND. What would you do?
FIRST. But I get spots before my eyes and I faint.
SECOND. It's a bad sign.
THIRD. Not necessarily.
(*Enter Marandro*)
SECOND. What's the news, Marandro?
MARANDRO. They've arrested the Peace Party leaders.
FIRST. Good. I've seen them. There was grease on their lips. I noticed. Don't tell me they join the Peace Party for nothing. Scipio gives them bread and cheese and wine and then they talk about peace while we're chewing hunks of timber, and my woman is dead sure enough and only one of the boys is left to me.
SECOND. I never saw grease on their lips.
FIRST. You got weak eyes.
THIRD. And *you're* out of your mind. (*To Marandro*) Are you sure?
MARANDRO. Sure I'm sure. They're all coming this way, t-t-tied together, Avarus in front. Ret-t-t-ogenes will tell us why.
THIRD. Retogenes likes to give us shows.
SECOND. They're coming this way?
MARANDRO. On the way to jail.
SECOND. Another trial, I guess.
THIRD. And more executions. It never fails. It hasn't failed yet.
FIRST. Traitors all of them.
THIRD. You're a damn fool.
FIRST (*a flicker of strength*). Who? Me?
THIRD. That's right. You.
FIRST (*down again*). They'll arrest you too.
THIRD. Let them.
MARANDRO. What are you t-t-talking about?
SECOND. What's the good of quarreling? We ought to remain united.
THIRD. United dead in a ditch. If the Romans don't do it, Retogenes and his gang will. I've heard him and Caravino. "Not an infant left in Numantia for Scipio to show off on his next triumph in Rome."
FIRST. Everybody dead. I like that.
MARANDRO (*seeing Audax*). There's Audax! Poor man....
SECOND. Must be hard when a fellow sends his own son off to die.
MARANDRO. I wouldn't put it that way.
THIRD. Why in God's name should they have arrested the Peace Party?
FIRST. Because they've got a bellyful of Roman dinner in them.

THIRD. I'll swear they've had terms from the Romans! And that's why—that's why these politicians will murder them!

SECOND. Terms—I'll say! Give up the city! Move your baggage out! Pay tribute! Settle in the sand two hundred bitter miles away! Not me! Leave my house to the first hooligan that comes and demands it of me? A Roman dog sleeping in my bed? I tell you the hot days have come and they'll rot down to their bones.

THIRD. The hot days have come and you'll be stinking in the grave with the rest of us and the Roman dog will sleep in your bed all the same.

SECOND. You're a maniac! I tell you the hot days are on our side, and in another month we'll be seeing a Pallantian army on the hills. Wait and see.

THIRD. Thank you, say my bones. Five more years of the same.

FIRST. They'll arrest you.

MARANDRO. No no, they won't. Don't t-t-t-talk so much, my friend.

THIRD (*laughing*). It's better than listening to my belly making speeches. Damn, now my eyes are rolling too. (*He leans against a wall and sits down*)

SECOND (*helping him*). Talking uses you up.

MARANDRO. We'll fight together to the bitter end.

(*Enter Lira and Julia*)

MARANDRO (*to Lira*). Good afternoon, madam.

LIRA. Good day, Marandro.

(*Lira and Julia step away*)

MARANDRO (*to the men*). A fine woman. I used to supply the family with wine. She danced in the chorus with Audax's wife.

SECOND. Isn't the other his sister in law?

MARANDRO. I don't know.

FIRST. She'll die anyway.

JULIA. Audax. (*Audax turns around*) What's the use? Don't look....

AUDAX. It's where I saw him for the last time....

JULIA. I know.

AUDAX. I keep saying the same thing, don't I! But I can't take my eyes away. Lira, I'm glad to see you.

LIRA. We wondered if we could help. At your house, perhaps.

AUDAX. Yes—at my house—thank you. Fortunately, I'm on duty day and night. My house.... Julia, what about Marcellus?

JULIA. It will be over soon. My husband today, myself tomorrow.

AUDAX. I'll try to bring some food again after dark.

(*Meanwhile, a number of citizens have appeared. An officer enters and approaches Audax*)

OFFICER. Reporting, general.

AUDAX. Yes—what is it?

OFFICER. The governor requests that you join him. He is coming this way and the prisoners after him, but he would like to be met and attended.

AUDAX. I'll go meet him. Let him know. (*The officer leaves*) Retogenes is delivering the prisoners to jail in person. But I don't know why he is coming on before them.

LIRA. Roman prisoners? What do you mean?

AUDAX. Oh. You haven't heard. Our own Peace Party is going to jail. It's a wonder Retogenes waited until now.

LIRA. I don't understand.

AUDAX. You're lucky. Well, I have to leave you. I advise you not to stay.

LIRA. Isn't there anything we can do for you?

AUDAX. Yes, of course. Tell the housekeeper I'll come home in two or three days, and not to worry about me.

LIRA. We'll do everything.

JULIA. Audax, please, for your own sake—don't look any more.

(*Audax presses her hand and leaves*)

LIRA. God knows what the men are up to again.

JULIA. Murder, what else?

LIRA. But why? Because they couldn't agree? I don't understand.

JULIA. Who knows?

LIRA. Maybe we shouldn't stay.

JULIA. It hurts, but I want to see it.

(*Now they are swallowed up by the crowd of ragged citizens. A few soldiers are among them. Most of the people sit quietly on the ground. Some listless conversation. A late citizen asks whether this is the place where "he" will speak. Then the fourth citizen suddenly accosts the fifth*)

FOURTH. Why're you staring at me?

FIFTH. Staring at you?

FOURTH. Yeah. Staring at me.

FIFTH. I've been staring at you?

FOURTH. That's what I said. You've been staring at me.

FIFTH. So I've been staring at you. But not because you're a picture of Apollo.

FOURTH. What do you mean? Is there something funny about me? (*To the sixth citizen*) You too? Anything funny about me?

SIXTH. No. Nothing funny about you. I ain't laughing. Nothing except what everybody knows.

SEVENTH. All right. That's enough.

FOURTH. What everybody knows? What does everybody know, you bastard? I'll kill you.

SIXTH. You call me bastard?
FOURTH. That's what I call you. And anybody else that stares at me.
SEVENTH. Come on, that's enough.
FOURTH. Because there's nobody in this town got a human right to stare at me. That's right. I was a soldier in the service twelve years.
FIFTH. Sure. Raiding the stalls in the market.
FOURTH. You stinking bastard!
FIFTH. That's enough. (*They fight*) You ain't fit to be seen among decent people.
FOURTH. I'll show you who's fit.
(*Others try to interfere, but the fourth citizen has the upper hand*)
EIGHTH. For shame! Retogenes himself is coming to speak to us.
FIFTH. Let go! Let go!
FOURTH. Twelve years in the service while you was putting on weight and now you think you got the right to stare at me. Bastard, bastard, bastard!
SEVERAL. Let him go! You're choking him! God damn you! There's an assembly of the people here!
(*But the fifth citizen has finally disengaged himself. He strikes a violent blow. The fourth citizen falls backward*)
FIFTH. Cannibal!
(*Suddenly everybody falls silent. The fourth citizen slowly picks himself up. He is sobbing. He drags himself away*)
FIFTH. He provoked me. Leave me alone.
EIGHTH. Forget it.
SEVENTH. Yes. Forget it.
SIXTH. He provoked you.
NINTH. Anyway, I think Retogenes is bringing good news.
TENTH. Me too.
ELEVENTH. I think we can manage another go at the wall. Masses of us. Torches. Ladders. And when that's done we'll talk peace.
TWELFTH. They'll have to carry you into battle on a stretcher.
ELEVENTH. Maybe you'd like to join the Peace Party. There's rope enough for everybody's neck.
TWELFTH. You don't scare me. I've got my thoughts.
EIGHTH. Don't start another quarrel, if you please.
(*Various remarks and grumbles. The group subsides. During this episode, Marcius has come in with a friend*)
MARCIUS. Is he here?
FRIEND. I'm looking. Yes, he is. Don't look now. But in a moment turn casually to the left and glance at the Tax Collector's house. The man standing

up is Marandro.
MARCIUS. The one in black? With the finger in his ear?
FRIEND. That's the man.
MARCIUS. All right. Stay here. (*He walks casually*) Are you Marandro?
MARANDRO. Marandro, import and export; in the good days, alas.
MARCIUS. May I have a word with you—on the side?
MARANDRO. At your service. (*They walk aside*)
A WOMAN IN THE CROWD. Give us soup instead of fighting like dogs!
A MAN. Back to your kitchen.
MARCIUS. I'm told you've got food stored away.
MARANDRO (*frightened*). Who t-t-told you this trash? Food? In Numantia?
MARCIUS. Calm down. We're safe in the crowd.
MARANDRO. Who are you?
MARCIUS. I'm somebody whose children are hungry. I'm nobody else. And I'll pay you whatever you want for whatever you've got. Caro told me about you.
MARANDRO. What did he t-t-t-tell you?
MARCIUS. That you sit like a dragon on a heap of victuals.
MARANDRO. It's not t-t-true. Like a what? Do I look like I have food? Why did Caro tell you this trash? You're from the police, that's clear enough.
MARCIUS. If I were from the police I'd be searching your cellar. Come on, Marandro, talk business or else the police *will* hear from me. (*Grim*) Besides, I'll kill a man for a piece of bread. What have you got and how much do you want?
MARANDRO. I haven't got anything. But I might get in t-t-touch with somebody. Maybe!
MARCIUS. What has your somebody got, and how much does your somebody want?
MARANDRO. A pound of flour for sixty silver denarii.
MARCIUS (*quietly*). Your somebody is lower than a dead stinking mongrel. What does he hope to do with silver? Bribe an eagle to fly him out of Numantia?
MARANDRO. That's his business. Good bye.
MARCIUS. Wait. I'll pay. Sixty in silver. For *two* pounds of flour.
MARANDRO. A pound and a half.
MARCIUS. It's children, Marandro; not myself, children. What kind of animal are you?
MARANDRO. All right. T-t-two pounds. Let it be.
MARCIUS. Where and when?
(*Marandro takes him aside. His answer is drowned in shouts from the crowd.*)

VOICE. Here they are!
VOICE. Retogenes!
VOICE. Speech! Hurrah! Hang Scipio!
VOICE. Where are the prisoners?
VOICE. Action!
VOICE. They'll sell us to Rome for a pound of meat!
(*Audax and escort enter*)
AUDAX. Peace! Silence! Order!
VOICE. Bravo for the general!
AUDAX. The prisoners—(*uproar*)—silence! The prisoners are being taken to jail. No violence will be tolerated.
VOICE. Are you going to feed them in jail?
VOICE. Make them starve!
(*Shouts of approval*)
AUDAX. Peace everybody! Let them plead their case in court!
VOICE. The Romans don't let traitors plead. Why should we?
VOICE. Did they allow your son to plead?
(*Voices silence him*)
VOICE. Forget the prisoners! Give us bread!
(*Shouts of approval, "Food, food," etc.*)
AUDAX. Make way for the governor!
(*Enter Retogenes, Caravino, soldiers, escort. Retogenes leaps up some steps. Caravino is at his side*)
RETOGENES. Numantians! The Peace Party is under arrest at last!
VOICE. Good work!
VOICE. Is it because they made peace, or didn't make peace, or what?
VOICE. I'm for peace, and I don't care who hears it!
VOICE. Your knees wobbling?
VOICE. Coward!
VOICE. Shut your mouths, all of you, and let the leaders speak!
RETOGENES. Friends, friends, friends! Let me say my word for God's sake! The law is the law. We catch Avarus and his friends sending secret messages to the enemy and getting secret replies. The law strictly forbids unauthorized contacts with the enemy! In defiance, they negotiate behind our backs as if they had authority.
CARAVINO. And negotiate for special terms for themselves. We strongly suspect it. We have evidence. Once they're in jail, we'll pry loose the truth.
VOICE. Make them sweat!
CARAVINO. You are the people! Decide for us! What shall we do with a gang that bargains in secret with Scipio?

TWO OR THREE VOICES. Hang them!
CROWD. Hang them!
VOICE. Let's do it ourselves!
VOICE. These men should be heard by our judges.
VOICE. The people are the judges!
VOICE. Ropes! Ropes!
VOICE. Here they come!
(*Uproar. Refrain of "Hang them, hang them!"*)
AUDAX (*To Retogenes and Caravino*). There's going to be a massacre! Have the prisoners moved back and taken another way!
RETOGENES (*through the noise*). Don't be a child, general.
AUDAX. I won't allow it! Call for calm!
AN OFFICER. Stand back everybody! Make room for the prisoners!
AUDAX (*to his men, drawing his sword*). Make a circle around the prisoners! (*They hesitate*) A circle around them, do you hear? Keep the mob away! No violence! Hands off! Back! Back!
THE CROWD (*continuing*). Hang them! Hang them!
VOICES. The prisoners!
(*Four gagged and bound prisoners are brought in. The mob surges against them, still shouting, but is tentatively held back by Audax's men*)
VOICES. Justice! Justice!
AUDAX (*waving his sword*). Let no one dare!
VOICE. Show some pity, you beasts!
VOICE. Peace and food!
VOICES. Grab those bastards!
A MAN. Here's pity for you!
(*He hurls a stone. One of the prisoners stumbles to the ground. A woman screams and rushes to the fallen victim*)
WOMAN. Let me through! Let me through! They stoned my husband!
(*The crowd falls silent*)
AUDAX. Arrest that man! That one—there—grab him.
(*A soldier seizes the stone thrower*)
THE STONE-THROWER. Somebody help me!
AUDAX. Get back, all of you! Away with him!
WOMAN. My husband is hurt!
VOICE. Leave her alone for God's sake!
VOICE. Hang her with the rest of them!
(*Audax helps the woman*)
AUDAX. The next man who throws a stone is dead!
VOICE. Don't be too rough on us, general! (*Laughter*)

RETOGENES (*to Caravino*). Wait.

THE WOMAN (*shaking her fist*). Rabble! Rabble! Retogenes, tell them! Tell them you and him are on Scipio's blacklist! (*Her husband tries to stop her*) You want the people to bleed with you! You're going to kill my husband—let me talk, let me talk!—you're going to kill my husband so—

CARAVINO. General! One of the prisoners is freeing his hands!

RETOGENES. Hold him!

AUDAX. Nothing's happening! Make room!

RETOGENES. All right! Let the prisoners march quietly.

WOMAN. Take me along.

RETOGENES. Yes, take her along, the witch, take her along. Open a way for them.

AUDAX. Make a circle. Keep out—you! Away! (*To an officer*) Your responsibility. On your life.

OFFICER. Make way. March. March.

(*The mob grumbles but allows the prisoners, the woman, and the escort to pass and leave*)

CARAVINO. People of Numantia, rest assured, the prisoners will be tried fairly, and they will not escape. Meantime, gird yourselves—the struggle continues. Our allies are arming. We are strong. The summer heat is sapping the Roman army. Shall we ever surrender? Shout it with me so the Romans out there can hear you: Never!

THE CROWD. Never!

RETOGENES. Never!

THE CROWD. Never!

(*The crowd slowly breaks up. A few people are left, among them Marandro, Julia, and Lira. Retogenes is gone, but Caravino lingers*)

CARAVINO (*privately to Audax*). You were a trifle uncooperative—

AUDAX. Don't make me raise my voice, Caravino. I saw your agents in the crowd. They've earned their pay. But murder is not *my* duty.

CARAVINO. Murder? General, if I were you I'd think of murder elsewhere. (*He gestures toward the ramparts*)

AUDAX. What I think of is my business.

CARAVINO. Is it? We are all extremely interested in your thoughts.

AUDAX. Here's one of them. Why was I kept in the dark about these so-called secret meetings and messages?

CARAVINO. Not guilty! So were we in the Council.

AUDAX. Kept in the dark? How did the meetings come to light?

CARAVINO. They were revealed to us.

AUDAX. By whom?

CARAVINO. They were revealed.

(*Audax looks at him*)
AUDAX. By Avarus himself! That trusting simpleton! I should have guessed!
CARAVINO. Let him prove it. And let him learn that we are the government, not he. Good day, general.
(*Caravino goes. Audax deep in thought, then notices the two women*)
AUDAX. Were you two watching this pathetic circus? You shouldn't have stayed. If you approved of it, you're fools; if you didn't, you're suspects.
JULIA. Audax—
AUDAX. Yes?
JULIA. Be careful....
AUDAX. Ha! Just what Connoba said to me.
LIRA. We mean well, and we're concerned for you. I've been a friend of the family so long—
AUDAX. I am thankful, Lira, don't misunderstand.
JULIA. Audax, I don't know what right I have—I want to ask you a question —not an easy one—
AUDAX. Ask me anything my Cornelia might have wanted to know.
JULIA (*low*). Why haven't you resigned? I'm terribly afraid....
AUDAX (*low*). Because the next day I'd be arrested, and the day after hanged; along with Avarus and the rest.
(*Julia looks into his face, and then lowers her head*)
JULIA. They do horrible things—but how can anyone keep decent and sane—with all this? And when all's said and done—
AUDAX. It's us. I understand.
JULIA. This is our home. I was married here. You too. You and Cornelia....
LIRA. And how else can they act? You can't win a war with prayers. I'm sorry for these people. I don't think Retogenes is always right. But people who go in for secret meetings—
JULIA. We mustn't stay any longer.
AUDAX. Thank you, both of you.
LIRA. We'll look after everything.
(*As the two women move away, the death-bell is heard off stage*)
JULIA. Come the other way....
(*Julia and Lira leave. A tumbril now rattles on stage. It is drawn by two men between the traces, and is loaded full of bodies. The gravedigger walks behind ringing the death bell. At one of the windows a woman appears. She speaks in a forlorn blank voice*)
WOMAN. Here.
GRAVEDIGGER. Age and sex? (*No answer*) Age and sex, up there?
WOMAN. A little boy. Eleven years and two months old.
GRAVEDIGGER. Bring him down.

WOMAN. I can't.
GRAVEDIGGER. Why can't you?
WOMAN. I can't.
GRAVEDIGGER. All right. Keep him.
AUDAX. Wait. (*To the woman*) We'll fetch him down, and decently. Open the door for us. (*He sees Marandro*) You there, citizen. Come with me.
MARANDRO. Me, general?
AUDAX. Yes, you. What's your name?
MARANDRO. Marandro, sir.
AUDAX. Come along, Marandro. Don't dawdle.
(*Marandro reluctantly follows him into the house. A few moments later they reappear carrying the dead boy on a plank. Marandro is nauseated and tries to avert his face*)
AUDAX. Lift up. He'll fall. (*Impatiently*) Up!
(*He manages to place the boy carefully in the wagon*)
GRAVEDIGGER. There's usually something for us.
(*Marandro has stepped aside. Audax looks at the window, which is empty, then gives the gravedigger some money*)
GRAVEDIGGER. Thank you, general.
(*The cart moves off to the shaking of the bell*)
MARANDRO. Some people get used to it. I can't.
(*He and the one or two remaining citizens move off. The bell is heard to the end of the scene. Audax is alone. He remains in deep reflection, looking again toward the plain below. Julia returns by herself*)
JULIA. I didn't want to leave you with her words, as though *I* meant them.
AUDAX. I know you better, Julia. Sister....
JULIA. Yes?
AUDAX. I was going to tell you tonight. I am leaving soon.
JULIA (*frightened*). What do you mean?
AUDAX. What can I mean? Leaving.
JULIA. Leaving for where? (*Whispering, as he gestures toward the plain*) Going to Scipio? You can't—your own child—you can't.
AUDAX. I'll be an example to Numantia.
JULIA (*incredulous*). Your own child.
AUDAX. I had chosen him—in my mind, you understand—I had chosen him to survive. Now the last one is myself.
JULIA. Scipio murdered him!
AUDAX. Scipio? He had no reason to, and was even honest enough to return our bribe after that miserable brawl. No. The war murdered my son.
JULIA. And suppose we win the war?
AUDAX. I've lost my taste for victory. The old soldier has had enough.

JULIA. I'm trembling. Are you in serious danger?

AUDAX. Yes, but that doesn't count.

JULIA. You're not going to lead the Romans against us?

AUDAX. No, Julia. Never.

JULIA. Is there something I don't know? Has it all been wrong?

AUDAX. Nothing you don't know. And as for what's right and what's wrong, I'm done with that. I'm sick of being right, I want this people of mine to give in to the wrong and live. The wrong isn't all that wrong, and the right isn't all that right.

JULIA. You destroyed Aemilius and Brutus in the field before Scipio became consul. You could destroy Scipio himself.

AUDAX. In three years? five years? ten years?

JULIA. I don't know.

AUDAX. In three years of fighting and siege, might a child die? Yes, a child might die. It isn't worth it.

JULIA. Your city.

AUDAX. I would like it to remain standing. But Julia....

JULIA. Yes?

AUDAX. You'll be left alone soon. Marcellus is dying.

JULIA. Yes.

AUDAX. You have no children.

JULIA. I have no children.

AUDAX. Fortunate woman. The unborn don't die. If the worst should happen—

JULIA. What then?

AUDAX. There will be a great self-destruction here.

JULIA. I know.

AUDAX. Julia, listen to me. I beg you. If the day comes—*if* it comes, maybe it won't—play dead in your cellar, take whatever food you can find, don't stir, lock the door, answer to no one, and wait until the Romans are in possession. If they let me live I will find you again; if not—(*Julia is crying*) Julia....

JULIA. Is that your advice to me? Welcome the first soldier that knocks down the door? Allow them to sell me? Become a charwoman in a Roman kitchen? Or worse? I'd rather die, it's ten times easier, I'll go with Marcellus, I'll kill myself when he is dead....

AUDAX. Julia—

JULIA. And you're running away, oh my God, my God....

AUDAX. Julia—how can I say it?—there's always time to make an end of it, don't you see? If you can bear it no longer—God knows it's easy, nothing else in this dirty world is easier. Don't die as a precaution, Julia, it's too absurd—promise—swear—raise your hand to me and swear!

JULIA. I can't. I'll be alone now. I can't bear it. My God, where are you, where are you, God, and why do we suffer so much? (*She is sobbing*)

SCENE SIX: AMONG THE DEAD

(*The ruins of Numantia. Three elderly citizens—two men and a woman—crouched in the rubble, tied up and guarded by a Roman soldier. Enter Polybius. He walks slowly, as though looking for something. He stares at the prisoners awhile. Enter Buteo*)

BUTEO. Polybius. I'm glad to see a friend.
POLYBIUS. Anything? Anyone?
BUTEO. Plenty of broken shoulders, scratched faces and bleeding hands.
POLYBIUS. What do you mean?
BUTEO. I mean our men digging into the rubble. We're taking losses without meeting an enemy.
POLYBIUS. Other than that?
BUTEO. Children. They seem to have spared the children here and there.
POLYBIUS. No one else?
BUTEO (*pointing to the prisoners*). More of those. More raggle-taggle odds and ends that were spared or couldn't afford the knife to stick into their gut; and more children, starved and too astonished to be scared.
POLYBIUS. Will I ever forget that first child? You and your legionaries at one end of the street, swords, spears, helmets, breastplates, and that child at the other end, wondering whether all this was for her.
BUTEO. I'm grateful for one thing.
POLYBIUS. What's that?
BUTEO. The men aren't hungry for females. Otherwise, pah! Scipio was right, as usual. Our whores were bugled out the front door with great ceremony, and whistled back through the cellar with greater discretion. I know why you're smiling.
POLYBIUS. How your military purity was offended when you first met our harlots! And how your manly integrity was affronted when you saw Scipio winking! We couldn't calm you down!
BUTEO. Have you seen my uncle?
POLYBIUS. Oh yes.

BUTEO. How is he?

POLYBIUS. Wild. Keep searching, Buteo. He *demands* prisoners.

BUTEO. Well, mine's only one sector. Maybe the others will dig up some flesh for him. Has anyone found Retogenes yet? There's my great hope.

POLYBIUS. Killed in state and lying in the middle of the Council Chamber all by himself. He fooled us. Not like Hannibal, who went down with his ship, and came up again into ours.

BUTEO. And the others?

POLYBIUS. The others too. When Scipio saw them—

(*A shout in the distance*)

BUTEO. What's that? What are they shouting about? Good news maybe.

(*Another shout*)

POLYBIUS. Can't you make it out?

BUTEO. No!

POLYBIUS. They're crowning Scipio and giving him a new name.

BUTEO. What name?

POLYBIUS. He is now Scipio Numantinus, in honor of this victory.

BUTEO. Not bad. Whose idea was it?

POLYBIUS. Mine.

BUTEO. I shouldn't have asked!

POLYBIUS. I thought it might distract your uncle. Perhaps give him something to tell the Senate. I whispered the hint to Maximus, who passed it on to the tribunes and down the ladder. All quite spontaneous.

BUTEO. Never mind. He deserves it. I tell you he does.

POLYBIUS. I don't deny it.

(*Enter a soldier*)

SOLDIER. Beg your pardon, sir.

BUTEO. Yes?

SOLDIER. Audax is requesting permission to look for some of his people in the city.

BUTEO. Why not? Keep two men with him.

SOLDIER. Right, sir. (*He leaves*)

POLYBIUS. I hope he finds somebody.

BUTEO. Isn't his wife dead?

POLYBIUS. Yes. She died in one of the epidemics. Look!

(*Enter Scipio hurriedly, followed by Maximus and several officers. He wears a crown of laurel which he angrily throws aside*)

SCIPIO. Prisoners! Give me prisoners, not crowns! Look at this! this! this! Shambles! Think of the promises I made to my men! (*Looks at his officers*) And you! What are you staring at? Don't follow Numantinus about! Go to Fulvius Flaccus! Or get me some prisoners! Scatter and find me some prisoners! Scratch the rubble!

BUTEO. Uncle—

SCIPIO. And keep the children away from me! (*To the soldier who is standing guard over the old prisoners*) You—what are you doing with these people?

SOLDIER. This is a temporary receiving point, sir. I'm supposed to collect a dozen prisoners before I carry them away.

SCIPIO. Cut their ropes.

SOLDIER. Yes, sir.

SCIPIO. Tying up old people! Have I come to this? Shame.... There, let me do it myself. Old fellow, don't be scared. What's your name?

OLD WOMAN. He's hard of hearing, my lord.

SCIPIO. Give them something to eat, for pity's sake, and let them sit or stand.

OLD MAN. Thank you, your excellence.

SCIPIO. He thanks me. And the city is broken, the temples down, the citadel burned, the people dead. Worse than Carthage. Why did they kill themselves? Am I an ogre? Is this courage? Wasn't there a man among them man enough to throw the sword away? Insanity! Name it in your chronicle, Polybius: insanity! And write this in your chronicle: Scipio entered Numantia victorious again, and wept.

MAXIMUS (*aside to Scipio*). Brother, control yourself. You're making things worse for us. Proclaim it all went according to plan.

SCIPIO. Run away from me, Maximus. I'm done for. Give Fulvius a box of sweets.

MAXIMUS. What do you take me for?

SCIPIO. Where's Audax?

BUTEO. I allowed him to do a bit of searching on his own.

MAXIMUS. Under guard?

BUTEO. Sure.

MAXIMUS. Don't forget you've got Audax, brother. An authentic prize. The only survivor! It'll look dramatic in Rome.

SCIPIO. Dramatic! And I'll be the buffoon in the drama. (*Angry*) I had Rome knee deep in prisoners! Polybius!

POLYBIUS. Yes, sir.

SCIPIO (*taking him to one side*). I want you to keep looking for the gold, do you hear? I'll give you five hundred men to dig up foundations, debris, empty lots, anything. And we'll question every prisoner we get, babies, lunatics, cripples.

POLYBIUS. I'll keep at it, Scipio, but—

SCIPIO (*cold fury*). No buts. Find the gold.

POLYBIUS. I'll do all I can.
(*Enter a soldier*)
SOLDIER. Beg to report, sir.
SCIPIO. All right. What is it?
SOLDIER. Five more survivors in the south sector.
SCIPIO. What kind?
SOLDIER. A couple of them are old, but the others seem to be in pretty fair condition, sir.
SCIPIO. Bring them to me. I'll question them myself. (*The soldier leaves. To Polybius again, pointing to the survivors*) What information did you get out of these?
POLYBIUS. I haven't—
SCIPIO. Why not? Why not? (*He grabs the old man*) You! Try to remember— did you hear any rumors about the gold in the temple or treasury? Rumors!
OLD MAN (*frightened*). They burned the furniture.
SCIPIO. The gold!
OLD WOMAN. We don't know, my lord. He's a little deaf, and we made sandals, out by the gardens....
BUTEO. Uncle—
SCIPIO. Pah! (*He lets the old man go*) Where's Audax? Oh yes. Leave me alone! Stare at each other. (*He pokes in the debris*) Watch me returning to Rome now. Ah!
MAXIMUS. What's the matter?
SCIPIO. Nothing. A splinter. It's a foretaste, an omen. (*He sits down heavily and loses himself*)
BUTEO (*to Polybius*). What does he want you to do?
POLYBIUS. He wants me to find the gold.
MAXIMUS. The gold's melted down, gone, he knows it, damnation!
POLYBIUS. I know. But we'll keep digging.
SCIPIO (*looking at them suddenly*). Died for what? For the glory. But what's the use of glory you can't glory in? Idiots.
MAXIMUS (*to Polybius*). Go to him. All this talk about dying. It gives the wrong people ideas.
BUTEO. He owes it to the army to look cheerful.
(*A soldier has entered. He talks to Maximus*)
SOLDIER. A report from the western sector, general. May I hand it to Publius Cornelius Scipio?
MAXIMUS. Let me see it first. (*He reads it quickly. Polybius and Buteo look at him. He shakes his head*) Better not just now. I'll keep it. Go on back. (*Exit soldier*)
SCIPIO (*his back turned to them*). Yes, better keep it from Scipio. (*He rejoins the

group) All right, let's move along. I want to see every corner of the city. Buteo: the officers are to maintain absolute order, no grumbling, no petitions, no meetings. Let the prisoners be fed so they can be sold. Hands off the women and all officers to report under the citadel's ruins at sunset.
BUTEO. I'll see to everything.
SCIPIO. Where's Fulvius Flaccus?
BUTEO. Writing a dispatch.
MAXIMUS. Naturally.
SCIPIO. All right. You can go.
BUTEO (*to a couple of officers*). Follow me, please.
(*They leave*)
SCIPIO (*to Maximus*). What was that report?
MAXIMUS. From the western sector.
SCIPIO. Well?
MAXIMUS. Nothing.
POLYBIUS. Here's Audax now.
(*Enter Audax, escorted by two soldiers*)
OLD WOMAN (*whispers to the old man*) Look! Look! It's Audax!
SCIPIO. I need you to guide us, general. The important buildings we've searched. It's the private homes of the great ones we need to inspect from cellars to roofs. You know of course where they all are.
AUDAX. I do. (*To Scipio, then to Maximus, then to Polybius*). Have you found anyone?
POLYBIUS. Here and there, like those three over there.
AUDAX. Not even Marquinius?
SCIPIO. Marquinius?
AUDAX. Our high priest. I thought he at least might—
POLYBIUS. Lie on a heap with the others.
AUDAX. A few remain, thank God. My people.
(*He turns to the survivors. The second old man suddenly stands up*)
SECOND OLD MAN. Turncoat! Renegade!
OLD WOMAN (*terrified*). Hush, for pity's sake!
MAXIMUS. What's that?
SECOND OLD MAN. Renegade! Your woman had more guts than you, you slimy coward!
FIRST OLD MAN. I didn't say nothing!
SCIPIO. Take them away.
SOLDIER. All right, you. Get moving.
SECOND OLD MAN. Let the world know it! He knifed us in the back! He'll do the same for you, Romans! Renegade! May you rot like a leper!

OLD WOMAN. Hush up—oh God—
FIRST OLD MAN. I didn't say nothing!
SOLDIER. Go on, damn you, shove off, on your feet, all three of you!
SECOND OLD MAN. You're a mongrel without race—
POLYBIUS. Away!
SOLDIER. Move!
SECOND OLD MAN. I spit on you!
(*The survivors are gone but we still hear the old man bellowing*)
SECOND OLD MAN. I spit on you!
SCIPIO. Pay no attention, general. What do they know? That you tried to save them, that you did your best?
AUDAX (*low*). Give me your dagger, Scipio.
SCIPIO. I need you here and in Rome, general. Afterward....
AUDAX (*frantic*). Kill me!
(*The guards hold him*)
SCIPIO (*discreetly*). Guards, take General Audax back to the camp. Keep him safe for us.
GUARD. Come along, general.
AUDAX (*struggling*). I have a right to my sword!
GUARD. That's enough.
AUDAX. Give me a sword! Hands off! Respect! (*Sobbing, as the guards lead him away*) Kill the scoundrel! Kill me! (*He is gone*)
SCIPIO (*looking after him*). Once a victor in the field, then a trophy behind my chariot in Rome, finally a slave. So the wheel turns, Polybius. Note it in your chronicle.
MAXIMUS. What next, brother?
SCIPIO. Next? To my own hole, down with the wheel. Come here, Polybius. If I don't keep you busy you'll be running to Audax to hold his hand. Gold, Polybius, I need gold for the Senate, fasten your mind on that.
MAXIMUS. What about the troops?
SCIPIO (*wearily*). The troops. Make more promises. Organize thanksgiving services to the gods.
MAXIMUS. Why not athletic games, too? But try to look satisfied, Publius, that's what matters the most. Come on, give us a hearty word.
SCIPIO (*picking up the laurel crown he had thrown away*). There's my crown, brother. Keep it for your grandchildren. Tell them fine stories....

SCENE SEVEN: THE SLAVE

(The setting of Scene One again)

AUDAX. My life nauseated me. I thought the ghost of my son would rise—with such hatred in its face.... And still so, after all these years.... Not so my wife. Her look is gentle...I think.

MARANDRO. Ghosts are good company, old soldier.

AUDAX. Old soldier. Strange to meet somebody who remembers. My life went into another language, and now I'm hearing the old tongue again.... When I remind the young rascals hereabout who I was, "Run for your lives," they cry, "the old man's off on his old horse again!" All in fun, maybe, but Tuccia gives them a scolding anyway.

MARANDRO. T-t-tuccia? Oh yes, T-t-tuccia.

AUDAX. She's no queen or princess, but I've learned not to be fastidious. So has she! Look at me! She's as cozy as an old pillow, a good cook besides, and the children, well, they're not mine, but—I'm what they have, and that's a good feeling. I recite Homer to them:

> And if some god torments me
> Far out on the wine-dark sea,
> I shall endure it.

MARANDRO. If the t-t-townspeople could have guessed you'd be here with your T-t-tuccia, and reciting Homer to the children in your lap, they'd have howled twice as much as they did.

AUDAX. I wanted to give an example.

MARANDRO. That's a good one! There was a wild panic, I t-t-tell you, when they missed you.

AUDAX *(flaring up)*. It didn't keep you from struggling another six weeks and then killing and dying like drunkards. I watched it. I was in Scipio's camp, don't forget, I sent messages, talked to envoys, pleaded, but to no avail. Retogenes won. "Death before slavery!" And on the last day—

MARANDRO. Don't t-t-talk about it.

AUDAX. I entered Numantia with Scipio. Like a madman. Bellowing for life, looking for—looking for those I knew. Even Scipio broke down and wept.

MARANDRO. Well, Scipio is dead, you're telling stories—

AUDAX. Spain is a Roman province—

MARANDRO. And the farmer went back to his plough.

AUDAX. If he survived.

MARANDRO. Thank God, a few of us did. You know, to carry on the name of Numantia.

AUDAX. Don't talk rot, Marandro. Oh! I beg your pardon, sir. (*He rises*)

MARANDRO. Never mind. Sit down, sit down.

AUDAX. I forgot....

MARANDRO. That's all right.... How things do turn around, though....

AUDAX. You don't know the tenth part of it, Marandro. I saw Scipio lying in a bloody heap in Rome. And was I glad? Not even. A slave doesn't care. I've learned to dig in the fields and I've built bridges for armies and I've carried stones for monuments to governors and heroes, usually dead ones, and I've been struck in the mouth and I've bowed to idiots and I've had three ribs smashed and I've been sold and sold again and now I'm a broken old man.

MARANDRO. With T-t-t-uccia in a cabin.

AUDAX. Yes. To be sure. And now and then a good year or two. Which reminds me; I ought to be on my way attending to my duties. (*He doesn't move. Long silence*) Once I had a master eighty-seven years old. I don't remember where. I think in Smyrna. I fed him, dressed him, combed his three hairs, wiped the drool off his lips, sat him on his chamber pot, and scratched his back. That was the only pleasure left to him—so I scratched. But those were the good days. Look—(*he shows Marandro his ankle*) wait—here too. (*He shows his neck*) See the dent? Go on, touch it!

MARANDRO. I don't have to. I see it.

AUDAX. The ankle is from working in a chain gang in the fields. And in silence, or else, clak! Chained up at night, too. But that was pleasant compared to the neck. In Brundisium, in a bakery. They put a wooden saucer round your neck—I suppose you've never seen one?

MARANDRO. No—I—

AUDAX. They clap it around your windpipe — about this wide around so you can just see over the edge to work the dough, but you can't lift any of it to your mouth.

MARANDRO. Why remember those awful times? A quiet night like this. If I t-t-t-ake this place, I'll let you stay home nights, not like now.

AUDAX. That will be a good thing, though to tell you the truth—

MARANDRO. What?

AUDAX. One Numantian to another?

MARANDRO. Of course.

AUDAX. I don't really stay up all night. About midnight something comes over me and I creep back under the covers with Tuccia.

MARANDRO *(laughing)*. Old horse thief!

AUDAX *(chuckling)*. No harm done, you know. And if a tramp makes off with a few chickens now and then, well, the chickens are as happy with him as with the master. But it doesn't happen much. Mummius is in the house. Mummius is the lad with the serious face who takes care of you here.

MARANDRO. Yes, I know.

AUDAX. We're friends. He sleeps light, and he tells me to go home and warm my feet.

MARANDRO. So there it is.

AUDAX. So there it is. Oh well, I'd better be going. The horses don't sleep easy until I've gone by the stable.

MARANDRO. Yes, time for bed. *(They rise)* Good night, old soldier. It was a good t-t-t-talk. With luck, we'll meet again.

AUDAX. I'll be a faithful servant to you, sir.

MARANDRO. I'm sure of it. *(He presses some coins on Audax)* Here....

AUDAX. Oh no, sir, I won't—

MARANDRO. For the children. Not a word. I'm off.

AUDAX. For the children. Thank you.

MARANDRO. Not a word.

AUDAX. Thank you.

(Marandro is gone. Only his voice is heard)

MARANDRO. Oh, Audax.

AUDAX. Sir?

MARANDRO. There's some fruit on the t-t-table. T-t-take everything home.

AUDAX. I will, sir. *(Alone, he looks at the coins)* Shoes this winter, little devils! *(He takes one coin away and hides it)* You never know. *(He draws near the table)* Three peaches! Should I? *(He drops two peaches into a scrip and contemplates the third)* Beautiful.... I'll take a mouthful, and Tuccia will eat the rest. It isn't every day. *(He bites into the peach)* A rivulet of juice.... Enough. *(The half peach goes into the bag. He picks up his lantern, kneels at the fountain, wipes his mouth and drinks. He plays with the water)* Smile for me, affectionate water.... The moon winks in it.... Rivulet down the mountain. Juice of a peach. Sap in a tree. Moistness on a stone. Rain, rain and rain. The sea, and Venus rising from it. And the living body! Tears and blood, urine and milk, male seed and woman's secreted answer. A drooling baby.... *(He chuckles)*

(Mummius appears)

MUMMIUS. Where have you been, general? Did our guest keep you?

AUDAX. He did, but I'm on my way, trust me, friend.

MUMMIUS. I do. All the same, don't forget to lock the greenhouse.

AUDAX. I'll lock the greenhouse.

GENERAL AUDAX

MUMMIUS. And make sure the lamp by the master's door—
AUDAX. Has enough oil for the night. I'll see to it.
MUMMIUS. He doesn't like the dark.
AUDAX. I know. Neither do I.
MUMMIUS. Nor I. Good night, old friend.
AUDAX. Good night, Mummius.
(*Mummius vanishes. Audax picks up the lantern, looks at it, and starts to go. Darkness all around*)
AUDAX. Shine, little light, shine while you can....
(*He disappears*)

The End

Notes

General Audax saw the light in *First Stage* in 1967 (see my Note to *The Fatal French Dentist*) after having *nearly* been produced at the Lincoln Center in New York. It resurfaced as one of the works in my 2-volume *Collected Plays* of 1971-1972. Retitled *The Fall of Numantia*, it became one of the four *Reinventions* of 2002, where it was preceded by a Foreword concerning its sources in the *Numancia* of Cervantes and the Sixth Book of Appian's Roman History. Now it reverts to its original title, but in much altered shape since its earlier manifestations.

The citation from Jorge Guillén translates (as best I can) into "To be. Nothing else. It will do."

III

AMPHITRYON

(after Molière)

CHARACTERS

Amphitryon
Sosia, *his servant*
Alcmena
Cleanthis, *her servant*
Jupiter
Mercury
Night
Naucrates, *a Theban officer*
Argatiphonditas, *another Theban officer*

Except for the Prologue, the action throughout takes place in front of Amphitryon's house, the latter built with an upper-floor balcony

PROLOGUE

(Mercury is lolling in a cloud. Enter Night, in a chariot pulled by two horses. She lights the stars)

MERCURY. Stop, dear Lady Night. Jupiter has sent me to have a word with you in private. We need your help.
NIGHT. Oh, it's you, Lord Mercury! I'd never have known you, stretched out like a pasha.
MERCURY. Running fool's errands for Jupiter has worn me out. So I decided to snuggle into a cloud while waiting for you.
NIGHT. I hope you're being funny, Mercury. A god oughtn't to say he's worn out.
MERCURY. Gods aren't made of steel, you know.
NIGHT. That's true. But divine decorum must be kept up all the same. When a word threatens our sublimity, it should be left to mankind, where it belongs. Gods may rest, but only men are worn out.
MERCURY. It's easy for you to talk, pillowed in your carriage and pulled along by a couple of thoroughbreds. But look at me: a pedestrian divinity! And whose fault is it? The poets', damn their cheek, who gave each god a comfortable situation in life, but left me on my feet like a village mail-carrier. Is this justice? I am Jupiter's own messenger: an acknowledged celebrity. And in all modesty, considering the work I do for him, I deserve a coach more than anybody else on Olympus.
NIGHT. What's to be done? But why are you down on the poets? They've tied the dearest wings to your heels.
MERCURY. True. Now I fly faster. Does that wear me out any less?
NIGHT. Have it your way, Lord Mercury. What can I do for you?
MERCURY. Oh—I'd almost forgotten. It's about Jupiter. He has found a new love and asks you please to spread your dark cloak over it. I imagine you have heard that Jupiter is sometimes in love. You may even have heard that he sometimes neglects the theological virtues, turns as human as Tom, Dick and Harry, and practices tricks, I hate to say it, to seduce the girls if they happen to be reluctant. Tonight it's Alcmena's turn. While her husband, General Amphitryon, is out of town with the Theban army, Jupiter, disguised as that same Amphitryon, is relieving his godly urges in

AMPHITRYON

Alcmena's arms.

NIGHT. How very odd. I never heard of a lover masquerading as a husband.

MERCURY. As a rule there are more effective ways of pleasing a lady. But Amphitryon and Alcmena are newlyweds. She is still aflame over the idea of a spouse.

NIGHT. Well, bravo for Jupiter, but I'll never understand the reason for these disguises of his.

MERCURY. He wants to taste a bit of everything. It's divine wisdom, make no mistake about it. Because it's a bore to be always the chief, the terror of the underlings, looking as if a mosquito wouldn't bite you. And how do you make love with a crown on your head that weighs a ton, and a thunderbolt in each hand? No, Jupiter is a connoisseur of pleasures and knows how to stoop for them. In order to penetrate wherever he pleases, he gives himself the slip, so to speak, and runs about in disguises.

NIGHT. Fair enough, if he only paraded as a man. But when I see him turn into a swan, a serpent, or a bull, I think it's downright unrefined, and I don't wonder that it makes people talk.

MERCURY. Let the fools talk. These transformations are delightful in their own mysterious way. What do your prudes understand? Jupiter understands. He is a gourmet, I tell you. He knows that our dumb creatures aren't half as dumb as people think.

NIGHT. Well, let him be careful. One of these days he'll be turned out to beg in the street by some thin god who works hard, makes large promises to the mob, and stays clear of women. (*Mercury groans*) You'll be retired too. Mark my words.

MERCURY. And you?

NIGHT. I am the night. I'm always needed.

MERCURY. Shall we get back to the present and be cheerful?

NIGHT. By all means. But if the girl is making Jupiter happy, what else does he want, and how can I help?

MERCURY. Keep the darkness dark a bit longer. Tell your horses to go slow. Give him time to display his talents. And delay his rival's return.

NIGHT. Thank you very much! A respectable job for a lady! Do you know what they call this?

MERCURY. Don't be prissy. What we ask of you is low only when the low-born do it. *We* are in a position, I hope, to give fragrant names to anything we choose to do.

NIGHT. So be it. You know more about these matters than I. I'm an innocent. I bow to your experience.

MERCURY. Tut tut tut. Your reputation doesn't bear looking into either, my sweet. You've covered up more than your share of dubious enterprises. I don't think we two need to stand on ceremony with one another.

NIGHT. Enough! We are what we are. Period. Let's not give mankind a chance to laugh by flinging unsavory truths at each other.

MERCURY. My lips are sealed. Well, my dear, you know what to do. *My* next assignment is to change from Mercury into Sosia.

NIGHT. Sosia?

MERCURY. Amphitryon's lackey. What a come-down!

NIGHT. As for me, I'll find a snug place in this hemisphere and just hover for a while.

MERCURY. I'm off!

NIGHT. Good night, Mercury.

ACT ONE

(Before Amphitryon's house. Enter Sosia carrying a lantern)

SOSIA. Who's there? Whew! Every step I take my tremors get worse. Gentlemen, I'm everybody's friend! It takes a moron to walk the countryside this time of night. My master Amphitryon, after defeating the enemy, what's their name again? decided to turn against me, his own servant. Because if he knew the meaning of love thy neighbor, would he have sent me off on a night as pitch black as this? Besides, it's a weird kind of night that seems to go on and on. Simply my coward's imagination, of course. And yet he might have waited until daytime to send me home with the details of his victory. Sosia, you're nothing but a miserable slave. Oh, it's a hard life, serving the rich and mighty. Everything has to revolve around them. Nature itself has to kneel to them. Night or day, hail or wind, storm, heat, frost—when they say run we run, when they say jump we jump. And after twenty years of running and jumping we're grateful if we squeeze a thankyou out of them. They bawl us out if we scratch an earlobe or burp after dinner. But like idiots we go on serving them. Why? The fact is, even a flunky likes prestige. The fellows who wait on the bourgeoisie look up to us. Hey, isn't that our house at last? Good. Suddenly I feel plucky again. Now to report to Alcmena. I'd better work out a professional account of the battle that knocked out the enemy. But how the Furies can I do it if I wasn't there? Never mind. I'll talk about cuts and thrusts, charges and melees, as if I'd been in the heat of the action myself. I won't be the first who gave a thrilling account of a campaign he never saw. I'll rehearse my speech before going in. Here's the room to which I'll be led as messenger. My lantern is Alcmena. "Madam, General Amphitryon, my lord and your master, his mind forever dwelling upon your ravishing charms, has chosen me over all the others of his entourage to apprise you of his victory, and to utter in his place the urgency of his amorous impatience." Not bad for a beginning. I ought to write a book. Now for Alcmena. "Is it true, my good, my honest, my brave Sosia? My heart bounces with joy to see you again. I missed you horribly." "You overwhelm me, madam. But we must speak of the General." "Ah yes. And how fares Amphitryon?" "He fares as a man of courage, madam, if the occasion demands it." Unimpeachable, and yet sly. "And when will the dear man return to satisfy my desires?" "As promptly as possible, madam, and yet later than he wishes." Witty, witty! "But in what frame of mind has this war left him? What does he say? What does he do?" "He says little and does much. He is all military." You dog, where did you learn to make phrases? "Now brave Sosia, tell me all about the victory, and the part you played in it." "Gladly, my lovely lady; and, without boasting, I am in a position to give you an intimate account of the battle. Here, shall we say, is the town of Telebos. There we have the river. This is where our men are encamped. And this is a stretch occupied by the enemy. His infantry commands a height at this point here. His right flank is protected by his cavalry. After prayers to the gods on both sides—the same gods, of course—the trumpets sound. The enemy, panting after our blood, divides his force in three. He charges. But we promptly cool his fire, as I will show you next. Here you see our main body, mad for action; here King Creon's own archers; and here myself with the brave vanguard. We strike like a flash of—" (*He hears a noise*) What's that? The vanguard doesn't like noises. Who goes there?

(*Enter Mercury from Amphitryon's house. He looks like Sosia*)

MERCURY (*aside*). Let's drive this chatterbox away from the house. We don't want him troubling our lovers at their pretty conference, do we?

SOSIA (*aside*) Maybe it's a false alarm. But who knows? The world is full of cutthroats. It's so dark here, it feels like it's been midnight for three hours. Phoebus must be drunk in bed when he should be out driving the sun. I'll finish rehearsing inside the house.

MERCURY (aside). The rascal is abusing the gods! This calls for reprisals. I'll steal not only his appearance but his name as well. Oh, I'm going to enjoy this.

SOSIA. Ye gods! Who's that ugly brute standing in front of our house? I'm done for. My knees are giving way. Wait. I'll try singing a song and acting

AMPHITRYON

sure of myself. (*He sings*)

MERCURY. Who's the dog barking out there as if he owned the world? Does he want to feel the back of my hand?

SOSIA (*aside*). He doesn't like music.

MERCURY. I haven't broken any bones for a week. What I need is a head or a shoulder to exercise myself on.

SOSIA (*aside*). Is this a man or a devil? I've never been so scared in my life. But wait. Maybe he's faking. Maybe he's as frightened as I am. A low braggart! I won't have anybody call me chicken. I may not be brave, but I can at least look it. Remember, Sosia: he's alone; I'm pretty strong; I've a powerful master; and this is our house.

MERCURY. Who goes there?

SOSIA. Me.

MERCURY. Who, me?

SOSIA. Me. (*Aside*) Courage, Sosia.

MERCURY. Me master or me servant?

SOSIA. Servant to some, master to others.

MERCURY. Where are you heading?

SOSIA. To where I was going.

MERCURY. Your answers are offensive to me.

SOSIA. Delighted.

MERCURY. By fair means or foul, I must know, traitor, what you do, whence you come, whither you are going, and where you dwell.

SOSIA. What I do? Both good and evil. Whence I come? From a location. Whither I am going? Elsewhere. Where I dwell? At home.

MERCURY. You're a wit, are you, a man of consequence. I'd like to become more closely acquainted with you.

SOSIA. Thank you.

MERCURY. I believe in human contact.

SOSIA. Me too.

MERCURY. Here. (*He boxes Sosia's ear*)

SOSIA. Hey! This is no laughing matter.

MERCURY. Of course it is. I wanted to match your witticisms.

SOSIA. But you hurt me, damn you!

MERCURY. Impossible. This was one of my drowsy blows.

SOSIA. If I was as quick as you, the feathers would be flying by now.

MERCURY. You haven't seen anything yet. Why don't we take advantage of the last quiet minute of your life to continue our conversation?

SOSIA. I'm going.

MERCURY (*stopping him*). *Where* are you going?

AMPHITRYON

SOSIA. I'm going to have that door opened for me. Why are you stopping me?
MERCURY. If you take another step towards that door, I'll be obliged to pulverise you.
SOSIA. What's that? You dare prevent me from going home?
MERCURY. Home? What do you mean?
SOSIA. Home. I mean home.
MERCURY. You rogue! You call this home?
SOSIA. I do. Isn't this where Amphitryon lives?
MERCURY. What of it?
SOSIA. I'm his servant.
MERCURY. You?
SOSIA. Precisely.
MERCURY. His servant?
SOSIA. Positively.
MERCURY. Amphitryon's servant?
SOSIA. Amphitryon's top servant.
MERCURY. And your name is—
SOSIA. Sosia.
MERCURY. Would you repeat that?
SOSIA. Sosia.
MERCURY. Let's be calm. Do you understand that before the sun rises, your bones will be paving the road from here to Hades?
SOSIA. Why this tantrum?
MERCURY. How dare you presume to take the name of Sosia?
SOSIA. I'm not taking it, I always had it.
MERCURY. A lie! An impudent lie! You maintain to my face that Sosia is your name?
SOSIA. I'd rather be called King Creon, but I'm plain Sosia to my wife, my mother, and my tax collector.
MERCURY (*pulling out a stick*). Do you see this object?
SOSIA. I do.
MERCURY. What is it?
SOSIA. It's awfully dark. An emaciated tree?
MERCURY. It's a stick. I'm attached to it and I'd hate to break it.
SOSIA. Why should you break it?
MERCURY. Because I'm going to apply it to your backside, you infinite villain. (*He beats Sosia*).
SOSIA. Police! Citizens! Help!
MERCURY. What? Are you making noises?

SOSIA. You're beating me black and blue and I'm supposed to keep my mouth shut?

MERCURY. I've only begun—

SOSIA. Stop! Is it fair to strike a coward?

MERCURY. It's not fair but it's fun.

SOSIA. No, it isn't. A true sportsman wants a challenge that's worthy of him.

MERCURY. All right, I'll stop. Provided you admit you're not Sosia.

SOSIA. Your stick didn't change my name. The only difference is that now I'm Sosia plus twenty lumps.

MERCURY. A few more will improve your thinking.

SOSIA. No, no! Enough of your stick. I'm no match for you. My mouth is shut.

MERCURY. Are you still Sosia, though? Speak, you clown!

SOSIA. I am whatever you say I am. A stick always knows the truth.

MERCURY. Did you tell me that your name was Sosia once upon a time?

SOSIA. So I thought up to now, but your stick proves that I was mistaken.

MERCURY. I am Sosia.

SOSIA. You are Sosia?

MERCURY. Yes, and woe to anyone who denies the fact.

SOSIA. But will you permit me—in the name of our holy gods—to ask you a question?

MERCURY. Ask away.

SOSIA. But you promise to keep your stick to yourself?

MERCURY. I declare a truce.

SOSIA. Then tell me, what can anybody gain from a penniless plebeian's name? And furthermore, how can Jupiter himself prevent me from being me? And finally who put this bat in your belfry?

MERCURY (*raising his stick*). Say your prayers.

SOSIA. Truce! Truce! You promised!

MERCURY. Dog! Scoundrel! Impostor!

SOSIA. That's better. Bawl me out. Verbal blows I don't mind.

MERCURY. The truce is broken.

SOSIA. Very well. But I refuse to snuff myself out for your sake. I am, and stick nor stone can take myself away from me. Is not evidence evidence? Am I not awake and sane? Did not Amphitryon bid me report his victory to Alcmena and tell her he loves her more than his medals? Didn't I arrive here a short while ago? Am I not holding a lantern in my hand? Didn't I find you standing in front of our house? Didn't I address you politely? Aren't you taking advantage of my cowardice to keep me from going home? Haven't you batted me about like a tennis ball? I wish the facts were otherwise, but facts are facts, I worship facts, so let me go home.

MERCURY. Stay where you are! *I* make the facts. Everything you said I take for myself—everything except the knocks and lumps. Those are yours for keeps.

SOSIA. But Amphitryon sent me from the camp to Alcmena; I came ashore at twilight; I walked all night shivering and shaking. Ask this lantern, it's been with me every step of the way.

MERCURY. You're lying. *I'm* the man Amphitryon sent to Alcmena; *I'm* the man who's come to announce his victory; I'm Sosia, son of Davus, jailed for stealing sheep, brother of Arpagos the drunken tailor of Larymna; and husband to the prude Cleanthis whose nagging drives me to an early grave. I'm the Sosia who was flogged in Thebes for failure to pay his bills to the bartender, and branded on his right buttock for assaulting the poet Cylindrus with an uncooked halibut.

SOSIA (*aside*). I'll be damned. How could he know all this without being Sosia? I'm beginning to believe him. And now that I look at him, I see he's a lot like me—his height, his face, his gestures. I'll ask him a few questions to clear up the mystery. (*Aloud*) Tell me, what did Amphitryon receive as his share of the booty?

MERCURY. A ring set with five large diamonds, the favorite jewel of our enemy general—while he was alive.

SOSIA. What does he intend to do with this ring?

MERCURY. He intends to give it to his wife. Haven't you got some harder questions for me?

SOSIA. Here's one. Where is this ring now?

MERCURY. In a little casket sealed with my master's arms.

SOSIA (*aside*). All this is true. I'm losing hold of myself. I've already surrendered to the logic of power; now I'm beginning to yield to the power of logic. And yet, as I pinch myself and look over my memories, I'm still tempted to think that I'm me. How can I resolve the question once and for all? I have it. Something I did alone, something I did unseen by anybody, nobody can know unless he's me. My next question will strike him dumb. (*Aloud*) In the heat of battle, sir, what did you do in Amphitryon's tent to which you ran as quickly as your legs would carry you?

MERCURY. I pounced on a ham—

SOSIA (*aside*). Bulls eye!

MERCURY. Took it prisoner, executed it without a court martial, hacked two thick slices out of its hide, stuffed them bravely into my mouth, and washed them down with a wine reserved for our officers. This done, my courage rose and I began to think bloody thoughts on behalf of our fighting men.

AMPHITRYON

SOSIA (*aside*). This is conclusive. Aristotle himself couldn't refute him, unless he was hidden in the bottle. (*Aloud*) I give up. You've proved that you're Sosia. If anybody denies it I'll call him a nitwit. But now tell me, who do you want me to be? Because I must be somebody—I think.

MERCURY. I'll strike a bargain with you. The moment I decide to stop being Sosia, you can be him again. But until then, you're a dead man if you try to impersonate me.

SOSIA. I submit. Farewell. Nothing fatigues a man like not being who he is. I've also lost my faith in the laws of nature, and the best solution is to go to bed. (*He walks towards the house*)

MERCURY. You clown! I'll show you which way bed lies. (*He beats him again*)

SOSIA. Oh, ah, oh! I'll be in a wheelchair for a month! The devil take this errand, I'm going back to our ship.

(*Exit*)

MERCURY. Driven away at last, the stubborn rogue. I've punished him for a dozen pieces of skulduggery nobody knows about except us on Mount Olympus. Ah, here comes Jupiter, with his Alcmena clinging to him.

(*Enter Jupiter in the guise of Amphitryon, Alcmena, and Cleanthis*)

JUPITER. My Alcmena!

ALCMENA. My Amphitryon! Oh my valiant soldier, my proud general! Cleanthis, let the slaves bring torches so that I may feast my eyes on him.

JUPITER. No, no, forbid them, my dove, forbid them. True, to see you better would enchant me, but I must keep my visit a secret. I have been a truant from my duties in the field. I stole a few hours in order to rush into your arms. What would King Creon say if he discovered my absence? And wouldn't the soldiers grumble? Wouldn't the agitators point their greasy fingers at me? Let us allow no witnesses to our forbidden sport.

ALCMENA. My hero! Your triumphs, your glory, your prowesses in war fill me with pride. But the soldier robs me of the husband. The noises of battle alarm the whispers of love. I dream of blows, wounds, and shouts. I tremble for you during the day. At night I wake up with cries of terror.

JUPITER. Every word you speak lights a new fire in my heart. To love and to be loved in return is a joy unknown to the very gods. (*Aside*) God knows. (*Aloud*) And yet, the perfection of my happiness is marred by a single tiny consideration.

ALCMENA. What is it, my best?

JUPITER. Could it be that you embrace me only out of a sense of wifely duty? Oh Alcmena, I want to be desired for myself; I do not care to be loved because I hold the gloomy title of husband.

ALCMENA. What a strange apprehension! Being your wife allows me to perform all that my passion for you urges.

JUPITER. But *my* passion for you is that of a lover, not of a husband! My happiness is a delicate blossom; it shivers when a grain of dust touches it; every shadow makes it wince. In me you see a husband and a lover. But only the lover matters to me. The husband stands in my way. The lover resents the husband. I beg you to neglect the one and lavish yourself upon the other. The rites of love are desecrated when they are performed as a duty. No. Away with the husband. Grant him your duty, but give the lover your kisses.

ALCMENA. Hush, Amphitryon. If someone overheard you, it might be said that you were less than altogether wise.

JUPITER. No, I am wiser than you think. But now I fear we must part. I must count my survivors, sort out the spoils, decorate the officers, and dine with the king.

ALCMENA. Alas, why was this night so brief?

JUPITER. Promise, Alcmena, when you think of me—think of the lover, and forget the — you know what.

ALCMENA. What Jupiter has brought together I cannot separate. Lover and husband are one and the same in my heart.

JUPITER. But the lover gives you this parting kiss.

ALCMENA. And the wife, this.

(*She returns to the house. Jupiter watches her until she is gone*)

JUPITER. Am I ever glad I invented flesh and blood.

(*Exit*)

CLEANTHIS (*aside*). Heavenly days! I'd lick my fingers over such a husband. How he fondled her! How he kissed her! And what a contrast with the baboon I'm chained to.

MERCURY (*aside*). Jupiter enjoyed Alcmena, and I'm left behind with this. Which proves that there are menials even among the gods. It's all relative, you see. In the land of billionaires, a millionaire's a pauper. Let's see if I can sneak away to tell Madam Night it's time to let the sun out of the cellar.

CLEANTHIS. Don't move! Where do you think you're going on your tiptoes?

MERCURY. On my tiptoes? Oh, so I was! I thought Alcmena might have gone to sleep. Naturally, I have to follow Amphitryon. Duty, you know.

CLEANTHIS. What's the hurry, you lout? Why so anxious to get away from me?

MERCURY. Don't upset yourself, dearest. We've years and years of life together ahead of us.

CLEANTHIS. That's no reason to leave without a nice word, you tramp.

MERCURY. Devil take nice words! I've run out of them after fifteen years of wedlock. When a couple's been married that long, every conversation has been conversed.

CLEANTHIS. Look at Amphitryon, you dog; watch how he courts Alcmena; and then blush for the frozen fish you are to your wife.

MERCURY. But they're newlyweds; we're an old married pair. What would people think if they saw me mooning over you like a puppy?

CLEANTHIS. Are you saying I'm too old to be desired?

MERCURY. I wouldn't dream of saying it, but one year the cup runneth over, and another year the well goeth dry.

CLEANTHIS. You don't deserve a faithful wife like me, you louse.

MERCURY. Your faithfulness, hang it, hasn't added a day to my life or a penny to my bank account. I'll take less faithfulness, thank you, and more peace in the house.

CLEANTHIS. I don't believe it! The villain scolds me for being an honest wife!

MERCURY. What I like in a wife is a sweet disposition. Your virtue makes so much noise, it gives me a standing headache.

CLEANTHIS. You want the kind of wife, do you, who'll caress her husband with one hand and her lover with the other.

MERCURY. What I don't know doesn't hurt me; and come to think of it, what I do know doesn't either. My motto is, "Less virtue, more peace."

CLEANTHIS. You wouldn't object if I flung myself to a lover?

MERCURY. Not a bit, if it brought down your voice and improved your character. In short, I prefer easy-going sin to oppressive virtue. But now I must follow Amphitryon. Goodbye, wife of my loins, with a parting kiss.

CLEANTHIS. So-so, so-so. (*Exit Mercury*) Ha! What keeps me from planting a set of horns on that scoundrel's head? (*She pulls out a mirror and looks at herself*) Seductive wench! Oh how I hate my virtue!

ACT TWO

(*Enter Amphitryon and Sosia*)

AMPHITRYON. Do you realize I've cut a man's liver out for a tenth of the rubbish I've taken from you? You're lucky I'm an officer and can't dirty my sword by sticking it into a commoner's gut.

SOSIA. If you're going to fly off the handle every time I open my mouth, I

AMPHITRYON

won't say another word and you'll always be right.

AMPHITRYON. All right. I'll hold my temper down and question you for the last time before I go see my wife. Stand tall, you slouch, look smart, stomach in. Focus on the facts. Make your answers brief and to the point.

SOSIA. Before I begin, sir, and so we sing in the same key, if you know what I mean, please tell me, shall I reply as my conscience dictates, or as one usually does to a superior? Shall I tell you the truth, or make you happy?

AMPHITRYON. I want the facts, pleasant or unpleasant. I hate yes-men, bootlickers, and lickspittles.

SOSIA. I'm glad. Go ahead and question me again; I promise to be honest with you.

AMPHITRYON. Now then, when I gave you my verbal orders—

SOSIA. I left at once. The skies were veiled as if in a velvet of deep mourning—

AMPHITRYON. What? What? What?

SOSIA. It was dark. I set off, cursing you every step of the way for saddling me with this mission.

AMPHITRYON. Impudent rascal!

SOSIA. Just say the word, sir, and I'll tell you all the fibs you like.

AMPHITRYON. Oh how I long to find one loving slave! But go on. What happened on the way?

SOSIA. The branches kept cracking, the gravel kept crunching, and I kept jumping out of my skin.

AMPHITRYON. You're a snivelling coward.

SOSIA. Exactly. Isn't it funny how some people love to run into danger, and others enjoy running out of it? I wonder if it's heredity or—

AMPHITRYON. Get back to your story. You arrived where we're standing now.

SOSIA. No, sir.

AMPHITRYON. What do you mean?

SOSIA (*moves Amphitryon a foot*). Here's where I arrived.

AMPHITRYON. Jackass!

SOSIA. Yes sir. Before going in to greet Alcmena, I stopped inorder to prepare my speech. I wanted to strike the right note and do justice to your victory.

AMPHITRYON. Then what happened?

SOSIA. Somebody interrupted me.

AMPHITRYON. Who was it?

SOSIA. Me. Another Sosia, who insisted he was your emissary, and who knew as much about all our secrets as the me who's addressing you now.

AMPHITRYON. Extravagance!

SOSIA. The truth. Whether pure and simple is Jupiter knows. This other self had beaten me to the house. In short, I had arrived before my arrival.

AMPHITRYON. What am I supposed to make of this drivel? You were either dreaming, or drunk, or crazy.

SOSIA. None of these, I swear. I'm a solid citizen, a man universally trusted and loved, I never drink on duty, and I don't dream when I sleep. Believe me, I found two Sosias here. One of them is in the house right now, and the other is talking to you. The one who's talking to you is gentle, tolerant, and dead tired; the other is vicious, but hale and frisky, and has only one ambition in life: to break fifty bones a day.

AMPHITRYON. I must be some kind of saint: I am standing here and attending to this imbecile without bursting a blood vessel.

SOSIA. If you're about to lose your temper, let me know and I'll shut my mouth.

AMPHITRYON. No. I promised to listen quietly and I will. But tell me: in your own opinion, is this story of yours credible?

SOSIA. Not in the least. I rebelled against it like a man who knows a horse from an ass. I called my other self an impostor. But finally the evidence struck me so hard that I was compelled to recognize myself in him: handsome, a noble pride in his bearing, excellent manners, a trustworthy look—in short, unmistakably me from head to toe; and we'd have become fast friends if he hadn't been so unfriendly.

AMPHITRYON. Patience, patience! Did you go into the house?

SOSIA. Go into the house! That's a joke! How could I go into the house? Would I listen to reason? Didn't I slam the door in my face?

AMPHITRYON. What? What? What?

SOSIA. Didn't I give myself a terrible pasting? Look.

AMPHITRYON. Somebody hit you.

SOSIA. Somebody hit me.

AMPHITRYON. Who was it?

AMPHITRYON *and* SOSIA *together*. Me.

SOSIA. Not the present me. The other one, who's as strong as four of us put together.

AMPHITRYON. Let's get to the point. Did you see my wife?

SOSIA. No.

AMPHITRYON. Why not?

SOSIA. Do I have to repeat? I was turned away. Don't ask! By the me that barred the door; the me that made me change my tune; the me that monopolized me; the valiant me that vented his rage on the pitiful me; in short, the me who's sitting in your house, and probably drawing my meager wages.

AMPHITRYON

AMPHITRYON. I've heard enough. If I listen to your gibberish any longer I'll turn into a lunatic myself. Follow me. Stop! Here comes Alcmena. Radiant, beautiful girl! She doesn't expect me. I'll surprise her.

(*Enter Alcmena and Cleanthis*)

ALCMENA. Let us offer a sacrifice to the gods, Cleanthis, to thank them for granting my beloved Amphitryon a glorious victory and a safe return home. (*She sees Amphitryon*) Heavens!

AMPHITRYON. Greetings, beloved wife!

ALCMENA. Back so soon?

AMPHITRYON. What? Here's a strange how d'you do! "Back so soon" is not what I'd call a sentimental effusion.

ALCMENA. My dear—

AMPHITRYON. I was hoping for something more ardent; something like "away so long, my darling!"

ALCMENA. So long?

AMPHITRYON. I grant you that I haven't been absent forever; but I am told that even fifteen minutes of separation is a quarter of an hour too long for true-hearted lovers.

ALCMENA. I don't see—

AMPHITRYON. No, Alcmena. That was a cry from the heart, confess it. Had you been awaiting my return with the impatience of a loving wife, you wouldn't have greeted me with "back so soon." This is a blow.

ALCMENA. I'm speechless. What's the meaning of this tirade? If you're disappointed in me, frankly I don't know what satisfies you. Last night, when you returned from the wars, I greeted you, I hope, as tenderly as any woman ever welcomed a man.

AMPHITRYON. What's that?

ALCMENA. Indeed, you showed by word and gesture that you were more than delighted with me, and you left me at dawn like a man rising from a banquet.

AMPHITRYON. What are you saying?

ALCMENA. And since you've hardly left, I don't see how I'm to blame if your sudden return took me by surprise.

AMPHITRYON. I understand. Because you longed for me, Alcmena, you dreamed that I had come back. And having treated me kindly in your dream, you feel you have done your duty to me.

ALCMENA. Have you forgotten our night together? Are you running a fever, Amphitryon?

AMPHITRYON. A fever! A cunning invention, madam.

ALCMENA. As cunning, sir, as the dream you invented.

AMPHITRYON. I mentioned the dream, madam, in order to save appearances after your strange words to me.

ALCMENA. I alluded to the fever, sir, in order to place your outlandish remarks in a favorable light.

AMPHITRYON. Let us drop the fever, Alcmena.

ALCMENA. Let us drop the dream, Amphitryon.

AMPHITRYON. This is not a proper subject for banter.

ALCMENA. That is probably why I'm beginning to be angry.

AMPHITRYON. Let's be serious.

ALCMENA. I'm in no mood for jests.

AMPHITRYON. Are you maintaining to my face that I've been here before?

ALCMENA. Are you denying to my face that you were here last night?

AMPHITRYON. I? Here? Last night?

ALCMENA. Came last night and went this morning.

AMPHITRYON. Came and went? (*Aside*) I'm thunderstruck. My head is spinning. Sosia?

SOSIA. Yes, sir. Her mind is fuddled. She needs a laxative.

AMPHITRYON. Alcmena, in Jupiter's name, take hold of yourself and think before you speak.

ALCMENA. I will. The entire household saw you coming home, Amphitryon. And if more proof is needed, and if you're really suffering from amnesia, tell me where else would I have heard of your latest victory, the death of Pterelaus at your own hand, and the diamond ring you tore from his dead finger?

AMPHITRYON. How many diamonds?

ALCMENA. Five.

AMPHITRYON. And what did I do with it?

ALCMENA. You gave it to me, of course.

AMPHITRYON. Where is it?

ALCMENA. Here. Look at it.

AMPHITRYON. Sosia?

SOSIA. Impossible. The ring lies in this casket here which has never left my person.

AMPHITRYON. Break the seal!

SOSIA (*opening the casket*). It's empty, by god! Either a magician has robbed us, or the ring, knowing it was meant for Alcmena, broke loose from the box and flew to her.

AMPHITRYON (*aside*). You gods who preside over the earth, what is the meaning of this tangle? What is your secret purpose?

SOSIA. We're in the same galley now, sir; you've got a double too.

AMPHITRYON. Silence!

ALCMENA. What is the matter, Amphitryon? Please explain.

AMPHITRYON (*aside*). This is uncanny; my two feet are solidly planted on the earth, but what is the earth planted on? I must investigate. But do I really want to know the truth?

ALCMENA. You've seen the ring, Amphitryon. Do you still deny that you returned it to me?

AMPHITRYON. No, I do not. My apologies. But may I—will you be so kind as to tell me what happened?

ALCMENA. Are you still pretending it wasn't you?

AMPHITRYON. Forgive me, but the fever—remember, I had a fever.

ALCMENA. And it blotted out all that took place between us?

AMPHITRYON. Between us? Ah! Let me hear the whole story.

ALCMENA. It's not a long one. I ran forward to greet you, I took you in my arms, I cried with joy.

AMPHITRYON. (*aside*). And I burst with rage!

ALCMENA. You gave me this magnificent ring. You spoke of your love, the torment of separation, the violence of your desire, the impossibility of staying away from me. Never have I seen you so tender, so passionate.

AMPHITRYON (*aside*). Every word stabs me to death. (*Aloud*) And you?

ALCMENA. I took it all in. It was divine, Amphitryon.

AMPHITRYON. And afterwards, if you please?

ALCMENA. We asked each other a thousand anxious questions, each one interrupted by a kiss. Then dinner was served. A romantic tête-à-tête by candlelight. And then we went to bed.

AMPHITRYON. Together?

ALCMENA. How else?

AMPHITRYON (*aside*). I asked, and I was answered. Are you happy now, you cretin?

ALCMENA. Your face is purple, Amphitryon. Did I do wrong by lying down at your side?

AMPHITRYON (*bellowing*). It wasn't at my side! Whoever asserts that I was here last night is telling a bloody lie! (*Aside*) Ye gods, I am trumpeting my disgrace to the world. (*A soft bellow*) Trollop!

ALCMENA. Oh!

AMPHITRYON (*his voice gradually rises again*). No more sugared words! No more consideration! Fury and vengeance!

ALCMENA. Against whom? What have I done? How am I guilty?

AMPHITRYON. I don't know; but I wasn't here! And I'm capable of murder, I tell you!

AMPHITRYON

ALCMENA. Suddenly I see it all. What a fool I was! You're a villain, a schemer! You want to be free of me, you want to cast me off, so you pretend I was unfaithful to you. Well, you've succeeded. The chain is broken. I divorce you. You're free.

AMPHITRYON. That's the least of it! Count yourself lucky if I go no further. You've dishonored me. I'll prove it. Your own brother is my adjutant. He was at my side every minute of the day and night till I left him to come here. I'll call him and expose you; I'll find out who was tête-à-têting with you or I'll hang every lecher in Greece to make sure I'm avenged.

SOSIA. Sir—

AMPHITRYON. Don't move till I return. (*Exit*)

CLEANTHIS (*to Alcmena*). Your husband is mad!

ALCMENA. Don't talk to me and don't follow me! (*She returns to the house*)

CLEANTHIS (*aside*). I still say he's balmy. But the brother will put everything right again.

SOSIA (*aside*). Too bad for Amphitryon. I wonder if everybody alive has suddenly grown a double. Now the question is, if *his* second me helped himself to Alcmena, what did mine do? I'll approach the subject discreetly.

CLEANTHIS (*aside*). Let's see whether the brute is going to talk to me. I'll act indifferent.

SOSIA (*aside*). Why this thirst for knowledge, my boy? What harm does a little ignorance do? No; I can't stand being in the dark. It's a human weakness—this laboring to discover what you're better off not knowing. (*Aloud*) Nice sunny day, isn't it?

CLEANTHIS. Don't you come near me, you viper!

SOSIA. Hey, what's the matter? Always grouchy, always sulking over nothing.

CLEANTHIS. What do you call nothing?

SOSIA. I call nothing what is called nothing in rhyme or in prose; and nothing, as you know, means—precious little.

CLEANTHIS. You miserable leftover of a man, I should scratch your eyes out to teach you what a woman can do when she's been wronged.

SOSIA. What now?

CLEANTHIS. You call nothing the insults of last night?

SOSIA. Tell me more.

CLEANTHIS. Go on, play innocent. Tell me you didn't come back either, no more than your master.

SOSIA. No—I did, I *feel* I did. Would I try to fool you? But I caught the fever from Amphitryon, the one you heard about, and was smitten with amnesia too.

CLEANTHIS. You think you'll wiggle—

AMPHITRYON

SOSIA. No, I swear; believe me; I was in a fearful state; drunk too; I thought alcohol would bring my temperature down. I'm sure I did things I'm going to regret, but I don't remember what.

CLEANTHIS. I waited up for you half the night. Amphitryon had told me you'd be coming. But when you arrived, you were a block of marble. I had to remind you that you have a wife. And when I tried to kiss you, you ducked.

SOSIA. Good.

CLEANTHIS. Good, he says!

SOSIA. You don't know why, Cleanthis. I'd eaten garlic, and I thought I'd better breathe away from you.

CLEANTHIS. I whispered tender words of love in your ears; but you stood there like a stump. Not breathing a word.

SOSIA. The garlic, dear.

CLEANTHIS. And when I dropped my modesty, and offered you my all and my best, the marble turned to ice. You defied the laws of matrimony, and refused to join me in bed.

SOSIA. I refused?

CLEANTHIS. You did, you limp snake. You humiliated me.

SOSIA. Thank you, Sosia.

CLEANTHIS. Is that how you respond to my tears? You laugh in my face?

SOSIA. I'm grateful to me.

CLEANTHIS. Is this your remorse?

SOSIA. Who would have thought I'd be so good?

CLEANTHIS. Impotent worm! Take that grin to the devil!

SOSIA. Calm down, Cleanthis, calm down. I'll explain. The doctors say that a man should abstain when he's drunk, because his seed gets all mixed up with the grape juice, and the babies he begets die of the hiccups before they're two hours old.

CLEANTHIS. I don't want any doctors' advice. Let them pester the sick, leave healthy people alone, and stay out of sex.

SOSIA. Gently. Doctors are fine people, don't believe the rumors you hear about them. They never kill a patient without sound medical reasons.

CLEANTHIS. Don't change the subject, and don't put on your Sunday manners with me. I promise you I'll make full use of the freedom you gave me.

SOSIA. What freedom?

CLEANTHIS. You said in plain Greek that I should take a lover.

SOSIA. Whoa! There I went too far. I take it back. (*To the world*) Don't anybody step on my property, d'you hear?

CLEANTHIS. We'll see. If I can ever screw myself up to it—

AMPHITRYON

SOSIA. Quiet. Here comes Amphitryon again, and he looks happy.
(*Enter Jupiter, merrily whistling*)
JUPITER (*aside*). I've landed again to appease Alcmena, wipe away her tears, and enjoy an intimate scene of reconciliation. I can't help it if the gods are insatiable. (*To Cleanthis*) Is Alcmena upstairs?
CLEANTHIS. Yes, general; and so full of grief and anger, she demanded to be left alone.
JUPITER. This command was not meant for me. (*Exits into the house*)
CLEANTHIS. What a sudden change of mood!
SOSIA. A minute ago he was breaking the furniture, and now he's whistling!
CLEANTHIS. It goes to show that men are incapable of using their reason. They're all mood, emotion, hot and cold flashes. If we could only procreate without your help!
SOSIA. Not so loud. The gods might overhear you and grant your wish.
CLEANTHIS. If they do, good riddance to your primitive tools!
SOSIA. Be quiet, here they come.
(*Enter Jupiter and Alcmena. Sosia and Cleanthis withdraw discreetly behind a tree or a statue*)
JUPITER. You'll drive me to distraction, Alcmena. Stop, for pity's sake, don't run away from me!
ALCMENA. No, I don't want to be in the same house with my tormentor.
JUPITER. I beg you!
ALCMENA. Let me go!
JUPITER. I—
ALCMENA. Let me go I say!
JUPITER (*aside*). Charming indignation. (*Aloud*) Stay!
ALCMENA. No. Don't follow me.
JUPITER. Where do you want to go?
ALCMENA. Wherever you're not.
JUPITER. Impossible. I worship you. I'll go everywhere you go.
ALCMENA. And everywhere you go I'll fly from you.
JUPITER. Am I such a monster?
ALCMENA. Yes. A monster, a mad beast, the sight of which terrifies me. Name anything odious, infamous, execrable under the sky, and I'll prefer it to you.
JUPITER. These are strong words.
ALCMENA. Not half so strong as what I feel. Oh, I hate myself for not finding the words I need to express my loathing.
JUPITER. But what have I done to be called a monster?
ALCMENA. Heavenly gods! How can you ask? This is beyond belief.

JUPITER. What happened to the love you swore to me last night—the love that was never to change?

ALCMENA. Your cowardly insults murdered it. In its place, you'll find a hatred as ample as the love it replaced, and this means infinite.

JUPITER. No, no, not so. Your love was no great matter if it could die as the result of an idle jest.

ALCMENA. How little you understand the soul of a woman! How blind you are! Had you been truly jealous I would have forgiven you. Jealousy is an honest emotion, it's a child of love, and love is willing to excuse it. But to play games of jealousy, to pretend furious emotions in the way of sport, to berate a woman in order to experiment upon her—this is too cruel and too flippant to be forgiven.

JUPITER. You are right, Alcmena; I bow my head. The violence you were made to suffer was criminal. I can make no excuses for it. But who commited the crime? Whom should you revile? The husband, Alcmena, the husband is to blame.

ALCMENA. Again?

JUPITER. Yes. The lover had no part in this brutal scene. He is incapable of hurting you. Hurting you? With so much love in his heart, such deep respect, such boundless admiration? He would die if he thought he had, what shall I say, ruffled your toga. If a man behaves like a boor to a woman, you know he can only be her husband. So hate the husband, Alcmena, I hand him over to you. Tear him to pieces. But save the lover who is innocent and adores you.

ALCMENA. I thought you were a general; instead you're splitting hairs like a lawyer. Husband, lover—I don' t care—I hate them both.

JUPITER. Then I must perish. I cannot survive your hatred. Already the blood has left my face, a weakness comes over me, my heart slows down. Sosia!

SOSIA (*appearing, followed discreetly by Cleanthis*). Yes, general.

JUPITER (*drawing his sword*). Try my blade on your finger. Has it been blunted on too many enemies?

SOSIA. It's sharp enough to slice through granite. I began to bleed while it was still an inch away from my flesh.

JUPITER. Tell King Creon to name a new commander in my place.

SOSIA. Gladly.

JUPITER. What's that, you clown?

SOSIA. I mean, I'm always glad to obey your orders, sir.

JUPITER. Say to him that a man who could offend Alcmena is not worthy to lead the Theban army.

SOSIA. I'm sure he'll agree, sir. But what are you planning to do?

JUPITER. Here is a drachma for you.

SOSIA. Much obliged, sir. The army will miss you.

JUPITER. I am going, Alcmena; there is a clearing in the woods—do you remember it? That is where I wish to expiate and expire. (*He starts to go*)

ALCMENA. False, cruel husband.

JUPITER. What did you say?

ALCMENA. Must I be kind to you after suffering your taunts?

JUPITER. I offer you a lifetime of remorse.

ALCMENA. If you truly loved me, you would have killed yourself *before* hurting me, not after.

JUPITER. Do you really hate me?

ALCMENA. I am trying to; and I despise myself for not succeeding enough.

JUPITER. One word, and I shall die for you.

ALCMENA. If I cannot hate you, can I want you to die?

JUPITER. But if you no longer love me, can I wish to live? Look at me. (*He goes down on his knees. Then, to Sosia and Cleanthis*) Assist me, my faithful servants. (*They fall on their knees too*)

SOSIA. Ouch.

JUPITER. Punish, Alcmena, or forgive.

ALCMENA. What choice do you leave me? I have opened my heart too freely. When a woman says she cannot hate, does she not mean that she has forgiven?

JUPITER. Lovely Alcmena, my joy—

ALCMENA. Stop. Let me be. I have been too weak. I am vexed with myself. (*She returns to the house*)

JUPITER. Sosia, back to camp, on the double. Invite every officer you meet to dine with me tonight. (*Aside*) This way, I'm rid of him and Mercury will take his place again. And now—ah, this will be even more delicious than last night. (*He enters the house*)

SOSIA. You see the happy couple, Cleanthis? Why don't we follow their example and make up a little bit too?

CLEANTHIS. With the likes of you? Ha!

SOSIA. You don't want to?

CLEANTHIS. No. Aren't you going to commit suicide?

SOSIA. I can't today. I'm on duty.

CLEANTHIS. Come back here, you dog.

SOSIA. No; I feel like throwing a tantrum of my own for a change.

CLEANTHIS. Nonsense. Come here. You're a villain. But I'm tired of always being right.

ACT THREE

(Enter Amphitryon)

AMPHITRYON. Fate has hidden that miserable brother from me on purpose. I have run myself ragged looking for him. I'm so unhappy I could hang myself. I can't find the man I need, and I keep bumping into those I want to avoid. Every mother's son rushes up to congratulate me on my victory. They all mean well, but I hate the sight of them. I have to smile, shake hands, accept their toasts—all the while cursing them under my breath. All this affection is going to kill me. My victory in the field has turned to ashes in my mouth. How many successful men are there like me, I wonder—carried in triumph on men's shoulders, admired, envied, adulated—but eating their hearts out over a spat at the breakfast table. Foul jealousy! Another man in her bed! Confusion and chaos in my mind! True, the ring might have been stolen. Seals have been broken in such a way that no one was the wiser. But they say that I myself brought it to her! Grant that Nature produces weird resemblances; grant that a rogue can exploit them for his own benefit. But to be taken for a husband—that makes no sense. There are a thousand details a woman would notice. Would notice in a man like Amphitryon. Magic? Sorcery? No, this is Greece, the heart of the civilized world, we invented geometry, by thunder; wouldn't it be sad if, after trouncing the enemy, I'd allow myself to be taken in by a fairy tale? I'll question her again. I went too roughly about it yesterday. My absence could have unhinged her. That, at least, is a credible explanation. For my peace of mind, oh heaven, may she be deranged!

(Mercury appears on the balcony. At first Amphitryon doesn't notice him)

MERCURY. Not being a peeping Tom by nature, I'm getting bored while Jupiter and Alcmena are making love. To cheer up my spirits, I'll make Amphitryon sweat a little by playing a prank on him. It's not very kind of me, I know; but, as all the books say, the gods are cruel. I wouldn't like to disappoint the philosophers.

(Amphitryon tries to enter the house)

AMPHITRYON. Why the deuce is the door closed at this time of day?

MERCURY. Easy, down there! Who's knocking?

AMPHITRYON. Oh, it's you. Open the door.

MERCURY. Just like that? Who are you?

AMPHITRYON *(aside)*. It's a cloudy day; maybe he can't see me clearly. *(Aloud)* Sosia!

MERCURY. That's my name. Why were you knocking at the door, stranger?

AMPHITRYON

You're creating a disturbance.

AMPHITRYON. Stranger! You wait, my boy, in a minute I'll give you a knock on the head that'll teach you manners.

MERCURY. Attempted trespass. Threats of violence. I think I'll unleash our dogs.

AMPHITRYON. The nerve! A lackey! A tattered rogue! A civilian!

MERCURY. Say, have you stared your fill at me? Your eyes are popping out of your head. Ha—if looks could kill.

AMPHITRYON. I'm shuddering at the thought of what you're cooking up for yourself. There'll be blood on the floor, shreds of flesh draped over tables and chairs. It's begun: the servants are rising against their masters.

MERCURY. What masters? Who's my master?

AMPHITRYON. Scoundrel! You dare ask me who's your master?

MERCURY. The only master I recognize is Amphitryon.

AMPHITRYON. And who is Amphitryon, if not me myself?

MERCURY. You, Amphitryon?

AMPHITRYON. Who else?

MERCURY. Hey, what have you been drowning your sorrows in? I'd like to try a bottle myself.

AMPHITRYON. He's needling me!

MERCURY. On your way, friend. I respect a good drinking man. But enough's enough. I shouldn't like anyone disturbing Amphitryon in the midst of his pleasures.

AMPHITRYON. Amphitryon? Amphitryon is in there?

MERCURY. In there is right. He's in Alcmena's bed, celebrating a minor success in a skirmish.

AMPHITRYON. No.

MERCURY. Yes. Besides they're getting over a little quarrel and enjoying the sweets of reconciliation. (*Amphitryon groans*) I know you wish them well, but no drunken serenade, if you please, or else I'll let the dogs loose on you. (*Exit*)

AMPHITRYON. What shall I do? Throw myself into the nearest well? Turn myself in to the lunatic asylum? Unbelievable disgrace! Shall I make an outcry or keep my mouth shut? Spread my shame or hide it? It doesn't matter anymore. If I avenge myself, I'll be satisfied, and hang the consequences.

(*Enter Sosia and Naucrates*)

SOSIA. Sir, the only man who's available for dinner is Colonel Naucrates.

AMPHITRYON. So you slipped out of the house, did you? Say your prayers—this is the end.

SOSIA. What?

AMPHITRYON. You've spoken your last insolent word, you flea-bitten traitor!
SOSIA. What's happening? Why are you mad at me?
AMPHITRYON (*drawing his sword*). You really want to know?
SOSIA. Colonel, help!
NAUCRATES. Stay, general.
SOSIA. What have I done? (*He hides behind Naucrates*)
AMPHITRYON. You dare ask! (*To Naucrates*) Let me slit his throat, colonel; he deserves it; take it from me.
SOSIA. Wait! Before you slit a man's throat, don't you tell him why?
NAUCRATES. These are indeed the regulations, sir. Even men of rank like us must follow due process.
SOSIA. That's it. I ask for due process.
AMPHITRYON. The villain shut my own door in my face, called me a drunkard, threatened to unleash the dogs....
NAUCRATES. Due process is satisfied. Slit his throat.
SOSIA (*falling on his knees*). How could I have done all that if I was miles away drumming up dinner guests for you? Ask him.
NAUCRATES. To be sure. That much I can personally confirm. And by the way, Lieutenant Polidas sends his regrets. Nevertheless, if the rascal insulted you, his throat must inevitably be slit.
AMPHITRYON (*to Sosia*). Who told you to invite anyone for dinner?
SOSIA. You did.
AMPHITRYON. When?
SOSIA. After your reconciliation with Alcmena.
AMPHITRYON. Get up. I'm going to spare you until this mystery is cleared up.
NAUCRATES. It's probably a plot against the army.
AMPHITRYON. I'm glad you're here, colonel. You'll be able to help me. I must uncover the truth. (*He is about to knock. Aside*) Though I fear it worse than the plague. (*He knocks*)
(*Jupiter appears at the door*)
JUPITER. Who comes here disturbing the master of this house?
AMPHITRYON. What's this I see? Heavenly gods!
NAUCRATES. Two Amphitryons! This calls for a full report.
AMPHITRYON (*aside*). So here is the answer! The truth is out, and at last it's clear as daylight that I can make nothing of it.
NAUCRATES. The more I look, the more they resemble each other.
SOSIA (*going over to Jupiter*). Gentlemen: here is the real Amphitryon. The other one tried to kill me. Please punish him right away.

AMPHITRYON. My sword will put an end to this infamous plot.

NAUCRATES. Stop. (*He holds Amphitryon back*)

AMPHITRYON. Hands off!

JUPITER. Restrain him. Do. When a man takes to violence, it's a fair sign, is it not, that his cause is suspect.

SOSIA. He's a well-known tramp of an actor. I recognize him now; his special talent is impersonating important people.

AMPHITRYON. Oh, you'll regret this, you poisonous insect.

SOSIA. My master won't allow a stranger to molest his servant, will he? (*He brushes Jupiter's toga*)

AMPHITRYON. Step aside, colonel; this outrage has to be washed in blood.

NAUCRATES. No; I can't allow a combat between Amphitryon and Amphitryon.

AMPHITRYON. This is insubordination! Mutiny! Instead of rushing out to avenge me, you're hindering me, you're favoring the enemy!

NAUCRATES. Sir, I'm only doing my duty. I'm ready to shed my own blood for Amphitryon, but which is the true one? Undue haste may cause an irretrievable error. A commission will have to look into this.

JUPITER. Thank you, Colonel Naucrates. I for one appreciate your prudence and understand your uncertainty. As you can see, I'm not drawing my sword nor abusing anyone. There are more peaceful ways of settling this misunderstanding. And indeed, I intend to settle it before long. I shall make myself known, and known so clearly, that this gentleman himself will proclaim my identity. But I desire all Thebes to witness the truth. Alcmena must be exonerated in public lest her fair name be tainted. I shall proceed at once to assemble our dignitaries. In the meantime, colonel, do me the favor of accepting the dinner invitation which Sosia extended to you on my behalf.

SOSIA. That settles it, gentlemen. The true Amphitryon is the one who invites to dinner.

AMPHITRYON. I am beaten like a mongrel. The impostor has outmaneuvered me. All right. I am putting up my blade. But you'll be hearing from me.

NAUCRATES. You've no grounds for complaint, sir, whoever you are. Let's have his explanation, and then we'll consult the code and take appropriate action. Perhaps he's lying. But I must say that he speaks like a man who knows the regulations.

AMPHITRYON. Dine with him, weakling, flatterer, go on. I've other friends in Thebes, thank heaven.

JUPITER. Bring them. Let them witness the conclusion too.

AMPHITRYON. Don't try to escape.

AMPHITRYON

JUPITER. Tush. With three words I'll confound you when the time comes.
AMPHITRYON. Jupiter himself won't protect you from me.
JUPITER. Who knows? I'll pray to him.
AMPHITRYON. (*aside*). I know the man I want. I'd better hurry before this villain gives me the slip. (*Exit*)
JUPITER. No ceremony, if you please; come in, my dear colonel.
NAUCRATES. I'm in a daze; but the daze hasn't spoiled my appetite.
SOSIA. Forget this fool, gentlemen; think only of dinner. I'll set the table myself and sample a few of the dishes. (*Jupiter and Naucrates enter the house*) After that, in the kitchen, I'll tell the maids how I routed that ox. Away, vile impostor, or I'll kill you with one of my scowls! Gad, I'm in great form today.

(*Mercury comes out of the house*)

MERCURY. You! Are you here again? Of course, you heard the dinner bell and thought you might stick your nose into our saucepans.
SOSIA. Gently, gently.
MERCURY. I'll raise a camel's hump on your back.
SOSIA. Gently, brave and generous me; moderation, temperance. Spare Sosia, dear Sosia. Find other pleasures in life than trouncing me.
MERCURY. Haven't I forbidden you to use my name?
SOSIA. But why can't we both use it? I'll allow you to be Sosia, and you'll allow me to be Sosia too. Let's leave the arguing to the two Amphitryons. And while they quarrel, you and I can live together like birds in a nest.
MERCURY. No, I'm stubborn. I won't share with you.
SOSIA. I'll give you precedence. You'll be the elder, I'll be the baby. You'll take the drumstick. I'll eat the tail.
MERCURY. No, I want to be an only child.
SOSIA. Tyrant! At least, let me be your shadow.
MERCURY. No.
SOSIA. Not a long shadow. A shrinky, submissive shadow. You'll get to like me. We'll become inseparable.
MERCURY. No good. The law is the law. If you try to cross that threshold, I'll reduce you to a memory.
SOSIA. Poor Sosia.
MERCURY. You're abusing my name again.
SOSIA. No, no. I didn't mean myself. I'm talking about an old uncle, his name happened to be Sosia too, who was inhumanly deprived of his dinner in this vicinity—a long time ago.
MERCURY. Watch what you say if you value your life.
SOSIA (*aside*). I'd cut you to ribbons, you arrogant son of a whore, if I had

AMPHITRYON

any spunk.

MERCURY. I beg your pardon?

SOSIA. Nothing.

MERCURY. I thought I heard you speak.

SOSIA. Me?

MERCURY. Something about a son of a whore tickled my eardrum, I'm sure of it.

SOSIA. Maybe it was the parrot in our house.

MERCURY. In whose house?

SOSIA. In your house.

MERCURY. Thank you. Goodbye now. If your backside ever itches for my stick, here's where I live. (*Exit*)

SOSIA (*aside*). To be thrown out at dinner-time puts the final heart-rending touch to my tragedy. Oh! Here comes the other wretch again. I was thrown out, he was thrown out. I'm the real Sosia—conclusion, I'd better take cover for a while.

(*Enter Amphitryon, accompanied by Argatiphontidas*)

AMPHITRYON. My reputation is ruined.

ARGATIPHONTIDAS. I know how you feel, believe me.

AMPHITRYON. My plight is entertaining the whole army. Details have already come back to me which even I didn't know. And yet, the resemblance was so amazing, can I really say she's guilty?

ARGATIPHONTIDAS. Sure you can. Did she do it or didn't she?

AMPHITRYON. She did, but—

ARGATIPHONTIDAS. That's all that counts. Listen, I'm your friend, we rose through the ranks together, and I tell you—mistake or crime, she's made a jackass out of you.

AMPHITRYON. That's true, but—

ARGATIPHONTIDAS. Quibbling won't help—she didn't know any better, the room was dark, she's as sorry as you are, and all that garbage. Fact is fact; yesterday she was brand new, today she's second-hand.

AMPHITRYON. You're right, but—

ARGATIPHONTIDAS. If this reaches Creon's ears, you'll be sorting sandals in a supply room.

AMPHITRYON. I don't know what I'd do without you. Advise me. What's my next move? Do I launch an inquiry? That's what Naucrates suggested.

ARGATIPHONTIDAS. Hell and fury! I hate the word. Inquiry be hanged! Are you a bureaucrat? A notary public? Or a soldier? Look at me. I don't wait for an enemy to come to words. Show me where he is; I charge like a bull, I run the bastard through the gizzard, and then I ask him for his point

AMPHITRYON

of view. Come on, leave the scoundrel to me. I'll wind his gut around my sword. Don't deprive me of the satisfaction. After I've butchered him, you can kill him too.

AMPHITRYON. You're reviving me, my friend. Let's go.

(*Sosia comes forward and falls on his knees*)

SOSIA. Master!

ARGATIPHONTIDAS. A filthy spy!

SOSIA. Punish me, master, hit me, knock me down, pull my nose, break my head, tear my heart out. That's what I deserve for my impudence. Cut off my tongue. I won' t say a word.

AMPHITRYON. Get up; tell me what happened.

SOSIA. They turned me out on an empty stomach. The other me wanted to beat me again. The devil is after both of us, sir; and, to sum it all up, I have been unsosified, and you disamphitryonated.

AMPHITRYON. No more words. I'm going in.

ARGATIPHONTIDAS. Who's this? Oh. It's Naucrates with a frumpy female in tow.

SOSIA. That's my wife, captain.

(*Enter, from the house, Naucrates and Cleanthis*)

CLEANTHIS. Merciful gods!

AMPHITRYON. What's the matter? Are my horns showing?

CLEANTHIS. I've never been so startled in my life. I left you upstairs, and find you outside.

NAUCRATES. Stay where you are, sir. We've been promised a satisfactory explanation.

(*Enter Mercury from the house*)

MERCURY. And here it is. Learn, ye mortals, that he who was drawn to Alcmena's couch was neither more nor less than the god of gods, the lord of Olympus, Jupiter. And I, I am Mercury, who for lack of better employment gave a welldeserved caning to the clown whose name I took. But let him be content. To be clobbered by a god is a distinction he will undoubtedly cherish, and boast of to the stable boys until his dying day.

SOSIA. Thank you ever so much, sir god. But I could have survived without your distinction.

MERCURY. Let him be Sosia again. I am tired of wearing his grubby face. In heaven, thank heaven, I can scrub mine in ambrosia. (*He vanishes*)

SOSIA. Good riddance, and stay away from me in the future.

(*Thunder and lightning. Alcmena comes out on the balcony as Jupiter appears in a cloud, an eagle at his side, a thunderbolt in his hand*)

ALCMENA (*looking at Amphitryon and at Jupiter*). Amphitryon! Amphitryon?

JUPITER. Mortals! Kneel and behold the divine impostor. Even now I keep the appearance of general Amphitryon lest I should blind you all; but these tokens show you who I am; and that, I trust, will suffice to appease your wrath, Amphitryon, and restore you to conjugal bliss. My name, to which the earth sings an incessant hosannah, will stifle evil rumors and equivocal suggestions. To share with Jupiter is an honor; to call Jupiter a rival is sublime. And shall not I rather than you feel the pangs of jealousy in my divine essence? For Alcmena is yours. Behold where she stands. God himself could not entice her, except by appearing in the shape of her husband. And those ineffable delights which she granted me were bestowed on no one but happy Amphitryon.

SOSIA (*aside*). Our good Jupiter knows how to sweeten the pill.

JUPITER. Nor is this all. I bring you tidings of great joy. Unto her shall be born a son who shall be called Hercules, and he shall be the strongest hero who ever bestrode the earth. You, Amphitryon, will grow wealthier and happier from year to year, laden with spoils of battle and swaddled in Alcmena's love. And the sons of the Muse, reporting your deeds in many a noble Tragedy, both in rhyme and prose, shall carry your fame through the long avenues of Posterity. Let a clap of thunder engrave these words into the Book of Fate.

(*Thunder; he vanishes*)

NAUCRATES. General, I offer you my sincerest congratulations.

ARGATIPHONTIDAS. Shake here, Amphitryon; it isn't every day.

CLEANTHIS. I'll give baby Hercules his bottle.

SOSIA (*aside to the colonels*). Gentlemen, will you hear my advice? Jupiter has been devilishly kind to our house. We're going to be rich; we'll have a famous son; and we'll be turned into literature. No one could ask for more. All the same, the less said the better, eh?

(*He discreetly ushers the officers and Cleanthis off-stage. Amphitryon below and Alcmena on the balcony stare at each other. Long silence*)

AMPHITRYON (*bawls*). Damn damn damn!

(*A highly becoming light-beam descends from the heavens on Alcmena, accompanied by arpeggios on a harp. Alcmena opens her arms*)

AMPHITRYON (*subdued, abashed, and enamoured, walks toward the house, groaning*). Damn damn damn..........

(*He vanishes into the house, as does Alcmena from the balcony*)

The End

AMPHITRYON

Notes

Amphitryon, in a licentious translation from Molière, appeared in 1976 in a little book of 58 pages, deliciously illustrated by a reclusive artist I never met, Beth Arnett, daughter of my (and other professors') secretary at the California Institute of Technology. For a long time my "adaptation" (as such violations are called these days) was adopted by many college and university instructors, until Richard Wilbur made a fine, faithful translation of Molière's farce which deservedly blotted my egotistical one from classroom reading lists.

The present, gently ameliorated version of the 1976 play calls itself more boldly my own, because, if I am not mistaken, my distance from Molière is much the same as that which stretches between Molière's *Amphitryon* of 1667 and that of Jean Rotrou of 1636, which was the great man's "source"; and the great man did not hesitate to put his name to the play as his own.

My 1976 booklet contained a useful Foreword, from which I quote and slightly modify the following passage:

> Why is [Molière's *Amphitryon*] not regarded as one of his major plays? Because the tale as it stands is without philosophical significance whatsoever. This is in contrast with plays like *Tartuffe* and *Le Misanthrope*, where significance inheres in the action as such. *Amphitryon*, instead, belongs to the zany world of the *commedia dell'Arte*, whose breezes Molière had been breathing all his life. What application to real life can possibly be extracted from such a daffy farce of impersonations and substitutions? And yet this is not quite the end of the line. For if significance is denied to the action itself, an author can still pepper it with substantial little *incidentals*. When for instance Sosia obeys a command of his master's, why not let him mutter something about the haves and the have-nots of this world? That is how the *commedia* actors often sprinkled their "innocent" little farces. So did Molière in his *Amphitryon*. So have I, with abandon. Thus, when all is said and done, the insignificant trifle is less insignificant and less trifling than appears at first glance. Let this be said, at any rate, to commend *Amphitryon* to our heavy century.

THE SUMMONING OF PHILOCTETES

CHARACTERS

Heracles
Philoctetes
Odysseus
Demodocus
Medon
Chorus of ten soldiers

The action takes place in front of the cave of Philoctetes on the island of Lemnos

THE SUMMONING OF PHILOCTETES

(Enter Heracles to the sound of a drum)

HERACLES. Philoctetes! My voice fills this island, you do not hear it, yet soon you shall. Heracles returns to earth: your master and companion when I too knew the warm and cold of life; but now become among the gods another god, and still your master. And my word as god remains my word when I was man: War! Philoctetes! Forget that the Greeks banished you long ago to Lemnos ringed by the sea: a warrior, lord of seven ships, but useless to the them, your foot swollen with the serpent's venom, a coarse stench polluting the holy sacrifice, and your cries unbearable to the soldiers. Let it be forgotten, for your banishment must end. Troy stands unbowed. Its princes strut atop the unbroken battlements, and will not perish until pierced by the strong, strange bow you fashioned, Philoctetes, in the long hours we gods gave you to create it, foreseeing it all. Philoctetes! Unite with your brothers! On the plains of Ilium the son of Achilles, great Pyrrhus waits for you. His the hand that cracks the city open. Yours the weapon in his hand. Come, come from the hunting of birds. Hunt Troy! Two heroes have landed on Lemnos, charged by the oracle to summon you. You do not hear them, but they arrive to take possession of you. They have set foot on the beach, resolute. They have scaled the hill towards your cave, while elsewhere the string of your bow thuds and the wild birds, premonitory, die in the sky. Return to the war, Philoctetes, return to the war! *(He vanishes)*

(Enter Odysseus, Demodocus, and the soldiers)

FIRST SOLDIER. No one is here, Odysseus. Follow me.

ODYSSEUS. The old horrible stench. I remember it. All but unbearable. Soldiers, spread out and look for our man, each in a different direction.

(The eighth, ninth and tenth soldiers leave)

ODYSSEUS. The darkness of Lemnos under the heavy trees. Nature's stairway of rocks and caves. The inhuman silence. Here, Demodocus, I myself brought the unhappy man ten years ago at the command of Agamemnon.

FIFTH SOLDIER. My lord! Here's a cave, and the remains of a fire!

DEMODOCUS. This must be his shelter!

ODYSSEUS. Go in, my friend. Draw your sword. Caution!

DEMODOCUS *(within)*. It is the cave, men! Furnished. Almost a house.

ODYSSEUS. What do you see?

DEMODOCUS. Wonderful. Two couches covered with skins. Medon is still alive! Wooden utensils—table, benches, a few knives—bronze basins and pots—

ODYSSEUS. More than we left him!

DEMODOCUS (*emerging*). Stone tools. A hearth. Sunlight penetrates from a high opening in the rock. But why do you hang back, Odysseus, with your hand on your sword? Go in yourself.

ODYSSEUS. Soldiers, keep looking about. Too many trees for comfort here. A man might be concealed anywhere with a bow in his hands.

DEMODOCUS. Do you think he will be hostile to us, Odysseus? After ten years?

ODYSSEUS. Ten years may have made him forget, or they may have deepened his hatred. That is why the sword is in my hand.

DEMODOCUS. Still, capturing the bow may be easy; but taking him back with us—

ODYSSEUS. And voluntarily! Freely offering us his skill!

DEMODOCUS. I see great difficulties in that, Odysseus. Volunteer to join the atrocious miseries of the war?

FIRST SOLDIER. Don't dwell on difficulties and miseries, Demodocus; it's the wrong approach for a soldier. After all, if he won't come back of his own free will, I suppose we'll tie him up and argue with him later.

DEMODOCUS. Force him back with us, like an enemy; but I'm afraid he'll never reveal his secrets to us if we do.

ODYSSEUS. And yet force him back we must if he refuses to come. Have you considered, my friends, that the Trojans are sailing towards Lemnos too?

FIRST SOLDIER (*deeply alarmed*). The Trojans? How would they know about his weapon?

ODYSSEUS. Why, have the Trojans no oracles of their own? Are not the same gods in their sky as in ours? The danger is greater than you think. Perhaps they have landed already; perhaps they have made friends with Philoctetes, and learned from him how to make the bow.

SECOND SOLDIER. Odysseus, what are you saying?

ODYSSEUS. Calm yourselves. While we are here, the rest of our forces are quietly scouring the island, with instructions of their own. But I trust that we have landed first. And we too have our instructions. We must persuade Philoctetes to return with us. But what if he refuses? Shall we allow him to be approached by a Trojan delegation? In his bitterness against us he might yield to them, traitor, without so much as a bribe.

SEVENTH SOLDIER. What must we do, Odysseus?

ODYSSEUS. Persuade him if we can, compel him if he resists, keep him

THE SUMMONING OF PHILOCTETES

    away from the Trojans, and if worst comes to worst —
THIRD SOLDIER (*low*). Kill him?
DEMODOCUS. This was kept from us till now.
ODYSSEUS. Are you ready, each one of you, to carry out Agamemnon's orders?
SECOND SOLDIER. If we must, Odysseus, if we must.
FIFTH SOLDIER. Who can blame us for keeping this weapon out of the enemy's hands?
THIRD SOLDIER. God knows we are loyal. Yet God forbid we should pour out the blood of a fellow Greek.
FOURTH SOLDIER. God forbid. Yet you know best what fighters we have been, always at your side; and how else is this endless, sorrowful war to end?

(*Enter the eighth soldier hurriedly*)

EIGHTH SOLDIER. Odysseus, I found footprints!
ODYSSEUS. How far from here?
EIGHTH SOLDIER. About two hundred yards away; on a sandy spot; but leading down from the cave, not returning to it.
ODYSSEUS. One or two men?
EIGHTH SOLDIER. Two.
ODYSSEUS. Good. Medon is with him. Old or fresh?
EIGHTH SOLDIER. Fresh, Odysseus, fresh!
ODYSSEUS. Splendid! Go back, soldier, and look sharp. Give us a warning the moment you see him. (*Exit the soldier*) Men, are we ready to disappear at the snap of a finger?
FIRST SOLDIER. We are, sir.
ODYSSEUS. Now, Demodocus, the rest is up to you. Here he will find you, a poor lonely shipwrecked Greek.
DEMODOCUS. I know my part, Odysseus.
ODYSSEUS. You were not chosen for this mission without good reason. Myself and the other chiefs Philoctetes hates, as though we and not the serpent had bitten his ankle. But you are a lieutenant: noble in your own right, a man I have always placed near myself at my table, among my dearest companions, young as you are and not yet in the highest authority. You are a stranger to Philoctetes. He can hate you only as a Greek, but you will easily persuade him to like you as a man. Furthermore, you are skilled with your tongue. To whom else do we turn, after the fighting or during a feast, for a love ditty, or a hymn to battle, or a ballad of old heroes? Though even as a spearsman you are by no means a man whom the enemy would ignore. Your role it will be, therefore, to enchant the heart of Philoctetes

with sinuous, inveigling words and strong appeals. Urge him to return to us. Stir in his heart the emotion of kinship, the longing for one's own which makes even their sins bearable. But speak to him especially of the honors that await him upon his return to us. Make him weep; stir his pride!

DEMODOCUS. But what if he furiously reproaches us for casting him off on Lemnos?

ODYSSEUS. Swear to our innocence and our good will. Did we plot the serpent's bite? Did we bribe the oracle? He was one of ours, we loved the man! No; counter with a solemn chord: duty, Demodocus, duty to our nation and to our cause: the call to arms. What man shall disobey? Troy, sitting like a harpy across the Hellespont, cramming down our ships, our goods, our sailors, Troy must be, shall be cut down!

SIXTH SOLDIER. Grant it, o gods!

FIRST SOLDIER. This is soundly spoken, Odysseus. What a pity Philoctetes is not here now. You would have persuaded him already.

DEMODOCUS. Yes, your words carry a great deal of weight, as always, Odysseus. You are a king. It is only human to have misgivings, of course, but I will do my best to follow your instructions. Shall I let Philoctetes know that his father is dead, and that his son, like your own Telemachus, reigns while he waits for his father's return?

ODYSSEUS. Do so. Good thinking, Demodocus!

(*Enter in haste the ninth soldier*)

NINTH SOLDIER. Odysseus, away from here!

ODYSSEUS. Is he coming?

NINTH SOLDIER. Yes! I saw two men from my hill—still in the distance, but coming this way; one limping, carrying the bow—the bow, do you hear? The other walking two steps behind. Philoctetes and Medon, as sure as there is water in the sea!

ODYSSEUS. Good work. Recall the other men. Run. Demodocus, stand before the cave. Speak boldly to him. When he grows soft, suddenly I appear. I disclose the oracle's revelation. You and I, astonished to meet. Have we left traces here?

FIRST SOLDIER. I think not.

(*The ninth and tenth soldiers return*)

TENTH SOLDIER. We've signaled the other man, Odysseus; he'll be here in a minute.

ODYSSEUS. Good. Remember: not a word about the bow, the prophecy, and the Trojans. They're for me to manage. (*The last man arrives*) Hurry up, soldier. All present? No one missing?

FIRST SOLDIER. All present, Odysseus.

THE SUMMONING OF PHILOCTETES

ODYSSEUS. Withdraw to a safe distance but without leaving Demodocus exposed. (*To the tenth soldier*) You, follow me to the ship. (*To the first soldier*) You, deploy your men and send runners to report to me. Demodocus, good luck.

DEMODOCUS. Depend on me. (*Exeunt Odysseus and the tenth soldier*) Friends, I think I will stand a little farther off, and choose the best moment.
(*He leaves*)

THE CHORUS, with drum

SECOND SOLDIER. Does your heart beat like mine, comrades?

FIRST SOLDIER. Zeus! Be with us. Zeus! Now this man comes, and already the stench of him sickens us. Zeus! Make him pliant, bend him to us, let him shift his ways like the stream when it parts and yields before the commanding rock. Zeus! Sharpen the words of Demodocus, let each syllable be a hook to catch the soul of this man. Zeus! We are your people. Will you forsake us? Are we to die in the futile plain where bones of our brothers lie, men once ordinary, men once reasonably content, lying now where the oak, the tamarisk, and the myrtle grew, become a barren country, yellow with war, pocked with spears and rusted swords and shreds of armor, while the vultures scrape in the skulls for meat. Zeus! Give us this man and his weapon, and the end of this abomination!

SEVERAL. So be it!

THIRD SOLDIER. Men, do you know how old I was when I enlisted for the war? Twenty years old, having barely tasted the pleasure of being a man, of attracting a woman's sly glances, of taking my place in the Assembly, uttering my first words there, surprised almost that I was taken seriously, no longer a boy, beginning the best years of a man; and these years, oh my friends, these strong years in which I should have found a kind wife, in which I might have established a house and grown in wealth and reputation, I have spent them like a beast among beasts in the sand; yes, my mouth filled with sand when we crawled on the beach and drove back the Trojans in the first onslaught, like a beast sweating and growling, muck-covered, swearing over dice, scratching the blood off the rings I stole from the dead—I, the son of a good man, Schedios of Pronnoi, before whom even now I would blush to say a foul word.

FOURTH SOLDIER. This is my story too.

FIFTH SOLDIER. Fifteen years we are children, fifteen years we are old men; and the little space between, must we spend it howling in the attack, luckless if we die, luckless if we live, life either killed or wasted? And why? Why? What is it all to us, I ask, though timidly?

THE SUMMONING OF PHILOCTETES

SIXTH SOLDIER. Why are we driven and driven?
SEVENTH SOLDIER. Why?
EIGHTH SOLDIER. Why?
NINTH SOLDIER. Because.
(*Drum-beats*)
(*Demodocus appears*)
DEMODOCUS. He's coming! Scatter!
FIRST SOLDIER. We'll move a little way off, Demodocus, as Odysseus commanded.
(*All leave*)
(*Enter Philoctetes, bow in hand, and Medon, carrying dead fowl*)
PHILOCTETES. Let me stop awhile, Medon. The wheel of pain turns again. We could sit down awhile. (*Medon offers to help him*) No no; sit farther off. Why should you suffer my suffering? This stench oozes into my very sleep and pollutes my dreams; and you so patient, pretending not to mind. Let me rest. The breeze cools my wound and sings like an old nurse. Clean Lemnos. I feel better. Medon, I'll help you pluck our catch for the day. No masters and servants here. Philoctetes works with his hands. Look. Thick. Hard. Efficient. Did you see how I shot the wild geese? I hardly aimed. Oh, I could have been Troy's horror—all Troy a giant boar, and my uncanny arrow—now!—dying it falls, moaning, and then my knife violent in its belly. How did this ugly thought come to me?... How cool it is. If only I could smell the fragrance that must be here. Yes, I know, the birds must be plucked. I am so tired. Why should I lie to you? The venom is mounting again. God, what is the purpose of such pain? Go into the cave by yourself, Medon. Leave me. I had rather be alone.
(*Medon enters the cave. Philoctetes sits moaning, his bow across his knees, and loses consciousness. Demodocus appears. He stands motionless at a distance from Philoctetes. Gradually Philoctetes regains consciousness. He opens his eyes and sees Demodocus. He leaps up and aims an arrow*)
PHILOCTETES. Medon! Your sword! Men on the island!
(*Medon rushes out of the cave, armed*)
PHILOCTETES. Stand back!
DEMODOCUS. Peace, my friends. I am a man who can do no harm. A castaway.
PHILOCTETES. A liar, maybe. Stay where you are. Who is here with you?
DEMODOCUS. No one. I am alone. No one else survived.
PHILOCTETES. You were shipwrecked?
DEMODOCUS. Yes.
PHILOCTETES. Your clothes are dry. You don't look exhausted.

THE SUMMONING OF PHILOCTETES

DEMODOCUS. I had a calm journey of it on my raft for a whole day. And I slept a full night on the beach.

PHILOCTETES. Take his knife, Medon.

DEMODOCUS. You are welcome to it, my friends, whoever you are.

PHILOCTETES. What's your name? Where is your home?

DEMODOCUS. Demodocus, son of Terpius, a man of Argos. But your voice fills me with fear. Will you treat me as a guest, or will you injure me? I have neither money nor goods.

PHILOCTETES. You'll come to no harm unless you look for it. How did your ship go down? An enemy? A storm?

DEMODOCUS. A storm. Will you not tell me where I am? Did I land on an island? Tenedos, perhaps?

PHILOCTETES. This is Lemnos.

DEMODOCUS. Lemnos! Then you—is it possible? You are Philoctetes! Alive!

PHILOCTETES (*lowering the bow*). You know my name.

DEMODOCUS. Who doesn't? Philoctetes! Unbelievable! How many times your story has been retold around the campfire—you, lord of Malis—and I live to see you! Oh we have wondered and wondered, are they alive, he and his companion?

PHILOCTETES. What campfire is this? Not before Troy, surely?

DEMODOCUS. Troy too surely. Lucky man, not even to know. Yes, before Troy. Still before Troy.

PHILOCTETES. Amazing. And you, man of Argos, what are you? An officer?

DEMODOCUS. I am.

PHILOCTETES. I don't remember you.

DEMODOCUS. I was never among the first, and then ten years ago, Philoctetes, I was a mere boy. You couldn't have noticed me. And even now I am better known among the Greeks for my singing than for my fighting, though even as a fighter I am not helpless.

PHILOCTETES. And was it for singing a false note, my friend, that the honest Greeks set you on a ship and sent you off?

DEMODOCUS. No, I am not an exile. I was sent to levy a thousand men in Messenia, but the storm wrecked our ship, and I, perhaps, am the only survivor.

PHILOCTETES. The war is hungry.

DEMODOCUS. Too, too hungry. Last year—

PHILOCTETES. Tell me no stories. Keep your nightmares to yourself, and take advantage of your accident; explain it as intended by the gods. Come,

THE SUMMONING OF PHILOCTETES

sit down; stretch your limbs, and feel what peace is like.
(Medon brings a bowl of water and a dish of fruit)
DEMODOCUS. I feel it already in every bone, kind Philoctetes. The change is so sudden, I keep wondering, is it myself talking here? And to Philoctetes! Who would have thought it? Chatting under the trees. Trees! If you saw the plain before Troy. Scarred, sacked, cracked, every leaf and every blade of grass blasted. The heather uprooted. Bones and sand and mud. And now I sit here drinking clean water and eating figs.
PHILOCTETES. Tonight you will eat a curd of boar's milk and honey we call "the gift of Meleager." Other dishes too, oddities I promise you'll enjoy. Not a bad place is it, for a man who was drowning this morning?
DEMODOCUS. Yesterday, Philoctetes. Oh, this is Elysium.
PHILOCTETES. Later we'll walk halfway up a cliff to watch the night drifting in. Night without ambush. Night without blood. Take it: the island is yours. It lies in the Aegean like a pillow for the weary sailor.
DEMODOCUS. You are infinitely courteous. Ten years of solitude have not coarsened you. But tell me. I suppose that other men have landed here, recently perhaps.
PHILOCTETES. Perhaps.
DEMODOCUS. Who. When?
PHILOCTETES. I don't know. We've seen no one.
DEMODOCUS. No one? In all the years?
PHILOCTETES. Why do you ask so suspiciously?
DEMODOCUS. Not suspiciously, my friend, only with surprise. The Trojans, we understand, sail freely among these islands.
PHILOCTETES. They are welcome if they land here.
DEMODOCUS. The enemy?
PHILOCTETES. You are my enemy too. You are a Greek.
DEMODOCUS. Why such a cruel word, Philoctetes?
PHILOCTETES. Why such a cruel word! Medon, did you hear that? I thank you of course—you made a gesture—the stench—oh, I notice!—yet you mastered yourself. But your fellow Greeks did not make the effort. Let me tell you what they did. They manacled me. Me, Philoctetes, like a slave caught stealing a herring. Odysseus dragged me here manacled and threw me on the ground like a sack of garbage and hoped I would die. But I didn't die. I am alive to enjoy their dying. But my words are rash. This island has been my happiness. Never did I dream when I was a boy, wishing I could be like my master Heracles, that I should find this paradise. Yet I hate the Greeks who brought it to me. Take the paradox.
DEMODOCUS. I understand. It was not a paradise they meant for you.

And yet, let me ask you, is there not a thrust in your flesh toward your own brothers? Do you ever wonder, do you ever feel a small questioning ache, would you not like me to tell you whether your old companions are still alive, or how they fare—Agamemnon and pitiful Menelaus, the mountainous Ajax, Meriones, audacious Diomedes, old Nestor, Achilles perhaps, and his companion the generous Patroclus, or even, even Odysseus?

PHILOCTETES. Odysseus! That ragged, thirsty, patched-up king of little Ithaca! Ithaca, where people eat gravel for supper! Ithaca had a king! Don't I remember him in the early days, when he saw himself sitting in Troy on a red cushion, a leg of mutton in each hand, and ten coffers of gold stowed away in his ship! And Agamemnon—no fool, I'll grant him that—invincible Agamemnon had visions of himself Emperor of Asia, he envied the centipedes because he had only two feet for people to kiss. I was more modest. A little gold, a little reputation, a few slave girls, I didn't ask for much, I was a villain of the tenth rank.

DEMODOCUS. You are a hard man, Philoctetes. Are we all bandits? Wasn't there a shred of justice in our going against Troy?

PHILOCTETES. Of course there was! Plenty of justice, my boy, Troy was a nest of pirates. An avalanche of justice! There's the beauty of your human affairs, crime and justice are bosom friends, famous allies; why, nothing's more deadly than a cause stinking with justice; but I, Philoctetes, I shook it all off the way a dog shakes the water off his back after a dip in the sea. A man stops being a bandit only when he's alone.

DEMODOCUS. Your anger burns through me. It convinces me that I should not tell you anything about these men, these criminals. Not even who died.

PHILOCTETES. Ah? Some of them died? Some of the great ones, I hope.

DEMODOCUS. Can you expect otherwise, after ten years? But what of your own kin, Philoctetes?

PHILOCTETES. How would you, a man of Argos, know anything of them in faraway Malis?

DEMODOCUS. You are right, I don't positively know, but it seems to me I heard that your father is no more—

PHILOCTETES. He was old....

DEMODOCUS. Your wife?

PHILOCTETES. She died giving birth to my son.

DEMODOCUS. He must be—

PHILOCTETES. Old enough to have taken my scepter in hand.

DEMODOCUS. He must want you home.

PHILOCTETES. Perhaps. Perhaps not. Let them be.... I've become another man. Let them be. I will show you my world by and by and what I and

THE SUMMONING OF PHILOCTETES

Medon have accomplished. You will ask the questions, believe me. We've captured the sun's rays; a river moves wheels for me; I created this bow, this bow which could do, which could do—only Zeus and I know what; we have an orchard; the hedgehog and the mole give us their hides; we have hemp for our nets; the porcupine supplies us with needles. The wild olive grows here, and wild barley too. We gather saffron on the hillsides for spice. We baked our first bread from crushed acorns, will you believe it? Sometimes we kill a boar. From the sea we catch mullet, bass, bream, and tunny; from the air and ground pheasants, quail, geese, rock-doves. But greatest wonder of all, here where men left me to rot, in this silence I can think at last. I ask questions of the stream and the tree leaf, of the spider and the seashell. Shall I tell you? I send my spirit prowling the night sky among the stars, like a child in dark streets who sees lights in the windows and puzzles at who and what happens within. You, poor fools, with your "I am not paid enough!" and "Will the neighbors sneer?" and "My wife is growing fat!" Pah! Give me no news. And forget those Messenians they sent you to enlist.

DEMODOCUS. We don't hear words like yours from Agamemnon! (*Silence*) Agamemnon is still alive, you see.

PHILOCTETES. Ah?

DEMODOCUS. And Menelaus too.

PHILOCTETES. Achilles defending them, of course, with great bluster.

DEMODOCUS. No more, Philoctetes. Achilles is dead.

PHILOCTETES. Impossible. Achilles could die? Who killed Achilles?

DEMODOCUS. Hardly believable, but Paris did, with an arrow, by ignoble chance.

PHILOCTETES. And another chance will do for Paris. But you, I imagine, are still hungry. Medon! Bring our young officer a loaf of bread and a dish of plums. I talk like a lord! No wine, alas; but we do have bread of a kind. (*Medon serves and then reenters the cave and remains out of sight*) Barley, you see, unleavened, not fit for a young warrior.

DEMODOCUS. Excellent. Excellent. I marvel at you. The longer I am here—no, I daren't say it.

PHILOCTETES. Dare! Dare! I am perfectly meek.

DEMODOCUS. Then I will dare and tell you that I have a great wish, in spite of your anger, to lure you to Ilium with me—even if need be on a raft. We need your hundred skills, your godly genius. At every council you, Philoctetes, are openly missed. And think of it—Achilles dead, Patroclus dead, Idomeneus dead, Leucus dead, Orsilocus dead, Cretan dead, Menestheus dead—

PHILOCTETES. Yes yes yes yes, slaughter, dead dead dead. Enough, you are trying to make me weep; and I do, I do. Scoundrels! Yet there they lie on the sand, their brains smashed, their guts filling with maggots. And hated Odysseus, is he still alive? No, tell me no more; what is it to me?

DEMODOCUS. He is still alive, God be thanked, and you must not hate him, Philoctetes; he only obeyed the oracle; there was no other way.

PHILOCTETES. So be it. Come, Demodocus, forget them all. We have been two in this colony these many years, and now we 'll be three.

DEMODOCUS. How is this possible? I was sent on a mission.

PHILOCTETES. I spit on your mission. Digging a grave for a thousand men. Look about you, my friend, and thank the gods—ah, ah, ah (*he writhes in pain*).

DEMODOCUS. You're ill! What can I do?

PHILOCTETES. The pain again again again. Look at me! A prince plagued by a foot! No—don't call Medon. I have troubled him enough. Ah, ah, ah.......

DEMODOCUS. Tell me what I can do.

PHILOCTETES. Nothing. Hold me. No. Stay away. I fall down and die for awhile and foul my cave. Wait for me. I can bear it.

DEMODOCUS. Your bow is heavy. Let me hold it for you. I will be waiting here.

(*Philoctetes gives him the bow*)

PHILOCTETES. You are kind. Medon! Medon!

(*He stumbles into the cave*)

DEMODOCUS. The bow in my hands! Kindness is rewarded....

(*Most of the soldiers appear*)

SIXTH SOLDIER. Demodocus!

DEMODOCUS. Yes.

SECOND SOLDIER. Not so loud.

FIRST SOLDIER. We heard everything. Masterfully done!

SECOND SOLDIER. Masterfully!

FIRST SOLDIER. At first we worried. "Why doesn't he obey his instructions?" we asked each other. And suddenly you call out to him, "Give me the bow"—and he gives it to you like a child.

SECOND SOLDIER. You have to remember that he doesn't know how important it is.

(*Enter the third soldier*)

THIRD SOLDIER (*to the first soldier*). We've sent the man, sir.

DEMODOCUS. Where have you sent what man?

FIRST SOLDIER. One of our men to inform Odysseus.

THE SUMMONING OF PHILOCTETES

DEMODOCUS. Of what, busybody? Is it your duty to spy on me?

FIRST SOLDIER. No sir. My duty is to execute my orders. But why wait for Odysseus to come? We've got the bow.

THIRD SOLDIER. Now's the time to bolt.

FOURTH SOLDIER. But is this the bow we want?

FIFTH SOLDIER. Of course! Oh, I could dance and shout!

DEMODOCUS. Hands off! What I do with the bow concerns me.

FIRST SOLDIER. Do with the bow? What can you do with the bow? We have it! Have it!

SEVENTH SOLDIER. Why stand and wait here, Demodocus? Let's go and meet Odysseus halfway.

EIGHTH SOLDIER. I know why he hesitates.

SECOND SOLDIER. Why?

SIXTH SOLDIER. He has made friends with Philoctetes.

EIGHTH SOLDIER. No, I didn't mean that. Don't you remember that we really want Philoctetes himself? That we want his brain? Who knows whether we can copy his bow? Whether we can handle it? What's it made of? Why does it have that curious knob in the middle? What kind of arrows does it take? I wouldn't dare use it. And it's come into our hands too easily, that's all.

FOURTH SOLDIER. Are we sure this is really the bow itself?

FIFTH SOLDIER. Always a doubter in the crowd. Always a questioner.

FIRST SOLDIER. Demodocus, no more of this. Let's take the bow to the ship and reason with Philoctetes afterward.

SECOND SOLDIER. From a position of strength.

THIRD SOLDIER. A bird in hand.

DEMODOCUS. A man who trusted me in the middle of my lies gave me the bow to safekeep for him.

FIRST SOLDIER. You asked for it and took it.

DEMODOCUS. He gave it to me! What if I walked into the cave while you stare at me and placed it in his companion's hand, scoundrel that I am?

FIRST SOLDIER. And the war?

FIFTH SOLDIER. We've got orders, Demodocus.

SECOND SOLDIER. Demodocus has made friends with Philoctetes.

SIXTH SOLDIER. That's what I said before.

SEVENTH SOLDIER. Why not? Philoctetes is a Greek.

SIXTH SOLDIER. A Greek! Did you hear him talk about the Greeks? He would eat us all boiled and salted if he could. And Demodocus was supposed to win him over. Instead it was Philoctetes who won him over.

FIFTH SOLDIER. The Trojans will get the bow! I see it!

THE SUMMONING OF PHILOCTETES

THIRD SOLDIER. Yes, the Trojans! Why not? They'll send Pandarus or another one of their professionals, somebody who won't mind a few lies and a length of dagger in the back if that 's the way to purchase the bow.

FIRST SOLDIER. Demodocus, come with us, orders must be obeyed.

THIRD SOLDIER. Don't hesitate.

FIFTH SOLDIER. In another few minutes it will be too late.

SIXTH SOLDIER. Odysseus is your master.

SEVENTH SOLDIER. You'll repent it if he gets wind of this.

EIGHTH SOLDIER. And if you anger him.

SECOND SOLDIER. Stop! I hear steps.

(Enter, running, the ninth soldier)

NINTH SOLDIER. Here is Odysseus! Stand ready!

(Enter Odysseus accompanied by the tenth soldier)

FIRST SOLDIER. Odysseus, we've got the bow!

ODYSSEUS. Where is Philoctetes?

DEMODOCUS. He became sick. He's in the cave, unconscious.

ODYSSEUS. Medon is with him?

DEMODOCUS. Yes.

ODYSSEUS. What did you tell him?

DEMODOCUS. I served him the lie about the raft; I shrewdly aroused his longing for home and companionship; I successfully concealed your presence; I secured his sympathy by envying his manner of life; and I skillfully extracted the bow from his fingers. No, I did so well he foisted it on me.

ODYSSEUS. What have we here?

FIRST SOLDIER. See for yourself, Odysseus.

ODYSSEUS. An attack of sarcasm! What's the meaning of this? Hand me the bow.

DEMODOCUS. Why?

ODYSSEUS. Am I to give reasons? Hand me the bow!

DEMODOCUS. Odysseus, let me wait here until Philoctetes recovers. With your permission I shall reveal the truth to him and ask his pardon for my lies. I will even return the weapon to him. Then man to man, openly and clearly, you can summon him to Troy. This will be the real glory for us: to win over the man by honest persuasion.

FIRST SOLDIER. Don't stand for this, Odysseus. If you'd heard Philoctetes as we did, you'd know nothing will make him tell his secrets and fight on our side. He says "Greek" the way a tiger growls.

ODYSSEUS. Is this true?

DEMODOCUS. Let me speak with him again. Give me more time. Think of his gratitude when we return—

THE SUMMONING OF PHILOCTETES

ODYSSEUS. No. The man is obstinate. I know him well. The oracle's message must be conveyed to him without more preambles. I am glad you have the bow, however. I like him better disarmed. Take it back to the ship, my son. I'll wait here, talk to him as quietly as I am talking to you, and persuade him to return with us.

DEMODOCUS. And if he refuses? Even though I have made him helpless?

ODYSSEUS. Go back to the ship.

DEMODOCUS. What if, in his anger, he prefers the Trojans?

ODYSSEUS. Go back to the ship.

DEMODOCUS. I wish to stay here.

FIRST SOLDIER. This is open mutiny, Odysseus.

EIGHTH SOLDIER. Give us the bow!

ODYSSEUS. Patience, my friends. All will be done gently. I myself, as it happens, do not question the loyalty of Demodocus. I understand his scruples. And yet, I don't know, I am no weakling; and we are many against one. We might have a scrap, shed some blood, but we could subdue him.

DEMODOCUS. What are you saying? Would I fight you? Never! No, I ask you simply as a man—

ODYSSEUS (*changing his tone*). Ask me nothing. Men, draw your swords. Demodocus, I order you to take the bow to the ship. Stay back, men! (*He draws his sword. Demodocus half raises the bow. Odysseus slowly advances. Demodocus retreats as far as he can*).

DEMODOCUS. Stop! Stop! (*He leaps away and disappears with the bow in the direction of the beach, but leaving the arrow on the ground. Odysseus and the soldiers sheathe their swords*)

ODYSSEUS. The bow, at any rate, is ours. But it's Philoctetes himself we want. A willing Philoctetes.

SEVENTH SOLDIER. And Demodocus? Surely you will not tolerate what we have just witnessed!

THIRD SOLDIER. He is a traitor, Odysseus. Will you not arraign him before the Assembly?

ODYSSEUS. I, not you, shall decide who is a traitor.

NINTH SOLDIER. The point is: we have the bow!

FIRST SOLDIER. And now for Philoctetes.

ODYSSEUS. Now for Philoctetes. Stand aside, men. I will take my place here.

FIFTH SOLDIER. In the open?

ODYSSEUS. Man to man.

(*The soldiers go to one side, except for the tenth soldier whom Odysseus detains*)

ODYSSEUS. You, stay.

THE SUMMONING OF PHILOCTETES

TENTH SOLDIER. Yes, sir.

ODYSSEUS. I learned from Demodocus what I sent him for: how bitter the man is against us. I expected the worst; the worst is what I find.

TENTH SOLDIER. Yes.

ODYSSEUS. I will beg him again.

TENTH SOLDIER. God grant you success.

ODYSSEUS. I may fail. (*The soldier looks down*) Are you and the other three ready?

TENTH SOLDIER. My lord—

ODYSSEUS. Are you ready? God strike you! Speak!

TENTH SOLDIER (*low*). We are.

ODYSSEUS. Look out for my signal. This is what I will do (*he rubs one of his cheeks with his hand*). You see it?

TENTH SOLDIER. I do.

ODYSSEUS. If Zeus is merciful, I will not give it. If I give it, be prompt. The blood is on my head, not yours; but yours will answer if you disobey.

TENTH SOLDIER. You are the master, Odysseus.

(*He rejoins the other soldiers, but remains silently apart from them. Odysseus sits on a rocky ledge facing the entrance to the cave*)

THE CHORUS, *with drum*

FIRST SOLDIER. Let us speak in praise of our lord Odysseus. To speak his praise is a lovely task, because whatever the mind shapes privately concerning this man, the mouth is glad to utter, and not only in the house, to father or wife or children, but in the marketplace, in the Assembly, to all men. It makes a man happy when he means his praise, when he bows because of the veneration he truly feels, when he presses a hand because he loves. Now, as is fitting, I will be the man to begin.

SECOND SOLDIER. What will you praise in Odysseus?

FIRST SOLDIER. I will praise his rank among the Greeks. Though he rules a harsh land, Ithaca, which has not grain enough to feed itself, and where few trees grow among the many-colored rocks, he is the man most honored by Agamemnon. Achilles was the stronger man; but he was proud, fierce, and factious. Menelaus is Agamemnon's brother, but he is a weak soldier, one who always leans against another. Diomedes is supreme in the battlefield; but he fights even in his dreams, even in his tent at supper, even in the Assembly. To every concern brought forward in the Assembly, he answers, "Fight!" Idomeneus was the richer man; he was king of Crete; he could plunge a hand into the treasury of magnificent Egypt; his palaces were thick and strong, with deep foundations; he called us rustics; yet because of all this, one half of his mind stayed at home and only with the other half did he attend to our war. And still he died. No. Agamemnon's true brother is Odysseus, though Odysseus came to him with only twelve ships—he had no more. Odysseus is strong, wise, loyal: in the fight a fighter, in council a counselor, and, I will add, at supper a merry man. Agamemnon has said in public, "While Odysseus remains at my side, I will not lift the siege of Troy, I will never be disheartened. But if Odysseus chose to despair and withdrew from us, I too would give up." So much has Agamemnon himself said.

SECOND SOLDIER. Now let me speak of Odysseus the ruler of Ithaca. How did he come to rule? By means of conquest? By sly murder of his betters? By bribing the old men? By promising the riches of the Hesperides to our poor country? Not so. But by unanimous applause and election, promising nothing, threatening no one. And I ask you all, my friends, to recount his achievements.

THIRD SOLDIER. He taught us to build houses as fine as those of proud Argos.

FOURTH SOLDIER. He cleared the roads of bandits by hanging some and giving work to others.

FIFTH SOLDIER. He gave the poor bread without robbing the rich.

SIXTH SOLDIER. He proclaimed the festival of Pallas Athene, at which the young compete in the chariot race and the wrestling and the spear-throwing while the whole island, assembled, relaxes, takes sides, and is refreshed by holiday.

SEVENTH SOLDIER. He rescued the debtors from prison and in a lean year proclaimed a full remission of all unpaid taxes.

EIGHTH SOLDIER. He gave us courts of justice and made an end of private revenge and family vendettas.

THIRD SOLDIER. He gave us peace without sloth—

FOURTH SOLDIER. And prosperity without vice.

FIFTH SOLDIER. Let me speak in my turn of Odysseus the master. I was a smith in his household before I became a soldier. And you too, my friend—

SEVENTH SOLDIER. I was a farmer.

FIFTH SOLDIER. You shall witness the truth of what I say. Did he ever speak brutally to any of us? He did not. Did he work us half to death, so that we lacked the living life on which to spend our earnings? He did not. Rather he came among us, taught us what he knew, and amazing to us, the poor, he asked to be shown; took the hammer in his own hands, rolled back his sleeves, and worked.

SEVENTH SOLDIER. Once when my leg was lame he took the plow from me and turned the soil behind the ox all day long under the sun.

FIFTH SOLDIER. Singing—do you remember?—singing all the while! So that we glowed brighter than the hot iron and worked like Vulcan to please him.

SEVENTH SOLDIER. And he gave us sudden holidays. "Go, my lads," he said, "it's been a month since the harvest feast; time for a twelve-hour carouse!" Laughing as he talked, and going about boxing with the boys of the village.

EIGHTH SOLDIER. Now I will speak of Odysseus the husband and father. Noble Telemachus, his son, walks gravely by his side as he visits his people, or sits close by when he delivers judgment. He is less strong, less lively than his father; more sober, perhaps more delicate, more studious. But strong love binds these two men together. Have you seen Odysseus lean toward his son, whisper a question into his ear, receive a reply, and nod in approval? Wise is the father who knows how to flatter his son; who takes, or seems to take, advice from him. And from the day Telemachus was born, Odysseus himself raised him. He did not fear smiles by entering the nursery and seeing that the linen was washed. He was the boy's tutor, playmate, and guide; until it happened that, although Telemachus was only in his seventeenth year when his father sailed to the war, Odysseus gave him the rule of Ithaca with peace and trust in his soul.

SIXTH SOLDIER. While Penelope his wife, glad and proud, having loved no man before and no man since, waits for the kindest husband who ever lived, in mourning and solitude. And even as she weeps, she is happy in her unhappiness, because the weight of her present misery is the measure of her former joy. Luckless woman, whom the loss of a husband cannot make unhappy! And by this I judge the goodness of Odysseus, that those who knew him best lament his absence most.

THIRD SOLDIER. And in the camp, my friends? Whose tent is empty? That of Odysseus. A man without handy concubines, without purchased whores, without soft-lipped slaves. The others quarrel over a captive and threaten civil war for the sake of a naked woman. They wake at noon from their debauches too destroyed to fight. Only Odysseus keeps faith with his wife. He rises from the banquet merry but clearheaded: even-tempered, his mind firm, his body controlled, his gaze like a prong of light into the dense world.

NINTH SOLDIER. See him now, sitting patiently. His fingers hold the strings of destiny.

FOURTH SOLDIER. Almost a god.

THE SUMMONING OF PHILOCTETES

FIRST SOLDIER. Almost a god.
ODYSSEUS. Soldiers, I hear a stirring in Philoctetes' mansion. Be vigilant. (*He rises and shouts*) Philoctetes!
(*Philoctetes appears. He gives a shrill cry. Medon, armed with his sword, stands next to him*)
ODYSSEUS. I am Odysseus.
PHILOCTETES. I recognize you! And I see, I see it all! An army of Greeks! I should have known! (*He restrains Medon with his hand*)
ODYSSEUS. I greet you, and I greet Medon, with affection and respect. I thank the Gods who have kept you full of strong life. Give me a hearing, Philoctetes. Do not condemn us before we have spoken. We come as your brothers.
PHILOCTETES. Odysseus: the same old fox. He sends me a young hypocrite to disarm me, he stalks me with a brace of ruffians, he stands before me with his sword out and cries Brother!
ODYSSEUS. More gently, Philoctetes. We arrived in a strange land. Who could predict what we should find? We are accustomed to war. But I am reassured and I return my sword to its scabbard.
PHILOCTETES. Always the fox. What are you looking for?
ODYSSEUS. You.
PHILOCTETES. Has the oracle told you that Philoctetes must die?
ODYSSEUS. Far from it. Our solemn mission is to take you back to our ranks.
PHILOCTETES. That is what your accomplice hinted. How affable to poor Philoctetes! Fancy the Greeks at their Assembly one night, the place stinking with corpses. Agamemnon strokes his beard and says, "How I pity Philoctetes! Never has he had his chance of a nobly torn belly or a gloriously broken skull."
ODYSSEUS. Let me speak.
PHILOCTETES. Then they send Odysseus off with a friend, and all for pity and affection they lie to him, trick him, rob him of his weapon, and trap him in his cave. Now Odysseus, speak up, good and blunt, and if it's blood you want, spare me your apologies.
ODYSSEUS. You treat me, Philoctetes, as though I were childish enough to treat you as a child. I have not come for pity of you. If circumstances required me to eliminate you, I would do so. This we both know; no fooling between us. As it happens, the oracle declares that your good fortune is ours, and ours is yours. A common interest binds us. Will you hear what it is? Or will you bite before the hand is even stretched?
PHILOCTETES. Speak.
ODYSSEUS. The sentence came from Calchas the soothsayer. "Not by force

THE SUMMONING OF PHILOCTETES

alone shall the Greeks overcome Troy, but by force allied with immortal cunning. Let Pyrrhus, the son of Achilles, be the force. Let Philoctetes, King of Malis, be our cunning." Listen again. Calchas saw your invented bow in a vision: strong, far-shooting, unerring: its arrows deadlier than those of Crete or Thrace: your secret. Taught by you, and armed each one of us with this bow, we shall send into the bowels of Troy a panic like the trample of a falling mountain. And you, Philoctetes, you will live; you glorious to the end of time: cherished by Greece, your wound forgotten, a sage among men, one of us, Philoctetes, Greek again.

CHORUS (*low*). One of us.

PHILOCTETES (*shaken*). He saw my bow in a vision?

ODYSSEUS. Yes, my friend. Let this persuade you of the truth of all I have told you. How could I have known that such a bow existed? Who knows except you, your companion, and the gods?

PHILOCTETES. I can't answer you. I've become too simple here, I can't see behind your words.

FIRST SOLDIER. Noble Philoctetes, he speaks the truth.

PHILOCTETES. Well, the bow is in your hands. Demodocus stole it, if that's his name.

ODYSSEUS. Be indulgent with us, Philoctetes. The bow fell into our hands; we should have returned it to you; but we have been soldiers in the field too long; my men would not relinquish it.

PHILOCTETES. Keep it then, my friends, see if you can handle it, go back to your ships, let the pinewood oars fly, and good riddance to you all.

ODYSSEUS. And you?

PHILOCTETES. We stay here. I have my world. I need no other. I can remake my bow. The secret is in my head.

ODYSSEUS. The bow is not enough. We need Philoctetes himself.

PHILOCTETES. Away! Forget me!

ODYSSEUS. You have been alone long enough. Think. Medon may die.

PHILOCTETES. God forbid! I am the older man. I will be the first to die.

ODYSSEUS. Perhaps not. God may not forbid. And then what will become of you? You will howl on your knees and go mad. A man must live among his kind.

PHILOCTETES. Ruffian! Back to Troy! You are not my kind!

FIRST SOLDIER. Odysseus! I hear somebody running.

SEVENTH SOLDIER. There! There!

ODYSSEUS. Demodocus!

CHORUS. Stop!

(*Demodocus rushes up to Philoctetes and thrusts the bow into his hands*)

THE SUMMONING OF PHILOCTETES

DEMODOCUS. Your bow, Philoctetes! Forgive me!
(*Medon has quickly handed Philoctetes the arrow Demodocus had left behind; he rushes into the cave and brings out more arrows*)
PHILOCTETES (*aiming*). Back Odysseus, back! My bow doesn't know how to miss!
ODYSSEUS. Back, men!
CHORUS. Oh God, help us!
PHILOCTETES. Stand back! Medon, look sharp. Back! Back!
ODYSSEUS (*to the soldiers*). No violence, my friends. All in good time. I admire Demodocus in a way. I deplore what he did; I who thought he was speeding to our ships! But I admire him. It was his conscience.
DEMODOCUS. Why do you jeer, Odysseus? This is our war, not his. Or his if he sees fit. And besides: I am no boy for dirty errands.
PHILOCTETES. Hands off your swords, all of you! Eyes open, Medon. Odysseus, don't stand there. Call your heroes together and clear the island. The wind will be rising soon.
ODYSSEUS. We will remain here and wait till nightfall.
PHILOCTETES. But if by nightfall you're not sailing in your ship, I will shoot you straight and happy through the heart.
ODYSSEUS. Let that be as it will. Patience.
DEMODOCUS (*to Philoctetes*). I will try to protect you.
PHILOCTETES. What are you doing?
DEMODOCUS. Going where I belong.
PHILOCTETES. Don't be a fool, Demodocus; stay here. Odysseus is waiting to pounce on you. You're a traitor to Greece. Congratulations!
DEMODOCUS. I think otherwise. Odysseus, for once let a younger man persuade you. My tongue is cleansed. Allow me to plead with him. He trusts me now.
ODYSSEUS. Suit yourself, my lad.
(*Demodocus rejoins the Greeks*)
PHILOCTETES. Don't be a fool!
ODYSSEUS. Grab him! (*The soldiers leap at Demodocus. Medon, ready to rush to his help, is restrained by Philoctetes*)
ODYSSEUS. Hold the boy. From behind. Lock his arms. Bind his wrists.
DEMODOCUS (*groaning*). Fool, fool, fool.... (*He groans with pain as two soldiers force him to his knees*)
PHILOCTETES (*to Medon*). The other opening must be guarded. Go in and keep watch. (*Medon obeys*) Is that how you'll tempt me to return to Troy? Demodocus, keep heart. The game isn't finished yet. Bandits! Leap at me! Leap! Take my corpse to Troy! Manacle my corpse this time!

THE SUMMONING OF PHILOCTETES

ODYSSEUS. Philoctetes! Once more! Return with us! How easily we could capture you!

PHILOCTETES. You don't know what my bow can do. Go back without me, rascals!

DEMODOCUS. We can't, Philoctetes! We must kill you if necessary! We're afraid you'll cross to the Trojans! Come back to us, my friend!

ODYSSEUS. Damnation! (*He touches and rubs his cheek. The tenth soldier whispers into the ears of the seventh, eighth and ninth, and the four slip away*)

PHILOCTETES. The Trojans are coming too! Of course! Let Hector have the bow! I'll make my home with them!

ODYSSEUS. Poor Hector. Hector is dead! But you are right, the Trojans are coming. You are more than right: the Trojans have come!

FIRST SOLDIER (*dumbfounded like the others*). When did they land?

ODYSSEUS. Patience....

(*The scene goes dark. The drum marks the passing of hours. Then the light returns. Enter the four soldiers carrying two litters, each with a dead man on it*)

ODYSSEUS. Look, Philoctetes. There will be no Trojans to traffic with. I am going to teach you an unforgettable lesson. Look at your Trojan saviors. They are the last ones you will ever see.

FIRST SOLDIER. Odysseus, we are all amazed. What happened?

ODYSSEUS. One of our patrols found a small Trojan craft, and some twenty men ashore. We took them by surprise and killed them all.

FIRST SOLDIER. With losses on our side?

ODYSSEUS. Not a man. Come, Philoctetes, come and look.

PHILOCTETES (*without moving*). Odysseus, I tell you once again, take yourself and your henchmen away. My bow is hungry for you. Beware.

ODYSSEUS. I understand. And I give up. If I take you alive, you will kill yourself rather than tell your secret.

PHILOCTETES. Like a fly.

ODYSSEUS. Well, what matters in the end is that we shall have no competitors. There they lie. You can even keep Demodocus. (*He seizes Demodocus*) He's yours. (*He throws Demodocus down toward the cave. Still holding the bow, Philoctetes instinctively takes two steps toward Demodocus as if to help him up, but he has left the opening of the cave unguarded. At a signal from Odysseus, the fifth soldier rushes into the cave. Philoctetes utters a cry but hesitates*)

MEDON (*within*). Master!

ODYSSEUS (*shouting*). Kill him!

PHILOCTETES. No!

MEDON (*within*). Master!

PHILOCTETES. No!

THE SUMMONING OF PHILOCTETES

CHORUS, *with drum.* Kill!
(*Philoctetes is about to kill Odysseus with an arrow but Odysseus catches hold of Demodocus and uses him as a shield*)
ODYSSEUS. Bring Medon out!
(*The fifth soldier carries Medon's body out. With a mighty effort Philoctetes breaks his bow in two. He flings himself sobbing over the body. Odysseus hands Demodocus, still bound, to one of the soldiers*)
SIXTH SOLDIER. He broke the bow!
FOURTH SOLDIER. He broke the bow!
PHILOCTETES. In my brain too, the bow is broken. O Heracles, let them perish before Troy all of them, and you, Odysseus, may your corpse be left to the dogs, let them devour you and turn you into their excrement.
ODYSSEUS. Why do you rail at me, Philoctetes? It is you who killed Medon, not I. Your hatred for us has made you insane. We came here, Greek to Greek, brother to brother, offering you immortal glory, love and reverence. You raved at us as if we, not the serpent, had bitten your ankle that foul day in the grove of Chryse. I now abandon you to your wrath and your misery. I shall report you mysteriously dead amidst a crowd of Trojan corpses, and exhibit these poor victims for proof. The Trojans will not come again. Neither shall we. Never, never will you see a human being again. (*To two soldiers*) You. You. Take up Medon's body.
PHILOCTETES (*flinging himself on the body*). No, no, no!
ODYSSEUS. Take up the body I say! (*The soldiers push Philoctetes aside and take the body*) Back to the ship, men.
DEMODOCUS. I tried, Philoctetes. May the gods protect you....
(*Six of the soldiers now move off, carrying the litters and Medon. Another, holding Demodocus, moves out as well. The first to third soldiers remain*)
FIRST SOLDIER. Without him?
ODYSSEUS. Without him. He will never give us his secret.
SECOND SOLDIER. No pity for us?
THIRD SOLDIER. For us who have to do the fighting?
SECOND SOLDIER. For us who only obey orders?
THIRD SOLDIER. We never meant you any harm.
SECOND SOLDIER. Harm? We wanted to fall at your feet.
THIRD SOLDIER. The common soldier was always your friend.
SECOND SOLDIER. What have we got to do with oracles, higher strategy, new weapons, headquarters, military policy?
THIRD SOLDIER. It is us you punish, not Odysseus, not Agamemnon.
SECOND SOLDIER. And our wives, our children, who don't even know you.

THE SUMMONING OF PHILOCTETES

FIRST SOLDIER. Enough wailing, men!
ODYSSEUS. Away, soldiers. No tears. The bow doesn't matter if no one has it.
(*Exeunt the three soldiers*)
ODYSSEUS. How quiet it is. Nothing but my voice remains. And after me, nothing.
(*He draws a dagger, rises and advances toward Philoctetes*)
PHILOCTETES. You'll murder me?
(*Odysseus throws the dagger down*)
ODYSSEUS. Here. For the day you become sick of the silence, oh my brother, my brother....
(*He turns and leaves. Philoctetes is alone. He seems bewildered. He picks up the broken bow and throws the pieces down again. He enters the cave, and comes out again, a broken man, holding a few scraps of Medon's clothing. A long time passes, at first marked with the drum, but then comes total silence. More time. Suddenly he flings himself toward the far end of the stage, where the Greeks left, and utters a wild cry*)
PHILOCTETES. Take me! Take me! (*The drum beats wildly. The fourth soldier appears*) Take me! (*He is sobbing*)
FOURTH SOLDIER. Odysseus! Come back! Take him!
A VOICE (*in the distance*). Take him!
(*Philoctetes lies on the ground. His sobs diminish. Reenter Odysseus, Demodocus, and the first to sixth soldiers*)
ODYSSEUS. Zeus has spoken! (*To the fifth and sixth soldiers*) You two, conduct noble Philoctetes to our ship. The bitter words and the cruel acts are erased. The King of Malis is our savior. Treat him with awe and veneration.
(*The soldiers escort Philoctetes out*)
ODYSSEUS. Friends, our mission is accomplished; not without difficulties, not, alas, without bloodshed, but accomplished, I believe, in a manner which must satisfy the supreme command. Demodocus, you are pardoned. Unbind the young man. I forget what has no need to be remembered. Philoctetes is ours, body and spirit. Now let the Trojans land and look for him!
FIRST SOLDIER. The Trojans? But you killed them!
ODYSSEUS. No, my children. Sooner or later you must know. Harden yourselves against the inevitable. These two men were sailors on our craft. (*The Chorus cries out in grief*) Their lives were demanded of them, two for ten thousand. Alas....
FIRST SOLDIER. Odysseus!
DEMODOCUS. You murdered two of our men?
ODYSSEUS. When you failed us, Demodocus, when your conscience became

THE SUMMONING OF PHILOCTETES

petulant, you forced me to give the terrible command. With the bow in his fist, and Medon at his side, Philoctetes was intractable. I made an inhuman desert around him. I showed him the face of silence. I broke him.

FIRST SOLDIER. But then, surely, my lord, you never meant to leave Philoctetes behind, with the Trojans on their way even now! What if he had not cried out for us in the end?

ODYSSEUS. He would not be alive.

FIRST SOLDIER. I shudder at your cunning, Odysseus. Always in control, even when you are surprised.

ODYSSEUS. No gloating. Let us be soberly satisfied.

FIRST SOLDIER. Odysseus, blessing to the Greeks, wherever you go, it seems to us that a shimmer of divinity surrounds you.

ODYSSEUS. Wherever I go, I go knee-deep in dung and blood. Such is leadership. Come, children, away. Demodocus, are you ready?

DEMODOCUS. Leave me here.

ODYSSEUS. Leave you here?

DEMODOCUS. Yes.

ODYSSEUS. Alone?

DEMODOCUS. Yes.

SECOND SOLDIER. Don't be a fool, Demodocus. Come with us.

THIRD SOLDIER. No one will remind you of anything.

SECOND SOLDIER. Your place in the field is still your place.

THIRD SOLDIER. Do we speak for you, Odysseus?

ODYSSEUS. You do.

DEMODOCUS. Leave me here. (*Pointing to the cave*) A home is ready for me.

ODYSSEUS. Demodocus, we set off as soon as the wind blows into our sails. Come if you wish, stay if you wish. I have no time to give you.

(*He leaves*)

FIRST SOLDIER. Come with us, Demodocus. This is too horrible. You will babble at random and finally lose your language. You will crouch on all fours like a beast. Who knows? You will fornicate with an animal, and beget a monster. Demodocus, live among men. Even hate is better than solitude. We should huddle on this earth of ours and hold each others' hands and say goodbye to the dying, and kiss their lips with a last warmth. But you will die alone, growling vacantly, your head on a stone, and the wild pigs will eat you.

THIRD SOLDIER. Think of the cheering fire in the house. The open door, the embrace. "You've come back to us," they cry. They take off your cloak, they bathe your feet, they offer you wine and honey, they cry and fuss over you.

FOURTH SOLDIER. Once long ago I quarreled bitterly with my father because he loved my brothers, but me he neglected and even starved; sometimes he beat me; he called me a vagabond. And I left the house; I went to Corinth; I lived alone among strangers. At night I heard the voices next door to mine; during the day I saw people in the street: families, lovers, friends, or polite acquaintances—I envied them all, even the man who patted a dog; and now and then I saw a man alone, like myself, and that man wore the same expression as mine, a studied air of indifference to hide his despair. He looks around and seems to say, "Me? I am alone only for the moment! I am expecting a happy crowd of friends. Don't worry about me, I beg you." But inside he cries. He goes home and stares at the wall opposite his chair. He eats an apple. He writes a letter. He washes his face. And he sits again and stares. Presently he begins to talk to himself. Then he stops, because he is ashamed. What will he do? He is not tired. What can he do? He paces the floor, lifts a vase from a shelf, places it on a table, he doesn't know why, and sits down again. All he wants now is to see a human being. He knows one at the far end of the city. But this man has a wife and two small children, and it would be a disturbance to knock at his door. What excuse would he have for the visit? He could say, "Excuse me, I came to borrow the hand-saw you promised me." Perhaps the wife would ask him to come in and share their meal. But if she did, he would reply, "Thank you, but I must hurry, I have an appointment," lest they humiliate him with pity; and he would go home again, and sit, stare, and suffer. Oh Demodocus, believe me, I returned to my birthplace, I kissed the first friend I met in the street; he thought I was mad.

THIRD SOLDIER. And the war, for that matter, is that so bad after all?

SECOND SOLDIER. No! Better this war all my life, and to lose an arm, than another month of loneliness.

THIRD SOLDIER. A comrade keeps you warm too.

SECOND SOLDIER. In the heat of battle you hear and see your platoon.

THIRD SOLDIER. At night you roar out a song together.

SECOND SOLDIER. You share a bottle.

THIRD SOLDIER. A story.

SECOND SOLDIER. A woman.

FOURTH SOLDIER. For whom will you sing? How will you fare without us who are the listeners? When you sang, we sat still and yet we traveled; we were ourselves and yet we became other men; our lives multiplied; wisdoms not our own became ours. Such was your power over us. But without us, where is your power?

(*Silence*)

THE SUMMONING OF PHILOCTETES

SECOND SOLDIER. He won't say a word.
A VOICE (*in the distance*). Men! The wind is rising, hurry, hurry!
FIRST SOLDIER. Demodocus. If you came running after us, and caught the rope-ladder while the ship moved away, you might cut a shabby or laughable figure. Many a fool will die rather than cut a shabby or laughable figure. Don't be a fool.
(*The soldiers slowly leave. Drumbeats. Then a long silence*)
DEMODOCUS. Erased from the records of the city and the temple, I now become free and innocent, not rising, not sinking, dumb as the laurel, still as a rock, clean as a drop of rain, peaceful as the dust. I will stop singing, being perfect. I will be reticent. I will listen to the sea's liquid speech, not one a liar among all its syllable waves. Philoctetes, I see Troy in torment to the end of time, to the end of time I hear the scurrilous mirth of the conqueror, the unjust and the just; but to me the seagull will report only the fish dancing in the sea, innocently devouring, innocently devoured. Blessed silence.....

The End

Notes

The Summoning of Philoctetes was published under the title *Island* in the Winter 1961 issue of the *Massachusetts Review*. It was my first *published* play. A revised version appeared in the first volume of my 1970-1972 *Collected Plays*. Rebaptized under its present title, it became part of my *Philoctetes and the Fall of Troy: Plays, Documents, Iconography, Interpretations* (1981)—a volume which also included translations of André Gide's *Philoctetes; or the Treatise on Three Ethics* (1898) and Heiner Müller's *Philoctetes* (1961: the date, by coincidence, of the original publication of *Island*). The present final version has been extensively revised and, surely, improved.

AGAMEMNON TRIUMPHANT

CHARACTERS

Agamemnon
Achilles
Briseis
Diomedes
Odysseus
Patroclus
Dolon
Soldiers

Zeus
Thetis
The First Figure: War
The Second Figure: Vengeance
The Third Figure

SCENE ONE

(In Achilles' shelter. An altar in one corner. Night. By a dim light we see Achilles, Patroclus and Briseis. Achilles wears his sword)

BRISEIS. How can I, when I see you so somber, so unlike yourself?
ACHILLES. Sing, I tell you, sing of consolations....
BRISEIS. I'll try, my dear *(She sings)*.

>   Bridegroom, exult! Just as you prayed,
>   The rites are done and you are married.
>   The girl, just as you prayed, is yours—

(She stops) I can't sing, Achilles. Tell me what happened. Tell your Briseis, the woman who knows all your secrets. Patroclus, ask him for me.
ACHILLES. Better for you not to know.
PATROCLUS. Tell her, my friend. Let her be warned, let her be prepared....
BRISEIS. Oh God, it's something too terrible....
(Silence)
ACHILLES. They want to drag you from me.
BRISEIS. Why? Why?
ACHILLES. I rose in the Assembly. A newcomer to the siege, but the strongest, with ships and men nearly as many as his, and fresh, rested, eager. I had the right. And I was the only man not cowed by big Agamemnon. Why have the winds been dead for a month and not a sack of barley, not a barrel of wine delivered to the troops? Why are the supply ships rooted in Aulis, unable to set sail? Nobody dared speak up but I. Not Aias, not Diomedes, not even old Nestor—it seems a man is never too old to be afraid to die. Dead silence. And Calchas too, pale as milk. Soothsayers also know when to keep their tongues on a leash. It was the scared look he gave me that maddened me. I cut through the crowd of trembling heroes and took him by the throat—
PATROCLUS. Shook him like an olive tree ripe for harvesting!
ACHILLES. "Dog," I said, "you are a priest, a seer, a man who reads the guts of sheep and the flight of birds, the gods protect you and yet you daren't tell us what we all know that you know." And all that time I see

Agamemnon stiffen as I speak. "Tell us!" I yell, "tell *him!*"

PATROCLUS. Not a word!

ACHILLES. So at last it was I who had to say what there was to say. "You, Agamemnon, yes you! Lecher! Worse than your brother and his Helen! You kicked away the high priest of Apollo who came begging you for the daughter you had dragged from the temple like a brawling rapist. And the man cursed you; you and all the Argives. And Apollo heard him. Speak, Calchas, or I'll throttle you!" I pushed him to the tribune. "It's true, my lord," he brings out at last; "have pity on me"—his knees knocking together. Well, I had shamed one of them at last. Nestor moved his grey-bearded bulk towards his mighty majesty. "Let the girl go, my lord," he said as low as possible; "send her home to her father, send rich gifts, tripods, golden drinking bowls, beautifully woven cloth for Apollo's altar; and then may the angry god have mercy on us and send the ships a fair Western wind." Silence again. Agamemnon looked at the crowd and read their faces. And he stared at me when he spoke. "I will do as you say, wise Nestor, for you are my friend. But you, Achilles, rash ill-judging man, late-comer to our war, you have a desirable captive—"

BRISEIS (*moaning*). Stop....

ACHILLES. "Who will warm my bed when the other one is gone."

BRISEIS. You will let him? You, Achilles?

ACHILLES. "You dare!" I cried; and I did touch the pommel of my sword, whereupon I was pelted with cries from all sides. No, Briseis, I shall not let them touch you. But give me time to think. Do we sail home? Or do we beat him down? "Come the next full moon," he said, "I'll send the priest's daughter home with generous gifts; and then"—giving me a thundering look—"your own darling—"

PATROCLUS (*suddenly*). Who is out there?

(*The tent is flung open. Agamemnon enters with five soldiers*)

AGAMEMNON (*to the soldiers*). Go!

(*They seize Briseis and the unarmed Patroclus. Achilles draws his sword. Two soldiers hold him off with spears*)

AGAMEMNON. Drop your sword, Achilles, if you care for your friends.

PATROCLUS. Let him kill me, Achilles! Do what you can!

ACHILLES. In good time. (*He contemptuously throws his sword to the ground*)

AGAMEMNON (*to one of the soldiers*). Take her to my shelter. The next full moon is too far off, comrade.

BRISEIS. Scum! Achilles will throw you to the dogs!

SOLDIER. Shut your mouth, woman.

(*He drags her off sobbing*)

ACHILLES. You have her now, Agamemnon. For the moment. But mark my words. Briseis is mine. No slave, but my honored woman and my bride to be when I am home again, and that, I think, will be soon. Dare not, tyrant of Mycenae, approach her nearer than a sword's length. Remember who I am.

AGAMEMNON. Windy talk from a bully. Until I ship the priest's daughter home to him, one night I'll saddle her, and the other your favorite. And if she doesn't suit me, I'll throw her to one of *them (pointing to the soldiers)*.

ACHILLES. You must be drunk, or else some god has stolen your wits. Touch her and die. And ask yourself what you will do here without me. Hector laughs at you and your weakling of a brother. I see not so much as a stone missing from Troy's walls. Without myself, Patroclus, and my Myrmidons, you'll rot here until even the vultures won't want to look at you.

AGAMEMNON. That's as the gods will decide. In the meantime, Achilles, remember that *I* am the king. Keep your place. Don't bellow in the Assembly because you have more muscle than I, or because your men are fresh and ours are tired. If you have something to say, speak to me in private. *(To the soldiers, pointing at Patroclus)* Let him go. Patroclus, you're not a hothead like your master. Instruct him in the rules. Rules are not to be violated unless I say so. Farewell. *(As he leaves)* The commanders meet tomorrow at dawn, Achilles. Be there. We want to give you instructions about the use of your fresh soldiers.

ACHILLES. My fresh soldiers will sit in their tents unless you undo this hour's work, return the girl to me and bow low before me into the dust where you belong.

AGAMEMNON. You are wanted, Achilles, but not needed. Stay, leave, do as you please. *(To the soldiers)* You. Follow me.

(He and the soldiers leave)

PATROCLUS. I was unarmed, Achilles.

ACHILLES. Yes.

PATROCLUS. What will you do? Speak to me. Your face is on fire. Remember, we have three thousand men.

ACHILLES. They have five times that number. And I am not a Titan.

PATROCLUS. What are you saying, Achilles? Surely we're not sailing home like frightened minnows! And leaving Briseis to him!

ACHILLES. Calm yourself. Be patient. I may not, must not be as rash as that feeble bully. Our ships are safely anchored at the far end of the line; and we, at any rate, have what's needful to feed ourselves. Beginning tomorrow we shall drill the troops every morning, and after drill the men will roll dice, run races along the beach, sing ballads, and gaze at the Hellenes and

Trojans slashing at each other in the distance. We shall allow Agamemnon to bleed until it dawns on him that here, here stands a king above his kingship.
PATROCLUS. In it and yet not in it. You know best.
ACHILLES. I do know best. Go speak to the officers. Reassure them about what happened here. No demoralizing ideas. You understand me.
PATROCLUS. Perfectly.
ACHILLES. And prepare them for active inaction.
PATROCLUS. I will.
ACHILLES. Good night, Patroclus, and thanks.
PATROCLUS. I wish I could have done more. Good night. (*He leaves*)
(*Stillness. Achilles goes to the altar and raises his arms to it until a light begins to glow from it*)
ACHILLES (*softly*). Mother! Goddess! Thetis! Rise from the sea!
(*Thetis appears. Achilles kneels to her and embraces her knees. She strokes his head throughout*)
THETIS. O my son. I feel the blow, I feel it deep in my undying heart.
ACHILLES. Has Zeus begun to hate me, mother? Would any prayer of mine or yours be made in vain?
THETIS. Not so. Tell me your prayer, that I may wind it into mine.
ACHILLES. You know it already.
THETIS. I do. Speak it aloud, so it becomes a thing and has weight.
ACHILLES. May Agamemnon and all the Argives who stand by him be trampled into the dust by Priam's sons, until he makes amends to me, and more.
THETIS. This I will cry for, until the god of gods satisfies us.
ACHILLES. Do it, mother, since my hatred needs you, do it.
THETIS. I will do it, Achilles my son, weep no more, my child.
(*The light dims and she vanishes*)

SCENE TWO

(*Zeus on his throne. Flanking him, the grim Figures of War and Vengeance. Before him, Thetis as suppliant*)

ZEUS. Again this deafening noise of quarrels. Those animals! Agamemnon hates his too glorious rival and steals his concubine. Factions rend each other. The enemy rejoices. Complaints rise to my ears. Then the contraption turns around. Factions tear the enemy apart. The enemy's enemy rejoices. The opposite complaints belabor me. Miserable brood, cosmic blunder! Elsewhere the elements burst, bubble, seep, mix and transmute without dinning petitions into my ears. But here I am again, drawn by these dim-witted creatures (*pointing at the two Figures*) whose enslaved commander I am and who bark their claims at me. Now moreover you, Thetis, you who copulated with a mortal. Why?

THETIS. Because you made me, my lord. You gave me to King Peleus. I struggled. But you had decided.

ZEUS. I forget why. One day these scandals will cease. As for Achilles—

THETIS. Glorious Achilles, giant of the earth, insulted like a brat by godless Agamemnon—

ZEUS. I know, I know. How many times must I hear the noisy story? Why are you here, Nereid of the green sea?

THETIS. He is my son and your beloved, he who destroyed Lesbos and Colophon and Smyrna and Clazomenae and Lyrnessus.

ZEUS. Yes yes.

THETIS. And whom the Fates have chosen to capture Troy.

ZEUS. Leave the Fates to me, little Thetis; do not overstep the line.

THETIS. And now you allow him to weep in his tent, bereft of his bride, disarmed, dishonored. Be just, my father, restore my son and punish the Argives. May Hector who worships you decimate them!

ZEUS. Let the twosome speak. (*Turning to the Second Figure*) You, blood for blood and hatred for hatred everlasting in your craw.

SECOND FIGURE. Do as she demands, Zeus of the Thunder.

ZEUS (*to the First Figure*). And you, lover of warfare?

FIRST FIGURE. Do as she demands, Zeus of the Thunder.

THETIS. Your answer, father, your answer?

(*Zeus reflects*)

THETIS. You nodded, father.

ZEUS. Little daughter, you asked, and I consent. The Argives will be punished.

THETIS. Blessed be your name!

SCENE THREE

(Evening in Agamemnon's tent. Present are Agamemnon, Diomedes and Odysseus. Here too an altar stands)

DIOMEDES. They say that a goddess is his mother.
AGAMEMNON. They say, they say!
ODYSSEUS. What does the man do all day in his quarters? Brood? Is that an occupation for Achilles?
DIOMEDES. Patroclus tells me—
AGAMEMNON. You meet with Patroclus, Diomedes?
DIOMEDES. Have I not told you?
AGAMEMNON. So you have....
DIOMEDES. On the sly, to be sure. After sundown. Patroclus is unhappy. With us (*looking hard at Agamemnon*) naturally—but also with his master. "Let him choose" says he to me in a whisper; "either sail home or else make peace with you and fight." But of course the man will do neither until he's—well—
AGAMEMNON. Avenged.
DIOMEDES. Satisfied.
AGAMEMNON. And in the meantime?
DIOMEDES. He drills his men, keeps his ships neat and ready for anything, rolls dice with Patroclus, rumor has it he even composes ballads—love ballads, Agamemnon; I would laugh if it weren't sinister.
ODYSSEUS. I've heard a rumor more sinister than that one.
AGAMEMNON. Namely?
ODYSSEUS. The enemy seems to know.
AGAMEMNON. Know what?
ODYSSEUS. All about Achilles. Achilles and you. In short, Achilles removing himself.
AGAMEMNON. That is not surprising. If we have informers, so have they. They are no more stupid than we are.
DIOMEDES. Listen to me, Agamemnon.
AGAMEMNON. What?
DIOMEDES. The winds became favorable again for us. Supplies came in. So did a few more seaworthy ships. But none of this should blind us. We'll never starve out the Trojans. Truth is, their bellies are as full as ours. We can't be in all places at once to control them. We haven't enough ships and fighters, and thanks to you we've lost—

AGAMEMNON. We must try harder.

DIOMEDES. *You* talk to him, Odysseus.

ODYSSEUS. We believe they will try to break out of the city; and do it soon.

DIOMEDES. It's their great chance, you see.

ODYSSEUS. With Achilles out of the way, Hector is ready for a do or die onslaught. He'll open the gates wide one overcast night and try to overwhelm us, and especially set fire to our ships.

AGAMEMNON. That makes no sense.

ODYSSEUS. How not?

AGAMEMNON. Why would he try to prevent us from scrambling back into the sea and be gone forever?

DIOMEDES (*to Odysseus*). There I'm with Agamemnon. What makes you think—

ODYSSEUS. One of my lads has a cousin in Troy. Sometimes they talk quietly at night through a slit in the wall, like Pyramus and Thisbe. Mind you, the information that passes can be treacherous—on either side. Still, this much is believable—that Hector wants to set fire to a dozen of our ships, just enough to put the idea into a soldier's brain that he'd better embark and be off before they are all reduced to cinders; yet not so many, on the other hand, that the drowsing lion out there will become excited.

AGAMEMNON. Complicated strategy....

ODYSSEUS. And all this—

DIOMEDES. Over a girl, damn it.

AGAMEMNON. Damn *you!* Now I see what these tales of doom and disaster are aiming at!

ODYSSEUS *and* DIOMEDES. Not—

AGAMEMNON. Have we turned into babies because Achilles sings love ditties in his tent? Have I lost my skills or my wits? Have you two gone flabby? And what of my brother? What of Aias whose one finger is stronger than Hector's two hands? And Tlepolemos of Rhodes, who towers above us all and whose father was Heracles?

DIOMEDES. For each of us the Trojans have one of theirs.

AGAMEMNON. Not equal to us! As for Achilles, hear me out. He'll never fondle his Briseis again! Not, that is, until he crawls back to me on his knees and makes his voice as small as a child's.

ODYSSEUS. You have not touched the girl, Agamemnon?

AGAMEMNON. What business is that of yours? Who commands here?

ODYSSEUS. Listen. Two beggars were quarreling over a loaf of bread. They brought the case before a judge. One claimed that he alone had found the loaf in an abandoned basket. The other, who had seized the loaf, argued that his opponent owed him money and therefore he had a right to the loaf. The judge decided in favor of the first claimant. "Sue for the money," he said to the creditor; "but the loaf cannot be alienated from the man who found it." And he ordered the loser to surrender the loaf. "Too late," was the reply; "I ate it."

AGAMEMNON. Good night, comrades. I shall sleep, or wake, tonight with whomever I please. Give me your hands. Till tomorrow morning. The usual meeting.

(*Exeunt Odysseus and Diomedes. Agamemnon sits brooding for awhile, then claps his hands. A soldier appears*)

SOLDIER. Sir?

AGAMEMNON. Bring in the girl Briseis.

SOLDIER. Briseis?

AGAMEMNON (*angry*). You heard me!

(*Exit the soldier. Agamemnon paces up and down the tent. He pours himself some wine and drinks it*)

AGAMEMNON (*to himself*). At night, the lamp out, who cares? Some are fat, some are thin, that's all. I have hesitated too long.

(*The soldier brings Briseis into the tent, then, at a sign from Agamemnon, leaves again*)

AGAMEMNON. Beautiful, graceful daughter of King Eëtion. Agamemnon welcomes you. Here is a silver cup of wine for you. Sit beside me.

(*Briseis takes the cup and flings it to the ground*)

AGAMEMNON. I like that. Hot blood. But the time has come. Presently I will stifle your anger under my weight.

BRISEIS. You would dare, would you?

AGAMEMNON. What would a man not dare to possess a girl like you?

BRISEIS. Dare the vengeance of Achilles?

AGAMEMNON. Even that. Achilles is a man, and I am a man.

BRISEIS. And so is the buffoon Thersites. You are not worth the strap on Achilles' shield, Agamemnon son of Atreus. Achilles is my lord, my lover, my husband and my avenger.

AGAMEMNON. Lovelier than ever! Yet, say what you will, little Briseis is nothing but Achilles' slave and concubine. And soon, that of a better man.

BRISEIS. A better man! Is it you, Agamemnon, who conquered Cilicia?

AGAMEMNON. Is it I who killed your father there? No. Your lover did. Are you not ashamed to enjoy his kisses naked in bed?

BRISEIS. Achilles killed my father in fair combat, weapon against weapon. He spared my mother and my seven brothers. He gave my father the king a hero's burial. And myself, yes, he took me as booty, yet *he* did not force himself on me. He loved me, courted me, and won my consent.

AGAMEMNON. Your next experience will be different.

BRISEIS. As the gods decide. Beware.

AGAMEMNON. The gods are on my side, woman.

BRISEIS. Beware Achilles is what I meant. If the heavens do not smite you, Achilles will. But what am I saying? It's Hector, Hector who'll run his sword through your belly, because without my Achilles you're nothing.

AGAMEMNON. The more you taunt me, the more delectable you look, and the sharper my appetite. We shall see who is the greatest man here. (*He claps his hands again*) Philacos!

(*Enter the soldier*)

AGAMEMNON. Have the women make the girl ready for me. And then come back.

SOLDIER. Don't struggle, girl.

BRISEIS. I am not struggling. Hands off. I know the way. I shall live to spit on your grave, Agamemnon.

(*Exeunt Briseis and the soldier. Agamemnon drinks more wine, falls into a deep study, then rises and kneels at the altar*)

AGAMEMNON. Mighty Poseidon, ruler of the life-giving sea that girds our land, you who have stood by us in the past, intercede with your lord and brother. Beg Zeus not to turn his face from us. Is he incensed against me? Have I offended him? Oh, I know that what I have dared to do deserves some blame. Thousands of good soldiers suffer, and will suffer worse, because I am proud. But is it not my right, indeed my duty, to be proud? Is anarchy preferable? And what is soft leadership if not anarchy? Furthermore, is it not decreed since the beginning of time that Troy will fall and perish in its rubble? But when and how? Under Agamemnon or another, better man? Inscrutable decrees! But now, now that I have stretched the bow to the breaking point, shall I not speed the arrow home to its target? And yet... temerity you admire; but rashness—in a king! (*Low*) Rashness you despise and punish. I humbly need a sign, Zeus; oh give me a sign!... Nothing.... A man must be a lamp unto himself.

(*He broods in silence. Enter Dolon. The two men speak in low voices*)

AGAMEMNON. Dolon!

DOLON. Ready to report, my lord.

AGAMEMNON. Welcome. Sit down. Here is wine.

DOLON. Thank you. Ah, I needed that.

AGAMEMNON. I can imagine.

DOLON. It wasn't easy.

AGAMEMNON. I'm listening.

DOLON. By the looks of it, the Trojans are mustering for a serious assault.

More than serious, my lord. Decisive, they say. I'm also told that someone already informed Odysseus. Ask him. Apparently their priests are telling the fools that victory is sure, now that Achilles—you know what. They're assembling in the squares, every last man carrying weapons like quills on a porcupine. All the streets that descend to the Skaian gate have been cleared of stalls and rubbish for quick passage.

AGAMEMNON. Anything else?

DOLON. I don't think so. My informer whispered "Guard the ships"—that's all he had time to say. I heard him clearly enough, but I can't see what they want with our ships.

AGAMEMNON. Every wisp of intelligence counts. Anything else?

DOLON. Nothing else.

AGAMEMNON. Thanks, Dolon. (*He goes to a coffer and pays him*) Well done, as usual.

DOLON. Thank you, my lord. Any time, call me.

(*Exit Dolon. Enter the soldier*)

SOLDIER. I was waiting outside, sir. (*With a toss of the head*). She's ready for you, sir, and quiet. Shall I light your way?

(*Agamemnon hesitates*)

AGAMEMNON. No need to.

SOLDIER. You'll go alone, sir?

AGAMEMNON. Don't question me, soldier. Go to bed.

SOLDIER. Yes, sir.

(*Exit the soldier. Agamemnon sits in silence*)

AGAMEMNON. Rashness they despise and punish....

SCENE FOUR

(*Achilles' tent at night. Patroclus, showing battlefield dirt on face, hands and clothes, is eating ravenously, watched by Achilles*)

PATROCLUS (*eating, drinking and talking at the same time*). And finally there was no stopping them. Even though Hector had been thrown to the ground. A huge stone against his shoulder. Aias threw it. But now Aias and his men were standing on the decks, fighting off the rascals with pikes, swords, stones, hatchets, planks, whatever came to hand. Sarpedon the Lycian was savaging our ranks like a lion feasting on sheep. Their archers were shooting arrows standing on top of their chariots safe in the rear. Helmets, shields, weapons rolled on the ground; hundreds of our men lay in their blood, many of them crying out at friend and foe alike not to be trampled to death, and only the dead ones rested from the uproar, the din, the moans and groans that must have risen to the gods in heaven.

ACHILLES. I could hear it from where I stood—not in heaven, but in hell on earth.

PATROCLUS. How can you bear to hear it and not bestir yourself? Offspring of ice! You had no mother!

ACHILLES. Let them be glad I didn't stab at them from behind. What happened next?

PATROCLUS. Suddenly torches appeared. I could see one in Hector's own hand, another in Aeneas's, a third in Sarpedon's.

ACHILLES. The leaders wanted the honor, of course.

PATROCLUS. An even more terrible roar went up. The first ship began to burn. Then the second.

ACHILLES. I saw the black smoke.

PATROCLUS. I began to yell. "Where are Agamemnon and Menelaus? Where is Diomedes? Where is Odysseus? Where is the other Aias? Where are all the damned heroes?" The answer came from Eurypilos who came running to me, grimly wounded though he was. "They are all hurt," he cries out, "hurt or dead, I dont know which!" I became wild.

ACHILLES (*suddenly*). Show me your sword! (*Patroclus complies*) I thought as much.

PATROCLUS. I forgot to obey you. I forgot to stand aside. I plunged in and fought. Are you surprised? I killed Sarpedon.

ACHILLES. Well done. All the same, I had given you an absolute order—

PATROCLUS. Hear me, Achilles. I killed him after he stabbed to death—dare I tell you?—your friend and host in Rhodes—

ACHILLES. Tlepolemos!

PATROCLUS. Yes. (*He watches Achilles*) Not a word? Not a tear? Gone too are Orsilochos, Crethon, Asaios, Dolops—and many more I know nothing of. I see that's nothing to you. As for tomorrow morning, if Zeus continues angry, or asleep—I daren't dwell on what may happen. The men have gone crazy thinking that every last one of the ships will burn and there will be no escape for them. While you sit there, tearless, stubborn, evil-minded, instead of rousing our men to battle, you who could scatter an army by only standing on a mound and hurling a shout.

ACHILLES. Finish your meal, Patroclus, because guests are expected.

PATROCLUS. Guests? Now? At this hour of night?

ACHILLES. Inventive Odysseus and rough Diomedes.

PATROCLUS. Was I misinformed? Aren't they wounded after all?

ACHILLES. They are, they are. But the herald came and told me that in spite of pain they must see me in secret. Listen! That was the signal. (*He goes to the tent's opening. Grimly*) A splendid painting dominated by red! And outlined in crimson they painfully come.

PATROCLUS. Achilles, friend, master, benefactor: yield, don't stiffen your heart!

ACHILLES. Greetings, my friends. Come into warmth and safety.

(*Enter Odysseus and Diomedes, both wounded*)

DIOMEDES. Thanks and good evening to you.

ODYSSEUS. You were expecting us, were you not?

ACHILLES. I was. Eurybates told me you were coming. I see that you are in pain. Sit. (*He claps his hands. A soldier brings in fruit and more wine*) Take whatever your bodies need. No—let me serve you. You carry your wounds with the pride they deserve. Patroclus, rest.

DIOMEDES. Patroclus! Here is my left hand.

ODYSSEUS. And both of mine are alive and well to give you thanks. You fought like—like one not far behind Achilles in strength. And killed Sarpedon for us. (*To Achilles*) All of us Hellenes owe you a debt of gratitude for sending him to us. And how we needed him!

PATROCLUS. Eat and drink, comrades.

ACHILLES. Indeed, you should be resting in your own cots instead of roaming at night to seek out your friends—resting and praying to Hera and Athene to restore you in time for tomorrow's battle.

ODYSSEUS. Hera and Athene be praised, there will be no battle tomorrow.

PATROCLUS. Something new!

ACHILLES. May I be told how this came about?

ODYSSEUS. It came about as follows. After we finally held off the Trojans, and night was falling, Polydamas—

ACHILLES. Who is he?

DIOMEDES. A half-brother of Hector, as prudent as the other one is tough.

ODYSSEUS. Bless him! He talked Hector into falling back across the stream in order to catch his breath and give the troops some sleep. And then Helenus their priest joined with our own good Calchas to demand a ten-day truce to bury the dead with solemn rites and sacrifices, and time to tend the wounded on both sides.

DIOMEDES. In short, they intend to pick up their bodies and retreat into the city.

ACHILLES. Retreat into the city! Are they insane? After setting fire to half a dozen of your ships?

DIOMEDES. No more insane than you, Achilles. They took terrible losses, and now they want time to dispatch emissaries to Thrace.

ACHILLES. For help. I remember. They were promised help.

DIOMEDES. Which they need as sorely as we do.

ODYSSEUS. Because they understand that seeing our fleet in danger, you sent Patroclus and are about to come in yourself.

DIOMEDES. And that, of course, is what brings us here tonight.

ACHILLES. Speak freely; you are among friends.

ODYSSEUS. Agamemnon repents.

ACHILLES. Of?

DIOMEDES. His mistake.

ACHILLES. His insults.

ODYSSEUS. He understands that he misused his authority.

ACHILLES. Misfortune has improved the man's wits.

DIOMEDES. He has not touched the daughter of Briseus.

ODYSSEUS. As you will be able to have her confirm.

ACHILLES. How so?

DIOMEDES. Because he wishes to send her back to you.

ACHILLES. A noble thief, who drops his loot as he runs from the constable.

ODYSSEUS. Much more will be coming to you, Achilles.

ACHILLES. Namely?

ODYSSEUS. When Troy is taken—by you, by us—for surely it is decreed that it will be taken—and we march on Priam's treasure-house, Agamemnon will hold us back and form us in a half circle, while you, Achilles, alone, or with Patroclus at your side, cross the threshhold, and choose for yourself and your Myrmidons whatever has been heaped up for centuries by the Dardanians: gold, silver, bronze, jewels, crowns, tripods, cauldrons, vessels of every description, beyond what even the kingdom of Egypt can boast of. Choose whatever you like and bring it proudly to your father, long may he live and take pride in you, Peleus king of Phthia—all of it, to the last bauble if you wish, or else allotting to the rest of us what you judge to be fitting. But there is more. Go then to the palace grounds where the captive women will be held, and pick for yourself and your henchmen twenty-four of the youngest and most beautiful, even Helen! for Menelaus yields her to you, albeit with a groan. Furthermore, Agamemnon and Nestor will give you, near Pylos, seven citadels, Kardamyle, Enope, Hire, Pherai, Antheia, Aipeia, and Pedasos, controlling land, some rich in cattle-bearing meadows, some in rifts of ore, some in generous vineyards, where you will be honored as a god, you and your sons, and the sons of these sons. Apollo himself, who killed many of us when we landed in the Troad,

would have relented for half these gifts. Therefore you too be satisfied and relent. Excessive pride betokens a tyrant; moderation becomes a hero.
(*Silence. Patroclus looks anxiously at Achilles*)
ACHILLES. Grim indeed is the outlook, O my friends, if such bribes are slipped into my fist. Therefore take this back to Agamemnon king of Mycenae. The lands and the citadels that he and Nestor offer me I could take from them by force if my own dear country did not suffice me. The women, if I desired others than my Briseis, would fall to me at the nod of my crested helmet. Priam's treasures, were I greedy, I who am content drinking my wine from an earthen bowl, I could tear out of your hands, because I am Achilles. On your tablet of gifts I have not seen the gift I want.
DIOMEDES. What can that be other than our deaths?
ACHILLES. May you live forever, comrades! But let King Agamemnon call the princes to the Assembly, and there let him, with his right hand, place the royal scepter of command into mine and fall on his knees before me swearing an oath of loyalty and obedience as a mere prince among princes. Then I shall lead your armies, kill Hector, breach the walls, and put an end to Troy forever. The other gifts, excepting the return of Briseis, are his and yours to keep. I do not need them. Poor I came, and poor I shall return to my fatherland, poor fatherland, devoid of cattle, iron and vineyards and rich only in hard stones and proud men.
DIOMEDES (*springing up*). Proud peacock! Before long, Zeus will pluck your feathers!
ACHILLES. And in conclusion, tell Agamemnon this: yield, or else employ the ten days of lucky truce to load your remaining ships and make ready the sails that scoop up the wind and the oars that beat the harsh-minded sea. To permit his own royal ship to raise anchor, I demand only the woman he stole from me, or else he perishes before his foot strikes the deck.
(*Silence*)
ODYSSEUS. We shall faithfully deliver to him every word you have spoken.
ACHILLES. Do so. If he demurs, I think that only one resource is left to the Argives.
ODYSSEUS. And what is that?
ACHILLES. Your brain, brilliant Odysseus.
ODYSSEUS. I shall supplicate it for help, mighty Achilles. Farewell.
(*Odysseus and Diomedes leave*)

SCENE FIVE

(Zeus on his throne, flanked by the two Figures. Thetis as supplicant)

THETIS. But he deserves to be king of kings!
ZEUS. King over Agamemnon, my child?
THETIS. And why not over Agamemnon? Is he not the better fighter and the nobler man? Is he not the son of a goddess? He demanded what was his due.
ZEUS. So they all shout in that world of yours. They all deserve to sit *here*, do they not, flinging my thunderbolts and inhaling the perfume of hecatombs sacrificed below in their honor. He demanded what was his due! Why have I come again? You call me, and I return.
THETIS. We are your humble instruments, my lord.
ZEUS. Which you force into my hands! *(To the two Figures)* You and you, speak up, you know it all, arrogant slaves! *(The Second Figure is silent).* So. This one is mute. Vengeance is happy, fulfilled. *(To the First Figure)* And you, lover of war and ruin?
FIRST FIGURE. You have gone too far, son of Kronos. Who is this little goddess who sports with a few dolphins in the sea? Shall Hector the Trojan become king of Argos, Mycenae and Sparta? Will Hellas speak Asian? Have you forgotten your immutable decrees? Enough! Your pampered Nereid has received satisfaction. The small wheel inside the big wheel has spun out its spin. With Achilles or without, the final hammer is raised, and will strike. Dismiss her.
ZEUS *(to the Second Figure).* Your turn. Speak.
SECOND FIGURE. I am content.
(Zeus stares at Thetis, who lowers her head)
ZEUS. You are my beloved child, Thetis. But begone.

SCENE SIX

(In Agamemnon's tent. Agamemnon, Odysseus and Diomedes)

ODYSSEUS. It came to me in that half-dreaming, half-waking state when our thoughts run loose in the mind, and sometimes, as if by chance, knit into an interesting design. Yet surely this time they were guided not by chance but by the gods.

AGAMEMNON. To the point, Odysseus!

DIOMEDES. No. Let him tell his wonderful story step by step; you will like it.

ODYSSEUS. At first I was merely dreaming a remembrance—how, as I lay wounded on my cot, Idomeneus sat at my side, gave me water to drink, and told me other men's adventures of the day in order to distract me from my pain. And in my dream there came back with especial force his mirthful account of huge Aias who, as the Trojans approached his ship, sent a soldier down to the hold to gather up the javelins kept there in storage. The door stuck fast. Three soldiers couldn't pry it loose. So Aias himself came running down, and butted his helmeted head against the door, which flew open at the blow. I heard Idomeneus laugh again in my dream, and call Aias "bull-headed". Now, still dozing and dreaming, and repeating these words to myself in Idomeneus' voice, an image sprung into my brain, of a scene I witnessed long ago in Ithaca: a furious bull battering down a fence and almost killing two of my farmhands. Suddenly, by Athena's will, the fence, into which a little gate was set, became in my brain the massive Skaian gate of Troy. A huge bull-head, made of wood and snouted in iron, went crashing through the gate. And I woke up, dazzled, holding on to that vision as if for the breath of life.

AGAMEMNON. What do you mean? This huge bull-head made out of wood—

DIOMEDES. Explain, Odysseus, explain.

ODYSSEUS. A squad of sturdy men, real as my fist, will climb Mount Ida and chop down its thickest, straightest tree. Working behind cover, for there are spies among us, they will cap it in iron, suspend it by halyards from a roof in a wagon, set the wagon on a dozen strong wheels, hide the contraption until the truce is over, and that same night wheel it close to the gate.

DIOMEDES. And from there—*(he makes a crashing sound)*

AGAMEMNON. Won't the sentinels make it out in the dark, sound the alarm and fling down fire and pitch before it can act?

ODYSSEUS. Its house will be gabled and covered. Our bull will be neither burnt nor pierced. And the alarm will come too late. Thirty or forty men will swing the mast to and fro until, with a mighty slam, it will break the gate and let the rest of us in. And then! The story ends.

DIOMEDES. Well, Agamemnon, what do you say to that? Let Achilles sulk till he rots! We'll be rushing through that tunnel in the wall, three to one against them.

AGAMEMNON. Draw it for me, Odysseus. Here's a piece of charcoal, draw it on the table.

ODYSSEUS. At your service. Front and side. A rude sketch.

DIOMEDES. Rude? It seems to move already!

AGAMEMNON. I see. And here, I suppose, go the ropes.

ODYSSEUS. Exactly. But I had better erase my masterpiece. Secrecy is essential.

AGAMEMNON. Is it? I don't know. Let me think. Amazing Odysseus! And yet, how can such work be done by a squad of soldiers, even picked ones, in the seven days of the truce that remain?

ODYSSEUS. Difficult but not impossible.

AGAMEMNON. Why take the risk? No. Have two hundred men—everybody!—work at your wooden beast. Make them hammer and saw in broad daylight. Secrets are found out, so no secrets. Let the Trojans know that Agamemnon had a vision. In expiation for his misdeeds, he must burn a gigantic wooden bull as an offering to the gods close to the city walls. The only secret—and here, Odysseus, we'll call on those picked men of yours—will concern those cables. They will be prepared on the sly, and be affixed where they belong on the last night, at the last moment. Then only will the truth appear. Too late for *them*.

DIOMEDES. Is this a good idea, Odysseus?

ODYSSEUS. A capital idea. Furthermore, Agamemnon, I take it as an omen. When the gods give a man wisdom, he knows that they have returned to his side.

AGAMEMNON. May you be as good a prophet as you are a dreamer! (*In high good humor*) Men! I feel a penitent vision coming on! Go, while I summon Calchas. A vision requires a priest.

SCENE SEVEN

(*Achilles' shelter. It is empty for a few moments; then, in haste, enter Patroclus followed by a soldier*)

PATROCLUS. Drunk? Achilles drunk? You're raving! Where is he?

SOLDIER. I swear to you!

PATROCLUS. What happened?

SOLDIER. While you were gone for news, and never seemed to come back, people were running in every direction, shouting this and that, rumors, facts, miracles never seen since the world was created. Of course we could see the smoke rising from the city. Finally we stopped a mule-driver who looked reliable because he didn't seem to care. He told us about the Skaian gate battered open, the—

PATROCLUS (*impatient*). I know all that. But where in God's name is Achilles?

SOLDIER. Where should a man be when he's drunk? You'll find him on his cot. Go in and see for yourself.

PATROCLUS. Go in yourself. At once! Get him up and out! It's urgent, but I don't want him to see me looking at him lying drunk on his bed. Go, go!

(*The soldier leaves; Patroclus paces nervously*)

PATROCLUS (*to himself*). Hurry, hurry! (*He looks outside and groans*) Oh my God! Is it too late?

(*He turns to face Achilles, who totters in, holding a large bowl and singing*)

ACHILLES.
>   Hail! Hail! Hail!
>   Homebound we sail,
>   Loaded with rubies and pearls,
>   Fat oxen and slender girls!

Greetings Patroclus, greetings Agamemnon, greetings you—what's your name?

SOLDIER. Arcas, sir, whom you promoted two—

ACHILLES. Did you hear the news, my boy? They whittled an Achilles out of a tree and threw it at the Skaian gate! Hail, hail, hail!

PATROCLUS. Achilles! Take hold of yourself! Every minute counts!

ACHILLES. What do you want? Can't you see I'm busy celebrating?

PATROCLUS. Throw away that bowl, Achilles! Don't waste a second! Lead the troops, join the Argives in the attack while there's still time!

ACHILLES. What? What? Repeat what you said!

PATROCLUS. I'm begging you to join in while there's still work to be done, before it's too late, before they reach the citadel and we're left here in our tents like drunken idiots! Give me the bowl!

(*He tries to wrest it from Achilles, who violently pushes him back*)

ACHILLES. The idiot is yourself! Advice fit for a lickspittle, a clown in the market-place! (*He throws the bowl away but draws his sword*) Get out! Both of you! Out of my sight!

(*Patroclus and the soldier flee. Achilles collapses*)

ACHILLES (*picking himself up*). Mother, are you listening? I wish a vulture had ripped your womb open and eaten my flesh before I was born! Where are your promises? Liar! Whore! (*He sobs wildly*)

SCENE EIGHT

(Agamemnon, battle-scarred, standing on the rubble of Troy. Trumpets sound)

AGAMEMNON. Lords of Hellas! Welcome at this hour of our triumph. We have done at last what we came here to do. Down is the proud nation that dared to challenge us for the rule of the earth. But while the defeated are at rest forever, the victors must labor on, and must do so, I admonish you, in obedience to the laws of Zeus. First then, let us bury the dead on both sides without pride of place or denigration of the annihilated foe. Above all, let fallen Priam and his fallen sons receive the honors which are their due, even as we weep over our own many heroes slain in battle. Some of you stood at my side when Hector, struck by twenty arrows, fell at his father's feet. You saw white-bearded Priam, threatening with a useless sword, shed his last tear when I, Agamemnon, lord of Mycenae, more in pity than in wrath, slew him so he could fall over Hector's body. Let these dead be honored, not desecrated. Next, let the women and children—the widows and orphans—be led out of the city. Assembled in our encampment below, they will receive gentle and honorable treatment before they are allotted in just proportion and quality to the number of soldiers each of you has brought to the siege, except for Odysseus, to whom, as the genius of our victory, a double share of slaves and treasures will be assigned. Next, allow no looting! Looters are to be executed on the very spot where they are caught. Every man will receive his share. Hence every man who loots is guilty of robbing his comrades. Let the treasures be brought before my shelter in the open plain, so that, under every man's scrutiny, every soldier and every chieftain who fought with us in this final battle will be satisfied when he embarks for home. My share will be the same as every commander's; equal among equals in my reward as I have been, I hope, in merit. When the sharing is completed, I shall appoint a governor over this new Troy, one who will rebuild the city and make of it our own eternal guardian of the Hellespont. Many of our brave soldiers have already declared their wish to take Trojan wives and settle in this place, so rich, so tragic in their minds. However this may be, the children of Troy must not be separated from their mothers. I will not allow it. As for Troy itself, its fallen stones shall rise again, the citadel on which we stand shall command the Troad once more, while the rest of us, victorious and serene, sail home at long last, to the arms of our fathers, our mothers, our wives and our children, and inspire the bards to sing to the end of time the story of our great conquest of Asia.

Now, comrades and allies, let us disperse. There's hard work to be done till nightfall. We are to meet late this night at the altar of Zeus in our camp, where we shall offer holocausts of oxen, sheep and rams in thanksgiving, feast to our heart's content and further deliberate. Lords and friends: I am no long-winded talker; my speech is finished. Go, betake yourselves to your several duties.

(*Trumpets sound again. Agamemnon leaves. The place is empty for awhile. Silence. Then, enter Diomedes*)

DIOMEDES (*calling*). Odysseus! Let me talk to you.

ODYSSEUS (*off-stage*). Coming!

(*Enter Odysseus*)

DIOMEDES. I saw you climb to the top of the tower, or what's left of it, but hadn't a chance to ask you what you saw out there.

ODYSSEUS. Lucky I came down again without twisting both ankles or breaking my neck. What I saw? Well, I can tell you that he hasn't moved. I could see a puff of smoke, the kind that suggests dinner being cooked. Why do you look disappointed?

DIOMEDES. I expected—

ODYSSEUS. I didn't. Shameful it may be to be present and witness it all; but doubly shameful to swim away as if ashamed.

DIOMEDES. Still—

ODYSSEUS. Shall I tell you something else?

DIOMEDES. You had better!

ODYSSEUS. Agamemnon intends to summon Achilles—

DIOMEDES. Summon!

ODYSSEUS. Invite Achilles to his shelter tomorrow.

DIOMEDES. Really! That will be a spectacle for the immortals!

ODYSSEUS. Also for us humble mortals; because you and I, who were Agamemnon's ambassadors, will be asked to attend.

DIOMEDES. For this, I'd be willing to give up my share of the spoils, and empty my own coffers besides! I want to hear him beg, "Please, please, Agamemnon, allow me to plant a parting kiss on Briseis' honeyed lips"!

ODYSSEUS. Keep your imagination sober, my friend. Come, enough of that. We'll talk again tonight.

DIOMEDES. And drink till dawn!

SCENE NINE

(Agamemnon's shelter. Enter Agamemnon and Odysseus. Agamemnon, flanked by soldiers, seats himself on a chair that has been raised upon a platform)

ODYSSEUS. The dead are gone towards oblivion under the tough earth. Already, I could swear, the ruins of the city are showing an expectancy of stones put back in place, houses occupied once more, gardens reseeded, new children eager to lose their innocence. Our newly won gains—the luxuries of Asian Troy and its women—seem already absorbed into our ancient possessions and cozily at home with us. Our vessels rock at anchor like horses of the sea impatient for departure. I shall leave the plains of Troy happy in the knowledge that I have served you well to the best of my powers. Now, however, we play out the epilogue, as in the mummeries our poets put on once a year in the courtyards of Ithaca. Achilles comes. He has nothing. He is nothing. But this nothing is strong, proud and dangerous. Think of the fangs of a desperate lion. Diomedes and I, and these soldiers, are here to stand by you should your words and your greatness enrage him.

AGAMEMNON. That greatness, Odysseus, such as it is, owes its sap and marrow to you. May I perish if ever I allow your glory to be forgotten or diminished. Come next spring, I hope you will cross the slender arm of the sea that separates your Ithaca from our Peloponnese, and be my honored guest, mine and Clytemnestra's, in my palace at Mycenae. No slave-girl but my glorious wife herself will joyfully fill your golden goblet with Arcadian wine. But here comes Diomedes.

(Enter Diomedes)

DIOMEDES. Friends, the man is approaching, with no one but Patroclus at his side and neither one armed. Your men are making a hedge on either side of them, without uttering a sound. A strange, silent progress. Take my advice, Agamemnon, and that of Odysseus too: don't spare the rogue; treat him as he deserves.

AGAMEMNON. Stand at my side, brave Diomedes. Leave everything to me.

(Achilles and Patroclus enter, the latter remaining discreetly in the background)

AGAMEMNON. Greetings, Achilles, and welcome. And a kind welcome to you, Patroclus, as always.

(Patroclus bows)

ACHILLES. I have accepted your invitation, Agamemnon, first of all in order to salute your impressive victory and to convey my high, unenvious admiration. And second, in order to take my leave without rancor. We shall not meet again this side of the Elysian Fields. I sail to my fatherland tomorrow, bereft of my honor and a beggar for my bride. Glorious my past, inglorious my present, dim my future. Long ago it was foretold to my mother that I should either die young but covered with glory at Troy, or live out a long but obscure life in my father's small kingdom. It appears that the gods have decided. Zeus, who they say detests injustice and punishes it, has turned his face away from me, scorning my just cause and nodding you to victory. Who am I to guess the reason why? When Zeus chooses to be cruel, who dares to scold him?

DIOMEDES. Arrogant towards us to the bitter end, Achilles, blind to your own faults, and offensive to the gods.

ODYSSEUS. Will you not remember that we came to you contrite, offered you far more than mere compensation; but you would have none of it and sent us contemptuously out of your presence.

DIOMEDES. To go die by the thousands at the foot of the city.

ACHILLES. Venomous words. Your turn, Agamemnon. Do not spare me either. (*A long pause*) Why so silent?

AGAMEMNON. Whom and what the gods love and hate, Achilles, I know no better than you do. They speak shining words one hour, and clouded ones the next. They send thunder, and flights of birds, and other omens, and no man can tell what they truly and deeply mean. Our soothsayers claim they can read the mind of Zeus, and not long ago I thought I could do so as well, above all because I am a king, a great man in this little world of ours. Yet in the end, Achilles, I know only my own mind, that strange, turbulent universe enclosed in a box of bone. The light that shines there is not so strong as I should like it to be; but it suffices, I hope and pray, to guide my hand. By that light, my friend, I perceive that I wronged you with a gross injury. I insulted you. Unprovoked, blind with rage, I tore what was dearest to you out of your hands. Then came a mean and false remorse, when I sent these two stalwarts to your tent to plead with you and offer restitution with great additions of cattle, land, women, gold. False humility and false repentance wrung from me when Hector was setting our ships on fire and breaking our spirits, until it became urgent to crawl to you for help. You did right to lock the gates of your spirit to me. Perhaps in your anger you went too far, but that fault vanishes in mine. Now, in this solemn hour of triumph, when nothing mean and false whispers counsels into my ear, my mind urges me to return Briseis to you, unharmed, and furthermore to load you, as the ally I called into this war, with sufficient gifts to honor you when you greet your dear father. A hero you came, a hero you shall part from me.

(*Achilles is thunderstruck. Finally comprehending, he opens his arms to Agamemnon, who now descends from his chair*)

ACHILLES (*softly*). My brother! My better than myself! My lord! How you humble me....

(*They embrace*)

AGAMEMNON. Give me your hand, and let me take you to Briseis who knows that you have come for her.

(*Exeunt*)

(*Astonished silence*)

ODYSSEUS. Am I awake or did I dream what just happened?

DIOMEDES. The man has gone mad, mad I say, mad. Patroclus, you're our friend and his alike. Am I not right?

PATROCLUS. I don't know what to say. I am glad for Achilles, and, I confess, for myself as well; yet I too feel as though I were dreaming.

ODYSSEUS. Loaded with gifts! Embraced! So be it. Tomorrow I sail. I have bloody work waiting for me in Ithaca, and will not delay another day. Give me your hands. Diomedes, Patroclus, companions entrenched in my heart. No other farewells.

SCENE TEN

(*Zeus on his throne. The two Figures stand before him*)

ZEUS. When? How? Who? Speak one at a time, imps of disaster.

FIRST FIGURE. What disaster, my lord? All is hushed. We roamed quietly over the city, picking at the rubble, noted here and there a house or a temple lopsided yet standing—

SECOND FIGURE. Saw the first colonizers begin to arrive and displace the dead. Well done, we sang, new blood appears, the old is gone—

FIRST FIGURE. Gone and not gone: much of it still sopping the walls, blood on the kitchen utensils, the steps of the bathhouses, the altars—

SECOND FIGURE. Well done, we sang, no laziness here.

FIRST FIGURE. The rain began to fall, and everything became grey; dogs lapped up the water in the gutters; water seeped from the broken culverts.

SECOND FIGURE. A few wizened natives were left. The new people pushed them into the raw weather. Out, Trojans, out!

FIRST FIGURE. We heard a baby wailing somewhere between two walls—

AGAMEMNON TRIUMPHANT

SECOND FIGURE. And then, satisfied that your will had been done, my lord, we left the city by the great gash that had been the gate. A quiet scene, my lord, missing the uproar of armies, the clatter of helmets and swords, the yells of pain and victory.
FIRST FIGURE. We hovered over the plain, gazing at its crop of weapons, wheels, pieces of chariots, carcasses of horses, dogs gnawing at them, and leftovers of Argive tents and campfires.
SECOND FIGURE. And that is where—
FIRST FIGURE. Hard by Agamemnon's shelter, my lord; we must be precise.
SECOND FIGURE. We perceived the shape, the thing in white we spoke of at the start—
FIRST FIGURE. That wouldn't answer our questions, nor flee from us when we threatened it, and how we snarled! but shamelessly followed us when we decided to ignore it and look for you—
SECOND FIGURE. Knowing you had come, and required our presence, ever dutiful to you—
FIRST FIGURE. Ever at your feet, my lord.
ZEUS. Good. (*He seems to listen*) Stand aside. Crouch. Farther away.
BOTH FIGURES. As you wish, master.
ZEUS. Farther away I say! Give me silence so it can enter. It is looking for me.
(*When the Third Figure enters, white-clad and veiled, it pauses before Zeus with its back to us. Zeus slowly rises—for the first time—moves to the Figure and lifts its veil*)
ZEUS. Welcome on earth.
FIRST FIGURE. No welcome. Sweep it away, Zeus.
SECOND FIGURE. The earth is fine as it is.
ZEUS. I gaze at you with love, foreboding, sadness and invincible hope. Give me your hands.
(*He keeps gazing silently*)
THE TWO FIGURES. Who is it, Zeus? Speak to us. Send it away! What is it?
ZEUS. That is not for you to know.

The End

Notes

Agamemnon Triumphant was printed for the first time in my 2002 *Reinventions*. It is the last play I have written and will have written.

In the first scene, Briseis sings a few lines Guy Davenport (1927-2005) allowed me to take from his translation of Sappho 116.

My Greeks are called Argives, as in Homer, and sometimes Hellenes; but in production a director might be wise to drop the Argives and call them Greeks.

Except for Aias, I use the Greek or Latin names as they are commonly written and spoken in English, sometimes ending in -os and sometimes in -us. The reason for making Aias the exception is a bit comical, and, I hope, temporary. "Ajax" is so well known in my time as a cleansing powder for kitchens and bathrooms that it has become difficult to apply the name to a heroic warrior. As soon as this inconvenient association vanishes, the hero's better-known name can be returned to him in print and production.

AGAMEMNON TRIUMPHANT

IV

VI

AND THE LORD GOD PLANTED A GARDEN

CHARACTERS

God
Gabriel
Adam
Eve

The scene: The plot of cleared land where Adam and Eve dwell, with the entrance to their cave.

SCENE ONE

GOD. Eve and Adam!
EVE *and* ADAM. My Lord.
GOD.   Eve for you whom I created first of human creatures
        Mother of all the wise family male and female to come
        Until the day
        Yet may it never befall
        When I abolish you;
        Then Adam for you
        Sprung from Eve's belly womb and hollow
        Both of you my children made in my image
        Image too of Gabriel
        Image of all the angels unknown to you but wandering and dwelling
        All but numberless in the universe my home;
        For you delightful to me
        My darlings my special care my fond experiments
        For you female and male
        For you above my animals I made this Garden
        An island for you
        Fairest of all provinces of Earth
        The rest sour waters wild flames harsh noises
        Cloud-smothered mountains and stony soil:
        Untamed compounds of discordant elements
        To be by you and yours, mankind,
        In all their multitude understood and tamed:
        Such is the inner meaning
        Eve and Adam
        Of the gift of your being in the image of God.
        Tell me then: what are your tasks on earth?
GABRIEL. Speak woman my child.
EVE. To understand and tame.
GABRIEL. To understand and tame what? Adam my child reply.
ADAM. This Garden and the Earth. The Earth, my Lord?
GOD.   It is the vast round
        Of which your Garden Adam is a morsel.

AND THE LORD GOD PLANTED A GARDEN

It begins beyond the river Embracing this fair island
With its twinned and twining arms
And continues in unmeasured tracts of land
Weeks away months years of walking running or riding
Huge waters too shaking their dangerous waves
Yet not so dangerous but these too
Even the high waves you shall one day Understand and tame.
But here in your beginning my dears
This Garden where the lily grows
The rose the bluebell yes flowers and trees
All but innumerable
Fruit of the branch the twig the root
A river affable and beasts your friends and willing food
Above you mild sun mild clouds the rain a pleasing visitor
All this I made for your beginning
And does it please you Adam please you Eve
Shall I do yet more for you?
Wake yourselves questioning me
For wisdom begins in shrewd questions.

(*Adam and Eve kneel*)
ADAM. Wonder of beauty.
EVE. Splendor of power.
ADAM. Spring of cheer.
EVE. Marvel of abundance.
ADAM. We thank you.
EVE. And would like to bear you a gift of love.
GOD. Your gift oh my children is your best will
Seeking the utmost inward of things
In order to become their gods.
Yet ask. What more shall I provide?
ADAM. We need and desire nothing more my Lord.
GOD. Rise rise and sit with me.
Tell me what is here as yet obscure.
GABRIEL. Speak children do not fear.
EVE. The knife you gave us Gabriel and taught us how to make and use, and other tools for which we thank you:
ADAM. This knife cuts into a fig an orange;
EVE. And all is well.
ADAM. But when it stabs a calf a lamb a rabbit,
EVE. They cry as we do when by mischance it cuts our finger.

ADAM. They cry they struggle they shun their hated death.

EVE. And we do against them what none do against us.

ADAM. Hence we ask: is it right to harm and kill what is so terribly unlike the orange and fig?

GOD. It is right
       For though you are like them you are also unlike them.
       I have granted them suffering without sense of it
       As I have granted them reasonable action
       Without reasoning thought.
       To you I have given pain
       But also sense of it and reasonable action
       But also reasoning thought.
       Yet taking as I give
       For I would not be spendthrift for the lion and miser for the eagle
       I have left you naked saying to myself
       Your thought shall provide
       And has indeed provided leaves skins food
       And this I answer this is just.
       I commend your question and listen again.

EVE. Shall I who bore Adam bear all others male and female too, or shall he bear some and I others?

GOD. You shall bear all
       And in the time of your heaviness
       He shall provide for you.
       To this purpose he received his swiftness and his power.
       Ask again.

ADAM. The double river that enfolds us.

GABRIEL. How is it called Adam?

ADAM. I have forgotten.

GABRIEL. Eve how is it called?

EVE. I too have forgotten.

GABRIEL. We called it Hiddekel.

ADAM. So we did friend Gabriel it comes back to me.

GOD. What of the river child?

ADAM. Beyond it we can see trees bearing all manner of fruit—pears, cherries....

EVE. Peaches plums....

ADAM. Ever so rich! Today walking in our garden we asked each other seeing that we were falling short here and needed to wander farther and farther "Have we leave to cross the river and pluck the fruit beyond?" But we are afraid of the high water that seems to run and bite. Does the river signify *thus far and no farther?* Is it forbidden to cross it?

GOD. It is not forbidden my children but perilous.
    I have made you in my image
    But not of my inapprehensible substance.
    You are male and female I am not.
    Beware of death by falling death by striking
    And concerning the river Hiddekel
    Death by drowning.
    I am your creator and lover but not your guardian.
    Yet the angel Gabriel will teach you
    How you may cross the river and be safe.
    All fruit of this earth you Eve and Adam may pluck and eat
    Save one
    Of one fruit only you may not taste
    One prohibition and no other
    I set athwart your lives.
    Turn your eyes where Gabriel is pointing
    Rise and tell me what you see.

EVE. On that nameless tree.

ADAM. Fruitless till now.

GABRIEL. Apples now hang.

GOD. And those you shall not eat.
    Adam and Eve you shall not eat this fruit.
    It is forbidden.
    Shun it. Such is my command.

ADAM. We will shun it, o Lord of creation.

GOD. Should you not ask me why?

EVE. We forgot.

GOD. This fruit Eve and Adam
    Does not differ from others.
    It is neither sublime above them nor poisonous.
    It is forbidden in order to be forbidden.
    It is the sign the token of Majesty above you.
    Thought is invisible and mute.
    This token is seen touched smelled and can be tasted.
    So is obedience made visible and palpable to you.
    All else is love and gift permission and delight.

ADAM. My Lord, we shall obey you.

EVE. And our angel Gabriel and all good counsels and commands.

GOD. Return to your daily simple chores,
       Eat dance love sleep laugh
       For this is your beginning
       And the mere dear syllables you are now
       Shall become words when I return
       Then sentences then volumes as I return and yet return
       Hoping to remain father and mother to you
       Upon the track of time to which I foreordain no end.
(*Adam and Eve withdraw*)
GOD. Will the end be happy heaven-born Gabriel?
       Speak your thought.
(*Gabriel smiles*)
GOD. No Gabriel I do not see your thoughts!
       Smiling again? Mocking my question?
GABRIEL. You saw the thought you asked me to speak.
GOD. Oh misbelievers! No Gabriel again and again
       I tell you all I do not dive into your thoughts.
       Commanding Spirit I am.
       My powers immense my knowledge wide-arched
       And so I was in the beginning when out of force
       Force and light light and time time and void
       I sprang
       And you millions around me
       Yet why whence and whereto I do not know
       Nor think I ever will.
       In loving anguish and helpless longing
       I sense I guess a commanding spirit commanding mine
       Begun before my beginning and it perhaps commanded again
       Mysterious sphere into sphere until
       Centered and sealed there crouches perhaps
       Some compression of power beyond conception and worship.
       But let it go!
       I am too busy to be haunted!
       I journey to and fro from sky to sky
       Planting inventions exuberant
       Furnishing each globe with the enterprises
       Of my unappeasable joy.
       Yet athwart each invention advances
       A resistance hard or mild,
       Matter's obduracy to matter yet also to my spirit

AND THE LORD GOD PLANTED A GARDEN

        Another spirit opposing me
        And now it yields and now I bend.
        Such are the angels' thoughts and even theirs
(*He points toward Adam and Eve*)
        Which mine surround and often catch
        Yet sometimes miss as chittering swallows do
        That snap at insects in the darkening day.
        How then Gabriel I asked
        Shall it be with these in our image so beautiful?
GABRIEL. Beautiful image stuffed my Lord—
GOD.   With messes of male and female fat and bone
        And nerve and bile how else my dear how else
        Was I to animate that image?
        I am given no power to make another God or angel.
        Then how shall my image live?
        Dead images we see when we hover over lakes
        You and I preening in such mirrors.
        These new images I desired
        Knowing feeling growing adoring and inquisitive
        For albeit I have made many things that grow
        None yet have I created essential of myself.
        Think of it Gabriel: knowledge and its delight
        So far granted only to us will spangle this earth
        Like a glisten of infinite dews on its foliage.
        And if on this earth why not again and again elsewhere
        Among these generous galaxies our home?
        And at last why not the stones the clouds
        Why not the dust the fire the water
        All of it mindful all of it intelligence
        And every atom conversable with each
        In mutual infinite lucidity?
GABRIEL. Therefore may all be well with them.
GOD.   Smiling again?
        You believe that I know.
        But I speak like a hammer and tell you I do not know.
        Kneel Gabriel and believe.
GABRIEL. I do God my only God.
GOD.   Make them begin to learn
        As I soar and land among other beginning worlds.
(*God kisses Gabriel*)

SCENE TWO

(Eve is sharpening her stone knife against another and singing a two-note working song)

EVE.　　Pah-pah-pah-pah
　　　　Sharp-sharp-sharp-sharp
　　　　　　AND
　　　　Pah-pah-pah-pah
　　　　Sharp-sharp-sharp-BLUNT!
(She laughs uproariously)
ADAM *(offstage)*. What are you laughing at?
EVE *(baffled)*. I don't know. Is the meat hot?
ADAM. Hot hot hot.
EVE. And the fruit cold. *(She giggles, still puzzling things out)*
　　　　Tak-tak-tak-tak
　　　　Sharp-sharp!
(Adam enters with roasted meat and a heap of melons)
EVE. Good! Let me try. *(She takes her sharpened flint and whacks a melon open)* You see? Me first!
ADAM. That's fair. Your knife. You first.
EVE *(tenderly)*. But then you. Here's a fat slice.
ADAM. Thank you. Very nice. You're as nice as a melon, Eve. Let's play a little before eating the meat.
EVE. Before? Not after?
ADAM. Before, because after, we're full, we're tired, we'd rather sleep.
EVE. But before, we're hungry, and the meat is nicely hot.
ADAM. By God, you're right, Eve.
EVE. Yes, but Adam you're right too.
ADAM. That's right! I'm right too, you're right and I'm right! *(They laugh uproariously)*
EVE. You're so funny! Let's play before. Come on, help me get up.
ADAM. Ready?
EVE. Ready. But remember the new rule.
ADAM. Wait. What is it again? I know. No hands above the other's knees.
EVE. That's it. Here we go!
(They play a game. The aim is to catch the other's foot, ankle or shin and flip him or her over)
ADAM. I'll get you first!
EVE. No you won't but yes I will!

ADAM. Yes I will but no you won't!
EVE. Mouse!
ADAM. Mosquito!
(*They squeal, laugh, struggle and growl ad libitum; finally Eve flips Adam over*)
ADAM. Aaauw!
EVE. I win!
(*She dances around him and sings her two-note song*)
EVE. Win-win-win-win!
(*Adam catches her and she falls too*)
EVE. Aauw! Unfair! Unfair!
ADAM. Everybody loses, everybody wins!
(*They laugh uproariously and roll on the ground*)
EVE. Oh I liked that! My belly aches from laughing.
ADAM. But now we're too dirty to eat. Let's go wash in the river.
EVE. I don't know. There's almost no water in it this time of year.
ADAM. Almost no water is plenty. We're not *that* dirty, silly!
EVE. I was joking, silly! Me first!
(*She runs off*)
ADAM. Everybody first!
(*He follows her*)
(*Gabriel appears on the empty stage; Adam and Eve's laughter recedes*)
GABRIEL. My loved ones. (*He examines the meat*) They have forgotten that once upon a time they knew nothing of fire and cooking. (*He examines the tools*) Not so bad. Slow by slow things almost incredible come to pass, yet o my Sovereign—
EVE (*off-stage*) Clean to dinner!
ADAM (*singing the two-note tune*) Din-din-din-din!
GABRIEL. How many years shall they like that same raw song?
(*Enter Adam and Eve*)
ADAM. Our angel!
(*They kneel*)
GABRIEL. Greetings again. Rise my dears.
(*They rise and he kisses each on the eyes*)
ADAM. Always your lips like ours as if we were the same you perfect Majesty and mere she and I.
GABRIEL. I appear the same for your sakes though in your absence neither male nor female but like our God presented male to your infant imaginations.
EVE. Where have you travelled these many days dear angel?
GABRIEL. These how many days dear Eve?

EVE. These—these (*she looks at Adam*).
ADAM. Twenty?
EVE. Twenty-someghing?
ADAM. Many.
EVE. We have forgotten to place the little nicks on the branch every morning as you said.
GABRIEL. Will you do so from now on?
ADAM. We will.
EVE. If you tell us where you went and what you did!
GABRIEL. I sought out the fair and rough the wet and dry of this earth my domain and trust foreseeing that the Commanding Spirit (praise it forever and ever) will make it a garden like yours for your descendants to delight in. Now sit down my children and eat.
(*Adam and Eve begin to eat. She tentatively offers Gabriel some meat*)
GABRIEL (*shaking his head*). You are made in our image but only our image and more I may not tell you. But across the river—what is the river's name?
BOTH. Hiddekel!
GABRIEL. Across the river I saw the trees without their fruit. Have you plucked those trees bare in my absence? Have you savored all their fruit? Are the cherries there as delicious to the tongue and palate as they are here?
EVE. You are teasing us Gabriel.
GABRIEL. How so?
ADAM. When the trees were copious with all that tempting fruit the river ran high and swift and we could not cross to reach them. Now that the river is low the trees have long since dropped their fruit and I guess the animals have eaten it.
GABRIEL. Now that the river is low you should build a bridge of tree trunks across it you and Eve working hard together hard and many a day devising height thickness and strength against the current once it grows strong again.
ADAM. What is a bridge Gabriel?
GABRIEL. I will show you. (*He draws in the sand with a stick*) Imagine a bird looking at you two. Here you are Adam and Eve two dots.
ADAM. Two dots? I and she?
EVE. Silly! The two dots is supposing. Supposing says Gabriel supposing this is I and you.
GABRIEL. Do you understand?
ADAM. Of course!
GABRIEL. And here is the river.

ADAM. And the water?

GABRIEL. We will keep the water safe in our minds.

EVE. That's easy since the river's almost dry! (*They laugh*)

GABRIEL. Hush children listen to me and look. Now I draw a line across the river and if these dots were you and you why should not that line be the trunk of a tree that fell down?

ADAM. Lightning struck it!

GABRIEL. Yes. Or else you cut it down with your good stone axe. And now you are walking over it careful not to fall. Remember we are imagining the river is full. You are walking across it and now you reach the wonderful land on the other side. Why do you look puzzled?

EVE. How did the tree fall so courteously just where you wanted it?

ADAM. And when the river is full Gabriel won't the water cover it or carry it away or I don't know what?

GABRIEL. Your questions please me. Eve it did not fall out of kindness towards you for our Sovereign does not so dispose the world. You and Adam pulled it in place from the wood.

ADAM. From the wood? Thank you! Not I!

EVE. Nor I! Thank you!

GABRIEL. How spoiled you are darlings of sunshine and gobblers of perpetual feasts!

ADAM. Dear angel do not be angry with us. We will cut the tree and pull the bridge in place.

GABRIEL. Nevertheless you were right Adam saying the water would cover it and roll it away when you needed it most. How then shall we keep this from happening?

EVE. I am sleepy Gabriel. God will help.

ADAM. Spoiled! You're spoiled! And I am wide awake. We have to raise the tree trunk high above the water.

GABRIEL. But how?

EVE. And besides a tree trunk is too short. We will need two at least. The river is wide.

ADAM. Do we really want the fruit on that other side Gabriel? We have enough here. This is a game you're playing with us.

EVE. I do. I want it. And I know what to do.

GABRIEL. Tell us.

EVE. The river is full of flat stones.

GABRIEL. Good!

ADAM. I know! We pile—

EVE. I thought of it first! We pile the stones up in the middle of the river—

ADAM. Because it's dry! You forgot to say that! And we roll the trees—. Oh but they're going to be so heavy and make such a sweat on our bodies....

GABRIEL. To be sure Adam. Two or three tree trunks. And who knows? Two or three piles of stones.

EVE. That's what *I* thought.

ADAM (*glum*). So be it.

GABRIEL. But how will you keep the trunks from rolling off the stones? And how will you keep yourselves from falling into the water?

EVE. Slowly Gabriel slowly.

ADAM. Ask us again one question at a time.

GABRIEL. How will you keep the trunks from rolling off the flat stones?

ADAM. I don't know.

GABRIEL. Think. Eve?

EVE. Thinking takes time Gabriel and alone is best.

GABRIEL. All the same think of the round trunk and the flat stone. The trunk rolls. Do you see it in your minds? You don't want it to roll. You want it to stay where it is. You have means. You have tools. What can you do?

ADAM. Slice a flat place on the trunk?

GABRIEL. Do you see it Eve?

EVE. Yes I do and I could have thought of it too. Flat on flat will be steady. We'll do it Gabriel: You will praise us when you see how seriously we work.

GABRIEL. I hope I shall. But next. How will you walk on that bridge without falling off and the torrent of water swift under you?

EVE. I don't know.

ADAM. I do. Make the trunk flat again but this time on top all the way, like this.

GABRIEL. To be sure. But still that will be dangerous. Think how narrow the bridge will be! What if a safer way could be devised?

(*He shows them a couple of creepers*)

EVE. We tie a lot of creepers together! You showed us how knots are made. I haven't forgotten. Look. Strong, isn't it?

ADAM. Then what?

EVE. We tie one end to a strong bush, or else around a rock on one bank, and the other end on the other. The first time over we shall need to be very very careful.

ADAM. Wait. We gouge deep holes into our bridge and we put sticks upright into the holes. Then we tie the creepers to the sticks. Do you see what I mean Eve? We'll walk across and hold on the way monkeys do with their paws and tails. Get up! Let me show you. Give me your hand. This way, this way.

EVE. Don't fall off! (*They laugh*) And what else Gabriel? Give us more hard questions. Wait! We shall make the holes *before* we lay the trunks on the stones!

GABRIEL. And how high will you pile the stones?

ADAM. Higher than the water.

GABRIEL. But how high is the water?

ADAM. High Gabriel.

EVE. Stupid! That's not an answer!

GABRIEL. Doesn't the river leave its message somewhere?

ADAM. Its message? What do you mean?

GABRIEL. I will show you. Look at the far bank from here. Do you see a light part above and a darker part below?

EVE. Yes I do.

ADAM. So do I.

GABRIEL. This is the message the river leaves. Where the dark ends and the light begins is as high—

EVE. Gabriel! What are those animals? Look look!

ADAM. Three five six of them. Staring at us! How fine they are!

GABRIEL. They are horses.

EVE. Horses.

ADAM. Horses.

GABRIEL. Pleased with you pleased with your zeal our Lord has brought you his next gift.

EVE *and* ADAM. Our Lord be praised!

EVE. Now they're running and playing, all six of them.

GABRIEL. Six Adam and Eve? Count again.

(*They do so, pointing with their fingers and numbering. They have a little trouble and interfere with each other ad libitum*)

ADAM. Six, seven eight! Eight horses!

EVE (*at the same time*) Eight horses! Now we have it right!

GABRIEL. You shall befriend them you man and woman.

ADAM. They are leaving. May we cross the dry bed and follow them?

GABRIEL. Not now. I have summoned them in order to tempt you and encourage you. They will come again my beloved but only when the river is full and the trees are spangled again with delectable fruit. Then will you cross and the horses lovingly greeted shall be serviceable to you.

ADAM. How? Shall we eat them? Do they give milk?

GABRIEL. No. But they will allow you to ride them.

EVE. Ride them?

GABRIEL. As you have seen the little gibbon riding on his mother.

EVE. How strange!
GABRIEL. Sitting astride them you will gallop and travel and discover and make new homes in other lands you and your progeny ages to come.
ADAM. Gallop....
EVE. Blessed be the Father and Mother who gives us these treasures,
ADAM. Now and in ages to come. (*They kneel*)
GABRIEL. But you will not forget the bridge?
ADAM. No Gabriel.
GABRIEL. You will measure haul cut drill and fasten?
EVE. We will we promise dear angel.
GABRIEL. So be it. Our Lord is watching. Answer his love with yours and deserve oh deserve his care.

SCENE THREE

(*Night. The remains of a fire are smoldering. By the fire, a log bench is propped on two stones. God and Gabriel stand to one side.*)

GABRIEL. I saw Adam run to the riverbank with a straight stick and measure all by himself untold and unguided the height he needed ascertaining it by the watermark left on each bank.
GOD. And then?
GABRIEL. Then came a little piling of stones and a little hacking at a tree and then they forgot.
GOD. Forgot!
GABRIEL. They made themselves a bench however. See how they flattened both ends of the trunk so it would sit securely on the stones.
GOD. And in the middle two scooped-out places for the joy of their delicate little buttocks!
GABRIEL. In which delight all else was forgotten and the luxurious fruit on the other bank not seen no longer craved.
GOD. Where are they now?
GABRIEL. Within doing the merry act of love. Will you be granting them a brood soon my Sovereign? When shall the race of man begin?
GOD. Not yet. Must it begin? I have cancelled other beginnings friend Gabriel. Now however I shall leave their minds undiverted by mother-care and father-worry.

GABRIEL. With deference I ask: have you allowed them from your store mind enough to be and perform what you propose?

GOD. If not I will abolish them and begin again. Here they come hand in hand and in the flattering moonlight a handsome couple I would grieve to call a mistake though less beautiful than horse lion and nightingale.

EVE. Dearest and best. Sweet and violent. My restless fountain.

ADAM. My blessed chalice. Best and dearest. Violent and sweet.

EVE. The moon has kept its eye wide open for us.

ADAM. And whenever it does there is a bird that flutes its best unseen in its own warm foliage. Listen.

(*They sit on the bench*)

GOD. Yes I would grieve.... Gabriel who knows? That dull bridge! Bridge to what? More mere feeding! Perhaps some loftier task of the mind will animate them.

EVE. (*Singing the two-note tune*) Love-love-love-love.

ADAM. There's milk left in the shell and a bit of fire. Shall I warm it?

EVE. Do my pretty do, while I crack hazelnuts. Hard work has made us hungry.

(*They laugh while Eve cracks nuts with a stone*)

EVE. Me one you one.

(*God and Gabriel reveal themselves*)

GOD. Eve first created
    And Adam the strong: greetings again.

ADAM *and* EVE. Lord God, welcome and all blessings upon you! (*They kneel*)

GOD. Rise my children.
    I remember your house I remember your fire
    But I do not recall this strong bench.
    Well done! Well done my firstling architects!

GABRIEL. Tell your Sovereign nevertheless tell honestly what this wood was meant to be namely not for repose but crossing over.

EVE. As you said Gabriel.

ADAM. It wanted to be a—bridge.

EVE. We are ashamed but it couldn't be.

GOD. Why not?

ADAM. We ran to the forest

EVE. And we ran to the river

ADAM. We found a log

EVE. We piled the stones

ADAM. We rolled it here

EVE. We cut and levelled the ends

AND THE LORD GOD PLANTED A GARDEN

ADAM. And then the silly rains began to fall again
EVE. The river swelled
ADAM. The stones disappeared
EVE. The log was too short
ADAM. We made a bench of it
EVE. And we are happy my Lord happy enough without those other plums and pears and without elsewhere regions.
GOD. Didn't you know the rain would fall again?
ADAM. We did know. But why did it fall before we had finished Gabriel's bridge?
GOD. Every ninth month it falls Eve and Adam
      And falls for three months quenching and drenching
      The beautiful world: and you
      You must do your work quick or slow accordingly.
      Where tell me is your notched tree branch
      Upon which you tell the days
      According to the sun
      And months according to the moon?

(*Silence*)

GABRIEL. They lost it my Lord.
GOD. How many days my children does it take
      The full moon to be full a second time?
ADAM. Many....
EVE. Not so many....
GOD. How many days my children does it take
      To haul a felled tree to the river?
ADAM. I forget....
EVE. I don't know....
GOD. How many days my children does it take
      To set one pile of stones athwart the river?
EVE. Two?
ADAM. Twenty?
GOD. How many days my children does it take
      Until the river falls again and turns to sand?

(*Adam and Eve look puzzled*)

GOD. And when you have reckoned
      How long you need to haul the logs to bevel them
      To pile the stones to place the trunk
      To stretch the guiding handrail
      When you have added each to each and each

              Of all these things then tell me
              When will you need to begin the work
              That will take you in triumph to the golden fruit
              The horses the new so promising regions
              When the river is too dangerous to swim?
EVE. Mighty Creator of all we have, have we offended you?
ADAM. That you make it all so hard?
EVE. So full of dancing numbers?
ADAM. That dance us dizzy?
GOD. But it is a happy dance they dance
              And would you not like to know the steps?
              That dance of the numbers is the heartbeat of the universe
              And when you know the steps
              The steps that I and Gabriel dearly wish to teach you
              You two shall become little less than gods
              Who now are little more than apes.
ADAM. What must we do my Sovereign?
GOD. Begin again and having begun
              Let your hunger demand more and yet more
              And always between rest and play be restlessly demanding
              Of this so question-worthy world.
              Take this humble unwanted stick
              And with your knife mark it thus
              Signifying the moon is full.

(*Eve does so*)

GOD. Tomorrow this same time
              The moon still puffing its round cheek
              You shall mark the stick again
              Yet slightly short signifying
              The moon begins diminishing
              Down its monthly journey.
ADAM. Sometimes the moon shows half its face sometimes it disappears even when the sky is clear and sometimes or always I don't know it grows slowly—
EVE. Wait! It goes and comes by its number my Lord by its very own number!
GOD. And these numbers you shall mark
              And when the moon is gone the mark will be thus
              And when it is full again you shall count up the marks
              And mark them all together thus: one month.
              And month by month or day by day

>   You shall measure the river the work you do
>   The growth of your children when they come
>   And thereafter you shall learn steps
>   Yet more intricate dances more delightful
>   Adding multiplying dividing
>   Taking distance thickness height rapidity
>   Once you begin my children and adore
>   The dance of thought outward and outward unto me.
> ADAM. Tell us and teach us my Lord.
> GOD.　Here is a straight rod. Let it be called a span.
>   Here mark it with a notch. That is half a span.
>   Span the distance between your shelter and the forest
>   Then between your shelter and the riverbank
>   Then span upward your height and then the trees'.
>   Mark the number by your two hands
>   Which have five fingers each.
>   Record and remember.
>   Tell each measure of time each measure of distance
>   Over and over till you can no longer forget.
>   Look at the moon again my dears
>   Think how it walks from horizon to horizon.
>   After you have marked it full half full
>   And of that half another half then filling once again
>   You shall ask of it does it walk in the sky alone?
> EVE. No so do the stars.
> GOD. And now I tell you this: the sun too is a star.
> EVE. Like these?
> ADAM. And yet so different?
> GOD.　Different because nearer to us.
>   Think how this fire of yours diminishes
>   Seen from that hill many spans from here.
> ADAM. And the sun too walks from side to side because it is a star!
> GOD.　And yet my children it is not the sun
>   That walks but the earth turning upon itself
>   And as it turns you who stand upon it
>   Think it is the sun that moves but it is you
>   It is the earth on which you stand that moves
>   And moves by number hour by hour and they too
>   The hours will be known to you by and by.
> ADAM. Gabriel!

(*Gabriel takes his hand and Eve's*)
GABRIEL. Do not fear. That motion is sweet and soft and humankind shall never feel it.
EVE. The sky seems terrible tonight.
GOD. Meet it bravely. Meet by and by
        Galaxies immense whirlpools of stars
        Planets and meteors flights of great melted bodies
        Light spreading from star to star vast silences
        Lonely dust dense points that suck atoms and light
        Time that flames out and is born again
        Globes of power fists of matter outward outward
        Constituting in my great arms the Anthem of Existence.
(*In the distance a choir of voices is softly singing*)
ADAM *and* EVE. What are they?
GABRIEL. Listen.
EVE. Heavenly angels....
ADAM. Merciful heaven....
GABRIEL. They are frightened.
GOD. Frightened and joyful.
(*After a while, the music recedes and dies out*)
GOD. Fall asleep Eve first created of human beings
        And Adam strong father fall asleep.
        Of my words retain what is needed
        Let the rest be dreamed away
        But leaving in your minds a flavor of high longing.
        Have I created them sufficient Gabriel?
GABRIEL. Be merciful my Sovereign.
GOD. Farewell good angel. Continue. As always I will return.

SCENE FOUR

(*Adam is squatting in the sun, surrounded by several kinds of fruit, including apples. He sings the two-note song.*)

ADAM. Orange good melon good
        Good banana apple good
        Good good good!

AND THE LORD GOD PLANTED A GARDEN

(He cuts an apple in two and bites into a half. Suddenly perplexed, he stops. He takes another apple and also cuts it in two. He rises. Then he cuts a banana in two. He rises and fetches two long bones. He places the two bones before him on the ground, and then places the halves of apples and bananas alongside them. He falls into a deep study)

EVE *(offstage)*. Adam! Adam! *(She rushes in)* I need to tell you!

ADAM. Stop! Catch your breath, silly!

EVE. No, I don't want to catch my breath. I have a story!

ADAM. You're sweating, dirty, bleeding from your shins—what happened?

EVE. A glorious story!

ADAM. Good!

EVE. I was standing on our lookout rock near the river when suddenly I saw those horses again, those beautiful horses, and yet the river's almost dry! Strange, I said to myself, and then I said, why not dare!

ADAM. Dare what?

EVE. Why not cross to the other side and meet them?

ADAM. Down one steep craggy bank and up the other to greet a flock of speechless beasts? Well, why not. But that's why you're bleeding, my woman.

EVE. I don't care. I decided to try. And I did clamber down holding on to branches and roots and tufts and striking against a few rocks, and then I waded across the river up to my knees and then up again—not so easy, I can tell you, but I was laughing all the while—never mind the scratches—because one of them—I mean the horses—one of the horses was standing at the edge looking down at me and sure it must have been wondering what I was about.

ADAM. Yes, animals do wonder. They didn't bite you, did they?

EVE. Bite me? They looked more like galloping away in a panic. And to be sure most of them did, going hunh hunh hunh as they ran. But three or four remained and especially the one who'd watched me climb up from the riverbed.

ADAM. Weren't you afraid?

EVE. A little. But afraid was less than excited. Wait. I've told you only the beginning so far. I went up to the horse slowly, I'll show you, this way easy easy easy and saying in my nice voice—

ADAM. The one I like so much—the voice—you know—?

EVE. Of course not, silly! I have several nice voices and so have you. It was another one I used. Listen. Pretty pretty pretty I sing-sang. He never moved. When I reached him I began to pat him on the neck. At first he started and then I was truly scared. But I kept saying pretty pretty pretty and patting and then stroking his muzzle and I could tell he liked me.

ADAM. Liked you!
EVE. Yes! Liked me! What will you say when I tell you that I jumped on his back?
ADAM. As the angel said! Oh he knew it! He wanted it! What happened next?
EVE. He rode away with me. No! I rode away with him!
ADAM. God help you!
EVE. Rode away, Adam, holding on to his mane and neck, and I don't know how but such a wild adventure I never had riding far far and coming to that hill we always look at when the sun goes down, and behind it I could see a vast beautiful plain, another river, a row of mountains—was I dreaming?—the wind whipping my cheeks, riding riding.
ADAM. And then what happened? Thank God you're back.
EVE. Because after a while he turned and brought me back where I had begun and there he stopped as if he meant it kindly.
ADAM. Strange and wonderful. And that was all?
EVE. All and enough. Down his back I climbed. Then down the bank across the bit of water and up the bank to come and tell you my story and take you with me for you to try.
ADAM. I will, but first let me show you something here.
EVE. What were you doing, Adam?
ADAM. I was sitting down to eat when—wait, I'll show you. (*He cuts another apple in two*) Have we got two apples now?
EVE. Of course not! What a fool. This is half and that is half.
ADAM. So you say. Now look at the bones. How many are there?
EVE. Two.
(*Adam places the half apples parallel to the bones*)
ADAM. How is it we have two bones but not two apples?
EVE. I don't know. Who cares? Better give me my half and the banana too. I'm hungry. And then we'll gallop.
(*Both eat*)
ADAM. The horses, the halves. It's puzzling. Besides we keep eating these apples and—
EVE. And what?
ADAM. God said do not.
EVE. Years ago!
ADAM. Years?
EVE. Or months.
ADAM. I suppose so.
EVE. Let's go, Adam!
ADAM. As soon as I've wiped my mouth. Aren't you ever tired?

EVE. Never never!
(She runs away laughing, followed by Adam)
ADAM. I'll be there first anyway! Adam the strong!
(He vanishes. After a little while Gabriel enters. He looks around, picks up the notched stick, and shakes his head)
GABRIEL. After the quarter moon they gave up and forgot.
(Offstage Adam and Eve are heard singing to their tune)
EVE. Bad horse gone horse fled horse
  Klop klop klop.
ADAM. Wait horse stop horse
  Klop klop klop.
GABRIEL. And they have heard the angels sing!
(Enter Adam and Eve)
ADAM. Our angel!
EVE. Gabriel!
GABRIEL. Well met once more. You look excited my children. And singing your one and best worst song as always.
EVE. I sat on a horse today and ran and flew with it and I wanted my Adam to do it too but they were all gone. Oh now I *am* tired and look—my shins still bleeding.
GABRIEL. Have you forgotten the plant I showed you?
EVE. You showed us many plants dear angel.
GABRIEL. But now I mean the plant whose leaf can be placed—
EVE. On a wound to staunch the blood!
ADAM. I remember too!
GABRIEL. Where do you keep it? You were going to collect the plants that are good to eat in themselves those you could chop to season your meat those that heal wounds those that help the sick belly or the aching head and those to one side that are too sour or too bitter for any good. *(Adam and Eve hang their heads)* Come let me heal your little wound. Do you remember what the blood does in your body Eve?
EVE. It....it bleeds.
ADAM. You wanted us to build a bridge Gabriel so we could reach and ride the horses on the other side yet you see they came in the dry season without any bridge at all.
GABRIEL. I asked them to come Adam.
ADAM. Why?
EVE. Yes why?
(Gabriel picks up the notched stick, and lets it fall again. He picks up the halves of apple)
GABRIEL. This fruit the apple was forbidden Adam and Eve.

ADAM. Look Gabriel. When you cut an apple in the middle you get half apples but you also get two pieces and how can half and two be the same?

GABRIEL. Because two can be two anything. Two human beings two trees two lions two angels but also two halves.

EVE. Two half angels?

GABRIEL. Yes if you cut me. And two half Eves and two half Adams.

(*Adam and Eve laugh*)

GABRIEL. Laugh my dears laugh yet I am troubled for you. Fear our Sovereign's displeasure. He gives. But he can take away.

ADAM. You disliked.... (*he looks at the apples*) our song.

GABRIEL. Would you not like to sing a better one?

ADAM. We would but what is wrong with ours? It has served us very properly.

EVE. And we sing it better all the time. We put new words to it.

GABRIEL. Yet a thousand other songs and finer words are waiting for you to beget them. Have you forgotten the voices the wonderful voices not long ago?

EVE. When we fell asleep. How strange it was.

ADAM. Were they, were those *songs?*

GABRIEL. They were.

ADAM. But not for poor us.

GABRIEL. Why not try?

ADAM. I like trying! Show us.

GABRIEL. There are many notes. They go up but of course they come down too. It is like climbing up or down from one hill to another, and yet while you go up there may be little downs on the way and while you go down there may be little ups as you go. Listen! (*He sings*) And you can run your voices quickly or slowly, and sharply or smoothly. (*He sings, with extempore comments*) And finally you can go no higher or no lower. You are at the top of the hill or at the bottom of the valley. Let us do it together.

(*They sing scales with exclamations etc. extempore*)

GABRIEL. Stop now. Shall I make it a little more difficult?

EVE. Yes, do!

GABRIEL. Listen to me. (*He adds the minor key to his scale*) or else this. (*He varies his speed and rhythm*) But all these notes are like an immense but unkempt field full of flowers. You must cull the right flowers and arrange them properly. And these right flowers rightly arranged you shall call melodies, and to these melodies you shall fit words of your best choosing for your delight and consolation.

EVE. Make a melody for us Gabriel.

GABRIEL. Gladly. (*He sings*)

O Sovereign, how manifold are thy works! out of wisdom hast thou made them all: the earth is full of thy riches.
So is the great wide sea, wherein are things creeping and swimming innumerable, both small and great beasts.
O my Sovereign, thou art clothed in honor and majesty,
Light is thy garment; thou spreadest the heavens like a curtain;
Thou makest the clouds thy horses and walkest upon the wings of the wind.
Thou didst lay the foundations of the earth; thou sendest the spring into the valley;
Thou givest drink to every beast of the field; the earth is satisfied with the fruit of thy works.
Thy trees are filled with sap, and the birds make their nests therein;
The high hills are a refuge to the wild goats; and the rocks for the conies.
Thou didst appoint the moon for seasons and the sun for a daily measure.
And man goeth forth unto his soft labors until evening, culling fruit and shearing the lamb.
Therefore sing unto him, sing psalms unto him: converse unwearied of his munificence.
(*Adm and Eve are gaping*)
ADAM. "Thou makest the clouds...." How did it go again Gabriel?
GABRIEL. Thou makest the clouds thy horses and walkest upon the wings of the wind.
ADAM. The clouds are horses? The wind has wings?
EVE. Sing it again Gabriel.
(*Gabriel sings the line*)
EVE. And sing about man goeth forth.
GABRIEL (*softly*). You sing Eve.
EVE. You first.
(*Gabriel sings the line*)
GABRIEL. Now you.
(*Eve tries. Gabriel teaches her extempore. Finally she has it, sings the line triumphantly and laughs*)
EVE. I sang it! Now Adam.
ADAM. I'll do even better! Wait! Do the whole end for me Gabriel.
GABRIEL. Listen to me. (*He sings the last two lines*) Now join me.
(*Again extempore, a lesson, until Adam has the lines*)
ADAM. Now all together!
(*All three sing, and Gabriel slyly harmonizes*)
ADAM. What did you do? You sang differently this time!
GABRIEL. I will teach you that difference I hope another day. And another

day you two shall make up songs of your own choosing songs of your own devising will you not? Promise me.

ADAM. We promise.

EVE. We will make wonderful melodies and fit to them wonderful words.

ADAM. We promise.

GABRIEL. So be it. The Lord God hears and takes notice of your promise.

SCENE FIVE

(Adam and Eve are sleeping in the sun, sprawled a few yards from each other. Abundant remnants of eating and drinking lie all about them. Some remains of a roast can be seen on a spit over a fire. Time passes. Then Adam half awakens, reaches for an opened coconut and drinks from it. He notices that he is perspiring)

ADAM. Eve....

EVE. Mmmmmmmm.

ADAM. It's hot. Wake up.

EVE *(brushing away a fly)*. You're right. Oh, look!

ADAM. At what?

EVE. At the fire. It's smoldering. Take the spit off, will you?

ADAM. Why not you?

EVE. It was you who dropped our bench in the fire. Besides, I ate too much.

ADAM. How many times will I have to hear about that useless bench? Good God! I used our measuring stick to roast the lamb!

EVE. Our measuring stick?

ADAM. Don't you remember?

EVE. I guess....

ADAM. It's all blackened.

EVE. Oh Adam, please let me sleep.

ADAM. Well, I'm sleeping in the shade.

EVE. Me too.

(They drag themselves into the shade, then fall asleep again, snoring pleasantly. Time passes. Birds sing. The stage darkens. When the lights return, the stage is empty for a moment)

SCENE SIX

(God and Gabriel on stage. God is holding the measuring stick)

GOD.   I made for them with fibers in their billions
        A brain—o Gabriel a brain a mere brain
        Made of human flesh can never gather in the universe.
        Yet this brain I made for them
        Was like a bucket to a well decently sufficient.
        Impetuously I added food shelter sunshine rain
        Peace good health and furthermore kept offsprings
        Unborn to them so they might master before breeding
        That which the brain I made for them can hold
        And be to our universe responsive knowledge
        And indeed modest creator and minor god.
        But wretched me I failed. Oh I have failed before
        And wept before but now again. Humbled divinity.
        Some master of my mastery watches us Gabriel
        From a sovereignty impenetrable. So be it.
GABRIEL. What of them my Lord?
GOD.   What of you Gabriel?
        For you I have another world.
GABRIEL. But what of them?
GOD.   Another world new creatures to rule
        Made fresh out of new wisdom.
        I have discarded brain and all such engines
        And will show you from my fund of matter
        Better capabilities. This *(he looks at the stick)* is barren.
        I am almost ashamed and shall abolish it.
(Adam and Eve are heard offstage singing their two-note ditty)
ADAM *and* EVE.
        Peaches peaches
        Hey hey hey!
        Berries berries
        Hoo hoo hoo!
(Gabriel covers his face with his hands)
GOD.   I have failed.
        But perhaps shall not fail next time.
GABRIEL. What of your promise to them?

GOD. What of their promise to me?
(*He pokes with the stick at an apple on the ground and then angrily discards the stick*)
ADAM *and* EVE (*still offstage*)
>   Melons melons
>   Wah wah wah!
>   Apples apples
>   Yoh yoh yoh!

GOD. Adam and Eve! Stand before me!
(*Adam and Eve appear. The thundering voice has frightened them. They look apprehensively at God and Gabriel*)
ADAM. We obey you my Lord.
GOD.   No you do not obey me!
>   Refractory to our love dead to our teachings
>   Lazy guzzlers and gapers
>   Lipping juices and lapping sunshine
>   Given to you not as your end but for your aid
>   And by you indolently abused dead
>   Dead to my great purpose which again and again
>   He Gabriel and I your Sovereign entreated upon you
>   When you lapsed promised to rise and lapsed again.
>   What have you done with my gifts?
>   How have you not perverted them?
>   The apple you swore you would not eat
>   Heedlessly you ate meaning neither good nor ill
>   Lax lazy inert to my command
>   Heedlessly broke the covenant between us
>   The loyalty I made so easy to uphold
>   And biting that fruit you bit my gentle hand.

ADAM *and* EVE (*on their knees, sobbing*). Forgive us my Lord forgive us!
GOD.   In part Eve and Adam I shall.
>   I know you both grateful merry and affable
>   Therefore will not abolish your life
>   But lax lazy and inert I know you too
>   And therefore will forsake you.
>   Live but live without me.
>   Live but live without my angels.
>   The ministering spirits depart from you.
>   Earth is yours no longer mine: plough it destroy it
>   Thrive or die: yours alone yours fair or foul alone.
>   Us you shall dream of and pray to

But forever in vain.
(*God departs. Gabriel approaches Adam and Eve and places his hands on their heads*)
ADAM (*sobbing*). You too Gabriel?
EVE (*sobbing*). Forgive us, forgive us!
GABRIEL.   In God's sweet light you loved one another.
            Love one another in your bitter night.
(*Gabriel leaves. Adam and Eve leap up*)
ADAM *and* EVE. Gabriel, Gabriel, Gabriel!

SCENE SEVEN

(*Winter. Adam, clad in heavier skins, is studying and manipulating a variety of branches lying on the ground. Long ropes of creepers and stone tools lie about as well. Every now and then he warms himself at a fire, but he is clearly intent on his problem*)

ADAM. Eve? Are you back?
(*Enter Eve, carrying a rudimentary net with a fish inside it*)
ADAM. You did catch one! I take it all back! But what's the matter with you?
EVE. I'm exhausted, that's all.
ADAM. Exhausted from catching a fish?
EVE. I'm two people now, man; why do you keep forgetting? And it's a hard clamber down to the river, wading into the current, handling the net, trying not to slip, scrabbling back up with a squirming fish. *Now* do I have the right to be tired?
ADAM. I'm sorry....
EVE. And who thought of making a net?
ADAM. You did.
EVE. And who laughed at me?
ADAM. I did. But you'll get two shares of the fish out of three, first because you made the net, and second because you're making a child. Come closer to the fire and dry your shins. No question, this *is* a handsome fish!
EVE. I'm so cold, so bitter cold. I hope the cough won't be clawing at me again. And everywhere that hateful snow.
ADAM. Still, with your net in hand we'll fill our bellies every day for a change until we cross that miserable river.
EVE. Dreamer. You're fooling with your logs and branches cozy near the fire, but I saw again what's left of that bridge of ours. Nothing! Every splinter

and pebble carried off to perdition, and it's a miracle we remained behind.

ADAM. The stones sank, the wood floated.

EVE. What?

ADAM. That's what stuck fast in my mind. And the leaves float. And coconut shells float.

EVE. What are you stirring up this time, Adam? I'd better cut up that fish.

ADAM (*excited*). Eve, we'll float across the river too. Tell your fish to wait. We'll float sitting on a crisscross of logs. Look. I'll take four or five pieces to show you what I mean. We'll have to cut them so they match a little better, but that's nothing. One, two, three and a lot more side by side; then another row on top of them looking the other way. And we tie them at the corners—wait—like this, and this, and this, so they hold together when the current buffets them.

EVE. And we?

ADAM. We sit on top. What did you think?

EVE. Just sit?

ADAM. No, I don't mean just sit. How would we ever get across? And what would keep us from being swept away like the bridge?

EVE. *I* don't know, Adam. I'm tired. I made the net, and now I can't think anymore.

ADAM. But this time I can! We'll do it like the fish. Look at that tail. You should have thought of it yourself. I'll flatten out two good sturdy branches at one end like fishtails so they catch the water, and the upper end I'll keep small and round for us to clutch with both hands, and we'll push the water—push push push until we reach the other bank.

EVE (*laughing*). My heap of muscles is not so dumb!

ADAM. At last a good word.

EVE. At last?

ADAM. Yes, at last.

EVE (*after a silence, softly*). It's clever, my dearest. But—

ADAM. But?

EVE. Why not simply die?

(*Adam stares*)

ADAM. I don't know. All three of us?

EVE. Like that baby bird yesterday frozen to death. Then the snow will have it all. And God can be happy.

ADAM. God won't know. First let's see whether the thing will hold after I'm done making it.

EVE. Why not wait until the river goes down? I'm tired to death hauling and lifting. I've counted the notches. In a few months the water will be down to

where we can cross without a bridge or anything.
ADAM. We can't wait a few months, woman. The island is dried out.
EVE (*bitterly*). *They* dried it out.
ADAM. No, Eve. It went back to being...natural. But out there the horses live, we'll forage with them. It's huge, Eve. And if we die we die, but first we'll try not to. Leave the island! Cross the river! Night and day the words hammer at my brain. And as for you, two months from now, how will you run, how will you ride a horse?
EVE (*feeling her belly*). I suppose I'd better feed our guest.
ADAM. Make him strong.
EVE. Make him *smart*.
(*She goes into the cave. Adam sets to work on the raft or on a paddle. After a mighty whack with a cutting edge he stands back*)
ADAM. Not so dumb after all, you heap of muscles! Never mind!
(*He continues to work, trying to keep his hands from freezing, as the scene darkens and a cold wind blows. He stops working and listens to Eve singing mournfully but beautifully within the cave*)

EVE.   Down to the river
       We carry the stone
       Down to the river
       We bear it alone.
ADAM (*takes up the song*)
       Lift, humans, lift
       The heavy stone.
       Lift crying to heaven:
       We bear it alone.
(*He resumes his work, but sobbing*)
ADAM. Gabriel, Gabriel....
(*Eve appears, looking at him*)

SCENE EIGHT

(*Adam and Eve stand almost reverentially on either side of the finished raft, upon which we see a couple of crude paddles and small bundles of belongings. Snow. Cold.*)

EVE (*touching the raft*). Won't it sink? Won't it tip over and send us drowning in the current? Won't it carry us too far down where there are no horses?

AND THE LORD GOD PLANTED A GARDEN

ADAM (*touching the raft*). We built it, Eve, you and I.
EVE. Yes.
ADAM. The days are short, but if we start now, then tonight, if Fate is willing, we shall be camping on that first row of hills, where the land looks so rich.
EVE. And if Fate is not willing—
ADAM. Farewell Eve, farewell Adam, farewell world, prosper or perish without us, you do not need us, no you do not need us.
EVE. Give me your hand.
(*She leads him toward the cave, where they kneel*)
EVE. You parcel of earth, island of gladness and grief, root of our lives, garden that was, we thank you.
(*She kisses the ground*)
ADAM. Return to the plants and animals when Spring returns, but do not forget us, hold our love in your root.
(*He kisses the ground too. Both remain bowed low for a while, then rise*)
ADAM. I'll take this end, you the other. Grasp it as close to the corners as you can, like this. Ready?
EVE. Ready.
(*They lift the raft and start. Adam falters, as if to take a last look*)
EVE. Don't turn around, Adam. Walk.

The End

Notes

And the Lord God Planted a Garden appeared in the Spring 1985 issue of *The Kenyon Review*. I retouched it before including it in my *The Virgin and the Unicorn: Four Plays* volume of 1993, and have again retouched it for its final manifestation.

Its reception by *The Kenyon Review* is perhaps worth setting down because so unusual. The editor, the late Philip D. Church, wrote me, on his typewriter, a charming personal letter of acceptance, from which I quote: "I have read it and I think it is marvelous. It's one of the best pieces I've gotten since becoming editor of the Review. The verse-line and idiom is [*sic*] perfect; my ear cannot detect one false or tinny note or word. The dramatization is rich in thought, conception, and characterization. I would like to publish it...." and so forth. This was followed by four handwritten pages of comment and analysis! Of course I wrote a thank-you letter and was in fact deeply grateful, but my private note reads in part: "[Church] made a hash of [my play] in the long, erudite and partly unintelligible commentary.... Perhaps I'm wrong. Perhaps he read the play better than I do." And, "The enthusiastic letter of acceptance...showed me, once again, that no artist can ever hope to speak so plainly that his audience—the very audience he is aiming it, not some alien population!—will take his spade for a spade."

Production notes. Adam and Eve should be played by short actors, God and Gabriel by tall ones. This will give the right sense of scale. There should be nothing childish about Adam and Eve, even when they are playing games. On the other hand, there must be nothing erotic in the game they play in Scene Two. God and Gabriel are magnificently clad but without indication of sex; Adam and Eve wear skins. God must have a beautiful speaking voice, Gabriel must sing beautifully, and the composer should, I think, be at home with Bach and Handel.

AN UNPLEASANTNESS IN JERUSALEM

*And they compelled a passer-by, Simon of Cyrene...
the father of Alexander...to carry his cross.*

MARK 15:21

CHARACTERS

Simon
Alexander, *his son*
Ruth, *his wife*
Seron and Bacchides, *Phoenician merchants*
Ieshua
Petros
Iohanan
Gabinius and Marcellus, *Roman centurions*
Zadok and Mathias, *young Hebrews*
Two Pharisees, two servants, soldiers, a crowd

The scene throughout is before Simon's house in Jerusalem

(*Enter Seron and Bacchides*)

BACCHIDES. Here is Simon's house. I recognized it after all.
SERON. It looks very quiet. Do you suppose he is gone with the crowd to watch?
BACCHIDES. He is not the man to watch an execution. But it must be a sad day for him. He is like us, a man who is all for peace.
SERON. Old business friends like us will cheer him up.
(*Enter Mathias and Zadok*)
MATHIAS. I wonder if he's still at home. Or did his bleach-blooded father lock the door today?
ZADOK (*calling*). Alexander!
MATHIAS. Alexander!
(*Alexander appears on the roof*)
ALEXANDER. I'm still here. Wait in the street for me.
MATHIAS. We will, but let's try to hurry, shall we?
BACCHIDES. That was Simon's son. I recognize the name. I remember when he was born, and Simon was deciding what to call him. "I'll call him Alexander," he said, "not to commemorate that blood-soaked conqueror, but to perpetuate the name of Helen of Troy's lover." Or similar words. Those two don't like the looks of us, I think.
SERON. Sons of rich fathers, I'll bet. Shall we be casual and walk through them?
BACCHIDES. I'd rather wait till they go away with their Alexander.
(*Enter two dignified Pharisees*)
FIRST PHARISEE. My own view is simple. Seven (*he sneezes*) seven false Messiahs—seven, you'll recall, is the number of apocalyptic scourges—and then the true and final Redeemer appears and delivers us. Delivers us metaphysically, of course. I don't meddle in politics.
SECOND PHARISEE. But how will he do it? Isn't that the more important question? Will he destroy the world, God forbid, and then establish the heavenly kingdom? Or — what seems more humane to me — will he establish the heavenly kingdom on earth? "By these three trumpets the third part of the nation was killed," says the text; but what does it really mean?
FIRST PHARISEE (*plaintively*). It means a crowd: that's certain. Wherever

you look, in a text or in a street, there's sure to be a crowd, and when there's a crowd, *I* catch a cold. Like today. Oh God, I sweat when I think of that crucifixion. Nothing but rabble. (*Sneezes*) You see!

SECOND PHARISEE. "My wrath is upon all the multitudes." Ezekiel, seventh chapter.

SERON. Watch this.

ZADOK (*to the Pharisees, in an unpleasant manner*). Citizens.

FIRST PHARISEE (*a little frightened*). Are you talking to us?

ZADOK. Yes, to you. Are you on your way to the execution?

(*The two Pharisees stare at each other. They do not know what the right answer is*)

SECOND PHARISEE. What business is that of yours?

BACCHIDES (*to Seron*). A knife!

SECOND PHARISEE. We—

FIRST PHARISEE. We hadn't decided as yet. What do you want with us? We're standing peacefully in front of Simon's house.

ZADOK. Your business is to be at the execution. Aren't you Hebrews?

FIRST PHARISEE (*thoroughly alarmed*). What else?

ZADOK. On what side? Rome? The anointed rascal of Nazareth? or Hebrew liberty?

FIRST PHARISEE. Good grief! On what side? I—

SECOND PHARISEE (*has an idea*). How dare you ask us on what side? On what side are you? Both of you! I challenge you to tell me in the open.

ZADOK. I'll tell you what side we're against, yellow Pharisee; against you, against Rome, against that Ieshua preacher; and for our sacred people!

SECOND PHARISEE. And what do you think we're for and against? Are you going to start beating up your friends? Freedom for the Hebrews! Down with the appeasers! (*In a lower voice*) Down with Rome.

FIRST PHARISEE (*not too loud*). Freedom for the Hebrews!

(*He carries his friend away*)

MATHIAS. You're taking risks.

ZADOK. I hate the sight of them. Temporizers. They'd lick the devil's dung —like Simon. And who are those two skulking over there?

(*Enter Alexander from the house*)

MATHIAS. At last. We thought you might not be able to come.

ALEXANDER. Of course I'm coming. You don't imagine I'd miss that spectacle, do you? Only I can't right away. I'm—I must talk to my father.

MATHIAS. You make me laugh.

ALEXANDER. Besides, the whole procession is going to pass in front of my house, isn't it? But I tell you I *am* coming along! Meantime take my knife and slip it into one of your sleeves. I don't want it found on me.

MATHIAS. I'll take it.

SERON. Do they all carry weapons here?

ALEXANDER. Now listen carefully, both of you. Three men the Group wants us to find in the crowd. The first is Jonas. Show him the point of your dagger and tell him we know that he dines and drinks at the house of Caius Lutetius, and Caius Lutetius is a Roman, a Roman Roman. Next, find Daniel.

ZADOK. Which Daniel?

ALEXANDER. The son of Menelaus. Show him the point of your dagger and tell him we know that he has got in his possession a Spanish sword with the carved image of Mars on the hilt. Tell him also that he went to the bathhouse on the Sabbath, which things we account insults to the Law. And thirdly, find Eleazar. Show him the point of your dagger and tell him we know on the one hand he inclines toward the appeaser Ieshua the so-called anointed and on the other he spoke the following words last Tuesday in the open market: "We Hebrews will find a way of living with Rome."

MATHIAS. Living with Rome? Good.

ZADOK. Jonas, Daniel, Eleazar.

ALEXANDER. I will join you as soon as I can. Death to the appeasers.

MATHIAS. Freedom.

ZADOK. Under the Law.

ALEXANDER. Go quietly.

(*He returns to the house*)

BACCHIDES. Could you make out what they said?

SERON. No. But I could feel the texture, so to speak. They're coming this way.

BACCHIDES. Let's quietly cross them.

MATHIAS. Who are you, foreigners, and why might you be staring at us from your corner?

SERON. Who might you be to ask us, my boy?

MATHIAS. Don't boy me, foreigner. And answer straight. Crooked answerers don't live long in Judaea.

SERON. We are two Sidonian merchants. We deal with Simon, the Jew from Cyrene, who is an old customer of ours.

BACCHIDES (*calling*). Simon! Simon!

ZADOK. Phoenician merchants! Money-clinkers! Come along.

(*Zadok and Mathias leave*)

SERON. Knives in the open street!

BACCHIDES. Simon!

SIMON (*in the house*). I'm coming! (*He comes out of the house*) No!

BACCHIDES. Yes indeed! Old Simon!

SERON. Let me embrace you!

SIMON. Seron! Bacchides! Old pirates! Alive and in front of my house! Let me kiss you! Let me look at you! Unbelievable! My Phoenician seagulls! Wait! Don't say a word! Here's plenty of shade. You shall not come into the house without a libation to the gods. Ruth! Ruth! Where is the woman? Ruth!

BACCHIDES. Don't worry about the libation! Let's look at you and talk to you! And don't go upsetting your household for us.

SIMON. Upsetting! You'll be upsetting my miseries, aren't you ashamed? Ruth! Seron, you've grown stout! (*Enter Alexander from the house*) I told you to stay home.

ALEXANDER. I know you did.

SIMON. Just one moment. I said just one moment! (*Embarrassed*) Friends, will you find—of all times—wait—(*to Alexander*) Don't move. Ruth! (*Enter Ruth*) Here are Seron and Bacchides after two hundred years and you're off dawdling in the cellar.

RUTH. I am so pleased to see you again. Welcome to our house.

BACCHIDES. The blessings of God on you and yours.

SERON. And a kind afternoon as well.

SIMON (*to Ruth*). Let the servants bring a table, chairs, and refreshments at once! Seron—Bacchides—will you—? Let me hug you again. I am rude. But do excuse me while I say two words to my son. I must.

BACCHIDES. We are the ones who need to be excused. Come; Seron and I will go into the house. (*To Ruth*) Will you lead the way?

RUTH. With pleasure. (*Aside to Simon, in a whisper*) *Please* don't lose your temper.

SIMON. A few minutes, gentlemen, a few seconds. The servants will wash your feet. The Safed wine, Ruth.

(*Exeunt Ruth, Bacchides, Seron. During what follows, two servants bring out a table, chairs, wine, water, fruit*)

ALEXANDER. All right, here I am. You can let go my sleeve. Are you about to lecture me in Greek? I don't seem to be respectable enough to be introduced to your friends.

SIMON. I want you to stay in the house this afternoon.

ALEXANDER. Again! I'm a man, father, not a boy. Goodbye.

SIMON. Wait. Alexander, I said wait. Don't come back gleeful with the poor fellow's blood. He hasn't done you any harm.

ALEXANDER. I could spit when I hear you talk. In my lifetime God will send his Messiah, Judaea will smite Rome, and we shall stand in judgment over mankind; and there you lounge, loafing over your Epicurus and your Aristippus! God will tear them leaf by leaf out of your hands.

SIMON. Why do you talk so much nonsense?

ALEXANDER. "Cursed is the man who breeds swine and twice cursed the man who teaches his son Greek science." But no, you must always be smiling. Weren't you smiling when that counterfeit Messiah stood up—when he had the stomach to stand up, that blaspheming Nazarene peasant—and tell us "I am able to destroy your Temple and to rebuild it in three days." Weren't you smiling then too?

SIMON. Of course I was smiling.

ALEXANDER. I'm ashamed for you in front of my friends. I can't repeat what they say about you. But every time you talk about peace and every time you open your God-confounded Aristotle—

SIMON. Enough! The puppy is lecturing me! Stay home today, your father is speaking.

ALEXANDER. I am going to see that penny-Messiah put to death.

SIMON. What in God's name has the poor man done worse than crying "Give to the poor and heaven will reward you?"

ALEXANDER. My father is a child! Have you forgotten that when we asked him, in the Temple, "Are we yes or no obliged to pay taxes to the Romans?" he answered loud and clear "Give to Caesar what you owe Caesar"? I knew then he wouldn't live long. Now one of his own gang has sold him and no one's going to keep me from cheering when they shove the cross on his shoulders. But that's enough. I'll be late. You've seen it my way, I hope. Be glad you've got a son who has principles.

(*Goodhumored suddenly, he embraces Simon and leaves. Simon remains motionless for a moment, then follows with a few steps. Seron and Bacchides reappear*)

BACCHIDES. His son has left him to go to the killing.

SERON. It might not be tactful to transact business now.

BACCHIDES. I don't know. We might amuse him. Business was always halfway a game for him. Simon! (*Simon turns back to them*) Don't try to conceal your heaviness, old friend. We know what has happened.

SIMON. I'm glad that you know something, and that you've guessed the rest. Sit down. Here; in the deep of the shade. (*He pours wine*) My friends, you have aged a little. So have I, to be sure. I didn't remember you so stout, Seron. And I have been anxious about your traveling too much in your almost old age.

BACCHIDES. We are bachelors, alas, without sons who can travel for us.

SIMON. Yes, a man ought to have sons; sons who will travel for him. No. He ought to be free of his sons. Let a man travel by himself. Eat, drink, my friends.

SERON. Are you going to sit by while we feast? Come on, your turn. Here's to sound currency.

SIMON. And to all sweet useful traffic. Water for me, thank you. I have a large order to place with you. We'll dine, and then I will walk with you to your inn, tell your men to bring your bundles here and you will stay with us—of course.

BACCHIDES. It will be an imposition on you.

SIMON. You are a comfort to me, won't you believe it? Only—I should warn you—an unpleasantness in Jerusalem—but you say you've heard something about it.

SERON. Yes, we have. May I ask, is this man a relation of yours?

SIMON. Is that what you see in my face? No, he's only another prophet, and I've seen half a dozen Messiahs come and go in my own lifetime. The last one promised to cleave the Jordan and make a dry path for his disciples. And he would have succeeded if he hadn't drowned.

BACCHIDES. You Hebrews never cease to astound us with your antics. But what about this latest wizard?

SERON. Maybe the man preached against the law.

SIMON. Oh, of course! Here is what he preached: "The world is wicked, and the world ought to be good. Be kind and happy and innocent, and God will reward you. I know, because God sent me. So why won't some of you believe that I am the son of God? It is perfectly evident to myself, and you know I am honest!" One day, smiling at the poor man, who must have been a fisherman at home by his lake before God told him to save us, I helped him with a trifle.

BACCHIDES. Ah! You're involved.

SIMON. A trifle of money and a little protection. I have some influence here, not much.

SERON. With the governor?

SIMON. Yes. Our fifth since they removed Herod. He trusts me, because I mind my own affairs. I told him several times the man is a north-country villager; leave him alone; he eats meat with his hands, and the first time he saw a woman with cosmetics on her face, he thought she was being treated for an illness. But when he began to call himself King of the Jews, Pontius became alarmed. How does it sound in Rome, he asks me, to have a man in one of our—well, our colonies—going about calling himself King? A man who already has a following. Anyway, to make a long story short, he stood before Pontius and like an idiot he refused to take it back. His father wouldn't let him!

SERON. As Bacchides was saying, you Hebrews are full of antics.
SIMON. So we are. May I pour again?
BACCHIDES. Enough to fill a thimble.
SERON. For a fat finger.
SIMON. I have found your agents honest of course but hesitant. Your coming in person at last will expedite our affairs. We can settle the details and I can put an order in writing by tomorrow. Did you hear something? (*He stands up and peers*)
SERON. I didn't.
SIMON (*sitting again*). I sense noises in the distance. As I was saying—
BACCHIDES. If you require nothing unusual, we can promise delivery within three months, with God's help and quiet seas.
SERON. Will you want insurance for the whole?
(*Simon seems to be listening to something else. Bacchides and Seron exchange glances*)
SIMON. Insurance?
PETROS (*off-stage*). Simon! Simon!
SIMON (*rising, almost frightened*). Who is calling my name?
PETROS (*off-stage*). Simon! Don't run away!
SIMON (*to Seron and Bacchides*). Please stay here. They are the poor fellow's disciples.
(*Petros and Iohanan appear*)
SERON. Don't be afraid.
SIMON (*to Petros and Iohanan*). I can't save him.
PETROS. You must. Simon: you must. They have rammed the cross on his shoulders that two men couldn't carry. They are beating him with rods. They are tearing his skull with thorns. He is bleeding. Iohanan, speak to him. Simon, will you stand there like a pillar while they're killing him? You are a power here. Use the money that makes you so ugly. Give it to Pontius Pilatus.
SIMON. It's no use; let him go; he's dead. Pontius is helpless; *I'm* helpless; I'll be murdered if I lift a finger.
PETROS. God oh God, he's making speeches. Simon, our Savior is dying. Think of your eternal soul. Save him. What does it matter if *you* die? He is your master I tell you.
SIMON. Let me go, Petros; we're too old for these turmoils. My Savior! Let's keep—
PETROS (*on his knees*). Simon, save him. Bribe them. You befriended him. Save him, and me too, oh God, while there's a little time. (*Weeps*)
SIMON. You too? I don't understand. Who is harming you? Get up, man!
IOHANAN. Come away, Petros. (*To Simon*) I didn't want to stop here; my

master needs no help; he chooses his time to go.

PETROS (*rising*). Look at me. I will tell you something so hideous—

IOHANAN. All is forgiven, Petros, let's go away.

(*Gabinius has appeared in the street. He watches the scene, half-concealed, and tries to catch the words*)

PETROS. I betrayed him! As you see me here I renounced him! (*Simon shrugs his shoulders*) They took him before Pontius and then somebody looked at me in the light. "There he is," he said, and then the soldiers clutched me under the arms and said, "Are you the man who drew a sword when we arrested your Messiah?" and I said no, I don't know him, who is he, and they pushed me away. Simon, here's a coward begging you to save your soul! You've given us help before, you won't deny it; give Pilatus gold, he likes money!

IOHANAN. God forgive you, you're babbling.

SIMON. Go home. You're an old man and you shouldn't rush about the streets.

(*A clamor in the distance. Enter Ruth*)

IOHANAN. Too late. I see nothing as yet, but they are coming. God will crucify himself today for the sake of the world that shall be judged presently in mercy but in terror. (*He kneels to one side*)

RUTH. Why is that beggar kneeling in front of my house? Drive them away, Simon. Today's no day for trouble.

PETROS. Woman—

RUTH. Do you call me woman? I call you vagabond. You should be ashamed to carry on in the streets like an old rag-peddler. Leave us alone.

SIMON. Now....

RUTH. You're trouble, I tell you. They come to town without a pair of shoes to their feet, they take charity from families that work for their bread, and then they tell us how we should live.

SIMON. That will do. Go back inside, and peace! And you, believe me when I say nothing can save him. Don't endanger my house.

PETROS. I'm ready, Iohanan. There's no help for you or me. God's will be done.

SIMON. Don't watch him with the cross on his shoulder. If God loves him, he'll be dead before the nails cut him.

IOHANAN. Don't meddle with us.

(*Petros and Iohanan leave. Gabinius watches them go. Voices in the distance*)

SERON. Can we be of help? You look so troubled.

BACCHIDES. So troubled.

SERON. I suggest we retreat into the house for a while. As you said yourself

just now, why look? And they're coming closer and closer.
RUTH. You see, it's not a woman saying it, but your friends. Come into the house. (*To Seron and Bacchides*) He is rude to you, keeping you outside when you've traveled a long journey.
SIMON. Wife, *you* go in.
GABINIUS. Simon!
SERON. Who is *this?*
SIMON (*to Ruth, fiercely*). Away! Into the house!
(*Ruth withdraws but remains visible*)
GABINIUS (*laughing*). Away! Into the house! Away with the women when a Roman appears! Good day to you, my dear sir. And I greet your friends, the two strangers. I am Gabinius, a Roman. Now Simon, I couldn't help overhearing your little meeting with Petros and Iohanan on my way to duty. Yes of course we know their names. And who they talk to; and who gives them a little money now and then—out of charity of course! What a pity our Emperor doesn't like charity for rebels. He calls it collusion, conspiracy—well, *I* don't know what he calls it, I'm only a soldier. But *he* knows! Far away though he is, he knows, Simon, in spite of your influence with the authorities. Well then. Why don't you speak to me? And why do your friends stare at me? You *are* Simon, aren't you, the father of Alexander, yes? who snatched the emblem of Tiberius out of my hands, yes? and tore it up in the street? Let me warn you, merchant. Your friendship with Pontius Pilatus won't—
(*Enter Marcellus*)
MARCELLUS. Gabinius! I'm looking for you. (*Whispers aside to him*) Where in blazes have you been? You were supposed to assist me. There's an uproar and you're gossiping in the street.
GABINIUS. Shut up, you fool. I was after big game. Very well, let's go. Well, look who's here. The flaming patriots.
(*Enter Alexander, Mathias and Zadok*)
RUTH (*in anguish, from the doorway*). Alexander!
ZADOK. Marcellus and Gabinius. And without escort. You've left your moronic soldiers alone to guide the mob.
GABINIUS (*hand on sword*). But they're not far off. I think you're fond of your life. Clear the way.
ZADOK. There's three of us. Not helpless either. (*Produces his knife. Simon rushes in between and roughly seizes Alexander, while the Romans laugh*)
SIMON. Into the house! Away, all of you! Fight elsewhere! Ruth!
RUTH. Cushi! Gedaliah! Help!
ALEXANDER (*struggling*). Take your hands off me! (*But the two servants appear,*

AN UNPLEASANTNESS IN JERUSALEM

and along with Ruth and Simon manage to get Alexander indoors)
SIMON. Tell the servants to hold him! Tie him up if you have to!
GABINIUS. Wisely acted, Simon. Keep your puppy out of my way. *(To Mathias and Zadok)* I'll deal with you later. Clear the path. Clear the path I say! *(Mathias and Zadok stand aside and sullenly let the two Romans pass)* I'll see both of you in a noose.
(Exeunt Marcellus and Gabinius)
SIMON. Go away! Don't come near my house again!
ZADOK. You'll be asking us and your son to protect you when the time comes. We'll see you then. *(Another clamor is heard, much closer)* Come on, Matthias. Let's wait for the parade outside the gate.
MATTHIAS. Good idea.
(Zadok and Mathias leave)
BACCHIDES. Simon, my friend, you're trembling. Come into the house.
SERON. Come into the house.
SIMON. No. I'll see it all. Trouble and all. I'll stand aside but I'll see.
(Now the crowd is close)
GABINIUS *(off-stage)*. Soldiers! Keep them back!
(Enter Gabinius, Marcellus, soldiers, and Ieshua, exhausted and in pain, carrying the cross, which is indeed so heavy that it will take two soldiers to remove it from his shoulders)
MARCELLUS. Disengage! I want the man disengaged from the mob!
SOLDIER. Keep away, Hebrews!
SERON. God help us.
MARCELLUS *(to Ieshua)*. And you. Why don't you crawl? Gabinius, prod him. Push him, men, the man is a weakling.
GABINIUS. Go, King of Hebrews! What's the matter with him? He's stopped again.
SIMON. He can't, he can't....
RUTH *(at the door)*. Simon, don't look. Let me take you inside. Please!
MARCELLUS. Beat him, men, apply the Roman law to his back!
RUTH *(to Seron and Bacchides)*. A woman begs you, tell him to come in.
BACCHIDES. He won't. Simon! He won't....
MARCELLUS. Give him the mule treatment. Beat the mule. Make him move. Damn damn damn. Why did they put the cross on him? I'm sweating my guts out! Beat him, didn't you hear me? Is he moving?
GABINIUS. He can't feel those swords any more. We need a regular flogging here.
MARCELLUS. He's stopped again. Now what's he staring at?
GABINIUS. At his friend Simon!
MARCELLUS. Mother of my whore! He's paying a call on a friend. *(To*

– 572 –

Simon) No spectators, my dear sir. I assure you I'm not responsible. I'm on duty. And I'm avoiding all the good houses as far as possible. I'd carry the cross myself. Go into the house, all of you. Move! Move! Nobody's listening to me!

GABINIUS. He's about to open his mouth.

(*Ieshua collapses*)

IESHUA (*feebly*). Water.... A little water....

(*Simon takes a bowl of water from the table and rushes to Ieshua*)

RUTH. Simon! Come back! Oh my God!

(*Seron and Bacchides clasp each other, amazed and terrified. The two servants have appeared. The Romans are speechless for an instant while Simon makes Ieshua drink*)

BACCHIDES. Ruth, come inside with us!

RUTH. Simon! Simon! Come back!

(*Seron and Bacchides hold her*)

MARCELLUS. Out of the way, merchant! How can we get the fellow up?

GABINIUS. I know how. (*To the soldiers, pointing at Simon*) Put the cross on him! Let *him* carry it!

(*They do so with a mixture of shouts and friendly encouragement*)

RUTH. Have mercy! He's an old man! Let me fall on my knees!

BACCHIDES. Ruth, come away!

SERON. You'll make it worse.

MARCELLUS. Get that hysterical female out of the way! At once, I say, at once at once at once.

(*With the help of the servants, Seron and Bacchides succeed in pulling the sobbing Ruth into the house*)

MARCELLUS. We can move at last! (*To a soldier*) You, help the king of the Jews. Wipe the blood out of his face.

GABINIUS. On your feet, Simon! Move, move! (*He strikes Simon*)

MARCELLUS. Whores in hell! He's almost as weak as the other one. Let's walk; walk walk walk walk.

(*Simon begins to move. Seron reappears*)

GABINIUS. Soldiers! Form around them!

MARCELLUS. At last I see the light! March, march, march, march, march, march, march.

(*They are gone. Enter Bacchides*)

BACCHIDES. Alexander is with her. What happened?

SERON. They've led him off, not saying another word, under the cross, on his knees, crawling, his hair in his face. Oh that we have lived to see this!

BACCHIDES. That we have lived to see this....

(*Enter Alexander*)

ALEXANDER. Have they taken him away?

SERON. They have....

ALEXANDER. What will they do to him? He's not accused of anything. He never meddled. They'll release him and he'll come back.

BACCHIDES. And your mother?

ALEXANDER. She is unconscious. The maids are with her. But I won't leave her.

(*Seron and Bacchides sit down, exhausted*)

SERON. What can we do?

BACCHIDES. Oh God, oh God. Romans....

(*Alexander remains standing irresolutely*)

ALEXANDER. Is there something I should do?

(*They do not answer. A long silence, and then Zadok and Mathias appear, carrying Simon's body. They place it at the feet of Seron and Bacchides, who have risen in dismay*)

MATHIAS. Gabinius thought this would be a good joke, us carrying him.

ZADOK. He made five soldiers grab us out of the crowd, five against two, and told us to carry him back to his house.

MATHIAS. We would have done it anyway.

ALEXANDER (*kneeling beside the body*). He's only exhausted.

MATHIAS. No, my boy, he's dead. He's dead of volunteering for the Romans.

ALEXANDER. Maybe he's only hurt. They cut him with the swords.

MATHIAS. Not the swords. He broke down. His heart.

ZADOK. An old man, after all.

MATHIAS. You'll get even with them.

ZADOK. The day is coming, Alexander. You'll get a bucket of blood for every drop in his veins.

(*He and Mathias leave. Darkness falls. Seron and Bacchides are standing on either side of the body. Alexander kneels over it. What follows is spoken in almost total darkness*)

SERON. Oh Simon, reckless pity, erroneous death.

BACCHIDES. Care, cries your death, we must care.

SERON. I don't know.

BACCHIDES. I don't know.

ALEXANDER. I'll avenge you, father.

SERON. On an evil day we came.

BACCHIDES. On an evil day we leave.

The End

Notes

This is a revised, final version of a play I called *The Sensible Man of Jerusalem* when I printed it in the second volume of my 1970-1972 *Collected Plays*.

Whether or not the crowd is seen on stage will depend on the resources available. The play can certainly be staged with the noise but without its appearance.

V

PRINCE POUPON
NEEDS A WIFE

(after Marivaux)

CHARACTERS

Prince Poupon XVII, *ruler of Pouponaco*
Sylvia, *a village girl*
Robin, *a village lad*
Flaminia, *daughter of a deceased courtier*
Lisa, *her younger sister*
Trivet, *a trusted servant in the prince's service*

(The action takes place throughout in an elegantly decorated chamber of the prince's palace. A large grim painting of Poupon the First on horseback hangs above the mantelpiece)

ACT ONE

(Enter Sylvia and Trivet)

TRIVET. Won't you listen to me, Madame Sylvia?

SYLVIA. Don't bother me.

TRIVET. But shouldn't a person be reasonable?

SYLVIA. No, a person shouldn't.

TRIVET. And yet—

SYLVIA. And yet I don't want to be reasonable. You can repeat "and yet" fifty times if you wish. I'll still refuse to be reasonable. So what will you do about it?

TRIVET. You ate such a light supper last night, dear Sylvia, you'll become ill unless you take breakfast this morning.

SYLVIA. I despise health and I'm glad to be sick; so there. Don't trouble yourself, send everything back, because I'll have neither breakfast, nor lunch, nor dinner today; nor tomorrow either. You took me away from Robin, and now all I care to do is to be furious and to hate you one and all until I've seen him again. Those are my resolutions, and if you want to drive me insane, keep telling me to be reasonable and you'll soon have done it.

TRIVET. God help me, I don't intend to try; I can see you'll keep your word. And yet if I dared—

SYLVIA *(angrier)*. Another "and yet"!

TRIVET. Oh, I beg your pardon, this one was a slip, but it's the last one; I stand corrected. Only I should like you to consider—

SYLVIA. I thought you stood corrected! I don't want your considerations!

TRIVET. —that the man who wants to marry you is your prince.

SYLVIA. I can't keep him from falling in love with me; he's not the first! But am I compelled to love him in return? No, I am not; and why not? Because love can't be compelled. What could be simpler? And I—I will marry for love.

TRIVET. Love love love love! If our revered Prince Poupon the Seventeenth has chosen you among his humble subjects, he has done so, believe me, for the highest reasons of state, and not for puppy love.

SYLVIA. In that case who told him to choose me of all girls? Did he ask my opinion? Let him take his highest reasons of state to another victim.

Instead, he has a gang of masked men carry me off from the village, and never asks how I feel about it.

TRIVET. Confess that they carried you off with every mark of courtesy, set you down gently on cushions in a luxurious carriage, and landed you in one of Prince Poupon's grandest suites. Treated you, in short, like his future wife and Princess of Pouponaco.

SYLVIA. I want to be Robin's wife, not Princess of Pouponaco. Do you force people to take presents in spite of themselves?

TRIVET. But do consider, future Princess, how he has treated you in the two days you've been here. Aren't you waited on as though you were already his consort? Look at the tokens of respect offered you, the number of women in your retinue, the entertainments you've enjoyed at his command. What is this Robin—a farmhand, God help him!—next to a Prince who showers you with delicate attentions—a young, handsome Prince who will not even appear before you—who shyly hides from you—until you are willing to meet him? For heaven's sake, open your eyes to your good fortune!

SYLVIA. Tell me—you, and all the women who are giving me advice—are you being paid to irritate me with your babble?

TRIVET. I do what I can; that's the sum of my wisdom.

SYLVIA. Your wisdom has accomplished precious little.

TRIVET. But will you at least tell me where I am wrong?

SYLVIA. Yes, I'll tell you, yes. Why have your people set four or five geese to spy on me day and night under pretence of serving me? My love is taken away from me, I'm given these women to replace him, and now I'm expected to be happy! And what's all this music to me, all these singers and these dancers? Robin used to sing better than any of them, and as for dancing, let me tell you I'd rather dance myself than watch others doing it. A simple girl happy in her village is better off than a princess weeping in a palace. Is the prince running after me? That's not my fault. I didn't look for him, and he needn't have looked for me. Is he young and attractive? So much the better for him; I'm glad. Let him keep himself for his equals, and let him leave me my poor Robin, who is no more the fancy gentleman than I am the fancy lady; who is no richer, no vainer, and no better lodged than I am; who loves me without frills, whom I love the same way, and for whom I'll die of grief if I don't see him again. Poor boy! What have they done to him? What has become of him? Wherever he is he's wallowing in tears, I know it, because he's so kind, so good! Maybe he's being mistreated by those same masked villains.... Oh, I'm beside myself! Look here, Mr. Trivet, do you really want to please me? Take yourself away, I can't bear the sight of you. Leave me alone with my grief.

TRIVET. This is blunt and clear. But set your mind at rest—

SYLVIA. Go away!

TRIVET. I repeat, set your mind at rest. You want to see Robin, and Robin will stand before you before the day is over.

SYLVIA. I'm going to see my own Robin?

TRIVET. And talk to your own Robin, too.

SYLVIA. I don't know whether I ought to believe you. I'll go wait for him in my rooms. But if this is a trick, I'll claw my way out of here no matter in what dungeon you lock me up.

(*She leaves. From the other side, the Prince and Flaminia have entered and watched her go out*)

PRINCE (*to Trivet*). Well? Is there any hope? What does she say?

TRIVET. Nothing worth repeating, my lord. She adores Robin, she can't wait to see him again, she doesn't want to set eyes on you, and she prefers bread and milk in her village to becoming Princess of Pouponaco. Frankly, if I may express an underling's opinion, I would suggest putting her back where we found her.

FLAMINIA. I've suggested the same thing already. What, my lord, what happened to the inclination you used to show to my sister Lisa? Poor Lisa! Weeping in secret. Forsaken by a fickle prince....

PRINCE. Flaminia dear, I swear to make it up to her, and to you as well. But you know what Dr. Vascularius has said—Dr. Vascularius, my infallible court astrologer and physician. The Poupon line is growing feebler every generation. (*He points at the painting*) My ancestors were warriors with thick moustaches and grim helmets who hacked away at their enemies on the battlefield, whereas I, seventeenth of the line, play croquet on the lawn and when fatigued, which is much of the time, the viola in my apartments. The Poupons need new blood, and that new blood must come from the People—says Dr. Vascularius, and I believe him. You and Lisa, my dear, are the daughters of a nobleman, God forgive him even though he gambled his and your fortunes away in my casinos. And I absolutely must mate with the earth and beget a row of stalwarts worthy of Poupon the First. Besides, I'm falling in love with my Sylvia.

FLAMINIA. You're an incurable dreamer, my lord.

PRINCE. Remember how I met her. Looking for mushrooms in my usual incognito as Baron Belair, I met Sylvia and asked her for a cup of milk out of the pail she was carrying. She made the dearest curtsy as she offered it, almost stumbling in the grass. And after that I went mushrooming every day—if it wasn't raining—and drank her milk, her eyes, her healthy buxom figure, and the hope of our race.

FLAMINIA. After that, what can one say?

TRIVET. One can say that there's something uncanny about that girl. It isn't natural for a woman to reject wealth and power. This creature belongs to a species unknown to us. There's a warning here; we're dealing with a prodigy. Send her back to her pots and pans and hang Dr. Vascularius.

PRINCE. Don't be macabre, Trivet.

FLAMINIA. Since you insist, my lord—

PRINCE. Irrevocably.

FLAMINIA. We'll have to march firmly forward. The love that holds Sylvia and Robin together must be destroyed.

TRIVET. Impossible. I told you this girl is unnatural.

FLAMINIA (*laughing*). Don't listen to his unnatural, my lord; Trivet has been reading fairy tales. I promise to prove to you that Sylvia is as natural as the rest of us women; and that's all I need to bring her down to where we women live. But when shall we see Robin?

TRIVET. Very soon.

PRINCE. I'm afraid we're taking a great risk, Flaminia. Robin saw me several times as Baron Belair together with Sylvia. Besides, if she sees him, she will fall into his arms more passionately than ever.

TRIVET. True; yet if she doesn't see him, she'll go mad; she promised it herself.

FLAMINIA. Trust me, my lord, we need Robin.

PRINCE. Very well, keep him here as long as you can. Tell him I'll lavish gold and titles on him if he'll kindly marry somebody else.

TRIVET. And if he refuses, we'll hang him instead of Dr. Vascularius.

PRINCE. That is what my ancestors would have done but I am too soft and kind to do; another proof that I must reinvigorate my line. Let me hear from both of you that I can count on you to second my efforts.

FLAMINIA. I swear to help you with all my might.

TRIVET. And so do I.

FLAMINIA. Even though my sister and I will be the losers.

PRINCE. On no account. Let me succeed, stand by me, and I shall restore your fortunes as if your dear father—

ALL THREE. May he rest in peace—

PRINCE. Had never touched a card or seen a roulette table. You too, Trivet, if you are loyal, you'll not call me a niggard.

TRIVET. I am yours body and soul, my lord.

PRINCE. Fortunately, I am not bereft of ideas. Indeed, my mind has been furiously at work and I have hatched an idea worthy of Poupon the Eighth, he who introduced backgammon to Pouponaco. My idea is this: Flaminia, we must send your sister Lisa into the fray.

FLAMINIA. Explain, my lord.
PRINCE. Robin must marry her.
FLAMINIA (*appalled*). Sir!
TRIVET. Oh harsh declivity!
PRINCE. Not so. Lisa will not marry simple Robin, but Count Robinet; she will forget me in a flurry of receptions, balls, horse races and nights at the opera; and we shall be rid of Sylvia's lover without bloodshed. What do you think of this Machiavellian scheme?
FLAMINIA. Allow me to doubt—
PRINCE. Lisa is beautiful, voluptuous, a coquette, ambitious.
FLAMINIA. My sweet sister!
PRINCE. And I can rely on her to turn the farm-boy's head.
TRIVET. That farm-boy is raving for love of Sylvia.
PRINCE. Pish! No more objections! Your prince is speaking. Take care that you implement my decision.
TRIVET *and* FLAMINIA. We will, my lord.
PRINCE. And don't exhaust me with more objections, do you hear?
(*Exit the Prince*)
FLAMINIA. Our master has spoken, and we had better obey. Call my sister, Trivet.
TRIVET. No need, here she comes. I'll go meet Robin while you prepare her for her amorous conquest. (*He leaves*)
(*Enter Lisa*)
LISA. What are my orders, Flaminia? I met Poupon in the corridor. He averted his eyes but sent me to you for I don't know what instructions.
FLAMINIA. You are aware that our beloved ruler has put it into his brain to marry—
LISA. A goose from the village pond. It's the only topic from one end of the palace to the other. I'm being divorced before I'm married. What's going to become of us, sister?
FLAMINIA. Don't worry. We'll rise out of the rubble by another way. Your instructions are to turn Robin's head, marry him as Count Robinet, and enable the three of us to live happily ever after.
LISA. Well, why not. I've caught a glimpse of our potato digger, and he is as fit a biped as the others I've known. But do you think a helpless maiden like me can turn his head? Inspect me a little.
FLAMINIA. Hm. You're in excellent shape.
LISA (*laughing*). I know I am.
FLAMINIA. And you see to it that everybody's aware of it.
LISA. Thank you.

FLAMINIA. A little more mascara here; and here.

LISA. Done.

FLAMINIA. Let me see you walk. Powerful! But the voice must contribute its share. Say something.

LISA. Count Robinet, why are you persecuting me?

FLAMINIA. That should melt him. At least I hope it will. Use all your arts, by which I mean, be yourself; now vivacious and giddy, now nonchalant, now tender, now mincing; your eyes naughty, aiming to kill; your gait seductive and dissipated; your talk spiced with quips and nonsense. But don't overdo it. Our inexperienced rustic might not approve; your charms might be too strong for his taste. Imagine a man who has never drunk anything but clear fresh water; pour the champagne, but pour it carefully.

LISA. Somehow, the way you describe my charms, they don't sound as lovely as you say they are.

FLAMINIA. I was analyzing them; that's why they sound absurd. But with men you're safe.

LISA. One more item. What about my scruples? If I don't truly fall in love with our hero, I'll feel dishonest. Don't forget I'm a respectable girl.

FLAMINIA. You're a *ruined* respectable girl.

LISA. That does make a difference, doesn't it. I'll keep reminding my conscience. And to make a start, I'll go dream in my boudoir of receptions, balls, horse races and nights at the opera until the moment you tell me to open fire.

FLAMINIA. Here comes Robin; but it's too soon to start. Come, let's go the other way.

(*Exeunt Flaminia and Lisa. Enter Trivet and Robin*)

TRIVET. Well, Master Robin, how do you like it here? Isn't it a handsome house?

ROBIN. What in blazes have I got to do with this here house? And who are you? What do you want out of me? Where are we going?

TRIVET. Your prince has appointed me—his most reliable official—to be your servant as of today; and to answer your last question, we are going exactly to where we have now arrived.

ROBIN. Reliable official or rogue, you're dismissed and I'm going home.

TRIVET (*stopping him*). Just a moment!

ROBIN. What's that? Hey, ain't it rude to stop your master? Hey?

TRIVET. Let the two of us come to an understanding.

ROBIN. Why? Have we got anything to tell one another?

TRIVET. We have. About Sylvia.

ROBIN. Ah, Sylvia, ah me! I beg your forgiveness. It comes to me now that

I've wanted to talk to you all along.

TRIVET. You lost her two days ago, didn't you?

ROBIN. That's right. She was stolen by a pack of masked thieves.

TRIVET (*mysteriously*). I know where she is.

ROBIN. You know where she is, my friend, my valet, my master, my anything you like? Oh, what a pity I ain't rich, I'd give you all my income for wages. Tell me which way I should turn, my true hearted friend—to the right, to the left, or straight ahead?

TRIVET. You'll meet her right here.

ROBIN. How good and kind you must be to have brung me here! Oh, Sylvia, sweetest child of my heart, I'm crying for joy!

TRIVET (*aside*). This fool's prelude bodes no good. (*Aloud*) Wait—I've something else to tell you.

ROBIN. First I want to see Sylvia; take pity on me, I can't wait.

TRIVET. I told you that you'll be seeing her; but before you do I must have a talk with you. Do you remember a gentleman who called on Sylvia in the village five or six times, and whom you saw in her company?

ROBIN. Yes. He looked like a sneak.

TRIVET. This person found your sweetheart very attractive.

ROBIN. He found nothing new, by crickety crack.

TRIVET. And he told the prince about her, and the prince was impressed by his story.

ROBIN. I told you he looked like a sneak.

TRIVET. His Royal Highness wished to have a look at her, so he gave orders to have her brought here.

ROBIN. Good. Now that I'm here, let him return her to me and good bye.

TRIVET. Not so fast. There's a small difficulty. Prince Poupon has fallen in love with Sylvia and intends to marry her.

ROBIN. Can't be done. She's in love with me and me with her, period.

TRIVET. You're missing the point; listen to the end.

ROBIN. You've reached the end already. Is somebody trying to swindle me out of my property?

TRIVET. Are you aware that the prince has decided to take a wife of humble but healthy origins?

ROBIN. No, I'm not aware, and I don't care.

TRIVET. I'm trying to inform you.

ROBIN. I don't care to be informed. I enjoy knowing nothin'.

TRIVET. Naturally, Sylvia's little obligation to you stands in the prince's way.

ROBIN. Let him pick another girl. There's dozens in the village with origins so healthy they never so much as sneeze.

TRIVET. That may be true. But our court astrologer, Dr. Vascularius, insists that Pouponaco needs an alliance between our prince and Sylvia. Are you ready to sacrifice your selfish interests to the future of our nation?

ROBIN. You're talkin' way above my pumpkin. I can tell you about hoof and mouth disease but I don't know crickety crack about the future of the nation.

TRIVET. Let me spell things out for you; but keep it all to yourself, because what I'm going to reveal to you is a state secret. The house of the Poupons will perish—perish, do you hear? die out—if its prince fails to restore it to health by marrying into the people. And the people in this instance happens to be Sylvia. What glory is in store for you, Master Robin! The lass you kissed by the village pump is fated to beget princes of the blood for a princely house that goes back to King Tutmose who built the pyramids!

ROBIN. That's nice. But I want my girl.

TRIVET. As for the grateful nation and its prince, they will make you Count Robinet and bestow acres of land and cattle on you.

ROBIN. That's nice. But I want my girl.

TRIVET. And all you have to do is marry the most beautiful of the ladies in the palace.

ROBIN. That's nice. But I want my girl.

TRIVET. Keep in mind, besides, that Prince Poupon could have you strung up from the oaktree in the courtyard and do with Sylvia whatever he likes, with or without the blessings of the Church.

ROBIN. I'll take my chances; I've got a thick neck.

TRIVET. Finally, struggling is in vain. It's all been foretold in the stars. It's bound to happen, like it or not. It's written down in heaven.

ROBIN. In heaven they don't write that kind of drivel. Just to show you: supposing it was foretold that I would knock you down and stab you in the back, would it make you happy if I fulfilled the prediction?

TRIVET. Certainly not! One should never injure one's betters.

ROBIN. Who is my betters? I thought I was Count Robinet.

TRIVET. Not yet, my lad. But you will be. With plenty of money to spend.

ROBIN. That's of no use to a man who has his health, a sound appetite, and a job.

TRIVET. Town house, country house....

ROBIN. Who'll be living in my town house while I'm in my country house?

TRIVET. Your servants, of course.

ROBIN. My servants? I'm to get rich so those ruffians can enjoy themselves at my expense! But wait a minute: could I live in both houses at the same time?

TRIVET. I suppose not; you can't be in two places at once, you know.

ROBIN. Well then, you simpleton, what's the use of two houses?

TRIVET. Whenever you like, you'll go from one to the other.

ROBIN. So I should give up my Sylvia for the pleasure of moving every month?

TRIVET. Doesn't anything tempt you? Very strange. Anybody else would jump at these mansions, these servants—

ROBIN. All I need is a cottage; I don't like to support idlers; and I won't never find a servant more faithful to me and keener to serve me than me myself.

TRIVET. I admit you've got an attendant there you won't want to dismiss. But wouldn't you enjoy riding in a fine carriage drawn by the best horses, or being surrounded by luxurious furniture?

ROBIN. You are a great fool, my friend, to be comparing Sylvia with furniture and horses. What more can you do in a house than sit down, eat, and sleep? Give me a good bed, a solid table, a dozen straw-bottom chairs, and I'm as furnished and as comfortable as I want to be. Ah, but I ain't got a carriage! Well then, I won't tip over. (*Pointing to his legs*) And isn't this a team my mother gave me? Ain't they sound legs? As God is my witness, this carriage of mine ought to be good enough for you too. Away, you loafers! Turn your horses over to honest farmers what needs 'em. We'll all have bread on our tables, you'll walk, and the gout won't bite you.

TRIVET. Sharp! Sharp! If you had your way, there wouldn't be shoes enough to supply the world.

ROBIN. Let the world wear clogs. I've had enough of your chatter. You promised to produce Sylvia, and an honest man keeps his word.

TRIVET. Just a moment. You don't care for honors, riches, handsome houses, reputation, carriages—

ROBIN. All frippery—

TRIVET. But what about good food? Would that tempt you? Would you enjoy a cellar full of the best wines? Would you rejoice in a chef who prepared expert and plentiful dinners for you? Picture to yourself, if you please, the most savory meats and seafood: they're yours, and for a lifetime.... You're not answering me.

ROBIN. What you're talkin' about now sounds better nor all the rest because I admit I'm a glutton, but all the same my heart is bigger than my gut.

TRIVET. Come, come, Count Robinet, be a happy man, leave one girl and take another.

ROBIN. No. I'll stick to plain Robin, Sylvia, ham and eggs and a jug of beer.

TRIVET. Alas for the wines you would have drunk, the morsels you would have tasted!

ROBIN. I'm sorry, but that's how it is. The best morsel of all is Sylvia. Are you or are you not going to show her to me? My stick is beginning to itch.
TRIVET. She's coming, don't worry. Only it's a bit early yet in the morning.
(*Enter Lisa in a glamorous décolleté*)
LISA. Oh, there you are, Mr. Trivet. The prince is asking for you.
TRIVET. The prince? I'm off. Why don't you keep Count Robinet company while I'm gone?
LISA (*softly*). If he will allow me.
ROBIN. There's no need; I'm pretty good company to myself when I'm alone.
TRIVET. Oh no, you might get bored. (*Fake aside to Robin*) The very woman I was telling you about. Lucky dog! I wish we could exchange places. Yum, yum, yum. I hope she doesn't turn you down. (*Aloud*) I mustn't let the prince wait.
(*Exit Trivet*)
ROBIN (*to himself*). Let's watch her pitchin' herself at me.
LISA (*softly*). Sir, aren't you our dear Miss Sylvia's suitor?
ROBIN (*coldly*). I am.
LISA. She's very pretty.
ROBIN (*as before*). She is.
LISA. And enviable.
ROBIN. Why enviable? Because the prince wants to steal her from me?
LISA. No, that's not the reason.
ROBIN. Well, what's the reason?
LISA. Because she is adored by a person—a person—well—a person like yourself.
ROBIN. Oh, I ain't so special.
LISA. And modest too! We've all heard about your prowesses in the village.
ROBIN. As how I wrestled Hulking Tom to the ground at the fair?
LISA. Oh yes. But I'm not surprised. Such biceps, such sinews! May I? (*She comes very close to him and feels his biceps*) Goodness gracious! Our effeminate courtiers would give gold for these muscles. Lucky Sylvia! What else did you triumph in at the fair?
ROBIN. I won the footrace, that's all. The prize was a piglet.
LISA. With legs like yours, no wonder. (*She feels his leg muscles*) Hercules!
ROBIN. Hey! Hold off there!
LISA. I meant no harm, dear Robin. But would you do something very particular for me?
ROBIN. I doubt it, but go ahead and ask.
LISA (*aside*). What a beast! (*Aloud*) Lady Grissini has invited a small, select company to a party tonight in her palace. Would you consent to be my

escort? The prince's wardrobe will be at your disposal, so we'll make a stunning couple, you and I.

ROBIN. Thank you, but the girl I'm escortin' to any party is Sylvia.

LISA. Of course Sylvia comes first! But she was asked by Baron Belair, and having watched your love-bird cooing at the baron, I don't think she refused him.

ROBIN. Yes she did, yes she did! You're slandering her, that's what. Look here, Miss Lisa, you're nothin' but a—a Scarlet Woman.

LISA. Are you aware that this is no way for a man to speak to a lady? You're insulting me.

ROBIN. Why? It's the truth. There's too much sugar in your words for me, and nastiness about Sylvia. If I've turned your head because I'm sturdy and good lookin', say good bye right now so you can recover, because I'm spoken for, you know, and besides, I don't want no girl makin' advances at me, I want to make 'em myself. On top o' that, I'm no dummy, and I know why the prince is throwin' you at me. So I say shame, young lady, shame!

LISA. This is too absurd for words!

ROBIN. How can young men stand them fancy airs at court? God, but a woman's ugly when she's a flirt!

LISA. My poor man, you're raving.

ROBIN. You talk about Sylvia. *There's* charm for you! If I told you about our love, you'd be amazed to hear how shy she is. You should have seen how she avoided me the first days; and then how she avoided me a tiny bit less; and then, little by little, how she stopped avoiding me at all; and next how she gave me shy looks; and then how she was ashamed when I caught her doin' it; and how I was happy as a king to see her shame; and then how I snatched her hand, and how she allowed me to hold it; and then how she blushed; and how I talked to her; and how she wouldn't say a word, though I could see she was thinkin'; and then how she gave me looks instead of words, and then words she let go without knowing what happened, because her heart went faster than herself. There wasn't no touching after a first meeting, let me tell you.

LISA. You're very amusing. I'm laughing. Ha, ha, ha.

ROBIN. Me too. Ha, ha, ha. And now good bye. If everybody was like me, you'd catch a white crow before finding a lover.

(*Enter Trivet*)

TRIVET. How is the happy couple doing?

LISA. It seems that I'm a scarlet woman, while Sylvia is a pink angel.

ROBIN. I'm off to look for her, because I'm suspicionous that you're keepin' her hidden from me.

(*Exit Robin*)

TRIVET. Wait for me, Master Robin! There's a luscious lunch being prepared for you in the kitchen!

(*Exit Trivet*)

LISA. Good riddance to the clown; let him return to his piglets; but I'm as penniless as before.

(*Enter the Prince and Flaminia*)

PRINCE. Well, are we making progress? Have you got Robin snug in your nest?

LISA. To make a long story short, your highness, Robin heard me out and when I was done he ran looking for his Sylvia.

FLAMINIA. I hope he wasn't rude to you.

LISA. Oh no. "Shame, young lady, you are a tramp;" and "You'll catch a white crow before you find a lover." That's his style.

PRINCE. I'm sorry to hear this, Lisa; but don't be chagrined; you've lost nothing in my eyes. If the future of the house of Poupon didn't require me to look down rather than up—or sideways—

LISA. Thank you, my lord; a compliment doesn't come amiss, for now I have proof that I can be disliked. It's a proof we women prefer to live without.

FLAMINIA. My lord, will you allow me to remark that your plan has failed?

PRINCE. Of course it has. How tiresome! What! Am I to force the girl into my bed at dagger's point? I who hate melodrama?

LISA. You should do it.

PRINCE. Nonsense. My heirs must be legitimate.

FLAMINIA. Well, my lord, I can see that it's my turn to try.

PRINCE. I don't know. I'm discouraged. And to think I have to look cheerful this afternoon when I review the Guard!

FLAMINIA. Don't give up, my lord. Have faith in your Flaminia. But first: sister, will you yield Robin to me?

LISA. Yield him to you? Yes! Take him away as far as possible!

FLAMINIA. I like him and what's more, I intend to marry him. Surprised? I'm not a nun, you know, and older sisters ought to marry before younger ones. The Bible says so. Our brawny Robin suits me perfectly, though I may have to teach him a subtlety or two—suits me, that is, if you, my lord, will keep the promises you made to Lisa.

PRINCE. I will, and then do even more!

FLAMINIA. In that case, consider it all settled. You don't know me, my lord. Do you think for a minute that Robin and Sylvia can hold out against me? That I am incapable of regulating hearts like theirs? Sylvia must consent, and you shall beget upon her as many rugged princelings as you desire.

Wait, I hear a dulcet voice; it's Sylvia's; she is whispering "I love you, my own Poupon." I see the wedding—there, before my eyes, sweet vision!—you're man and wife. Count Robinet marries me. He and I take possession of the grounds you will bestow upon us. And Lisa marries the nobleman of her choice. End of story.

LISA. End of story? It hasn't even begun!

FLAMINIA. Silence, heretic. My first step is to call Sylvia; the time has come for her to be reunited with Robin.

LISA. Your vision will fall apart the moment they find each other again.

PRINCE. I think so too.

FLAMINIA. Splendid: we differ only over yes or no; nothing worth mentioning. Meantime, I've decided they'll see each other as often as they please. This is the first of several traps I intend to set for their love.

PRINCE. Well, do as you like. I feel a vile headache coming on. The burdens a prince has to bear! As Shakespeare observes—

FLAMINIA. Yes, my lord. But I hear Robin and Trivet. Let's vanish.

(*They leave. Enter Robin and Trivet*)

ROBIN (*looking back off stage*). All six of you! Stay where you are, you clowns and loafers, or go look for Sylvia! (*To Trivet*) Will you tell me why these uniformed gallows-birds are following me about? I can't lift a finger without being watched.

TRIVET. This is our prince's way of showing his regard for you. He wants these men to follow you in your honor.

ROBIN. Oh, you mean it's a honor to be followed?

TRIVET. Absolutely.

ROBIN. And tell me, who follows the men who are following me?

TRIVET. Nobody.

ROBIN. And you don't have nobody following you neither?

TRIVET. No, I don't.

ROBIN. You mean you people are not honored?

TRIVET. We don't deserve to be.

ROBIN (*showing his stick*). If that's the case, clear out! And take the whole crew with you! Away!

TRIVET. Why? What do you mean?

ROBIN. Get out! I don't like folk who don't deserve to be honored.

TRIVET. You don't understand me!

ROBIN (*beating him*). I'll talk more clearly.

TRIVET. Stop, stop, what are you doing? I'm black and blue—you're pummeling your best friend! And look! Here comes your beloved!

(*Enter Sylvia and Flaminia*)

SYLVIA (*running joyfully to Robin*). There he is! Oh, dearest, sweetest Robin, it's you! I'm seeing you again! My poor boy! Oh, I'm so happy!

ROBIN (*breathless*). And so am I. Oh, oh, oh, I'm dying, I'm too happy.

SYLVIA. There, there, my love, gently. How much he loves me; how wonderful to be loved like this.

FLAMINIA. My dear children, I'm overjoyed to see you so faithful to one another. (*False aside to Trivet*) I'm ruined if anybody hears me. But I can't help myself, my heart goes out to them.

TRIVET (*playing along*). I warn you not to betray our beloved prince by encouraging them.

ROBIN. Get out, you rascal, before I twist you into a pretzel.

TRIVET. I'm only doing my duty.

(*He runs away*)

SYLVIA. Oh, Robin, how wretched I've been.

ROBIN. Do you still love me?

SYLVIA. Do I still love you! Is that a question you should ask?

FLAMINIA. Oh, I'll bear witness to her love. I've seen her in despair, wailing over your absence. I almost cried with her. I couldn't wait to see you together, even if it costs me my prince's favor; and here you are. Good bye, my friends; I'm leaving you, because you bring tears to my eyes. Alas, you remind me of my love for someone—someone who perished fighting for our prince. He had something of Robin's expression. I'll never forget him. Good bye, Sylvia; I've been assigned to keep watch over you, but you can count on me. Love Robin, he deserves it. And you, Robin, whatever happens, look on me as a friend, a person who wishes to be of use to you.

ROBIN. You're a dear, and I'm your friend too. I'm so sorry your sweetheart got perished. I see you're unhappy, and so are we.

(*Flaminia leaves, dabbing her eyes with a handkerchief*)

SYLVIA (*plaintively*). Well, Robin, my love?

ROBIN. Well, Sylvia, my soul?

SYLVIA. How unhappy we are!

ROBIN. Let us love each other always; that will help us be patient.

SYLVIA. Yes, but what is going to happen to our love? I'm so worried. The prince is trying to inveigle me with all kinds of luxuries so he can rejuvenate Pouponaco or whatever.

ROBIN. And he's throwing titles and vamps at me in order to separate us.

SYLVIA. What? Are you going to leave me? Will you get used to life without your little Sylvia?

ROBIN. My dove, would I get used to fasting?

SYLVIA. I don't want you to forget me, but neither do I want you to suffer because of me. Who knows what the brutes will do to you? I love you too much, I'm in a daze, everything makes me wretched.

ROBIN (*crying*). Ay ay ay ay!

SYLVIA. Now I'm going to cry, too.

ROBIN. How can I stop crying when I see you so anxious? You wouldn't be shedding these tears if you pitied me.

SYLVIA. Hush; I won't tell you anymore that I'm unhappy.

ROBIN. But I'll guess the truth. Please promise to be cheerful.

SYLVIA. I promise. But you must promise to love me forever.

ROBIN. I'll love you, and nothing will shake my love, as long as there's a breath left in my body. I'm yours and you're mine, do you hear? Shall I take an oath? Tell me what to say.

SYLVIA. I don't know any oaths, and I trust you without them. And you can trust me too. All my love is yours. Who else should have any particle of it? Let's remain just as we are, and forget all about oaths.

ROBIN. In a hundred years we'll be the same as now.

SYLVIA. The very same.

ROBIN. And we'll show 'em this very night. Seems there's a party tonight to which a select few is invited, meaning you and me. I'll be your escort, and you'll be mine.

SYLVIA. Dear me! I promised a gentleman—but that was before you arrived. (*Merrily*) He'll just have to go by himself now that you're with me.

ROBIN. I knew it! You see? After a little misery, pleasure tastes all the sweeter.

SYLVIA. And yet I could manage to be happy without any misery at all.

ROBIN. How can I be miserable when you look at me as you're looking now?

SYLVIA. And where have you learned to say all these lovely things? There's only one of you in this world, and only one of me to love you.

ROBIN. Oh, the honey of your words!

(*Enter Trivet and Flaminia*)

TRIVET. It breaks my heart to interrupt this duet, young lady, but your mother has arrived by courtesy of our generous prince, and wishes to see you right away.

SYLVIA. Don't leave me, Robin. I have no secrets for you.

ROBIN (*taking her arm*). Let's go, my love.

FLAMINIA. Go meet your mother by yourself, dear Sylvia, it's more proper that way. Trust me—I have seen to it that you're both free to meet as much as you like.

ROBIN. Thank God, you're on our side. All right, dearest, go see your mammy, tell her I'm keepin' that sack of onions for her as promised.

SYLVIA. Very well, I'll go alone. Wait for me, my dear. Perhaps Flaminia will keep you company.

FLAMINIA. I don't know if I can.... But yes I will.

TRIVET (*to Sylvia*). I'll show you where your *mammy* is waiting for you.

(*Exeunt Sylvia and Trivet*)

ROBIN. Thank you, dear Flaminia. You're the only person I can stand to be with in this house.

FLAMINIA (*as though confidentially*). My dear Robin, I enjoy your company too, but I'm afraid *somebody* might notice how much I like you. And speak of the devil, here he is again.

(*Re-enter Trivet*)

TRIVET. Sir Robin, dinner is being served.

ROBIN (*gloomily*). I'm not hungry.

FLAMINIA. You must eat, I want you to, you need it.

ROBIN. Do you think so?

FLAMINIA. I do.

ROBIN. I don't believe I can swallow a morsel. (*To Trivet*) What's on for a start?

TRIVET. A gorgeous minestrone full of goulash.

ROBIN. Hm. We'd better wait for Sylvia. She likes a hearty soup.

FLAMINIA. I think she'll dine with her mother. You're the master, of course, but I advise you to leave them together, and to see her after dinner.

ROBIN. If you say so; but my appetite ain't ready yet.

TRIVET. A bottle of Chevalier-Montrachet 120 years old has been uncorked, and the roast sits on the table.

ROBIN. I'm so depressed.... Roast what?

TRIVET. Roast mutton swimming in gravy.

ROBIN. So much grief.... Well, let's go. It'd be a sin to let the meat get cold.

FLAMINIA. Don't forget to drink to my health.

ROBIN. What do you mean? You're comin' with me, by crickety crack, and we'll drink to each other's healths and loves. Why are you hesitating?

FLAMINIA. You know why. (*To Trivet*) Will you promise not to tattle to the prince?

TRIVET. What about my loyalty oath to the Poupons?

ROBIN. I pummeled your backside before; now it's the turn of your ugly face.

TRIVET (*running away*). I'll be keeping an eye on you, Flaminia!

FLAMINIA. Oh the villain! And would you believe that he pretends to be in love with me?

ROBIN. In love with you? Let's drown him in that bottle of Chevalier-Montrawhatever.

ACT TWO

(The next day. Enter Sylvia and Flaminia)

SYLVIA. Yes, I believe you. I think you do wish me well. That's why you're the only person I can endure in the palace; all the others I look on as my enemies, especially that vamp Miss Lisa whom the prince is throwing at Robin. But by the way, where is Robin?

FLAMINIA. He'll soon be here; he's still at table.

SYLVIA. What a miserable place this is! Never have I seen such polite ladies and gentlemen. Oh, the sweet manners, the bowing and curtsying, the compliments, the promises! You'd think they were the kindest people in the world. But not a bit! Because there isn't a single one who fails to whisper into my ear, "Miss Sylvia, believe me, you ought to give up Robin and marry the prince." And all this, mind you, without shame, in the most natural manner, as though they were urging me to do a good deed. "But I'm pledged to Robin," say I; "where's constancy, integrity, good faith?" That they don't understand; it's Greek to them; they laugh in my face, they tell me that I'm behaving like a baby, that a grown up girl ought to show more sense. Pretty, isn't it? Who are these people? Where do they come from? What clay are they made of?

FLAMINIA. Of the same clay as everybody, my dear Sylvia. Don't let it surprise you. And yet—they are also thinking about the future of Pouponaco; don't forget that; they love our country.

SYLVIA. But shouldn't a girl be faithful? Isn't that more important than all this palaver about the future of the country? More than that, isn't my faithfulness one of my charms?

FLAMINIA. Oh, it is! And I wish that Robin were back from feeding himself in order to hear you speak.

SYLVIA. Why doesn't the prince take a girl for his wife who is a real farmgirl? He forgets that I've gone to school, and that the nuns taught me how to read and write and speak and behave like a lady. Between you and me, my mother has just finished telling me for the twentieth time that I'm above Robin. Of course that doesn't matter to me in the least, but it proves that the prince shouldn't have picked me for his plans. He's wasting these concerts and plays, these dinners as lavish as wedding feasts, these jewels he keeps sending me. They must cost him huge sums, it's an abyss, he's ruining himself, and I ask you, what does he gain? If he gave me a whole dress shop, I wouldn't be as happy as with a ball of yarn I got from Robin on my last birthday.

FLAMINIA. I know. I've been in love too, and I see myself in that ball of yarn. That is why I'm so sorry for that lovely gentleman, Baron Belair, who is obviously smitten with you.

SYLVIA (*embarrassed*). Please don't mention him.

FLAMINIA. Why not? Has he offended you?

SYLVIA. Oh no! He's as sweet and handsome and genteel as a gentleman can be. Such refinements! And such white, soft, slender hands! Robin is lucky that—(*she stops*)

FLAMINIA. That what?

SYLVIA. Nothing.

FLAMINIA. Incidentally, I thought the baron looked very unhappy when he saw you holding hands with Robin at Lady Grissini's soirée last night.

SYLVIA. I noticed too.

FLAMINIA. And did you notice that I went over to him and made him dance with me? I think I managed to cheer him up.

SYLVIA. I didn't think so, not at all. But where is the prince all this time? How truly strange that he is hiding from me, as if I were the princess and he a village boy.

FLAMINIA. Prince Poupon is awfully shy, and terribly afraid you will not like him.

SYLVIA. Well, he's right to be afraid. Let him forget about his silly project and choose a wife in the palace, which is brimful with women who know how to flutter their eyes and pucker their mouths. They're far more attractive than a bashful thing like myself that doesn't dare look at people and that blushes if somebody says she's pretty.

FLAMINIA. Don't waste your breath praising our women, my dear, because they're miles away from praising you.

SYLVIA. Oh? What do they say?

FLAMINIA. They ridicule you, they taunt the prince, they ask him how is his rustic beauty. "Have you ever seen such a common face?" I heard one of them say yesterday. Then another one of them cried out, "Why isn't she in the kitchen downstairs churning butter?" and everybody laughed. Then somebody criticized your eyes, somebody else the way you walk, the way you talk—what do I know? I was so furious I could have choked!

SYLVIA. How I despise these women! If I'm such a clod of a girl, why did the prince select me of all the girls he could have chosen?

FLAMINIA. Oh, they're sure he'll send you back to the village before the week is over. He'll come back to his senses, they say. How I wish you could get even with these backbiters!

SYLVIA. So do I. It's lucky for them I'm in love with Robin; otherwise I'd show up these vipers.

FLAMINIA. And wouldn't they deserve it! I've told them: "You're doing all you can to get Sylvia dismissed and to take her place in the prince's heart; but if she were so inclined, she'd wiggle her little finger at him and he'd follow her to Timbuctoo."

SYLVIA. At least you know the truth; I could crush them if I wanted to. But I'm not interested in the prince.

FLAMINIA. Hush—here's somebody coming.

SYLVIA. Oh my God, it's Baron Belair! I asked him for pity's sake to stay away from me.

(Enter the Prince as Baron Belair, with Lisa as a lady in waiting. The Prince bows to Sylvia)

PRINCE. Forgive me for intruding upon you, Miss Sylvia. You asked me, alas, to stay away from you; and indeed, I wouldn't have dared to come if Miss Lisa hadn't asked me to escort her. She has obtained the prince's permission to pay her respects to you.

(Lisa and Flaminia exchange winks)

SYLVIA *(gently)*. I'm not unhappy to see you again, though I'm in low spirits just now. As for Miss Lisa, about whom I am well informed, I'm obliged to her for wishing to pay her respects to me. I don't deserve them, but if she wants to curtsy to me, let her go about it and I'll return the compliment as best I can; she'll excuse me if I do it badly.

LISA. Yes, my dear, I'll excuse you with all my heart; I don't ask for what's impossible. *(She curtsies)*

SYLVIA *(aside)*. The slut! *(She curtsies)*

LISA. Where did you learn such exquisite manners, my child?

SYLVIA. In my village, mother.

FLAMINIA *(to Sylvia)*. Good.

PRINCE. My dear lady, under pretext of paying a respectful call, you're abusing Miss Sylvia.

LISA. That wasn't my intention, I assure you. I was only anxious to see the village lass who has turned you-know-whose head. Perhaps I can find the secret of her charm. I'm told she's naive, and I suppose this creates an amusing pastoral effect. I should dearly love to see her dancing a country jig for us.

SYLVIA. I will oblige, madam, on the day you marry Robin.

LISA. Robin, my dear, is worthy only of you.

PRINCE *(to Lisa)*. Enough! Another word, and I will report these insinuations to our prince.

LISA. I'm going. I only wanted to see for myself with what sort of creature the prince wanted to sully his bed.

(*Exit Lisa*)

SYLVIA. Creature! Sully! If she hadn't left, I swear I would have scratched out her eyes.

FLAMINIA. Insults from her kind should be taken as compliments.

PRINCE. My beautiful Sylvia, this woman has misled both the prince and myself. Shocking behavior! You know my feelings for you; you know how deeply I respect you. The truth is that I came here to drink in with my eyes a person dearer to me than life itself, and to acknowledge in you—as unhappily I must—our future sovereign. But I shouldn't let myself go. Flaminia is listening; and you belong to someone else.

FLAMINIA. No harm done! Don't I know a person can't see her without loving her?

SYLVIA. All the same, I'd rather he didn't love me, because I'm sorry I can't reciprocate, truly sorry.

PRINCE. How kind you are, Sylvia! And how unfortunate I am! What is the love I offer you, what are the possessions I would spread at your feet, when I have two happy rivals flanking me, one humble and the other royal?

SYLVIA. The royal one need give you no concern. And you have my permission to love me, that's settled. I'll enjoy it, besides, provided you promise to take your grief patiently; because that's the best I can do for you. Robin came first, you know; nothing else stands in your way. If you had been beforehand—but what good are these ifs? Bad luck will have it so. You're unhappy, and I'm none too happy myself.

PRINCE. You be the judge, Flaminia. How can a man stop loving her? So tender, so generous! I had rather be pitied by Sylvia than adored by any other woman.

SYLVIA. I'll let you judge too, Flaminia. What should a girl do with a man who thanks her no matter what she says?

FLAMINIA. I would fall in love with him, that's what!

SYLVIA. Don't make things worse for us. (*To the prince*) Do try to love me peacefully, will you—but help me get even with that woman.

PRINCE. I'll do it at once, my beloved Sylvia. As for me, I don't care how you treat me, my mind is made up, and if our prince obtains your hand, I shall still have the pleasure of adoring you as long as I live.

SYLVIA. Oh, I'm sure of you. I trust you.

FLAMINIA. Go now, my dear baron; inform the prince against the lady in question. Let everybody comply with the respect we owe our Sylvia.

PRINCE. You'll hear from me presently.

(*Exit the Prince*)

FLAMINIA. And I'll go look for Robin, whom somebody must be keeping at table.

SYLVIA. When Robin is feeding himself, he doesn't need anybody to keep him company.

FLAMINIA. So I've noticed. In the meantime, why don't you try the brocaded dress that was made for you? I can't wait to see it on you.

SYLVIA. I'm sure it will fit me; and it's a lovely material. But I'd rather not take these dresses. The prince wants me in exchange, and that's a bargain I'll never agree to.

FLAMINIA. You're wrong there. Even if you keep refusing him, everything will still be yours. Really, you don't know our generous Prince Poupon.

SYLVIA. If you say so. But I hope he doesn't ask me afterwards, "Why did you take my presents?"

FLAMINIA. He'll ask you, "Why didn't you take more of them?"

SYLVIA. Very well: I'll help myself to as many presents as he likes; that way he won't be able to upbraid me.

FLAMINIA. Carry on. I'll answer for everything.

(*Exit Sylvia*)

FLAMINIA. Things are beginning to fall into place. I'd better go look for—but here he comes. If this magnificent hunk were to fall in love with me, and bring myself and Lisa an estate, I could forgive my father for ruining us at the roulette table.

(*Enter Robin, laughing, with Trivet*)

ROBIN. Ha, ha, ha! Hello, Flaminia.

FLAMINIA. Hello, Robin. Tell me why you're laughing, so I can laugh along with you.

ROBIN. Trivet's been showing me about the house. I noticed a tall rascal lifting a lady's dress from behind. Now here's a prank, says I to myself, and I tell him straight off, "Stop it, you low scamp; this trifling is indecent." But the lady overhears me. She turns around and says, "Can't you see he's carrying my train?" "You mean he's carrying your tail," says I. That's when the rascal started to laugh, then the lady fell to laughing, Trivet laughed, everybody was laughing; so to keep 'em company I decided to laugh too. But now I want to ask you, what was we all laughing about?

FLAMINIA. About nothing. You don't happen to know that what this lackey was doing was done according to custom.

ROBIN. You mean it was another honor?

FLAMINIA. That's right.

ROBIN. Well, I'm glad I laughed. It's a funny honor, by God, and a cheap one, too.

FLAMINIA. You're in a good mood. That's how I like to see you. How was your meal?

ROBIN. God love me! I wish you had seen the tasty concoctions! And the cook's fricassee! There's no fighting that cook. I drank so many healths to Sylvia and you, it won't be my fault if you ever get sick.

FLAMINIA. What? Did you think of me at all?

ROBIN. Once I've given my friendship to a person, I never forget it, especially at table. But what about Sylvia, has she gone to see her mother again?

TRIVET. Oh, Sir Robin, still thinking about Sylvia?

ROBIN. Hold your tongue when your master speaks.

FLAMINIA. You're overstepping the bounds, Trivet.

TRIVET. Me, overstepping the bounds?

FLAMINIA. That's right. Why do you try to keep Robin from talking about his darling girl?

TRIVET. His darling girl is it? I'm beginning to see how much you care for the prince's interests.

FLAMINIA. Robin, that man is going to make trouble for me on your account.

ROBIN (*angry*). No, my sweet, he won't. (*To Trivet*) Look here, I'm your overlord, you said so yourself, I didn't know a thing about it. Well, you loafer, if I catch you tattling, and if they so much as say boo to this fine girl, you'll be short two ears; I'll have 'em in my pocket.

TRIVET. I'll do my duty and live without my ears.

ROBIN. Two ears! Can they still hear me? And now clear out.

TRIVET. I will; but as for you, Flaminia, you'll be paying the fiddler.

(*Robin threatens him, Flaminia stops Robin, and Trivet leaves*)

ROBIN. This is too much. No sooner do I find an honest person in this house than some busybody sticks his nose into our conversation. But now, my dear Flaminia, let's talk about Sylvia as much as we like. It's only when I'm in your company that I can stand to be away from her.

FLAMINIA. How sweet of you! There's nothing I wouldn't do to make both of you happy. And you, well, you're already so dear to me that when I see anybody upsetting you, I suffer as much as you do.

ROBIN. How sweet of you! I feel calmer when you pity me. Already I'm only half as sorry to be miserable as I was before.

FLAMINIA. Who wouldn't pity you? Who wouldn't be interested in your fate? You don't realize what you're worth, Robin.

ROBIN. That's possible, you know. I've never taken that close a look.

FLAMINIA. It's terrible to be so powerless! If you could read into my heart!

ROBIN. What a shame; I can't read; but you'll explain it to me. I swear I'd like to be rid of my grief if only out of consideration for the way you worry about it; but everything will be settled by and by, you'll see.

FLAMINIA. No, I'll never be a witness to your happiness; it's all over for me. Trivet is going to denounce me, I'll be taken away from you. Who knows to what faraway land I'll be exiled? Perhaps I'm speaking to you for the last time, Robin, and there'll be no pleasure left for me in this world.

ROBIN. For the last time! Oh, I was born under a wicked star! I had one only love, they took her away, and now are they going to swindle me out of you too? Is this the way to treat a loyal Pouponian? Have they decided to kill me? Are they savages?

FLAMINIA. Whatever happens, I hope you won't forget Flaminia, who desired nothing so much as your happiness.

ROBIN. My dear good girl, you've won my heart. Advise me in my distress; let's put our heads together; what do you propose? I'm not very bright when I'm angry. Sure I love Sylvia, but I have to keep you too. My love shouldn't knock out our friendship, no more than our friendship should nibble at my love; and here I am all tangled up.

FLAMINIA. And here I am all unhappy! From the time I lost the man I loved, I've been at peace only in your company; with you I've revived a little. You're so much like him, sometimes I think he is speaking again. I've never liked anyone except him and you.

ROBIN. Poor girl! How inconvenient for you that I'm in love with Sylvia; otherwise I'd gladly offer you the likeness of your poor sweetheart. I guess he was a good looking fellow.

FLAMINIA. Didn't I tell you he was just like you? You're his living portrait, except so much stronger.

ROBIN. And you was crazy about him?

FLAMINIA. Look at yourself, Robin; see how much you deserve to be loved, and you'll understand how much I loved him.

ROBIN. Can a body answer more sweetly? Every word you say is downright friendly. I'd never have guessed I was that handsome; but since you loved the copy of me so well, I've got to believe that the original is pretty fair, too.

FLAMINIA. Life is so hard! And if only I hadn't been too homely to deserve either one of you.

ROBIN. Homely? Did you say homely? How dare you insult yourself like that! Don't take it lying down. Why, you're the most beautiful—I mean—you're a beauty—a regular goddess Aphrodisiac.

FLAMINIA. Stop, Robin, stop. I'm so troubled, I'd better leave you. It's hard, God knows, to tear myself away from you, but where would it all lead? Farewell. I must prepare myself for bitter exile. I don't know where I am.

Adieu.

(*Exit Flaminia*)

ROBIN (*gazing after her*). She's too good for this place, by crickety crack. If I had to lose Sylvia by some accident, God forbid, I think I'd take refuge with her in my despair.

(*Enter from another side Trivet in a long beard, disguised as Dr. Vascularius*)

TRIVET (*very deferential*). Dr. Robin, my respects. I hope I'm not troubling your repose. My name is Dr. Vascularius.

ROBIN. Where have I seen you before?

TRIVET. Nowhere, dear sir; we are strangers to one another.

ROBIN. No we ain't. I know it was you that advised the prince to marry my girl.

TRIVET. Advised him? Never! I was only reading the stars for his Royal Highness, and argue with them as much as we mortals will, they won't listen to reason. I humbly apologize for them.

ROBIN. Well, your stars are a pack of villains, so I won't hold them against you. What can I oblige you with?

TRIVET. I have come to beg a favor of you, Dr. Robin.

ROBIN. Always willin' to be of service.

TRIVET. I had the misfortune to speak lightly of you in the prince's presence.

ROBIN. You don't say! What did you tell him?

TRIVET. Oh, I only said—but ever so lightly—"I hear that Master Robin's grammar is not so highly developed as are his muscles."

ROBIN. Ha, ha, ha, ha! I like that! It's a fact that I don't exercise my grammar like I work out my arms and legs. What did the prince answer?

TRIVET. He became angry.

ROBIN. Good. He's an honest man; I'm glad. If he wasn't keeping my Sylvia from me, I'd be friends with him. But lemme hear what he said.

TRIVET. "Robin," he said, "is a man of honor. As I value him, I desire him to be respected. Grammar is for pedants like you, Vascularius. Instead, the frankness and simplicity of Robin's character are qualities I should wish to find in all of you. I stand in the way of his love, and it grieves me to the soul that a higher duty to our nation compels me to injure him."

ROBIN. Bless my heart, I'm beginning to take a fancy to the dear man, and I'm not half as mad at him as I thought I was.

TRIVET. Alas, my reply to his reply made matters worse for me.

ROBIN. Things are warming up, eh? What was your reply to his reply?

TRIVET. I said—but still ever so lightly, so very lightly!—that the prince shouldn't stand on ceremony and marry you off without ado to the village crone.

ROBIN. The village crone is it? Old Pamela Brittleback? Watch my stick!
(*Trivet throws himself at Robin's feet*)
TRIVET. Dear Dr. Robin, hear me out, I beg you! The prince is going to dismiss me from his service if you don't intercede for me.
ROBIN. Intercede for you! Ask the planets to intercede for you! Because *I'm* about to beat you black and blue.
TRIVET. Don't, Dr. Robin; wait, wait! You like Flaminia, don't you?
ROBIN. Hold your tongue! What's Flaminia got to do with this? Get up!
TRIVET. Flaminia is very poor, you know; her father ruined her before he decided to die. If you are kind enough to obtain my pardon, I will restore her fortune by marrying her to a wealthy cousin of mine who is court astrologer to the sultan of Mesopotamia.
ROBIN. Hang your cousin and your sultan! I won't have nobody marrying my friends from under me.
TRIVET. But I thought—
ROBIN. Stop thinking! Thinking will cost you a broken skull.
TRIVET. But what can I do to regain your friendship?
ROBIN. Stop talking about marrying people to people. And if you do, I give you my word of honor I'll make things right between you and the prince.
TRIVET. I promise to obey you, and I shall await the results of your embassy. Good day, Dr. Robin.
ROBIN. Your servant. (*Exit Trivet*) Well! I'm becoming a man of consequence; everybody obeys me, which feels pretty good. But I'd better not breathe a word to Flaminia about the cousin. There she is!
(*Enter Flaminia*)
FLAMINIA. My dear boy, I've brought Sylvia back to you. She just stopped for a moment to look at herself in a mirror.
ROBIN. That's your Sylvia for you! But why didn't you come sooner to tell me? We could have chatted while waiting for her.
(*Enter Sylvia*)
SYLVIA. Greetings, Robin dear. I've been trying on the most beautiful dress! How pretty I looked in it! Ask Flaminia. If I chose to wear any of these dresses and jewels, we'd see who was too clumsy to please anybody. But I'll say this—they have the cleverest seamstresses here.
ROBIN. My love, they're not as clever as you're tasty.
SYLVIA. If I'm tasty, Robin, you're very gallant to say so.
FLAMINIA. I'm glad to see you both a little happier now.
SYLVIA. Why not? As long as no one bothers us, and the prince stays out of the way, I'd as soon be here as any other place.
ROBIN. I'd like to see anybody bother us! They're sending folk in to me on

their knees left and right because they made some unrefined remark about me.

SYLVIA. To me too. I'm waiting right now for that wretched Miss Lisa, who has been ordered to repent before my eyes for calling me a village girl.

FLAMINIA. If anybody vexes you from now on, let me know.

ROBIN. Oh yes, Flaminia loves us both like a sister. (*To Flaminia*) And it's tit for tat as far as we're concerned.

SYLVIA. Oh, that reminds me. I want you to be friends with Baron Belair—you know the gentleman I mean; because he's been very kind as well.

ROBIN. Tit for that, I say, tit for tat.

SYLVIA. After all, what harm is there in his liking me? When all's said and done, the people who love us are better company than those who don't.

FLAMINIA. Quite right.

ROBIN. Let's add Flaminia, in that case; she cares for us; and that'll make a foursome.

FLAMINIA. It's a friendly thought I'll never forget, Robin.

ROBIN. Well, since we're all together, let's have a snack to cheer us up.

SYLVIA. You go, Robin. Now that we can meet as much as we like, we needn't be in each other's way. Don't worry about me.

ROBIN. All right. Are you coming, Flaminia? I hate to eat by myself.

FLAMINIA. I'll join you, especially as somebody is coming who'll keep Sylvia company.

(*Exeunt Robin and Flaminia. Enter Lisa from another side. She makes a number of ceremonious curtsies to Sylvia*)

SYLVIA. Not quite so many curtsies, madam, so I won't be obliged to return them. You fancy me too awkward to perform them, I know.

LISA (*in a sad voice*). Your merits have spoken here.

SYLVIA. Not for long, I'm sure, because I'm not putting myself out to impress anyone. I'm rather sorry to be as good looking as I am, and I'm sorry you're not quite pretty enough.

LISA. Ah, what a situation!

SYLVIA. Here you are sighing because of a little country girl. You're taking your time now. Where have you left your tongue, madam? Do you lose your gift for prattling when it comes to making amends?

LISA. I can't begin to speak.

SYLVIA. Then don't. Because you can moan until tomorrow morning, but you won't change my looks; beautiful or ugly, my face will remain what it is. But what brings you here? Haven't you scolded me enough? Well then, finish me off, help yourself!

LISA. Spare me, Miss Sylvia; my outburst has brought trouble on my whole family. Baron Belair compels me to apologize to you, because he flies into a passion if someone so much as ruffles one of your curls. He said he would make a report of me to the prince if I didn't beg you to accept my excuses.

SYLVIA. It's all over; I'm no longer angry. I'm sorry for you and I forgive you. But why did you provoke me to begin with?

LISA. Perhaps you know that the prince had chosen me to be his wife before he met you. Then he wanted me to marry Robin in order to free you for himself. And Robin rejected me too. Of course I took it badly when I found out that true charm doesn't always gain the upper hand.

SYLVIA. While ugly faces and bad figures do, because the upper hand is mine! I unforgive you!

LISA. Very well, I admit I'm jealous. But since you don't care to be our princess, and since you're devoted to Robin, why not help me regain Poupon's affection? If he returns to me, you will be perfectly free to marry your sweetheart.

SYLVIA. Why don't you lure him back by means of your own true charm, as you call it? Because I advise you not to count on me.

LISA. You are very sharp with me. Well, I've apologized as much as is necessary, and now it's open war. The prince hasn't lost all his senses, nor have I lost all my power over him. And believe me, once I sit on the throne, you'll be going back to hoeing potatoes in the fields.

SYLVIA. Once you sit on the throne! Watch out! I'll speak to the prince. He hasn't dared come near me as yet, because I'm cross with him; but I'll let him know he can be a little bolder from now on.

LISA. Do so. In the meantime, I'll report to Belair that he had better forget his passion for you, since you're about to inveigle the prince on top of your Robin. Good day, madam, and remember me in your prayers.

SYLVIA. Go your way, I don't even know you're alive.

(*Exit Lisa one way, enter Flaminia by another*)

FLAMINIA. What's the matter, Sylvia? You look upset.

SYLVIA. I'm simply boiling. That impudent Lisa woman came again to apologize; and I don't know how the hussy went about it, but she managed to infuriate me again. I can't begin to tell you what all she threw in my face! She even boasted that it was she who was going to marry the prince!

FLAMINIA. Did she now! Oh what a pity that your attachment to Robin prevents you from putting her and all the other scandal mongers in their place!

SYLVIA. You're right. And that reminds me. Where is the fellow? Every time I have news of him, he's sitting down to a meal, a drink or a snack.

FLAMINIA. Yes, I noticed it too. Please don't repeat my words, because we're talking among girls now. Tell me the truth, do you really love that boy so much?

SYLVIA. Oh yes, I do; I have to, you know.

FLAMINIA. Shall I tell you what I think? Confidentially now. You don't seem to be made for one another. You, Sylvia, have taste, intelligence, an air of breeding and distinction; while he—well, I don't want to spell out the obvious. Oh, he's a fine looking lad and truly unpretentious, but in all honesty I can't understand how you—well—I feel, as your mother does, that perhaps you're lowering yourself a little. It's easy to guess at any rate that this is what Baron Belair believes, even though he's much too delicate to breathe a word of his inner thoughts.

SYLVIA. Put yourself in my place. Robin was the most likable boy of the district; and he was my neighbor in the village. He followed me about because he was in love with me; and as I was used to seeing him day after day, I began to care for him too; but I always knew he was a glutton and had no education.

FLAMINIA. An uneducated glutton! Lovely qualities in the suitor of our charming and tender Sylvia! Come now, what have you decided to do?

SYLVIA. I don't know what to say; so many yesses and noes are whirling through my head, which should I listen to? On the one side, Robin is a gadabout who thinks only of his dinner; on the other side, if I marry him, these arrogant women will crow that I've gone back to where I deserve to be. And then there's something else.

FLAMINIA. Oh? What is this something else?

SYLVIA. You know....

FLAMINIA. No, I don't.

SYLVIA. Of course you do. Baron Belair....

FLAMINIA. What of him?

SYLVIA. This is in strict confidence too, Flaminia, please! I don't know what's happened to me since I saw him again; but he seems so sweet, he tells me such tender things, he talks about his love so nobly, so humbly, that I'm full of pity for him, and this pity keeps me from thinking as straight as I should.

FLAMINIA. Come! Tell me the truth! Your secret is safe with me. Are you falling a little bit in love with him?

SYLVIA. I don't think so, because I'm supposed to love Robin.

FLAMINIA. He's an excellent gentleman.

SYLVIA. I know.

FLAMINIA. And no pauper!

SYLVIA. I don't care.

FLAMINIA. It occurs to me that if the prince allowed you to marry the

PRINCE POUPON NEEDS A WIFE

baron and consented to look for another village girl to sire his future strong Poupons, you'd still be amply avenged and justified.

SYLVIA. I've been thinking the same thing, to be honest with you; and I would do it, maybe, if Robin wanted to marry another girl. I'd have the right to tell him, "You left me, I'm leaving you, we're even." Otherwise—dear me! Life is so difficult!

FLAMINIA. Your scruples do you honor, my dear. As far as delicacy of feelings is concerned, you and Belair are a match made in heaven! I doubt whether your Robin would indulge in these refinements of conscience if opportunity came his way. Heavens! Here comes the baron again.

SYLVIA. I look like a fright! Let me mend my hair and face!

(*She runs away as Prince Poupon enters from the other side*)

PRINCE. Why are you laughing, Flaminia?

FLAMINIA. No reason, my lord, no reason. But don't take another step; Sylvia will be here in a few minutes.

PRINCE. Good. I was looking for her. Are we making any progress?

FLAMINIA. Such progress, my lord, that when she comes, and I make a coy exit, you may as well reveal yourself to her and sweep her into your arms.

PRINCE. Not quite so fast, my dear. I want to examine my darling a little longer.

FLAMINIA. Say rather that you are enjoying yourself.

PRINCE. Always so clever! Yes, I am enjoying myself. It's a new pleasure; nothing like all those balls and banquets and three-act comedies that wear me out.

FLAMINIA. Have it your way, but don't—wait; here's Princess Sylvia.

(*Enter Sylvia*)

FLAMINIA. Come in, my dear; don't be afraid. I was trying to entertain the baron without much success. As he was anxiously looking for you and not for me, allow me to withdraw. Not another word!

(*Exit Flaminia*)

PRINCE. Dearest Sylvia, I was looking for you in order to ask whether Lisa has apologized to you as commanded. But why should I lie to you? I was looking for you in order to see you again—my only happiness on earth. But if my love wearies you, if I myself displease you and stand between you and a much nobler life, order me to hold my tongue and leave. I'll suffer without complaint, resolved as I am to obey you in all things.

SYLVIA. Just listen to you! How am I ever going to send you away? If I order you to be still, you'll be still; if I order you to leave me, you'll leave me; you won't dare complain, you'll obey me in everything. A fine way you've chosen to make me give you orders!

PRINCE. Can I do better than make you the mistress of my destiny?

SYLVIA. What's the use? Could I bring myself to make you unhappy? If I told you to go away, you'd believe I hate you; if I told you to be still, you'd believe I was cold; and all these beliefs would be untrue; I'd be distressing you without making myself a bit happier.

PRINCE. Well then, beautiful Sylvia, what do you want me to do?

SYLVIA. I don't know what I want! I'm waiting for somebody to tell me. I know even less than you about it. Robin loves me; the prince courts me; you deserve me; there are women here who insult me and whom I'd like to punish; I'll be humiliated if I don't marry the prince; Robin worries me; you trouble my mind because—because. Oh, I wish I had never met you; all this turmoil in my brain is making me miserable. If only you were the prince!

PRINCE. What if I were?

SYLVIA. I'd tell Robin you were the master, and it couldn't be helped. But I'd want to use that pretext only for you.

PRINCE (*aside*). Isn't she adorable? I ought to reveal myself now.

SYLVIA. And it's not because of power and possessions that I'd want you to be the prince, but because of yourself. But it mustn't be. No. I'm glad you're not the master after all; I'd be too tempted. And even if you were, I couldn't choose to be unfaithful; I love Robin; and that's my conclusion.

PRINCE (*aside*). Let's wait a little longer. (*Aloud*) All I ask, Sylvia, is that you continue to think kindly of me. The prince is preparing an entertainment in your honor. You are finally to meet him after the feast; and I am instructed to tell you that if you remain indifferent to him, you will be free to go home.

SYLVIA. Oh, I'll remain indifferent, and I'm as good as gone already. But once I'm home, you'll visit me again. Who knows what will happen then? No! I'll never be unfaithful. Do I hear steps? It could be Robin!

(*She runs away*)

PRINCE (*alone*). Fly, my dove!... Will marriage be as delicious as this?

ACT THREE

(*Later the same day. Enter the Prince and Flaminia*)

FLAMINIA. I agree, my lord; this delay doesn't spoil anything, but you've nearly reached your goal — and I mine.

PRINCE. Ah, Flaminia, how I thank Dr. Vascularius—or rather the planets. I started out dreaming only of renewing the Poupon line, and now I find myself in love like the most common of commoners.

FLAMINIA. Congratulations.

PRINCE. It is pleasant, of course, to have a countess or a duchess tell me distinctly that she adores me. And yet, Flaminia, this pleasure is pale and insipid compared to my joy when I listen to Sylvia's scruples and hesitations.

FLAMINIA. Dare I ask you to repeat something of what she tells you?

PRINCE. Impossible. I'm delighted, I'm bewitched; but that's all I can report.

FLAMINIA. The report is unusual but promising.

PRINCE. If you knew, says she, if you knew how wretched I am because I must not love you, because the prince wants me for himself, and because I must be faithful to Robin, and because I see you grief stricken! One moment more, and she would have cried, "Love me, love me, take me into your arms!"

FLAMINIA. We can dispose of the prince at any rate!

PRINCE. Yes; we have him in our pocket. Which leaves us with Robin outstanding. So hurry, Flaminia, hurry. Will you conquer him soon? You know I am determined not to use force against him. What does he say?

FLAMINIA. To tell you the truth, my lord, I think I have got him head over heels in love with me, only he doesn't know it yet. By calling me his dear friend, he is living at ease with his conscience, and enjoying his love gratis; but in our next conversation, I intend to let him become acquainted with the true nature of his intimacies with me. And between his weakness for me, which will not remain incognito for long, and your own gentle words to him, we'll be putting an end to your worries and completing my labors, from which, my lord, I will emerge victorious and defeated.

PRINCE. In what way?

FLAMINIA. Oh, it's a detail of small importance; namely that I've taken a fancy to Robin—only in order to add spice to my plot, of course.

PRINCE. And don't forget; the lad you've taken a fancy to will be Lord Robinet.

FLAMINIA. I haven't forgotten. But let's leave this room, my lord. Go find Sylvia. Here's Robin, and he mustn't see either one of us yet.

(*Exeunt Flaminia and the Prince. Enter Trivet and Robin, the latter looking gloomy*)

TRIVET. Well, what am I supposed to do with this writing desk and paper?

ROBIN. Silence, underling; give me time to think.

TRIVET. As much as you wish.

ROBIN. Tell me, who provides my board in this place?

TRIVET. The prince does, as you well know.

ROBIN. Deuce take it! All this tasty food is beginning to worry me.
TRIVET. Why?
ROBIN. I'm afraid of being charged without my knowing it. What are you laughing at, you oaf?
TRIVET. I'm laughing at your funny notions. Go on, Count Robin, eat and drink without fear.
ROBIN. I'm enjoying my meals in good faith, and I'm hanged if I want to be handed a bill when I go; but I'll take your word for it. Tell me, though, what's the title of the man in charge of the prince's official business?
TRIVET. You mean his secretary of state?
ROBIN. That's right; I want to send him a letter. I'll ask him to notificate the prince that I'm collecting dust here and that I want matters settled once and for all, as my dad is at home all by hisself and needs help in the stable.
TRIVET. And then?
ROBIN. And after that, me and Sylvia must hear the wedding bells. Go on, start writing. Begin with "Sir".
TRIVET. Stop! The correct form is "Your Excellency".
ROBIN. Put both and let him choose.
TRIVET. If you say so.
ROBIN. "This is to inform you that my name is Robin."
TRIVET. I'm writing. "This is to inform you that my name is Robin." What next?
ROBIN. "And that I am courting a girl whose name is Sylvia, and who is a respectable girl from my village." Have you got that?
TRIVET. Yes, sir.
ROBIN. "And also that I have recently made friends with a girl that's called Flaminia who can't live without us, nor us without her; wherefore, upon receipt of same—"
TRIVET. Flaminia can't live without you? Ay, the pen drops from my hand.
ROBIN. And what's this insolent swooning all about?
TRIVET. For two years, Sir Robin, I've sighed in secret for Flaminia.
ROBIN (*producing his stick*). I don't think a corpse does any sighing.
TRIVET. Wait! Put that stick away! Suppose I'm in love with Flaminia? What's that to you? You like her, that's all, and when you like somebody you don't feel jealous.
ROBIN. You're mistaken; my liking doesn't like trespassers. (*Beats him*)
TRIVET. Damn your liking!
(*He runs away. Enter Flaminia*)
FLAMINIA. What's going on? What's the matter, Robin?
ROBIN. The rascal was telling me that he's in love with you.

FLAMINIA. I know he is. Don't you see—that's why he wants to report my friendship for you to the prince. He's hoping that I'll be disgraced, so he can take my hand, slip a ring on my finger, and call himself my savior.

ROBIN. And you, my dear, what do you say?

FLAMINIA. What can I say? And to whom can I turn if I am disgraced?

ROBIN. To me, d'you hear? And I don't want to share our friendship with nobody, and least with that no-good Trivet.

FLAMINIA (*gently*). Robin, do you realize that you're quite ruthless with my heart?

ROBIN. Me? What harm am I doing?

FLAMINIA. If you don't stop speaking to me the way you do, soon I won't be able to tell what kind of feeling I have for you. The truth is, I'm afraid to examine myself on this matter. I might find more than I wish.

ROBIN. Well then, don't never examine, Flaminia. Just let things be. And don't look for a man. I have a girl and I'm keepin' her; but if I didn't have one, I wouldn't go lookin'. What would I do with a girl as long as you were about? She'd be in my way.

FLAMINIA. She'd be in your way! After that, how can I be a mere friend to you?

ROBIN. Well, what else do you want to be?

FLAMINIA (*softly*). Not second to Sylvia....

ROBIN (*uneasy*). Side by side?

FLAMINIA. Hush. I'll send her to you if I find her. Will that make you happy?

ROBIN. Don't go yet, don't send nobody, don't go!

FLAMINIA. I must, dear Robin. The prince's personal secretary has asked for me, and though I tremble, I must see what he wants. Good bye, Robin, I'll be back soon.

(*Exit Flaminia. Enter the Prince*)

ROBIN. Who the devil is coming now? Ha, it's that baron. I've been meaning to look for you, sir. I didn't like the way you leered and moped and grumbled when you saw me and my woman together at Mrs. Grissini's party. Once I become Count Robinet, I might just exchange this stick for a sword and run you through the windpipe, by crickety crack.

PRINCE. Calm down, my good man. The prince has ordered me to talk to you.

ROBIN. You're free to talk, but nobody ordered me to listen.

PRINCE. I see that in order to curb you I must tell you the truth at last. Know then that I am not Baron Belair, as both you and Sylvia believe; I am the Prince himself.

ROBIN. No foolin'?

(*Enter Trivet holding up a large painting of the Prince on horseback*)
PRINCE. Read what is says, my lad.
ROBIN. I can't read, but it's a picture of you, and no mistake. Nice horse, too.
PRINCE. It says, Prince Poupon the Seventeenth. Do you believe me now?
(*He strikes the same pose as in the picture*)
ROBIN. I do, I do. (*He falls on his knees*) My lord, forgive me for blathering like a muck headed fool.
PRINCE. Gladly, my boy. Stand up! I forgive you with all my heart, provided you don't reveal to anyone what I have told you.
(*Trivet trips off with the painting*)
ROBIN. I promise to keep my mouth shut. But since you bear me no grudge, my lord, won't you take care that I bear none against you? I ain't strong enough to stand up to a prince, but you should pity me, bein' so powerful, because I know you don't want to rule over the land like a tyrant.
PRINCE. I am too soft, too weak, and you all take advantage of that.
ROBIN. How can I answer you, my lord? I have only one girl to love me, but you, your house is full of high born ladies, and yet you take my one and only girl away from me. Suppose I was a poor man, and that all my property amounted to a penny. Then suppose you come along, worth a silver mine; you fling yourself on my poverty and you tear the penny out of my hand. Isn't that a sorry thing to do?
PRINCE (*aside*). He is right, and I am touched by his grief.
ROBIN. I know you're a kind-hearted prince, everybody says so; I'm the only one who won't be able to agree with them.
PRINCE (*aside*). How can I answer him?
ROBIN. Come, my lord, ask yourself: "Shall I harm this simple fellow because I have the power to do so? Isn't it up to me, his master, to protect him? Shall I be unjust to him now and repent of it later? Who will fill the office of prince if I don't? No, I shall order Sylvia to be restored to him."
PRINCE. Always the same idea! Remember that I am your monarch and could make you and Sylvia tremble. Instead, though our country needs her, though you are obstinate, and though you have shown me scant respect, I take an interest in your grief and try to alleviate it. Indeed, I want to ennoble you, grant you estates out of my own possessions, and give you Flaminia for your wife. But still you resist like a stubborn peasant.
ROBIN. Oh, life is so difficult!
PRINCE. However, I confess that I have been unjust to you. Let Pouponaco suffer. Sylvia belongs to you. Go back to your village with her. And since Trivet has asked me a thousand times for permission to marry Flaminia, I will finally give my consent and let them be man and wife. Good bye,

Robin. I shall order a cart to take you back to your farm.
ROBIN (*choking*). Wait, wait.
(*But the Prince has left*)
ROBIN. Flaminia and Trivet! Did I hear what I heard? This is an emergency. I'd better find her right away. But what am I going to tell her? That I'll twist Trivet's neck? And that I'll give up Sylvia? Is that possible? Am I the Robin I used to know? No, Robin is my name but I've turned into somebody else.
(*Enter Flaminia, looking unhappy. Long, tragic silence*)
ROBIN. Talk to me....
FLAMINIA. Adieu, Robin.
ROBIN. What do you mean—adieu?
FLAMINIA. The prince is ordering me either to marry Trivet or else to take perpetual vows as a Sister of Chastity on the island of Saint Barrabas. And I'm past caring which of the two horrors I'll pick, because as in a bolt from heaven it was revealed to me that I'm being rightly punished.
ROBIN. For what?
FLAMINIA. For not concealing that what I felt for you wasn't friendship.
ROBIN. What was it?
FLAMINIA. You name it. I can't.
ROBIN. ... Love?
FLAMINIA. Oh don't say another word, Robin, let me fly to my destiny.
(*She takes a couple of steps*)
ROBIN. Stay! Don't leave me!
FLAMINIA. Let me go; I have said too much.
ROBIN. Stop! Because that bolt from heaven just hit me too. I love you! There, that settles it, and I don't know what I'm saying. Uff!
FLAMINIA. Are you sure, Robin? Or are you deluded?
ROBIN. Sure I'm sure!
FLAMINIA. What a predicament!
ROBIN. I'm not married, fortunately.
FLAMINIA. That's true.
ROBIN. Sylvia will do her duty to Pouponaco and marry the prince, as is right and proper.
FLAMINIA. And a blessing to our dear country.
ROBIN. After which, since we miscalculated and love each other by mistake, we'll reach an understanding and somehow make the best of it.
FLAMINIA (*softly*). Do you mean that you will visit me in my convent?
ROBIN. No, by crickety crack, because I'll visit you in my bed.
(*He swoops on Flaminia and embraces her*)
FLAMINIA. Count Robinet! What are you doing to me?

ROBIN. What about you? Why didn't you warn me from the start that you was going to turn my head?

FLAMINIA. And you—did you send out a warning that you would captivate me? Kiss me again.

(*They kiss*)

ROBIN. Uff! You ladies sure know what's what! But hadn't I ought to talk to the prince afore he hands you over to that rascal Trivet? Give me courage to do it, my pigeon. (*They kiss again*) Who would've thought this would taste so good? I don't know whether I'm comin' or goin'.

FLAMINIA. Go to the prince, my darling. I'm sure you'll find him accomodating.

ROBIN. All right; but you—don't tell Sylvia that I love you. She'll think I'm guilty of somethin', when it's plain as sunshine that I'm innocent. After all, ain't I giving her up because when the good of 'umanity is at stake, a man shouldn't be selfish?

FLAMINIA. A noble thought, my lord. But now go, go!

(*Exit Robin*)

FLAMINIA (*looking up*). Papa! (*Changing her mind, she looks down*). Papa! Forgive me for marrying beneath my rank, as I forgive you for preferring the gambling table to your family. Besides, wherever you may be now, a blue-blood in either place (*imitating Robin*) ain't no better nor a farmhand. Lo and behold, here's the other one.

(*Enter Sylvia*)

FLAMINIA. What are you dreaming about, fair Sylvia?

SYLVIA. About something I don't understand, namely myself.

FLAMINIA. What's so incomprehensible about yourself?

SYLVIA. Do you remember how I wanted to be avenged on that Lisa girl and the other envious women? Well, that's all over.

FLAMINIA. You're not vindictive, you see.

SYLVIA. And I loved Robin, didn't I?

FLAMINIA. So I vaguely remember.

SYLVIA. I think I don't any more.

FLAMINIA. That's no calamity.

SYLVIA. And if it were a calamity, what could I do about it? When love came along, I loved him; now that it's going away, I *don't* love him. Love came without my bidding, and it leaves in its own good time; I don't believe that I'm to blame.

FLAMINIA (*aside*). I'll needle her a bit. (*Aloud*) When we look into ourselves, we rarely find anything to blame.

SYLVIA. What kind of insinuation is that? I order you to agree with me without afterthought. Really! The women they send after me in order to nag the life out of me!

FLAMINIA. Don't lose your temper; I was only joking, Sylvia. I truly believe you're not to blame in the least. But who is it you're in love with? Is it Baron Belair or the prince?

SYLVIA. How can you ask? You're joking again, when I'm in torment. The prince is determined to revive the Poupons by marrying me. What will he say when instead of refusing him for Robin, I reject him for one of his own vassals? If he is even a tiny bit of a tyrant, he'll throw me into a dungeon instead of sending me back to my sheep and cows.

FLAMINIA. This is worrisome, I admit. But I'll let you in on a secret.

SYLVIA. What is it?

FLAMINIA. Dr. Vascularius took me aside an hour ago and whispered that a tremendous revelation is at hand for you.

SYLVIA. What sort of revelation? Revelations can be good or bad.

FLAMINIA. He wouldn't tell me. But by his wink and his grin I gathered it will be a gratifying one.

SYLVIA. I don't know. Maybe it will be revealed that I've behaved like a slut toward Robin. How can I help fretting myself about him? Will I be making him very miserable? What's your opinion? But don't go putting a lot of scruples into my head.

FLAMINIA. Don't worry about Robin; he'll be easy to console.

SYLVIA. Thank you! Thank you very much! To listen to you, it doesn't take much to forget me. Don't tell me he's found someone else in the palace!

FLAMINIA. Nonsense. I don't know what I was saying. Forget you? You'll be lucky if he doesn't go mad with despair.

SYLVIA. Now why did you say *that* to me? You and your mad with despair! You've made me hesitate again.

FLAMINIA. What if he no longer loved you. What would you say?

SYLVIA. I'd say... that you should keep the news to yourself.

FLAMINIA. But you're annoyed because he does love you! What do you really want?

SYLVIA. You can laugh, but I'd like to see you in my place.

FLAMINIA. Here's your admirer. Take my advice—settle with him, don't worry about dungeons, and remember what I said about the revelation.

(*Exit Flaminia. Enter the Prince*)

PRINCE. Sylvia—won't you look at me? Your face becomes overcast every time I come near you. And yet I had the temerity, a while ago, to hope—

SYLVIA. Continue.

PRINCE. That you could love me.

SYLVIA (*sadly*). How can I allow myself to love you, when on the one side stands Robin and on the other the prince?

PRINCE. What if I could sway the prince? We are blood relations, and I have some influence over him.

SYLVIA. And Robin? Tell me, you who are a man of principle: you know how I stand with Robin. Suppose I felt like being in love with you. Suppose I gave way to my feelings. Would I be acting right? Or wrong? There now, give me your disinterested advice.

PRINCE. Consider this. A man is riding a horse westward at a modest canter. Lightning strikes in front of him. The horse takes off eastward at a wild gallop. Is the rider to blame? Of course not. And so it goes for us lovers. Passion races us whither it will, and only the devil would be mean enough to blame us for being carried away by it. Such, adorable Sylvia, is my verdict, and King Solomon couldn't do better.

SYLVIA. I bow to your wisdom, and will love you as much as I like. But now another scruple gnaws at my spirit.

PRINCE. My dearest girl has as many scruples as the rose has petals. Tell me what this one is, and promise me it will be the last.

SYLVIA. I promise. What if people accuse me of being a fortune hunter?

PRINCE. They cannot make that accusation.

SYLVIA. Why not?

PRINCE. Because, if you had been a fortune hunter, you would have chosen the prince rather than one of his subjects.

SYLVIA. You are wise, my lord. But perhaps I failed to choose him because he never showed himself to me.

PRINCE. Now I tremble again. What if he suddenly appeared? Appeared and dazzled you?

SYLVIA. I'll make you so happy you'll never have to tremble again. Step back, my lord, and hear my solemn oath, which is (*she raises her hand*) that to my dying day I shall never love the—

PRINCE. Stop, Sylvia, stop, stop, stop! Don't complete your oath!

SYLVIA. Strange man! Why not?

PRINCE. Shall I let you swear against myself?

SYLVIA. Against yourself? Baron Belair, what do you mean?

(*Trivet trips in with the painting again*)

PRINCE. Do you recognize Poupon the Seventeenth?

SYLVIA. The revelation!

(*She kneels. Exit Trivet*)

PRINCE. Rise, Sylvia; rise, fair promise of Pouponaco. I concealed my rank up to this moment, so that I might come to know the real person you are, and owe your love only to my own.

SYLVIA. Oh, my prince, what an oath I was about to take! But now you are sure that I loved you for yourself, without mean ambition.

PRINCE. These words seal our marriage.

(*He kisses her. Enter Robin and Flaminia*)

ROBIN. I overheard you, Sylvia.

SYLVIA. Well then, I won't have to tell you what happened. The prince—yes, this is our prince—he will talk to you, because I am too troubled. Please come to an understanding. Explanations are beyond me. What would you tell me? That I've left you. What would I answer? That it's true. Let's pretend that you've said it and that I've answered, and then—console yourself as best you can.

PRINCE. Calm yourself, beloved. Flaminia, I place Count Robinet in your hands. Count, take Flaminia, marry her, and enjoy the good will of your prince forever. Yes, dearest Sylvia, that is how our whirling hearts and our uncertain destinies have finally come to rest.

ROBIN (*to Sylvia*). Shall we shake hands and be friends, you snake?

SYLVIA. Let's be friends and shake hands, you serpent.

(*They shake hands, look at each other, and run away in opposite directions*)

PRINCE. Flaminia, look on your prince as your eternally grateful benefactor.

(*Flaminia kneels and kisses the Prince's hand*)

FLAMINIA. It pleases me no end that my little... arrangements succeeded all around. (*She rises*) Go, my lord, go find your princess, and I my spouse.

(*Exeunt separately the Prince and Flaminia. The stage is empty. Enter Lisa*)

LISA. Is this any way of ending a comedy? Succeeded all around be hanged! What about me? I'm the prettiest girl in Pouponaco, bar none, if you know what I mean, and yet I have nothing whatever to show for it. My clever sister is flying so high, of course, that she forgets her poor—

(*Reenter Flaminia*)

FLAMINIA. Lisa dear!

LISA. Yes, sister.

FLAMINIA. Come here.

LISA. Yes, sister.

FLAMINIA. You look a little pinched. But I have an idea. Shall I marry you to, let me see, to Trivet?

LISA. To Trivet? How dare you!

FLAMINIA. Not so loud. Poupon is about to surprise him. In reward for his services, Trivet will be named tomorrow Lord Chamberlain of the realm, with an income of twenty thousand ducats. Good bye, Lisa; my big man is waiting for me.

(*Exit Flaminia*)
LISA. Hm.
(*Enter Trivet, wailing*)
TRIVET. Ay, ay, ay!
LISA. Trivet! What's the matter with you?
TRIVET. The matter with me is that I'm destined to stand at the precise spot where blows are handed out.
LISA. Poor man, let me rub your shoulder. Tell your Lisa what happened.
TRIVET. I ran into Dr. Vascularius, armed with his cane and spitting mad because I impersonated him. Feel the bump on my head. Ooooy!
LISA. Poor Trivet. I'll kiss it away. There. Come with me, I have something magical in my room that will heal you.
TRIVET. Have you? Ooyooyooo!
LISA. What now?
TRIVET. It hurts all over. Oh, I'll need large helpings of that magic!
(*Exeunt*)

The End

Notes

Lovers of French classic comedies will recognize that *Prince Poupon Needs a Wife* is unequivocally a reconception of *La Double inconstance* (1722), one of Marivaux's brilliant early plays. I translated *La Double inconstance* faithfully and literally many years ago for inclusion in my *Seven Comedies by Marivaux* (Cornell University Press), the first collection of his comedies ever published in the English language. That translation is the bedrock on which *Prince Poupon* is built. But built with enough differences to take its place, like my *Amphitryon*, among my own plays. *Prince Poupon Needs a Wife* was first published in my *Reinventions* (2002). It is presented here in a lightly improved version.

Production hints

Sylvia is beautiful, of course, but the audience must be made to feel at once that she will give Pouponaco the sturdy babies it wants. Flaminia is a few years older than Robin, but well under 30. Trivet is the oldest member of the cast. The comedy will be sharper if he is shorter than Lisa.

One expects a bevy of servants to come, go, announce, escort, and fetch and carry in any self-respecting princely palace. I have dispensed with them in the interest of thrift, but directors are to consider themselves free to call in as many of them as they please and can afford.

THE VIRGIN
AND THE UNICORN

(a fable with song and dance)

CHARACTERS

Umfrey, *Earl of Dumfrey*
Robert, *Baron Theefton*
Margaret, *the Earl's wife*
Basset, *the Earl's steward*
Clotilda Bennyworth, *daughter of the earl's late chamberlain*
Leofa, *the People's Delegate*
Peter, *a servant*
Gareth and Dagonet, *minstrels*

The action takes place in the Earl of Dumfrey's castle, during the reign of King Stephen the Second. The Earl, the Baron and Margaret are all in their early thirties; Clotilda is in her twenties; Basset is in his late fifties or early sixties.

SCENE ONE

(A large room, warmly and cheerfully furnished, in the ancestral home of the Earl of Dumfrey. One glimpses a balcony overlooking the grounds. The curtain rises on a tableau: Peter, the servant, is exhibiting a gored poodle to the Earl of Dumfrey, Baron Theefton, and Ralf Basset. Far away is heard the ugly trumpeting of the unicorn)

EARL *(appalled)*. Another one!

BARON. Very strange indeed. I must believe you now, my dear Umfrey. But do pull yourself together.

EARL. How can I? Wherever I turn, nothing but gored poodles, gored kittens, gored cows, horses, sheep, we even found a gored canary. God only knows how it happened. *(Trumpeting again)* Listen to the horrible beast.

BASSET *(gloomily)*. Two thousand gored chickens. Our farmers are being pauperized. Whose poodle is it this time, Peter?

PETER. Lady Ann's, Master Basset.

EARL. Oh no! My wife's best friend. Has she been told?

PETER. Indeed she has, my lord. Lady Ann is in bed under sedation.

EARL. Oh my God, my God. Take the horrible thing away.

BARON *(who has been examining the poodle)*. A clean penetration through the abdomen. A circular perforation of an inch and a quarter on one side of the poodle, and of something less than an inch on the other. This is no rapier thrust, Umfrey.

EARL. Robert—

BASSET *(to the baron)*. My lord Theefton, allow Peter to take the poodle away. His lordship cannot bear—

BARON. Oh, of course, of course. *(Basset motions Peter away)*

EARL *(weakly)*. And bring us something to drink, Peter. Something strong.

PETER. Yes, my lord.

(He leaves with the poodle)

EARL. So there it is. I'm deadly white from head to toe, my hands are chilly. I'll have grey hair before my time.

BASSET. Not so, my lord. A cup of wine will restore you.

EARL. Good Ralf Basset. I'm beginning to understand it your way. And mark my words. If all men, bar none, had resembled you in this miserable earldom of mine, the unicorn would never have appeared to make life bitter to me.

BARON. What on earth do you mean, Umfrey? What has Master Basset got to do with the unicorn?

BASSET. Nothing, my lord.

EARL. No, tell him, let him understand it too.

BASSET. It's only a personal notion.

EARL. Personal nothing. When our common everyday wickedness rises, says Basset, when people become even less tolerable than they usually are, a sort of malevolence accumulates, like a foul pressure on the heavens, and then—it's happened before, you know—read the chronicles.

BARON. My friends, this animal has really gone too far if it has gored your brains as well.

EARL. You don't understand, Robert—lucky passer-by—you come and pay us a visit—jolly, dressed to kill, swimming in perfume, the song leaping from your lips like a kitten off a window-sill—you don't know the darkness of it all.

BARON. Nonsense, I'm still waiting to hear how this unpleasant unicorn is connected with our good Ralf Basset.

EARL. Good Ralf Basset—there's your answer. If we were all as good as he — don't you understand?

BARON. No, I don't.

BASSET. Perhaps later, my lord. I am deeply embarrassed.

EARL. Let the wicked be embarrassed, and in the highest places, not you! Wicked deeds, wicked thoughts—greed, ambition, envy, lust (*he groans*)—they begin to exceed the permitted excess—no innocence is left except here and there (*taking Basset's arm*)—and suddenly the unicorn appears, someone sees his long thin horn peering into a farmyard, the alarm is sounded, mothers call their children indoors, everyone is afraid of the dark—and yet for some reason the unicorn never kills people, he kills their livelihood, their pets—like the poodle....

BASSET. He exists because there are people; perhaps that's why he spares us.

EARL. Who knows? But when he arrives, the world becomes unhinged. Wives murder their husbands. People refuse to pay taxes. Rain falls on my fireworks. Merchants break contracts. Poverty spreads over the land. King Stephen demands fresh levies. Thank God, here's Peter again.

(*Enter Peter with refreshments. He serves the Earl and the Baron*)

EARL. Where is my wife, Peter?

PETER. Lady Margaret is in her Garden of Exotics, my lord, but she intends to call on Lady Ann as soon as Lady Ann regains consciousness. Water as usual, sir Ralf?

THE VIRGIN AND THE UNICORN

(*He pours water for Basset and exits*)

BARON. Water, Master Basset? The man who oversees the barrels in the earl's cellar? The lord of spigots?

BASSET. It's not that I'm not fond of wine, my lord; nor that I *am* fond of water. The truth is, I used to press the grape rather too freely, if anything.

EARL. Couldn't bear to see the wicked lot of us, that was why.

BASSET: Really, my lord! I simply swore to my poor wife on her deathbed to give it up. It's an old story, not worth telling.

BARON. Very touching, my dear Basset. I adore principles! Well, Umfrey, let the two of us sinners drink to the downfall of the unicorn. One of your men is bound to catch him sooner or later, and you'll be nailing his horn over your mantelpiece before the month is out.

BASSET. A man can never catch the unicorn, my lord.

BARON. Nonsense. And if one man can't, a dozen will.

BASSET. Not a dozen, nor a thousand. Only a virgin can.

BARON. A what?

BASSET. A virgin. Carrying a mirror in her hand, and walking at random in field or forest. She prays to the Holy Mother of God, and perhaps the unicorn appears. If he does, she turns the mirror to the beast, its face is caught, and it cannot move away from its image. Then she walks backward, holding the mirror steady to the unicorn, and the beast follows, fascinated. It is the purity of the glass and the virgin's purity it follows, and it follows wherever she goes until she leads it to the men who kill it. But all this happens only perhaps.

BARON. Only perhaps what? Why haven't you sent a battalion of virgins out, for God's sake, each one holding up a dressing-room mirror?

EARL. Oh, the things he doesn't know!

BASSET. Only a virgin can catch the unicorn, my lord, but a virgin does not *necessarily* catch it. God must decide. Do you see the difficulty? You send a girl out, mirror in hand. A girl with a reputation. A marriageable girl. But suppose she fails to catch the unicorn. Perhaps the time had not come. But perhaps, on the other hand—

BARON. I see. (*A light comes*) I see!

BASSET. Now everybody wonders—is she, or isn't she? Father and mother lose their sleep, enemies chuckle, fingers are pointed, quarrels break out. One daren't ask any girl—almost (*the Earl looks uncomfortable*).

BARON. I have an idea!

EARL. I'm sure we've tried it, Robert; he's *our* unicorn, you know.

BARON. Don't you want to hear it?

EARL (*wearily*). Of course we do.

BARON. Why not send out a girl ten years old? It's so simple, and so sublimely obvious, that it probably never occurred to any of you. A ten-year-old girl, carefully chosen, is sure to be immaculate, and would certainly not object to being thought so.

BASSET. I'm afraid—

EARL. Poor Robert, do you take the unicorn for a fool? A ten-yearold girl!

BARON. Or nine.

EARL. I'd laugh if I weren't on the edge of a breakdown. Leave me to my gloom. (*To himself*) My guilty gloom.

BASSET (*low*). Your idea is astute, my lord—

BARON. But?

BASSET. Ten-year-old, or nine-year-old girls have no effect on a unicorn. For him, a virgin is a girl who might be no virgin if she chose. You see the point, my lord: there has to be merit in it. Otherwise it's like asking a cat not to bark.

BARON. I give up. Maybe I shouldn't have come.

EARL. Don't say that, Robert. You're my best friend, you know. We'll go hawking again together.

BASSET. My lord—

EARL. Oh God, I forgot, the hawks are gored. As for the foxes—I shouldn't have written you at all.

BARON. Tush. I wanted to help. Provide you with ideas. When you sent a message about the unicorn, and about Lady Margaret's favorite greyhound—remember, I have known Margaret forever, we grew up together—I dropped everything, I rushed here with hardly an attendant. I am at your service, Umfrey; the ancient oath, baron to earl, and all the rest.

EARL. Have another cup of wine, Robert.

(*He sits down heavily in a chair. Loud boos are heard outside*)

EARL *and* BARON. What's that?

BASSET. I'll go see. (*He goes out to the balcony*) Merciful heavens!

EARL. What now? And do I have to know it?

BASSET. It's Clotilda!

(*The Earl gets up as if stung, then doesn't know what to say*)

BARON. Clotilda?

EARL (*feebly*). Bennyworth. The daughter of our late chamberlain....

BARON. I must see this. (*He rushes to the balcony*). Ha! Why is that mob booing her? Somebody threw a lump of mud!

EARL. No....

BARON. Handsome girl! Look at her! Watch her walking absolutely *through* them! Magnificent! (*Shouting*) Rabble! Umfrey, do something! Wait—I think she's come in at the gate. I can't see her anymore.

BASSET. Yes, she has come in.

(*Both have now re-entered the room*)

EARL. Is she safe? Where's the crowd now? What are they doing?

BASSET. They have dispersed, my lord.

BARON. You look petrified, Umfrey. What is going on? I insist on being told.

BASSET (*discreetly*). A very sad affair, my lord. Bennyworth, our chamberlain, clamored to have his daughter dispatched to find the unicorn. It was a point of honor for him. Perhaps ambition. And we dispatched her. Lord Dumfrey was most reluctant—most, most reluctant: he has such delicate feelings. He struggled, but to refuse outright was impossible—as bad as expressing an open and official doubt about the purity of the Bennyworth family. Well, she was dispatched, and she returned without. It means nothing, you understand, the Immaculate Saint Hilda, our patroness in heaven, might have failed too, if I may so express it, but the people do not make fine discriminations—and even in better circles—in short, a few well-bred snickers killed our chamberlain. The mother, thank God, had been mercifully dead for years. (*To the Earl*) My lord, calm yourself, I beg you. You are not even remotely to blame; on the contrary, everyone knows how generously, how persistently, you opposed poor Bennyworth, how you begged him not to send the girl.

BARON. It's obvious you did your best, old man. Come on, what's done is done. The storm will blow over; it's only the first—

(*Enter Clotilda Bennyworth. She glides in with a look of mournful reproach, and sits down on a stool in a corner. General silence. Then Basset rushes over to her and kisses her hand*)

BASSET. My poor dear child.

CLOTILDA. Always kind, Master Basset. There's a tear in your eye! You at least are a man I can count on.

BASSET. Always, my dear; I look on you as my adopted daughter.

CLOTILDA. For everybody else I am a nuisance, or worse.

EARL (*softly*). Did anyone hurt you, Clotilda?

CLOTILDA. Since when does it matter?

BASSET. Shameful, shameful.

CLOTILDA. No one raised his voice to protect me.

BARON. It came and went so fast—I—

EARL. Oh, Robert, Baron Theefton, my oldest friend. Mistress Clotilda Bennyworth, daughter of our late chamberlain.

BARON. Honored.

CLOTILDA. I am happy to meet you, my lord. I knew you had arrived.

BARON. Look on me, my dear lady, as a champion ready to defend your fair

name against any dastardly imputations.
CLOTILDA. Thank you, my lord.
BARON. The Turks, I assure you, have more than once felt my—
(*Another clamor outside*)
EARL. What now? What now?
(*The Baron and Basset rush to the balcony again. Their backs are turned to Clotilda and the Earl*)
EARL (*pathetically*). Clotilda....
CLOTILDA (*fiercely*). Kiss me.
BASSET (*leaning over the balcony*). What happened? Leofa, I see you! I'm holding you responsible! You were dispersing five minutes ago. What did you say?
(*Meanwhile the Earl, one eye to the balcony, embraces Clotilda with passion and reluctance*)
CLOTILDA. Again. Villain! Again. Coward!
BASSET. Speak up down there!
A VOICE. It's the unicorn!
BARON (*turning about, but the Earl has jumped away in time*). Another killing!
EARL. Oh no!
BASSET. I am afraid so. The man Leofa is coming up.
BARON (*still on the balcony, joyously*). And I see my Lady Margaret!
EARL. I don't want to know what happened.
(*Enter Leofa*)
LEOFA. She done it again, and here she is, the vamp, and she done it again. Your lordships, I saloote you with respeck.
BARON (*coming into the room*). Who is this oaf?
LEOFA. This oaf is sincerely yours, Leofa, the People's Delegate, and I ain't come to see your worship but the Earl of Dumfrey, head of the legally constitooted government of this here earldom.
EARL (*weakly*). Well, I insist that you speak courteously to everybody in this room, and everybody means everybody.
LEOFA. In that case and speakin' courteously to everybody in this room, I announce that your lady's favorite foal, my lord, was gored till death ensued a half hour ago, and standin' for the people I say that if it wasn't for the unsavory likes of her, (*pointing to Clotilda*) still speakin' courteously to everybody, we wouldn't have no bleedin' unicorns running through the edibles of the land. The people has spoke.
EARL. The white foal is gored?
LEOFA. Yes, sir. Till death ensued.
CLOTILDA. Is that all you can think of, my lord, a stupid horse, while this baboon stands here insulting me?
EARL. I'm sorry....

LEOFA. "Baboon" is undemocratic.

BARON. I'd gladly have one of my footmen thrash him, madam, but alas, I have come here practically unattended, and my rank prevents me from doing it myself.

LEOFA. Excuse me, sir, but no stranger 'as the right to thrash the common people; that's the prevocative of 'is own beloved overlord.

BASSET. All right, Leofa, but you've gone too far this time. What on earth has Mistress Clotilda got to do with the unicorn? You know as well as I do that the unicorn appeared weeks before she—to make a long story short, one thing has nothing to do with the other. I have explained the logic of it a dozen times.

LEOFA. Nevertheless we the people has got a feeling that wickedness and wickedness goes hand in hand.

BASSET. What wickedness? For the life of me, use logic, man!

LEOFA. Logic is all right for them what can afford luxuries. The people has got feelings, and the feeling today is that it's time the land was purgated. We demand morality in 'igh places. And there's some in our midst that mutter still worse.

EARL. What do they mutter?

LEOFA. I'm not with 'em, mind you, I'm just reportin'.

EARL (*anxiously*). Well, out with it.

LEOFA. Look at 'er smilin' while the people manhandle her. Anybody but a witch would have a good cry and run for her life. That's what some of 'em are sayin'.

CLOTILDA. Will you tolerate this, my lord?

EARL. Certainly not.

BARON. Scandalous!

LEOFA. I was only reportin', your lordships, and all inside the circle of respeck I owe to one and all.

BARON. The ruffian!

BASSET. Here's half a crown, Leofa. Now go away.

LEOFA. You're a sensible man, anyway, Master Basset. I meant no 'arm. Hoo, here's Lady Margaret now; watch your manners, everybody.

(*Enter Lady Margaret*)

LADY MARGARET. Simply incredible!

EARL. We've heard the terrible news, my dear.

BARON. My dear Lady Margaret, I was struck dumb. Your favorite foal. I feel as though a child of mine had been gored. I could weep.

LEOFA. Me too.

CLOTILDA. Please accept my condolences, Lady Margaret. (*Lady Margaret snubs her*)

LADY MARGARET (*to the Baron*). Thank you, Lord Theefton. Peacefully at pasture she was, in the innocent blue of the day: then all of a sudden gored to oblivion. Is there a God, I ask you? As for Lady Ann, she has simply taken to her bed. What do you mean to do about it, Umfrey? The cup is overflowing at last.

EARL. I'll call another meeting of my knights—an urgent session.

LADY MARGARET. I give up. And why is this peasant allowed in the castle? Mud wherever he has set his boots.

LEOFA. Honest earth, my lady.

BASSET. That's enough, Leofa. Out you go.

LEOFA. The people condole, my lady, but they want a return to morality, and causes removed. Your lordships—

(*Exit*)

LADY MARGARET. Something to drink, if you please. I can't breathe.

(*The Baron rushes a refreshment to her*)

BASSET. If only people were a little kinder. I speak in general.

CLOTILDA. If they were kinder to defenseless girls.

LADY MARGARET (*under her breath*). Hah, this is too much! (*Aloud*) Umfrey, a person doesn't know where to turn anymore. Do you realize that I saw Princess born and that I could practically *talk* to her? It's as if the only creature who ever loved me had died.

EARL *and* BARON. Come now, really!

LADY MARGARET. Honest animal affection, without deceit, without secrets.

EARL. Still, you have your hothouse of Exotics to distract you, my dear. (*He nudges the Baron*)

LADY MARGARET. The simple love of an uncomplicated beast.

BARON. I've longed before everything to be allowed a peek at your famous hothouse, Lady Margaret. These violent plants, these poisonous flowers, these crawling grappling choking vines—what splendid lessons they teach us.

EARL. You really must show them to Robert, my dear. It will take your mind off the tragic event. And the best time is now.

BASSET. It is indeed, my lady.

LADY MARGARET. Are you really interested?

BARON. Interested, interested? Lady Margaret, a higher gratification mortal man could not endure.

LADY MARGARET. Very well. (*In a different tone*). Yes! It *will* distract me a little. Yes! By all means.

EARL. And by tomorrow, after my nap, you will see measures taken. An iron fist—
LADY MARGARET. Yes, dear. Call your lazy knights again. The unicorn will be terrified. Follow me, Lord Theefton.
(*The two leave. There is a moment of silence. Churchbells ring*)
BASSET (*going to the balcony*). Another penitential procession. The good people assembling before the church. (*He returns to the room*)
CLOTILDA. The good people. I still shudder at the words I heard. They're ready to burn me as a witch.
BASSET. My dear Clotilda, no harm will come to you, believe me. The people are a little excited, of course. But I myself, with my lord's permission, stand between your innocence and the world. And I sincerely hope that Lord Dumfrey is your protector as well.
EARL. Of course, of course.
BASSET. My lord, I am going to speak frankly before Clotilda. I am disappointed in—how shall I put it?—in your inaction.
EARL. I am calling a meeting to—
BASSET. No, my lord, you know perfectly well that I am not talking about *that* inaction, but about your immobility with regard to my adopted Clotilda. (*The churchbells ring again*) She is being treated rudely—beyond toleration—by the common folk in the streets—and by persons of higher rank—in this very room, I'll make bold to say—but, be that as it may, I look in vain for a firmer stand on your part, a public declaration of your faith in the young lady's innocence. Listen to these bells, Lord Dumfrey. Think of your father who wore the cross under the gates of Jerusalem. Think of the founder of your line who baptized the heathen Saxons. Think of our faith in you, and then call out to the people, "As you love me and as you take pride in my righteousness, so shall you believe in her chastity!"
EARL. Why doesn't lightning strike me now?
BASSET. Strike *you*, my lord? Our beloved ruler?
EARL. Stop, stop....
BASSET. Have I said too much?
EARL. Too much, oh too much! I must speak.
CLOTILDA (*frightened*). Umfrey!
BASSET (*staring at Clotilda*). "Umfrey"?!?!
EARL. Basset—Clotilda—I warned you many times—it can't be hidden forever! My righteousness, her—! Daggers into my flesh! Clotilda and I—I and Clotilda—yes—
BASSET. No.
EARL. Thank God, I've told you, of all men. I feel better already, but the

unicorn is my fault, I bear the guilt. I know I'm not the only transgressor in the land, but I am the ruler, in me it counts more heavily. What can I do? I am bewitched by the poor girl, I tremble when I see her—love and desire tear me to shreds, I wrong my wife, my innocent wife—

CLOTILDA. Umfrey, this is too much!

BASSET. This is a nightmare....

EARL. It is. Oh Basset, I know I am the most hell-ridden man of the kingdom.

CLOTILDA. So! Now your steward knows it all. I hope you're happy. But what good it will do me I don't know. *(She sits down with her back to the men)*

BASSET. I wish I had died ignorant of this. I who loved and respected you, my lord. I'm in a daze. Bennyworth! My lord, you knew all the time—to put it mildly!—and yet when Bennyworth made his daughter look for the unicorn, you relented and let her go.

EARL. I had no choice! I would have insulted the poor misguided man beyond recovery if I had refused to send her out. I didn't know then that people would hound her to the stake with evil suspicions. *(Resolutely)* My friend, I have not made my confession in a fit of weakness. Here is my unshakable decision. You shall tell me and Clotilda what to do.

BASSET. Undo the sins you have committed. Be sinless and kill the unicorn. But first, my lord, allow me to speak alone with Clotilda.

EARL. By all means; an excellent first step. Clotilda, look at us, and see that you obey Master Basset, no matter what.

(He leaves. Clotilda and Basset stare at each other. Basset looks for words)

BASSET. Clotilda, have you ever been to Paris?

CLOTILDA. No, sir.

BASSET. Paris is an extremely remarkable city. Infinitely more diverting for beautiful young women than our obscure earldom of Dumfrey. We have heard of Paris, but has Paris heard of us?

CLOTILDA. I don't suppose it has.

BASSET. Now as my lord's chief steward, I think I can promise you the most comfortable conveyance to the French capital, and the richest entertainment upon your arrival. You will lodge with the Comtesse du Jolimot, who is our blood relation there.

CLOTILDA. Thank you, but no.

BASSET. Why not? Hers is one of the finest houses in Paris.

CLOTILDA. Thank you, but no, I'm not going to Paris, Master Basset.

BASSET. Dresses, servants, balls, opportunities for an advantageous marriage, what more can a girl want? You are an orphan, my dear.

CLOTILDA. I am not leaving the earl.

BASSET. This touches me, Clotilda. A charming first love! It is something I respect and even envy a little, being an old man. But alas, my child, you cannot love the earl without wounding his wife.

CLOTILDA. His wife! It's a pleasure to wound her, it's my one consolation.

BASSET. Isn't she a little jealous of you? Even without knowing? These are feelings that bestir themselves within us sometimes before our conscious minds are alerted. But let us leave Lady Margaret aside. You are harming the earl, you are harming yourself, and didn't your hidden deeds help bring the curse of the unicorn on our heads? Because the earl is right. The sins of the great weigh more heavily. Believe me, my child, you will love again. It seems impossible to you now, you feel that all you possess of love has gone irrevocably to his lordship, but you will be surprised, I promise, one year, two years from now, (*Clotilda yawns discreetly*) when you discover that a new power to love has replaced the old; the dry well has slowly and imperceptibly replenished itself. Go, my child, leave us for three months, try, and then we shall consider again what to do.

CLOTILDA. No, Master Basset, your words sound like a very beautiful book, but I am attached to the earl; here I am, and here I stay. I have my reasons.

BASSET. Something I don't know? Are you—?

CLOTILDA. No I am not.

BASSET. Anything else? This amazing passion—

CLOTILDA. Why amazing? I love the earl, I am all his, he is mad about me, and I won't budge, I am going to make my way right here.

BASSET. Make your way?

CLOTILDA. I mean, love where I love.

BASSET. But suppose a terrible scandal breaks out?

CLOTILDA. I don't care.

BASSET. How can that be?

CLOTILDA. Please, Master Basset, you who handle deeds and contracts and settlements all day long! The earl loves me so tremendously, and I love him too with all my might, isn't he bound to do something for me? Even if there's a scandal? Especially if there's a scandal?

BASSET (*groaning*). Heavenly angels.

CLOTILDA. Now you'll go and misunderstand me again. I would die for the earl, I'd do anything for him, I'm sure I can never love anybody again, exactly as you said, but I'm an orphan, you made a very special point of that yourself. Who knows what would happen in Paris-the earl might forget me. No, I don't like to gamble.

BASSET. Whereas here you hold the trump card in your hand.

CLOTILDA. Here I know the rules of the game.

BASSET. What are you hoping for?

CLOTILDA. As the earl's mistress—
BASSET. Brazen girl!
CLOTILDA. I don't care. I have my dreams. An orphan has to protect herself. Everybody hates me. (*Almost whispering into Basset's ear*) But one day I shall live in my own manor.
(*She glides out*)
BASSET. I have heard too much today.... I wish I were a hundred miles away.... Poor Lady Margaret! Peter! What now? What now?
(*Enter Peter, holding a gored sheep in his hand*)
PETER. The last sheep of the earl's last flock.
BASSET (*sinking into a chair*). I am no longer surprised.

SCENE TWO

(*The hothouse of Exotics. Lady Margaret is guiding Lord Theefton*)

LADY MARGARET (*snipping a leaf off a flowering plant*). It has the softest fur. There. (*She rubs it against the Baron's cheek*)
BARON (*ravished but nervous*). Amazing. Yes. Again....
LADY MARGARET. Isn't it?
BARON. Yes. One hardly—it's altogether.... What is the plant?
LADY MARGARET. The *Kalosperma impudens*.
BARON (*wiping his brow*). Kalosperma..... How do you do. (*He titters*)
LADY MARGARET. Observe its flower. These long supple filaments, reaching anxiously over the corolla.
BARON. What are they, Lady Margaret? I am full of scientific wonder.
LADY MARGARET. They are simply the stamens. The male organs.
BARON. Oh yes.
LADY MARGARET. The flower is a sexual animal, why deny it? Even we women learn to speak with erudite detachment, we name the parts, we observe the actions—well, perhaps we do feel a tiny shiver trespassing on our composure—but we no longer blush—that is the beauty of science.
BARON. Admirable.... Science doesn't blush.... (*He feels the stamens with his palm*)
LADY MARGARET. They tickle. (*He giggles*) Look close. (*She bends close to him over the flower*) Each filament bears its bud, swollen, distended with the male particles, the pollen, and waiting for a touch to break open, and to pour

itself out. Poof!

BARON. The little rogue!

LADY MARGARET (*moving to another flower*). And yet this one is even more fascinating. Really shameless. Look at this elongated pistil, erect in the calyx. For a flower!

BARON. Yes, for a flower—quite shameless—

LADY MARGARET. We call it the *Priapisca vehemens*. But I'll surprise you, my lord. This is a female flower.

BARON. This? This.... thing? Female?

LADY MARGARET. Nature is a brawl, a tumult, Lord Theefton. Expect anything. The pistil contains the flower's womb. Feel it. Do, my lord.

BARON. Almost —ye gods—

LADY MARGARET. Like flesh. (*The Baron wipes his brow*) When the plant is ready, when the time of desire comes upon it, the time of fruition, why not call it the time of love?

BARON. Exactly—the scientific term.

LADY MARGARET. The pistil grows, it lifts itself stiffly and yearningly, it seeks and we might even say it calls for the pollen, namely through the perfume it secretes. There is no modesty, no hypocritical reticence here. Come to me, the flower cries. I want you to stroke the tip with your finger, Lord Theefton.

BARON. Oh!

LADY MARGARET (*laughing warmly*). What you feel is the pistil's secretion over its thousand fine hairs—the damp warm cushion which retains and sucks in the pollen. As for the pollen itself—but you're uncomfortable, my dear friend, your face is flushed—perhaps—?

BARON. No—not at all! Margaret—Lady Margaret—go on!

LADY MARGARET. I hardly know—should we?

BARON. Yes yes! You were saying....

LADY MARGARET. Something about the male granule that lies here. Suddenly it wakes into activity, it sends a long slender finger deep into this pulp until it meets the ovule in its sack. And there the impregnation occurs, the sweet consummation blessed by Nature.

BARON. Dear Nature! (*He leans over another flower*)

LADY MARGARET. Not so close, my lord!

BARON (*jumping back*). What did I do?

LADY MARGARET. You were inhaling the *Iasonus sceleratus*. Some say one shouldn't....

BARON. Shouldn't? Why not?

LADY MARGARET. Its perfume.... What shall I say?... The Persians chew its petals for—for unmentionable purposes. It seems to me that merely breathing it—(*She breathes it*)

BARON (*weakly*). Merely breathing it—like this—

LADY MARGARET (*weakly*). The people call it St. Anthony's bane.

BARON (*weakly*). St. Anthony's bane?

LADY MARGARET (*weakly*). They say that St. Anthony himself couldn't have resisted the fragrance. Even I....

BARON. Even you?

LADY MARGARET. Perhaps I shouldn't have come so near. If only.... But we must be detached, we must.

BARON. Must we? Margaret....

LADY MARGARET. And yet, if one could be like this exotic twiner, the *Lekkerkuss gloriosus*. Watch the curling tendrils, see how they reach out towards a stem as if in adoration—and when they find it—

BARON. And when they find it? What then?

LADY MARGARET. They grasp it quickly, violently—because they are fearless—because they know no law or prohibition—because they need-need-need, and what they need—

BARON. They take!

(*He flings himself on Lady Margaret and kisses her passionately*)

LADY MARGARET. My lord!

BARON. Margaret! My Margaret! I am your tendril! I need you and I take you!

LADY MARGARET. Robert!

BARON. Yes, call me Robert, and you—my love, let me kiss you again, my flower, my nectar, my perfume—

LADY MARGARET. Robert, if I had known... What is happening? Where am I? Robert! Since when?

BARON. Since always! Can you ask? I could bear it no longer at Theefton. Surely you know why I came here. The unicorn was a pretext. Too many years had gone by. Oh Margaret, Margaret, Fate came between us.

LADY MARGARET. Not so loud, my friend, hush, there are people nearby.

BARON. My goddess, confess it now that you love me. Ah these blessed flowers! You answered my kisses, you didn't thrust me away, you wanted me to grasp you in my arms! "What they need, they take!"

LADY MARGARET (*weakly*). No, Robert.... I meant the plants....

BARON. Didn't we play together as children, years before Umfrey saw you, and hadn't we celebrated a solemn mock wedding in the rose garden, you were eight, I was nine....

LADY MARGARET. How was I to know this meant anything to you? Or that you'd remember these childish promises?

BARON. Oh Margaret, that was the culmination of my life—at nine—I have remembered nothing else. You were my wife from that holy afternoon forth. You the heiress of Wyngham, Brigsley, Tuckbetter and Glaswin Epton, I heir to the barony of Theefton—our lands, too, lying amorously flank to flank. But then—miserable times—you were orphaned. King Stephen gave you to Umfrey—to my friend! I bowed, I wept, I withdrew, I decayed. But now—look down, ye gods, Margaret is in my arms again.

LADY MARGARET. A married woman, Robert.

BARON. Bitterness! And I must think of you lying in his bed at night—or day!—oh God!—

LADY MARGARET. You mustn't torment yourself, Robert; and you needn't. But hush, we were looking at my specimens. My lovely flowers, my only consolations....

BARON. Wait, Margaret. You said, "you needn't." Why "you needn't"?

LADY MARGARET. It must have escaped me. Don't probe, Robert, for the sake of our happy childhood. Leave an aging woman to tend her griefs alone.

BARON. Griefs? You *will* tell me! I'm on fire, I could smash walls with my bare fists, I am Hercules, confide in me, here, rest your marvelous head on my shoulder.

LADY MARGARET. Oh Robert, if only I had a trusted friend.

BARON. Look at me. I would leap into a gulf full of crocodiles to rescue a hairpin that belonged to you! Tell me, tell me what it is that weighs on your soul, beautiful Margaret.

LADY MARGARET. Hide my face.... Robert, listen....

BARON. Speak to me.

LADY MARGARET (*in a whisper*). I am not my husband's wife.

BARON (*astounded*). What are you? Who is your husband's wife? Tell me! Tell me, do. Who is his wife?

LADY MARGARET. Clotilda.

BARON. Clotilda Bunny, Benny—the girl?

LADY MARGARET. Yes.

BARON. Is his mistress?

LADY MARGARET. His wife.

BARON. I'm lost. Are they secretly married?

LADY MARGARET. No, they are not married, and yet she is his wife, and his only wife.

BARON. His only wife! And you?

LADY MARGARET. I am the maiden Countess of Dumfrey.

BARON. Maiden!

LADY MARGARET. Maiden.

BARON. And I am Robert newborn, newborn this instant! I am forming my first thoughts on this earth! I will liberate you! Before God, you are not married, and never were. You revert to me! Exact an annulment at once.

LADY MARGARET. Umfrey will fight it. He has my lands, Robert, he is in love with my lands.

BARON. Villain! I had forgotten your lands.

LADY MARGARET. I could prove his—but that's too loathsome—a medical inquiry—reports to the Pope—

BARON. Odious! I forbid it. But something must be done! I am lashing my brain. Sooner or later it will produce ideas. It always does.

LADY MARGARET. I have had years to produce ideas.

BARON. Margaret! Your eyes tell me you have found the way.

LADY MARGARET. Perhaps. The way—a difficult way—I would need all your courage, your—

BARON. Love! My love! My invincible love! Into my arms! (*He kisses her*) Use me, I am but the extension of your thought and the execution of your will.

LADY MARGARET. Dear, dear Robert. Could it be that we are meant to be happy yet?

BARON. Here is my oath. By all the saints, Robert shall be twined about Margaret like the—name it for me, my soul.

LADY MARGARET. The *Lekkerkuss gloriosus*.

BARON. Amen. Now; what must I do?

LADY MARGARET. Nothing. The first action is mine, and I have the courage for it at last. Oh I was so miserably alone!

BARON. Angel!

LADY MARGARET. But now all is changed. I shall go into the forest with a mirror in my hand—

BARON. And hunt the unicorn! Divine virgin, the unicorn will be yours. How did I fail to think of it! You will capture the unicorn, you of all maidens will not fail! Destiny speaks! And the world will know that you are no man's wife. Your false husband will be unmasked. The false marriage will be dissolved. Margaret and her true Robert will be joined, stamen to pistil. The archbishop will bless their union. And happiness seasoned with revenge shall fill the bowl of our lives. My wife! (*They embrace*)

LADY MARGARET. Be careful! Somebody is approaching. It's our steward. Here is a little door. Do nothing, and above all, say nothing to anyone; leave everything to me.

BARON. I will, I will. Once more? (*He offers to embrace her*)

LADY MARGARET. Patience.
(*With a finger across her lips, she leaves*)
BARON (*alone*). Heavenly Margaret is mine! Wyngham's grazing lands are mine! The mills of Brigsley are mine! Tuckbetter's corn is mine! The waters of Glaswin Epton are mine! Glaswin Epton, where Ecgfrith defeated Wulfhere in the year 671, and where Theefton overthrows Dumfrey today. Baron cuts down earl, oh savory hierarchical revenge, and even better, I best my best friend. I can't stand the joy of it, I want to write epics, I could drink the North Sea, I'll sneeze a mountain away. Whom can I tell? Halloo, here comes the dear honest fellow. Ralf Basset, here I am, were you looking for me?
(*Enter Basset, very glum. The Baron sings*)
        This way, fair maiden, to your lover's arms.

BASSET. I was looking for Lady Margaret.
BARON. The divine Margaret has just left, after giving me a lesson in rare plants I shall never forget.
(*Singing*)
        This way, fair maiden, to your lover's arms;
        Your lover with impatience sighs.

BASSET. You seem very happy, my lord.
BARON. I seem because I am and I am because I love.
BASSET (*more glum than ever*). You too. The place is being smothered with love. (*Sarcastically*) I suppose, my lord, you will tell me that you are in love with Lady Margaret, who has adored you since childhood.
BARON. You knew it? Ay! (*Putting his hand over his mouth*)
BASSET. What??! I was joking!
BARON. Ha ha ha, you drew it out of me without even trying! No, Basset, you were not joking, it's the power of your famous honesty, my friend, it gives you prophetic gifts in spite of yourself. Extend your hand to the happiest man in England!
BASSET (*pulling his hand away*). Is this *your* joke?
BARON. Joke? Let the world hear it is no joke. I mean to proclaim my love from this *Priapisca lekkerpuss* to the farthest star, not forgetting the Earl of Dumfrey on the way.
BASSET. I'll be insane before the day is out. However, love as much as you like, my lord; congratulations; but I trust my poor Lady Margaret has sense enough to see with her own eyes the difference—I say no more.
BARON (*stung*). Don't, my friend, because you happen to be right again, I

return the congratulations; she does see the difference with her own eyes—and with her own fresh lips—and with her own plump arms—here in the greenhouse she saw it ten minutes ago.

BASSET. Lady Margaret?

BARON. Lady Margaret.

BASSET. I don't believe it. But I admire your telling these stories to me, who have served Lord Dumfrey from the time he was a child.

BARON. Why shouldn't I? I know enough to freeze you all in your shoes. I have plucked the secrets of this house. I was not in the diplomatic corps for nothing. When I served in Norway—

BASSET. Bluff. You know no secrets—there are no secrets to know.

BARON. My dear Basset, your loyalty amuses me. But I know as well as I hope you do what connection exists between Lord Dumfrey and the sham virgin Clotilda.

BASSET (*astonished*). Who told you?

BARON (*laughing*). An angel—Lady Margaret.

BASSET. She knows? She knew? And she told you?

BARON. She knows, she knew, and she told me.

(*Singing*)
> Your lover with impatience sighs.
> Fair maiden, swiftly yield your charms—

Hmm, that heavenly fragrance. Marvelous flowers—the Arabs chew them for—for unmentionable purposes. I must have them at my wedding. Yes, Basset, I have culled the secrets of this house. Your loyalty is useless. Remember, I know who is the true virgin in this house, and I know who is the false virgin.

BASSET. I don't follow you.

BARON. Useless discretion. At the hour of my choosing, the public will be invited to inspect Umfrey's bedchamber. And I shall address them as follows: "Your master, good citizens and reverent judges, has failed to perform his conjugal duty even once in the five vacant years of his spurious marriage. Here, however, is Mistress Clotilda." And all the rest.

(*Singing*)
> Fair maiden, swiftly yield your charms,
> Else your woeful lover dies.

BASSET. Excuse me.... Failed to perform?.... Lord Dumfrey?

BARON (*suddenly solemn*). A crime, Basset; his soul and body are sold out to that witch Clotilda. Because of his greed for land and yet more land he tears Margaret from the bosom of her doting parents. Then he violates the sacrament for five unholy years—refuses to consummate—allows her to wither. Thank God the poor orphan preserved her purity, which now devolves on me.

BASSET (*weakly*). How, on you? What do you intend to do?

BARON. That is my secret. But as sure as the Pope and King Stephen are alive, Margaret will be mine, along with Wyngham, Brigsley, Tuckbetter, and Glaswin Epton.

BASSET (*flaring up*). This is plunder! Wyngham, Brigsley—vulgar plunder!

BARON (*offended*). Vulgar?

BASSET. Why didn't I see it before? The unhappy woman looking for comfort, staggering in the darkness, and stretching out her innocent hand to a smiling claw! However, there's still Ralf Basset. I'll make your designs public, Baron Theefton.

BARON. Piffle. Say one word, and I fling your master to the mob. But you misunderstand me. My designs are pure. I love Lady Margaret. We played together as children—this is sacred—I knew her long before Umfrey set eyes on her—we had exchanged oaths in a bower, she was seven and I was eight, the spirits of the woods were undoubtedly listening, we were Aeneas and Dido, only younger; the nymphs and the goblins declared that we should ultimately be united; for these lands, I ask you to note, these lands border upon mine, they are my natural extension. I am amputated without them.

BASSET. They also border upon this earldom.

BARON. But they bordered on me before Umfrey knew Margaret. No, my good Basset, this is the beginning of my ascent. The Theeftons are destined to eclipse the Dumfreys. Three weeks and two days after I was born, a bolt struck down the church steeple in Dumfrey Bottoms. The heavens don't speak in vain.

(*He sings*)

>Dame Fortune can whirl
>Baron to Earl,
>And one more fluke
>Turns Earl into Duke.

Shall I make cottage laws, do cornfield justice, educate muddy shanked milkmaids and build rotten windmills when I could be multiplying my estate and branding my name into the chronicles?

BASSET. My lord, I ask you to excuse me. You want no company just now to keep yourself entertained.

BARON. Wait. Let you and I be friends, Basset; I'm in a temper to have no enemies; may the sun shine on all men alike. Perhaps you should do something underhanded too, like the rest of us sinners. I think you'd feel more at home among us if you did.

BASSET. In plain words, are you suggesting an alliance between yourself and me?

BARON. Why not? I need good men. The Theeftons are obviously in the ascendant. And your master is beyond help. Oh you can warn him about me—much good may it do him! I'm galloping into the future; saddle your horse and ride after me before I'm out of sight.

BASSET (*going*). Excuse me.

BARON. Right you are; time to join our good friends again. I promised Umfrey I'd go trotting with him about the countryside. We might catch a glimpse of the unicorn. (*He laughs and puts his hand on Basset's shoulder*) Coming, Basset?

BASSET (*disengaging himself*). I was about to forget—I promised Lady Margaret to label a few of her plants. Go without me, my lord.

BARON. I will. Think of the Theeftons while you label away.

(*He leaves singing*)

BASSET (*watching him through the window*). Ruffian! Dancing down the path. What now? He's stopped by the roses. Plucks a rose and puts it in his sleeve. Sting him? Not Theefton, it wouldn't! Theefton is in the ascendant! Ha! He's leaping over the hedge with his arms out like a pair of wings! Enough, enough. (*He turns away and sits on a stool*) I've lived too long, I've heard too much.... Poor Lady Margaret, poor suffering woman....

SCENE THREE

(*Same as Act One. Next evening. The room is even warmer and more lovely in the evening than it was during the day. The Earl, the Baron, and Clotilda are playing cards*)

EARL. Don't we need more lights?

BARON (*ogling Clotilda*). Not in the least. This half darkness is enchanting. It sets a man dreaming. Perhaps a lady too?

CLOTILDA (*flirtatious*). Ladies have to be careful about dreaming, Lord Theefton. I open with six.

BARON. Charming!
EARL (*annoyed*). Well, I think it's getting too dark. Peter! More lights.
BARON. Three of spades.
CLOTILDA. I take two. My lord?
EARL. Snip with a jack.
BARON. Not bad. Another card for me.
(*Enter Peter with lights*)
EARL. Set them here, Peter. Is Lady Margaret still up and about?
PETER. I believe she has retired, my lord, but I'm not sure. Shall I inquire?
EARL. No, never mind.
PETER. Thank you, sir. (*He leaves*)
CLOTILDA. Double-hook and beat seven. Your turn, my lord.
EARL. Oh yes; I flip a queen of hearts.
BARON. I pass.
CLOTILDA. My lord?
EARL. Oh, one whiskey with the king.
BARON. I place five in a dash.
CLOTILDA (*triumphant*). Snip-snap!
EARL *and* BARON. Again!
EARL. The pot is yours.
(*Clotilda rakes it in and carefully puts the money in her purse*)
CLOTILDA. You're allowing your minds to drift tonight, gentlemen.
EARL. Oh, I don't know.
BARON (*ogling Clotilda*). I plead guilty. My mind is drifting, guess where? Mistress Clotilda, your bracelet is a marvel. May I?
(*He leans over her forearm*)
CLOTILDA (*charmingly*). Do you really like it? It's perhaps too brilliant for an orphan. A friend gave it to me. A *former* friend.
BARON. A friend who would resign himself to being your former friend, Clotilda, must be an unfeeling clod.
EARL (*extremely annoyed*). The game's over for tonight and thank God it's almost time for bed. Margaret must be waiting up for me.
BARON (*sarcastic*). Impatiently, I'm sure.
(*Enter Basset, carrying papers*)
BARON. Basset my friend, would you take Lord Dumfrey's place at the card table?
BASSET (*joylessly*). No thank you. I am working on the Dumfrey tercentenary celebrations.
EARL (*gloomily*). Celebrations.
BARON. They'll cheer you up, Umfrey. Your house is almost as ancient as

ours of Theefton. That's something to be proud of.

BASSET. A couple of minstrels have asked to be heard tonight, my lord. As they looked hungry, I took it upon myself to say yes.

EARL. A little music before bedtime can't do any harm. Or maybe it can. What else, Basset?

BASSET. Nothing, my lord. Leofa is down in the kitchen, grumbling among the cooks and the maids.

BARON. Why don't you hang the rascal, Umfrey?

CLOTILDA. That's what *I* would like to know.

BARON. I don't tolerate grumblers on my lands.

EARL. Good. But I'll thank you not to hang my taxpayers for me. (*Sound of the unicorn*) Oh my God, listen!

BARON. Fairly close, I'd say.

EARL. Merciful heaven, take this plague away and forgive us our sins.

BASSET (*muttering*). Deserve it first.

EARL. What did you say?

BASSET. Nothing, my lord. Allow me to work quietly in a corner.

EARL. In the dark?

BASSET. The darker the better.

(*The unicorn's trumpeting again, now very close indeed. Everyone is startled*)

EARL. Listen! The beast is in my park! Practically under the walls! Robert, go see. Basset—

(*The Baron and Basset rush to the balcony*)

EARL. This is for my sins. Witch! And flirting under my nose. But I'm sending you away.

CLOTILDA. You'll never send me away!

EARL. I will, I will!

(*Exclamations from the balcony*)

BARON. There! There! By the hedge! Beyond the basin!

EARL (*rising*). What? What do you see? Basset! (*re-enter Basset*) Your face is white. What did you see? Don't tell me....

(*Clotilda runs to the balcony*)

BASSET. My lord—the unicorn—

(*Clotilda screams*)

EARL. What? What?

(*The Baron re-enters, followed by Clotilda*)

BARON. The unicorn is caught!

EARL. Who—?

BASSET. Your wife....

BARON. Caught by Lady Margaret! Caught by a virgin! Tremble, Lord

Dumfrey!
CLOTILDA. This is a dirty scheme to ruin me, Umfrey! Your wife is leading in the unicorn and holding up a mirror as though she had caught him.
EARL (*choking*). Where is she going?
CLOTILDA. She's coming here. This is a plot devised against me.
BARON (*with a laugh*). On the contrary, my dear Clotilda; we're going to help you; be patient.
BASSET. He knows everything, my lord. So does your wife.
EARL. How?....
BARON. Brace yourself, Umfrey. Your unmarried wife has confessed herself to me. Leofa is in the house. Capitulate, or in a few minutes your People's Delegate will trumpet the news that Lady Margaret is a virgin.
EARL. Capitulate?
CLOTILDA. Umfrey, do something!
EARL. The world is coming to an end. How does Robert come into this? How did Margaret—? Explain, Basset, for the love of God! And why does this blackguard keep chuckling in my face?
BASSET. My lord, I too know more than what you chose to tell me. You kept the worst from me. Your neglect of Lady Margaret. The unhappy woman wants to save herself from all of you—villains—yes—I open my mouth and cry villains. You Lord Dumfrey—a shameful alliance—you Clotilda—
CLOTILDA. Nobody wants your sermons, my good man. Do something, Umfrey. She's in the castle now with the unicorn.
BARON. There's nothing to do for anyone.
BASSET. You, woman, seducing Lord Dumfrey to serve your ambition. And you, Lord Theefton—
BARON. I'm a guest.
BASSET. Playing with Lady Margaret's affections to swallow her estate—
EARL. My lands! He wants my lands! Never!
BARON. Too late, Umfrey, Margaret is mine!
EARL (*drawing his dagger and going for the Baron*). Not for long.
(*Clotilda screams and Basset interposes*)
BASSET (*loud*). Who are you to punish a man, sinner? (*The Earl's arm falls*) There is only one innocent being here—your wife—fumbling to save herself from the wolves!
CLOTILDA. Fiddlesticks!
EARL (*sinking into a chair*). Where is she? Go look, somebody. Oh God, what have I done with my life? Robert, what have I done to you?
BARON. You have done that you stole Margaret from me.
EARL. Villain!

BARON. I love her, she loves me, we were pledged to each other years before you knew her—I was twelve, she eleven—children, pure and prophetic. All is fulfilled. Umfrey, the time has come to yield up your so-called wife, declare the so-called marriage null, and restitute the lands you took from her. If you refuse, out with it all, the whole revolting story, your sordid affair with Clotilda—

CLOTILDA. Protect me!

BARON. All of it conveyed to King Stephen. You'll roll from your chair of state straight to the Tower.

(*The door opens. Enter Lady Margaret*)

EARL (*with his last breath*). Where is the unicorn?

LADY MARGARET. In the wardrobe. (*She shows a key*)

EARL. Who saw you?

LADY MARGARET. Nobody.

EARL. Who saw the unicorn?

LADY MARGARET. Nobody.

BARON. Margaret. Heroine!

LADY MARGARET. Not yet.

BARON (*low*). But why at night? Why in secret? I don't understand.

LADY MARGARET. You will.

BASSET. My dear lady, are you quite safe? Did the beast try to harm you?

LADY MARGARET. Thank *you* for asking, Basset. I had a moment of terror, for he was growling and ready to thrust at me. But I held the mirror steadfast, and lo! he became meek, and gently followed me. I have not even a stain on my dress, not a spot on my hands, nor a wrinkle in my purpose.

BARON. Miraculous woman.

EARL. Margaret, speak to me.... I *am* concerned for you.

LADY MARGARET. And I for you, my husband. I set you free to marry Clotilda.

EARL (*groaning*). You knew.

LADY MARGARET. From the start. (*Clotilda faints*) The little toad has decided to faint. Umfrey, you know the rules of chivalry; help your mistress.

(*Basset attends to Clotilda*)

EARL. Margaret, I don't want to be set free. I was bewitched. You belong to me.

LADY MARGARET. You mean Wyngham, Brigsley, Tuckbetter and Glaswin Epton belong to you.

BARON. Precisely.

EARL. This is unjust. We've lived together for five years—peacefully—you accepted my deep respect—you can't wish a scandal to break over my head, surely.

BARON. What scandal? We'll do it quietly.

EARL (*furiously*). Stay out of this, mongrel—

BARON. By thunder, I'll call Leofa! Here I fret over your reputation—

CLOTILDA (*who has unfainted herself*). Umfrey, my lord, listen to him, do as they say, we're powerless against them....

BARON. That's a sensible girl. She's all yours, Umfrey. You can afford to marry whomever you wish, you're not a lowly baron afraid of a misalliance. A man like you is immune to whispers. Take Clotilda—the poor girl loves you and you're ever so devoted to her. Nobody will be told that Margaret caught the unicorn, it could have been the work of a stray virgin happening by. Or the unicorn, having completed his mission, could have drifted into the wardrobe by himself. Leave it to my diplomatic experience. All that's required of you is a friendly settlement with Margaret, a donation to the church, and a gift to the Pope. I have it! You'll send him the unicorn's tusk in a velvet case, and the story ends in a flurry of toasts and violins.

EARL. I'm dizzy.

CLOTILDA. Here, let me take care of you. (*She tries to give him some wine*) You see, the evil wind has blown some good to us after all.

EARL (*weakly*). Go away....

LADY MARGARET (*offering her hand to the Baron*). My lord....

BARON (*devoutly*). My own!

BASSET (*throwing himself at Lady Margaret's feet*). Dearest lady, listen to me, listen I beg you, don't take refuge with Theefton of all men! If you knew his real purpose!

BARON. The man is lying!

BASSET. Your husband has done you an immense wrong, I know it, but he repents. Look at his face! While Theefton comes here lusting only after your lands—he told me so himself!

BARON (*laughing*). Told him so myself! Very likely! Congratulations on your mouthpiece, Umfrey—he deserves his wages—but here, thank God, no one is fool enough to believe him.

LADY MARGARET. Rise, Master Basset, rise. *I* am fool enough to believe you.

EARL *and* BARON (*contrasting pitch*). Margaret!

BASSET. Lovely lady, I've opened your eyes. I've saved you.

EARL. At least you've seen through this puppet. So far I'm happy.

BARON. Margaret!

LADY MARGARET. I see through all of you.

BARON. This is a dream. Margaret! I adore you. You fell into my arms

yesterday afternoon—
EARL. That's a lie.
LADY MARGARET. Thank you, Umfrey.
BARON. Why did you hunt the unicorn if you weren't—
LADY MARGARET. In order to crush you all. Basset, you didn't open my eyes. I know how to open them on my own, thank you. I understood Theefton's greed from the beginning. He stole my favorite puppy when I was ten.
BARON. He ran away! Finders keepers!
LADY MARGARET. And I knew my husband's deceit, and I knew Clotilda's ambition. But I waited for my day. Which came. Now I shall make you all cringe. Umfrey, choose; either you drive your mistress out, come to my bed, and give me my rights as Countess of Dumfrey, or else I leave you demolished in your ruins and marry myself and my lands, eyes wide open, to your enemy Theefton.
BASSET. She loves her husband, you see!
LADY MARGARET. My friend, you'll die the same baby you were born. But phrase it as you like, I'll love my husband, so be it, from the moment he does my will, my justice, my good. And do or don't, by all the saints in paradise who have witnessed my patience—
EARL. What, my dear?
LADY MARGARET (*fiercely*). I'll be avenged!
BASSET. God save us!
CLOTILDA. Protect me, my lord. Show her what you are. Protect the defenseless.
LADY MARGARET. Peter!
(*Enter Peter*)
PETER. Madam.
LADY MARGARET. Warn Leofa to be here in exactly ten minutes; not nine and not eleven; ten minutes from this. (*She snaps her fingers*)
PETER. Yes, madam. (*He leaves*)
LADY MARGARET. Speak, Umfrey.
EARL. Clotilda will leave.
CLOTILDA. Oh!
BARON. Wait! You're not rid of me yet. Umfrey, I order you to keep Clotilda. Like it or not, Margaret will be Baroness Theefton! Or else Leofa, the people and the king will be told how you and Clotilda have broken the sacrament, poisoned the land, and inflicted the unicorn on it. I will ruin you. You will end your days on a pallet in King Stephen's clammiest dungeon. Robert Theefton has played his trump card.

LADY MARGARET. And what if I refuse to become your mate? What will you have gained?

BARON. Vengeance. Like yourself.

LADY MARGARET. What if, instead of vengeance, I were to offer you land?

BARON. Land? Where and when?

LADY MARGARET. Tuckbetter and its corn; at once.

BARON. Hm.

LADY MARGARET. Besides, remember where you are.

BARON. Where I am?

LADY MARGARET. Namely in Lord Dumfrey's stronghold, with few retainers at your side.

EARL (*delighted*). That's true. I'll try him on the spot for plotting against the earldom, and have his head before he can open his mouth.

CLOTILDA. But I'll cry his story from the rooftops.

LADY MARGARET. Shut your mouth, my child; we'll come to you in a minute. Well, Robert? Think of the axe. And think of Tuckbetter's cornfields.

BARON. I'd prefer the mills of Brigsley.

EARL. They're yours.

BASSET. My God, where are you?

LADY MARGARET. Allow me, Baron Theefton.

(*She pours him some wine*)

BARON. Thank you. Political questions can always be settled, provided there's a little good will all around, a touch of genuine sincerity. Here's my hand, Umfrey.

EARL. What about the falling into your arms yesterday afternoon?

BARON. A diplomatic fiction.

EARL. Here's mine. Brigsley is yours. Basset will draw up the charter tomorrow in good Latin. And Margaret—Margaret—come here—my wife (*kissing her hand*) a great stone has been lifted from my chest. The earldom is saved, my soul perhaps too.

CLOTILDA (*throwing some pewter on the floor*). Brutes! Brutes! Plotting together to tear me to pieces. But I'll get even with you! (*Suddenly remembering*) Wait! Wait! (*To the Earl*) King Stephen asked you for a hundred-twenty knights on horse-back for the French expedition and you gave him only thirty, you pleaded this and that, you lied and you bribed the king's clerk! I know all your secrets! I'll expose you! Leofa is coming, good! I'll make you grovel!

(*Basset is thunderstruck*)

BARON. Gently, Clotilda, this needs to be discussed.

EARL. My life is over.

LADY MARGARET. Not so. Dear Clotilda, what will mere revenge get you?

You who will be enjoying the glory of having caught the unicorn.

ALL. What?

LADY MARGARET. Why do you all look surprised? Clotilda went into the forest early this evening—

(*Enter Peter*)

PETER. Leofa, the People's Delegate!

(*Enter Leofa, Peter exits*)

LADY MARGARET. Leofa, how good of you to come; come in, come in.

(*Leofa kneels before Lady Margaret and kisses her hand*)

LADY MARGARET. Stand, excellent friend, and attend to my words. Mistress Bennyworth left the castle this evening longing to succeed where she had failed before, and anxious to restore her reputation in the eyes of the people she loves. She found the foul unicorn—yes! she caught him; she led him back—

LEOFA. The unicorn is caught! Where is the fiend?

LADY MARGARET. In the wardrobe. And here is the key.

LEOFA (*taking the key*). Heaven be thanked!

LADY MARGARET. Heaven be thanked, of course; but heaven's instrument as well.

LEOFA (*kneeling before Clotilda and kissing her hand*). Mistress Bennyworth, the sweet saints in heaven rain their goodness on your pretty head. Our progenitors will be told the inspirational story of your lily life. You have justified the people's confidence.

CLOTILDA. I've always loved the people, Leofa.

LEOFA. No 'usband will be too great for you. Kings will ask for your 'and from Asia to Constantinople.

LADY MARGARET. That will do, Leofa. Go tell the people the happy tidings.

LEOFA. At once. Long live the house of Dumfrey!

BARON. Amen. (*Exit Leofa*) He's right, Clotilda, you will find a choice husband as soon as the news has spread.

CLOTILDA. Well, I hope nobody here expects me to be grateful.

EARL (*low*). Do take the girl away, Basset.

BASSET. No, I am sick at heart. The brazen hussy. And you, Lady Margaret, cold from your brains to your womanhood. You, Lord Theefton, false friend and plunderer. You, my lord, false vassal, liar and adulterer. And myself, a grey-haired baby.

EARL. I'm afraid we *are* a fearful lot. On the other hand, we're friends again, Basset, and are we any worse than the rest of the world?

BARON. Rather better, if anything.

LADY MARGARET. Look at other places.
CLOTILDA. Paris, for example, where Master Basset has promised to send me.
BARON. Are there not clouds in the sky?
CLOTILDA. Does it not rain in June?
LADY MARGARET. Don't swans for all their beauty honk?
EARL. And didn't Christ himself lose his temper?
(*Enter Peter*)
PETER. The minstrels attend in the antechamber!
EARL. What minstrels?
PETER. The two Master Basset invited, my lord.
EARL. So he did. Well, let them play, let them sing! Why not, after all?
PETER. This way, lads; here is a place ready-made for you.
(*Enter a Gareth and Dagonet, the latter holding a lute. They bow*)
GARETH. Greetings lords and ladies! We thank you for your welcome and hope to please you by performing the very latest song we composed for the court of King Stephen the Second.
EARL. Sing away!
(*Gareth sings, Dagonet accompanies*)

> When God said
> Let us make the earth
> What did he do
> He took a heap of dirt
> He took a heap of dirt
> And made a muddy ball
> And that is why oh why
> We're muddy one and all!

(*Applause*)
EARL. The clever things they think up in London!
SINGER. My lord, it is the custom, in the capital, to dance to the song, all in a round.
BARON. Hand in hand, all in a round! Mistress Bennyworth, may I?
CLOTILDA. Of course.
EARL. Margaret?
LADY MARGARET. With pleasure.
(*The minstrels repeats the ballad, and all dance except Basset who has bitterly removed himself*)
EARL. Enough, enough! Let the ladies breathe! Peter, more wine! Ah, my

spirits are reviving at last! I propose a toast. Friends! We are reconciled!
BARON. Reconciled!
CLOTILDA. Reconciled!
LADY MARGARET. Reconciled!
EARL. Basset, where are you? Hang it, come here; I—
BASSET (*in loud agony*). I am NOT reconciled! (*He rushes to the balcony*) I've had enough! Dance without me!
EARL. Peter, stop him!
(*Peter catches hold of Basset already standing on the balustrade and ready to jump off*)
PETER. Don't jump! Don't disobey Lord Dumfrey!
BASSET. Let me go, for pity's sake! Lie and cheat without me!
EARL. Basset, Ralf my good friend, come away for God's sake. I need you. The land needs you. The world needs you.
CLOTILDA. We all love you, Master Basset.
BARON. I told you yesterday: you're one of us!
EARL. Listen to me. I shall double those acres you own near Pitmarsh.
BARON. Excellent idea.
EARL. And ask King Stephen to make you a baronet.
BARON (*aside to the earl*). Are you mad? His great-grandfather was a woodcutter!
BASSET. Spare me, my lord, let me die.
LADY MARGARET. Stand aside, all of you. Peter, you too, let him go.
EARL. Margaret will do it, of course.
LADY MARGARET. Basset!
BASSET. Yes, Lady Margaret.
LADY MARGARET. Turn around again. Yes, away from me. Look down into the park, look towards the forest. What do you see?
BASSET. What do I see? I see darkness.
LADY MARGARET. Tell me the weather of that darkness, Basset.
BASSET. The darkness is cold.
LADY MARGARET. I felt it too, face to face with the beast. The cold of that corpse you seem in such a hurry to become. Tell me, Basset—because *I*, poor woman, don't know—tell me who or what rules over us when we are cold. Is it as the Church teaches us?
BASSET. It is! (*Pause*) I don't know....
LADY MARGARET. Will you fall straight into Hell, having taken your own life?
BARON. Infallibly. Holy Scripture requires it.
EARL (*crossing himself*). God preserve you.
LADY MARGARET. Or will the angels welcome you after all? Or will you be scattered into the void?

BASSET. I don't know.
LADY MARGARET. And yet you will make that discovery soon enough, Basset; because you are old.
EARL. Margaret....
LADY MARGARET. Old, Basset, old. Why such haste? Self murder is not for the old, my friend; self-murder is unseemly when Death stands at the door uncalled, about to knock.
EARL. Margaret will do it, I said so.
LADY MARGARET. Turn back to me, dear Master Basset. (*Basset does so*) Oh, I find in your eyes the wish that you could wish to live.
BASSET. You do?
LADY MARGARET. You are looking at me, and what do you see? A wicked beautiful woman. Around my neck and arms jewels happy to circle them. On my body soft silk resting against the softer flesh. In the room warm candles, silver shimmering, homely oak of tables and chairs, foolish deceitful familiar people, and the wine more purple than the grape it came from. And what do you hear, Basset?
BASSET. Human words swimming towards me like a school of sirens singing.
(*Basset reenters the room*)
EARL. A bowl of wine this once, Basset. For a token.
BASSET. I don't know, my lord. I am astray. (*He drinks*)
EARL (*embracing him*). Forgive me, Ralf.
BASSET. Pay no attention to me....
(*The Earl and Basset withdraw to one side of the room*)
BARON. Lady Margaret, my hat is off to you, so to speak.
CLOTILDA. I have always admired you so much. May I...?
LADY MARGARET (*friendly and regal*). Of course.
(*She offers her hand for Clotilda to kiss*)
CLOTILDA. Thank you!
BARON. My dear Clotilda, you of all people should comfort our desponding steward.
CLOTILDA. You are ever so right, my lord.
(*She flies to the other side of the room*)
BARON. Lady Margaret, a word with you.
LADY MARGARET. Yes, baron.
BARON (*low*). Surely you won't allow a steward to turn baronet for trying to jump off a balcony?
LADY MARGARET. Don't be apprehensive, Robert. The king will laugh in my husband's face.
BARON. Well....

LADY MARGARET. And if he doesn't, keep something else in mind.
BARON. Namely?
LADY MARGARET. There is rank and rank. Rank of the moneybag and rank of the sword. Rank of today and rank five hundred years old. Rank ridiculous and rank sublime.
BARON. You reassure me dearest Margaret. (*He turns*) Look here, friend Basset—
(*Leofa rushes in, holding a gored chicken and rabbit in his hands*)
LEOFA. My lords, treason, a new unicorn in the woods!
ALL. Oh!
LEOFA. Look! Gored, gored again, everything is starting all over. When will it end? Lord Dumfrey, say something!
EARL. I'm calling a meeting of the council tomorrow! I'll name a commission! I'll launch a massive inquiry! Basset! Suggest something.
BASSET (*bitterly*). Sing and dance! Sing and dance till doomsday!
GARETH. An excellent suggestion, my lords, my ladies. Our repertory is immense, but our Ballad of Sir Blot is most fitting, because it alludes to the unicorn that was ravaging Cornwall before it came hither. The Prince of Wales danced it to our music last month and gave us a guinea for it, he was that pleased.
BARON. Let's hear it and let's dance to it.
EARL. So be it.
LADY MARGARET. So be it. Take your places, everybody!
(*The minstrels sing and play as everybody except Basset dances. During the dance Basset stealthily leaves the room*)
GARETH.
>Sir Blot, come hither and declare aloud,
>"I am a landlord rich and proud."

DAGONET.
>I am a landlord proud and rich,
>Ten serfs relieve me when I itch.

GARETH.
>Sir Blot, come forth and say with me:
>"To dukes and kings I bend my cunning knee."

DAGONET.
>The knee I slyly bend to dukes and kings
>Is bent to me by trembling underlings.

GARETH.
>Sir Blot, who is the lucky maid you'll wed
>And tumble in your bouncy bed?

DAGONET.
>   The lucky lass I mean to marry
>   Must bring me field and mine and quarry.

GARETH.
>   Sir Blot, proclaim both left and right,
>   "I slew the unicorn tonight."

DAGONET.
>   I hate to boast, and fibs I scorn:
>   Yes I slew the unicorn!

EARL. Lively work, minstrels! You have exhausted us. Enough for now. I feel the breath of midnight in the land. Master Basset will give orders for a warm supper below, clean bedding, and something of substance for your purses tomorrow morning.

MINSTRELS. Our humble thanks, my lord.

LADY MARGARET. Where *is* Master Basset?

EARL. He was here just now!

PETER. My lord, Master Basset withdrew while your worships were dancing.

LEOFA. So 'e did, I seen 'im slink off lookin' like 'e'd swallowed a rat—no offense meant to nobody.

BARON. I never saw such aversion to merriment!

EARL. Well, call him back, Peter; tell him he is wanted here.

PETER. Very good, my lord. But here he comes.

(*Enter Basset, carrying a pilgrim's staff, a scrip, and a thick leather-bound folio. Everyone stares. He walks up to the Earl*)

EARL. What does this mean, Basset?

BASSET (*offering the folio*). My lord, Lady Margaret, your next steward, whoever he may be, will find the accounts of the estate in order.

EARL. Where are you going? Put those damned accounts on the table.

(*Basset does not obey*)

BASSET. As I believe you know, my lord, my lady, the abbot of Newminster is my cousin on my mother's side. I shall ask him for shelter. Allow me to take my leave.

EARL. Certainly not! In the middle of the night!

LADY MARGARET. We do not allow it!

EARL. Neither do I.

BARON. Obedience, my worthy friend, obedience.

CLOTILDA. Do remain, Master Basset; I shall continue to need your guidance.

EARL. As for the unicorn, Basset, you know how it is. God chooses at random.

Remember what the saintly Richard Rollo wrote me: "God moves in mysterious ways". *Deus absconditus*. The beast will be migrating in good time to other shires, probably to Theefton's very soon.

BARON. Nonsense!

BASSET. Let the beast go where it pleases, my lord; I shall not hear it in my cell.

EARL. Your cell is in this castle, Basset.

BASSET. Thank you, Lord Dumfrey, but no.

EARL. But yes!

DAGONET (*striking up*). Yes, yes, yes! Dance to our music, sir!

GARETH. Dance all, dance all! Dance to the great Yes!

(*All but Peter and Leofa, who watch from a corner, surround Basset in a dance*)

ALL. Yes!

BASSET. No!

ALL. Yes, yes, yes!

BASSET. No.

ALL. Yes!

BASSET. No!

ALL. Yes!

(*They dance Basset—clutching his folio—off-stage, led by the minstrels. The Yes and No end in an indistinguishable blur. Peter and Leofa remain alone on stage. Peter stretches his body to listen*)

PETER. What in the devil's name was the last word, yes or no?

LEOFA (*busy wrapping the chicken and rabbit in a tablecloth*). How should I know? And what's it to me? Hey! Looks like their lordships left most of their wine in the cups. That's nobility for you.

PETER. Yes no yes no yes no. I'll worry and worry.

LEOFA. What do you project to do with all that wasted wine twiddling its thumbs in there?

PETER. What did you say?

LEOFA. I asked, what are you going to do with all that wasted wine?

PETER. I don't know. (*Drinking*) Here's what.

LEOFA (*falling to*). That's my boy. Here's how.

PETER. And you, what are you going to do with *those*?

LEOFA. Those chicken and rabbit?

PETER. Yes.

LEOFA. Give 'em to the wife for cooking, what did you think? I've got five children to feed.

PETER. And the hole in them?

LEOFA. Dummy! I've got 'oles in my shoes, 'oles in my pocket, 'oles in my

roof, there's a steady dumb 'ole in my stomach, and another waiting for me by the church. Why should I mind a hole in my boiled chicken? Drink up.
(*A new unicorn is heard in the distance*)
PETER. Might as well.
LEOFA. Cheers!
(*The unicorn once more*)
PETER. Cheers? I'm not so sure. But—might as well.
(*They clink and drink up*)

The End

Notes

The Virgin and the Unicorn: a Miraculous Drawing-Room Comedy made its debut in the *Minnesota Review* in 1967. It reappeared in Volume I of my *Collected Plays* of 1970, then again in *The Virgin and Unicorn: Four Plays* in 1993, and now for the last time, with a different subtitle. It has undergone revisions at each of these stages.

THE FRIAR, THE PEDDLER AND THE WITCH

CHARACTERS

Hunter
Peddler
Friar
The Witch
Idiot
Monkey

THE FRIAR, THE PEDDLER AND THE WITCH

PROLOGUE

(A wild, wooded hill. Enter the hunter, armed)

HUNTER.　Who I am, and what I am,
　　　　　Ladies, children, gentlemen,
　　　　　Let me gradually disclose
　　　　　In honest English and plain prose.
　　　　　And first, to make no mystery,
　　　　　I am not what I seem to be.
　　　　　My open hides a hidden smile,
　　　　　My genial quip, dyspeptic guile.
　　　　　Round about me, as I go,
　　　　　Grass hides its head under a snow,
　　　　　The tiger shivers, and the mole
　　　　　Declines into a deeper hole.
　　　　　Only the spider with some glee
　　　　　Lifts one leg to wave at me
　　　　　(I taught him all his strategy).
　　　　　He catches flies, and I catch men,
　　　　　For each mouth gobbles what it can.
　　　　　Nature is that awesome harmony
　　　　　Where each harms each in due degree,
　　　　　And I, Nature's own patriot,
　　　　　By doing harm, fulfill my lot.
　　　　　Doing harm? Not quite. I grant
　　　　　All men the very harm they want!
　　　　　But here I might become abstruse,
　　　　　And my audience, or myself confuse.
　　　　　Instead—stop! What are these sounds?
　　　　　A pair of lungs, a heart that pounds,
　　　　　Two legs lifting a bulk uphill
　　　　　With feeble muscles, and feebler will:
　　　　　It is the peddler, jolly, fat,
　　　　　The merry mouse to my grim cat.
　　　　　Here is set our rendez-vous;
　　　　　He does not know it, but you do.

(Exit)

SCENE ONE

(Enter the peddler, large pack on his back. He deposits it, sits, wipes his face, sighs)

PEDDLER. This is a memorable sweat. Every faucet of my body is leaking. However, I believe I have reached the top of the mountain at last. It is true, as they said in the village, that it's an odd heap of a mountain. I passed a lizard bleaching himself on a stone who pricked up his ears when he saw me, and slowly turned his head to watch me go by. A bird wearing a monocle beat the air in front of me, winked, grinned with his whole beak, and flittered away. Heaven be thanked, I am steeled by ignorance and will assume that science has discussed the habits of these animals with reassuring Greek words. Little flask, pretty flask, where are you? *(Drinks)* Oh my, I love to fatigue myself for the sheer pleasure of resting afterward. My poor outraged pump, don't I know that uphill is the wrong way for a man? Am I not the flower of cowards and a worshipper of sofas? Come, on my way down I'll deliver myself into the hands of Nature, and let gravity do the work. *(He sings)*

> Fiddle-high and fiddle-low,
> The sea be salt
> The sand be dry,
> Heaven be a barrel, O!
>
> Falalol and falali,
> A child's a cup
> A man's a bowl,
> Heaven be a barrel, Ay!
>
> Diddle-di and—

(A shot off-stage)
Don't shoot, I haven't got a penny, take it all, it's a mistake, I have a wife!
(He hides behind a tree or a rock. Enter the hunter)
HUNTER. I thought I heard something human snivel. Oho, a fat man. Your credentials, flesh?
PEDDLER. I am a proletarian, sir. I am a peddler, a negligible peddler not worth the attention of a bullet.
HUNTER. Well, let me look at you. Stand up. I'm not a thief. I am a hunter. And I was after a doe, not flabby peddler steak. Blow your nose and let's

be friends.
PEDDLER. Did the beast go the other way?
HUNTER. Yes, I missed her, but on purpose. It was our first meeting, and I thought a hint of her future was enough. I like a bullet to be the last rebuttal in a long, familiar discussion. But tell me, my friend, can I make up in any way for the little fright I gave you?

>   You are a stranger, I know,
>   While I am at home with these boulders,
>   I dwell among wolves, I throw
>   A bearskin over my shoulders—

PEDDLER. A bearskin!
HUNTER.   I sleep on leaves, I dine on rabbits,
           Rough in my speech, gruff in my habits —
PEDDLER. Granted, but a bearskin!
HUNTER. Why not a bearskin?
PEDDLER. In this age of luxury? You shock me into a state of compassion.
HUNTER. You say you are a peddler?
PEDDLER. A merchant. In good standing with the Council for the Propagation of Prosperity, in whose Annual Index I am marked with two stars and an exclamation point.
HUNTER. A clothes-peddler, perhaps.
PEDDLER. Yes. I am glad you wormed the fact out of me. A bearskin in our age is a sign of antiquated thinking. You must have a wife?
HUNTER. Not today.
PEDDLER.   In that case, alas, I needn't show
           My muffs and lace and bibelots,
           Gloves dying to be dropped by flirts
           And squeezed by playboys, Cleopatra's bow,
           Salome's veils, Bathsheba's skirts;
           And, how sad! You won't care to see
           Stoles of paramecium hair, chemisettes
           Of felted cobwebs, impudent corsets
           Amused with sequins, hoses, filigree,
           Threads spun of April air, frilled hairnets,
           Or my silky Sinkiang cloth,
           My Bechuanaland brocades,
           My satins light as eyelashes of maids,
           My chintzes woven out of Dnieper froth,

My woolens dyed in Patagonian shades.
Women grow faint when I name my wares. For hunters, however, I carry a serviceable coonskin jacket. Its calm solidity is matched only by its unforgivable cheapness. Allow me to open my store at Point 46, Hunters' Jackets.

HUNTER. Stop! What I want is the richest lady's scarf you sell. There's a woman not far from here I want to pay for—for favors.

PEDDLER. So, there is something here besides bears! Interesting. Scarfs, scarfs. Undies, slippers, bosom-holders—here we are. No. This one—no. I will not sell it. I meant to hide it. Never. Oh, these golden threads! Unique!

HUNTER. Then show me another.

PEDDLER. I cannot sell it because the Countess Melibella of Magrigento once wept into it. It is, in other words, second-hand merchandise, though I have washed it. An ancestress of the dear countess waved it toward her husband departing for the eleventh Crusade and dropped it in despair when the ship melted into the horizon. To me it must ever be treasurable far beyond the three-thousand ducats' worth of gold threaded into its tissue. Oh sweet perfume, incumbent yet!

HUNTER. Here; this is all I have.

PEDDLER. Money! I will take three out of your three coins as a token of your interest, and then give you the scarf gratis. I will not sell it.

HUNTER. So much for that.

PEDDLER. Yes. But you have aroused my curiosity. This deserving lass—I am thinking now of your wish to compensate me for startling me a little with your musket. She is fond of gifts? And has a willing disposition?

HUNTER. Indeed.

PEDDLES. Where might a traveller with a bulging stock find her?

HUNTER. I'll gladly show you where. Climb on this rock. (*Helps the peddler*) Stoutly, boulder of a man! Now tell me, what do you see?

PEDDLER. A heap of shrubs and other nondescript vegetables. Wait, there's a path! An angular, a guilty-looking path! Where does it go?

HUNTER. It sneaks to a hut a day's walk away;
A jumbled, limping, scrabbled hut
In a thing you'd call a clearing
Except none ever cleared it,
But trees have better taste than growing there.
The house is a sty; no door; spiders haunt it
With their gallop, and termites wade neck-high
Into its floors. You hear beam and board
Sigh, and spinelessly agonize
While the wind nubs his head through the walls.

THE FRIAR, THE PEDDLER AND THE WITCH

An idiot rules the mansion—cries,
Groans and jabbers in the breeze.
He is overlord of mice and rats,
Of moles, porcupines, asses, goats,
Grunting pigs, braying donkeys,
And—unbelievably—a daughter.

PEDDLER. The story has a happy ending.
HUNTER. Yes. The idiot has a beautiful daughter.

>Here is a woman who could turn the dead
>To lechery, and the meager saints
>To the reconsideration of their prudence.
>Oh nothing paints her but herself
>In the embrace of amorous breezes—
>Lips that leap, eyes that bite,
>Shoulders like peaches rounded
>Where a peddler's palm can nuzzle home,
>Breasts that melt to the finger's dance—
>Oh and what else? I blush;
>Thighs straining like two thicker arms—
>And this queen, diamonded in a hut,
>This danger to melancholy, this patch
>Of pleasure on the world's sour face
>Could be the flame burst from your match.

PEDDLER. Help me down this boulder, friend.
HUNTER. Wait!

>It happened that the moon caught sight of her
>Between two parted elbows of an elm one night
>When, her daily misery accomplished,
>She freed the tides of her black hair
>And made her body ready for her nightly bath.

The moon stood still. Time gave one cry, and fainted.
The wind, its finger fidgeting a leaf,
Hung mid-air; all life—the very ants that trot
And fuss with midget speed—
All life broke off and stood solidified.
And now the moon sent down two rays

To cup the girl's enchanted face,
He gazed at her with white surprise
And love, such love as arid moons can feel.
At last he set her free, slung time
Over his shoulder, and pushing stars aside,
Marched out the night.
And then the woman bathed,
Neither she nor any animal
Remembering the miracle, except
She sang, and the creatures of the bearded wood
Were less ferocious for a night; there seemed
A heartbeat in the sod, all sensing it.
Beauty strikes such awe into the universe.

PEDDLER. Help me down this boulder, brother, you have wiped twenty years off my passport. This moon-stopper, you say, lives a day's walk from here, and she will do the foul, exquisite deed?
HUNTER. Yes, if properly rewarded.
PEDDLER. But what about the blabbering father? Bless my soul! To be lunged at by an idiot in a fit of outraged paternity!
HUNTER. Undo your bundle for her! It will do. As for the man, she will put him to sleep with his jug of wine, though for that matter he can't distinguish you from a monkey. Wait! I think I hear something. Listen.
PEDDLER. I don't hear a thing except the usual jingling of the leaves.
HUNTER. But I do. Stop. Up the mountain-side. He's coming our way.
PEDDLER. Who is that?
HUNTER. I can hear him. He is praying. Can you see him now?
PEDDLER. I do.
(*Enter the young friar, carrying an umbrella and psalming to himself*)
FRIAR.   Nine thousand fifty-seven
            Names of God, help for evil,
            Balm and spell,
            Nine thousand fifty-seven
            Avenues from Hell—

Ah! God's peace upon you, gentlemen, and good afternoon. I am a child of God and a pilgrim to anywhere.
PEDDLER. And I am a merchant, sir, seeking an honest living among the native populations.
FRIAR. A very warm afternoon, is it not?
PEDDLER. So it is. I recommend a little rest on this very spot. A breeze is

strolling here of whose services I have just now availed myself. I am, in fact, refreshed enough to be leaving again. I take this very unpleasant, spiny and potholed way behind the boulder to visit a remote customer, but I will no doubt have the pleasure of meeting you again on the main road. (*Picks up his bag*) Hunter, farewell and thank you for your guidance.

PEDDLER. A pleasure, sir.

FRIAR. God bless your enterprise, sir.

(*Exit peddler. The hunter has secretly dropped the scarf*)

FRIAR. It is good to sit down. I am not yet accustomed to long walks. Do you live here, sir? Please excuse my curiosity.

HUNTER. With pleasure. Yes, I live here. I am a hunter by profession and keep the woods free of immortality.

FRIAR. I am a friar. Not a very modern thing to be, but it is an honest occupation.

HUNTER. And one, I understand, that promises a considerable future.

FRIAR. He, he! Yes indeed. We used to say just that at the seminary; in jest, you know.

HUNTER. You have recently taken your vows? I am guessing because of your youth and your brand new cloak.

FRIAR. One week ago. This is my first enterprise among people. I am a little frightened by it all, though everybody has been very kind.

HUNTER. Most people indulge in kindness to strangers. It is so easy. But tell me, where will you spend the night? You too must forgive my questions, but this is quite the wilderness.

FRIAR. It is a kind curiosity. I sleep on the ground, anywhere, with my head on my satchel. Animals mistake me for a lump of matter, and men see at a glance that I have taken the vow of pauverty. I am quite safe and comfortable.

HUNTER. Even so, allow me to make a suggestion. It is late afternoon, you are tired, and the country is new to you. I cannot offer much—I live alone and simply in a small cabin not far from here. But there is solid food, respectable wine—I should say clear water for you—and fresh straw to sleep on. Stay for the night, and start again tomorrow.

FRIAR. I accept with gratitude, and I should be glad to pay you, but, as I have just said, I have nothing of value, except, perhaps, prayers.

HUNTER. I will take one of medium intensity and count myself well paid. But I am really very curious about you. May I ask what brings you to these uncanny mountains?

FRIAR. I will be happy to answer you, but it is difficult. How shall I put it and not be laughed at? The church has made of me a child. I see those who see, but what they see I have not seen. Do you understand? It is not much to know by rote as I have always done; nor to hate sin by sermon and scripture. One must touch knowledge. And I am an uncooked, unsalted and unpeppered dish of a lad. I needed to meet misery. But you're smiling.

HUNTER. *Sympathetically.* To meet misery! It's a thought that doesn't come to worldly men like me.

FRIAR. Yes! Fill as it were my book with indecent illustrations,
 Take the size of scoundrels with my actual hand,
 Dip my sandal into the bloody inundation
 Of sin on earth, weep, and think, and faintly understand.

HUNTER. Better be careful every moment not to become your own subject, my friend. If evil were to study evil, its conclusions would be inexact, would they not?

FRIAR. I pray to be helped against temptation.

HUNTER. But can you tell a temptation from an opportunity? Do you know a sin when you meet one?

FRIAR. I think the old catalogues are still reliable.

HUNTER. Therefore, I take it, no wines, perfumes, featherbeds and women. You hate them.

FRIAR. They distract. I am afraid I sound a bit starched, and even presumptuous.

HUNTER. Not a bit. But alas for the wines, perfumes, featherbeds and women!

 Oh give the world a chance
 To dance,
 And give us a little sin
 To be happy in!

But I'm joking. Are you rested enough to follow me home?

FRIAR. I am, thank you. But are you sure I won't intrude?

HUNTER. You will give me a great deal of pleasure, I assure you. Oh, what's this? *(He picks up the peddler's scarf)* A lady's scarf! And an expensive one! Look, these are golden threads. And that design of bold-faced roses! The peddler must have dropped it. This will be a serious loss for him.

FRIAR. Poor man. Is this a lady's scarf, really? Such a beautiful thing! It may be worth a whole day's work to him, or a whole day's walk to come back for it. Wait! He can't be very far, carrying his heavy load. I'll catch up with him in an hour. Well, I am very thankful for your invitation, and perhaps we shall meet again.

HUNTER. No doubt. But I still urge you to stay. I know the house our friend is going to. Spend the night here, leave fresh at dawn tomorrow, and if you follow my directions you will have the scarf in his hands that same night. And, incidentally, the house in question is well worth a detour. An old witless man lives in it with a daughter and a curious assortment of animals. Our friend was anxious to see the whole family. He seems to be drawn to animals. Be that as it may, you are sure to find him there.

FRIAR. I *will* stay, then, and be on my way refreshed in the morning.

HUNTER. Splendid! My weapon. Are you ready? I look forward to fine talk over the fire.

I want you to remember the hunter you met—

FRIAR. Oh, I will.

HUNTER (*aside*). And the day you stumbled into his net.

SCENE TWO

(*Next evening. A clearing, though there are trees at the edge, and a good deal of shrubbery. A shoddy hut, one side open so that the interior is partially visible. No one is on stage as the curtain rises, but various animal noises are heard. A monkey wanders out of the hut, jumps about, and vanishes. Soon after, the idiot slouches out with a bottle and a cup, and helps himself liberally. Finally the friar appears, chanting*)

FRIAR. Wheel of wheels,
Ray of rays,
Sublimity of sublimities,
Father of fathers—

Good evening. (*The idiot grunts*) I am a friar traveling in the name of God, and I am looking for a peddler who lost a scarf. Is this the house where he stopped? (*The idiot offers him wine and begins to weep*) My poor man, what is the matter? Do you understand me? Oh what a miserable creature, and what a miserable house. Has God directed me to the beginning of my work? (*Loud*) Is anyone here? (*Only the noise of animals answers*) The hunter spoke of animals. This must be the place. (*Loud again*) Is—oh! (*The music of a plucked instrument is heard within, and the voice of a Witch*)

WITCH (*sings*). Long will be brief,
One becomes two,

> Time is a thief
> But death is true.
> How will a mortal lover last?
>
> The roses ebb,
> The kings dismount,
> And step by step
> They reach the ground.
> How will a mortal lover last?

FRIAR.   Seek one immortal,
    But I should almost sin, and say,
    At your own lips is the music
    Angels for angels play.

(*The music stops. He calls inside*) May I come in? I am a harmless friar, please don't hide.
(*The Witch appears. She is about twenty years old and is of course bewitchingly beautiful*)
WITCH. Beautiful person! Who are you? Welcome until you dissolve. Perhaps I am dreaming you. If I gaze at you too happily, will you turn into smoke and vanish?
FRIAR.   Perhaps. For I am smoke in the mind of God,
    And my hardest bone is no more than dust.
    Strange person. May I, shyly, applaud
    What you sang, the strings your fingers trod,
    And the violas and oboes you spoke.
WITCH. Smoke would not pay me a compliment. But will you melt if I kiss you? (*Kisses him*) You are still here!
FRIAR. How bold you are. But I must remember to thank God before I go to sleep because He improved nature with such a creature as you are.
IDIOT. Greeshur! Greeshur! Greeshur! Liquor! (*Drinks*)
FRIAR. The poor old man. How pitiful. But please let me state my business. I am looking for a peddler who lost this scarf on the road. A hunter told me that I should find him here.
WITCH. No, I have seen no peddler.
(*Enter the monkey. Seeing the friar, he leaps upon him playfully, snatches the scarf and jumps up and down hugging it*)
FRIAR. Oh my God, he will destroy the scarf!
WITCH. Go back to the house, monster. (*Exit the monkey, squealing and dancing*) This is my family. Oh I am so ashamed before a stranger. You are the most

beautiful being I have ever met. Stay with me.

FRIAR. I must find that poor peddler, but I won't go away at once. He may have stopped somewhere else on his way. And here is a poor soul that needs the word of God.

WITCH.   It is my father; I am its child.
I do for it the best I can,
Giving bread and drink. I keep
Harmless animals who entertain me
With their simple inapprehensions;
I have my garden, at whose breasts I feed.
Our house died long ago, we live in its corpse,
I nail and saw all year, but clumsily,
Until I am exhausted of all skills
Except the skill of crying on the shoulders
Of the wood, where no heart beats at all
And all my joy is not to be rebuked.

But I am boring you, and how rude to let you stand. Please come in. No, please don't! It's so grim inside. I don't know what to say.

FRIAR.   I'll stay outside then. How can I help you?
I will teach you how a prayer is a bird,
And it and good deeds, lighter than the frankincense,
Fly godward. Let me wash your father's face.

(*The Witch goes into the house and returns with a basin and a rag. While the idiot grunts in annoyance, the friar washes him*)

IDIOT. Wine! Hooo! (*He slops the whole bottle over his face*)

WITCH. Oh! It's never any use, no use ever. Let me take him inside.

FRIAR. I am afraid I irritated him.

WITCH. No no. (*To the idiot*) Give me your hand, nicely now, give me your hand, Stand up, it's good night now. Good night. (*She takes him inside*)

FRIAR. Please don't scold him! It was my fault. (*Alone*) How gentle this girl seems, and how patiently unhappy. What are the loveliness of the thin, smoking cascade and the rumored supremacy of the spirits? Beside a twenty-year-old girl nothing seems alive to a young man. This is what the prior hinted. And I do not forget his documented advice.

I should like to know the use of beauty.
It seems so incidental to the stuff
And purpose of the world. Why should creation

Sing when it could grumble? (*Pause*) Now let me think
High thoughts and place a strong hand on my brain
Because it is when mind relaxes
That the body snaps the man and God is lost.
Come, thoughts! The topic: Beauty.
For one it is a hospital: ill from the ache of blueprints,
Ledgers and percentages, he betakes himself to lyric poetry,
Or plunks two roses on his desk,
Or lets the meadows cure him and the mountains nurse.
For some, beauty dwells in strict Reality,
The order of the speeding stars,
The dance and music of inexorable numbers.
But for most, what is beauty
But a merest humblest annex to their house,
A pattern on their butter, rouge on a girl,
Daffodils or shepherds stitched in tablecloths.
Oh friar, collar your thoughts! Arrange!
Topic, topic, topic, lucid, excellent;
My subject, Beauty, in the clean abstract.
Is Beauty a bed for the lounging of idlers
A noble excuse for shiftlessness,
An invitation to neutrality?
"A still life of a loaf of bread! Away with your brush!
Give bread to the starving nations!"
And some have entered beauty like a church—
Is she coming? I am troubled because of this girl.
She kissed my lips, and then what argument
Appeases or outsmarts the gorgeous blood?
When she returns, oh I must press her for a longer kiss.
How sweet, how good the night seems, as though
From the shrubs, hidden flowers were singing!
She is here!

WITCH. I have put him to bed. Dear young man, will you eat something with me?

FRIAR. Yes. Thank you. And I must recover that scarf from the monkey, and then go find the poor peddler. He may have come by and never stopped.

WITCH. But it's too dark to find a poor peddler. Sleep here, please stay, and entertain me. Don't answer! Sit here, and drink and eat. Here is a clean cup for your wine.

FRIAR. I don't drink wine.

WITCH. Why not?

FRIAR. God tells us beware of drunkenness. Wine is a mitigated evil; that is to say, it is not scandalously bad, and several minor saints have praised it. But because it is the first step to luxury, I had rather drink water.

WITCH. What a funny speech! Well, here is water. (*He drinks*) Now let me drink from your cup, the way lovers always do. Will you have meat, vegetables, and bread?

FRIAR. I am not allowed meat.

WITCH. Why not?

FRIAR. God tells us not to kill life. Eating the meat of an animal accustoms us to the mutilation of life. I myself, quite privately, believe that a soul dwells in all beings endowed with eyes. Therefore I will eat only a little bread and these beans.

WITCH. You speak so strangely.

FRIAR. I am very sober.

WITCH. Sober indeed!

>   You are like the red tempest
>   Hesitating one instant
>   Astraddle two waves.
>   You are like the violent falcon
>   Deceiving the sky with stiff
>   Horizontal wings.
>   You are like the tilting steed
>   Stunned in his rampage by fear
>   Of one new noise.

Friar, are you afraid of me? (*She takes his hand*)

FRIAR (*standing up*). No! We are under God. (*He sits down again*) I shall eat another piece of bread.

WITCH. Who is God? You have mentioned the name several times. And you took your hand away.

FRIAR. My poor absent sister, is it possible? And do I have to speak of Him while munching bread? He is the invisible terrible No between yourself and sin, and the nebulous Yes which fumbles us to heaven, we hope.

WITCH. Is it he who told you not to drink wine and eat meat?

FRIAR. Yes. Invisibility has written books on such matters.

WITCH. I think invisibility is very silly. I should be sorry if *I* were invisible. Shouldn't you?

FRIAR. Yes.

WITCH. Am I beautiful?

FRIAR. Every star in the sky, I think, is an eye admiring you.

WITCH. What pretty things you say! I shall reward you by excusing you from meat and wine. And to thank me for the reward you may kiss my lips.

FRIAR. I may not kiss a woman.

WOMAN. Why could that be?

FRIAR. Because all philosophy and religion regard woman as a great distraction to accurate thought.

WOMAN. But what if the woman is beautiful?

FRIAR. Why then she ought to be especially feared and avoided.

WITCH. And if she is ugly? Can you kiss her then?

FRIAR. Then the danger, I suppose, is less. But I am not sure, because our books and priests seem to be concerned most of the time with beautiful women.

WITCH. But if you may not kiss a beautiful woman, may you touch her with your hand?

FRIAR. By no means. We are much warned against it, except in greetings, like good morning or good evening.

WITCH. Then good evening and good morning and forever good morning and good evening! I knew your priests would find some way out of all that grumpiness. (*She takes his hand again*)

FRIAR. You are laughing at me a little.

WITCH. They are the whitest hands I have ever seen. I will call them pilgrims, and me their shrine!

FRIAR. Pilgrims and shrines! You know something about the world after all!

WITCH. I do? What curious things hands are. They have a hundred little private syllables to say "I don't know" or "I am afraid" or "I protest" or "I am angry", and then there are the eyes, by which lovers' hearts travel when the words don't dare as yet. Please don't frown! You are disappointed because my hands are not as white as yours. But my heart is as soft as your palm.

(*The friar rises in great agitation*)

FRIAR. This is wrong. I have to be on my way. The peddler.

WITCH. If I were a horrid leper you wouldn't go.

FRIAR. Now you are crying! What shall I do? All this is *so* unbecoming. We are strangers, after all.

WITCH. Then sit down again and tell me who you are. I forgot to ask you.

FRIAR. I am a very young man not worth anybody's attention. I was weaned from the seminary a week ago to try the world and to make certain

observations upon it which demand an absolutely clear mind. My biography, so far, would read, "He was born and raised."
WITCH. That is so marvelously simple!

> Thank you for being born,
> For I was born as well, and so there's hope,
> Since I have seen the most eccentric birds
> Meet on a single thorn.
>
> Thank you for being raised,
> You might have died, and I too, on the way,
> We might have lain together grave by grave,
> And never faced.

And now we are getting to know each other. You have even met my family.
FRIAR. Why do you keep all these animals?
WITCH. They come to me, and stay.
FRIAR. Is your father kind to you as far as he can be?
WITCH. As kind as the moss: indifferent but soft.
FRIAR. Is your mother dead?
WITCH. I don't know. What is this on your forehead? So deep a canal my little finger goes swimming in it!
FRIAR. Here? Why, I'm not sure. It feels like a furrow.
WITCH. The first whipmark of time, and you didn't know it. Don't you gaze at yourself in the mirror?
FRIAR. No, of course not. Why should I?
WITCH. Because your beauty would fill you with reverent pleasure. I am bewitched by that little sluice between your nose and the middle of your upper lip. And bedeviled by your green eyes and the long lashes that make awnings over them. But now I want you to attend to me. Do you see this monstrous spot on my cheekbone? I would like to know whether it reminds you of a cockroach or some other ugly insect.
FRIAR. A pretty insect; a pretty ladybug dozing on a white leaf.
WITCH. Is it? I will tolerate it from now on for your sake.
FRIAR. Sing for me.
WITCH.   But I am singing all the while!
               How deaf you must be
               When all my nerves
               Sing in love's incalculable style.

THE FRIAR, THE PEDDLER AND THE WITCH

        Why did you wait so many years,
        My unforgivable? I begged you
        To hurry, the wind heard,
        Only you covered your ears.

        So now at last let fingers clutch,
        Our limbs be neighborly,
        Breath dive into breath,
        Shoulder and shoulder touch.

Why are you afraid, when the very sparrows eat out of my palm?
FRIAR. Sparrows! Sparrows indeed! If I were a sparrow I too would nest in your hand. Who ever heard of a moral sparrow? I want to sleep. I've a long journey tomorrow, and I intend to dream of peddlers. Good night. Why don't you speak frankly and say good night?
WITCH. But, dearest, do you go to bed without bathing?
FRIAR. Bathing! I have not enough philosophy left to turn a gnat from a spider web—I would kiss you if half a crumb less than God himself stood between us—and you talk of scrubbing backs and soaping faces!
WITCH (laughs). My strange lover!

        I am not sure at all I know
        What you say,
        But neither do I know
        Why the branches row
        And why the squirrels don't pray,

        And why my love is rougher
        Than the sudden undertow
        That pulls the swimmer in the bay
        And deep, beneath its cover,
        Makes his woebegone body play.

Come with me, friar, by the pool, where no one watches, neither above nor below. Come with me, let go your dusty fear. Come.
FRIAR. Take your bath! I want to be alone.
WITCH. What a pity! I had such games in mind for the moon in the water and you and me.
FRIAR. What are you doing?
(*The Witch begins to undress among the shrubs*)

WITCH.   Poor moon! He never says a word and acts quite cold,
                But at my touch he bursts into a hundred drops of gold,
                Yet though he's shattered the moment I come near,
                His higher self gives me a circular sneer —

FRIAR. You don't mean to undress completely before me?
WITCH. I always undress here because I can hang my clothes on the twigs.
    You can go inside the house if you wish, my sweet.
FRIAR. Why should *I* go inside the house? Have *I* anything to be ashamed of?
WITCH. Perhaps you do. Sweetest, won't you come with me?
FRIAR. Don't step nearer! I ask you.
WITCH. Wait for me! (*Exit, singing*)
                My rose will endure,
                An angel is man,
                Kings will be poor
                And three shall be one.
                Then, then my mortal love will last.
FRIAR (*on his knees*).
                My first night, my God, and I am slipping
                Out of my innocence glance by glance,
                Nothing by nothing. I should have been blind.
                And they needed a man to count the loaves
                And sell our garden's carrots.
                I might, by mere neglect of life,
                Have got myself a nook in Paradise.
                This girl and my first night—my first night,
                Stupid with desire. I will be surely grasping her,
                And lust away my mind. I, study evil!
                The hunter was right.
                Corruption in its carcass pondering corruption,
                Is that science? Too hard for me. Let me go home.
                The stillborn cell for me, and the heart ticking as even
                As the clock of the refectory. Up! (*He rises*)
                This is much better. But oh won't it be rude
                To leave without thank you, goodbye, a blessing,
                And maxims recommending God in time of trouble?
                And the peddler, and the scarf!
(*Enter the monkey, pulling the peddler's bag. The scarf hangs around his neck*)
FRIAR. The peddler's bag! And the scarf! Monkey, where is the peddler?

(*The monkey makes frantic noises at the friar*) What does this mean? Yo ho, old peddler, are you there? What is the beast trying to say? I've heard stories of men murdered and faithful animals leading the law to their bodies. Yes, yes. What are you trying to tell me, poor squealer? Here is my hand. Yes, tell me all, or take me to the poor man. He seems to understand me! He is putting the scarf into the bag as if he had seen the peddler do it. As if it were his own. As if—(*all the unseen animals suddenly make their noises*) My God, my God—can it be true? Are you the—? And the other animals, are they—? A witch! God save me! Ah! Don't touch me! My umbrella!
(*He runs away. The monkey dashes after him, then returns disconsolately and putters with the clothing. The animal noises die out, and all is silent when the woman returns. The monkey tries to embrace her*)

WITCH. Away, lecher! Away lecher, away! (*Exit the monkey, weeping and dragging the bundle*) Hunter, I have done your bidding. Time, gallop, time, grizzle that friar! Old he came and old he becomes.

SCENE THREE

(*Same as Scene One. Next afternoon. The hunter sits bathing his feet in a large basin as the friar appears on a height, transformed into an old man*)

FRIAR. Hunter! Hunter! (*He leaps down a ledge and almost falls*)
HUNTER. Slow and easy, granddad. At your age one doesn't go diving like a chamois.
FRIAR. "At my age?" Hunter, look at me—we met yesterday! I'm the innocent friar.
HUNTER. My word, so you are! Let me rub my feet dry. (*He slips into his boots and rises*) Oho, I understand. It's a disguise. Shrewd, sir friar!—a disguise to inquire into the evils of the wicked world without falling into temptations on the way.
FRIAR. I don't know what you mean. But I'm dreaming. I don't recognize my own voice, I have aches in my waist and in my legs, I walk doubled over, and you—hunter, who are you? And who am I? Why did you pretend not to recognize me? Why do you babble about disguises?
HUNTER. How in the devil's name should I recognize you? This is no place for a costume party, you know. Here's a basin—pardon a few specks of muck in the water—look at yourself!

FRIAR (*at first speechless*). It's a dream. I am twenty years old. (*Shaking his head*) I have no wrinkles. I have no wrinkles at all. And my hands don't tremble. (*Puts down the basin*)

HUNTER (*sententious*). Live and change, change and live.

FRIAR. Now I begin to understand the truth.

> And I know you—a farcical spirit that fools
> Between the first and fortieth wink of God.
> Therefore before you rub your hands
> Or oil your mind for your next prank,
> Let me assure you that I am not frightened,
> And distinctly not tempted into anger.
> All I ask of God is to wake up—
> That is how sublimely simple it is.
> He will not let me creep at an angle
> Through the woods, and speak like sandpaper,
> My mouth between two corrugated cheeks,
> Laughed at by some minimal devil.

HUNTER. Minimal!

FRIAR.   Was I too slow hating the woman?
> Pardon me, pardon me. But I ran!
> I am not an animal. Sweet God,
> I need so many, many years to find
> Your face among the sins.
> As I stand,
> As I curse you, I never touched the girl.

HUNTER. What a pity you didn't! If I had been twenty....

FRIAR. Prayers, fasts, and abstinence will remind Him he has overlooked an accident here. I have forty, fifty years to go. My health is superb! I could work another sixty years.

HUNTER. At your age?

FRIAR. You're an illusion! A warning! A trial! Devil, I exorcise you!

HUNTER (*half-aside*). It's been tried before.

FRIAR.   Total of sums,
> Period of phrases,
> King of ministers,
> Truth of opinions,

Save me, cleanse me, harbor me, cure me, praise me, hold me, remember me, remember me.....

THE FRIAR, THE PEDDLER AND THE WITCH

(*Exit*)

HUNTER. What a lot of mumbling! (*He takes his boots off and starts to wash his feet again*)

> The sun warms his toes,
> The moon duly moons.
> Matters stand as matters should,
> And each thief has his spoons.
>
> The soldier has his gun,
> The sailor has his boat.
> Bird flies, fish dips, hare jumps,
> And gangsters vote.
>
> I like to do a touch of right,
> I like to do a bit of wrong.
> The two together make a rhyme,
> With which, good souls, I end my song.

The End

THE FRIAR, THE PEDDLER AND THE WITCH

Notes

The original title was *The Monk Who Wouldn't*—an attractive one, but at the time I wrote the play (probably in 1955), and for many years to come, "monk" and "friar" were words hardly differentiated in my mind. As a matter of course, they became clear to me when I began to work on *The Art of Alessandro Magnasco* and looked into his many depictions of friars. Be that as it may, *The Monk Who Wouldn't* was published in the Summer 1962 issue of *First Stage: a Quarterly of New Drama*, then again, revised, in Volume Two of my *Collected Plays* (1972), and thoroughly bettered for the present volume. As mentioned in the Foreword, it is the earliest of the plays I have allowed to survive.

The Friar, the Peddler and the Witch is based on a Kabuki drama by Kyoka Izumi, *Kohya-No-Hijiri* ("The Holy man of Mount Koya") which I saw staged in Tokyo in 1954, while stationed there as a private first class in the U.S. Army. I recollect only that the Japanese play was built around the Circean motif I used for my own purpose.

VI

IV

THE KUKKURRIK FABLES

≈≈

43 mini-plays

TABLE OF CONTENTS[3]

The sociable swallow, 690

Agamemnon's cupbearer, 691
A banquet in Venice, 694
A bone of contention, 696
The caterpillar and the leaf, 697
The conceited minnow, 698
A conference of kings, 698
A conversation between a bulldozer and a mouse, 699
The crow and the beggar, 701
The dragon of Helgoland, 701
The eagle on the mountain, 702
The faithful gardener, 703
The farmer, his son and his mule, 704
The flattered hippopotamus, 706
A flea protests, 706
The fox and the crow, 707
Hank the salesman, 708
How God bested the Devil, 710
How God learned what measure is, 711
In the belly of the whale, 713
The innovation, 715
The journey of a cow, 715
Kukkurrik triumphant, 718
Landscape with cloud and dunes, 720
The lucky pebble, 721
The lunatic pigeon, 722
The moth who disguised himself as a dragon, 723
The nameless tree, 725
The owl who didn't like long necks, 726
The parliament of animals, 727
The perfidious spider, 729
The pony who came to a stream, 731
The queen and the poodle, 732

---

[3] The first fable stands as prologue, the last as epilogue. The others are in alphabetical order.

The rich ibis and the pauper thrush, 734
The rock and the sea, 737
The spinster, the canary and the cat, 738
The squirrel who was caught in a war, 739
The stubborn cobbler, 741
The termite and the ant, 742
Three revolting animals, 744
The tiger who became humane, 746
The two mice, 747

Aesop's apology, 748

Notes, 751

THE SOCIABLE SWALLOW

Characters: Narrator, the Swallow, the Seal, the Leader of the swallows

NARRATOR. A flock of migrant swallows had landed at break of day on a small island in the ocean. One of the swallows, more sociable than the others, decided to strike up a conversation with a seal nearby.

SWALLOW. Ah what a flight we had last night!

NARRATOR. Said the swallow for a beginning. The seal, however, was half asleep, so he lifted only one of his two eyelids and said as vaguely as possible...

SEAL. Oooo....

SWALLOW. Oh yes! A thick fog came in maybe a hundred miles from here, we lost sight of the stars, and if we hadn't put a fairly clever leader in charge, we might never have landed here for our rest.

SEAL. Oooo....

SWALLOW. Oh yes! Not that I for example couldn't have found the way as well as he. But I'm one of the younger ones, I have to keep my place. However, once we land in the north, I'll find a healthy wife, make a few babies, and become top-swallow in my turn.

SEAL. Oooo....

SWALLOW. Oh yes! Of course it's a long way from here. Hundreds of miles, more fog, storms, nasty wind currents, gulls and boobies that cross your flight line. But we know what we're doing and we know where we're going. It's been in our blood for millions of years, swallows are smarties.

SEAL. Oooo....

SWALLOW. Oh yes! Look at me for instance. Notice this metal strip around my ankle?

SEAL. Grrumph....

NARRATOR. The seal thought he was having a noisy dream.

SWALLOW. Some fool of a fellow took me in his hands when I was an infant and slipped this ring on for me. Thanks, I said. Somebody makes me a present, I don't ask why. It looks distinguished, don't you agree? Maybe I can pass it on to my children. Heredity, you know. This is known as a decorative mutation.

SEAL. Oooo....

SWALLOW. Oh yes! Of course everybody is used to seeing it by now and it doesn't flutter feathers anymore. But on the return trip at the end of the season, when it's always more crowded, I'll attract a lot of attention with this bauble flashing in the sun. It will help my career. To be sure we travel mostly by night, but even then there's the occasional lighthouse. Did you know that lighthouses are dangerous?

SEAL. Oooo....

SWALLOW. Oh yes! Fools rush into them and then it's a short plop to kingdom come. The trouble is we fly low, most of the time we skim the waves. And we're crazy about light, we're sun-worshippers, though we do fly at night, I'm not sure I know why, maybe because the stars are useful, who knows?

NARRATOR. Just then the leader of the swallows called his flock together.

LEADER. Away, away, let's make up the time we lost in the fog, away away!

NARRATOR. After they had been aloft for a while, the leader turned to the sociable swallow.

LEADER. Why were you wasting your breath talking to that lump of a seal, when you ought to keep it for the journey?

SWALLOW. Because I for one have an alert mind and like to stay in touch.

LEADER. Stay in touch with a blubbery seal?

SWALLOW. What do you mean, blubbery? Let me tell you that this seal happened to be one of the most interesting personalities I have ever met.

NARRATOR. So spoke the sociable swallow, not without a touch of indignation.... And now that I think of it, I too am utterly fascinated by anyone willing to listen to me.

AGAMEMNON'S CUPBEARER

Characters: Narrator, Agamemnon, Alycus, Sinon, Diomedes, Ajax, Nestor, Odysseus.

NARRATOR. Agamemnon and his generals were considering for the thousandth time how to set about capturing Troy. Achilles was dead, the city was standing as tall and stiff as it had stood ten years before, and it seemed that everything had been tried—

AGAMEMNON. Catapults, battering rams, showers of fire, volleys of treachery, even negotiations.

NARRATOR. What to do next? The warriors thought and thought as hard

as warriors can, but Diomedes had no special ideas except...
DIOMEDES. How about a bigger ram?
NARRATOR. Ajax scratched his head and said...
AJAX. Why not send another thousand footsoldiers out to have a bash at the gate?
NARRATOR. Odysseus just looked wily; and Nestor stroked his beard and observed...
NESTOR. Let us be wise.
NARRATOR. Finally they decided to shoot a few more arrows into the town, and then the meeting broke up. Now Agamemnon was alone with his servants, and he sat in his tent a weary man.
AGAMEMNON (*to himself*). The only way out, I suppose, is to send for Sinon...
NARRATOR. The famous military expert from Macedonia.
AGAMEMNON. It's a humiliating step to take—an expert from the provinces!—and it's going to be damned expensive, but what else is left? A final retreat? Become a clown in the history books? Give Homer a chance to sing scurrilous ballads about me?
NARRATOR. His mind still far away, Agamemnon noticed that his sixteen-year old cupbearer, Alycus, was standing timidly before him, waiting for a pause in the hero's thoughts to speak to him.
AGAMEMNON. What is it, Alycus?
ALYCUS. My lord, you should build a great wooden animal on wheels, hollow inside, and fill it with our best soldiers, and then pretend to break up camp and sail home. The Trojans will be sure to tow the animal into the city, and then at night our men can climb out of it and open the gate so the whole Greek army can pour in.
AGAMEMNON (*smiling*). Lovely; you are one smart little boy; but now go tell Glaukos that he might as well serve; I am dining alone tonight. And bring me quill and tablet before you go.
NARRATOR. That night, Agamemnon wrote to Sinon and summoned him to the Greek camp. Two weeks later Sinon stood before him.
SINON. I'll do my best, general, but it will cost you eight talents.
AGAMEMNON. Eight talents? That's half the booty we've taken in ten years of victories!
SINON. Eight talents for my services, two more if I succeed, and three if I fail.
AGAMEMNON. Why?
SINON. To compensate me for the injury to my reputation.
NARRATOR. Agamemnon almost choked. But there was no bargaining.
AGAMEMNON (*aside*). Damn damn. What if the son of a whore signs up

with the Trojans?
NARRATOR. As soon as he was hired, Sinon began to poke—
SINON. Allow *me*.
NARRATOR. Of course, sir.
SINON. I poked at the Trojan battlements, looked for secret drains, measured the walls, counted Greek heads, examined supplies and equipment, reassessed the lines of communication, and even infiltrated Troy itself by disguising two assistants as old Cappadocian crones peddling sausages.
NARRATOR. After four months...
SINON. May *I*?
NARRATOR. Sorry, sir.
SINON. After four months, I submitted my full report, over a thousand tablets long, containing, among others, chapters on Background and Prospects, Tables of Casualties, Losses of Equipment, Forces Committed, Temporary and Permanent Allies, Deficits Due to Desertion, Analysis of Strategy Shifts, and Recommendations for Actions in the Light of Existing Conditions.
NARRATOR. The report was read to the assembled chiefs.
SINON. To conclude, I recommend that a horse be built of wood, filled with seasoned infantrymen and planted in front of Troy while your main body feigns a withdrawal. The Trojans will beyond a doubt lead the horse into the city to rejoice over, and that same night your men will issue forth, open the city's gate, and, together with the main body, overwhelm your foe.
AGAMEMNON. An idea worthy of the gods!...
NARRATOR. Cried Agamemnon. Odysseus chimed in...
ODYSSEUS. I adopt it, I make it mine!
NARRATOR. Ajax was brief and to the point...
AJAX. Smashing!
NARRATOR. And wise Nestor gave his assent too...
NESTOR. The contrivance of a sage.
NARRATOR. The poor cupbearer, who happened to be present, didn't dare remind even himself that he had thought up the selfsame stratagem half a year before, and gratis at that.
ALYCUS (*to himself*). I must have said something different with a stupid twist to it.
SINON (*frostily*). Gentlemen, I am glad you are satisfied. The task of implementation is yours. Tomorrow I return to Macedonia.
NARRATOR. The Greeks paid him, built the horse, took Troy...
AGAMEMNON. And sacked it to the last footstool.

DIOMEDES, AJAX, ULYSSES, NESTOR. AGAMEMNON
>   (*singing*)
>   Fly over Troy, victorious flags,
>   And brawny boys, shout hail!
>   With booty bulging in our bags,
>   Stoutly home we sail.

NARRATOR. The story of Agamemnon's cupbearer may be unfamiliar to you. I have it from Arctinus of Miletus, who wrote fables a long, long time ago, and who adds his own curious comment to this one.

ALYCUS. "What father," says Arctinus, "will listen to the advice of his son, what professor will heed a pupil's hypothesis, what millionaire will adopt the faith of his mechanic? We Greeks, I am afraid, weigh the man instead of the idea: we had rather keep our heads empty than stoop to be instructed."

A BANQUET IN VENICE

Characters: Narrator, the King of Podolia, the Doge, the Overseer of Public Charities, the Cripple.

NARRATOR. The young king of Podolia was traveling to broaden his views and make friends for Podolia. In Venice he was received with satisfying pomp and shown the wonders of the city, its art treasures, its dungeons, and its famous Arsenal. One late afternoon, after several hours of banqueting in the Ducal Palace, the king turned to the doge who was sitting to his right and said...

KING. My friend and venerable host, tomorrow I must pursue my journey. Allow me therefore to make a last request of you. Bring before me two citizens of Venice. Let one of them be the happiest, and the other the unhappiest man in the state. For to climax the memorable entertainment I have enjoyed in your city, I wish to ask your happiest Venetian for his secret, and help your most wretched citizen out of his misery—if any misery be allowed in your fair republic.

DOGE. A charming request, your majesty, and unmistakably Podolian!

NARRATOR. Now the whispers went eagerly back and forth among the senators and councillors, and a good-humored contention took place, until the doge's own advice prevailed and two messengers were dispatched into very different districts to summon the chosen men. An hour later the two citizens appeared. The contrast between them was unsurprising, for one man was smiling, arrayed in the richest furs, silks and jewels imaginable, while the other was clad in malodorous rags, he tottered along by leaning on a stick, and a nervous anxiety contorted his wrinkled face.

DOGE. Your majesty's wish is granted.

KING. Indeed it is. Ah, my lord, how awesome is the distance from happiness to misery when they stand so nakedly illustrated before our eyes. (*Turning to the two men*) You, sir, shall tell me whether riches alone have made you happy; and you, my poor man, may ask me for a modest sum that shall enable you to make a new and fairer beginning in life.

NARRATOR. Before either of the men could answer, the guests all began to titter, and the doge spoke as follows...

DOGE. Your highness is mistaken. This beaming citizen, our Overseer of Public Charities, happens to be the most miserable creature in Venice. And the happiest Venetian is yonder unwashed and fidgeting beggar.

KING. How can this be? The rich man is all smiles, the poor man looks wretched. All is as it should be, unless a comedy is being played at my expense.

OVERSEER. No, no, your highness, this is no comedy!

NARRATOR. Cried the Overseer...

OVERSEER. I am smiling because, on the way to the palace, I was informed that your majesty had promised to relieve the unhappiest man in Venice, and now, when I stood before you, I heard the confirmation from your own munificent lips. (*He prostrates himself*)

KING. What ails you? Rise, rise.

OVERSEER. I owned ten galleons trading with the Orient. News came this morning that three are lost at sea. My credit is fatally hurt, I am compelled to dismiss half my cooks and lackeys, and I must either commit suicide, or else suffer the jeers of my hated rival, the Director of Urban Works.

NARRATOR. Hot tears spurted out of the Overseer's eyes, moistening the carpet under him. But now the king turned toward the poor cripple.

KING. And you? If you are the happiest man in Venice, why these rags, why this tormented expression?

CRIPPLE. Um, um, um!

DOGE. He is mute, your majesty, but I shall reply for him. The man was born on the pavement and has slept all his life on cold flagstones. This morning he inherited from a thief we hanged a pallet filled with worms and rotten straw, and tonight he will sleep in a bed for the first time since he was born. My messenger hauled him away as the sun was going down; he longs for his cot; he had been the blissfullest man in Venice, perhaps in the whole

world, and will be so again if your highness will detain him no longer.
NARRATOR. The young king waved his hand in dismissal, and as the doge had foretold, a joyful smile drew itself out on the poor man's face, and he hobbled away on his crutch as speedily as he could.
(*The beggar leaves with smiles and thankful noises*)
KING (*to the Overseer*). As for you, I should like to relieve you, but three galleons are two galleons more than Podolia owns. Here, however, is a garnet ring. Wear it; you are now a Knight of the Pewter of Podolia.
NARRATOR. This was no common distinction...
OVERSEER. Oh, thank you, your highness, thank you!
NARRATOR. And the Overseer departed a little less distraught than he had arrived.
DOGE (*smiling*). My royal friend, you forgot to ask the happiest man for his secret.
KING. I think I know it already, your excellency. To be happy is to take a leap forward, though it be from nothing to little; and to be miserable is to be thrust backward, though it be from very much to merely much.
DOGE (*lifting his glass to the king*). There is great wisdom in Podolia.
KING (lifting his glass to the doge). It lay dormant until Venice brought it out.

A BONE OF CONTENTION

Characters: Narrator, the Fox-terrier, the Spaniel, the Hawk.

NARRATOR. A fox-terrier and a spaniel were fighting over a steakbone. Merciful heavens, they went for each other with teeth, claws, shoves, barks and kicks.
FOX-TERRIER. Get away from my bone!
SPANIEL. This bone belongs to me!
FOX-TERRIER. Mongrel!
SPANIEL. Flotsam!
FOX-TERRIER. I'll throttle you with your own tail!
SPANIEL. I'll throw you to the cats!
FOX-TERRIER. Oaf!
SPANIEL. Fleaface!
FOX-TERRIER. Lickspittle!
SPANIEL. Perpetrator!

NARRATOR. It was a fearful spectacle, for both dogs were bleeding out of a dozen wounds. Considering this opportunity, a young hawk, inexperienced in the sad ways of the world, came down from a tree in order to pick up the bone for himself. The dogs stopped fighting at once.
SPANIEL. Who's this?
FOX-TERRIER. A foreigner!
SPANIEL *and* FOX-TERRIER. Brother dogs, unite!
NARRATOR. And both dogs flung themselves on the bird.
HAWK. Help! They're murdering me!
NARRATOR. The hawk was lucky he escaped alive that day with a small loss of feathers. But what would have happened if *I* had reached out a hand for the bone?
SPANIEL, FOX-TERRIER *and* HAWK. Brother animals, unite! Down with man!
NARRATOR. Stop, my friends, stop! I was only pretending! But wait. Suppose a Martian were to land and take a fancy to our bone. What then?
ALL FOUR. Earth-brothers, chase the Martian!
NARRATOR. For there isn't *anybody* with whom we couldn't make a faction. In the meantime, the hawk went for other game, the spaniel chewed one end of the bone, and the fox-terrier nibbled the other. They were still bleeding, but they were bleeding in peace.

THE CATERPILLAR AND THE LEAF

Characters: The Caterpillar, the Leaf.

(*The caterpillar is munching on the leaf*)
LEAF. Why are you nibbling me up? cried the leaf to the caterpillar. It hurts; I am bleeding; I will die.
CATERPILLAR. Believe me—answered the caterpillar—I have nothing against you personally.
LEAF (*weeping*). Then why don't you go elsewhere?
CATERPILLAR. Because I have nothing for you personally either.
(*He takes another bite. The leaf cries out*)

THE CONCEITED MINNOW

Characters: Narrator, the Fisherman, the Minnow.

NARRATOR. A fisherman had already caught three handsome trout—they were lying in a basket next to him—when he hooked a minnow.
FISHERMAN. My lousy luck!
NARRATOR. He was about to throw it back into the stream when the minnow, catching sight of his grimace, cried out...
MINNOW. And what's the matter with me, if I may ask? Let me inform you that I'm as good as any trout that swims in these waters. I'm small, but I am good looking, smart, and appetizing. In short, I resent your gesture of contempt and demand to be treated with the respect I deserve.
FISHERMAN. Oh well, if you insist.
NARRATOR. And he tossed the minnow into his basket.
(*The Narrator inspects the basket*)
NARRATOR. I don't know about people, but in minnows, once the ego breaks loose, there's no telling *where* it will stop.

A CONFERENCE OF KINGS

Characters: Narrator, the First King, the Second King.

NARRATOR. Two kings had met to argue over a border dispute. One was clothed in gold and silver, the other was dressed in rags, and his face was full of cuts. The king in gold and silver was shocked.
FIRST KING. Brother, what has happened to you? Look at your rags, look at those bruises, I can't stand it!
NARRATOR. And he forgot all about the border dispute.
FIRST KING. What did they do to you, brother?
SECOND KING. Don't ask. I've been all but hacked to death. I'm a good king. I raised everybody's wages and salaries and commissions and deductions and dividends and pensions and royalties, and the people got used

to enjoying money, so they asked for more, but the treasury was empty, I sold the queen's jewels, the rich denounced me, the rabble besieged me, everybody threw stones at me, and if it hadn't been for our blessed border dispute they would have murdered me to pieces. While look at you, oh look at you! Gorgeous and peppery, without a wrinkle anywhere on your face. Brother, how do you do it?

FIRST KING. If only you'd asked before! Unlike you, I made my ministers impose a tax on my people so heavy it would have ruined five generations to come. At the last moment, when all you heard in the realm was the noise of sobs and groans, I made an unforgettable gesture from my balcony and reduced the tax by one entire tenth. And now, brother, what do you think?

SECOND KING. That you're rich enough to buy Mammon, and that the people, though hungry, bless you everywhere you go. (*He sobs*)

FIRST KING. My dear, dear people.

A CONVERSATION BETWEEN A BULLDOZER AND A MOUSE

Characters: Narrator, the Bulldozer, the Mouse, the Mother Mouse.

NARRATOR. A large bulldozer was tearing up a field in which a family of mice had made its nest. As the bulldozer carved its way nearer and nearer to their home, the mice could hear the groans of wounded bitterweeds and the gasps of slain beetles rising from all sides of the field.

MOTHER MOUSE. What shall we do?

NARRATOR. The mother was crying, hugging her miceling.

MOTHER MOUSE. Look at those terrible jaws gnashing away at the earth! Do something, daddy! Go talk to him!

NARRATOR. So her husband leaped forward and ran up to the machine, which he addressed as follows.

MOUSE. Lord Bulldozer, spare my little family; we are poor but honest mice that have lived in this useless lot for many years without disturbing the peace.

NARRATOR. The bulldozer paused.

BULLDOZER. And what makes you think that I have come to disturb the peace?

MOUSE. Well——

BULLDOZER. Nonsense! You are thoroughly mistaken. I am leveling the ground for an eighty-five-story apartment house as a special favor to you mice.

MOUSE. As a special favor to us mice?

BULLDOZER. Yes, sir. You have been disgracefully happy in a sordid nest with an occasional dandelion in your gullet; but after I have finished my work, you will take your pick of a hundred rooms, each one overflowing with bread and cheese, potatoes, and lamb chops. The nation of mice will thrive. You will erect a monument to me.

MOUSE. I am very glad that the nation of mice will thrive; but what about us?

BULLDOZER. Who is us?

MOUSE. Us, me, my woman, and my two miceling.

BULLDOZER. I don't know 'us'; I deal in principles. Excuse me, but I have work to do.

NARRATOR. The mouse ran back to his family, and said as cheerfully as he could...

MOUSE. The bulldozer brought me good news: he is growing an apartment house here especially for the nation of mice, and we will live in whipped cream to the end of time.

NARRATOR. And before the mother mouse could make a comment (a pity, because she was a sensible beast)...

MOTHER MOUSE. Look out!

NARRATOR. A ton of earth fell on top of them, and the bulldozer churned on. (*Pause*) Let you be more careful than these mice, and when you see progress coming your way...

THE TWO MICE (*feebly, from under the pile of earth*). Jump aside in time....

THE CROW AND THE BEGGAR

Characters: Narrator, the Beggar, the Crow.

NARRATOR. A beggar was standing with his cap in his hand far from the road, all alone in a field of boulders and stubble. A cold wind crept from gray horizon to gray horizon. Puzzled by the sight, a crow landed among the weeds a few paces from the man.
CROW. Beggar, no one will give you anything in this desert.
BEGGAR. Crow, no one will deny me anything in this desert.

THE DRAGON OF HELGOLAND

Characters: Narrator, the Dragon, the Badger

NARRATOR. We harm those we hate; we also hate those we harm; otherwise our conscience would sting us, and who likes to be stung? Not, at any rate, the dragon who lived in Helgoland.
DRAGON. I am the dragon of Helgoland, and I have taken a vow to exterminate all the raccoons of the realm.
NARRATOR. And may one ask why?
DRAGON. One may not, but I have my reasons, and history is on my side. Now I know there are raccoons in this impenetrable forest and—ecod, I can see one in yon undergrowth. With one belch of flames (*huge noise*) I have now laid waste five acres of land. Good. I hear a feeble lament in the ex-undergrowth which means another raccoon bagged. I'll go over and pay him off with a final burst. Ye gods! What have we here?
NARRATOR. The disappointment was a grave one, for instead of a raccoon, he found a litter of badgers, all burned to death, except for one who was just alive enough to despond.
BADGER. Why did you kill us? What harm did we do you in our short small lives? Why did you strike us down who are innocent?
DRAGON. Innocent devils! I hate you weasels; all the world knows you've

been plotting against me with the raccoons!
BADGER. But we are not weasels; we are badgers.
DRAGON. Well, I hate badgers too. They're always standing in the way of my fire.
NARRATOR. The last of the badgers did not live to hear this stiff accusation. But from that time on, the dragon never thought of badgers without spitting a flame of disgust.
DRAGON. Everybody is against me........

THE EAGLE ON THE MOUNTAIN

Characters: Narrator, the Mountain Climber, the First Eagle, the Second Eagle.

NARRATOR. Five sportsmen were climbing a huge mountain no human being had ever scaled. The gales blew and whistled between the crags, on all sides chasms opened, the air was thin, the men gasped and tottered into hurls of snow, three were buried in an avalanche that tore the mountain's face, a fourth lost hold of a ledge and fell headlong to his death, and at last the fifth—

(*The mountain climber appears*)

THE MOUNTAIN CLIMBER. Stumbled to the top, where, under a cold sun, I planted the flag of my beloved country. (*He salutes and sings*)
   From scaling this here mountain
   My heart it gallops like a nag.
   But twice as fast, believe you me,
   It thumps to see my country's flag.
NARRATOR. And down the mountain he tottered. An eagle, attracted by this colorful arrival, descended upon the flag.
FIRST EAGLE. I don't know what it is, but it certainly cheers things up around here. I wonder if it tastes as good as it looks.
NARRATOR. And he took a few nibbles.
FIRST EAGLE. No; this will never replace rabbit giblets. Let's see what happens if I nip it away from the stick it's attached to.
NARRATOR. Nip away he did, and the flag landed on one of his wings.
FIRST EAGLE. Gorgeous! Elegant!
NARRATOR. Just then another eagle flew by.
SECOND EAGLE. Hey Frizzle, what have you got there?

FIRST EAGLE. Oh, a new outfit, something stylish for my feathers.
NARRATOR. His friend was strongly impressed.
SECOND EAGLE. How did it come your way?
FIRST EAGLE. I hate to boast, but do you see that fellow all dressed up scrabbling down the mountain?
SECOND EAGLE. I do.
FIRST EAGLE. He brought it up specially for me.
SECOND EAGLE. Specially for you?
FIRST EAGLE. Can't you see?
NARRATOR. The other eagle could hardly deny the evidence. Word soon spread, and the happy bird draped in the flag became the most admired eagle of the range.

THE FAITHFUL GARDENER

Characters: Narrator, the Gardener, Death.

NARRATOR. An old gardener was shearing and trimming a privet hedge in a nobleman's park, when, looking up from his work, he saw a dark figure standing beside him.
GARDENER. Who are you?
NARRATOR. Asked the gardener. The figure replied...
DEATH. I am your death. Your time has come, gardener. I must take you away.
NARRATOR. For a few moments the old man was unable to speak. But then he said...
GARDENER. My hedge is unfinished. Look, I have evened it here as smooth as a baby's cheek, but yonder it is as wrinkled and rough as my own. Let me finish my work, it will not take me long; I wish to leave the park in order.
DEATH. Why care about leaving it in order? Presently, when I extend my long fingers into your old heart, you will have ceased to care.
GARDENER. I have been the duke's gardener for sixty years. What will he think of me if I leave him with a rough privet hedge?
DEATH. What will he think of you? Fool! I repeat that in another heartbeat there will be no *you* to care about privets and trimmings and masters.
GARDENER. But I care now! I care, I do! Let me finish my work!
DEATH. Death delays for nothing and no one.

GARDENER. Yes it does! We're debating, so you've delayed!
NARRATOR. And with his long fingers he took the gardener's life.
DEATH. You are mistaken. The moment hadn't come. Now it has.
NARRATOR. And he extended his long fingers into the old man's heart.

THE FARMER, HIS SON AND HIS MULE

Characters: Narrator, the Farmer, the Farmer's son, Four philosophers

NARRATOR. A farmer had loaded two sacks of potatoes on his mule and left for the market-town, accompanied by his little son. After selling the potatoes, feeding the mule, and stopping at a tavern with his boy for a loaf of bread, a hunk of cheese and (*for himself*) a mug of ale, he spoke as follows...

FARMER. Son, the road home is a long one. As I'm feeling my age and a heaviness in my head, I'll ride our Meg till we reach the stone bridge over the creek. By that time I'll be my chipper self again, we'll change places, and it'll be your turn to ride her as far as the roadside chapel to Our Lady. After that, we'll reward old Meg for carrying our potatoes and you and me, and let her trot home light and easy on her own.

NARRATOR. The lad happily agreed, and so, I think, did the mule, who had her own way, after so many years spent together, of understanding her master. Homeward they went, with the farmer astride the mule and singing a ditty, and the boy walking at his side, now hopping on one foot, now on the other. Presently they came across a philosopher and his disciples who were walking toward that same market-town for a convention of sages.

FARMER (*raising his hat*). Good day to you all, gentlemen...

NARRATOR. Said the farmer, bending down from his mule. And on he rode, the little boy at his side. The philosopher was above answering, but he turned around to watch the farmer, the lad and the mule ambling on their way until they were out of earshot, and then he said to his disciples, who had, of course, turned around with him...

FIRST PHILOSOPHER. There goes a fine lesson in selfishness! The coarse-grained father, smelling of cheap beer, takes his ease on the mule, while the delicate boy must drag behind him on the gravel. Let the child sweat! Let his soles bleed! The old ruffian is comfortable and that is all he cares about.

NARRATOR. Upon reaching the stone bridge over the creek about an hour later, the farmer got off the mule as promised and said to his son...

FARMER. Your turn, my boy! Let me seat you on old Meg. Oopsy-daisy, up you go!

NARRATOR. And off they went again, the farmer singing another ditty as he walked, and the mule in a good mood because of the lighter load he was now carrying. After another hour or so, they met a second philosopher on his way to the sages' convention. This one was alone, muttering aphorisms to himself.

FARMER (*raising his hat*). God be with you, sir.

NARRATOR. Again he received no reply, but the philosopher turned around to watch the little group moving off. Then he took out a note pad and scribbled...

SECOND PHILOSOPHER. The world has gone topsy-turvy at last. The child rides the mule, the old man trudges on foot. Soon, to complete the picture, the man will be carrying the beast on his shoulders.

NARRATOR. After reaching the chapel, where father and son crossed themselves and the mule uttered a pious bray, the farmer said...

FARMER. All right now, Meg has been a good girl; let's set her free; we'll walk on either side of her and try to reach home before supper.

NARRATOR. Off they went again, the mule ambling contentedly, the farmer singing and the boy hopping now on one foot and now on the other. They were nearing home when they crossed the path of two more philosophers on their way to the convention.

FARMER (*raising his hat*). Gentlemen, I bid you a good evening.

NARRATOR. The same thing happened as before. The philosophers said nothing to the farmer, as they were in the middle of a disputation about Being and Essence, but both turned around to watch the little family down the road and away.

THIRD PHILOSOPHER. Remarkable sight. It teaches us that folly is congenital in mankind and education cannot root it out. Two supposedly rational creatures walk alongside a mule, and to neither, it seems, does the idea occur that one of them, or both, could ride the animal.

FOURTH PHILOSOPHER (*with a sigh*). One does despair at last, does one not?

NARRATOR. Presently the farmer and his son got home, stabled the mule, and sat themselves down to the supper the farmer's wife had prepared. The boy had been itching to ask a question of his father.

BOY. Dad, who was all them fancy gentlemen you raised your hat to on our

way home and who never said nothin' to us?
FARMER. They are philosophers, my lad.
BOY. Philosophers? What are they?
FARMER. Philosophers are folk who understand things which the likes of us ain't likely to ever fathom, and that's why, when I pass them on the road, I raise my hat, and so must you, my boy, when you grow old enough to wear one.

THE FLATTERED HIPPOPOTAMUS

Characters: Narrator, the Hippopotamus, the Crocodile

NARRATOR. The hippopotamus was delighted.
CROCODILE. What are you delighted about?
NARRATOR. Asked his best friend, the crocodile, who was chagrined to see him so happy.
HIPPOPOTAMUS. Why, when the lion spoke to us last night on behalf of the pension for retired lions, he smiled at me and said in the hearing of all present: "Without Handsome Hippo's assistance, I am powerless here."
CROCODILE. Ha! I hate to disillusion you, my dear friend, but you make me laugh. Handsome Hippo! Are you truly taken in by this obvious piece of flattery?
HIPPOPOTAMUS. No, I am not. I am not flattered by what the lion said; but I am flattered to be the one he chose to flatter.

A FLEA PROTESTS

Characters: Narrator, the Dog, the Flea

DOG. I despise you.
NARRATOR. So said the dog to the flea as he lifted his indignant rear leg to scratch his flank.
DOG. You parasite!
NARRATOR. The flea happened to be a reasoner.

FLEA. You call me a parasite...
NARRATOR. He squeaked from behind a tuft of bristles which the dog could not reach...
FLEA. But don't you live off rabbits, don't cats live off mice, don't people live off chickens, don't lions live off zebras? Why does everybody hate us so?
NARRATOR. Unfortunately, the dog was a reasoner too.
DOG. We despise you because you live off those who are bigger and stronger than yourself. That makes you a parasite. We live off those who are smaller and weaker than us. That makes us normal.
NARRATOR. What could the flea reply? Rules are made by rulers, and those who bother the rulers must not expect to be called by pretty names.

THE FOX AND THE CROW

Characters: Narrator, the Fox, the Crow

NARRATOR. A crow was sitting on a branch with a cheese in his bill when a hungry fox, drawn by the smell, stopped under the tree and spoke as follows...
FOX. Master Crow, the beauty of your voice has enthralled me for many a year. I have never before dared to speak up. I am shy in the presence of a master, but how grateful I should be if you deigned to sing me a brief ditty!
NARRATOR. This was a most attractive speech! The crow opened his beak, dropped the cheese, and krawked his uttermost, high, middle, and low.
CROW. Kraw kraw kraw!
(*The fox applauds*)
FOX. Bravo! Enchanting!
NARRATOR. Our fox didn't like to make enemies.
FOX. My eyes are filled with tears. But—what is this lying in the grass?
CROW. This? Oh, it's a cheese; I was about—
FOX. A cheese? Ye gods! A greasy Gorgondola! It must not beslobber your windpipe!
NARRATOR. And, picking up the cheese with all his teeth, he gulped it down in a wink.
FOX. There. I have removed the temptation. Your voice is saved.
CROW. You mean it? Thanks a million, mister Fox.
FOX. It is for me to thank *you*, O precious friend. You have given me everything

I came for. Farewell!

NARRATOR. The fox was chuckling under his breath. But wait! The crow was happy too...

CROW. Kraw kraw kraw!

NARRATOR. And why not? The fox had won a savory meal, the crow a delicious compliment. And neither is easy to come by in this world.

HANK THE SALESMAN

Characters: Narrator, the President, the Chairman, First Director, Second Director, Third Director.

NARRATOR. Above all the salesmen working for him, the President of the company loved and prized a man whose name was Hank. Hank had eyes that made the ladies dream of naughty adventures in ancient Samarkand. Beneath his comely nose a long black moustache pointed to the right and left like a pair of wings. His hair was curly and neatly trimmed around his well-washed ears, his cheekbones looked like small ruddy apples, and his arms seemed to have been forged to carry the helpless out of fireswept buildings. He was, furthermore, a man of merry monologue who believed in the quality of the product his company sold (I forget just now what this was)—

PRESIDENT. Tiger Detergent: the Suds that Roar into Dirt.

NARRATOR. Thank you, Mr. Weamish. Well, Hank believed in Tiger Detergent as devoutly as the Pope believes in the Trinity. As a result, he scoured his territory like a conqueror, selling more boxes of Tiger Detergent than anyone the company had ever employed. No wonder he was the President's favorite...

PRESIDENT. Oh Hank!

NARRATOR. And the darling of all the Directors too. And no wonder, either, that one morning, as the meeting of the Board of Directors was getting under way, the Chairman of the Board confronted the President with rage exploding in face, gestures and words.

CHAIRMAN (*thundering*). The news has come to me that our President has fired Hank. Why, Mr. Weamish, did you fire Hank?

NARRATOR. The Board was dumbfounded. The President said lividly nothing.

CHAIRMAN (*shouting*). Why, why, why? What made you do it?
NARRATOR. And still the President was silent. But now the Board was finding its voice.
FIRST DIRECTOR. Confess...
NARRATOR. Said one director.
FIRST DIRECTOR. Wasn't it envy? Was Hank too successful? Did he steal the sunlight from you?
PRESIDENT. Oh no! I? I envy Hank? I who admired him so? I who gave him raise after raise?
SECOND DIRECTOR. What then?
NARRATOR. Asked another director.
SECOND DIRECTOR. Did he debauch the secretaries?
PRESIDENT. He did; but that was stipulated in his contract.
NARRATOR. As you can see, he was beginning to weep. Another director spoke up.
THIRD DIRECTOR. Did he peculate and malversate?
PRESIDENT (*blubbering*). Hank malversate or peculate? Hank? Oh Hank, you who lunched on yogurt when you traveled in order to save the company's pennies! I never knew a boy as honest as you, except my grandmother in heaven.
NARRATOR. The chairman was losing patience.
CHAIRMAN (*bawling*). Enough! Mr. Weamish: you fired our most brilliant salesman, though you knew that the competition was after him day in day out with offers I myself couldn't have resisted: stock options, limousines, holidays in Bermuda. One last time, tell us the cause, or else you in turn— the rest is blank, but as you all know, my silences are even more terrible than my howls.
PRESIDENT (*whispering*). Mister Chairman, forgive me, but you named the cause yourself.
CHAIRMAN. Fiddlesticks! Where? When?
PRESIDENT. The offers from our competitors.... Every day a new one, grander than the last.... Oh, I was so afraid that he was about to leave us.... so nervous, so terrified....
CHAIRMAN. That you fired him?
PRESIDENT. That I fired him.
NARRATOR. And there my story ends. Hank, as you might guess, went on to sell innumerable units of the next product...
PRESIDENT (*wretchedly*). Goop Brothers Miracle Fertilizer: The Dirt That Grows on You.
NARRATOR. While the President was condemned to wrap parcels with twine

and tape in the stockroom. There, for years to come, he would impart to newcomers and old-timers alike a settled conviction of his...

PRESIDENT (*old man wrapping a box*). Let me tell you that doing mischief in order to prevent it is a very sad mistake. Another stretch of tape, my boy.

HOW GOD BESTED THE DEVIL

Characters: Narrator, the Devil, God, the Physicist, the General

NARRATOR. Some people believe that the devil is busy night and day tormenting mankind. But that's a pretty medieval way of thinking. Actually, the devil turned the whole machinery on, so to speak, right from the start; I mean, he made people as ornery as he could and then he left them to their own devices. Now and then he lands here to make sure that everything is going wrong, but then he goes about his interests elsewhere, or else between trips he relaxes on the homestead in Gehenna.

On one of his tours on earth the devil happened into the troposphere just when a few physicists and generals were trying out a hydrogen bomb.

DEVIL (*Explosion*). What in blazes is this? (*Explosion*) Fantastic! My hair's on fire and every bone in my body is broken. This is better than the time Woozis exploded and every pottlewibblet on it was exterminated.

NARRATOR. But the devil's a tough piece of steak as you can imagine, so the jolt didn't shake him for long, and down he went to talk to the generals and the physicists.

DEVIL. Something new is cooking, I see.

PHYSICIST. Yes...

NARRATOR. Said the chief physicist...

PHYSICIST. We're pretty proud of it, it's a ball of fire.

DEVIL. Tell me all about it.

NARRATOR. So the physicist gave him the lecture.

PHYSICIST. Hydrogen isotopes, tritium and deuterium, critical mass, self-sustaining reactions, annihilation of matter...

DEVIL. Excellent, excellent. Here's the Nobel Peace Prize. (*The physicist counts and then pockets the money*) But what do you propose to do with this gadget? Seems a pity just to let it drift.

NARRATOR. A general chimed in.

GENERAL. Don't worry, sir; we've got plans to blow the stuffings out of the enemy and to leave nary a child standing up to tell the tale. That'll teach them to be nice to us.

DEVIL. Lovely, lovely; but are they going to wait for you without playing a trick or two of their own I hope?

GENERAL. No sir; you can rely on those hooligans; they intend to split each freedom-loving one of us from tip to top to punish us for our free enterprise.

NARRATOR. At that point the devil became a little worried.

DEVIL. Tell me, what about the rest of the world?

GENERAL. What rest? There ain't no rest on *my* radar screen.

PHYSICIST. Perhaps, sir, there might be a rest, I don't know, people who just sit around and live. With geranium pots. Of course, I don't know who they are.

DEVIL. Neither do I!

NARRATOR. The devil was in a black panic that was a pity to see. The truth is, Lucifer needs people for his mischief, because, you see, there's no such thing as disembodied mischief, mischief is absolutely void until it gets into living creatures. So the devil flew like a bullet to the mansion of the lord, where he didn't even announce himself...

DEVIL. Out of my way, you flunkeys...

NARRATOR. He just plunged in and broke into God's private cabinet.

DEVIL. Murder! It's murder! It's massacre! It's a plot against me, and don't tell me it isn't, I ought to know a plot when I see one, and what in hell am I going to do without people?

NARRATOR. The lord chuckled. He'd never seen Lucifer in such a broil.

GOD. At last! At last and at long last I have found the way of besting you. The forces of evil are smashed. Hang up your pitchfork, Satanas, I've outsmarted you, I'm almighty after all.

DEVIL. You mean——?

GOD. I do. From now on, it's cosmic dust for you. Enjoy it if you can.

NARRATOR. And that is the story of how the devil left the earth forever.

HOW GOD LEARNED WHAT MEASURE IS

Characters: Narrator, God, Gabriel, Abel, Cain

NARRATOR. When Jehovah began his career, he really enjoyed tossing his mighty thunderbolt around.

GOD. The point, my dear Gabriel, is that I have standards.
GABRIEL. Yes, your Infinity.
GOD. In fact, and this is a mystery I don't impart to the first-come archangel, me and the idea of standards erupted together out of nothing: we *were* the Big Bang.
GABRIEL. Yes, your Magnipotence.
GOD. And ever since, I've zoomed and zapped about the universe making my standards stick. Here on earth, for example—(*he tosses his thunderbolt*)[4]
GABRIEL. What was it this time, my Lord?
GOD. You didn't notice?
GABRIEL. No, your Splendor.
GOD. That, Gabriel, was a rebellious electron.
GABRIEL. How did it sin, your Excellence?
GOD. It refused to whirl. It stood and dawdled. Look closer.
GABRIEL. Heavenly angels! It's whirling like mad! But, my liege, wouldn't a poke with your pinky have sufficed? Because—
GOD. Wait! (*He tosses the thunderbolt*). While you were admiring that particle—
GABRIEL. No, I noticed, I noticed! That pebble falling up instead of down! When you bashed it, it stopped mid-air in the silliest way I ever saw, and did it ever turn around and fall down!
GOD. The rules, you see.
GABRIEL. Still, wouldn't a word—a simple word from you—because your thunderbolt—for instance, this little caterpillar—
GOD. What about it? Let me take a look. No!
GABRIEL. Alas!
GOD. Dummy! You're supposed to eat that leaf, *it* isn't supposed to eat you! (*He hurls the thunderbolt*). Report to me, Gabriel.
GABRIEL. All I can say about that geranium leaf, your Majesty, is that it was.
GOD. God be praised, forever and ever, amen. But who comes here?
GABRIEL. Your friends, Abel and Cain.
GOD. My masterpieces. I hope they at least will behave. Let's become invisible.
(*Enter Abel and Cain*)
ABEL. I can't help it, my sweet brother, if my burnt offering to our Father and Lord sent its smoke straight up into the sky, while yours fizzled and sputtered and sent the smoke into your eyes.
CAIN. My eyes are clear enough to see a scoundrel who fools with my burnt offering every time it's time for one.
ABEL. And where is this scoundrel, my sweet brother? Aside from our aged

---

[4] Gabriel will be picking up the bolt each time, and returning it to God when needed.

parents, there is only you and me in the whole wide world.
CAIN. And in a second, me will be all. (*He strikes Abel*) That will teach you to be funny.
ABEL. Jehovah, avenge me! (*Cain drags Abel's corpse off-stage*)
GOD. Did you see that?
GABRIEL (*sobbing*). I did, I did; it's the worst, the vilest, the cruelest—
GOD. This, Gabriel, calls for a punishment like none I've ever inflicted. Hand me my thunderbolt!
GABRIEL. Oh, your Grandeur, your thunderbolt is so worn out with use—
GOD. Is this the time to criticize?
(*He flings his thunderbolt. A yell off-stage*)
GOD. It didn't kill him though. It was worn. Blunt at the edges....
GABRIEL. I feel weak...
(*He sits heavily down and jumps up again*)
GABRIEL. My lord!
GOD. What now?
GABRIEL. Nothing, your Magnificence, but sitting down—or trying to—well—the grass wouldn't bend under me. It—how shall I put it with sufficient dignity—it stung—my—
GOD. Curse this earth! Fetch me my—give me my tweezers, Gabriel.
GABRIEL. Tweezers should do it nicely, your Immensity.
(*God works at the grass*)
GOD. Thunderbolt for Cain; tweezers for grass: make a note of that, Gabriel.

IN THE BELLY OF THE WHALE

Characters: Narrator, Six herring.

NARRATOR. A whale had opened his jaws and swallowed a row of herring. The unfortunate fish were flopping about helplessly in the vast stomach, each looking with anguish at the others for signs of help or hope. Instead, one of them began to cry...
FIRST HERRING. Oh my God, oh Jesus in heaven, we are all undone! Don't you see the hole gaping at the end of this cavern? There begins the gut, thither we are bound, and beyond we shall be digested into herring paste!
NARRATOR. The other herring made an uproar at this. On every side, in

the dark, came shouts of...
SECOND HERRING. Alarmist!
THIRD HERRING. Rumor monger!
FOURTH HERRING. Ignoramus!
NARRATOR. Then, looking about in the faint phosphorescent glow, they severely contradicted the craven herring.
SECOND HERRING. Gentlemen, the indisputable fact is that we have slipped, somehow, into a quiet restful place.
THIRD HERRING. Almost a resort.
FOURTH HERRING. Say rather a haven, a vault under which neither sharks nor fishing nets are to be feared.
FIFTH HERRING. A new life is beginning for us, gentlemen!
SECOND, THIRD *and* FOURTH HERRING. Hear, hear!
NARRATOR. At that moment, they heard a familiar voice from afar. It was that of a fellow herring the whale had missed in his gulp.
SIXTH HERRING. Do you hear me down there, all you herring?
THE OTHER HERRING. Yes, we hear you, Ferdinand!
SIXTH HERRING. Good! The monster has fallen asleep. You can all swim out again, but do it quietly!
NARRATOR. Well! The herring forgot their fine words, and with a terrified...
THE FIVE HERRING. Hush hush! Let's get out! Don't push! Here's the exit! Shhhh!
NARRATOR. They darted and scrambled all over each other to the outside world. Safe again, they happily swam home to their families, each one crying to his kith and kin...
SECOND HERRING. Listen to what happened to me!
THIRD HERRING. Less than an hour ago—
FOURTH HERRING. I who am hugging you now—
FIFTH HERRING. Was staring Death—
(*Pause*)
FIRST HERRING. In the face....

THE INNOVATION

Characters: Narrator, Farmer Jake, Farmer Pete.

NARRATOR. Farmer Pete and Farmer Jake were looking at a strange new apple tree.

FARMER JAKE (*scratching his head*). Sure is the oddest apple tree I ever run up against.

FARMER PETE. My landlord invented it. He's a famous experimentalizer with ten framed diplomas on the wall.

FARMER JAKE. Who ever seen an apple tree with a purple trunk?

FARMER PETE. Nobody, that's who. And instead o' leaves it grows feathers.

FARMER JAKE. *Yeller* feathers! And dang me if the apples ain't square instead o' round!

FARMER PETE. Yep, they're uncommon all right. Try one. Nice and ripe.

FARMER JAKE. Thanks. Ouch! I'm bleedin'!

FARMER PETE. Yep, cuts your lips like a razor.

FARMER JAKE. Not much of a tree, I guess.

FARMER PETE. Not much of a tree? What do you mean, not much of a tree! Don't tell me *you* could have growed it!

FARMER JAKE. Nope, I couldn't. I'm stoopid; and some jackass notions it takes a genius to dream up.

THE JOURNEY OF A COW

Characters: Narrator, the Philosophical Cow, the Carinthian Cow, the Indian Cow, the Indian.

NARRATOR. In a charming meadow of lower Carinthia the cows were feasting on the sappy grass with joy in their souls.

CARINTHIAN COW. And why not? There's no better meadow in Austria, no jollier cowherd, no friskier dog, and no happier fate. Most of the day we eat dinner, from time to time we take a walk—two steps or three—and then we lie down for a sunbath and a sleepy friendly confabulation.

NARRATOR. One of these cows, however, was a different sort. She had acquired a little philosophy, I don't know where, and this had got her to grumbling a good deal about life, and also—to speak the whole truth—about death. Now and then she would allow the other cows to partake of her thoughts.

PHILOSOPHICAL COW. Oh sisters, sisters, I admire your serenity, I envy your bliss. Do you think that this cowherd, whose face you lick, and for whose handpats you compete, bestows his good will on you because he loves you? I am sorry indeed to disabuse you, I wish I could leave you ruminating with a grateful heart, but you must be told that this cowherd and his rich employer are merely fattening you for the kill. The kill, my sisters! For your death! You listen complacently to the bells around your necks, but these bells do not peal for you; they peal to cheer the cowherd; for you there is only the eternal nothing; and yet you graze, you smile, you grow fat in order to be condemned the sooner, and you dare to be happy!

NARRATOR. The other cows listened as carefully as they could, but it is not easy to pay close attention to metaphysics on a full stomach, and these cows had a full stomach most of the time.

CARINTHIAN COW. Thank you, dear.... You're telling us awful things we shouldn't forget. It's so very sweet of you to want to keep them from us... But you know best... How beautifully you talk!... I always say, education is a wonderful thing.... On the other hand, the grass *is* luscious, and as for the cowherd, well, he's always been a gentleman to me. It's time for our nap now, but as soon as we wake up, or maybe after a snack, we want to chew over all the stories you told us.

PHILOSOPHICAL COW (*to herself*). These animals are hopeless. I must look out for myself. Each cow is alone in her universe. We can only make a pretense of communicating. We moo in the void. One of these days I shall go to India, where cows, I hear, are worshipped instead of broiled.

NARRATOR. She revolved this notion in her mind for a long time, and even inquired of a flock of migrant geese in what direction India lay. And then, one morning, when her companions looked more paunchy than the philosophic mind could bear, she set out without farewells on the long and dangerous road to India.

PHILOSOPHICAL COW. I took the side roads, ate the wild grass along their borders, slept among strange herds in alien fields, but I advanced with a hopeful heart through the dust, the cold, the windstorms, the rain, the heat, I don't know how many months or years, until at last I came to a village, look! a village in which the cows are roaming at will in the streets, without a dog to bark at them or a herdsman to march them back and forth!

NARRATOR. And she asked joyously of the first cow who crossed her path...

PHILOSOPHICAL COW. Am I in India?

NARRATOR. The Indian cow, who was pale and thin, and walked slowly with lowered head, looked up in surprise.

INDIAN COW. Poor wretch, you are. But you—where do you come from? Because one look at your girth is enough to tell me that you are not one of us.

PHILOSOPHICAL COW. I come from Carinthia.

INDIAN COW. Carinthia? I don't know where that is, but oh it must be heaven. You are the chubbiest cheeriest cow I have seen in my whole fly-bitten life. (*She sobs*)

PHILOSOPHICAL COW. What's the matter with you? Why are you crying? I came here to live among you. In Carinthia men fatten us for the slaughterhouse, we die butchered in the flower of our youth. I came here to be a goddess and to live out in peace the years which nature counted out to me.

NARRATOR. Before her new friend could answer, a man with a stick approached.

INDIAN COW. Run, run! I'm too weak, but you can run before he beats you half to death!

NARRATOR. But it was too late. The man swung his stick.

INDIAN. Out of the way, you loafers! Here! Here! Here! (*He beats them*)

NARRATOR. Our cow had never been struck, so now she dodged this way and that, her head in a whirl, mooing bitterly at each blow, until she found herself in another street, where the man didn't bother to pursue her. After she had recovered herself a little, she looked for her companion among the other cows in the street; and in fact the Indian cow painfully rejoined her after a while.

PHILOSOPHICAL COW. What happened? Why did the man beat us? And why does everybody look as sick as you? I see nothing but skin and bones and drooping muzzles! Was it all a mistake? Are you not goddesses after all? Was I misled?

INDIAN COW. No, you were not misled, my dear; but when goddesses swarm in their thousands, even goddesses starve. If we chance on a rich man's field, his servants fall on us with sticks. If we walk in people's way, they beat us breathless. So we return broken-hearted to our daily stubble, rice husks, and refuse which the very beetles disdain. Once in a long while our worshippers squeeze three drops of milk from our wrinkled udders.

They love our dung better than our souls. They groan when we are too weak to give them a baby ox. At long last we drop with our jowls to the earth, and expire knowing that our hides will be turned into common purses. Let them! But shall I die of old age without once curling my tongue around a plentiful meal like the thousands, forgive me for weeping, the thousands you have surely enjoyed?

NARRATOR. The philosophical cow was dumbfounded. For many a day she said nothing, only snatching at a tuft of grass now and then, and, because she was stronger than the others, shoving them away from the better morsels.

PHILOSOPHICAL COW. Shoving them away? Oh God, in Carinthia we invited each other to partake! What shall I do? What shall I do? Shall I remain where I am, live out my natural life as a goddess but live it out in misery? Or return to the bliss of Carinthia, so sure but ever so brief?

NARRATOR. I have heard that she is in India to this day debating with herself, because she cannot decide. And neither can I.

KUKKURRIK TRIUMPHANT

Characters: Narrator, Kukkurrik, the Chiffchaff.

KUKKURRIK. Kukkurrikkukkurrriku!

NARRATOR. Every day before dawn, the rooster Kukkurrik uttered a mighty volley of crows, watched the sun come up, and said to himself...

KUKKURRIK. I've done it again!

NARRATOR. For he believed that his crowing made the sun rise. Once, however, it happened that his chum, the chiffchaff, risen from his twigs before his usual time, overheard Kukkurrik.

CHIFFCHAFF. What d'you mean, "I've done it again." What've you done again?

KUKKURRIK. It's really none of your business, little friend, because my sacred mission in life is my private affair.

CHIFFCHAFF. What sacred mission?

KUKKURRIK. Making the sun rise every morning. There! You've wormed the truth out of me.

NARRATOR. The chiffchaff ought to have been impressed, but...

CHIFFCHAFF. You superstitious henpecker, you arrogant eggnog—*you* bring out the sun? Ha, ha, ha! Go on and prove it to me.

KUKKURRIK. I don't know why I should bother; but even a fool like you must have heard of logic.

CHIFFCHAFF. Logic?

KUKKURRIK. Yes, logic. Every morning I crow, and every morning, as soon as I have finished crowing, the sun rises. Cause and effect. Logic. Ergo probatus est.

CHIFFCHAFF. It so happens that the sun comes out in the morning because a god, whose name if you please is Fibbus, takes it out for a ride. Did you say logic? I drank FACTS with my mother's milk.

NARRATOR. And there the quarrel ended, because the sweet voice of his favorite hen was calling Kukkurrik to business.

KUKKURRIK. Coming, dearest...

NARRATOR. One winter night, however, Kukkurrik and that same hen (her name was Mistress Pertelote) had a falling out, and Kukkurrik left her roost in a huff.

KUKKURRIK. Women!

NARRATOR. It was long past midnight and very frosty, and poor Kukkurrik caught a ferocious cold. He could feel the fever burning up his lungs, his head was in a whirl, he coughed grit and gravel, he cursed Mistress Pertelote...

KUKKURRIK. I've spoiled the little—

NARRATOR. And, as the time to crow came on, he found that he couldn't bring out so much as a semiquaver.

(*Kukkurrik tries and tries*)

KUKKURRIK. I don't care; it'll be dark for once.

NARRATOR. And he staggered up his loft, where he fell into a deep sleep. Hours later, the chiffchaff woke him up. It was bright day.

CHIFFCHAFF. Friend Kukkurrik, wake up, it's me, your best friend, you've been furiously sick, your wives tell me you couldn't crow, and yet here's the blissful sun blushing all over the world, and to add insult to infamy, there's not a cloud to be seen from poop to stern.

KUKKURRIK (*half asleep*). What's that?

CHIFFCHAFF (*shouting into Kukkurrik's ear*). You didn't crow and the sun is up! Pray explicate.

NARRATOR. He thought the hour of victory had struck and the Fibbus hypothesis was confirmed forever. But not at all!

KUKKURRIK (*in a hoarse whisper*). I guess—I guess—I crowed so long yesterday that it carried for two days.

CHIFFCHAFF. I'll be damned!

KUKKURRIK (*coughing and wheezing*). In fact—I wouldn't be surprised—if I lasted the sun—a week.
(*Exit, chuckling*)
NARRATOR. And he left the chiffchaff agape at the compelling power of logic.

LANDSCAPE WITH CLOUD AND DUNES

Characters: Narrator, the Cloud, the Wind, First Dune, Second Dune, Third Dune, the Cactus, the Rock.

NARRATOR. A benevolent cloud which had spent its life wandering above tender meadows and fruitful valleys turned one day to the wind with the following surprising words.
CLOUD. I am sick at heart, oh my friend. The world is not all tender meadow and fruitful valley. I have had glimpses, in the farthest distance, of a wretched desert deprived of all life except a few bristles of heartless vegetation. Send me, I beg you, to that pitiful sand; I have in me rain, milk, blood, call it what you will, to bring the desert to life.
WIND. Think twice, my sweet friend. Not in a hundred years have I driven a cloud over the barren region you're speaking of. Why choose to hover over a desert instead of billowing gracefully above green grass and buttercups?
CLOUD. I am different. The grass and the buttercups do not need me. The poor desert does. Lead me to the desert, my friendly wind.
NARRATOR. The wind, who is an intelligent spirit, said nothing more, and blew soft and steady until the cloud had her wish and stood high over a burning tract of dunes that seemed never to end. The dunes looked up in horror.
FIRST DUNE. What is this thing?
NARRATOR. Cried the highest of them, as if choking in its sand. The wind replied...
WIND. What you see there is a cloud.
ALL THE DUNES (*with hatred*). A cloud, a cloud, a cloud!
FIRST DUNE. What are you looking for, stupid cloud? You're sitting on our sun. Don't bully us. Go home!
CLOUD. Gently. I am your sister. I have come to quench your terrible thirst. I am here to die for you. And afterward, you will turn to grass and trees, to

fruit, to fountains and brooks, to barley, wheat and corn.
NARRATOR. A heap of sand replied...
SECOND DUNE. Nobody is thirsty here. Die for somebody else!
NARRATOR. A cactus shouted defiance...
CACTUS. Take your barley to the North Pole!
NARRATOR. A half-buried rock bawled upward...
ROCK. Ugly bundle of fumes, we'll burn up your rain if you dare touch us.
NARRATOR. And a hiss came from a cunning little dune.
THIRD DUNE. Wind, wind, blow up a nasty storm, whisk us aloft, we'll scratch her face and blot out her rain.
NARRATOR. Such, and rougher, were their words, which the kindly wind tried in vain to scatter. For a few hours, the cloud moved about undecided; but finally she turned to the wind and said...
CLOUD. Guide me back to the land of meadows, my friend. Ah bitterness: the desert is the desert it wants to be.

THE LUCKY PEBBLE

Characters: Narrator, Robin, Colin, the Prince.

NARRATOR. Two peasant lads named Robin and Colin were sitting at the edge of a footpath, chewing grass and tossing pebbles into the meadow which lay before them. One of Robin's pebbles happened to strike a hunter who was asleep behind a clump of bushes. The hunter gave a cry...
PRINCE. Ouch! Hey!
NARRATOR. Leaped up, and strode toward the boys.
PRINCE. Who threw that pebble? I demand to know who flung that pebble!
NARRATOR. The two boys were terrified.
COLIN. He threw it, sir.
ROBIN (*at the same time, but piteously*). I threw it, sir.
PRINCE. Wonderful boy! You saved my life! Look at me; don't you recognize me? I am none other than your Prince. I was pursuing a fox with my retinue, but I galloped so nobly that I lost my way. Exhausted, I lay down and fell asleep. Your blessed pebble woke me. I saw a deadly snake on my breast ready to strike. I killed it, and thanks to you, my dearest and patriotic boy, our country will continue to rejoice in my rule.
ROBIN. I was glad to do it, sir.

PRINCE. I know you were, O charming and loyal youth. All the same, I intend to reward you. What is it you would like of me? Name anything within reason.

ROBIN. A sling maybe?

PRINCE (*laughing*). You will have a sling of ivory with a golden handle. But in addition, I will take you to my palace forthwith; I will ennoble your parents (if any) and give them twenty thousand ducats for vestments and furnishings; and when you grow up, I shall make you Captain of my Dragoons.

ROBIN. Sounds yummy.

PRINCE. Come, mount my steed behind me.

NARRATOR. For, I am happy to report, the Prince's horse had been grazing nearby.

PRINCE. And let us rejoin the hunting party—made frantic, I daresay, by my absence.

NARRATOR. However, as they were about to gallop away, Colin tugged at the Prince's spur, which he could just reach.

COLIN. What about me? I was throwing pebbles too!

NARRATOR. The Prince nipped his spur out of Colin's reach.

PRINCE. How *dare* you compare your vulgar pebble-throwing with his? (*To Robin*) Your playmate has shifty eyes.

ROBIN. Upstart! (*He pulls his tongue*)

NARRATOR. And the horse sped off, covering Colin in a great cloud of dust. What remains to be said? Colin went home to spend the rest of his living days planting turnips and beans, and Robin grew up to become a rich, pampered, and dreaded Captain of Dragoons.

THE LUNATIC PIGEON

Characters: Narrator, First Pigeon, Second Pigeon, Third Pigeon.

NARRATOR. Two tubby pigeons were sitting on the gravel in a park, when a third one came strolling by. After a few words of polite greeting—they had not seen each other for a while—the newcomer could not contain himself.

THIRD PIGEON. What happiness it is to possess a magnificent tail like mine!

NARRATOR. His friends were puzzled.

FIRST PIGEON. Magnificent tail?

SECOND PIGEON. What magnificent tail?

THIRD PIGEON. Look behind me. Behold the luminous expanse of green and blue.
NARRATOR. And now he began to strut about the gravel, wagging his bare little behind.
THIRD PIGEON. Admire if you please the shimmering discs, praised by the better poets.
FIRST PIGEON. You are out of your small mind. The tail you are talking about belongs to the peacocks who live in the park with us. I wish you could turn your head and look at your own rear.
THIRD PIGEON. So do I; but my consolation is that I can watch the children who surround me, hoping to catch one of my feathers. I take delight in their innocent pleasure.
NARRATOR. The two other pigeons stared at each other, excused themselves, and walked away.
SECOND PIGEON. Strange lunacy...
NARRATOR. Said one of the normal pigeons.
FIRST PIGEON. All the stranger...
NARRATOR. The other normal pigeon added...
FIRST PIGEON. When you consider that just as God made us, and never mind these useless peacocks, we pigeons are the most bewitching birds in the world.
SECOND PIGEON. As everybody knows.

THE MOTH WHO DISGUISED HIMSELF AS A DRAGON

Characters: Narrator, the Moth, the Snail, the Grasshopper, the Horsefly, the Bluejay, the Owl.

NARRATOR. Said the moth to himself one day...
MOTH. Why did Mistress Nature make us so very frail, I wonder? We're at the mercy of a thousand large and brutal animals, like titmice and chickadees, that fly faster than we do, and have teeth and claws to torment us with. Thank God, *I'm* nobody's fool, I've mutated, evolved and painted huge dragon's eyes and stripes on my wings. I hope they work.
NARRATOR. He didn't wait long to find out.
MOTH. Stand aside. Here's a snail I want to send galloping away. Boooo!

(*He rushes at the snail, spits, and displays his wings*)

SNAIL. What in blazes—? (*Rolls off-stage*)

NARRATOR. Bravo! The snail sucked his head back into his shell so fast, he rolled all the way down the hill. The sight of that dragon took five years off his life.

MOTH (*chuckling*). Pretty good for a beginning. Aha! There's a grasshopper. Out, out, brave wings! Boooo!

GRASSHOPPER. Help!

NARRATOR. The poor beast leaped seven feet over a fence, never to be heard from again.

MOTH. Here comes a bully horsefly. Boooo!

HORSEFLY (*making the sign of the cross*). Jesus protect me!

(*He flees; a thump is heard off-stage*)

MOTH. Heart attack. Better and better.

NARRATOR. But finally came the real test, in the shape of a hungry bluejay.

BLUEJAY. Twiddle, twiddle! Ha, what's this? An insect, brand unknown, but I'll make an antipasto of him all the same. Here goes my world-famous indirect dive.

NARRATOR. But the moth was ready.

MOTH. Now or never.

NARRATOR. At twelve inches, out went the wings, the ghastly eyes stared at the bluejay like a fiend out of hell—

MOTH. Boooo!

NARRATOR. The bird stopped dead in the air—

BLUEJAY. Damn!

NARRATOR. And vanished over the horizon, pursued by the moth.

MOTH. I'll find you, twiddle-beak! (*Exit*)

NARRATOR. It was a triumph on every front. Presently the moth became the terror of the neighborhood. (*Reenter moth*) He grew fat, as befits the terror of a neighborhood, and became reconciled to the workings of Mistress Nature.

MOTH. It isn't size that counts; it's brains.

NARRATOR. After a while, he took to frightening the larger birds, and even cats and dogs, for the sheer sassy sport of it. He'd creep up on a pigeon or a schnauzer, erect his monstrous wings, and go...

MOTH. Boooo!

NARRATOR. It never failed, and the moth grew ever fatter and sassier. One day, however, he ran up against an owl, which is a bird that doesn't see much of anything, at least in daytime. Only the moth didn't know it, so he thought he'd have one more laugh.

MOTH. Another feather in my cap. Boooo!
NARRATOR. The owl was half asleep, but the sound interested him.
OWL. Eh?
NARRATOR. And he opened his eyes in a tiny slit. All he saw, though, was a blur.
OWL. Who goes there in the shimmering sun?
MOTH. Boooo!
NARRATOR. Owls, it so happens, work mostly by ear.
OWL. Would you mind repeating?...
MOTH. Boooo!
NARRATOR. That last booo did it. The owl made a dart...
OWL. Gulp!
NARRATOR. And gobbled up the disappointed moth, whose final thought on this earth was...
MOTH. Ye gods, I must have slipped.
NARRATOR. Truth is, one usually does in the end.

THE NAMELESS TREE

Characters: Narrator, the Pine Tree, the Nameless Tree.

NARRATOR. In a faraway corner of the world no human being has ever visited, there flourished a species of trees which, as no one has ever seen them, I'm unable to describe to you, though I like to imagine them as thick cabbages sitting on long trunks, and why not? I do know, however, that one day a seedling was wafted into their midst from western Oregon. The seedling rooted itself next to one of these trees, and it too flourished. First a sapling came up, and then, many years later, a pine tree mature enough to know the rules of civility and to greet its neighbor with a mellow...
PINE TREE. Good morning to you, neighbor!
NARRATOR. The tree it thus addressed responded with an equally cordial...
NAMELESS TREE. And a sunny day to you, young stranger. It's been my pleasure to watch you pushing up season after season. Now that you've reached ripeness and wisdom, let me wish you hundreds more years of the same.
PINE TREE. How very kind of you...
NARRATOR. Exclaimed the pine tree.

PINE TREE. I owe it to you to introduce myself: I am a pine tree, at your service. And you, my friend?

NAMELESS TREE. And I? I am who I am. What else can I say?

PINE TREE. Forgive me! I was simply asking for your name, without intending, I assure you, to press beyond the margin of a decent curiosity.

NAMELESS TREE. Your curiosity is welcome, but I know nothing about names; what is a name?

NARRATOR. The pine tree was surprised.

PINE TREE. A name is, well, a name, something you call something. As I told you, I am not only a tree, like you, I am a pine tree, as they say in Oregon, or a *Tannenbaum* in German, or, better still, a *Pinus ponderosa* in Latin.

NARRATOR. At this point it was the native's turn to be surprised.

NAMELESS TREE. Alas, I am nothing but what you see, and so are my relatives who live all around us. We have no names that I know of. Tell me, what good are names?

PINE TREE. I'm not sure, but I can inform you that without a name, one doesn't know who or what one is; perhaps one doesn't even altogether exist—if you'll forgive my mentioning it.

NAMELESS TREE. How very awful; and I suppose that if you lack a name you stop growing, you lose your leaves, your roots wither, and the creatures give up on you and fly elsewhere?

PINE TREE. Oh no! Please don't be frightened! No such thing! Just look at yourself! Any mother-tree would be proud to call you her own!

NAMELESS TREE. Then may I be your friend without a name?

PINE TREE. You may be and you are...

NARRATOR. Said the pine tree, shaking all his needles.

PINE TREE. Besides, I give you permission to forget mine; for the more I gaze at your head of leaves, the more I feel that I too shall prosper without it.

THE OWL WHO DIDN'T LIKE LONG NECKS

Characters: Narrator, the Stork, the Goose, the Owl.

NARRATOR. In their Academy of Science, on the shore of a pretty lagoon, the animals were debating the question of long necks. The stork, it turned out, was an expert on the subject.

STORK. Briefly, fellow members of the Academy: by means of a long neck we can keep our bodies in place and send our faces ahead to look for worms and frogs practically anywhere we like. We can graze in every direction there is, we can peck our own tails clean—if I may say so without offense—we can rest our weary cheeks on our own bosoms, and best of all, we can enjoy our meals longer, for it takes a morsel a delightful time to travel down the œsophagus into the *stomachus*, vulgarly known as the stomach.

NARRATOR. In my opinion it was a good and scholarly speech. But suddenly a noise was heard in the reeds. A silly goose who had eavesdropped on the proceedings was madly clapping her wings. The stork's discourse had quite carried her away.

GOOSE. Honk honk! Me too! Honk honk! Me too I like long necks—honk honk!

NARRATOR. It was most embarrassing for the stork. And now the owl spoke up. He hadn't liked the speech about long necks for reasons of his own.

OWL. I for one do not see eye to eye with a goose, but I am glad that our esteemed colleague has found someone—unacceptable to the Academy, to be sure—to honk in support of his theories.

NARRATOR. All the Academicians snickered except the stork, who blushed to the tip of his beak, and found his way to the exit while the animals decided unanimously in favor of short necks. For a goose can be as right as Aristotle, but no one cares to be right in her company.

THE PARLIAMENT OF ANIMALS

Characters: Narrator, the Rabbit, the Uncle, the Lion, the Elephant, the Bear, the Cobra.

NARRATOR. The white rabbit was showing his country off to his uncle who lived across the river. He took his uncle to the Parliament of Animals, where they crouched in the gallery with the other small creatures while the leaders of the animals spoke and debated.

UNCLE. What a glorious institution you are showing me...

NARRATOR. Said the uncle.

UNCLE. All these wonderful animals speaking their minds! On our side it's hold your snout or else. Look at that majestic lion in the center!

RABBIT (*proudly*). He's our king, but all the same we tell him off any hour of the day. But hush up now; the session is about to start. Here comes our dear elephant.

NARRATOR. And indeed, an elephant was lumbering to the rostrum, where he trumpeted a greeting, and said...

ELEPHANT. Mr. Lion, king or no king, I am sick of your reckless policy of cutting down banana trees, and I demand drastic reforms.

UNCLE (*whispering*). Oh my God, now surely a pride of lions is going to tear the poor elephant to shreds.

RABBIT. Not in the least, the elephant can say whatever he pleases.

UNCLE. Can he? Can he?

NARRATOR. And his nephew was right, for the lion replied...

LION. I am making a note of your interesting objurgation, Lord Tusky.

NARRATOR. The elephant having returned to his place, he was followed by a cobra, who wound himself around the speaker's platform.

COBRA (*hissing and spitting*). Banana trees or no banana trees, the time has come, say I, to think of taking our kings from another species.

LION. Thank you; it is very helpful to get a number of constructive views.

NARRATOR. The visiting rabbit could hardly keep from dancing with pleasure and clapping his paws.

UNCLE. The beauty of it, oh the beauty of it! "A number of constructive views!" What a king, what a country!

NARRATOR. And now a bear stood up.

BEAR. I do not necessarily support Sir Scales; but I want to make it perfectly clear that unless you lions subsidize the culture of honey bees, I might subject his proposal to a sympathetic examination.

LION. I do trust that we can satisfy you; in the meantime I want to thank you for your important contribution to this debate.

UNCLE. He thanks him, he thanks him! But nephew, surely this is all a game! It can't be serious. They're all in a plot together, so to speak, and they're pulling our legs.

RABBIT. Pulling what? I'll show you, and when I've shown you, you can cross the river again and give your spineless friends a report about us.

NARRATOR. And leaving his uncle speechless, he leaped into the midst of the assembly. The uncle thought he was dreaming when he saw his own kinsman stride to the platform and heard him state with great dignity...

RABBIT. And I the rabbit am dissatisfied with the way you lions and elephants and bears trample all over our cabbages without any regard for our interests. I demand that you guarantee the integrity of our fundamental vegetables.

LION (*politely*). I believe your speech is out of order...

NARRATOR. Said the lion. The bear added...

BEAR. He certainly failed to follow parliamentary procedure.

NARRATOR. The serpent declared...

COBRA. The rules are clear: a *cuique suum* petition must be filed *ad usum* with the clerk.

ELEPHANT. And filed with the clerk before the opening of the session under subsection 16b.

LION. I am indeed sorry...

NARRATOR. Concluded the lion. And—

UNCLE. Wait!

NARRATOR. He gobbled up the white rabbit. The uncle wanted to shout...

UNCLE. They've eaten my nephew!

NARRATOR. But he looked around him at the little animals who were in the gallery with him. Nobody seemed to have noticed a thing. Then he looked at the Parliament: the lion, the bear, the cobra, the panther, the orangutan, the elephant, the rhinoceros—

UNCLE. Heavenly gods, they're huge! I think I'll go home.

NARRATOR. And he went back to his side of the river. He was used to keeping quiet. (*Pause*) As for me, rather than give you my opinion of the case, I'll sing you a few couplets as follows:

> Rule the happy realm who will,
> Master Jack or Mistress Jill,
> Haughty captain, sober prelate,
> Jeweled king or bearded senate —
> Brother, mind this homely truth:

LION (*growling*). **VAIN IS THE BITE WITHOUT A TOOTH.**

THE PERFIDIOUS SPIDER

Characters: Narrator, the Fly, the Spider, the Fly's Cousin.

NARRATOR. Evil is what others do. What you and I do is irreproachable, and we are ready to prove it. So it was with the spider who caught a fly in his web.

FLY. Yipes!

NARRATOR. As he was running toward his prey on all eight legs, the fly went on his knees (as far as the web allowed him) and cried...

FLY. Mercy! Mercy!

NARRATOR. But the spider was not to be moved.

SPIDER. Why should I let you go? The law of nature demands that I eat you; and on top of nature I'm hungry.

FLY. But I don't want to die!

SPIDER. Neither do I. I am eating you, my dear, in order to keep alive.

FLY. Of course, you have the right to live too. But if you'll let me go, I promise to send another fly your way. Your web hangs in a dark corner (God knows how I fell into it) but I'll send somebody on an errand straight into your clutches, word of honor, my own sister if necessary.

SPIDER. Well, I'd be a bit of a fool to free you on the basis of a promise. But I'm not heartless either. Call over one of your friends, tell him you've found a piece of meat in this corner, and the moment he is caught I'll release you.

NARRATOR. It was not the best bargain in the world—the fly would have preferred his own offer—but what could he do? So he sang as bravely as he could...

FLY. Dinner's on the table!

COUSIN. Where? Where?

NARRATOR. Called out a cousin of his, and flew straight into the web.

COUSIN. You son of a cockroach, why did you lure me into this trap with you?

FLY. In order to save my life. There never was a better reason. (*To the spider*) Well, sir, I've lived up to my part of the bargain. Unbind me at once.

SPIDER. Unbind you—a cowardly scoundrel who lures a neighbor to a cruel death in order to save his own skin? I could never look at myself in the mirror again!

NARRATOR. And in the name of decency he gobbled up both flies. (*Pause*) Evil is what others do. What you and I do is always, as I said....

THE PONY WHO CAME TO A STREAM

Characters: Narrator, the Pony, the First Trout, the Second Trout.

NARRATOR. A very young pony who was traveling to enrich his life found himself at the edge of a rapid stream.
PONY. Looks like water, and looks like it's in a hurry. How do I hoof it across to the other side?
NARRATOR. After thinking it over for a few minutes, he cautiously dipped one foot in...
PONY. Cold!
NARRATOR. Then another, then his third, and then his fourth. Presently he was standing up to his nostrils in water.
PONY. What next, I wonder.
NARRATOR. Two good-natured trout came swimming down the current.
FIRST TROUT. Is anything the matter, my friend?
NARRATOR. Asked one of the trout.
PONY. Nothing much, thank you for asking, and good morning to you both. I'm obliged to cross to the other bank in order to enrich my experiences of the world, but I'm afraid of drowning.
FIRST TROUT. Come now! It's a well-known fact that all mammals, with the exception of man, swim by instinct.
PONY. Swim by what?
FIRST TROUT. By instinct, or inborn disposition, or congenital ability. I thought everybody knew it.
PONY. Oh, of course...
NARRATOR. Said the pony, ashamed of his ignorance; and so encouraged, he lurched into the middle of the rapid. The current toppled him at once...
PONY. Help! Help!
NARRATOR. And carried him off.
PONY. Help! I'm drowning! (*Vanishes*)
FIRST TROUT. Hm. I really thought that all mammals can swim.
NARRATOR. The trout who had been silent so far spoke up.
SECOND TROUT. All mammals can swim in quiet waters. One should always speak in full sentences, my dear.

THE QUEEN AND THE POODLE

Characters: Narrator, the Queen, the Poodle, the The Minister of Transportation, The Minister of Information, The Minister of Culture, The Minister of Foreign Relations, The Mutt, the Footman.

NARRATOR. A poodle had strayed into the boudoir of the Queen of Paphlagonia. She was beautiful, her eyes shone like two pearls, and her skin was the color of early morning. The poodle was greatly impressed, for this was the first queen he'd ever met. But the queen too was delighted.

QUEEN. Come here, pretty pretty poodle; welcome and sit on my lap; how sweet! Here's a piece of sugar for you from my own silver dish, and wait! hold still, my darling, because I'm going to tie this blue ribbon around your neck.

NARRATOR. And she kissed his cold nose a dozen times. The poodle licked her hand in return as daintily as he could...

POODLE. Allow me...

NARRATOR. First scraping his tongue against his teeth in order to make it perfectly clean.

NARRATOR. That same afternoon the queen was presiding over a meeting of the Paphlagonian cabinet.

QUEEN. A dreadful affair! Nothing but urgent business, crises, catastrophes.

NARRATOR. First came the Minister of Transportation...

MINISTER OF TRANSPORTATION. Our camels are wearing out, your majesty, I must have new camels immediately!

NARRATOR. Then the Minister of Information...

MINISTER OF INFORMATION. When in Christ's name will Paphlagonia adopt the telephone?

NARRATOR. Then the Minister of Culture...

MINISTER OF CULTURE. The peasants are using bad grammar in the fields again!

NARRATOR. And then the Minister of Foreign Relations...

MINISTER OF FOREIGN RELATIONS. Just as I feared! The Americans have never heard of Paphlagonia!

NARRATOR. Seven bundles of documents lay before the queen. She had to read them all, sign them...

QUEEN. And understand them too.
NARRATOR. Just at that moment the poodle ran into the Council Room—the footman had left the door ajar in order to listen—and blissfully wagging his tail, he jumped onto the queen's lap again and raised his muzzle to her face.
POODLE. Here I am again! Woof!
NARRATOR. He was still wearing his blue ribbon.
QUEEN (*shouting*). Who left the door open? Who let this mongrel in?
NARRATOR. The terrified footman came running.
FOOTMAN. Your majesty called?
QUEEN. Throw out this dog; is this a cabinet meeting or a zoo?
FOOTMAN. Yes, your majesty.
(*He throws the poodle out of the palace*)
POODLE (*wailing*). What happened? What did I do wrong?
MUTT. Excuse me for noticing your grief, but I'd like to help if I can—with good advice...
NARRATOR. Said a philosophical mutt who found the poodle wandering near the ditch where he lived. So the poodle told him the whole fearful story. The philosophical mutt listened carefully.
MUTT. Don't you know the saying of the wise men? That there is a time and a place for everything?
POODLE. But not for love!
MUTT. Even for love.
NARRATOR. A few days went by. The poodle could hardly eat. Now and then he chewed listlessly on a worn-out bone, because he was really famished, but he paid attention only to his disappointed heart.
POODLE. I can't bear it. I must see her again. She does love me.
NARRATOR. So he ran back to the palace, and without hesitation, without a single wrong turn, he found his way once more to the queen's boudoir.
NARRATOR. The queen was reading a romance when she saw the poodle at the foot of her couch.
QUEEN. My pretty poodle is back! Come here, my poor darling, forgive me for being mean to you, it was such a dreadful day! And look! My ribbon is still tied around your neck, but ever so wilted, ever so besmudged, and I'm sure you haven't swallowed a morsel in days!
NARRATOR. The poodle was beside himself with joy and frisked in his queen's arms as happily as a lamb in clover. But when a footman arrived carrying a dish of delicacies for him, he remembered his hunger and fell to eating with loud, voracious gulps. It was the finest meat in the palace. Even the footman ogled it with envy. As for the queen, she was delighted

to see her pet enjoying the dinner she had given him. But after a while she grew impatient.

QUEEN (*mirthfully*). That's enough! Now I want to play with you.

NARRATOR. And she bent down to take the poodle's dish away. Imprudent queen! A gobbet of meat was left in the dish. The poodle bit her hand and snatched up the meat. It was gone in a second.

QUEEN. My hand is bleeding!

FOOTMAN. Shall I destroy the hound, your majesty?

(*The queen and the poodle look at each other*)

QUEEN. No; please bandage the wound.

NARRATOR. After the footman had left, the queen took the poodle into her arms again. He licked her hand remorsefully.

POODLE. I'm nothing but a beast....

NARRATOR. But the queen gently stroked his head.

QUEEN. Never mind. I should have remembered that there's a time and a place for everything.

POODLE. Even for love...

NARRATOR. Thought the poodle.

THE RICH IBIS AND THE PAUPER THRUSH

Characters: Narrator, the Ibis, the Thrush, the Thrush's Wife.

NARRATOR. The ibis and the thrush had been good friends in their student days, long ago. They had shared their meals...

IBIS. Here's a leg of spittlebug, old man.

THRUSH. And I brought two slices of cold frog.

NARRATOR. And they had warbled all night in praise of ladies they were too poor to entertain.

IBIS and THRUSH (*singing*).
>>Of all the birds that I hold dear,
>>Phyllis my robin hath no peer;
>>There is no bird so fair, so fine
>>Nor yet so fresh as this of mine.

NARRATOR. Today they were still friends—friends, of course, as one is friends when one is quite grown up, has married, brought children into the

world, and learned to look at life maturely. The ibis had become extremely rich...
IBIS. By working hard.
NARRATOR. And the thrush had remained poor...
THRUSH. Also by working hard.
NARRATOR. The thrush lived with his family—
THRUSH. Tell them! In a messy mass of decayed wood and cowdung, that's where, next to a factory that makes stinking carburetors.
NARRATOR. The ibis, on the other hand, had just acquired a magnificent hideaway made of the finest Amazonian twigs.
IBIS. Let's not exaggerate....
NARRATOR. One of its two nests sheltered the young ones; it faced the mountains and overlooked a lovely ground of roses, azaleas, and camellias. The other, quite close to the first, yet snuggled in a delicious rash of leaves which gave it privacy, housed the ibis couple and faced a lake—
IBIS. A pond, a simple pond!
NARRATOR. Over which the orange rays of the setting sun gently laid themselves to sleep.
IBIS. Cheap purple prose.
NARRATOR. The thrush and his wife never visited the ibis, you can imagine why, but the ibis liked his old friend and now and then flew over for an informal visit. But it was becoming harder all the time. Every other topic of conversation seemed to depress his old *camarade*—not to mention the sour-faced wife. All that was left was reminiscing.
IBIS. Do you remember the day you dressed up as an owl?
THRUSH (*depressed*). Sure I do. We laughed and laughed.
IBIS. And the time I miaowed behind your back and you almost fainted?
THRUSH (*glum*). Oh yes. It was fun.
IBIS (*to himself*). What shall I do? What shall I do?
NARRATOR. The ibis didn't want to give up his dear friend. He thought and thought, and finally an ingenious idea occurred to him. On his next visit, after the greetings and a sip of stale apple juice, the ibis produced a deep sigh that couldn't be ignored.
WIFE (*distrustfully*). What's the matter with you tonight?
NARRATOR. How she hated those visits!
IBIS. The matter is that I sit here and envy both of you.
THRUSH. *Envy* us?
WIFE. Envy *us?*
IBIS. Indeed I do. Oh, you don't feed on imported snails, I know, and carburetors have their drawbacks, but you love one another, your children

respect you, you lead your quiet unruffled lives, singing much better than any ibis ever will, and ever would, do you hear, even if he owned all the gold mines of Araby. No, my old friends, believe me, it is not possessions that make a bird happy, happiness is not purchased.

NARRATOR. The two thrushes began to look more cheerful than they had in months.

THRUSH. Is anything specific the matter?

IBIS. I shouldn't worry you with my troubles.

WIFE. Of course you should. We've been your friends long enough, I hope.

IBIS (*groaning*). What shall I say? Living with my wife has become intolerable.

THRUSH *and* WIFE. We had no idea—

NARRATOR. Both were becoming hugely interested.

IBIS. We spend entire evenings not exchanging a single word. She demands fur-lined nests, flights over the Pacific, lotions for her feathers, God knows what else, while all I want from life is a dish of worms every day and a good chat with friends like you. We haven't a thing in common. And the children—I haven't told this to anyone—but our girl has taken up with a stork who cackles in free verse and drinks. She intends to live with him on top of a chimney. As for the boy, he keeps saying he wishes he'd been born something with four legs and a set of teeth. I don't know how much longer I can bear it.

NARRATOR. This was all news to the thrushes. They were amazed. But they consoled their friend as best they could...

THRUSH. Things will get better.

WIFE. You must look at the bright side.

NARRATOR. And dolefully shook their heads.

THRUSH. You see...

NARRATOR. The thrush said to his wife after the ibis had left them...

THRUSH. Haven't I always told you? It takes the rich to be really wretched in this world. Come here and give us a peck.

WIFE. Poor ibis...

NARRATOR. She kissed her husband and they spent a happy evening together. Meantime the ibis had flown back in haste to his nest, where he embraced his wife, folded their young under his wings, and sat down with them for a late supper under the moon, in full view of the agreeable lake.

IBIS. A perfectly ordinary pond, I do assure you.

NARRATOR. When his wife asked him what he had done that day, he only said...

IBIS. I have done a good deed.

NARRATOR. But later that evening, over a rare nectar of chrysanthemum, he spoke again.

IBIS. The fable has it, my dears, that the rich are unhappy. It is a fable we the rich should cultivate. We must pay priests, philosophers, and novelists to spread it. For it cheers up the world a little, and it buys us (I hope) time to endure.

THE ROCK AND THE SEA

Characters: Narrator, the Rock, the Sea, the Seagull.

ROCK. I stand with hard torso, high forehead, and headstrong pride...
NARRATOR. Said the rock to the sea.
SEA. And I am flexible and insinuating...
NARRATOR. Replied the sea to the rock.
ROCK. When you come leaping at me, I hold out my fist and split you into a hundred splinters.
SEA. When I leap at you, I deviously divide myself and erode you with a hundred fingers.
ROCK. I shake you off, poor fool, every time you advance.
SEA. I leave off, proud imbecile, only to attack again.
ROCK. You attack me with the chips of myself, because you are too weak to do your own mischief.
SEA. I use you against yourself instead of wasting my own substance.
ROCK. I have proved that I am better than you...
NARRATOR. Concluded the rock.
SEA. My superiority over you is established...
NARRATOR. Settled the sea. At that moment, a seagull landed on the rock.
ROCK. You heard us!
SEA. Yes, you heard us! Which one of us is right?
SEAGULL (*singing*). Everybody is always right; isn't that what words are for?
NARRATOR. And away he flew.

THE SPINSTER, THE CANARY, AND THE CAT

Characters: Narrator, the Spinster, the Cat.

NARRATOR. A spinster was living quietly with her cat and her canary. One day she left the bird cage unlatched by mistake, and while she was busy in her kitchen boiling a chicken for dinner, the cat put his paw into the cage. But the canary was no fool, and the moment he saw a claw where a claw had never appeared before, he began to chip-chip like a maniac and to shake the cage by flying against its bars. The spinster came running in.

SPINSTER. You horrible thing!...

NARRATOR. She cried, pulling the cat away.

SPINSTER. You mean, horrible, cruel thing, you were going to murder an innocent little bird!

NARRATOR. And, though she was a lady, she gave her cat a memorable whack on his rump. That evening, as she was putting fork and knife into her meal, the cat sat himself down on a chair by the table and said...

CAT. What are you eating there, my mistress?

SPINSTER. Chicken.

CAT. Isn't chicken a bird?

SPINSTER. I suppose it is.

CAT. Why do I get punished for wanting to eat a bird and why don't you punish yourself for eating another?

SPINSTER. That is not a nice question. You were going to devour the little bird practically in front of me. Dear Jesus, I would have seen the feathers in your jaw and the blood on the kitchen tiles. Whereas the chicken was scientifically processed a hundred miles from here, so that I never saw nothing.

CAT. Why didn't you tell me before? Leave the cage open again, and I promise I'll eat the canary clean and quiet while you're away.

SPINSTER. You wicked animal...

NARRATOR. Said the spinster, biting into the chicken's thigh...

SPINSTER. You don't want to understand. The canary is a pet, the chicken is food.

CAT. Not for me; for me the canary is food too.

SPINSTER. Very well, but as I nourish you loyally and plentifully, and at no

small expense to myself, there's no reason why you need a canary.
CAT. Yes there is.
SPINSTER. No there ain't.
CAT. Yes there is; canary is caviar for us cats, and that's more than I get loyally and plentifully around here.
SPINSTER. Enough!—(*she stands up and shakes a chicken leg at the cat*) That canary is mine, mine, mine, and you won't touch him!
NARRATOR. Mine, mine, mine! Cats and you and I know when we come to the unanswerable argument. The cat slunk off the chair and went to lap up his nuggets of tripe, and he never ogled the canary again.

THE SQUIRREL WHO WAS CAUGHT IN A WAR

Characters: Narrator, the Squirrel, the first General of the Gibbons, the second General of the Gibbons, another Gibbon, a Buzzard.

NARRATOR. Though much is better than little, little is better than nothing.
(*Noise of warfare*)
NARRATOR. The gibbons were making war on each other and raising a tumult in the forest. One day, as they were pelting each other with coconuts from adjoining trees, a missile struck a squirrel who was bringing the afternoon's harvest home to his family, and stretched him stiff and dead at the feet of his spouse.
SQUIRREL. My husband! The gibbons have killed him! They killed my provider! What will happen to our children?
NARRATOR. Sobbing all the way, she herded her young into a hollow of her tree and ran up to gibbon headquarters a dozen branches higher, jumping out of the way of the coconuts and pineapples that flew all about her. When she reached the gibbon general, she raised a pitiful clamor about her dead husband and her unprovided children, holding the fatal coconut in her paws.
SQUIRREL. That coconut was meant for one of you! We squirrels have nothing to do with your war, we don't even know what it's about.
NARRATOR. Here the general interrupted her.
FIRST GENERAL. It's about ideals, madam, and it might not be amiss if you learned something about the important issues of our world.

SQUIRREL. I don't care about ideals, my husband is dead of a mortal wound, my children are going to starve, and I demand compensation, namely a winter's supply of cashew nuts and an escort out of this infernal tree.

FIRST GENERAL. You're out of your mind. I'd like to know how we could carry on a decent war if every time a bystander was hit we were obliged to dip into the treasury to compensate him. Get out of here, and next time tell your husband to duck. Besides, he was hit by the enemy and not by us, I can tell by looking at the coconut, so take your complaint to the next tree.

NARRATOR. With this, the squirrel was booted off the branch, and the gibbons went back to their affairs. The squirrel stopped by the hollow to see that her children were safe, and then, taking advantage of a lull in the bombardment, she ran across to the tree where the enemy was lodged. She quickly made her way to the general of the hostile gibbons, and reported her complaint, exhibiting the coconut once more.

SQUIRREL. Look at the weapon, you can't deny that it's yours, it killed my innocent husband and left my children without provision. I demand that you make some restitution to us, namely a month's supply of cashew nuts.

SECOND GENERAL. Are you on our side in the fight?

NARRATOR. Asked the general.

SQUIRREL. What do you mean on your side? I'm a squirrel, a different species and a mother of three, I'm a neutral, I have no ideals, I don't belong to any side.

SECOND GENERAL. God strike you, we don't like neutrals around here. Get out of my tree before I have you clobbered to death as a spy.

NARRATOR. Terrified, the mother squirrel ran away as fast as she could. On the way down, a kindly old buzzard who had watched the scene took her aside and whispered into her ear...

BUZZARD. Go back to your children, madam, take them away while you can, and don't make trouble merely because you are right. You must always smile; smile at everybody, and keep saying thank you.

NARRATOR. With this, the widowed squirrel went back to the hollow, and began to move out her children and three or four berries she still had in a hutch. As she was hurrying down the trunk with her brood, an armed gibbon stopped her.

GIBBON. Where do you think you're going with all these supplies?

SQUIRREL (*smiling and curtsying*). To the authorities, in order to help the brave soldiers.

GIBBON. That's enough. Just hand those berries over to me, I'll take 'em to headquarters, let's see you out of here by the time I've swung my tail around this branch.

SQUIRREL. Thank you, sir...
NARRATOR. Said the widow, and she left the tree with the little squirrels, bereaved, battered and robbed, but alive.
(*Noise of bombardment; the narrator and squirrel flee*)

THE STUBBORN COBBLER

Characters: Narrator, the Cobbler, the Cobbler's Wife, Donald, Chorus.

NARRATOR. A cobbler whose name was Barnaby lived with his wife Alice in a deep, narrow valley, in a country of which I know only that it was excessively damp. One unlucky day, when it happened to be raining ten times as hard as usual, this cobbler got horribly angry with his wife.
COBBLER (*hammering away at a shoe*). Twelve hours a day I fix lousy shoes to keep a roof over our heads, and what do I get? Cold soup and stringy meat.
NARRATOR. The alarm had sounded in the village, and the people were running toward high places.
CHORUS (*outside*).
        Neighbor, oh neighbor, pack up and away,
        Or surely you'll drown by dark of the day.
NARRATOR. And Alice was pleading with her husband...
WIFE. Dearest Barnaby, relent, for God's sake, and forgive me this one time for the cold soup and the stringy meat. The streets are flooding, our neighbors are running away, let go that shoe and—
COBBLER (*hammering at the shoe*). Silence, you bitch! I work my nails off to support you and when I'm hungry I can't even get an honest meal out of you!
WIFE. Forgive me, forgive me! You can't tell that I'm kneeling because the water has come up to my bosom, but I beg you to postpone your anger long enough to run away with me. Take the shoe along, it belongs to neighbor Donald, who has already escaped. You can beat me with it once we're safe.
NARRATOR. And still the other villagers were running for their lives.
CHORUS (*outside*).
        Neighbor, oh neighbor, pack up and away,
        Or surely you'll drown by dark of the day.
NARRATOR. But the cobbler thought of nothing but his anger.
COBBLER (*hammering away*). Damn, damn, damn!

NARRATOR. So Alice ran away by herself, and reached a high place where she met her neighbor Donald.
DONALD. Greetings, my sweet Alice! As you can see, I ran for safety with only one shoe for my two feet.
WIFE (*tearful*). I apologize, but my husband is still working on your other shoe.
DONALD. Where is the dear man?
WIFE (*sobbing*). Steady at his work-bench, in spite of the flood.
DONALD. Do tell! Well then, come with me into this cave, pretty Alice. I've lit a fire, and we'll let it dry us together.
NARRATOR. When the waters subsided at last, the cobbler was found stubbornly drowned beside his work-bench.
DONALD. My shoe was ruined, but I married my sweet Alice instead.
NARRATOR. And many a time, as the years went by, they shook their heads together over the deceased Barnaby.
WIFE. Solid as a rock he was.
DONALD. And so fond of his soup and meat.

THE TERMITE AND THE ANT

Characters: Narrator, the Termite, the Ant.

ANT. What are you doing in that hole?
NARRATOR. Asked a pretty ant of a burly termite as she was strolling on an old log.
TERMITE. I live here, my dear...
NARRATOR. Replied the termite.
ANT. How odd! Do you enjoy it down there? And what's it like?
TERMITE. I enjoy it very much, and it's like safe and peaceful and comfortable; my pantry is always full of delicacies; and I'm not mauled like you by nasty winds, ugly frosts, flaming suns, marauding enemies, and beastly men.
ANT. It does sound jolly. Did you say a full pantry?
TERMITE. I did indeed say a full pantry. Would you like to come and see?
ANT. Why not?
NARRATOR. And down she went into the hole. It was awfully black at first, and when she got used to it, it was still awfully black; but she could feel that she was in a gallery.

ANT. Where are you, friend termite?

TERMITE (*touching her nose*). Right here, my dear; follow me and make yourself at home. I don't get many visitors, you know.

NARRATOR. And they walked down the gallery. It was not too difficult, because the gallery was so narrow that you couldn't get lost in it, it led you onward all by itself. But the blackness was giving the ant terrible flashes, and she became anxious to arrive at a respectable room. After a dreadfully long time, she heard the termite say...

TERMITE. Well, here we are. This is my dining room. Feel the antique paneling and the sturdy furniture. Relax, my dear, and let me fix you a timber sandwich.

ANT. Where am I? Where am I? I'm going blind. It's as black here as in your hallway. I can't see a thing.

TERMITE (*surprised*). Why would you want to see things? What good would it do you down here? Seeing's all right where there's danger, but down here we don't need all these glares and shadows and visions. Enjoy yourself, my dear, sit down, here's a comfortable splinter.

NARRATOR. But the ant was terrified. She almost wept, and the flashes were getting worse.

ANT. I don't want to sit down! I want the light! Oh, where's the way out?

NARRATOR. And she ran around groping for the opening to the gallery, bumping here and bumping there, so that the termite was quite bewildered.

TERMITE. I'll help you, my dear. But why don't you like it here? Didn't God make the darkness for his creatures to enjoy?

ANT. It's not true! It's not true! God made the darkness to punish horrible animals like you. Where's the light? Oh where's the light?

NARRATOR. The termite was so dumbfounded by what the ant had said that for a while he forgot to move. But the ant was still crying with terror, so he finally caught her and guided her into the gallery.

TERMITE (*sadly*). Shall I see you out, my dear?

ANT. Let me go!

NARRATOR. And she ran and stumbled toward the blessed hole—ah there, after a twist in the gallery...

ANT. There it is at last!

NARRATOR. And she jumped out into the world, upon which a quiet moon was shining. Joyously she exclaimed, sitting on her hind legs as though she wanted to embrace it...

ANT. Heavenly moon! Sweet shapes of the world! Take me back!

NARRATOR. As for the termite, he remained behind to puzzle over the miserable novelty he had heard.

TERMITE. Did God make us his good termites to enjoy his darkness, or was she right, did he make the darkness to hate us with?
NARRATOR. He was still thinking about it as he ate his dinner, and the question ran after him even on his snug little plank, as he was falling asleep. But next morning, when the blackness seemed to be laid fresh and thick in every cranny, he rose from his sleep invigorated again.
TERMITE. To work!
NARRATOR. He cried, and, biting with relish into the log, he dug a deeper room for yet a darker, darker night.

THREE REVOLTING ANIMALS

Characters: Narrator, the Rat, the Skunk, the Porcupine, the Jackal, the Lion.

NARRATOR. A rat, a skunk, and a porcupine were bemoaning their evil destiny.
SKUNK. I have lost my appetite for life...
NARRATOR. Said the skunk.
SKUNK. I am hated and shunned. My name is used for petty ridicule. Fame, honor and affection are forever denied me. Why, last week, when I waved a friendly tail at a little impertinent monkey, he put out his tongue and flung me an obscene grimace.
NARRATOR. The porcupine joined in.
PORCUPINE. And I? Though I lack your beauty, master skunk, I am an honest family man, a decent provider, in my ribcage beats a simple heart. And yet for every quill on my body the world has stung me with a barb of derision. Yesterday I gave a kindly greeting to a gazelle, who tittered in reply, 'A genteel porcupine! I've seen everything now!' and ran laughing into the woods.
RAT. Gentlemen...
NARRATOR. Said the rat in his turn...
RAT. They may laugh at you or avoid you, but they do not loathe you as they loathe me, the rat, whom they call plague, vicious killer, lover of sewage. My intellect and my agility only excite their horror. Last month I nodded at a rabbit—
SKUNK (*sarcastically*). Everybody loves a bunny!
RAT. I nodded at a rabbit, and he screamed 'A rat! A disgusting rat!' as only

a rabbit can scream when he sets his mind to it.

NARRATOR. Putting their heads together, the three unhappy creatures decided to complain to the lion, who was king of the animals. They arrived at court as the monarch was dining, and were greeted by a jackal, who was the king's majordomo.

JACKAL. You may watch his majesty at his repast, and present your petition after dessert. You are not among his favorites, but his majesty gives a hearing to even the lowest.

NARRATOR. The lion was sitting at table with an enormous bib under his beard.

LION (*roaring*). What's after soup, stoopid?

NARRATOR. The majordomo lifted several silver covers.

JACKAL. Your majesty, here is a homely but excellent rabbit stew, a superb *émincé de gazelle*, and *singe en brochette*, the chef's specialty.

LION. *Singe en brochette?* What's that?

JACKAL. Monkey on a spit.

LION. Hand it over!

NARRATOR. After the lion had finished eating, and as he was wiping the grease off his whiskers, the jackal told him...

JACKAL. Your majesty, here are three of your citizens, the skunk, the porcupine and the rat, who say they wish to file a claim.

LION. A claim? What kind of a claim? Step forward, don't dawdle, speak up and have done.

NARRATOR. The three animals had watched the lion's dinner with wide open eyes and mouths. The rat, who was indeed no fool, cried out...

RAT. A misunderstanding, your highness! Not a claim, your majesty, but acclaim, oh king, enthusiastic acclaim!

NARRATOR. And he led his friends in a round of applause for the king. This done, they bowed to the ground and left the supreme presence as hastily as their legs would move.

LION. Revolting beggars. I was glad to see them go before the cognac.

NARRATOR. Our three citizens ran and ran until they arrived in a far-away field.

PORCUPINE. Oh God, I feel faint when I think of that sweet gazelle, that droll monkey, and that cuddlesome bunny.

SKUNK (*whispering*). Turned into main courses.

RAT. Yes, but turned into main courses, my friends, because they were not repulsive enough.

NARRATOR. And from that time, not one of them ever complained of his fate again.

THE TIGER WHO BECAME HUMANE

Characters: Narrator, the Tiger, a Boy, the Hunter.

NARRATOR. If only the world would see me as I see myself! There was a tiger once who decided to become humane against the advice of all his friends.

TIGER. I want to show the world that in spite of our sharp teeth, our ferocious growl, and the cruel traditions of our race, some few of us are not beyond redemption.

NARRATOR. "But what about our nature?" his friends objected.

TIGER. We must overcome it.

NARRATOR. And so this tiger gave up killing people and animals. Instead he ate bunches of forget-me-nots, he picked up bananas and mangos, and occasionally he even grazed like a cow. It was not much fun....

TIGER. Awful alfalfa.... But....

NARRATOR. But he made up for his discomfort by his moral satisfaction.

TIGER. I am truly nice.

NARRATOR. One day, alas, a crowd of hunters spotted him as he was licking at some mushrooms.

BOY. There's the killer!

NARRATOR. Whispered a boy, and one of the hunters raised his rifle. But the tiger looked up at that moment and cried out...

TIGER. Stop! I am the kindly tiger, the famous tiger who has become peaceful!

HUNTER. I'll show you what a peaceful tiger is...

NARRATOR. Said one of the hunters, and he shot the good beast dead between the eyes. Ah, if only the world would see me as I see myself!

THE TWO MICE

Characters: Narrator, the Country Mouse, the City Mouse.

NARRATOR. The country mouse was spending a holiday with his cousin the city mouse. Though he didn't come exactly from the country, but from a decent, small town in Ohio where life burns slow, if steady. Now he was in Greenwich Village, where his cousin had taken up painting. Most of the day the cousin mashed cream cheese on pieces of cardboard, and the other Village mice thought he was doing pretty powerful work. The country mouse, however, had other interests.

COUNTRY MOUSE. Oh if I could only find a really nice girl to settle down with!

NARRATOR. So he didn't say much about the cream cheese on the cardboard. But he did tell his cousin that he was a little shocked by the pace of life about him.

COUNTRY MOUSE. Goodness gracious, cousin, the words you use, the notions you throw around, the magazines you read, the friends you run around with—they all make my fur stand up on my back. And the females—well, they're no different. You and them—you talk about funny things—weird situations—private doings—sometimes not even normal doings—and not only sometimes, but almost all the time.

CITY MOUSE. In short, you're getting a free education at my house like nothin' they taught you back in Ohio. I hope you're enjoying it.

COUNTRY MOUSE. Oh yes, thank you. But maybe I'm not enjoying it as much as I ought to feel that I should be enjoying it.

CITY MOUSE. You're nothin' but a limp lollipop, but stick around; I used to be a choir mouse too.

NARRATOR. One evening they were disarraying themselves for a trend-setting party where they had been promised electronic guitars, communal sniffing of Tibetan floor wax, and the unmentionable poems of a rat on parole.

CITY MOUSE. Now listen; I'm taking you to this party because our mothers know each other. But for God's sake don't make me look like a fool by staring and fidgeting if a couple of mice go off into the bednook, or if a mouse is using the needle to get more *with* the music, you know, into the gut, where it's alive, or if some girl rodent shows her—you know what I mean. We live the free life, if a mouse wants to feel unconstrained, who the hell are we to butt in with middle-class prejudices, so for God's sake don't act like a forlorn cheesehole.

COUNTRY MOUSE. You mean that some girl mouse might—might—?

CITY MOUSE. That's the true innocence, *mon cher.*

COUNTRY MOUSE. I know, but wouldn't it be nicer to have a quiet type of party? A little talk, a little singing, lemonade, cookies, musical chairs maybe, because all this freedom, you see—

CITY MOUSE. Freedom ain't the kind of thing you turn off and on. When you're free, you've *got* to be free, or else the other mice put the hex on you.

COUNTRY MOUSE. You mean if I'm not free tonight—?

CITY MOUSE. If you're not free tonight like the rest of us, whether you like it or not, we'll be hooted and cackled at till I'll never dare show my whiskers out of this hole again.

COUNTRY MOUSE. Oh cousin, is that what freedom is? I see you are as much a slave as I, and if slave I am and slave must be, I'd rather be a slave where I feel at home.

NARRATOR. And instead of going to the party, he ran all the way to Ohio, where soon afterwards he married the daughter of a Presbyterian churchmouse, and begot, in the most conventional manner possible...

CITY MOUSE. Once a lollipop always a lollipop...

COUNTRY MOUSE. A happy litter of miceling, both boys and girls.

NARRATOR. And was he not right in his way? Freedom, he had found, is but the slavery we happen to enjoy.

AESOP'S APOLOGY

Characters: Narrator, Aesop, King Croesus.

NARRATOR. One afternoon, as Aesop was playing a game of chess against himself on a terrace belonging to his master, King Croesus of Lydia, the latter, fresh from the hunt, sat down with the fabulist in order to tease him a little.

CROESUS. My dear Aesop, I'm afraid you're something of an idler.

AESOP. Why, my lord? Because I am refining my chess game instead of galloping after a boar?

CROESUS. Never mind galloping, friend Aesop. Instead, take a look at your fellow bards and philosophers. Our young Greek world is teeming with geniuses who ascend one breathless height of Mount Parnassus after the other, each man determined to reach closer to the divine sun than his rival. Look at the great Peisander...

AESOP (*sighing*). I am looking, my lord.

CROESUS. How he ravished us with the ten thousand lines of his *Cnossiad* ! Five days in a row he held us spellbound.

AESOP. Five long, unforgettable days, my lord.

CROESUS. And what about Phrynichus, that master of the stasimon, whose *Phoenician Virgins* we saw on our stage last spring? Did he not make man, woman, slave and even myself weep a flood of tears?

AESOP. He did, my lord, and afterward all of you made so merry with him in your palace that the walls shook with your laughter.

CROESUS. Because he deserved it, Aesop. When did you ever write a trilogy?

AESOP. Alas, alas.

CROESUS. And last night, as we sat banqueting, none other than Anaximander was nourishing our spirits with the sixty-eighth chapter of his *Treatise on Wind*.

AESOP. He was, my lord, and praise God, we are to have the sixty-ninth tonight.

CROESUS. Those, my lazy friend, are the immortals. Those are the visionaries whose works our descendants will be reading and revering. While you—

AESOP. Spare me!

CROESUS. Whom I noticed at the lower end of my table manhandling a side of pork, you mope and dream between meals, play games, throw bread at the ducks in my pond, and whenever the fancy takes you, humor those ducks into some fable three hundred little words long; more, I do believe, would exhaust you. What do you say in your defense, you pigmy?

AESOP. In my defense? When you have crushed the breath out of my body?

CROESUS. Have I? You appear to be breathing normally.

AESOP. In that case, if your royal highness will allow me to vent a tiny parable—

CROESUS. With chattering foxes and contentious cows again?

AESOP. No, no, my lord, nothing low; everything properly human.

CROESUS. On that condition, parable away.

AESOP. Thank you, my lord. You and I, my lord, know that the grandest, vastest kingdoms, like Persia, like China, like Egypt, must be governed by extremely wise men. And they, being as wise as their nations are immense,

deserve our humble admiration. However, the world has its little kingdoms too, like your own prosperous Lydia, or that modest island of Samos where I was nursed. Shall these be governed by nitwits, my lord, to correspond with their few acres? Or is it your opinion that small kingdoms should be abolished altogether? Shall we make a gift of Lydia to Emperor Cyrus?
CROESUS. Not likely, you rascal.
AESOP. Well then, mine, like yours, is a small principality. You would like to shame me into enlarging it. I, however, only wish to rule it well. Yet this is where I tremble. Have I, have I ruled it well?
CROESUS. Were I to deny it, I would be lying instead of teasing. Master Aesop, you have been a wise governor of your few acres.
AESOP. If this is your true opinion, my lord...
NARRATOR. And now the fabulist kissed his master's jeweled hand....
AESOP. Good luck, Cyrus, adieu, pharaohs. The monarch who governs my little realm is happy.

The End

Notes

Far more than conventional—or even unconventional—plays, these fables invite directors, actors, musical accompanists, and set, costume and prop designers to *invent*. Shall the production be rich or sober? How many of the fables will be selected—fifteen minutes' worth, an hour's, more? How many actors will be cast—a single one, two, three, four, ten? What mix of male and female? What sort of musical effects, if any? Will the show be a dramatized reading or a fully acted production?

A number of parts for which I routinely used the masculine (e.g. the lunatic pigeon, or the trouts in "The pony who came to a stream") can readily be shifted to actresses. Here and there, furthermore, a line need not be spoken by the character to whom I have assigned it.

The role of the ubiquitous narrator can be assigned overall to a single actor or actress, or it can be assumed by all the actors and actresses in turn as the show progresses. It is a part as attractive to actors, in most of the fables, as the character-roles.

The narrative versions of these fables, called *Gobble-Up Stories*, are published in my *Otherwise Fables*, together with my other works of fiction.

APPENDIX
Plays translated by the author

In *Five Comedies of Medieval France*, New York: E.P. Dutton, 1970:
Anon: **Peter Quill's Shenanigans** [*La Farce de Maître Pierre Pathelin*, 1485?]
Jean Bodel: **The Play of Saint Nicholas** [*Le Jeu de Saint Nicolas*, ca. 1200]
Adam de la Halle: **The Play of Robin and Marion** [*Le Jeu de Robin et Marion*, ca. 1285]
Anon: **The Washtub** [*Le Cuvier*, 15th century]
The Chicken-Pie and the Chocolate Cake [*Le Pâté et la tarte*, 15th century]

In *The Theatre of Don Juan: a Collection of Plays and Views 1630-1963*, Lincoln: University of Nebraska Press, 1963:
Tirso de Molina: **The Playboy of Seville** [*El Burlador de Sevilla y convidado de piedra*, 1630]
Lorenzo da Ponte: **The Punished Libertine or Don Giovanni** [*Il Dissoluto punito ossia il Don Giovanni, 1787*]—with Adrienne M. Schizzano.

In *Thomas Corneille's Ariadne, followed by an essay on French classical tragedy*, Gainesville: University of Florida Press, 1982:
Ariadne [*Ariane*, 1672]

In *Seven Comedies by Marivaux*, Ithaca: Cornell University Press, 1968:
Robin, Bachelor of Love [*Arlequin poli par l'amour*, 1720]
Double Infidelity [La Double inconstance, 1722]
Money Makes the World Go Round [*Le Triomphe de Plutus*, 1728]
The Game of Love and Chance [*Le Jeu de l'amour et du hasard*, 1730]
    —with Adrienne S. Mandel.
The Wiles of Love [*L'Heureux stratagème*, 1733]
Sylvia Hears a Secret [*Les Fausses confidences*, 1737]
The Test [*L'Epreuve*, 1740]—with Adrienne S. Mandel.

In *Ludwig Tieck: The Land of Upside Down*, London: Associated University Presses, 1978:
The Land of Upside Down [Die verkehrte Welt, 1799] — with Maria Kelsen Feder.

In *August von Kotzebue: the Comedy, the Man*, University Park and London: The Pennsylvania University Press, 1990:

APPENDIX

The Good Citizens of Piffelheim [*Die deutschen Kleinstädter*, 1801]

In *Two Romantic Plays*: Los Angeles: Spectrum Productions, 1996:
Prosper Mérimée: ***The Spaniards in Denmark*** [*Les Espagnols en Danemarck*, 1825]

In *Prosper Mérimée: Plays on Hispanic Themes*, New York et al.: Peter Lang, 2003:
The Opportunity [L'Occasion, 1829]
Carvajal's Family [La Famille de Carvajal, 1829]
The Gilded Coach [Le Carrosse du Saint-Sacrement. 1829]
Inès Mendo [Inès Mendo ou le Préjugé vaincu and Inès Mendo ou le Triomphe du préjugé, 1825]

In *Philoctetes and the Fall of Troy*, Lincoln: University of Nebraska Press, 1981:
Heiner Müller: ***Philoctetes*** [*Philoktet*, 1965]—with Maria Kelsen Feder.

www.ingramcontent.com/pod-product-compliance
Lightning Source LLC
Chambersburg PA
CBHW010718300426
44114CB00023B/2891